KU-690-534

THE BEGINNINGS OF QUAKERISM

PUBLISHED BY
THE SYNDICS OF THE CAMBRIDGE UNIVERSITY PRESS
Bentley House, 200 Euston Road, London, N.W. 1
American Branch: 32 East 57th Street, New York 10022, N.Y.

Standard Book Number 521 04308 5

First Edition (published by Macmillan & Co. Ltd.) 1912
Reprinted 1912, 1923
Second Edition (published by the Cambridge University Press) 1955
Reprinted 1961, 1970

Previously printed in Great Britain at the University Press, Cambridge
Reprinted by William Lewis (Printers) Ltd, Cardiff

THE BEGINNINGS OF QUAKERISM

BY THE LATE

WILLIAM C. BRAITHWAITE

SECOND EDITION REVISED BY

HENRY J. CADBURY

CAMBRIDGE

AT THE UNIVERSITY PRESS

1970

BY THE SAME AUTHOR

THE SECOND PERIOD OF QUAKERISM

FOREWORD TO THE SECOND EDITION

By L. Hugh Doncaster

At the time of his death in 1905, John Wilhelm Rowntree had collected much material to enable him to write a history of the Society of Friends "which should adequately exhibit Quakerism as a great experiment in spiritual religion, and should be abreast of the requirements of modern research."[1] Subsequently his friends Rufus M. Jones and William Charles Braithwaite agreed to carry out this task, and the Rowntree Series of Quaker Histories, edited by Rufus M. Jones, was published during the next sixteen years as follows:

Studies in Mystical Religion by R. M. Jones, 1909. Reprinted: 1909, 1919, 1923, 1936 and 1944.
Spiritual Reformers in the 16th and 17th Centuries by R. M. Jones, 1914. Reprinted: 1928.
The Beginnings of Quakerism by W. C. Braithwaite, 1912. Reprinted: 1912 and 1923.
The Second Period of Quakerism by W. C. Braithwaite, 1919. Reprinted: 1921.
The Quakers in the American Colonies by R. M. Jones, Isaac Sharpless and Amelia M. Gummere, 1911. Reprinted: 1923.
The Later Periods of Quakerism (2 vols.) by R. M. Jones, 1921.

The series is the fullest historical study of the Society of Friends yet made, and traces the story from mystical predecessors of Friends to about 1900.

The first two volumes may be regarded as introductory, and *The Beginnings of Quakerism* may be seen as the foundation volume of the series. It is an intensive study of the first years of Quakerism, up to 1660, based on the extraordinary amount of manuscript and printed material left by the first generation of Friends.

[1] *The Beginnings of Quakerism*, 1st ed., p. v.

William Charles Braithwaite brought to his task great gifts, and his mastery of detail and ability to order and interpret it, combined with "high thought and beauty of language,"[1] make this the outstanding volume of the series. A. Neave Brayshaw, who was well qualified to make the judgement, wrote of this work, "The result of many years' study and research, it is one of the most valuable of all the pieces of Quaker history that have ever appeared."[2] Largely on account of this scholarly work, the University of Marburg conferred on the author its honorary degree of Doctor of Theology in 1922, saying,

> he has rendered signal service to Church History, both as a scholar and in research work, by his profound books, *The Beginnings of Quakerism* and *The Second Period of Quakerism.* He has laboured indefatigably in education and popular instruction; also in social problems and for the restoration of justice and fellowship in the intercourse of nations. In him we thankfully honour, at the same time, the actively applied brotherly love of the Quakers, of whom he has shown himself a worthy representative.[3]

Few books of historical study stand the test of being reprinted forty years later, but those responsible for the Rowntree Series have no doubt about the rightness of making *The Beginnings of Quakerism* once more available. Much has happened since it was written. Scholars on both sides of the Atlantic have been at work, and much new material is now available. Emphases have been changed and fresh facts have emerged. We see more clearly, for instance, the content and the relevance of the Puritan background to the early Friends, and we know much more of contemporary movements and their influence on Friends. But while there is room for fresh interpretation in the light of recent research, the main body of *The Beginnings of Quakerism* remains by far the

[1] A. Neave Brayshaw, *The British Friend* (1912), p. 70.
[2] *The British Friend* (1912), p. 68.
[3] A. Ll. B. Thomas and E. B. Emmott, *William Charles Braithwaite* (1931), p. 77.

most adequate study of its subject, and no further valid interpretation is likely to be made without building on this foundation.

The present volume is not, however, simply a reprint of the last edition. As it remains the standard work on this subject, certain minimum changes have been made to bring it up to date.

First, in the earlier editions there was an introduction by Rufus M. Jones, linking Quakerism to the mystical movements studied in his introductory volumes, and interpreting the religious experience of Friends. This interpretive chapter has regretfully been omitted on the ground that recent studies have, in the minds of a number of scholars, put Quakerism in a rather different light.

Second, about one hundred and fifty small alterations have been made in the text, the great majority being additional references or corrections in the footnotes.

Third, a new appendix has been prepared in the form of additional notes referred to by asterisks (*) in the text, bringing bibliographical references up to date, embodying a few manuscript notes left by William Charles Braithwaite, and incorporating such other supplementary material as will make the volume as accurate and "abreast of the requirements of modern research" as possible.

Henry J. Cadbury, Professor at the Harvard Divinity School, has been responsible for the textual revision and for the additional notes. A scholar in the field of New Testament study, he is also an authority on Quaker history, and the reader will at once be conscious of the skill and scholarship which he has brought to his task. It is also clear that such a one is gravely limited in such work. William Charles Braithwaite himself set limits to his work, particularly in the field of interpretation; and Henry J. Cadbury in his revision and notes has accepted those limitations.

A number of people have contributed suggestions, but one has contributed so much that he must be mentioned by name. Geoffrey F. Nuttall, especially in his *Early Quaker Letters*, 1952, being a calendar of the Swarthmore

Manuscripts with annotations and indices, has made available a wealth of material which has repeatedly been drawn on in the revision notes, and to him special acknowledgement is gladly made.

L. HUGH DONCASTER

WOODBROOKE COLLEGE
SELLY OAK
BIRMINGHAM
February 1954

PREFACE TO THE FIRST EDITION

The standard *History of the Rise, Increase, and Progress of the Christian People called Quakers*, by William Sewel of Amsterdam, was published in Dutch in 1717, in English in 1722, and in German in 1742. It had been preceded by a much inferior work, Gerard Croese's *Historia Quakeriana*, printed in Latin in 1695, and in German and English in 1696, and was succeeded in 1789–1790 by John Gough's *History*, which in the earlier period is a mere compilation. Sewel's book is a conscientious and well-written piece of work for its day, but necessarily falls far short of present needs. Of shorter histories, *The Rise of the Quakers*, by T. Edmund Harvey (1905), *The Story of Quakerism*, by Elizabeth Braithwaite Emmott (1908), and the article on "Friends, Society of," by A. Neave Brayshaw, in the new edition of the *Encyclopædia Britannica*, may be consulted with advantage.

My friend the late John Wilhelm Rowntree planned a History which should adequately exhibit Quakerism as a great experiment in spiritual religion, and should be abreast of the requirements of modern research, and he was gathering materials for the work during the last year of his life. To us who knew him intimately he seemed admirably qualified for the task, alike by his acuteness of intellect and width of outlook, his clear understanding of the genius of Quakerism, and his brilliance of style; and the lectures on "The Rise of Quakerism in Yorkshire," in his *Essays and Addresses*, give a taste of what he might have accomplished had he lived.

The execution of his plan has fallen to friends who shared his conception of the significance of the Quaker movement in its bearing upon spiritual religion; and Dr. Rufus M. Jones, the editor of the series, has already published two volumes, *Studies in Mystical Religion* and *The Quakers in the American Colonies*.

In writing the present history of the Beginnings of Quakerism, I have endeavoured to make good use of the unique treasury of MS. and printed materials in the Library of the Society of Friends at Devonshire House, Bishopsgate, E.C.; and I also owe much to the publications of the Friends' Historical Society, which are continually making fresh portions of this material readily available. I wish to acknowledge much help from the Librarian, Norman Penney, who is also editor of the *Journal of the Friends' Historical Society*, and has contributed a mass of valuable notes to the Cambridge edition of Geo. Fox's *Journal*, now being published. I am much indebted to Dr. Rufus M. Jones especially for his Introductory Chapter[1]. I have also had valued help in various ways from A. Neave Brayshaw of Scarborough, Gilbert Gilkes of Kendal, Chas. E. Gillett of Whittington, Wilfrid Grace of Bristol, Dr. J. Rendel Harris of Selly Oak, William F. Miller of Winscombe, Pastor D. Mulder of Herwen, Holland, Joseph Rowntree of York, Constance M. Rowntree of Scalby, Abraham Shackleton of Dublin, and Ernest E. Taylor of Malton. The Index has been prepared by Elizabeth Foster Brown of Croydon.

Prior to 1752 the year in England began on the 25th March, which month accordingly became the first month of the Quaker calendar, falling partly in one year and partly in the preceding year, while January and February formed the eleventh and twelfth months of this preceding year. Hence has resulted much chronological confusion. I have given the month and year of all dates according to the modern (New Style) calendar.

The map of the Preston Patrick district, made with help from Ernest E. Taylor, is intended to assist Friends and others who desire to visit for themselves the places in this district whose historical associations are recorded in the following pages.

W.C.B.

34 WEST BAR, BANBURY
September 1911

[1] Omitted from the present edition.

NOTE

DATES, so far as month and year are concerned, are given according to New Style, but the day of the month is left unaltered.

Quotations are corrected as to spelling and punctuation; omitted words are indicated by ...; words added to complete the sense by square brackets.

The following contractions are used in the notes:

A.R.B. Colln. A collection in Dev. Ho. (see below) of about 250 letters of early Friends. See Appendix B.

Besse, *Sufferings*. *A Collection of the Sufferings of the people called Quakers*, from 1650 to 1689, taken from original records and other authentic accounts, by Joseph Besse. In two folio vols. London, 1753.

Camb. Journ. Edition of Spence MS. Journal of Fox, two vols. Cambridge, 1911. See Appendix A.

Dev. Ho. for MS. materials preserved in Devonshire House, now in the Library, Friends House, Euston Road, London, N.W. 1.

Extracts from State Papers, First and Second Series. Supplements to *J.F.H.S.*

F.P.T. *The First Publishers of Truth*, being early records of the introduction of Quakerism into England and Wales. Edited for the Friends' Historical Society by Norman Penney. London, 1907.

Hist. of the Commonth. and Prot. *History of the Commonwealth and Protectorate, 1649–1656*, by Samuel Rawson Gardiner, four vols. London, 1903.

Inner Life. *The Inner Life of the Religious Societies of the Commonwealth*, by Robert Barclay. London, 1876.

J.F.H.S. *Journal of the Friends' Historical Society*, begun 1903. Edited from Dev. Ho. (see above).

Journ. or *Ellwood Journ.* Ellwood edition of the Journal of George Fox, originally printed in 1694. References are to Bi-centenary edition in two vols. London, 1891. The text of quotations is corrected to the 1694 edn.

Letters of Early Friends, edited by Abram Rawlinson Barclay. London, 1841.

Life (or *Journal*). Journals and lives of the following Friends published under various titles: William Caton (1689 edn.), Richard Davies (1771 edn.), William Edmondson (1715 edn.), Thomas Ellwood (1714 edn.), Gilbert Latey (1707 edn.).

Sewel. *History of the Rise, Increase, and Progress of the Christian people called Quakers*, by William Sewel, two vols. London, 1811 (5th edn.).

Short Journ., by George Fox. See Appendix A.

Smith's *Catalogue*. *A Descriptive Catalogue of Friends' Books*, by Joseph Smith, two vols. London, 1867.

Spence MSS. vol. iii. Described in Appendix B.

Swarthm. Colln. Swarthm. collection of MSS. at Dev. Ho. (see above). See Appendix B.

Works. Collected writings of following Friends published under various titles: John Burnyeat (1691 edn.), Edward Burrough (1672 edn.), Steven Crisp (1694 edn.), William Dewsbury (1689 edn.), Margaret Fell (1710 edn.), Francis Howgill (1676 edn.), Richard Hubberthorne (1663 edn.), Charles Marshall (1704 edn.), James Nayler (1716 edn.), James Parnell (1675 edn.), Isaac Penington (1784, 3rd edn.), Thomas Taylor (1697 edn.).

CONTENTS

CHAPTER I

THE PURITAN REVOLUTION

CHAPTER II

THE FOUNDER OF QUAKERISM

CHAPTER III

PIONEER WORK

(1649–1652)

CHAPTER IV

THE PEOPLE IN WHITE RAIMENT

(JUNE 1652)

CHAPTER V

SWARTHMORE

(1652)

CHAPTER VI

FURTHER WORK IN THE NORTH

(1653–1654)

CHAPTER VII

QUAKERISM AT THE BEGINNING OF 1654

CHAPTER VIII

THE MISSION TO THE SOUTH

(1654)

CHAPTER IX

FURTHER WORK IN THE SOUTH

(1655)

CHAPTER X

THE WIDER OUTLOOK

CHAPTER XI

NAYLER'S FALL

(1656)

CHAPTER XII

CONTROVERSY

CHAPTER XIII

CHURCH ORGANIZATION

CHAPTER XIV

ITINERATING WORK OF THE LEADERS IN GREAT BRITAIN, 1656–1660

CHAPTER XV

SURVEY OF THE GROWTH OF QUAKERISM

(1656–1660)

CHAPTER XVI

WORK BEYOND SEAS

CHAPTER XVII

RELATIONS WITH THE STATE

CHAPTER XVIII

THE RESTORATION YEAR

(1660)

CHAPTER XIX

FRIENDS IN PRIVATE LIFE

CHAPTER XX

QUAKERISM AT THE END OF 1660

APPENDICES

MAPS

(*At end of Volume before Index*)

CHAPTER I

THE PURITAN REVOLUTION*

No greater moral change ever passed over a nation than passed over England during the years which parted the middle of the reign of Elizabeth from the meeting of the Long Parliament. England became the people of a book, and that book was the Bible. . . . Elizabeth might silence or tune the pulpits; but it was impossible for her to silence or tune the great preachers of justice and mercy and truth who spoke from the book which she had again opened for her people. . . . The whole temper of the nation felt the change. A new conception of life and of man superseded the old. A new moral and religious impulse spread through every class. . . . The whole nation became in fact a Church. The great problems of life and death, whose questionings found no answer in the higher minds of Shakspere's day, pressed for an answer not only from noble and scholar but from farmer and shopkeeper in the age that followed him.—JOHN RICHARD GREEN, *Short History of the English People*, chap. viii.

THE Puritan Revolution, which covered the period from the Petition of Right in 1628 to the Restoration in 1660, was concerned on the one hand with the dominance of Parliament, and on the other with the dominance of the great type of religion which we call Puritanism. It was successful in assuring the supremacy of Parliament, to which the restored monarchy and episcopacy of the later Stuarts were dependent in a way which would have been abhorrent to Charles I. or to Laud. With respect to Puritanism, the measure of success was less complete, and it was not until the struggle for the special domination of Calvinism had failed that after a generation of bitter persecution of Nonconformists under Charles II. the truer ideal of religious toleration for all forms of faith was substantially achieved in 1689.

The present book is an attempt to rewrite, from original sources, the early history of the important spiritual movement which was inaugurated by George Fox, and as the necessary background to our study, some understanding of Puritanism, both on its political and on its religious side, is essential. But while the political system of the Commonwealth and the Protectorate gave Friends, as we shall see, the opportunity of publishing the truths for which they stood, the religious side of Puritanism is more vitally important, for the whole atmosphere of life in England was charged with its penetrating influence.

The name Puritan, like that of Quaker, was at first a term of reproach. It began to be used, shortly after the accession of Elizabeth, of the party of English Protestants who regarded the reformation of the Church under Elizabeth as incomplete, and urged its further "purification" from unscriptural and corrupt forms and ceremonies.

> "This name," said Whitgift in 1572, "is very aptly given to these men, not because they be pure, no more than were the heretics called *Cathari*, but because they think themselves to be *mundiores ceteris*, more pure than others, as *Cathari* did, and separate themselves from all other Churches and congregations as spotted and defiled." [1]

Many of the reformed clergy, in exile during Mary's reign, had come under the spell of Calvin's great dogmatic and ecclesiastical system. On their return, however, they found that a Protestantism was being established in England which was characteristically English. Instead of rejecting, with Calvin, everything which could not be established from scripture, it was disposed to retain everything which scripture did not disprove. There was little logic in the English system, and some compromise, but it had the merits of being more comprehensive and more practicable than a narrow Calvinism would have been. To the earnest-hearted Protestant, steeped in the Genevan teaching, it seemed sadly invertebrate, especially for the decisive hour of conflict with the Papacy. Gardiner describes the fighting qualities of Calvinism in a powerful passage. He says: [2]

[1] See *The Oxford English Dictionary*, sub voce "Puritan."
[2] *Cromwell's Place in History*, p. 5.

Every spirit must take to itself a form, and the spirit of Protestantism took to itself a form in its struggles against the papacy and the secular authorities by which the papacy was supported. Wherever Protestantism was on its defence, it developed intellectually the Calvinistic creed, and where, as in Scotland, Protestantism was threatened not merely by invasion from abroad, but by attack from the ruler in whose hands lay the reins of government, it adopted the Presbyterian organization as its best means of presenting a firm front against the assaults of a government working in the papal interest. . . . This creed and discipline were offered to the world, not as mere temporary expedients, but as immovable pillars of the divine temple, without which perhaps no real Christianity could exist, and which must therefore be imposed on all men without consideration of their wishes. Clad in the armour of the Calvinistic creed, the more religious of the Elizabethan Protestants defied the missionaries of Rome and the fleets of Spain.

The system of Calvin claimed to exercise entire supremacy over the lives of men. Based originally on the appeal which scripture made to the heart by the witness of the Spirit,[1] it had tended more and more to erect the scheme of doctrine and the Presbyterian form of church-organization which the logical mind of Calvin drew from scripture into a thing of authoritative institution. The Bible was to be read by the common people, and to make its own appeal, but it would be a marked Bible, with the proof texts of Calvinism annotated, and continually reiterated from the pulpit. In an age which exalted doctrine, and was impatient of theological twilight, a logical scheme of Divine truth which satisfied the intellect compelled the enthusiastic acceptance of multitudes, and, if circumstances served, would not hesitate to claim for itself universal obedience. Accordingly, during the reign of Elizabeth, there was not only the struggle between the supremacy of the Crown and the supremacy of the Pope, but there was also in preparation the struggle, which the pedantry and pretensions of the Stuarts precipitated, between the Divine right of a theocratic Presbytery and the Divine right of Bishops and Kings.

[1] See Auguste Sabatier, *Religions of Authority and the Religion of the Spirit* (English translation), pp. 160-163.

The practical sagacity and untheological temper of Elizabeth had at first enabled her to keep within the episcopal establishment many Puritan-minded clergy. She had succeeded in maintaining bishops and the Book of Common Prayer, but the doctrine taught by the most earnest of her clergy was the doctrine of Calvin, and she had not insisted on full conformity[1] to the rubrics of the Prayer Book in the country parishes. But the zeal and bigotry of Thomas Cartwright, the English champion of the Calvinist system, alarmed Elizabeth, especially his fanatical advocacy of Presbyterian church-government, to the absolute exclusion of the State.[2] He taught that the ministers, through their classes and synods, were to wield full spiritual power and jurisdiction. Their weapon was excommunication, and they were responsible for its use only to Christ. The civil power was "to see their decrees executed, and to punish the contemners of them." Other forms of faith—Papal, Episcopalian, or Sectarian—should be ruthlessly suppressed, and all heresy should be punishable with death. Richard Hooker controverted Cartwright with the stately English and the large-hearted reasoning of the *Ecclesiastical Polity*, while this crude assertion of extreme Calvinism checked any further reform of ritual in the English Church, and caused increasing harshness towards nonconforming ministers. By the establishment, on a permanent basis, of the Ecclesiastical Commission in 1583, the supremacy of the Crown in ecclesiastical matters was asserted in the most systematic and despotic fashion. The steady pressure of the Commission effected an artificial uniformity of worship. But it could not in any way settle the conflicting issues of ritual, doctrine, and church-government which were in debate.

The Puritan movement continued to grow in strength, and to become more definitely hostile to episcopacy, and at the same time Separatist Churches sprang up, opposed

[1] Persons within the Church of England who failed to give this full conformity were the original Nonconformists. Those who separated from religious communion with the Church of England were called Separatists.

[2] It was in 1572 that the first English presbytery was set up at Wandsworth.

both to presbyters and bishops. The beginnings of the Anabaptists in England have been sketched in clear outline by Dr. Rufus M. Jones in *Studies in Mystical Religion*, chap. xvii. We are told of the little groups of "brethren" who claimed the attention of Archbishop Warham in 1511, and were probably Lollards who had reached independently the position taken by the continental Baptists. We are given evidence of their more definite establishment about 1538, when a policy to "repress and utterly extinguish these persons" was set on foot, but with little success. Anabaptists at Faversham in Kent and Bocking in Essex,* about 1549, were the first that made separation from the Reformed Church of England, and gathered congregations of their own. They grew in strength during Elizabeth's reign, in spite of vigorous persecution, and there were several of their conventicles in London in the year 1589. But the permanent settlement of Baptist communities belongs to the early Stuart period.

With the Independents the case is similar. Robert Browne is generally regarded as the founder of Independency, though he afterwards conformed to the English Church. With Robert Harrison he formed a "Church" at Norwich about the year 1581, opposing himself equally to prelacy and presbytery. Driven to exile in the Low Countries, he produced in 1582 his *Treatise of Reformation without Tarrying for anie*, which was a strong plea for the Church's independence of the State. Bound up with the treatise was a Catechism which set out the character of the Church he desired to see established. While agreeing in many points with the Presbyterian ideal, from first to last the people of the Church were made supreme. Every one was a king, a prophet, and a priest under Christ to further the Kingdom of God and break down the kingdom of Antichrist, and all officers were appointed by the Church and controlled by it. Brownism of this type became the accepted basis of all the early Separatists. It could only at first establish itself precariously in England, and persecution drove its adherents oversea to Holland, then the chief home of religious liberty. The martyrdom of Barrow, Greenwood, and Penry in 1593 was followed by the Act "to retain the Queen's Majesty's subjects in their due obedience" (35 Eliz. cap. 1), which dealt with the "wicked and dangerous practices of seditious sectaries," and punished persons resorting to conventicles with imprisonment until they conformed, with a proviso for their abjuring the realm. The Act had an apparent success in silencing the Presbyterian element within the English Church and forcing avowed Separatists into exile.

The accession of James stirred the hopes of all sections of the Puritans. Bred a Presbyterian, he had given it as his opinion that their Church was the purest in the world, and that the service of the English Church was "but an evil-said Mass in English." He seemed likely, therefore, to be prejudiced in favour of Puritan ideas. Accordingly on his way up to London in 1603 he was presented with the "Millenary" petition, representing the views of 800 of the English clergy. It was couched in language of studied moderation, without abuse of Episcopacy or advocacy of the Presbyterian system. James, in the autumn, summoned the Hampton Court Conference, which met at the beginning of 1604, and was convened in order to provide him with materials for correcting all abuses in the Church. It was a golden moment when men were in a mood for conciliation. But the King threw it away. He would have nothing to do with Presbyterian ways: they agreed with monarchy no better than God with the devil. He would make these Church-reformers conform or harry them out of the land. The Canons of Convocation of 1604 followed, and some three hundred nonconforming ministers, who refused to accept the tests, were deprived of their cures.

The Separatists had also presented their petition for greater liberty of worship, recalling their hardships through exile and through persecution at home. It was slighted by a monarch who found the inviolable bases of Church and State in a Divine right of Bishops and a Divine right of Kings.

The Parliamentary struggle against the arbitrary

government of James and Charles was mainly in the hands of men of Puritan sympathies. And when the attempt was made, with the help of the Crown, to force Laud's anti-Presbyterian policy on the whole people of England, the fusion of the Puritan and Parliamentary movements, one aiming at an exclusive type of religion and the other at control over government by a popularly elected House, became for the time complete. As Gardiner points out,[1] so close was the union that, when Charles in 1634 resolved for the necessary defence of the country to levy ship-money rather than summon Parliament, his arbitrary action was caused by the knowledge that Parliament would refuse to grant a penny except on condition that Laud's system should be swept off the face of the earth.

When at last in November 1640 the Long Parliament met, the King's interference with the Presbyterian system in Scotland had resulted in the invasion of England by a Scottish army. The English Parliament could, therefore, set about redressing grievances without fear of dissolution since the King must have money for paying the Scots, and meanwhile the Scottish army was virtually at its disposal. Accordingly it was able to sweep away the Star Chamber and the other special courts, to imprison Laud, and to send Strafford to the scaffold. The issue between King and people culminated in the Grand Remonstrance of December 1641, which again shows clearly how, in Gardiner's phrase, "the spear of Parliamentarism was tipped with Puritanism." In this document, reform of the Church on Puritan lines went hand in hand with demands for a continuance of Parliamentary government. A new conformity arranged by a general synod of divines, with the approval of Parliament, would purify the Church. It was far from their purpose, they say (sect. 184), to let loose the golden reins of discipline in the Church, to leave private persons or particular congregations to take up what form of Divine service they please. They held it requisite that there should be

[1] *Cromwell's Place in History*, p. 11.

throughout the whole realm a conformity to that order which the laws enjoin according to the Word of God. They desired to unburden consciences of superstitious ceremonies, to suppress innovations, and to take away the monuments of idolatry.

When the Civil War broke out in the following year, the threatened failure of the Parliamentary arms threw Pym in 1643 on the support of the Scots, and the price that had to be paid for this support was the Solemn League and Covenant. Parliament by this Covenant swore to preserve the reformed religion in Scotland and to reform religion in England and Ireland, according to the Word of God and the example of the best Reformed Churches, in doctrine, worship, discipline, and government, and to endeavour to bring the Churches in the three kingdoms to the nearest conjunction and uniformity in religion, confession of faith, form of church-government, directory for worship, and catechizing. They further swore to endeavour the extirpation of popery, prelacy, superstition, heresy, schism, and profaneness. In effect, then, the Solemn League and Covenant involved the imposition upon England of the full Presbyterian system, with its intolerance, its doctrinal rigidity, and its exacting discipline. The menace of this system continued to lie on England, even after the crisis in the fortunes of the Parliamentary cause had passed away with the victory of Marston Moor in July 1644. It caused great misgivings in the practical mind of Cromwell, bent on the surest means of achieving military success. In choosing his officers he refused to reject one man as an Independent and another as a Baptist, and, after the victory of his New Model army at Naseby in 1645, he urged Parliament to grant liberty of conscience to the "honest men" who had been fighting. "He that ventures his life for the liberty of his country, I wish he trust God for the liberty of his conscience, and you for the liberty he fights for." The impending establishment of Presbyterianism also led to a division of opinion in Parliament and to great controversy in the country, and in revulsion against it a strong body of opinion, especially in the army, attached itself to the Independent system.

Independency in exile during the reign of James had already had some notable developments. Its numbers had been reinforced from England, especially as a result of the Canons of Convocation of 1604. About the end of 1607 a large band from Gainsborough, part of the famous Congregational Church formed five years earlier at Scrooby Manor House, fled to Holland, settling after a time at Leyden, with John Robinson as their pastor, and in 1620 these Pilgrim Fathers established a colony in New England at Plymouth. Thenceforward New England received constant accessions of Puritans from the mother-country. In 1629 a charter was granted establishing to the north of Plymouth the Colony of Massachusetts Bay, just at the time when the King was announcing his resolve to govern without Parliaments. As Green says:[1]

> By the Puritans at large the grant was at once regarded as a providential call. Out of the failure of their great constitutional struggle, and the pressing danger to "godliness" in England, rose the dream of a land in the West where religion and liberty could find a safe and lasting home. . . . Puritan emigration began on a scale such as England had never before seen. The two hundred who first sailed for Salem were soon followed by Winthrop with eight hundred men, and seven hundred more followed ere the first year of the king's personal rule had run its course. . . . As the contest grew hotter at home the number of Puritan emigrants rose fast. Three thousand new colonists arrived from England in a single year. . . . Between the sailing of Winthrop's expedition and the assembly of the Long Parliament, in the space, that is, of ten or eleven years, two hundred emigrant ships had crossed the Atlantic and twenty thousand Englishmen had found a refuge in the West.

Of these two colonies that of Massachusetts soon showed a spirit of intolerance, which resulted in the establishment of the Colony of Rhode Island on the principles of absolute religious freedom. We shall find that several of the ministers who most zealously opposed

[1] *Short History of the English People*, chap. viii. sect. 4.

Friends in the North of England had lived in Massachusetts.[1]

Meanwhile in England the Independents were attracting some of the best elements in the Puritan party. Their congregational system allowed an elasticity of development better suited to the Puritanism of England than was a rigid Presbyterianism. When the yoke of this seemed falling on England about the year 1644, Independency sprang into national importance as the system which by contrast with the bonds of episcopacy or of the presbytery was the natural religious home for men of free spirit.

The tendency of English Independents was in favour of some degree of religious liberty. When the army in 1647 began to take a part in politics against the Presbyterians, it made proposals to the King which would have left episcopacy in being, except as regards any penal jurisdiction, whether direct or through the civil magistrate, but it insisted on a repeal of all acts enjoining the use of the Book of Common Prayer, or imposing a penalty for not coming to church or for meetings elsewhere, desiring that provision should be made in some other way for discovering Papists and disabling them from disturbing the State. It also proposed the repeal of all ordinances imposing the taking of the Solemn League and Covenant. If the King had been willing to accept these terms the religious peace of 1689 might have been anticipated by forty years. But in this as in other respects the proposals were too far in advance of the times to win acceptance After the further period of civil war produced by the King's secret engagement with the Scots, the army ejected his supporters in Parliament by Pride's Purge, and procured the passing of the Ordinance which led to his trial and execution. During these proceedings, in anticipation of their issue, it promulgated a document compounded out of the proposals mentioned above and a scheme put forward in October 1647 by a knot of men, led by John

[1] I may mention Francis Higginson, Thos. Weld, Saml. Eaton, and Christopher Marshall.

Lilburne, who came to be known as Levellers. As now proposed, supreme power was to be placed in the hands of a Parliament elected every two years on a basis of household suffrage, and sitting for seven months. The Executive was to consist of a Council of State, chosen by Parliament and under its control. One important reservation to the power of Parliament was proposed: there was to be a religious settlement on the basis of an established Puritanism, not compulsive, but with liberty for those who professed faith in God by Jesus Christ to worship according to their conscience, in any place except those set apart for the public worship, "so as they abuse not this liberty to the civil injury of others, or to actual disturbance of the public peace." This religious liberty, however, was not to extend to popery or prelacy, which were politically obnoxious.

It was, however, natural that, while the Rump of the Long Parliament was ready to abolish Kingship and the House of Lords, it did not consent to abdicate in favour of the new Parliament proposed by the army. Cromwell persuaded his brother officers to be content with presenting the document to the House, without expecting it to be immediately passed into law. The situation gave an obvious opening to Lilburne and the Levellers. A third version of his scheme was issued, and was taken up by some of the soldiers; but Cromwell declared in support of the Rump, and crushed the mutinous regiments at Burford in May 1649.

It will be clear from the foregoing that, although there had been no formal settlement of religion on the basis of liberty of conscience for all except Episcopalians and Roman Catholics, the pressure of the army and the leanings of the English Independents had practically secured this for some years. There was religious liberty *de facto*. Indeed, from the time when the Long Parliament began to sit, religious refugees had been pouring over from Holland to reinforce the persecuted sects at home. During the years from 1643 to 1649 London became a cauldron of seething Puritan causes.

Apart from the Presbyterians and the Independents,

one or other of whom was seated in the place of power, the chief of these sects was the Baptist. The permanent settlement of Baptist Churches in England has been carefully traced by Dr. R. M. Jones,[1] who describes the founding of the first General Baptist Church about 1612 by Thomas Helwys, who had belonged, with his leader, John Smyth,* to the Scrooby Independent congregation. By 1626 there were at least five other General Baptist Churches. They promulgated in 1614 the earliest plea for full liberty of conscience.* These General Baptists were Arminian in faith, that is to say, they maintained the general salvability of mankind and rejected the Calvinist dogmas of original sin and predestination. Nearly at the same time, however, Particular or Calvinistic Baptist Societies arose. The first of these arose in 1633 in Southwark following a Congregational Church led by Henry Jacob. By 1644 there were seven congregations in London and forty-seven in the rest of England. In this year they carefully defined their position in a Confession of Faith, which impressed their contemporaries with the orthodoxy of their theology. They were persecuted and ridiculed, especially for their lay-preachers of mean origin. They desired the complete separation of Church and State, and a wide religious toleration, and greatly expanded the rights, privileges, and functions of the laity, even to the allowance of women-preachers. They opposed tithes and "hireling ministry," and had their itinerating "messengers of the Churches." Denne, the most powerful preacher among the General Baptists, advocated the doctrine of the Inner Light in *The Drag-net*, *etc.*, a book published in 1646, before Fox had begun his public preaching. The points of contact between the early Baptists and the early Friends are indeed numerous, and I shall show in a succeeding chapter that it was a "shattered" Baptist Society at Mansfield, in 1648, which first supplied George Fox with congenial religious fellowship, and, under his leadership, developed into the earliest Quaker congregation.

[1] *Studies in Mystical Religion*, pp. 407-427.

London, during the years of toleration, became, in the opinion of men like Thomas Edwards, the author of *Gangræna* (1646), and Ephraim Pagit, the author of *Heresiographie* (1645), a hot-bed of pernicious and heretical sectaries. Pagit, whose animus must be allowed for, speaks of a numerous company of heretics suddenly descending on London like locusts—the unpure Familists, who pretend to be godified like God; the illuminated Anabaptists; the Independents with their excess of liberty; the Sabbatarians, who are for keeping the old Jewish Sabbath; the Anti-Sabbatarians, who say every day is a sabbath to a Christian; the Traskites, who would observe many Jewish ceremonies; the Millenaries, who believe in the reign of Christ and His saints on earth for a thousand years; the Etheringtonians, with a hodge-podge of many heresies; and an atheistical sect, who affirm that men's souls sleep with their bodies until the Day of Judgment. He also mentions in the body of his book a number of other sects; indeed, "since the suspension of our church-government," he says, "every one that listeth turneth Preacher, as shoemakers, cobblers, buttonmakers, ostlers, and such-like, take upon them to expound the holy scriptures, intrude into our pulpits and vent strange doctrine, tending to faction, sedition and blasphemy." "Heresy," he urges, "is as dangerous as fire: use your best endeavours to quench it, before it consume us."

Of this confusion of sects, with their discordant voices, we get perhaps the best idea by reading the experiences of those who were out on the troubled ocean. In 1641, for example, a gentlewoman of Puritan convictions, named Mary Proud, married Sir William Springett, a young man of twenty, who shared her zeal. They refused the use of a ring, and during their short married life scrupled many things then in use amongst those who were counted honest people, as, for instance, singing David's Psalms in metre, and when, like others, they tore out of their Bibles the Common Prayer and forms of prayer at the end of the book, they tore out also the singing Psalms as the inventions of vain poets. They were also brought off from the

Bread and Wine, and, looking into the Independent way of worship, saw death in it, nor did baptism with water answer the cry of their hearts. At this time, about the year 1643, her husband died, and when their child was born Mary Springett would not allow her to be baptized, though Puritan preachers were sent to persuade her. "Through this," she says, "I waded, after some time, but soon after this I went from the simplicity into notions, and I changed my ways often from one notion to another, not finding satisfaction." She had been a Puritan, zealous in what were called the "duties," keeping the Sabbath, fasting often, praying in private thrice a day, hearing sermons and "lectures" daily, and reading much in scripture. "I was so vehement in prayer," she writes, "that I chose the more remote places to pray in, that I might not be heard to pray, and could not but be loud in the earnest pouring out of my soul." Now, in her weariness of heart, she became disgusted with all religious exercises, and abandoned their use, both in her family and in private. She consorted with persons of no religion, and grew to loathe outward profession; and in this restless state let in every sort of notions that rose in that day, and tried in turn to get good out of them, but only sorrow and trouble were the end of all, till she came to the conclusion that though God and His truth existed they were not known to any on earth, and so gave up the search in despair. A time of frivolity followed, "carding and dancing, singing and frequenting music meetings," but with much trouble of heart. She believed that there was no revelation since the Apostles' days—nothing that she knew to be of God so certainly that she could shed her blood in defence of it. Once, watching the vanity of a Lord Mayor's show, she asked a Puritan bystander, "What benefit have we by all this bloodshed, and Charles's being kept out of the nation, seeing all these follies are again allowed?" He answered, none that he knew of except the enjoyment of their religion, to which she rejoined that that was a benefit to those who had a religion, but none to her. Through all her darkness, however, she held a trust in the Lord, even when she owned herself to have no religion which she could call true: she could not, indeed, call God Father, but cried to Him as her Creator, and when melted into tears at such times supposed it must be some influence from the planets that made her tender, for she could not own anything in her to be of God. In this state she married her second husband, Isaac Penington, in 1654, a man like herself, "who saw the deceit of all notions, and lay as one who refused to be comforted by any appearance of religion." A few years later both husband and wife found in the Quaker experience of an indwelling Christ that for which their souls had been thirsting.[1]

London, at this period, contained many persons who were adrift from their spiritual anchorage. The authority, usually so powerful, of the established institutions of religion had been destroyed, for in 1643 prelacy had been abolished, and in 1645 the Book of Common Prayer, while the substituted Presbyterian system established by the Ordinance of 1648 had failed to plant itself securely in England. Gardiner sums up the situation carefully. He says:[2]

> Even in Lancashire, where the system obtained the greatest acceptance, it was hampered by the reluctance of parishioners to elect elders and deacons; and after the defeat of Charles at Worcester [3rd Sept. 1651] it was still more hampered by the knowledge of the leading ministers that they had become obnoxious to the Government as supporters of the royal claims. The weakness of the London Presbytery was no less manifest. In an appeal made by the Provincial Assembly early in 1652, fears were expressed of "the utter dissolution of Presbyterial Government." The Minutes of the Classes of Manchester, Bury and Wirksworth tell the same tale. Ordinations and the examinations of candidates for the ministry are frequently mentioned but it was difficult and often impossible to fill up the elderships, the mainstay of ecclesiastical discipline.

[1] The account of Mary Penington's religious *Experiences* was written by her about the year 1668, and completed in 1680. It was not put into print during her life, but has since been published, the latest edition appearing in 1911, with Introduction and Notes by Norman Penney. The text is not in a satisfactory state; see note, *post*, p. 503.

[2] *Hist. of Commth. and Prot.* ii. 86.

Presbyterianism, as a clerical system, with its jealous safeguards of learning and character in its ministers, met with no serious opposition. Its jurisdiction over the morals of the laity was an exotic which took no root on English soil.

As early as 1649 an adverse writer speaks of "the heavy judgment of God upon [the Presbyterians] in so speedy snatching the power from them when they thought themselves so securely the lords of all," while about the same time their own ministers and elders say, "as for the Presbyterial Government itself, we may justly say of it, as the Jews did upon another occasion, 'We know that everywhere it is spoken against.'"[1]

With Episcopacy dethroned and Presbyterianism neither popular nor established in any effective sense, the force of institutional religion was at its lowest point. There was, on the one hand, an "outburst of unrestrained sectarianism,"[2] and, on the other, a singular variety in the denominational persuasion even of the parish ministers. Patrons still presented to benefices, and tithes were paid, though where the patron was the Crown or some delinquent, the choice was usually left to the parishioners. Accordingly besides Presbyterians there were many Independents and a few Baptists who became incumbents, and these naturally impressed their own views on the parishes in their charge. The Commonwealth authorities never reduced this confusion to any orderly system, and though tithes maintained a precarious existence, it is clear that there was nothing that could be called a national Church. With respect to the Church as with respect to the monarchy the old order was gone, but nothing stable had taken its place.

Yet, on the doctrinal side, religion exerted triumphant authority. The episcopal system had disappeared for the time with its votaries, without leaving a great void in the hearts of the nation, because the current Calvinism of the day had become the religion of the

[1] *The Rebels' Looking Glasse*, 1649, and *A Vindication of the Presbyteriall Government and Ministry*, London, printed for C. Meredith, 1650; quotations furnished me by A. Neave Brayshaw.

[2] *Hist. of Commth. and Prot.* ii. 86.

people, and it mattered little whether it came from the lips of an Episcopalian or Presbyterian or Independent or Baptist divine. Laud had appealed, indeed, from the dogmatism of Puritanism to the cultivated intelligence for the solution of religious problems;[1] but those whom he reached were in exile, and the multitude regarded religion as a thing of doctrinal profession. The authority of doctrine, or what the first Friends called "notions," held sway as it has not done in England before or since. In the first half of the seventeenth century men seemed under a compulsion to construct a scheme of Divine truth which should satisfy the intellect. The new translations of the Bible had fertilized the world with Bible knowledge and given many an education in religious things which, in the zest of the fresh study, seemed to make them masters of Divine truth. The Bible was regarded as the one authoritative Word of God, which contained a full provision of infallible truth, and doctrinal theology became every man's occupation. We shall remember William Tindale's rejoinder to one of his acquaintances a hundred years earlier: "If God spare my life, ere many years I will cause a boy that driveth the plough shall know more of the scripture than thou doest." This general knowledge of the Bible was now diffused, and accordingly when the era passed in which the State repressed schisms and sects, it was at once succeeded by an age of controversial warfare between conflicting opinions. Polemic replaced persecution, and its virulence was at least better than the fires of Smithfield. In the keen doctrinal atmosphere of the time, a day's dispute in public between opposing combatants was the most delightful and improving of pastimes. A Puritan divine, for example, at Henley-in-Arden, would take up the cudgels against preaching without a call and argue his case with five private preachers—a nailer, a baker, a plough-wright, a weaver, and a baker's boy.[2] When Thomas Taylor, who afterwards became a Friend, disputed at Kendal in 1650 on

[1] Gardiner, *History of Great Civil War*, iii. 108.
[2] "The Pulpit guarded with XVII Arguments," London, 1651.

the subject of infant-baptism in the parish church against three other ministers, and had got the better of them, his hearers ran up Kendal Street crying, "Mr. Taylor hath got the day! Mr. Taylor hath got the day!" with an enthusiasm now reserved for the result of a game of football.[1]

With the sudden increase of polemical literature the question of the liberty of the Press sprang into importance. The Long Parliament in 1643 passed an Ordinance for the regulating of printing which called forth the most splendid of Milton's prose tracts, the "Areopagitica."

> "Though all the winds of doctrine," he says in a famous passage, "were let loose to play upon the earth, so truth be in the field, we do injuriously by licensing and prohibiting to misdoubt her strength. Let her and falsehood grapple, who ever knew truth put to the worse in a free and open encounter."

The overthrow of authority and the intense religious earnestness of the times combined during the years of toleration to produce a number of quick-growing but usually short-lived sects. We have already noticed the rise of Independency and the expansion of the Baptist movement: we must now refer to some of the less stable products of Puritanism.*

We may begin with the Fifth Monarchy men,* who pressed for the establishment of the Fifth Monarchy of Dan. ii. 44; that is, the reign of Christ and His saints, which, according to their interpretation of Daniel, was to supersede the four monarchies of the ancient world. A petition from Norfolk and Norwich was addressed to the Council of Officers in February 1649 to this effect. Gardiner says:—

> What the petitioners meant was that, as only the godly were fit to govern, the Church should be the sole depository of civil authority. Independents and Baptists were to combine to choose delegates, who were in turn to elect "general assemblies or Church Parliaments, as Christ's officers and the Church's representatives, and to determine all things by the Word, as that law which God will exalt alone and make honourable."[2]

---

[1] *Works* of Thos. Taylor, Testimony to him by R. Barrow.

[2] Gardiner, *Hist. of Commth. and Prot.* i. 29, and references elsewhere in the work.

These persons, whose ideas were embraced by a man of the importance of Major-General Harrison, were by virtue of their ruling principle opposed to Parliamentary institutions of a representative kind, but the Nominated (Barebone's) Parliament of 1653 was an attempt with modifications to put Harrison's views into practice. Cromwell, indeed, did not desire an assembly of fanatics, but a gathering of patriotic and godly Puritans. When the experiment broke down and the Nominated Parliament dispersed at the end of the year, Cromwell, now Protector, was virulently assailed by the Fifth Monarchy preachers, who had been the backbone of the advanced party in it. They continued in open or covert hostility to the Government through the rest of the Commonwealth period, and sometimes involved the Quakers in discredit, though Friends had in reality no sympathy with their views or methods. The Fifth Monarchy movement had originated among the Baptists, many of whom, especially in the army of Ireland, continued to favour it. The supersession of Fleetwood by Henry Cromwell in 1655 was aimed at the Baptists in the Irish army, whom Fleetwood, a Baptist himself, had notoriously patronized, and showed Cromwell's distrust of those officers who, in Gardiner's phrase, "arrogated to themselves the title of 'the godly.'"

The Fifth Monarchy men were the political zealots of Puritanism, but their extravagance appears sobriety compared with the obscurantist convictions of the Muggletonians, who nourished their faith out of the Apocalypse. The rise of this strange sect illuminates the situation as clearly as the early experiences of Mary Penington have done. Lodowick Muggleton was a London tailor, who became a zealous Puritan much in fear of hell-fire. He would listen to none but Puritan ministers with short-cut hair. "For," says he, "if a man with long hair had gone into the pulpit to preach, I would have gone out of the church again, though he might preach better than the other." When the Civil War began, there was, he says, a great upheaval among the religious societies. Many fell away, and declined in love towards one another. Some turned Presbyterian, others Independents, others became Ranters, and some fell to be mere atheists.

I was altogether at a loss, for all the zeal we formerly had was quite worn out. . . . For I had seen the utmost perfection and satisfaction that could be found in that way, except I would do it for loaves, but loaves was never my aim, but a real rest in my mind I always sought after, but could find it nowhere.

A year or two after the King's execution, Muggleton heard of several prophets in London, and of two persons who claimed to be greater than prophets—John Tannye, who declared himself the Lord's High Priest, and was to gather the Jews out of all nations; and John Robins, who claimed to be God Almighty and to raise the prophets from the dead. "I have had," he says, "nine or ten of them at my house at a time, of those that were said to be raised from the dead." John Robins greatly impressed Muggleton, especially by the power which he claimed for his prophets to damn any who opposed or spoke evil of him. Soon after this Muggleton and his cousin John Reeve began to have revelations of their own, and in 1652 announced themselves as the two witnesses of Revelation xi., sent, they said, to seal the elect and the reprobate with the eternal seals of life and death, after which Jesus would visibly appear in power and great glory. They add, with an earnestness insensible to humour, that "if any of the elect desire to speak with us . . . they may hear of us in Great Trinity Lane, at a Chandler's shop, against one Mr. Millis, a Brown Baker, near the lower end of Bow Lane."[1] The self-confidence of the two prophets, and the assurance with which they pronounced curses against those who rejected them, enabled them in that age of religious confusion to found a sect which lingered on as late as the year 1868, and is not yet quite extinct.[2]

[1] See title of *A Transcendent Spiritual Treatise, etc.* (1652). Smith's *Bibliotheca Anti-Quakeriana*, pp. 300-332, contains a useful bibliography of Muggletonian books.*

[2] See *The Oxford English Dictionary*, sub voce "Muggletonian," and *J.F.H.S.* vii. p. 62. For the Muggletonians see *Dict. Natl. Biography*, articles

They made headway among the religious extremists of ill-balanced minds, who were at this time numerous in London. An encounter with some Ranters shows the way in which their propagandist work was done.

"One of those Ranters," says Muggleton, "kept a victualling house and sold drink in the Minories, London, and they would spend their money there. So John Reeve and myself came there, . . . and many of them despised our declaration. . . . So John Reeve gave sentence of eternal damnation upon many of them . . . but one of them, being more offended at his damnation than all the rest, he was moved with such wrath and fury . . . that five or six men could hardly keep him off, his fury was so hot. Then John Reeve said unto the people standing by, 'Friends,' said he, 'I pray you stand still on both sides the room, and let there be a space in the middle, and I will lay down my head upon the ground and let this furious man tread upon my head.' . . . So the man came running with great fury, and when he came near him, lifting up his foot to tread on his neck, the man started back again and said, 'No, I scorn to tread upon a man that lieth down to me.'"

John Reeve died in 1658, but the other prophet lived on and, as we shall find, issued his condemnations freely against his rivals, the Quakers.

The two men whom Muggleton names, John (more correctly Thomas) Tannye and John Robins, were among the most extravagant fanatics then in London. Tannye claimed to be a Jew of the tribe of Reuben, and proclaimed the rebuilding of the temple with himself as the High Priest; he also called himself "Earl of Essex," heir to the throne and King of France. In 1651 he was imprisoned in Newgate for blasphemy, and a few years later disappeared. Muggleton says that he made a little boat to carry him to Jerusalem, and going to Holland to call the Jews there, he was cast away and drowned. John Robins is classed as a Ranter. He was a small farmer, who had sold his land and come to London, where he claimed power to raise the dead, and from

"Muggleton" and "John Reeve," and essay by A. Jessopp, "The Prophet of Walnut Tree Yard," in *The Coming of the Friars.* My details are taken from *The Acts of the Witnesses of the Spirit,* by Muggleton, 1699 edn. It is divided into chapters and verses like the Acts of the Apostles.

his extravagant claims was known as "the Ranters' God."

The Ranters* represented the revolt against authority in its extremest form. Dr. R. M. Jones, in his study of the movement, says:[1]

> Ranterism was to all intents and purposes a revival of the doctrines of the "Free Spirit." . . . There was in England in the Commonwealth era a real *contagion* of the idea of God as indwelling. Some of the stronger minds who were *possessed* with the idea were able to hold it in balance with other ideas equally true; but some unstable, ill-balanced men and women were swept quite off the poise of sanity by it, and large groups of the common people (this was essentially a movement of the common people) were carried into a cheap, half-digested "spiritualism," which bristled with dangers; as, in their ignorance of history and sound psychology, they were almost bound to be, at that stage of thought. They fell into a vague pantheism, which blurred the distinctions between good and evil, and which landed them in a moral (or immoral) topsy-turvy.

The moral laxity charged against the Ranters, no doubt with some exaggeration, brought them into much disrepute. It sharply distinguished them from the Quakers, even in the mind of so bitter an opponent as Baxter. He says:[2]

> The Quakers were but the Ranters turned from horrid profaneness and blasphemy to a life of extreme austerity on the other side. Their doctrines were mostly the same with the Ranters.

The fact is that the Ranter position afforded no test by which the individual could distinguish between the voice of the Spirit and the voice of his own will. The Quakers, on the other hand, were "Children of the Light," and insisted that there could be no guidance of the Spirit apart from a walking in the light. Accordingly their message became an antidote to Ranterism, and reclaimed many of the Ranters themselves to a truer type of spiritual religion.[3] It also supplied the need of many who might otherwise have become Ranters.

The Familists were a sect much more truly akin to

[1] *Studies in Mystical Religion*, p. 469.
[2] *Reliquiae Baxterianae* (1696 edn.), i. 77.
[3] See, *e.g.*, Geo. Fox, *Journ.* i. 95.

the Quakers.[1] Originating in Holland about 1530, they reached England about the middle of the century. Henry Nicholas, the apostle of the movement, had an experience of spiritual illumination not unlike that which came to Fox. In the Family of Love*there was an insistence on real righteousness and actual holiness, as contrasted with the fiction of a merely imputed righteousness.

"The true Light," said Nicholas, "is the everlasting life itself and . . . shows itself through illuminated, *i.e. godded* men, for through such persons the Most High is *manned* [incarnated]. The true Light therefore consists not in knowing this or that, but in receiving and partaking of the true being of the Eternal Life, by the renewing of the mind and spirit and by an incorporation of the inward man into this true Life and Light so that the person henceforth lives and walks in the Light in all love."

In addition to this common element of a deep inward experience, the Familist, like the Anabaptist and the Quaker, rejected oaths and war and capital punishment, and his position towards the Bible and towards outward rites and ceremonies was substantially the same as that taken by Friends. Moreover, like Fox, Nicholas made much of quiet waiting in silence. An extract from a statement made before a Surrey Justice of the Peace in 1561 shows a similarity also in the matter of simplicity of language, "They may not say, 'God speed, God morrow, or God even.' When a question is demanded of any, they stay a great while ere they answer, and commonly their word shall be 'Surely'[2] or 'So.'" They held that no man should be put to death for his opinions, and believed that ministers should itinerate from place to place. They believed in perfection, much as Fox did—"The same perfection of holiness which was in Adam before he fell is to be attained here in this life."

It is obvious that the Familists and the Quakers had a close affinity to one another. They were not strong in

[1] My account is abridged from Dr. R. M. Jones, *Studies in Mystical Religion*, pp. 428-448.

[2] Compare Fox's habit of using "Verily," *Journ.* i. 3. In both cases there may have been an intention to follow the example of Christ, in His characteristic use of the word "Amen."

numbers, judging from their petition to King James, which says that they are "few in number, and poor in worldly wealth," upon which Rutherford makes the comment, "Would God they were few in number, yet they are pestering twelve counties of England." We hear of them as the Etheringtonians in London, as the Grindletonians in Yorkshire, also later in the century as a small sect of threescore persons in the Isle of Ely. The channels through which they influenced George Fox* have not yet been discovered.

There is, however, at least one case of a Grindletonian afterwards becoming a Friend. Thomas Barcroft, of Colne, about the year 1656 wrote a treatise, preserved in manuscript in the Swarthmore Collection,[1]

> . . . chiefly for the service of those with whom I have had in times long past sweet society and union in spirit, in the days of that glimmering of light under the ministry of Brierely, Tonnan, and some few more, whose memories I honour,—called then by the professors of the world Grindletonians, Antinomians, Heretics, Sectaries, and such-like names of reproach, as in these days by the men of the same generation of Cain, that was a murderer, the Children of Light are in scorn called Quakers.

Roger Brereley,* perpetual curate of Grindleton Chapel, some nine miles from Colne, had been tried at York for Antinomianism but acquitted. It is clear from Barcroft's treatise that under his teaching men had been brought to a living spiritual experience very much deeper than the doctrinal religion of the day, although during the intervening twenty-five years Barcroft says that he "fed on dead things, excellent at the time of their appearance, bearing the shadow, the substance being passed." The views of the Grindletonian Familists even in the envenomed pages of old Ephraim Pagit[2] are evidently consistent with a spirituality closely resembling Quakerism. They held, for example, that "when God comes to dwell in a man, he so filleth the soul that there is no more sinful lusting."

Penn, in his Preface to Fox's *Journal* (p. xxv), classes

[1] Swarthm. Colln. i. 174.

[2] *Heresiographie*, 3rd ed. 1647, p. 101.

the Familists with the Seekers. After speaking of the rise and degeneracy of the Puritan movement, he says:

. . . that many left them, and all visible churches and societies, and wandered up and down, as sheep without a shepherd, and as doves without their mates, seeking their beloved, but could not find Him (as their souls desired to know Him), whom their souls loved above their chiefest joy. These people were called Seekers by some, and the Family of Love by others, because, as they came to the knowledge of one another, they sometimes met together, not formally to pray or preach, at appointed times or places, in their own wills, as in times past they were accustomed to do, but waited together in silence, and as anything rose in any one of their minds, that they thought savoured of a Divine spring, so they sometimes spoke.

The Seekers were, however, the product of the religious travail of the age rather than of any one religious sect, and were recruited also from Independents and Anabaptists, and from the Presbyterian and Anglican churches. As Dr. R. M. Jones says:[1]

Such persons always appear in epochs of religious unsettlement, persons who are "like doves without their mates," and who seek in earnestness for the Beloved of their souls. As soon as faith in the authority of the Church grows faint, and the sufficiency of established forms and rituals is seriously questioned, the primal right of the soul to find God Himself is sure to be asserted.

Similar tendencies in Holland produced the parallel contemporary movement of Dutch "Collegiants,"[2] the connection of which with the English Seekers is at present the subject of research by Dr. R. M. Jones, whose results will, it is hoped, appear in another volume of this series.

The term Seekers[3] is first used in England in 1617, and in 1648 we have a clear statement of their religious position from John Saltmarsh, who had himself found the deep spiritual experience of which they were in search.

[1] *Studies in Mystical Religion*, p. 452.

[2] See *Friends' Quarterly Examiner*, 1910, pp. 298-302, a summary by Isaac Sharp of Pastor Theodor Sippell's articles on the Origin of Quakerism in *Die Christliche Welt* of Marburg. Cf. *post*, p. 409.

[3] I make use of Dr. R. M. Jones's account in *Studies in Mystical Religion*, p. 452-466.*

They believed that in the Spirit-filled Apostolic Age all was administered under the anointing of the Spirit, clearly, certainly, infallibly. But now, in this time of apostasy, there were no such gifts, but only an outward ceremonial administration. Accordingly, much in the spirit of the circle of souls waiting for the redemption of Israel, among whom Christ was born, they "waited" for power from on high, finding no practice of worship according to the first pattern. They waited in prayer, not pretending to any certain determination of things, nor to any infallible interpretation of scripture. They waited for a restoration of all things, and a setting up of a Church according to the pattern in the New Testament. They waited for an Apostle, or some one with a visible glory and power, able in the Spirit to give visible demonstration of being sent.

It was Cromwell, we shall remember, who wrote in 1646 respecting his favourite daughter, Lady Claypole, "she sees her own vanity and carnal mind; bewailing it, she seeks after (as I hope also) what will satisfy. And thus to be a Seeker is to be of the best sect next to a Finder, and such shall every faithful, humble seeker be at the end."

These Seekers or Waiters, who felt the insufficiency of the current doctrinal and external religion, and were not yet brought into a deeper soul-satisfying experience, afforded the most receptive soil in England for the message of Fox. Some of them won their way for themselves into the consciousness of the indwelling Light of Christ, and on meeting with Fox or some other Quaker "Publisher of Truth,"[1] at once claimed spiritual relationship. More often the Quaker message proved like a spark falling in prepared tinder. As we shall see, the first strong group of Friends at Balby near Doncaster consisted of such a community, and the great Quaker convincement in Westmorland and North Lancashire six months later, in June 1652, was, in fact, the acceptance

[1] This title will be frequently used for the itinerating Friends with the gift of ministry who spread the Quaker message.

of Fox and his message by the important community of Seekers which had its centre at Preston Patrick. The expansion into Cumberland in the following year was largely done with the help of Seekers, and when the Quaker Publishers came south in 1654, it was from Seekers, and to a less extent Baptists, in London, Bristol, and many other places, that they gathered many of their most stable adherents. Indeed, it is not too much to say that over the part of England where Quakerism planted itself most readily the communities of Seekers had already prepared the way.

On the other hand, as Penn points out, the Seekers sometimes developed into Ranters, and it must not be supposed that the Quaker movement, except in certain districts, absorbed the Seekers *en masse*.

Friends who had been Seekers did not altogether reject the name after their convincement. Thus Francis Howgill, in reply to a violent petition to the Protector from one Thos. Ellyson, says:

> I am one thou calls a Quaker and Seeker, and blessed be the Lord for evermore that ever I was found worthy to bear the name in truth, for they that seek shall find and they that wait shall not be ashamed.[1]

The two movements, indeed, were continuous with one another. Under the new conditions of religious freedom on the one hand, and active religious controversy on the other, which prevailed in England from the assembling of the Long Parliament, there had been a sudden growth of sects, which took their shape from the light, airy imaginations, or the deep spiritual yearnings of their votaries. There were thousands of honest-hearted persons who used their freedom to make a quest after truth, and many of these found no rest either in forms or in doctrines, and whether they called themselves Seekers or not were weary with their travelling through the sects and athirst for the gospel of a living Christ. The religious climate was thus singularly favourable to the growth of Quakerism.

[1] Howgill's *Works*, p. 13.

CHAPTER II

THE FOUNDER OF QUAKERISM*

George Fox, the weaver's son, apprentice to a shoemaker and dealer in wool, had little book-learning beyond the Bible, but he had as a young man acquired first-hand knowledge of varieties of religious experience by walking through the Midlands to seek out and converse with "professors" of Puritanism in all its forms. Thus trained, he was better suited to found a new religion that should satisfy the desires of the soul than if the academic study of Hooker and Calvin had accustomed him to regard the organization of Churches and the details of dogma as matters of spiritual importance. His views, which he drew from obscure corners of his own country, had come from distant lands and ages. . . . These ideas . . . he alone was able to impress upon a large portion of mankind by the fire of his living genius.—GEORGE M. TREVELYAN, *England under the Stuarts*, p. 312.

RELIGIOUS movements develop with the help of a favouring environment, but they spring out of great personal experiences. The fresh truth roots itself in life before it can be uttered in a message. This is certainly the case with the Quaker movement of the seventeenth century. It sprang directly from the vital and vitalizing experience of its founder, George Fox,* whose purity and sincerity of nature gave his witness extraordinary force.

Fox was born in July 1624 at the little village of Fenny Drayton,* on the Leicestershire border of Watling Street.[1] His father, Christopher Fox, was a weaver, a man of standing and capacity, filling the office of churchwarden,[2] and worthily known to his neighbours and to us

[1] Most of the facts in this chapter are taken from Fox's *Journal*, as edited by Thos. Ellwood in 1694. This *Journal* ranks among the religious classics of the world. My references are to the convenient Bi-centenary edition, London, 1891, but I have corrected the text to that of the 1694 edition. Vol. i. pp. 1-41 contains Fox's early experiences. They are not in the Cambridge edition of the *Journal*, which begins, as now extant, at a later point. See Appendix A on *Journals of Geo. Fox*.

[2] *J.F.H.S.* i. 10.

by the name of "righteous Christer." His mother, whose maiden name was Mary Lago, came of good family,[1] and was "of the stock of the martyrs"—a pregnant phrase which may denote descent from one of the martyrs out of the next parish of Mancetter, Robert Glover, burnt at Coventry in 1555, or Mrs. Joyce Lewis, burnt at Lichfield in 1557.

Fox speaks of his father as "an honest man, and there was a seed of God in him," and describes his mother as "an upright woman," and they were evidently persons of consistent Christian life and character, who would train their family of five or six children in the fear of the Lord. They understood their boy's grave and serious nature, and, under sympathetic handling, the lad's character developed early.

"When I came to eleven years of age," says Fox, "I knew pureness and righteousness; for while I was a child I was taught how to walk to be kept pure. The Lord taught me to be faithful in all things, and . . . I was to keep to 'Yea' and 'Nay' in all things; and that my words should be few and savoury, seasoned with grace, and that I might not eat and drink to make myself wanton, but for health, using the creatures in their service, as servants in their places, to the glory of Him that hath created them."[2]

This agrees well with an account given of him when a man of twenty-eight:

. . . in his behaviour very reserved, not using any needless words or discourses that tended not to edification . . . very temperate in his eating and drinking, his apparel homely yet decent.[3]

He learnt self-control early, and we may think of him as a lad who had been taught to watch his words and actions carefully, and had been thrown much into communion with himself. His parents at first designed him for the ministry,

[1] Letter of Joseph J. Green, in *Friend*, 2nd Feb. 1906. A Lieutenant-Colonel Lagoe is mentioned in *Clarke Papers*, iii. pp. 74, 212, and a Colonel Lego, iv. pp. 25, 188. Joseph J. Green suggests a possible connection with the Purefoy family, whose monuments are found in the parish church. (See *George Fox*, by Dr. Thos. Hodgkin, p. 10.) Colonel George Purefoy, the squire of the parish, seems to have taken an interest in young George Fox (see *Journ.* i. 48). Possibly George had been named after him.

[2] *Journ.* i. 2.

[3] *An Encouragement early to Seek the Lord . . . in an Account of the Life and Services of Thomas Thompson*, 1708.

but finally put him to work with a shoemaker, who was also a grazier and dealer in wool, probably George Gee of Mancetter.[1] He learnt the trade of shoemaking, and, as we shall see, followed it for a time when living at Mansfield; but his master made use of him in other parts of his business, especially with sheep, "an employment," says Penn, "that very well suited his mind in several respects, both for its innocency and solitude, and was a just figure of his after ministry and service."[2]* Fox, even as a 'prentice, acquired a character for plain dealing. The people with whom he did business learnt to know that "if George says 'Verily,' there is no altering him."[3] Clearly there were the makings of a singularly pure-hearted and truth-loving character in the young man. He was laughed at sometimes, but held his way, and became esteemed for his innocency and honesty. Such a man was already sensitive to the light of truth, and when the fuller revelation came would not be disobedient to the heavenly vision.

The hour of decision came through a simple incident, momentous in its issues. When about nineteen, and on business at a fair, two Puritans, one of them a relative, asked his company over a jug of beer. After satisfying their thirst, they began drinking healths, calling for more and agreeing that whoever refused his turn should pay all. This habit of drinking others' healths to impair our own, as Camden calls it, had come into vogue, with other drinking customs, through the intercourse with the Low Countries in Queen Elizabeth's reign. In the Long Parliament days it became the custom to drink to every one at the table, and this grew into one of the chief vices of the age. Fox had never before been asked to do such a thing, least of all by high religious professors, and the inconsistency of their profession and their conduct grieved him to the heart. In his straightforward fashion, he laid

[1] See Wm. Rogers' *The Christian-Quaker*, part v. p. 48. I suggest that we should correct Rogers' Manchester to Mancetter, formerly spelt Mancestre. Cf. *J.F.H.S.* iv. p. 86; vi. p. 143; vii. pp. 2, 44, 86. In Foxe's *Book of Martyrs* the place is called Manchester.*

[2] *Journ.* Pref. xliv.

[3] *Ibid.* i. 3. See *ante*, p. 23 *n*.

a groat on the table to pay his share of the reckoning and went away, but that night he could get no sleep, and walked up and down his chamber, praying and crying to the Lord. Then a voice spoke in his heart, saying to him, "Thou seest how young people go together into vanity, and old people into the earth:[1] and thou must forsake all, both young and old, and keep out of all, and be as a stranger unto all." "Then," says Fox, "at the command of God, on the ninth day of the seventh month [Sept.] 1643, I left my relations, and brake off all familiarity or fellowship with young or old." There was a holy compulsion on his soul, driving it to leave the low levels of religious life around it, and to fulfil itself in the society of the Divine. And so in 1643, during the first doubtful years of the Civil War, Fox began his solitary quest. For the next four years he moved about from place to place, shunning as a rule both professor and profane, for fear of receiving spiritual hurt. We know little of Fox's outward circumstances, but he seems to have had some income of his own, for he says, "I had wherewith both to keep myself from being chargeable to others, and to administer something to the necessities of others."[2] His relations wanted him to marry, hoping, we may suppose, to settle him at home, but he told them he was but a lad and must get wisdom. Others thought he should join the Parliament army; one clergyman bade him take to tobacco and psalm-singing, "but," says Fox, "tobacco was a thing I did not love, and psalms I was not in an estate to sing: I could not sing." Another prescribed physic and blood-letting, but his body was so dried up that they could get no blood from him.

During these years of quest, as throughout his life, Fox showed genuine attachment to his relatives, although their wishes could not control his work. When he heard that they were troubled at his absence he returned home for a time, and a little later spent about a year in his own country. Here he had much converse with the minister Nathaniel Stephens, a Presbyterian divine eighteen

[1] It has been suggested that when Fox spoke of "old people going into the earth," he used the word in the same sense as in his letter to Ministers in America quoted in *Second Period of Quakerism*, p. 436; cf. *ibid.* pp. 410, 439.

[2] *Journ.* i. 7.

years his senior, who was a stanch defender of tithes and infant baptism, a thorough Calvinist and great in apocalyptic literature.[1] He was a man of character with the courage of his convictions, and was ejected for his nonconformity in 1662. Stephens was struck with the insight of Fox, and at first thought highly of him. The *Journal* gives one "very good, full answer" which the young man made to the question, "Why Christ cried out upon the cross, 'My God, my God, why hast thou forsaken me?'" Fox said that at that time the sins of all mankind were upon Jesus, which He was to bear and to be an offering for, as He was man, but died not, as He was God, and so dying for all men He was an offering for the sins of the whole world. But when Fox, instead of attending church, went into the orchards or fields with his Bible, Stephens lost confidence in him "for going after new lights," and his relations were distressed, "though they saw beyond the priests." It was, of course, one thing for his parents to have a deeper experience of truth than the minister of the parish, and another thing for them to dissociate themselves from public worship or approve their son's doing so. They watched his career at times with grave anxiety, but son and parents seem always to have retained their mutual affection, and when the mother died long after, in 1674, Fox was sorely stricken.

"For," he says,[2] "I did in verity love her as ever one could a mother; for she was a good, honest, virtuous, and a right-natured woman, and, when I had read the letter of her death, it struck a great weight upon my spirit and it was in a travail for a quarter of an hour, and there being people in the room saw some sudden travail upon me, though they said nothing, and when my spirit had gotten through [the travail of soul] I saw her in the resurrection and the life, everlastingly with me over all, and father in the flesh also."

---

[1] For Stephens see *George Fox*, by Dr. Thos. Hodgkin, pp. 12-14, and Joseph Smith's *Bibliotheca Anti-Quakeriana*, p. 412, and authorities there quoted; also article in *Dict. Natl. Biography*, and note in *Camb. Journ.* i. 394.*

[2] This is taken from a copy by A. R. Barclay (now in Dev. Ho. Portfolio 31) of a paper respecting the death of Mary Fox in George Fox's handwriting. See the paper in *J.F.H.S.* vii. p. 79. Fox had been in America, and had been taken to prison while on his way to visit his mother.*

The experiences of the young seeker after truth threw him more and more upon communion with God. At Barnet he often walked solitary in the Chace to wait upon the Lord. In London he found "all was dark and under the chain of darkness," and could not unburden himself even to his uncle Pickering, who was a Baptist, "and," says Fox, "they were tender then." At Mancetter he found the minister "angry and pettish"; at Tamworth the priest was accounted "an experienced man," but proved only like an empty hollow cask. At Coventry, while discoursing with Dr. Cradock, Fox chanced to set his foot on a flower-bed, at which the man was in a rage, as if his house had been on fire, and all their talk was lost.

His religious experiences he calls "openings," a significant word which shows how deliverance came to his shut-up and burdened soul by fellowship "with Christ, who hath the key, and opened the door of light and life unto me. . . . He it was that opened to me, when I was shut up and had not hope, nor faith."[1] These openings soon took him beyond the current outward religion of his day. Profession was not enough: the true believer was one who was born of God, and had passed from death to life. Learning was not enough—though commonly supposed to be—for, as he was walking in a field one Sunday, "the Lord opened unto me that being bred at Oxford or Cambridge was not enough to fit and qualify men to be ministers of Christ, and I stranged at it, because it was the common belief of people." Church-going was not enough, for though men called the churches holy ground and the temples of God, He dwelt not in temples made with hands but in men's hearts—His people were His temple and He dwelt in them.[2] The reception of ideas like these, which ran counter to the main current of thought round him, shows the sincerity and open-mindedness of Fox; but when we find that he not only entertained these revolutionary truths, but proceeded to act upon them to the full, separating himself from the organized Churches, and becoming an iconoclast, we gain some

[1] *Journ.* i. 12. [2] *Ibid.* i. 7.

measure of the simplicity and courage of the man. He was not afraid to be in a minority, if only the truth were on his side. It would, however, be a profound mistake to suppose that the convictions which were forming in Fox's mind were mere negations; on the contrary, if there was an annulling of the old, there was a bringing in thereupon of a better hope through which to draw nigh unto God. We must examine the obverses of these negations. The true believer must be born of God; the minister must have the Lord's own teaching; the place where God dwelt and manifested Himself was in men's hearts. When his relations at this time were grieved at his absence from church, he "brought them scriptures and told them, There was an anointing within man to teach him, and that the Lord would teach His people Himself."[1] Here, in the year 1647, when Fox was twenty-two, we reach the central experience out of which the Quaker message sprang. Fox now tells us that he began to regard the priests less and to look more after the dissenting people, for they had some "openings." But none among them all could speak to his condition. He continues:

> When all my hopes in them and in all men was gone, so that I had nothing outwardly to help me, nor could tell what to do, then, O then I heard a voice which said, "There is one, even Christ Jesus, that can speak to thy condition," and, when I heard it, my heart did leap for joy. . . . My desires after the Lord grew stronger, and zeal in the pure knowledge of God and of Christ alone, without the help of any man, book or writing. For though I read the scriptures that spake of Christ and of God, yet I knew Him not, but by revelation, as He who hath the key did open, and as the Father of Life drew me to His Son by His Spirit. And then the Lord did gently lead me along, and did let me see His love, which was endless and eternal, and surpasseth all the knowledge that men have in the natural state or can get by history or books: and that love did let me see myself as I was without Him. . . . I found that there were two thirsts in me, the one after the creatures to have gotten help and strength there, and the other after the Lord, the Creator, and His Son, Jesus Christ. And I saw all the world could do me no good: if I had had a king's diet, palace and attendance, all

[1] *Journ.* i. 8.

would have been as nothing: for nothing gave me comfort but the Lord by His power. And I saw professors, priests and people were whole and at ease in that condition which was my misery, and they loved that which I would have been rid of. But the Lord did stay my desires upon Himself, from whom my help came, and my care was cast upon Him alone.[1]

A passage like this takes us back to the primitive Christian experience of union with Christ. We are where Paul was when it pleased God to reveal His Son in him, and where John was when he wrote, "he that hath the Son hath the life." But in 1646 the doctrine of the great Puritan Churches—the Presbyterians, Independents, and Particular Baptists—left little room for a first-hand experience of this kind. They held that God had spoken to man through the scriptures and in the finished work of Christ; they believed that He would speak again in judgment at the second advent; meanwhile man ought not to look for further direct communication. The scriptures were the one sufficient rule of faith; no further light was needed or to be expected. The day of immediate revelation was past. But now one man in England, driven by his passion for reality, was demanding and receiving a direct experience of truth. He had sought it at the hands of man, but the sincerity of his own heart had laid bare the religious insincerity about him, and he had perforce turned from man in order to keep the integrity of his pure and tender spirit. Then in communion with his deepest self he made his great spiritual discovery. He found in his own spirit the place where a seed of Divine life was springing up, the place where the voice of a Divine teacher was being uttered, the place that was being inhabited by a Divine and glorious presence. It was the recovery for himself and for England of that immediate contact of the soul with God which had been the living experience of Jeremiah, and the early Church, and the saints of all ages. He could say with the Christian Psalmist, "the Most High clave my heart by His Holy Spirit and searched my affection towards Him, and

[1] *Journ.* i. 11.

filled me with His love. And His opening of me became my salvation . . . and I drank and was inebriated with the living water that doth not die . . . and I forsook the folly which is diffused over the earth, and I stripped it off, and cast it from me, and the Lord renewed me in His raiment and possessed me by His Light."[1] As we have seen, there were many others in England who had reached or were seeking after this experience, but here was a man who, having won truth as the prize of a great quest, would hold it precious, and give his life in glad devotion to the mission of spreading the light.

At this point in his *Journal*, Fox, quite naturally, begins to speak of his experience under two images, as a living in the light, and as a growth of the seed of God in him. The "opening" came to him,

> . . . that every man was enlightened by the Divine Light of Christ, and I saw it shine through all, and that they that believed in it came out of condemnation and came to the Light of Life, and became the children of it; but they that hated it, and did not believe in it, were condemned by it, though they made a profession of Christ. This I saw in the pure openings of the light, without the help of any man, neither did I then know where to find it in the scriptures, though afterwards, searching the scriptures, I found it.[2]

This great affirmation, that every man had received from the Lord a measure of light which, if followed, would lead him to the Light of Life, was in conflict with the current Puritan conceptions of the nature of God and of human nature. One-sided doctrines of election and reprobation had obscured the Fatherhood of God and had magnified His sovereignty at the cost of veiling His love. And, on the other hand, the line was drawn sharply between the human and the Divine. The natural man belonged to an undivine order of life, marred by the Fall, and under the dominion of Satan. In agreement with this "dualistic" conception of the universe, the Calvinistic sects of the day held that during life there was no escape from the body of sin. These ideas of the

[1] *Odes of Solomon*, No. 11, translation of Dr. J. Rendel Harris.

[2] *Journ*. i. 34.

age were part of Fox's mental environment, and had their influence, as we shall see, on Quaker thought and practice; it speaks strongly for his singleness of purpose and strength of soul that they could not assert their authority against the living witness of the Light within.

The preparation of a religious leader goes forward through much sorrow and tribulation.

"When I had openings," says Fox, "they answered one another, and answered the scriptures, for I had great openings of the scriptures; and when I was in troubles, one trouble also answered to another."[1]

A brief reference to these times of conflict* may be made. Sometimes there seemed to be two persons pleading in him, but his secret faith was firm, and, anchored on Christ, he found himself swimming above the world and its temptations. After this, he found a pure fire within him, by which he could discern what veiled him and what it was which opened him. The groans of the flesh that could not give up to the will of God or endure the cross, these had veiled him; but in the groanings of the Spirit he had been opened and had known true waiting upon God for the redemption of the body and of the whole creation. At another time in Nottinghamshire all evil natures, as those of dogs, swine, and vipers, revealed themselves in the heart of Fox, and he cried to the Lord in dismay, having never been addicted to these evils. The Lord answered him that he must have a sense of all conditions, if he was to be able to speak to all conditions.

"In this," he says,[2] "I saw the infinite love of God. I saw also that there was an ocean of darkness and death; but an infinite ocean of light and love which flowed over the ocean of darkness. And in that also I saw the infinite love of God."

A "great work of the Lord" fell upon him,[3] so that for some fourteen days he seemed to be dead, and his face and person became changed, as though his body had been remoulded. He felt that he had been brought through the very ocean of darkness and death, and through and over

[1] *Journ.* i. 9. [2] *Ibid.* i. 19. [3] *Ibid.* i. 20.

the power of Satan, and by the eternal power of God had come out of it into the power of Christ. At another time in the Vale of Belvoir, or Beavor, a great cloud came over him and shut him in with the material universe till his heart seemed to say, "all things come by nature," that is to say, according to the mode of thought of the age, there was nothing Divine about them. But as he sat still under the temptation, and let it alone, a living hope arose in him, and a true voice which said, "There *is* a Living God who made all things."[1]

Amid these chequered experiences one passage of extreme beauty reveals the ecstatic condition into which Fox was lifted by his vivid consciousness of the indwelling life of Christ.[2] It belongs to the year 1648, when he would be twenty-four years old, and is on several accounts of great importance. In reading it, we are reminded of the similar Familist and Boehmist teaching with respect to perfection.

> Now was I come up in spirit [that is, renewed up in nature[3]] through the Flaming Sword, into the Paradise of God. All things were new, and all the creation gave another smell unto me than before, beyond what words can utter. I knew nothing but pureness and innocency and righteousness, being renewed up into the image of God by Christ Jesus, so that I say I was come up to the state of Adam, which he was in before he fell. The creation was opened to me, and it was shewed me how all things had their names given them, according to their nature and virtue. And I was at a stand in my mind, whether I should practise physic for the good of mankind, seeing the nature and virtues of the creatures were so opened to me by the Lord. But I was immediately taken up in spirit to see into another or more stedfast state than Adam's in innocency, even into a state in Christ Jesus that should never fall. And the Lord shewed me that such as were faithful to Him, in the power and light of Christ, should come up into that state in which Adam was before he fell, in which the admirable works of the creation and the virtues thereof

[1] *Journ.* i. 26. See Whittier's poem on this experience, entitled "Revelation." Muggleton also was tempted to believe that "there is no God, but all things come by nature." See *The Acts of the Witnesses of the Spirit*, 1699 edn. pp. 18, 19.

[2] *Journ.* i. 28.

[3] Cf. *Ibid.* i. 41. "Christ . . . who renews up into the image of God, which man and woman were in before they fell."

may be known, through the openings of that Divine Word of wisdom and power by which they were made. Great things did the Lord lead me into, and wonderful depths were opened unto me, beyond what can by words be declared, but, as people come into subjection to the Spirit of God, and grow up in the image and power of the Almighty, they may receive the word of wisdom that opens up all things, and come to know the hidden unity in the Eternal Being.

Such a passage helps to explain much that is extraordinary in the character of Fox, the commanding impression produced by his personality, the air of authority which habitually accompanied his words and actions, the claim to an inner spiritual knowledge which he confidently made. It is clear that he regarded himself as kept through the power and light of Christ in a state of perfection like that of Adam in paradise. One significant proof of this is found in the device on his favourite seal —G. F. and the Flaming Sword.[1] To understand the passage, we must disentangle the experience from the phrases used to explain it. These illuminated the experience to the mind of Fox, with its seventeenth-century cast of thought, but somewhat darken knowledge now. He possessed as the surest fact of his consciousness a wonderful newness and purity of life, which had come to him through the indwelling life of Christ. At the same time he shared the preconceptions of his age as to the undivine order to which the natural life belongs. The Divine teaching and the Divine perfecting within him conflicted with these preconceptions, but he avoids having to surrender them by regarding his new experience as an altered human nature, renewed up into its condition before the Fall, and in that renewed state once again possessing the capacity for Divine fellowship and the innocency which fallen man had lost. If this is understood, the artificial mode of statement will no longer obscure the freshness and vividness of this culminating passage of Fox's spiritual autobiography.

We have now traced in bare outline the experience

[1] See Fox's Will, in which this seal is left to Nathaniel Meade, *Camb. Journ.* ii. 355.

that transfigured the life of the Apostle of Quakerism. Those who have read the first volume of this series[1] will be aware that the illumination which came to Fox had not been withheld from other men of transparent purity. The quest after the living God, for which the Reformation had liberated the souls of men, was continually penetrating beyond the letter of scripture to the inspiring Spirit, and bringing into the religious life of England mystical elements which went far beyond the doctrinal systems of the age. I am disposed to agree with Dr. R. M. Jones in believing "that the teachings of the Family of Love had as much to do with producing the general mystical atmosphere as any one influence had." It seems also probable[2] that the influence of Jacob Boehme's writings, which were put into English in successive volumes between the years 1644 and 1662, was considerable. The resemblance between these teachings and those of the Friends did not escape contemporary writers. Henry More, for example, the Cambridge Platonist, in his *Enthusiasmus Triumphatus* (1656), says,[3] "Ranters and Quakers took their original from Behmenism and Familism"; and Baxter, in his *Quakers' Catechism* (1655), couples together Quakers and Familists in one place and Quakers and "Behmenists" in another.[4] Thos. Taylor, who, prior to joining Friends, had been minister to the great community of Westmorland Seekers, was an admirer of Jacob Bewman, as he calls him, and in 1659 wrote:

> There is that in his writings which, if ever thy eye be opened, will appear to be a sweet unfolding of the mystery of God and of Christ in divers particulars according to his gift.[5]

But no direct contact of Familist or Boehmist influences with Fox has yet been established, nor would be likely to have been alluded to in his *Journal*, had it occurred. He may most probably have come into some knowledge of their ideas, but it is important to bear

[1] Dr. R. M. Jones, *Studies in Mystical Religion*. See, *e.g.*, p. 494

[2] *Ibid.* p. 494.

[3] 1712 edn. p. 49.*

[4] Preface B and C, 3 b.

[5] *Works*, p. 86.

in mind that these would be to him like other "notions" until they became matters of heart-experience, and when he had thus made them his own he would think no longer of their human origin, and would speak of them as "openings" of light to himself. Boehme, who died, a man of forty-nine, in the year of Fox's birth, had been, like Fox himself, born in a village, educated in the simplest way, and apprenticed to a shoemaker. Unable to endure the ribaldry of his shopmates, he had been turned out by his master, and had travelled about among the Babel of warring sects which made up the Protestant Germany of his time. Like Fox again, his experience came to him in visions and what he called "openings." He, too, had come into Paradise through the Flaming Sword, and when replenished with Divine knowledge, had sat down, "and viewing the herbs and grass of the field in his inward light, he saw into their essences, use and properties."[1] As Dr. R. M. Jones points out,[2] any knowledge of Boehme or of the Familist principles which came to Fox through the small mystical sects and the current mystical literature of the time might readily act on his spirit by way of "suggestion" and be reproduced in a vivid psychic experience which would be in his mind the sure evidence of its truth. The strong probability of influences of this kind having reached Fox does not prevent Wm. Penn's statement from being substantially true, that[3] "as to man, he was an original, being no man's copy." The religious life of the time had repelled and isolated him, and so little conscious influence was exerted upon his experience. He felt that was from no outward source, for he had turned away from men and from institutions.

[1] See Barclay's *Inner Life of the Religious Societies of the Commonwealth*, pp. 214, 215. The passage respecting the Flaming Sword is in a treatise of Boehme's published in England in 1641, the other quotation is from W. Law's *Life of Behmen* (edn. 1764). Dr. R. M. Jones promises a study of Boehme in a volume of the present series, which will no doubt deal at length with his relations to Quakerism. A good summary of Boehme's life and teaching is to be found in G. W. Allen's article on "Boehme" in Hastings' *Encyclopaedia of Religion and Ethics*, vol. ii.*

[2] *Studies in Mystical Religion*, p. 495.

[3] Preface to *Journ.* p. xlvi. Penn, however, had no personal knowledge of the early years of the Quaker movement.

It formed itself, as purely as any experience can, through meditation and the direct intercourse of his soul with God. But no man can fail to be in manifold ways the child of his age, and the religious movement which Fox began would prove itself a noble expression in life of the ideals of Puritanism and of the Reformation.

We now turn to the small beginnings of this Quaker movement. At what point, we ask, did the disciple of the Light become an apostle? In a document, written in 1676, Fox says that the Truth sprang up first in Leicestershire in 1644, in Warwickshire in 1645, in Nottinghamshire in 1646, in Derbyshire in 1647, and in the adjacent counties in 1648, 1649, and 1650.[1] In another paper he speaks of business meetings concerning the poor and to see that all walked according to the Truth, held earlier than 1650 in Nottinghamshire, Derby, and Leicester, where there was a great convincement.[2] The *Journal* again says[3] that many were turned from darkness to light in the three years 1646, 1647, and 1648, and meetings were gathered in several places. It is clear, however, from the reference to practising physic in the passage about the Flaming Sword already quoted, that as late as the year 1648 Fox was in doubt as to the work of his life, and, indeed, in one of the documents just mentioned, an experience of this year is referred to as taking place "before the Lord did send me forth to preach His everlasting gospel."[4] The beginning of propagandist work may be dated back to 1647, but not earlier. To this year apparently belong the visits to Dukinfield and Manchester, where Fox first speaks of himself as "declaring truth."[5] According to Sewel, his preaching at first chiefly consisted of a few powerful and piercing words, which might take

[1] George Fox, *Epistles*, p. 2. Also in *Camb. Journ.* ii. 338-344.

[2] Document by George Fox, "Concerning our Monthly and Quarterly and Yearly Meetings," printed in part in Barclay's *Letters of Early Friends*, p. 311. The MS. conclusion of this document, signed "G. F. Kingston-upon-Thames, 6mo. 1689," belonged to my father J. Bevan Braithwaite, but has since his death been given to the Devonshire House Library.

[3] *Journ.* i. 28.

[4] MS. conclusion of 1689 document, "Concerning our Monthly and Quarterly and Yearly Meetings."

[5] *Journ.* i. 18.

root in hearts already prepared to receive them.[1] A little later he attended a great meeting of Baptists at Broughton on the border of Leicester and Notts, which was held "with some that had separated from them, and people of other 'notions' went thither."[2] Here his mouth was opened, truth was declared, and the power of the Lord was over them all. Fox at this time seems to have been living at Mansfield, where he was following his trade,[3] and we shall hardly be wrong in connecting these separated Baptists with the community of "shattered" Baptists in Nottinghamshire, with which, as we shall see, he was now associating himself. After the Broughton meeting, he began to attract attention, and one Brown on his deathbed prophesied great things of him.[4] Fox at this time "saw the harvest white and the seed of God lying thick in the ground, as ever did wheat that was sown outwardly, and none to gather it."[5] Next year in Nottinghamshire great meetings began, and there was a mighty work of God amongst the people. At Mansfield, on one occasion, he was moved to pray in the church, and the Lord's power was so great that the house seemed to be shaken.[6] In Leicestershire several "tender" people were convinced, and many in the Vale of Belvoir, where he stayed some weeks, preaching repentance as he went.[7] We now come to his association with the "shattered" Baptists in Nottinghamshire, on which much new light is thrown by papers recently unearthed at Devonshire House.[8] A Baptist community had existed in Nottingham and the neighbourhood, which, before Fox came, had lost its spiritual life and become scattered and broken. One portion continued to meet together on the Sunday, "to play at shovel-board and to be merry," the rest became,

[1] *History* (1811 edn.), i. 23.
[2] *Journ.* i. 19.
[3] Jno. Whiting, *Persecution Exposed*, 1715 edn. p. 208, speaks of Fox working at his trade at Mansfield.
[4] *Journ.* i. 20.
[5] *Ibid.* i. 21.
[6] *Ibid.* i. 24.
[7] *Ibid.* i. 26.
[8] "Children of the Light," papers at Devonshire House (Box A, Portfolio 10). The papers were prepared for the use of the "Morning Meeting" in 1687, in order to establish the origin of the name "Children of the Light." Two of them are extracts from a work otherwise unknown to me, Oliver Hooton's *History*. As Oliver Hooton was a son of Elizth. Hooton, he was in a position to know the facts.*

like so many other groups of dissatisfied persons, a company of Separatists, unaffiliated to any sect. As early as the beginning of 1647 Fox had been attracted to these Separatists, and found them a "tender people," especially one of their number, Elizabeth Hooton of Skegby, near Mansfield.[1] The Baptists, as we have seen, allowed women to preach, and, since we are told that after leaving them she "testified against their deceit," it is probable that she had been a Baptist preacher before she became the earliest woman-preacher among Friends. She may indeed be the person referred to in Edwards' *Gangraena*[2] as follows :

> In Lincolnshire, in Holland [the low-lying district round Spalding] and those parts, there is a woman-preacher, who preaches (it's certain), and 'tis reported also she baptizeth, but that's not so certain.

She was at this time in middle life, and became one of the stanchest supporters of the new movement. In 1648 Fox came among this community, and he says:

> Returning into Nottinghamshire, I found there a company of shattered Baptists and others, and the Lord's power wrought mightily, and gathered many of them. Then afterwards I went to Mansfield and thereaway, where the Lord's power was wonderfully manifested both at Mansfield and other towns thereabouts.[3]

Oliver Hooton describes the coming of Fox from his mother's point of view. He says:

> The mighty power of the Lord was manifest that startled their former Separate meetings, and some came no more: but most that were convinced of the truth stood, of whom my mother was one and embraced it.

The community, as a whole, seems to have accepted the message of Fox, and to have formed a new association together under the appropriate name of "Children of the Light." The choice of this name—the earliest by which Friends were known—was due to Fox preaching the light of Christ as the guide to eternal life: they had not been using it as Baptists or Separatists, although

[1] *Journ.* i. 9.
[2] 1646 edn., Second Division, p. 29.*
[3] *Journ.* i. 27.

the name had been used before by some continental Baptists,[1] and was used by some of the Seekers.[2] Fox also went among the Baptist remnant who played shovel-board on Sundays. He cried against their laxity of conduct, and at last many of them were convinced, including their leader, Rice Jones.[3] These facts respecting the Nottinghamshire Children of the Light are of cardinal importance. It becomes clear that Fox, at the outset of his mission, found material ready to his hand in this broken Baptist community, and, in the most formative and plastic period of his life, impressed his influence on its members, and, in turn, was no doubt himself impressed by the Baptist point of view in matters of church-life. We have discovered the channel along which many of the Baptist influences which affected Quakerism probably came.

Rice Jones, though joining the Children of the Light for a time, was a man of unstable character, and soon returned out of the light to "dark imaginations." He went as a soldier to Worcester fight, and afterwards brought scandal upon Friends by going to Fox in Derby prison and saying to him, "Thy faith stands in a Christ that died at Jerusalem, and there was never such a thing." A false report about Fox and his followers was spread abroad in consequence of this which did great harm, though Fox "brought the power of the Lord over his imaginations and whimseys."[4] Rice Jones now drew off from the Children of the Light, carrying many of the Baptists with him. He was personally jealous of Fox, prophesying in 1654 that he was then at his highest, and would fall down as quickly as he had risen.[5] This earliest of Quaker separations is thus described: "Through neglecting the cross which the light led to, many got into an exalted spirit, and denied George Fox's testimony, and spurned against the effects of it." They considered themselves Quakers, but shirked

[1] See Barclay's *Inner Life*, pp. 262 *n.*, 273 *n.*

[2] *Studies in Mystical Religion*, p. 460.

[3] For Rice Jones (Rhys Johns) see note in *Camb. Journ.* i. 396.

[4] For this episode see the "Children of the Light" papers, *Journ.* i. 69, and *Camb. Journ.* i. 10. Cf. *post*, p. 119.

[5] *Journ.* i. 194.

the consequences of public avowal; or, as William Smith of Besthorpe wrote in one of his epistles, "these people have taken up a belief that they may keep their inward unto God, and yield their bodies to comply with outward things."[1] They became known for a time as "Proud Quakers," and for some years held their meetings at Nottingham in the Castle Yard. Friends frequently laboured with them, Nayler, George Whitehead, Hubberthorne, and Fox, but Rice Jones was generally hostile, and condemned Friends for declaring truth in the markets and churches. He grew lax in conduct, using profane language, taking the oath of abjuration, and developing Ranting tendencies, while many of his followers "were turned to be the greatest football players and wrestlers in the country." Before the Commonwealth period was over this least robust of all types of Quakerism had been re-absorbed either by Friends or by the world. Several "came to see their uncertain standing and [their] being exalted above the cross of Christ, and did really bow to the requirings of truth as it was manifest in them, and came again into sweet fellowship." Rice Jones grew poor and set up an alehouse, and John Trentham of Mansfield, who had been the other leader of the separation, turned a drunkard and died miserably.[2]

At some point, not precisely dated, in the early life of the Nottinghamshire Children of the Light, say the end of 1648 or the beginning of 1649, Fox tells us that he was commanded to go abroad into the world, which was like a briary, thorny wilderness, and when he brought the word of life to the world it swelled and made a noise like the great, raging waves of the sea.[3] He marks the period as an epoch in his life by devoting the next few pages of his *Journal* to a summary account of his message. The scope of this, as it came to him in the fresh morning of life, was much wider than has been generally recognized, universal rather than sectarian, social as well as religious, wider

[1] *Few Words unto a Peculiar People*, 1669, p. 1.*

[2] See "Children of the Light" papers; also *Journ.* i. 416; George Whitehead's *Christian Progress*, p. 121; Nayler to Fox (undated), Swarthm. Colln. iii. 75; and *Camb. Journ.* ii. 314.*

[3] *Journ.* i. 35.

than even the energy and confidence of Fox was able to compass, the programme not of the founder of a sect, but of the prophet of a new age. What did this young apostle of twenty-four set himself to do?[1]

> "I was glad," he says, "that I was commanded to turn people to that inward light, Spirit and grace, by which all might know their salvation and their way to God—even that Divine Spirit which would lead them into all truth, and which I infallibly knew would never deceive any."

And with the help of this Divine power he was to bring men off from the world's ways and worship, including "prayings and singings, which stood in forms without power," and "men's inventions and windy doctrines, by which they blowed the people about this way and the other way, from sect to sect," and "their beggarly rudiments, with their schools and colleges for making ministers of Christ," and "their images and crosses and sprinkling of infants, with all their holy-days (so-called)." But his gospel was not only a call to a living experience of Christ, which swept away the insincerities of religion; it was also a call to reality in every relation of life.

> When the Lord sent me forth into the world, He forbad me to put off my hat to any, high or low, and I was required to Thee and Thou all men and women, without any respect to rich or poor, great or small. And, as I travelled up and down, I was not to bid people "Good morrow," or "Good evening," neither might I bow or scrape with my leg to any one, and this made the sects and professions to rage.

It takes a brave man to engage in a crusade against the conventional insincerities, which we call the civilities of life, and there is no part of Fox's witness which reveals his dauntless passion for truth more clearly than this uncompromising refusal to bow down before the manifold pride of life of that ceremonious age. The emphasis laid on these matters by the early Friends may seem to us exaggerated, but we do well to remember that the discourses of our Lord include a sermon against religious ostentation (Matt. vi. 1-8), and that class distinctions are still the chief

[1] *Journ.* i. 35-41.

barrier between the organized Churches and the masses. We shall see in a later chapter how great was the cross borne by those who maintained this testimony.[1]

The spiritual illumination and downright sincerity of Fox led him to attack not only the social unrealities, but also the social abuses of his day. He had a wonderfully clear perception of moral issues, and was far before his age in denouncing prevalent forms of injustice and oppression. Accordingly, side by side with the other parts of his message, he tells us:

> About this time I was sorely exercised in going to their courts to cry for justice, and in speaking and writing to judges and justices to do justly, and in warning such as kept public-houses for entertainment that they should not let people have more drink than would do them good, and in testifying against their wakes or feasts, their may-games, sports, plays and shows, which trained up people to vanity and looseness, and led them from the fear of God—and the days they had set forth for holy-days were usually the times wherein they most dishonoured God by these things. In fairs also and in markets I was made to declare against their deceitful merchandize, and cheating and cozening, warning all to deal justly, and to speak the truth, and to let their yea be yea and their nay be nay, and to do unto others as they would have others do unto them, and forewarning them of the great and terrible Day of the Lord, which would come upon them all. I was moved also to cry against all sorts of music, and against the mountebanks playing tricks on their stages, for they burdened the pure life and stirred up people's minds to vanity. I was much exercised too with school-masters and school-mistresses, warning them to teach their children sobriety in the fear of the Lord, that they might not be nursed and trained up in lightness, vanity and wantonness. Likewise I was made to warn masters and mistresses, fathers and mothers in private families, to take care that their children and servants might be trained up in the fear of the Lord, and that they themselves should be therein examples and patterns of sobriety and virtue to them.[2]

In this important passage we find, mingled with some Puritanical disparagement of the healthy play of body and imagination, a true discernment of the principles of justice, temperance, commercial honesty, and religious

[1] See chap. xix.

[2] *Journ.* i. 39.

education. The enforcement of these principles was a definite part of Fox's mission to England. At Mansfield[1] he spoke to the justices against the oppression caused by fixing a legal wage for farm-labourers below what was equitable. The Statute of Apprentices (1563) had required the justices to do this every year at the Easter quarter-sessions, and, in so far as it was put in force, it lent itself to great oppression, although originally intended to bring the statutory wages into correspondence with the increasing cost of living.[2] When a prisoner at Derby in 1650-51 Fox saw the iniquity of the criminal law, which, among other savage features, put men to death for small thefts. He wrote to the judges, and was under great sufferings about it ; but, says he,

> . . . when I came out of it, the heavens was opened and the glory of God shined over all. And two men suffered for small things, and I was moved to admonish them for their theft [and] to encourage them concerning their suffering—it being contrary to the law of God—and a little after they had suffered, their spirits appeared to me as I was walking, and I saw the men was well.[3]

Fox, again, frequently issued warnings, especially in the early years of his work, against drunkenness and dishonesty. Copies of some of these have come down to us. One is addressed to drunkards, liars, swearers, brawlers, and those who follow dice and cards and tables and shovel-board, and tells them that they are acting contrary to the light that comes from Christ Jesus, and are condemned by it. The placard was set up at some church door or in some market-place by the itinerating enthusiast, for at the foot are the words, still vivid after two hundred and fifty years :

> Let this stand where it is stuck up, I charge you in the name and fear of the Living God, lest the plagues of God come upon you, and you that can read, read it to the people.[4]

---

[1] *Journ.* i. 27.

[2] Michael Dalton, *The Countrey Justice*, 1643 edn. p. 96, says: "The Justices of Peace (at their Easter quarter-sessions) shall do well to assess the wages in such manner as that servants, etc., may reasonably maintain themselves therewith, and that their masters should in no wise exceed or give above such wages by way of contract."

[3] *Camb. Journ.* i. 13.

[4] Dev. Ho., Boswell Middleton Colln. p. 48.

Another, addressed to fishermen, boatmen, watermen, and carpenters, and all tradesmen and professors who swear, drink, fight, and cheat, is couched in similar terms and ends very much in the same way.[1] A third warning is to be set upon the doors of steeple-houses, "which the world calls their church," and says in blunt language:

> God is not worshipped here: this is a temple made with hands: neither is this a Church, for the Church is in God. This building is not in God, neither are you in Him, who meets here.[2]

We must think of Fox, then, as finding in the indwelling life of Christ which came to him a light which gave a new illumination and interpretation to all the facts of life. The experience involved a readjustment of all other knowledge; it scattered shams and falsehoods, and left the young prophet face to face with realities, till he saw that every relation of life was religious, every act sacramental in its significance. He combined in a singular degree the burning zeal of the enthusiast with the magnetic force of a born ruler of men, and though he would not be able to realize his spiritual vision on the universal scale, he would succeed in embodying it, with wonderful completeness, in the lives of thousands, who, under his teaching, would become "Children of the Light."

[1] Dev. Ho., Saml. Watson Colln. p. 25.
[2] Dev. Ho., Boswell Middleton Colln. p. 113.

CHAPTER III

PIONEER WORK

(1649–1652)

The Quaker religion which [Fox] founded is something which it is impossible to overpraise. In a day of shams, it was a religion of veracity, rooted in spiritual inwardness, and a return to something more like the original gospel truth than men had ever known in England. So far as our Christian sects to-day are evolving into liberality, they are simply reverting in essence to the position which Fox and the early Quakers so long ago assumed.—WM. JAMES, *Varieties of Religious Experience*, p. 7.

There is room yet for the teaching of the Inward Light, for the witness of a Living God, for a reinterpretation of the Christ in lives that shall convict the careless, language that shall convince the doubting. The dust of a busy commerce hides the Cross. The Christ of the people is but a lay-figure draped in a many-coloured garment of creeds, and, worshipping the counterfeit of its own creation, the world sins on.—JNO. WILHELM ROWNTREE, *Essays and Addresses*, p. 75.

WE have now reached the opening year of the Commonwealth, 1649. Fox has already become the leader of the Nottinghamshire Children of the Light, and is about to address himself to the harder work of proclaiming his message to a scoffing world. It is not surprising to find that his first strength was directed against what he felt to be the crying evil of the day, religious insincerity. It outraged his whole being, and, in hot revolt against it, he forgot his charity.

"The black earthly spirit of the priest," he says,[1] "wounded my life, and, when I heard the bell toll to call people together to the steeple-house, it struck at my life, for it was just like a market-bell, to gather people together that the priest might set forth his ware to sale."

And so it came to pass that, as he went to a meeting

[1] *Journ.* i. 41.

at Nottingham one Sunday morning, and saw the town from the top of a hill, the church of St. Mary seemed to him as a great idol against which he must cry.[1] The mighty power of the Lord was amongst the Friends in their meeting, but Fox after a time went off to the church. The congregation seemed to him like fallow ground, and the minister stood in his pulpit above like a great lump of earth. His text was from 2 Peter i. 19, "We have also a more sure word of prophecy; whereunto ye do well that ye take heed, as unto a light that shineth in a dark place, until the day dawn, and the day-star arise in your hearts." The preacher, fairly enough, explained the sure word of prophecy as the scriptures, and went on to say that they were the touchstone and judge, and were to try all doctrines and appease and end controversies.[2] At this the young enthusiast, carried away by "the Lord's power," as he styles it, cried out, "Oh no, it is not the scriptures," and with rapt voice spoke of the Holy Ghost, that gave forth the scriptures, as the judge and touchstone of them, greatly to the amazement of the congregation, who "could not get it out of their ears for some time after, they were so reached by the Lord's power in the steeple-house."

The law as to the disturbance of public worship was much less stringent than is the case to-day; it did not extend to remarks made after the sermon was over—a licence often made use of by Friends and others—but an act of Mary (1 Mar. st. 2, cap. 3) punished the malicious disturbance of a preacher in his sermon, and accordingly Fox was had before the magistrates, who committed him for trial at the assizes. It is interesting to note that the sheriff, John Reckless, in whose custody he was placed, became a Friend.[3] When the assizes came on, some one, whose name is not given, was moved to offer up himself body for body on behalf of Fox, the

[1] *Journ.* i. 42.

[2] I take this sentence from the (so-called) *Short Journal*, 1, 2, in the Devonshire House Library. As to the nature of this document see Appendix A on *Journals of Geo. Fox.*

[3] *Journ.* ii. 78. For Reckless see note in *Camb. Journ.* ii. 405.*

first of a series of similar acts of self-sacrificing love which adorn the early annals of Quakerism. The offer was superfluous, for by an oversight Fox was not brought into court till the judge was risen, and soon after the assizes he was released. He was still a good deal at Mansfield, where the meetings of the Children of the Light were much disturbed by "wild people,"[1] who joined with the Puritans in accusing them of witchcraft and of being false prophets and deceivers.

The new movement, with its unsparing iconoclasm, its shakings and tremblings of those under the power of the Lord, its strange cases of healing, and, above all, the occasional raptures of its young leader, gave colour to this opinion. Fox, for example, at Atherstone, within a few miles of his birthplace, goes into the church, and,

> ". . . as I stood among the people," he says,[2] "the glory and life shined over all, and with it I was crowned: and, when the priest had done, I spake to him and the people the truth and the light . . . and it set them in a hurry and under a rage, and some said I was mad, and spoke to my outward relations to tie me up, and set them in a rage, but the truth came over all, and I passed away in peace."

At Mansfield-Woodhouse, near Mansfield, when he spoke in the church, the congregation fell on him in a great rage, beat him with their hands, Bibles, and sticks, and nearly smothered him. They then put him in the stocks, and afterwards stoned him out of the town.[3] He soon found himself in more serious trouble. On Wednesday, 30th October 1650, Fox attended a "lecture" at Derby, and when the minister had done, spoke "of the truth, and the Day of the Lord, and the light within them, and the Spirit to teach and lead them to God."[4] He and his two companions were taken into custody, and charged with blasphemy before two magistrates of high standing, Gervase Bennett and Colonel Nathanael Barton,* the two men who became Members for Derbyshire

[1] See incident in *Short Journ.* 2.
[2] *Short Journ.* 13, and, less fully, *Journ.* i. 48. Cf. Mark iii. 19–21.
[3] *Journ.* i. 45.
[4] *Short Journ.* 4, 5, and *Journ.* i. 50.

in the Nominated (Barebone's) Parliament of 1653.[1] Under the Blasphemy Act of August 1650,[2] which had just come into force, an offence was committed where any person (1) affirmed himself or any other mere creature to be very God, or to be infinite or almighty or equal with God, or that the true God or the eternal Majesty dwelt in the creature and nowhere else, or (2) affirmed that acts of gross immorality were indifferent or even positively religious. Fox was examined for eight hours, mainly under the first branch of this Act. He says:

> The power of God was thundered among them, and they flew like chaff, and they put me in and out from the first hour to the ninth hour at night in examinations, having me backward and forward: and said that I was taken up in raptures, as they called it, and so at last they asked me whether I was sanctified? And I said, Sanctified? Yes, for I was in the paradise of God. And they said, Had I no sin? Sin? said I, He hath taken away my sin (viz. Christ my Saviour), and in Him there is no sin.[3]

The magistrates, relying probably on unguarded phrases which Fox may have used, and strongly impressed with the dangerous tendency of his opinions, held that he had confessed an offence, and, under the powers of the Act, committed him to prison for six months, which extended to nearly a year till the early part of October 1651, as he would not allow his relatives to become surety for his good behaviour. During this year he was offered a captaincy, a striking tribute to his qualities of leadership, and on refusal was put for a time into the dungeon, a low place in the ground, amongst the rogues and felons. His answer to this offer gives shortly the ground of the well-known Quaker testimony against war.

> "I told them," he says,[4] "I knew from whence all wars did arise, even from the lust, according to James his doctrine [Jas. iv. 1, 2], and that I lived in the virtue of that life and power that took away the occasion of all wars."

---

[1] The mayor also took part, though he did not sign the "mittimus," or commitment warrant, given in *Journ.* i. 51.

[2] 1650, cap. 22. Scobell's *Collection of Acts and Ordinances*, London, 1658, pt. ii. p. 124.

[3] *Camb. Journ.* i. 2.

[4] *Journ.* i. 68.

Later in the year, when Charles and the Scottish army were marching south to their defeat at Worcester, Fox was pressed for a soldier, and again refused to serve.

The imprisonment at Derby had some notable effects. The odium of the charge against Fox had greatly troubled his relations,

> "for," he says,[1] "they looked upon it to be a great shame to them for me to be in gaol: and it was a strange thing to be imprisoned then for religion, and some thought I was mad, because I stood for purity and perfection and righteousness."

Many who had been impressed by his message[2] turned aside because of the persecution, amongst others, his fellow-prisoner, John Fretwell of Stainsby (between Chesterfield and Mansfield), who, however, revived his service with Friends at a later date.[3] Margaret Fox says,[4] "Very few . . . stood firm to him when persecution came on him." The new movement, indeed, had as yet little strength. The Children of the Light in Nottinghamshire were discouraged, but Fox himself only gathered intenser spiritual fires from his enforced quiescence. The current teaching about sin especially stirred him, and he writes:[5]

> I saw that when the Lord should bring me forth, it would be as the letting of a lion out of a den amongst the wild beasts of the forest. For all professions [that is, religious sects] stood in a beastly spirit and nature, pleading for sin and for the body of sin and imperfection, as long as they lived.

The idolizing of churches was also much on his mind as a thing which he must publicly protest against.[6] When Fretwell forsook him his spirit was "doubled" upon him, and he felt himself as a king set for the defence of the faith that gives victory, the hope that purifies, and the belief that brings men from death into life.[7] His exalted spiritual condition is shown in the strange episode that followed the

[1] *Camb. Journ.* i. 10.
[2] *Journ.* i. 61. Fox uses the word "convinced," but he seems often to use this of the immediate impression made rather than of a permanent and settled convincement.
[3] Farnsworth to Fox, 1653, in Swarthm. Colln. iii. 52; cf. *Short Journ.* 5.*
[4] Testimony to Fox in *Journ.* ii. 511.
[5] *Journ.* i. 76.
[6] *Ibid.* i. 90.
[7] *Short Journ.* 4 and *Camb. Journ.* i. 3.

Derby imprisonment.[1] Walking in a close one winter's day with some friends he saw the three spires of Lichfield Cathedral, and they struck at his life.* As soon as his friends had left him he went by eye over hedge and ditch till he came within a mile of the city, and there leaving his shoes with some shepherds, went on in his stockings* up and down the streets and through the market—it being market-day —crying, "Woe unto the bloody city of Lichfield."

"And," says Fox, "no one laid hands on me, but as I went thus crying through the streets, there seemed to me to be a channel of blood running down the streets, and the market-place appeared like a pool of blood. Now when I had declared what was upon me and felt myself clear, I went out of the town in peace, and, returning to the shepherds, gave them some money, and took my shoes of them again. But the fire of the Lord was so in my feet and all over me that I did not matter to put on my shoes any more, and was at a stand whether I should or no, till I felt freedom from the Lord so to do, and then, after I had washed my feet, I put on my shoes again."

Fox says that at the time he did not know why he had been sent to cry against Lichfield, but when he afterwards learnt, out of John Speed's *Chronicle* or some such source, that a thousand Christians had been martyred there* in the time of the Emperor Diocletian, then he understood. This *ex post facto* explanation, with the help of a piece of unreliable history, is of course worthless. The fact would seem to be that, as had been the case at Nottingham, the sight of the spires threw him into a fever of spiritual exaltation, and the nearer view of the cathedral, scarred and ruined from the Civil War, suggested to his deeply sympathetic nature the blood-guiltiness of the city. The woe he uttered was more dramatic in its setting but not more unsparing in its language than the woe which he had given forth from his prison against the pride and vain profession of Derby.[2] A great judgment

[1] *Journ.* i. 77. The *Camb. Journ.* adds one or two details, i. 15.

[2] *Journ.* i. 76; and passage in *Camb. Journ.* i. 9. My friend, A. Neave Brayshaw, suggests that he had a subconscious horror of Lichfield, dating from his early childhood, when his mother, Mary Lago, "of the stock of the Martyrs," must have told him of the martyrdom there of Mrs. Joyce Lewis (see *ante*, p. 29), and probably of Wightman, burnt in the same city only twelve years before Fox's birth.

he had then felt was upon the town, and he had seen the power of God go away from it, as the waters ran off from the town dam when the flood-gates were up. Fox, indeed, at this period felt himself arrayed in the light and truth and glory of the Lord against a hardened world, and, like Jeremiah (xx. 9), could have said, "There is in mine heart as it were a burning fire shut up in my bones, and I am weary with forbearing, and I cannot contain."

Before leaving the Derby imprisonment there is one last point to note. When examined before the magistrates Fox and his followers were called Quakers by Gervase Bennett, and the derisive name at once came into vogue. We find the word used as early as the year 1647,[1] not of Friends, but of

> . . . a sect of women (they are at Southwark) come from beyond sea, called Quakers, and these swell, shiver and shake, and, when they come to themselves,—for in all this fit Mahomet's Holy Ghost hath been conversing with them—they begin to preach what hath been delivered to them by the Spirit.

Fox says that Justice Bennett gave the nickname because Fox had bidden them tremble at the name of the Lord.[2] Barclay, on the other hand, tells us that the name came from the trembling of Friends under the powerful working of the Holy Ghost.[3] There is no real inconsistency between the two accounts. Fox gives the words of his own which led to Bennett's retort, but Barclay correctly states, as the 1647 extract shows, what must have been in Bennett's mind when he applied the scornful epithet to Fox. The name almost at once found its way into print in a tract

[1] Cited from Clarendon MSS. No. 2624, per *The Oxford English Dictionary*, sub voce "Quaker." Tradition records that when questioned on the subject of inspiration Mohammed said that sometimes it affected him "like the ringing of a bell, penetrating my very heart, and rending me as it were in pieces." See Smith and Wace, *Dict. of Christian Biography*, iii. 963.

[2] *Journ.* i. 58. But in *Great Mistery*, pp. 61, 110, he accepts the word as meaning "tremblers," saying that Bennett first gave the name, "though the mighty power of the Lord God had been known years before," and "quaking and trembling we own, though they in scorn calls us so." In the *Cambridge Journ.* i. 5-8 there is a strongly-worded letter from Fox to Bennett as "given up to misname the saints." Cf. *post*, p. 119.

[3] *Apology*, prop. 11, sect. 8; cf. Wm. Penn, *Serious Apology*, 1671, p. 12.

published in London early in 1652 called "The Pulpit guarded with XVII Arguments."[1]

Wider service in the North of England now opened before Fox. He tells us that after his release from Derby, his relations, presumably his parents, were offended at him.[2] The Fenny Drayton minister, Stephens, had before the Derby imprisonment spread a wild rumour to the effect that he had been taken up into the clouds with a whirlwind, and afterwards had been found full of gold and silver,[3] which had caused his relations to write asking him to come and show himself. They had visited him at Derby, and had tried to take him home with them, offering to be surety for his good behaviour.[4] They had come again to see him when he was thrown into the dungeon among rogues and felons, and were clearly much distressed at his proceedings,[5] as were also some of those with whom he had associated in religious fellowship.

It is probable that this closing of doors for work in Nottinghamshire and Leicestershire may have influenced Fox in going north into Yorkshire, and there is some evidence that when in Derby he had been in correspondence with the group of Seekers near Doncaster, at Balby, Warmsworth, and Tickhill, who now gave a welcome to the new movement.[6] I have called them Seekers, but the name is hardly emphatic enough, for they had already found the light. It was from Scrooby, ten miles south of Doncaster, that the Pilgrim Fathers had sought in Leyden, and afterwards in the American "wilderness," the religious freedom that was denied them at home, and now

[1] P. 15, "We have many sects now abroad, Ranter[s], Seekers, Shakers, Quakers, and now Creepers"; and p. 29, "Enthusiasts, Seekers, Shakers, Quakers, Ranters, etc." Cf. Alex. Gordon in *J.F.H.S.* ii. 70. The preface is dated Jan. 1, 1651, that is, 1652 New Style.*

[2] *Journ.* i. 79. His parting letter to them is perhaps preserved in Fox's *Epistles*, No. 5.

[3] See *Short Journ.* 4, *Camb. Journ.* at the beginning, and cf. *Journ.* i. 206. His relations seem to have known that when he left them he had a great deal of gold and silver about him.

[4] *Journ.* i. 62.

[5] *Ibid.* i. 69.

[6] The Swarthmore Colln. iii. 53, contains a letter from Farnsworth to Fox early in 1653, which says: "I sent those letters to thee that thou desired to have, which was written when thou was in prison at Derby." Jno. Leake of Selby had visited him there. See *Journ.* i. 80.

from the same district Quakerism was furnished with its first strong centre of life. Fox simply tells us that, passing into Yorkshire, he preached repentance through Doncaster and several other places, and afterwards came to Balby. The chief persons in the group that now accepted his message were Richard Farnsworth, Thomas Aldam and his wife Mary, and John and Thomas Killam and their wives Margaret and Joan, who were both sisters of Thomas Aldam. Farnsworth became, next to Fox, the chief leader in the North of the new movement. He came from Tickhill, and was a man of good education. When a lad of sixteen the Lord's work began in him,[1] and he became zealous in hearing sermons and in Bible reading and prayer. He learnt chapters of the Bible by heart, wrote out sermons, and repeated "duty" at night, and, he says, "could have persecuted even unto death those that were licentious and did not walk exactly as I did." In his early manhood there was no more ardent Puritan and Roundhead in the district. But, when about twenty or twenty-one, questions began to arise in his mind and disturb his religious complacency. Through the light of God in his conscience and the concurring testimony of scripture he came to see that the Church was not a house built of stone but was made out of living stones, and that the ministers were often merely formal in their prayers and sermons, so that their preaching was "as the telling of a tale, or a boy that saith over his week's work at the school." After this he saw that the sprinkling of infants was a carnal thing, and, though he continued to take the communion, he found no benefit in it, and his soul longed after the living Bread. He was now called Independent, Brownist, Separatist, and the like, and was in great spiritual conflict for nearly a year. He ran after priests, high in "notion," but found no peace. The righteous law was set up in him, and the curses rang in his ears, "Cursed, cursed, cursed art thou ; for thou dost not continue in all things that are written in the book of the law,

[1] The name is sometimes given as Farnworth. For his early spiritual experiences see *The Heart Opened by Christ*, May 1654.

to do them." The ministers condemned him and other tender persons, soldiers and others that feared God, and when they found them speaking two and three together called them Independents, Sectaries, and Tub-preachers. Farnsworth left off going to church, and began to wait upon the Lord for teaching, counsel, and direction.

Thomas Aldam of Warmsworth had a somewhat similar experience. He, too, had been a zealous Puritan, but had become a Separatist, waiting on the Lord. Then the revelation came to him. The power and spirit of God caused his bones to shake and his limbs to tremble. He saw how formal his religion had been, and felt himself a child of wrath. After this a promise of mercy came to him if he repented. He laid hold on the promise, and, as he gave himself up to be guided by God, it was shown him "that the Lord alone was the teacher of His children, that the word was in my heart, and that the scripture was the testimony of that word."[1] It is evident that Farnsworth and Aldam, and probably the other members of the group, had reached the Quaker experience before Fox came among them. This strengthens the likelihood that they had invited him into Yorkshire, having met him or heard of him in the adjoining county of Nottingham. They threw themselves earnestly into the new movement, and seem to have organized meetings at once, if, indeed, they were not already banded together as a community of Children of the Light.

It was no doubt at the instance of this Balby group that Fox now went on by Cinderhill Green, near Sheffield, to Lieutenant Roper's house near Stanley, a few miles north of Wakefield.[2] Here James Nayler and Thomas Goodaire* came to see him, and at one evening meeting William Dewsbury and his wife Ann came, and afterwards joined Fox as he walked in the fields in the moonlight and confessed Truth and received it.[3] These accessions

[1] See *Biographical Memoirs of Friends*, by Edwd. and Thos. J. Backhouse and Thos. Mounsey (1854), pp. 64-69, and *Short Testimony*, by his son Thos. Aldam, 1690.

[2] Fox's Testimony to Wm. Dewsbury in Wm. Dewsbury's *Works*. Thos. Stacey, of Cinderhill Green, was probably convinced at this time.

[3] *Ibid.*

were as important as those at Balby. James Nayler's career, both in its lights and shadows, is of the utmost significance to any one who desires a true understanding of early Quakerism, and until his fall he was the ablest speaker and one of the most trusted leaders of the movement. His final repentance and recovery rank among the great personal experiences in Church-history. Nayler came from the neighbouring village of West Ardsley or Woodkirk, and belonged to the yeoman class.[1] He was some eight years older than Fox, and during his eight or nine years in the Parliamentary army had served as quarter-master under Major-General Lambert in Scotland, who found him "a man of a very unblameable life and conversation."[2] There is a singular anecdote of his earnestness, which, if correctly reported, shows that he made Quakers before he was one himself.[3] One of Cromwell's officers, riding in Scotland at the head of his troop after the battle of Dunbar (3rd Sept. 1650), found Nayler preaching to the people,

> ". . . but with such power and reaching energy," he says, "as I had not till then been witness of. I could not help staying a little, although I was afraid to stay, for I was made a Quaker, being forced to tremble at the sight of myself. I was struck with more terror before the preaching of James Nayler than I was before the battle of Dunbar. . . . I clearly saw the cross to be submitted to, so I durst stay no longer, but got off and carried condemnation for it in my own breast. The people there, in the clear and powerful opening of their states, cried out against themselves, imploring mercy, a thorough change and the whole work of salvation to be effected in them."

It is not surprising that to a man of this fervency of spirit the call of the Lord to service came after he had left the army and resumed his yeoman life. The story of this immediate revelation of God to his soul was told in January 1653 to the astonished Puritan magistrates at

[1] *Journ.* i. 107, and *F.P.T.* 291; also Nayler, *Works*, p. 14. He was son of goodman Nayler, "goodman" being the regular designation of a yeoman. He calls himself a husbandman, *Works*, p. 12.

[2] At Nayler's Trial. See Burton's *Diary*, i. 33.

[3] In Jas. Gough's *Memoirs*, 1781 edn. p. 56 (ex relatione James Wilson of Kendal), cited in Barclay's *Diary of Alexander Jaffray* (2nd edn.), p. 543.

Appleby, who had not believed such an experience possible, and one of them, Anthony Pearson, was convinced as he sat on the bench.[1] It runs as follows:

Nayler. I was at the plough, meditating on the things of God, and suddenly I heard a Voice, saying unto me, "Get thee out from thy kindred and from thy father's house." And I had a promise given in with it. Whereupon I did exceedingly rejoice, that I had heard the Voice of that God which I had professed from a child, but had never known him.

Col. Briggs. Didst thou hear that Voice?

Nayler. Yes, I did hear it, and when I came at home, I gave up my estate [and] cast out my money, but, not being obedient in going forth, the wrath of God was upon me, so that I was made a wonder to all, and none thought I would have lived. But, after I was made willing,[2] I began to make some preparation, as apparel and other necessaries, not knowing whither I should go, but, shortly afterward, going agateward[3] with a friend from my own house, having on an old suit, without any money, having neither taken leave of wife or children, not thinking then of any journey, I was commanded to go into the west, not knowing whither I should go, nor what I was to do there, but, when I had been there a little while, I had given me what I was to declare, and ever since I have remained, not knowing to-day what I was to do to-morrow.

Col. Briggs. What was the promise that thou hadst given?

Nayler. That God would be with me, which promise I find made good every day.

Col. Briggs. I never heard such a call as this is in our time.

Nayler. I believe thee.

In another place he says that he was "sent out without bag, or scrip, or money, into the most brutish parts of the nation, where none knew me, yet wanted I nothing."[4]

We notice no special reference to Fox in the above account, and it seems likely that Nayler also was travelling for himself the pathway of Quaker experience, and was ready at once to take up fellowship with the Children of the Light. When he joined the new movement he was

[1] Nayler's *Works*, pp. 12, 13. Also in Besse, *Sufferings*, ii. 4.
[2] I conjecture that Nayler's talk with Fox came at this point.
[3] *I.e.* "on the road."
[4] *Works*, p. 186.

excommunicated by the Independent Church to which he had belonged.[1]

Dewsbury, perhaps the sweetest and wisest of the early Friends, was a man of about the same age as Fox. When a boy of eight,[2] he became aware of his moral responsibility, and began to read the Bible and to mourn and pray to God, thinking Him without in the sky, but feeling His hand within executing judgment upon the evil in him. In vain he sought relief from this condemned state by the way of strict religious observance. The lad was a native of Allerthorpe, in the East Riding, and, like Fox, was put to mind sheep, where he was left much to himself and found his great ease in mourning to a God whom he knew not. Hearing of strict Puritans at Leeds, he gladly went to Holbeck as apprentice to a clothmaker. He found much preaching and profession, but met with none who could tell him what God had done for their souls. He went to hear one man after another, without finding peace, and the Flaming Sword, the righteous law of God, still cried in him for a perfect fulfilling of its requirings. He took the Bread and Wine, but the evil of his heart still stood before him, and he believed himself a traitor to his Master like Judas, until it was showed him that the seal of the covenant was the Spirit of Christ, and not the outward elements, and the true Supper was the body and blood of Christ of which the world knew nothing. The same overpowering sense of evil in his heart silenced his Psalm-singing, for he was not in David's condition. His inward struggles so prostrated him that he was unable to do his full work, and his master thought he was fallen into a consumption. The Civil Wars were now beginning, and the ministers were crying, "Curse ye Meroz, because they went not forth to help the Lord against the mighty." Young Dewsbury joined the army, willing to give his body to death in obedience to God, so that he might free his soul from sin and escape the wrath

[1] *Journ.* i. 107. Nayler addressed a letter to them, given in his *Works*, p 697. See also *Congregational Historical Society Transactions*, March 1903 article by Rev. Bryan Dale on "James Nayler, the Mad Quaker." *

[2] *Works*, pp. 45-55, annotated carefully with scripture references.

under which he lay. But in the army no one told him of the true gospel, of Christ who is the glad tidings to sinners; but the letter of scripture was their gospel, and his soul found no rest. Then he heard of the Reformed Scottish Church, and travelled to Edinburgh, but only found formality. Next he sought the Anabaptists and Independents, yet still the witness of Divine love for which he yearned was wanting. And now the Lord discovered to him that His love could not be attained in any outward ways, as though the Kingdom of Heaven came by observation or the Word of the Lord was to be had from men. His mind was turned within to the light in his conscience, to hear what God Himself would say. And he was taught that the Kingdom of Christ was within, and the enemies were within and were spiritual, and must be fought spiritually with the power of God. He could no longer fight with an outward sword against an outward king in defence of an outward gospel, and left the army, returning to his trade. His will was brought into subjection, he says,

> . . . for the Lord to do with me what His will was, if He condemned me, He might, and, if He saved me, it was His free love. . . . And the cry of my condemned soul was great, and could not be satisfied, but breathed and thirsted after Christ to save me freely through His blood, or I perished for ever, and in this condemned estate I lay waiting for the coming of Christ Jesus, who, in the appointed time of the Father, appeared to my soul, as the lightnings from the east to the west, and my dead soul heard His voice and by His voice was made to live.

This was in the year 1645. He still found himself under the power of sin, feeling, like Paul, a law in his members warring against the law of his mind, until in the year 1651, perhaps through help from Fox, he knew the power of the Lord to free him, by purging away the evil nature that held him in bondage, and leading him into the new Jerusalem, "where," he says in apocalyptic phraseology, "my soul now feeds upon the tree of life, which I had so long hungered and thirsted after, that stands in the paradise of God, where there is no more curse nor night, but the Lord God and the Lamb is my Light and Life for ever and ever." As we read this artless autobiography of a soul's search after a living God, the uncompromising sincerity of the man shines out as clearly as in the case of Fox, and though there is a much stronger consciousness of sin, the issuing experience is all the greater for the long discipline of self-humiliation and patient endurance of darkness which had preceded it. Dewsbury, too, had won his way for himself to the Quaker experience.

From Lieutenant Roper's Fox rode to Selby, visiting John Leake, who had been to see him in Derby prison, and was convinced. At this place he left his horse, feeling it to be his duty to go to some of the principal houses to admonish and exhort the people to turn to the Lord.[1] It was now the month of December 1651, and during the weeks that followed the young prophet trudged with untiring energy over the East and North Ridings, urged forward by the compelling force of his great message. Although Carlyle, with some truth, says of Fox, "George dates nothing, and his facts everywhere lie round him like the leather-parings of his old shop," there is evidence at this period that his *Journal* is based on well-kept memoranda, which allow us, with the help of one or two clear dates, roughly to trace his itinerary week by week.[2] We can follow his travels by Selby to Beverley and Cranswick, then through York to Borrowby, and so by Stokesley through Cleveland to the coast at Staithes, after which he passed to Whitby and Scarborough and over the Wolds to Malton and Pickering, going from Pickering among the Moors to the place where he sat on a haystack and spoke nothing for some hours for he was to famish his hearers from words, then

[1] *Journ.* i. 80.

[2] The certain dates are: (*a*) Monday 22nd Dec., Fox lies out all night on a haystack, the day before he reaches York, *Journ.* i. 83. (*b*) March 1652, he is at Oram or Ulrome, *Journ.* i. 96; and for the date, *F.P.T.* 293. (*c*) May 1652, Thos. Aldam's imprisonment, *Journ.* i. 106, determined by fact of his release after two years and seven months confinement on 7th Dec. 1654; Aldam to Margt. Fell, Swarthm. Colln. iii. 37. (*d*) Whitsunday, 6th June 1652, Fox is at Sedbergh; see *F.P.T.* 242. For Stokesley, see *Short Journ.* 9; for Scarhouse, *F.P.T.* 305; for Dent and Garsdale, *F.P.T.* 329.

again to Cranswick, and so to the coast at Ulrome and through Holderness, that "dark corner of the world,"[1] to the land's end, then back by Hull to Balby, and, after a short round in Lincolnshire, back a third time to Balby, and on by Wakefield and Bradford to Pendle Hill and the people beyond who were to be gathered. From Pendle Hill he passed into the Yorkshire dales, preaching repentance through Wensleydale, Langstrothdale (where he stayed at Scarhouse), Dentdale, Garsdale, and Grisedale, till he entered on a new era of work at Sedbergh. He must have travelled on horseback or afoot some seven hundred and fifty miles, and often roughed it at night, so that, he says, a report was raised "that I would not lie on any bed, because at that time I lay many times without doors."[2] His privations were great: a night in a haystack in rain and snow, a day's journey through deep snow, a vigil sitting among furze bushes till it was day, another night under a haystack, footsore and weary, a night with three companions under a hedge,—such were some of the experiences of these months. He was dressed in leathern breeches and doublet,[3] and a white hat, the leathern dress being chosen for its simplicity and durability. The rhapsody of Carlyle in *Sartor Resartus* somewhat exaggerates the singularity of this dress, but it no doubt heightened the effect that was produced by Fox's extraordinary personality. An intense spiritual vitality possessed him, so that when he spoke in Beverley church it seemed to one of the hearers as though an

[1] So styled by Dr. Richd. Fiddes, Rector of Halsham, 1696; see Poulson's *Holderness*, ii. 383.

[2] *Journ.* i. 98.

[3] See a paper in Dev. Ho., Portfolio 10, No. 41, which is now printed in *J.F.H.S.* vii. p. 78; also Croese, who, in his *Historia Quakeriana*, 1695, pp. 34, 35, says, "Ac tanquam si sui calciolarii et coriarii operam pristinam oblivisci aut nequiret aut nollet, visus ad multum tempus obambulare, ac suum concionandi opus peragere, vestitus totus coriaceus, ob quam rem ei diu adhaesit nomen 'viri coriacei.'" Sewel, *History*, 1811 edn. i. 20, confirms this. For the leather breeches see further *Journ.* i. 89; *Camb. Journ.* i. 52, 170; and *An Answer to John Wiggan's Book*, 1665, pp. 123, 136, 137. For the hat see *Camb. Journ.* i. 52. Leathern garments were not so singular as has sometimes been supposed; see *Journ.* i. 89 *note.* We may also recall the Danby Quaker of fifty years ago, in Canon Atkinson's *Forty Years in a Moorland Parish* (1908 edn. p. 112 *note*), who said, "Mak' things last what they will, is my advice to this meeting; and old-fashioned homespun and good leather breeks is baith very lasty."*

angel or spirit came into the church to declare the wonderful things of God, and then passed away,[1] and in York, as he talked to people, he says:

> . . . the very groans of the weight and oppression that was upon the Spirit of God in me would open people and strike at them, and make them confess that my very groans did reach to them, for my life was burdened with their profession without possession and words without fruit.[2]

Often the ministers were afraid to face him. He says that the power of the Lord "shook the earthly and airy spirit in which they held their profession of religion and worship, so that it was a dreadful thing unto them when it was told them, 'The man in leathern breeches is come.'"[3] There were wild rumours about him. Christopher Marshall, the minister of the Independent Church at Woodkirk of which Nayler was a member, had been trained in New England under John Cotton,[4] and believed that Fox carried bottles about with him which bewitched people into following him*and rode a great black horse which spirited him away threescore miles in a moment.[5] As he went along in Holderness and elsewhere,[6] he spoke like another John the Baptist of the Day of the Lord that was coming upon all unrighteousness, uttering his message through the towns and by the seaside and to the people at work in the fields. At Tickhill, after being mobbed in the church, he mounted a wall and declared the word of life in such authority and dread that the priest began trembling himself, so that one of the crowd said, "he is turned a Quaker also."[7] Fox during these months illustrated in his own person the truth that came to him, that a single man or woman living in the spirit of the apostles and prophets would shake all the country in their profession for ten miles round.[8] At Wakefield, indeed, the people said that he and his companions made more noise in the country than the coming up of the

[1] *Journ.* i. 81.
[2] *Camb. Journ.* i. 20.
[3] *Journ.* i. 89; not in *Camb. Journ.*
[4] *Congregational Historical Soc. Transactions*, i. p. 224, and note in *Camb. Journ.* i. p. 402.
[5] *Journ.* i. 107.
[6] *Short Journ.* 6; see *post*, App. 1.
[7] *Journ.* i. 105.
[8] *Journ.* i. 109.

Scottish army.[1] He behaved on all occasions with confident boldness and unflinching personal courage. At Warmsworth he and Thomas Aldam roused the anger of the minister and his parishioners.[2] The priest shook him, and the people beat him and threw clods at him and struck him with their crab-tree staves and threw him about. Thomas Aldam was arrested and taken to York for a long imprisonment of two years and seven months, and a warrant was out against Fox, to be executed in any part of the West Riding. But, says Fox, "I saw a vision, a man and two mastiff dogs and a bear: and I passed by them and they smiled upon me."[3] And so it proved, for the constable that took Aldam deliberately refrained from taking Fox, being loath to trouble strangers. Other grave perils were avoided by what seemed to Fox interpositions of Providence, or were averted by his resolute bearing. A commanding authority attached to his personality which seems to have shown itself through his eyes: Prof. W. M. Ramsay suggests that Paul's fixed steady gaze was one chief source of his influence over men, and the same may be said of the piercing gaze again and again attributed to Fox. A man's soul speaks in his eyes, and the intense sincerity of Fox made his look carry the sentence of condemnation to those who were turning away from the truth.[4]

On certain clergymen and justices in Yorkshire the inspired earnestness of the strange itinerant made a deep though not always a lasting impression. There was Philip Scafe, minister at Robin Hood's Bay, who joined the new movement.[5] Another clergyman, named Boyes, a charming old man of whom we would fain know more, went with him from place to place near Pickering, and took him to his own church on the Moors. He called

[1] *Camb. Journ.* i. 38.

[2] *Journ.* i. 103.

[3] *Short Journ.* 11. Cf. *Journ.* i. 106.

[4] See Prof. W. M. Ramsay's *Paul the Traveller*, p. 38. For Fox see, *e.g. Journ.* i. 167, 473; ii. 401; and *Camb. Journ.* i. 42, 185; *post*, pp. 475, 411, 84, 201.

[5] *Journ.* i. 57; Sewel, *History* i. 76 (identifying him with Philip Scarth, who is mentioned in *F.P.T.* 296, and frequently in Besse's *Sufferings*). Croese, *Historia Quakeriana*, p. 57, is the authority for Robin Hood's Bay.

Fox brother, and evidently realized that the spiritual life of the young Quaker transcended all his own learning and experience.[1] He was chaplain to Justice Luke Robinson of Thornton Risebrough, near Pickering, who was a leading man for the Commonwealth in the North of England, and a member for Scarborough in the Long Parliament. Robinson treated Fox with favour and afterwards spoke highly of him among his fellow-members of Parliament at Westminster, and in 1666 Fox called on him and found him still very loving.[2] In Nayler's trial before Parliament in 1656 Robinson behaved moderately. Justice Hotham* of Cranswick, who may probably have been related to the famous Sir John Hotham, was another prominent man who gave Fox a warm welcome, and was of opinion that his teaching of light and life was raised up as a bulwark against Ranterism.[3] Fox calls him a pretty tender man that had some experience of God's working in his heart, and Hotham said that he had known the principle of the Inward Light for ten years.[4] His estimate of Fox shows the essential sanity of Fox's behaviour in spite of his fervour of spirit and the occasional extravagances into which he was betrayed. This sanity showed itself whenever he was in contact with Ranters. In Cleveland he had come among a people who had formerly known a genuine religious experience, but were shattered to pieces, and their leaders had turned Ranters. They still held some kind of meetings, but took tobacco and drank ale in them, and so had grown light and loose.[5] Fox dealt with them, as he had no doubt formerly dealt with the shattered Nottinghamshire Baptists, by urging them all to come together again and wait to feel the Lord's power and Spirit in themselves as the power which would gather them to Christ, and enable them to be taught of Him. Afterwards, if any one declared what the Lord had

[1] *Journ.* i. 90, 92-94, and *Camb. Journ.* i. 29. Boyes is also mentioned as following Farnsworth in a similar way in a letter written by Farnsworth in the autumn of this year 1652 (Swarthm. Colln. iv. 229). See *post*, p. 76.

[2] *Journ.* i. 92, 123; ii. 76.

[3] *Journ.* i. 95.

[4] *Ibid.* i. 81.

[5] *Ibid.* i. 84, etc.

opened to him, it would be a message to be received and lived in the power of. These people, who had their centre at Stokesley, mostly received "Truth," and became a strong meeting. At Staithes also the Ranters were greatly stirred by Fox's visit.[1] Their leader, Bushel, pretended to have had a vision of his coming, and was to doff his hat and bow down to the ground before him as he sat in his great chair. When he proceeded to put his flattery into practice, Fox checked him roughly with the words, "Repent thou swine and beast."[2] A few months later, at Gainsborough, Fox was publicly charged with saying that he was Christ, and seems to have narrowly escaped being lynched by the enraged people. Thereupon,[3] in the eternal power of God he was moved to stand on the top of a table and declare that Christ was in them unless they were reprobate, and that, at the moment when he was speaking, the power in which he spoke was Christ and the power of Christ. His words and the authority with which he uttered them demonstrated the truth at once to the people, and they went away satisfied.

The work in Yorkshire at once resulted in the formation of groups of Children of the Light in many of the places visited. The Balby group was the first and most important. At Wakefield the members were in part drawn from the Independents; at Selby, York, Borrowby, Stokesley, Staithes, Liverton, Malton, Ulrome, Patrington, and probably in some other places, Fox left behind him groups of convinced persons who, in accordance with his advice at Stokesley, began at once holding meetings of a very simple character. The following account, from Kelk Monthly Meeting, in the East Riding, relates to the first months after his visit.

Now, though many were convinced and did believe the Truth, and divers did no longer join with the priests of the world in their public worship, yet we had no settled or appointed meetings:

---

[1] *Journ.* i. 86.

[2] The full phrase is taken from the *Short Journ.*

[3] *Journ.* i. 101, 102. The man who originated the rumour was Cotten Crosland; see Fox's *Great Mistery*, p. 298. I have taken the substance of Fox's defence from the *Camb. Journ.* i. 34, which is clearer than the Ellwood *Journ.*

but on the first days of the week it was the manner of some of us to go to some town where were friendly people and there sit together, and sometimes confer one with another of the dealings of the Lord with us.[1]

In such gatherings together of a separated and convinced people for fellowship with each other and with the Lord we see the first tentative beginnings of a Friends' meeting.

Fox had received a welcome from many influential leaders of Puritanism in Yorkshire. We have already spoken of Robinson and Hotham. Lieutenant Roper of Stanley must have been almost a Friend; Captain Richard Pursglove of Cranswick certainly was; Colonel Overton was much impressed.[2] But if Fox started out with the expectation of winning the Puritan leaders of the county, he must be held to have failed in his enterprise. His success lay rather in bringing priests and people wherever he went face to face with the tremendous demands of vital religion and in securing the acceptance of these demands by a large number of honest-hearted men and women, who were thenceforth consecrated to a new way of life.

Fox passed on in May 1652 to further strenuous and fruitful service, but, under the leadership of Richard Farnsworth and William Dewsbury, the work in Yorkshire continued to make wonderful progress. About August 1652 there were memorable developments at Malton, where Fox had already convinced Roger Hebden, the woollen-draper, Christopher Halliday, William Pearson of Setterington, and others.[3] Upon Roger Hebden was poured out the spirit of prayer and prophecy,[4] and a great work of the Lord took place, which recalls on a small scale the *autos-da-fé* by which luxurious Florence paid homage to the holy zeal of Savonarola. "The men of Malton," with,

[1] *F.P.T.* 293.

[2] For Pursglove see *Journ.* i. 81-83, 95; *F.P.T.* 293, letter to Fox (Swarthm. Colln. iii. 119); and references in Best of Emswell (Surtees Socy.), 175, 176. For Col. Overton, see *Dict. Natl. Biography* and Gardiner's *Hist. of Commth. and Prot.* and Firth's *Last Years of the Protectorate*. A *Journal* of Nayler's, about 1654 (Swarthm. Colln. iii. 6), mentions Robinson, Hotham, and Overton. Overton had Fifth Monarchy leanings.

[3] *F.P.T.* 295.

[4] See *A Plain Account of Roger Hebden*, 1700, Isaac Lindley's Testimony and p. 7.

we opine, the sturdy woollen-draper at their head, burnt their ribbons and silks and other fine commodities, "because they might be abased by pride."[1] Aldam was now in York Castle, and had already written to Fox of the great power of the Lord which had broken forth at Malton.[2] He now writes that Jane Holmes had been there, and the power of the Lord was mightily with her. She had been ducked as a scold for crying her message through the town. Afterwards fifty persons were wrought upon and shaken, and, says Aldam, "some shopkeepers was caused to burn a great deal of ribboning of silks and braveries and such things."[3] Young Thomas Thompson of Skipsea hears of it, and writes:[4]

> About the sixth or seventh month [August or September] we heard of a people raised up at or about Malton, that were called Quakers. . . They were by most people spoken against, but . . . I met with none that could justly accuse them of any crime, only they said they were a fantastical and conceited people, and burnt their lace and ribbons and other superfluous things which formerly they used to wear, and that they fell into strange fits of quaking and trembling.

Jane Holmes was taken to York Castle, where she contracted a fever, and afterwards fell into a "wild, airy spirit, which was exalted above the cross, which kicked against reproof and would not come to judgment."[5] The limits imposed by the frailty of human bodies and minds upon the Quaker experience of the indwelling Spirit emerged thus early and divided into two parties the little flock of seven prisoners in York Castle. Both Farnsworth and Dewsbury visited the prison and reasoned with her, but they and Aldam could effect nothing, for

[1] See one of the earliest Anti-Quaker Tracts, "The Querers and Quakers Cause at The Second Hearing. . . . The Quaking and entransed faction discovered to be a new branch of an old root, revived by Satan, etc.," 1653, p. 39, itself an answer to some queries by an advocate of the Quakers. It is clear from the evidence adduced in the text that Barclay, *Inner Life*, p. 301, and Jno. W. Rowntree, *Essays and Addresses*, p. 16, are wrong in dating the Malton awakening in 1653.*

[2] Dev. Ho., A.R.B. Colln. No. 16 (to be dated July 1652).

[3] Aldam to Fox, Swarthm. Colln. i. 373. To be dated July 1652.

[4] *An Encouragement early to Seek the Lord*, 1708 edn. p. 16.*

[5] Aldam to Friends, Swarthm. Colln. iii. 40. Farnsworth refers to Jane Holmes, Dev. Ho., Saml. Watson Colln. p. 36.

"the wild nature was exalted in her above the seed of God."

When Jane Holmes was brought to York, she found two other women prisoners already there: Elizabeth Hooton, who had been in prison at Derby in 1651 for reproving a minister,[1] and was now at York for a like offence at Rotherham;[2] and Mary Fisher, who had spoken to the Selby minister. She had been a servant with Richard Tomlinson of Selby,[3] and we shall hear of her fearless witness again in persecuting New England and in the camp of the Sultan. Aldam thinks[4] that the Yorkshire authorities supposed that the work would cease if they had a few of the leaders fast and close locked up, but, instead of this, persecution drove Friends nearer together, and the work went on powerfully. We note that he says, "Our Friends are driven in union more close together," and he also speaks of Jane Holmes and her party having "no freedom to come amongst any Friends very little."[5] As early, then, as 1652 the title "Friends" began to be used.

Aldam himself knew something of the strange excitement or "power" which in those days so commonly justified the nickname of Quakers. Major-General Harrison, a man, as we have seen, of advanced views, came into the castle-garth for the purpose of holding a great court. Aldam was moved to warn him against partiality and taking bribes, and says,[6] "I was taken with the power in a great trembling in my head and all of the one side all the while I was speaking to them, which was a great amazement to the people, and they was silent."

The burning of ribbons at Malton was still fresh in men's minds when in October 1652 the call came to William Dewsbury to leave wife and children, and "to run to and fro to declare to souls where their Teacher is —the light in their consciences."[7] He went through

[1] Besse, *Sufferings*, i. 137, and her letter to the mayor in Swarthm. Colln. ii. 43.
[2] Besse, *Sufferings*, ii. 89.
[3] Aldam to Fox, Swarthm. Colln. i. 373.
[4] Swarthm. Colln. iii. 36.
[5] Aldam to Friends, Swarthm. Colln. iii. 40.
[6] Aldam to Fox, Swarthm. Colln. i. 373.
[7] *Works*, p. 94.

Selby, lodging with the Tomlinsons,[1] and the mistress of the house was made to go out into the streets under the mighty power of the Lord, which carried her almost off her feet, and to cry, "Repent, repent, for the Day of the Lord is at hand. Woe to the crown of pride: woe to the covetous professors: woe to the drunkards of Ephraim," a proceeding which struck a great astonishment through the people. The young apprentice who tells us the story of Dewsbury's visit was so cut to the heart by his message that he fell on the floor "as dead to all appearance as any clog or stone," and when he came to his senses again found himself in Dewsbury's arms. The ardent apostle of Quakerism passed on into the East Riding, travelling much from town to town, and sounding the trumpet of the Lord. Fifty years afterwards[2] the power which accompanied him at this time stood out vividly in the memory of those who were reached.

> "His testimony," they say, "was piercing and very powerful, so as the earth shook before him. . . . Oh, it was a glorious day, in which the Lord wonderfully appeared for the bringing down the lofty and high-minded, and exalting that of low degree. Many faces did gather paleness, and the stout-hearted were made to bow and strong oaks to bend before the Lord."

Dewsbury went chiefly to the places where Fox had been received, from Holderness to Malton and on through Cleveland, and a list is recorded of forty-three "first-fruits" of his ministry, among many others whose names might have been added.[3] Here we can only mention a few: John Whitehead, the Puritan soldier of Scarborough Castle, a short, thick-set man, whose spiritual experience closely resembled that of Dewsbury; Robert Fowler of Bridlington Quay, master-mariner, and afterwards owner of the famous *Woodhouse*; Marmaduke Storr of Owstwick, who would share Dewsbury's imprisonment at Northampton; and young Thomas Thompson of Skipsea,[4] who went at night by rough country ways to the house where Dewsbury was staying, and found him writing, while the rest of the company

[1] *F.P.T.* 289, 290. [2] *Ibid.* 294. [3] *Ibid.* 297.
[4] *An Encouragement early to Seek the Lord*, 1708 edn. p. 17.

sat in great silence and retirement of mind, until "after a little time William ceased writing, and, many of the town's people coming in, he began in the power and wisdom of God to declare the Truth."

Farnsworth also did diligent work. He had travelled with Fox in May for a few days from Bradford to Pendle Hill and on towards Wensleydale. A little later, in July, he and Nayler followed Fox to Swarthmore, but in the autumn he returned to Yorkshire.[1] A letter which he wrote to Fox and Nayler gives a graphic description of his service.[2] At Stanley, near Wakefield, many were "wrought on" by the power of the Lord, including a captain's wife, and, while Farnsworth was speaking next day to the crowd in Wakefield market, she came up, and was "wrought on" in the tumult, and cried out, "This is the power of the Lord," and, though very proud, was humbled and ripped off her silver lace. Farnsworth was followed by the people into the house of a Doctor Hodgson, and in the house four or five others were "wrought on," to the general amazement, until he mounted a table, and held the people silent by his message. At night the Quakers were stoned as they left the town, "stones flew as fast as bullets in a battle," but no one was hurt. After visiting the prisoners at York, the party, which included some Balby Friends, went on to Malton, where they had powerful meetings for two nights and a day, "the one night," he writes, "we were up till one o'clock, and the next day the power of the Lord was among us all the day. I was made to let forth my life unto them, and the very life in them were raised up: we was together that night till twelve o'clock." The party then left for York, accompanied on the road by many of the Malton Friends. "We came into the fields that night like an army, [and] had very much ado to part:

[1] *Journ.* i. 107-110; *F.P.T.* 291; *Journ.* i. 123.

[2] Swarthm. Colln. iv. 229, printed in part in *Letters of Early Friends*, p. 216. The date is ascertained by the fact that it is evidently the first letter to Fox and Nayler since Farnsworth left them, and by the dates of Wm. Sykes' imprisonment referred to in letter, as these dates are given in Besse, *Sufferings*, ii. 90, and in a MS. account of his grand-daughter, Esther Morris, in Dev. Ho., Portfolio 11, No. 6.

some of them came on with us half the way to York, and old Boyes the priest." They reached York before sunrise and pushed on by Selby back to Stanley, where they had a great meeting on the Sunday morning. Farnsworth adds ardently:

> So I see the Lord glorifying Himself every way to His own praise: but the world is all on a fire. I am much threatened of my life, but I fear not what man can do: I hear that there is warrants out as for blasphemy, that I should say, "I am the light of the world." Ah, dear hearts, be valiant: the Lord rides on triumphantly.

In December we find him at work round Balby,[1] with a book in print, which "Friends" are made bold to read out to the people, in the churchyards after service, and at the market-crosses on market-days, soldiers going along with them and standing by while they are reading, a significant hint as to the religious leanings of the army. He adds, "The priests is all on fire, their kingdom must down." A few days later he took part in another remarkable meeting at Malton, where the Pentecostal manifestations that marked this early work in Yorkshire reached their culmination.

> "There was," he says,[2] "at Malton, at the time called Christmas, nigh two hundred Friends met to wait upon the Lord, and did continue three or four days together, [and] did scarce part night or day I was with them, and twice the mighty power of the Lord was made manifest; almost all the room was shaken."

William Dewsbury came to the latter part of this memorable meeting, and the rumour of it reached London and was used against the Quakers in the pamphlet already referred to, which asks,[3] "Whether, when about Malton, there are towards 200 or 300 neglecting their callings, young and old, to compare notes of their entranced madness, it concerns not a Church, nay, a Commonwealth, if it

[1] Farnsworth to Margt. Fell, 2nd Dec. 1652, Swarthm. Colln. iii. 45.

[2] Farnsworth to Margt. Fell, 7th Jan. 1653, Swarthm. Colln. iv. 83. For Dewsbury's presence see Thos. Thompson's Testimony concerning Jno. Whitehead.

[3] "The Querers and Quakers Cause," p. 44.

were no more than pagan, to look to it, and prevent the growth of further mischief?"

The strong religious excitement which attended the work at Malton was not altogether healthy. Nayler, I think in 1654, visited the town, and wrote that "much deadness is got amongst them." [1] George Emmot of Durham, after leaving Friends, wrote with much scorn of his experiences with his "quaking companions amongst their Setteringtonians, Maltoneers, Paludarians." [2] Setterington, near Malton, was the home of William Pearson, and a Friend named Story was a Paludarian, that is, a native of Marishes, another neighbouring village. There was, however, a strong growth of Quakerism, which quickly outgrew the early extravagances,[3] and there can be no doubt as to the permanence of much of this pioneer work in Yorkshire. The East Riding, as early as December 1652, had a meeting, settled by the wisdom of Dewsbury, for Friends in general, "to be kept on the third day of the week, and to continue for a General Meeting, once in three weeks." [4] While this was primarily intended for waiting on the Lord, it must have afforded opportunity for conference among Friends on matters of necessary arrangement, and is accordingly not without interest as a first step towards organized church-life.

[1] *Six Weeks' Journal*, Swarthm. Colln. iii. 6.*

[2] "A Northern Blast, or the Spiritual Quaker Converted, Being Soul-saving Advice to the giddy people of England, who are running headlong to Destruction. Wherein are shewed the manner of their Meetings in the County of Yorkshire and Durham, their Quakings, Shreekings, and ridiculous Actions, etc." (1655), p. 6.

[3] In G. Lyon Turner's *Original Records of Early Nonconformity*, i. p. 165, the entry against Malton in the Episcopal Returns, 1669, runs, "Quakers very numerous, sometimes 300, mean quality."

[4] *F.P.T.* 295.

CHAPTER IV

THE PEOPLE IN WHITE RAIMENT *

(JUNE 1652)

It pleased the Lord in His infinite [mercy to] visit a people in the latter age of the world. . . . So in that age there were many in a fervent [desir]e after the Lord and the way of worship that might be the [mos]t acceptable to Him, which caused many to leave off the [for]mal dead way of worship then professed amongst a people notionally professing Christianity, [and] under a deep sense of the want of the enjoyment of that we made profession of, caused us to separate ourselves from among them, so that it pleased God to look down upon us with an eye of pity, and He sent His servants amongst us to preach the glad tidings of the gospel of peace, which directed our minds to the measure of grace or light manifested within our hearts and consciences: notwithstanding many and great were the sufferings we underwent for the same.—*First Publishers of Truth*, p. 57 (Cumberland account).

WE now return to the end of May 1652 and resume the narrative of Fox's pioneer work. He is travelling with Farnsworth, and has eaten and drunk but little for several days together.[1] They come to Pendle Hill in the edge of Lancashire, and Fox is moved of the Lord to go up it, which he does "with much ado, it was so steep." The local proverb with pardonable exaggeration said:

> Ingleborough, Pendle, and Pen-y-ghent
> Are the highest hills between Scotland and Trent.[2]

A mount of vision is an inspiration to the Seer; it uplifts his heart and supplies the ample horizons which his soul requires. On another occasion, near Dolgelly,[3] Fox came to a hill, presumably Cader Idris, which the people told him

[1] *Journ.* i. 109, and parallel passage in *Camb. Journ.* i. 40.

[2] Cited from Harland and Wilkinson's *Lancashire Folk-lore*, p. 204 *n.* Pendle rises 1831 feet above the sea-level, Ingleborough 2373 feet, Pen-y-ghent 2250 feet. Whernside is 2414 feet in height, and several others of the Yorkshire Fells are higher than Pendle.

[3] *Journ.* i. 376.

was two or three miles high, and from its side he could see a great way, and was moved to sound the Day of the Lord there, and to set his face several ways, and tell his companion in what places God would raise up a people. So, from the bleak moorland brow of Pendle, with the Irish Sea in view, Fox sounded forth the Day of the Lord,*and had a vision of places where there was a great people to be gathered. That night, at the alehouse where he stayed, still clearer vision came to him, and he saw a great people in white raiment by a river's side coming to the Lord, and so he gave forth papers to that country for the ale-wife to disperse, which she did.[1] The *Journal* gives the contents of this paper: The Day of the Lord is at hand, Christ is come to teach His people Himself and to bring them off from the world's ways and teachers to His own free teaching. In an exalted frame of mind Fox passed on northward, soon parting from Farnsworth, and it is evident that the fires of an intense zeal were burning in the heart of the young visionary. He came to a house, and the man would have given him money, but he shook his hand at it and told the man to mind the Lord. That night he lay out on the fellside, and so came into Wensleydale, and declared the truth through all the towns as he went. We are told that he advised those he met "to fear God, which, together with his grave look or countenance, did much alarum the people, it being a time that many people were filled with zeal."[2] Some persons took him for a madman and distracted, and would have locked him up; at one house he was moved to say[3] that he was the son of God and was come to declare the everlasting truth of God, and so he was had down to some Puritans, who received his message and directed him to others of their way of thinking. In this manner he passed on through the dales, till he reached the town of Sedbergh, in the north-west corner of Yorkshire, a place with fourteen alehouses and a clergyman who was a common frequenter of them.[4] Sedbergh, or, more pre-

[1] *Short Journ.* 16. [2] *F.P.T.* 311. [3] *Short Journ.* 17.

[4] I take this detail from a paper of Gervase Benson's in Swarthm. Colln. IV. 258.

cisely, Brigflatts, above the river Rawthey, proved to be the place of his vision of a people in white raiment. It lay on the eastern edge of a district which already contained a people who were organized as a community of Separatists, and were in a large degree prepared for the message of Fox. We know a few particulars of their earlier history from papers preserved by Philip Swale of Hartforth, near Richmond in Swaledale.[1] They had grown into strength under the ministry of Thomas Taylor,[2] a man eight years older than Fox, and an Oxford graduate, who came, it would seem, from Carlton, near Skipton. As a boy he had a sense of sin and the need for righteousness, and for several years was under great fears lest he should miss of eternal salvation, and his brother tells us that he thus came to be a "true Seeker and inquirer after the best things, and the Lord was good unto him in a preparative work, before he came to know the Sabbath of eternal rest in Christ Jesus." In course of time he became a public minister, but still showed himself a Seeker, says his friend Robert Barrow, "having real desires to understand the things of God, and the mysteries of His kingdom, and was a man of an honest life and clean behaviour, and in his preaching and judgment was more refined than the rest of his neighbouring priests." He proved his sterling character by refusing to receive his maintenance from tithes, when he became convinced that they were popish and anti-Christian. In this way he became minister to persons at Preston Patrick, a few miles south of Kendal, who were separated from the national worship, and took for his support only what his hearers were willing freely to give him. Greatly beloved and esteemed by his congregation for his sincerity and godly living, he gained a wide influence, and the Chapel at Preston Patrick became the centre of a community of Seekers, who came to the General Meeting held

[1] See my paper on "The Westmorland and Swaledale Seekers in 1651" in *J.F.H.S.* v. 3-10.*

[2] For Thos. Taylor see his Works, called *Truth's Innocency* (1697), especially Testimonies at beginning by his brother Christopher Taylor, his son Thos., and his friend Robt. Barrow. Also *F.P.T.* 214, 244, 253. For Carlton, see Swarthm. Colln. i. 18, Taylor to Margt. Fell.

there once a month from Sedbergh in Yorkshire, Yealand and Kellet in Lancashire, and Kendal, Underbarrow, Grayrigg, and Hutton in Westmorland. They were the most zealous and religious Roundheads and Puritans in the district, and, as the newly discovered Swaledale Papers[1] show, provided Taylor with a stipend of fifty pounds a year. The community had a vigorous spiritual life, with a ministry springing up in its midst, and Taylor would sometimes let two of these ministers, John Audland and Francis Howgill, preach in his pulpit. His prowess as a divine is shown by his victorious dispute at Kendal against infant baptism, referred to in a previous chapter.[2] Taylor did not entirely confine himself to his own district. He was evidently well known in Swaledale, forty-five miles away, and in February 1651, while Fox was lying in prison at Derby, a group of Seekers who lived there were in correspondence with their "dear Christian friends in and about Preston Patrick" for a share in his services. They would have liked him to come and live at Richmond, but are grateful to the Preston Patrick community for condescending to their desires so far as to allow him to give them part of his ministrations, and hope to contribute at least twenty pounds a year towards his maintenance. The concluding paragraph of this letter comes so near to Quakerism, both in its conception of ministry and of the indwelling Christ, as to deserve reproduction in full.

"We take notice," they say, "that God seems to call to distance from you some of those that were a mouth in public to you, by which we also perceive that a remna[nt], according to the good pleasure of His will, is remaining with you; and believes the other either by word or letter will be remembering you, and that out of that Divine fulness some will be enabled to comfort the weak. But all we—and it is His mercy we are so—are weak ones, and have not any to administer a word of comfort to the weary soul, till the Lord make strong for Himself in Christ some to perform the same: besides the inward and outward

---

[1] See *J.F.H.S.* v. 3-10.

[2] *Ante*, p. 17.

oppositions still strongly perplexing and opposing: but stronger is He that is in us than he that is in the world, and He will not cease till He have brought forth judgment unto victory for us all, to the praise of His grace."

There was at this time a movement, with which the great name of Richard Baxter, of Kidderminster, became associated, for a closer union between Presbyterians, Independents, and others, and in his desire after unity Taylor was prevailed on to resume the practice of infant baptism, although it was a thing that "he and his hearers had seen beyond and the emptiness thereof." This retrogression on his part was a "condescension" which the zealous Westmorland Seekers could not approve,[1] and, accordingly, the Swaledale Seekers had their wish, and Taylor removed to Richmond, as a "Lecturer," that is, an approved preacher without a settled charge or a State maintenance. The Preston Patrick community were left to their own resources in the matter of ministry, relying chiefly on Audland and Howgill, but having help from several others. They are described[2] at this time as separated from the world's worship and empty dry forms of religion, and fostering their fellowship and spiritual life by frequent meetings, sometimes sitting in silence, often having times of fervent prayer, sometimes engaging in religious conferences. Several of the Seekers had openings from the Lord, "from which they could have declared excellent things, having some sight or comprehension thereof, yet wanted the inward possession of the virtue, life and power of what they declared of, and in this state continued many days."

It was at this point in their history that the Westmorland Seekers came into contact with George Fox.

[1] See *F.P.T.* 253.

[2] For these paragraphs see Thos. Camm's Testimony to Camm and Audland in *The Memory of the Righteous Revived* (1689) and the notice of Ann Camm in *Piety Promoted*, pt. iii. p. 199. The opening sentences of the preface of *Saul's Errand to Damascus* give a similar account and draw no distinction between the meetings of these Seekers before and after Fox's visit. Cf. *F.P.T.* 244, "Preston Patrick, where the said ff. H., J. A., and several others did usually preach to the congregation there met."

They were, indeed, a people in white raiment, waiting to be gathered. As we tell the wonderful story of the next few weeks, we shall see how the solitary enthusiast found himself rapidly surrounded by an eager band of disciples, indeed the whole community seems to have received joyfully the new message. He had been in Garsdale at Major Bousfield's,[1] who had directed him to a meeting of the Seekers, on Whitsunday, 6th June, held at Borrat, near Sedbergh, at the house of Gervase Benson, a man of note.[2] A number of the Seekers were convinced at this meeting, and Fox stayed on for the fair-day on Whit-Wednesday, when, after a meeting with some Puritans in a house in Sedbergh, he went into the open church-garth, holding a public meeting there though the church was prepared for him. He stood on the bench under the yew tree in his leather dress with its alchemy buttons and his hair hanging in ringlets, contrary to the Puritan fashion. There for several hours he "preached to a great auditory his testimony concerning the new way of the Light of Christ Jesus leading to the Kingdom of Heaven, more clearly than heretofore had been preached." He showed that the Lord was come to teach His people Himself, and exposed the emptiness of the Puritan ministers. He urged his hearers to come off from the temples made with hands, so that they might know themselves to be the temples of God. None of the ministers present had power to open his mouth, but at last a captain asked why Fox would not go into the church, for that was the proper place to be preaching in. Fox told him[3] that it was only a place of lime and stone and wood, for the true Church was in God (1 Thess. i. 1). Howgill, who was listening to Fox for the first time, answered the captain, and said to the people, "This man

[1] *F.P.T.* 329. For a later and less favourable glimpse of Miles Bousfield see Wm. Edmondson's *Journal* (1715), pp. 10-12, cited *post*, p. 210.

[2] There are several accounts of these Sedbergh meetings, viz. *Journ.* i. 112; *F.P.T.* 242, 243; *F.P.T.* 329, 330; *F.P.T.* 333. The yew tree became a mere shell, and was blown down in January 1877. See *Sedbergh, Garsdale, and Dent*, by W. Thompson, 1910 edn. p. 115. A portion of it is preserved at Brigflatts Meeting-House. Borrat was near Cautley Crag, a few miles from Sedbergh, up the Rawthey valley. See Geo. Whitehead's *Christian Progress*, p. 22.*

[3] *Short Journ.* 18.

speaks with authority and not as the scribes." A number of persons were convinced, including Capt. Henry Ward of Sunnybank, near Grayrigg, who told Fox that his very eyes had pierced through him.[1] Fox went home with two of the convinced Seekers, Thomas Blaykling and his son John, to their house at Draw-well,[2] a mile and a half away, and on the following Sunday was taken by the son to the great meeting which the Seekers were holding that day at Firbank Chapel, a place of far-stretching views high up the steep fell on the Westmorland side of the Lune, of which only the burial-ground is now left. Howgill and Audland were the two preachers for the day.[3] Fox waited till they had done, walking about the chapel door, and when the meeting broke up, gave notice of one on the fellside in the afternoon. Howgill thought that Fox looked in at the door, who, he said, might have killed him with a crabapple, the Lord's power had so surprised him. It was an intensely expectant and receptive company of about a thousand persons that listened to the Quaker message that afternoon, though they thought it strange that a man should preach on a hill and not in the church. Fox had gone to the top of the mass of rock, hard by the chapel, still known as Fox's Pulpit.* The word of the Lord had come to him that he must go and set down upon the rock in the mountain, as Christ had done before. After some time he stood up, with his rapt face and piercing gaze, and for three hours declared himself. The fellside, he told them, was as holy as any other ground, for did not Christ meet with His disciples on a mountain; he was there to tell them that Christ Himself was now come, who had ended both the temple and its worship, and the priests and their tithes. All were to hearken to Him. Christ was their Teacher

[1] *Camb. Journ.* i. 42.

[2] *F.P.T.* 243. For particulars of Draw-well see *J.F.H.S.* ii. 22.

[3] For the Firbank Meeting see *Journ.* i. 113, with additions in *Camb. Journ.* i. 43, and *Short Journ.* 18, *F.P.T.* 243, and Fox's Testimony to Camm and Audland in *The Memory of the Righteous Revived* (1689), p. 326. For Firbank Chapel see *Sedbergh, Garsdale, and Dent*, by W. Thompson, 1910 edn. pp. 68-70. It was standing in 1837, but fell into ruins a few years later, and the congregation moved down to a lower and more sheltered site.

to instruct them, their Governor to direct them, their Shepherd to feed them, their Bishop to oversee them, and their Prophet to open Divine mysteries to them. They were to know their bodies to be prepared and sanctified and made fit temples for God and Christ to dwell in. Fox said that it was his mission to bring them off from the temples, tithes, priests, and rudiments of the world, which had been instituted since the Apostles' days, that they might come to the Spirit of God in themselves and to Christ the Substance. Many hundreds were convinced under the inspired power of this message, including all the teachers of the Seekers' community.

Audland took Fox home with him to his house at Crosslands, and, says George, with his quiet humour:

> . . . there came John Story to me, and lighted his pipe of tobacco, . . . saying, "Come, all is ours," and I looked upon him to be a forward bold lad, and tobacco I did not take,* but it came into my mind that the lad might think I had not unity with the creation,* for I saw he had a flashy, empty notion of religion; so I took his pipe and put it to my mouth, and gave it to him again to stop him, lest his rude tongue should say I had not unity with the creation.[1]

Audland, on the Wednesday, brought Fox to the General Meeting which the Seekers held once a month at the Preston Patrick Chapel. Thomas Camm, then a schoolboy of twelve, gives a vivid account of this meeting in his important narrative of the first publishing of Quaker truth in Westmorland.[2] Audland, it seems, would have had Fox go up into the pew where the preacher usually sat, but he refused, and took a back seat near the door. There he sat,

> . . . [in] silent waiting upon God about half an hour, in which time of silence F[rancis] H[owgill] seemed uneasy, and pulled out his Bible and opened it, and stood up several times, sitting down again and closing his book, a dread and fear being upon him that he durst not begin to preach. After the said silence and waiting G[eorge] F[ox] stood up in the mighty power of God, and in the demonstration thereof was his mouth opened to preach

[1] *Camb. Journ.* i. 44.

[2] *F.P.T.* 244.

Christ Jesus, the Light of Life, and the Way to God, and Saviour of all that believe and obey Him, which was delivered in that power and authority that most of the auditory, which were several hundreds, were effectually reached to the heart, and convinced of the truth that very day, for it was the day of God's power.

Fox went on to Kendal, where a meeting had been appointed for him in the moot-hall, and several were convinced or favourably inclined. One Cock, he tells us, met him in the street and would have given him a roll of tobacco, so he accepted his love but declined the gift.[1] From Kendal he visited Underbarrow, still within the area of the Seeker community, reasoning in the way with his companions, especially with young Edward Burrough, of whom we shall hear again. Next morning his Puritan comrades roughly rebuffed some poor travellers who asked relief, and Fox ran after them and gave them some money. The Puritans, coming out from their breakfast, saw him a quarter of a mile off, and said that he could not have gone so far in so short a time without wings. They were filled with strange thoughts about him, and were doubtful about allowing the meeting which had been arranged, but it was finally held in the chapel, and many were convinced. From this place Fox passed on with an aged man, named James Dickinson, to his house at Crosthwaite, and so forward into Cartmel and Furness.

This crowded fortnight was the creative moment in the history of Quakerism. In the freshness of his powers and of his experience Fox had a living message, which he uttered with prophetic authority, and both the message and the prophetic messenger answered the yearnings and the hopes of a strong community of earnest-hearted Seekers. Under the influence of half-a-dozen powerful meetings and of the personal intercourse with Fox enjoyed by his hosts and their friends, a great company was gathered in. Many of these became the heroic pioneers of the new movement, overcoming the buffetings of opposers and persecutors by their invincible faith. We

[1] *Journ.* i. 116. For Underbarrow see also *F.P.T.* 245.

must interrupt the course of our narrative for a few pages to make their acquaintance.

Howgill and Audland, as the spiritual leaders of the community—men of proved gifts and power—claim first notice. Francis Howgill, born in 1618, was the older man. He lived at Todthorne, near Grayrigg, and had been a tailor and farmer.

A crumbling wall still shows where the farmhouse stood, amid green pastures, just below the place where men have broken the rule of the heather, and by a beck which comes rushing down from the spacious fells—a beautiful, wide-viewed country, yet with an underlying sternness in it.[1]

He tells us his early experience in "The Inheritance of Jacob Discovered after his Return out of Ægypt,"[2] dated from Cork, 18th January 1656. From twelve years old he set his heart to know God, and followed the strictest Puritan ways. He read much, and often prayed three times a day, but, imagining God to be at a distance, failed to find Him. Growing in knowledge, he became admired and puffed up, and posted up and down after the most excellent sermons, but only gained more words. During this time, the light in his conscience often judged him for wrong-doing, but he was taught to slight it as only a natural conscience, and was told that the man who had nothing but this "restraining grace" was but a tame devil. The guilt of his heart was not taken away by all his outward belief in Christ and partaking of the Lord's Supper, but, he says:

. . . when I could sorrow most, I had most peace, for something spoke within me from the Lord, but I knew Him not then, and they said That it was heresy to look for the word of the Lord to be spoken now in these days, but only the letter, and so I regarded it not much.

Then he turned to the Independents, spent all his spare money on books, and joined with them as being more separate from the world. He also tried the Anabaptists,

[1] *Francis Howgill*, by Ernest E. Taylor (Friends Ancient and Modern Series, 1906), which also contains illustrations of the yew in Sedbergh churchyard and Fox's "pulpit" on Firbank Fell.

[2] *Works*, pp. 37-64.

but found both these sects worshipping the letter and a merely historical Christ, and still failed to win peace.

"Then," he says, "some preached Christ within, but they themselves were without, had but words, and yet they said, All must be within,—unto which my heart did cleave—and spoke of redemption, and justification, and all within, and of God appearing in man and overcoming the power of the devil. And then that in my conscience bore witness it must be so . . . but still I saw . . . that they enjoyed not what they spoke."

At last, after much hurrying hither and thither, Howgill had it revealed in him that the Lord would teach His people Himself, and so he waited in the expectation of a time of revelation near at hand. As his mind turned to the light, he had many truths opened to him, and caught them up in the wisdom of the flesh, going up and down, preaching against the ministry, and running out with the things revealed to him, so that he says he was wondered after and admired by many as he "preached up and down the country [out] of the fulness that was in the old bottle." But when the day he had waited for came, and he heard the message of Fox, his foundation was swept away, and all his righteousness and unrighteousness was judged and weighed, and all was found too light.

"As soon as I heard him declare," says Howgill, "that the Light of Christ in man was the way to Christ, I believed the eternal word of truth, and that of God in my own conscience sealed to it: and so, not only I, but many hundreds more, who thirsted after the Lord . . . we were all seen to be off the foundation, and all mouths were stopped in the dust."

The dreadful power of the Lord fell upon him—all that ever he had done was judged and accursed—and, after a time, as he gave up all to the judgment, he saw the cross of Christ and stood in it, and saw the enmity slain upon it, and a new man was made in him, and peace came, and eternal life was brought in, and thus it pleased the Father to reveal His Son in him and to give him true rest, to "lie down in the fold with the lambs of God, where the sons rejoice together, and the saints keep holy days."

John Audland, born about 1630, was at this time a

young man of twenty-two. He was a linen-draper, and lived at Crosslands, near Preston Patrick. His strong understanding and great memory made him early proficient in scripture, and by the time he was twenty he had become an eminent preacher among the Westmorland Seekers, and sometimes preached to crowded congregations in other churches and chapels. The message of Fox reached his heart at once: he saw, like Howgill, the emptiness of his great profession and high-flown notions, and used to say, "Ah! . . . what have we been labouring for? . . . All our building tumbles down; our profession is high as the wind; the Day of the Lord is upon it, and His word as a fire consumes it as dry stubble: . . . we must forsake the world and all its glory: . . . 'tis a Saviour that I long for: 'tis Him that my soul pants after: oh! that I may be comprehended into His life and overshadowed with His glory, sanctified throughout by His word and raised up by His eternal power."[1] Such earnestness of spirit brought him into a rich experience which fitted him for service and filled him with spiritual strength beyond his bodily powers. He became an eager pioneer of the new truth, wearing himself out to an early death, a man "of a sweet, ruddy and amiable countenance, and of a cheerful spirit: . . . immortality shined in his face and his voice was as thunder."[2] Howgill and Audland, on their convincement, felt it right to return money which they had received from the parish and people for preaching at Colton-in-Furness, a course which Fox tells us[3] made the priests and professors more to rage.

With their names we may fittingly couple those of the two men—Edward Burrough and John Camm—who in future years would be their yoke-fellows in the work. The Publishers of Quaker Truth went forth, in most cases, after the manner of the Seventy, two and two, as, for example, Howgill and Burrough, Camm and Audland, Wilkinson and Story, Stubbs and Caton.

[1] Ann Camm's Testimony to Camm and Audland in *The Memory of the Righteous Revived* (1689). Audland died 22nd March 1664.

[2] Chas. Marshall's Testimony in *The Memory of the Righteous Revived.*

[3] Testimony in Howgill's *Works.*

Burrough was just turned nineteen,[1] and came from Underbarrow, between Kendal and Windermere. He was brought up[2] well and piously, and Howgill says of him:

> In his natural disposition he was bold and manly, dexterous and fervent,—and what he took in hand he did it with his might, —loving, kind and courteous, merciful and flexible and easy to be entreated. His whole delight was always among good people, and to be conferring and reading the scriptures, and little to mind any sports or pastimes, which there is an incidency unto in youth, but his very strength was bended after God.

Burrough tells us how he became a Puritan and Roundhead, having much religious knowledge, but little of the living truth. When he was about seventeen, he had some true sight of God, and separated himself more from the vain ways of the world, and found the preaching he had delighted in listening to withered and decayed, and began to have openings of truth. Then he became puffed up, not knowing the cross, "and here," he says, "I lived pleasantly, for I had the true God and the true truth in my comprehension, which by my wisdom in the Light I had comprehended, and I had the world in my heart." He fed himself with the past experiences which he had formerly enjoyed, and said to himself, "Whom God loves once, He loves for ever," but the witness in his heart, which the earthly nature made merry over, would give him no rest. Then Fox came, speaking a language which he knew not, for all his high talking, and he saw that he was in the prodigal state, and above the cross of Christ, and in bondage to his own will. A day of thick darkness and trouble came upon him, until he separated from all the glory of the world and joined the Quakers, "and now," he says, "I am despised of my neighbours and carnal acquaintance, and is not greater than my Lord, who was

[1] The Westmorland Registers at Dev. Ho. give his birth as 1st March 1632, son of James; that is, 1633 New Style; baptized on 3rd, which was a Sunday. *F.P.T.* p. 263, says he was born in 1635; and Howgill, in his Testimony, says he was sixteen or seventeen when he met Fox. The year 1633, however, agrees well with the account of his spiritual experience at the age of seventeen, *i.e.* 1650, allowing two more years before he knew Fox.

[2] See Howgill's Testimony and Burrough's Tract (1654), "A Warning from the Lord to the Inhabitants of Underbarrow," both in Burrough's *Works*.

called a blasphemer and a deceiver, as now I am . . . in whom my soul hath full satisfaction, joy and content." His parents, indeed, turned him out of their house, and, an outcast from his home, he threw himself with single-hearted devotion into the pioneer work of the Quaker movement, so that Howgill tells us that during the ten years of his brief life-work, he never spent one week to himself. This explains a passage in one of his letters from London (24th Sept. 1658)[1] which would otherwise seem wanting in natural affection. He writes:

> The old man and old woman, my father and mother according to the flesh, is both departed this world, ten days one after the other, and I am sent for down, but truly I cannot go: it is only pertaining to outwards, and I feel no freedom to it at present.

Camm was a man of about fifty, of great zeal and weak constitution, who had an old family estate of his own, and lived at the house, still standing, which he had built for himself at Camsgill, Preston Patrick. His son[2] tells us that his religious earnestness led him to see beyond the ministers and their empty forms, and so he separated from them, "still pressing forward towards a further manifestation and revelation of the way of salvation, which his soul hungered and thirsted after." He sometimes preached to the Westmorland Seekers, and when the message of Fox came home to him, bowed under it, and at the cost of much sacrifice—for he was a capable and prosperous man of business—he devoted himself to spreading the truth.

The community of Seekers contained a number of other men with gifts of leadership, who threw in their lot with the Quaker movement. From Sedbergh there were the Blayklings, young George Harrison, and Gervase Benson, a man of wide influence. He had been Mayor of Kendal, 1643-44, and prior to the Civil War was Commissary of the Archdeaconry of Richmond, the chief ecclesiastical office under the Bishop of Chester. A Proctor at Civil Law, a Justice of the Peace, and a

[1] To Howgill, Dev. Ho., A.R.B. Colln. No. 40.
[2] Thos. Camm's Testimony in *The Memory of the Righteous Revived.*

Colonel, he was at this time one of the leading men of affairs in the North of England, and a principal man among the Seekers and one of their free preachers. As a Friend he was noted for his plainness in dress, apparel, and manners, calling himself husbandman, and rejecting all titles.[1]

Kendal, the chief town of the district, supplied some notable disciples—the weaver Thomas Holme, who became the apostle of Quakerism in South Wales ; Thomas Willan, a future treasurer of the Kendal fund for the "service of Truth" ; and Christopher Atkinson, who would prove himself unworthy of his call as a minister. From Grayrigg, besides Howgill, came the schoolmaster Ambrose Rigge, then a youth of eighteen, who was made, like Burrough, an outcast from his parents and friends ; Thomas Robertson, "an innocent, faithful, patient man" ; Captain Henry Ward of Sunnybank ; and Thomas Ayrey of Birkfield, a man of excellent gifts but weak faith. At Preston Patrick, in addition to Camm and Audland, there was John Story, a poor man of large understanding and memory, who had good service for many years with John Wilkinson of Millholme, near New Hutton, though both Friends afterwards became arch-Separatists. Underbarrow, besides Edward Burrough, contributed Miles Halhead of Mountjoy, "a plain, simple man," about ten years older than Fox ; "little" Miles Bateman of Tullythwaite, who turned apostate ;[2] and Miles and Stephen Hubbersty.

From the Lancashire end of the district came Robert Widders* of Over Kellet, six years older than Fox, "a grave solid man, and had a great discerning of spirits, and was sharp against deceit and hypocrisy,"[3] a man whose face was a refreshment and whose words were few. Lastly, there was young Richard Hubberthorne, the only son of a Yealand yeoman, who was little in stature, of weak constitution and slow in speech, yet of great

[1] *F.P.T.* 242, 250. Consult *The Ejected of 1662 in Cumberland and Westmorland*, i. 75, by B. Nightingale. This gives additional information as to the pre-Quaker careers of John Camm and Gervase Benson. For most of the particulars of the other Seekers enumerated see *F.P.T.* pp. 241-273.

[2] See Annals, 1657, in *Camb. Journ.* ii. 337. There was also a Miles Bateman, senr. ; see *F.P.T.* 245 *n.*, and note in *Camb. Journ.* i. 405.

[3] John Whiting's *Persecution Exposed* (1715 edn.), pp. 168-171.

reliability and sound judgment.[1] He had been a captain, and sometimes preached among his sincere and sober companions, who loved him well. Writing as I suppose for the first time to Fox, he says:[2]

> The eye being opened which was blind now comes to witness thee and reads thee within me. I was in prison and thou hast visited me . . . and I live in thee in measure. . . . Weeds and pollutions are often wrapped about my head, even these things that thou said, lust and thoughts fleshly. . . . Pray for me that that which is pure may draw me out of all (which is the true Son of the Eternal God): but there is the bondwoman and her son, and he pleads for freedom because he is of Abraham, but [pray for me] that he may be cast out, and the true seed, the pure birth, may grow. Pray that I may be keeped not to boast above my measure, but may walk in the easy and gentle leadings of the Lamb, and may drink of those rivers in which thou swims.

Besides the above, there were many women, especially John Blaykling's sister Ann, Audland's wife Ann, two young women, Jane and Dorothy Waugh, who were serving maids at John Camm's, Elizabeth Fletcher, and Elizabeth Leavens, afterwards wife of Thomas Holme.

Thomas Taylor himself did not meet Fox during these momentous weeks. He visited him, however, at Swarthmore in September, and was convinced,[3] preaching on the following day as "a tender spring of life sprang up in him." He showed his sterling character by giving up his benefice as a lecturer at Richmond, not consulting what he should do for a livelihood, but trusting to the Lord to provide for himself, his wife, and their family of five small children. A letter written to Fox[4] nine months later shows the beauty of his spirit:

> Blessed be the Lord that did not suffer thee from the beginning to flatter me but [caused thee] to deal faithfully with me in that great business of my soul. O what a loss suffers every one when pillows are sewed under men to sleep more securely in a way of

---

1 Burrough's Testimony in Hubberthorne's *Works* (1663). *Richard Hubberthorne*, by Ernest E. Taylor (Friends Ancient and Modern Series, 1911), gives a careful sketch of the man. He was born in 1628.*

2 Swarthm. Colln. iv. 4; undated, but endorsed 1652.

3 See Testimonies by Fox and Thomas Taylor, junr., in Taylor's *Works*.

4 Swarthm. Colln. iii. 29, dated 18th May (1653).

ignorance and opposition to the pure truth. Truly, friend, I find through the great grace of my God a principle springing up in my soul that doth really give evidence against all the world. . . . I have been a soarer up in the first nature high, but the Lord hath been good to bring me somewhat low, and, though He hath visited me with His love, and given me refreshment from His presence in it, yet dare I not boast of myself in anything. . . . I perceive the way of God's leading His people under the cross is the way that the pure love of the Lord saw only safe and certain to bring us out of the pit to Himself by.

Such a letter sums up the deep experience which seems to have come upon the Westmorland Seekers as the result of the messages given to them by Fox. He brought them not only under a sense of the indwelling life of Christ, he also brought home to them the absolute claim of their Lord to that whole-hearted discipleship which consists in taking up the cross daily and following Him. In the good soil of these honest Seekers' hearts the message bore fruit a hundredfold.

It is evident that the accession to Quakerism of this vigorous community of Seekers greatly enriched the intellectual and spiritual forces of the movement, and made possible its further extension on a large scale. The new Publishers of Truth were in most cases men of competent Bible knowledge and religious training, according to the standards of the time, having been carefully taught in these respects before they became Friends. They were men, moreover, of a singularly advanced religious experience, for their intense sincerity of purpose had carried them beyond the doctrines and professions which satisfied others till they felt themselves like prodigals, who had spent all and were in want, and they had then been brought into the abiding bliss of the Father's house through the eternal life which sprang up in their hearts and brought them into union with Him. Finally, they were for the most part young men in the prime of their ardour and strength, who would follow the movings of life rather than the counsels of prudence in shaping the new religious movement to which they had vowed their service.

The profound significance of these features of the

situation will not be lost on the student of Quakerism. Had there been the same combination of intellect, heart, and youthful vigour at other epochs of Quaker history, the record would have been very different from what has been the case. It is, indeed, probable that at no other period did England provide in equal richness the mass of eager and spiritually minded seekers after truth that existed in those days of triumphant Puritanism. The Quaker message appealed with greatly reduced force to the Laodicæan spirit of a later age, but, allowing for this, the failure to secure a succession of men with the fire and gifts and first-hand experience of these early pioneers was a chief reason for the gradual declension of power.

The absorption of the Westmorland Seekers* was important in another way. It provided the new movement with a type of meeting out of which the Friends' meeting could naturally develop, and with an existing organization, immature no doubt, but sufficiently established to provide corporate fellowship to a number of groups of persons who met in their own meetings, but also kept in touch with one another throughout a wide district, as the existence of the General Meeting once a month at Preston Patrick shows. It was accordingly easy for Fox, a few weeks later, to go from place to place and settle meetings at Sedbergh, Preston Patrick, Kendal, Underbarrow, and Hutton, and soon afterwards at Grayrigg.[1] Westmorland thus became at once a strong centre of Quakerism. Howgill gives us a charming glimpse into the warm fellowship of those early days:[2]

The Kingdom of Heaven did gather us, and catch us all, as in a net and His heavenly power at one time drew many hundreds to land, that we came to know a place to stand in and what to wait in, and the Lord appeared daily to us, to our astonishment, amazement, and great admiration, insomuch that we often said one unto another, with great joy of heart, "What? Is the Kingdom of God come to be with men? And will He take up His tabernacle among the sons of men, as He did of old? And what? Shall we, that were reckoned as the outcasts

[1] *F.P.T.* 246. [2] Testimony in Burrough's *Works*.

of Israel, have this honour of glory communicated amongst us, which were but men of small parts, and of little abilities in respect of many others, as amongst men?"

From that day, he tells us, their hearts were knit to one another and to the Lord in fervent love, not by any external covenant or form, but in the covenant of life with God, and they met together in the unity of the Spirit, treading down all contentions about religion or its practices. The more they found opportunity for waiting together, the more were they strengthened in their hope and faith, and holy resolutions were kindled to serve the Lord and declare His message by word and life. Burrough, in similar language,[1] speaks of their frequent meetings, their waitings on the Lord in pure silence from their own words and from all men's words, their sense of the word of the Lord in their hearts, burning up and beating down all that was contrary to God, and their baptism with the Spirit, making their hearts glad and loosing their tongues. The new experience brought with it a fresh glow of spiritual life and a fresh fervour of fellowship, which filled men with wonder and joy. The fellowship of Pentecost and the fraternal joys of the early Franciscans were reproduced among the simple-hearted "statesmen" of Westmorland.

It is worth our while, before closing this chapter, to consider for a moment in what respects a devout member of this great Seeker community fell short of the full experience which afterwards came to him under the preaching of Fox. The experiences of Howgill, Audland, Taylor, Burrough, and Hubberthorne, already recorded, throw light on this question, and Howgill deals with it at length in one of the finest of his tracts, which was addressed to Seekers, and is called "A Lamentation for the Scattered Tribes, etc." (1656).[2] The separated fellowships, he says, had a zeal which showed them that the national way of worship under Prelacy and Presbytery was not according to the mind of the Lord. They had sought to

[1] Preface to the Reader at the beginning of Fox's *Great Mistery*.

[2] Howgill's *Works*, pp. 65-88, especially pp. 67-71.*

conform themselves to the practices of the primitive Church, and had there set up their rest, walking according to the most exact pattern that was visible or written. But in so doing they became ministers of the letter, and in their very conformity to the first Apostles were departing from their ministry, for they had been ministers of a living experience which they had themselves tasted. By thus gathering men into a conformity to the letter and to that which was visible, they were missing Christ the substance and teaching a religion which was all at a distance, grounded on the report of Christ dying at Jerusalem, and the belief in this report they called faith. They boasted themselves in their ordinances, the water and the bread and wine, which were but elementary and never anything but a sign, and in the day of appearance of Christ the elements would melt with fervent heat. He goes on to say in words of rare spiritual beauty:

If you build upon anything or have confidence in anything which stands in time and is on this side eternity and the Being of beings, your foundation will be swept away, and night will come upon you, and all your gathered-in things and taken-on and imitated will all fail you. . . . Why gad you abroad? Why trim you yourselves with the saints' words, when you are ignorant of the life? Return, return to Him that is the first love, and the firstborn of every creature, who is the Light of the world. . . . Return home to within: sweep your houses all, the groat is there, the little leaven is there, the grain of mustard-seed you will see which the Kingdom of God is like . . . and here you will see your Teacher not removed into a corner, but present when you are upon your beds and about your labour, convincing, instructing, leading, correcting, judging, and giving peace to all that love and follow Him.

CHAPTER V

SWARTHMORE *

(1652)

Oh, the love which in that day abounded among us, especially in that family [at Swarthmore], and oh, the freshness of the power of the Lord God which then was amongst us, and the zeal for God and His truth, the comfort and refreshment which we had from His presence, the nearness and dearness that was amongst us one towards another, the sights, openings and revelations which we then had. . . . And hence came that worthy family to be so renowned in the nation, the fame of which spread much among Friends, and the power and presence of the Lord being so much there with us, it was as a means to induce many even from far to come thither, so that at one time there would have been Friends out of five or six counties.—WILLIAM CATON'S *Life*, 1689 edn. chap. iii.

WE left Fox on his way into Lancashire, going towards that remote district of Furness, which down to the last century remained insular in position and character. "A stranger was promptly detected, and without much ceremony made aware that he was regarded, in the local phraseology, as an 'outcome.'"[1] Accordingly, at Staveley (Lakeside) on the Sunday (20th June) following the Underbarrow meeting, Fox was subjected to a Furness welcome when he spoke "the word of life" to the people, after the minister was done. The rough crowd, with the churchwarden at their head, dragged him out of the church, gave him a beating, and threw him headlong over a stone wall. A youth in the chapel, who was taking down the sermon, John Braithwaite by name, came to be convinced, and became one of the Quaker Publishers of Truth.[2]

[1] Paper by John Fell in *Transactions of Cumberland and Westmorland Archaeological Society*, xi. 360, cited from Dr. Thos. Hodgkin's *George Fox*, p. 64 *n*.

[2] *Journ*. i. 118. *Short Journ*. 19 supplies the name of the place. Cf. Margt. Fell in *Journ*. ii. 512. For Braithwaite see note in *Camb. Journ*. i. 406.

He now comes to Swarthmore Hall, near Ulverston, an Elizabethan manor-house, still standing, where there was a great profession of religion*and open house was kept for travelling ministers. These "lecturing ministers" would often have prayers and religious exercises in the family. "This," says the mistress, Margaret Fell, "I hoped I did well in, but often feared I was short of the right way."[1] The master, Thomas Fell, member of the Long Parliament, Judge of Assize of the Chester and North Wales Circuit, Vice-Chancellor of the Duchy and Attorney for the County Palatine of Lancaster,[2] was away at the time—a man of about fifty-four and a pillar of the State, though he afterwards withdrew himself from public life, disapproving the Protector's assumption of authority. The mistress, Margaret Fell, was sixteen years younger than her husband and ten years the senior of Fox. She belonged to an old county family, the Askews of Marsh Grange, but her descent from the martyred Anne Askew is most improbable, though frequently asserted.[3] Writing in 1685 to Lord Ancrum,[4] she said:

> For my own self, I have very few [relations]: my father was a gentleman living in Furness, behind the Sands, his name was Askew, and had a good estate as it was counted in his time, and he had children only me and another daughter,*and he left us as good as £6000, when I was married to my first husband.

The father, John Askew, brought her up at Marsh Grange according to her rank, till she was between seventeen and

[1] *Works* (1710), p. 2.

[2] *Dict. Natl. Biography.*

[3] Dr. Thos. Hodgkin, *George Fox*, and Maria Webb, *Fells of Swarthmoor Hall*, both give currency to this idea, and the latter (p. 39) also wrongly gives Fox's visit as "the winter of 1652." Joseph J. Green, one of the most accurate of our Quaker genealogists, writes to *The Friend* of 2nd February 1906: "As a collateral descendant of John and Rachel Abraham of Manchester, whose son Daniel married Rachel Fell of Swarthmore Hall, I have frequently been favoured with the correspondence of their descendant, Miss Emma C. Abraham of Liverpool, on historical subjects. She informs me that the statement made in . . . 'The Fells of Swarthmoor Hall' . . . is non-proven and has probably no foundation in fact. The name of Askew, Ascough, or Ayscue is of frequent occurrence in the early Ulverston parish registers." See also reference in *J.F.H.S.* vi. 179, to a paper by John Brownhill, M.A., of Lancaster, making it quite clear that there was no relationship.*

[4] Dev. Ho., A.R.B. Colln. No. 105, dated 31st January 1685.

eighteen, when she married Thomas Fell, and as the years passed became the mother of nine children, of whom seven daughters and one son were living at his death in 1658.[1] She describes herself as having been a Seeker for the twenty years from her marriage to the year 1652, being one that sought after the best things and was desirous of serving God, and went often to hear the best ministers that came into Furness; but it is clear that she was not a Separatist, and continued diligent in her attendance at the Ulverston church.

She had already heard of a people that were risen up, and some of them imprisoned at York, and did very much inquire after them.[2] She also seems to have had a vision of a man in a white hat who should come and confound the priests.[3] But she knew nothing of Quakers till she heard of Fox coming towards them, when he was twenty miles off, presumably at Kendal.[4] It does not appear that Fox went to Swarthmore at her express invitation; she simply says:[5] "Our house being a place open to entertain ministers and religious people at, one of George Fox's friends brought him hither, where he stayed all night."

Judge Fell was away on the Welsh circuit, and Margaret Fell was also out, but William Lampitt,[6] the Ulverston minister, came up to the Hall and had a long talk with Fox, who perceived he was a Ranter in his mind, talking of high notions and perfection, and so deceiving the people. "He would have owned me," says Fox, "but I could not own nor join with him, he was so full of filth."[6] In the evening Fox had much conversation with Margaret Fell, who had been distressed to hear of his disagreement with Lampitt. The next day there was a "lecture" by Lampitt at Ulverston[7] to which Fox

[1] See Margt. Fell's *Works*, pp. 1, 2.
[2] Testimony in Fox's *Journ.* ii. 512.
[3] *Camb. Journ.* i. 52.
[4] Address to Reader in Spence MSS. iii. fol. 132.
[5] Testimony in Fox's *Journ.* ii. 512.
[6] *Journ.* i. 119. In Calamy's *Ejected Ministers* he is spoken of as "a warm and lively preacher."
[7] I follow Margt. Fell's account in *Journ.* ii. 512.

was invited, but he walked in the fields until the word of the Lord came to him to go to the church. When he arrived, they were singing before the sermon, and, to quote Margaret Fell's account,

> . . when they had done singing, he stood up upon a seat or form, and desired that he might have liberty to speak, and he that was in the pulpit said he might. And the first words that he spoke were as followeth, "He is not a Jew that is one outward, neither is that circumcision, which is outward; but he is a Jew that is one inward, and that is circumcision which is of the heart." And so he went on, and said how that Christ was the Light of the world, and lighteth every man that cometh into the world, and that by this Light they might be gathered to God, etc. And I stood up in my pew, and I wondered at his doctrine, for I had never heard such before. And then he went on, and opened the scriptures, and said The scriptures were the prophets' words, and Christ's and the apostles' words, and what as they spoke they enjoyed and possessed and had it from the Lord. And said, "Then what had any to do with the scriptures but as they came to the Spirit that gave them forth? You will say, Christ saith this, and the apostles say this, but what canst thou say? Art thou a Child of Light, and hast walked in the Light, and what thou speakest is it inwardly from God, etc.?" This opened me so, that it cut me to the heart, and then I saw clearly we were all wrong. So I sat me down in my pew again, and cried bitterly: and I cried in my spirit to the Lord, "We are all thieves, we are all thieves, we have taken the scriptures in words, and know nothing of them in ourselves."

Weeping in her pew among her children, she heard little more of the address, having her own thoughts, but when a Puritan magistrate, John Sawrey, ordered Fox to be taken away, who was by this time declaring with his usual vehemence against false prophets, Mistress Fell called out from her place, "Let him alone, why may not he speak as well as any other?"[1] That night he spoke in the Hall among the servants of the Fell family, and they were all impressed and afterwards convinced: Thomas Salthouse and Ann Clayton, who became Publishers of the Quaker message, Mary Askew, and,

[1] For this see *Journ.* i. 120.

chief of all, William Caton, then a lad of sixteen, companion to the young squire George Fell.*

As for Margaret Fell, she was struck into such a sadness that she knew not what to do, her husband being from home. She saw the truth and could not deny it; indeed she says, "I had never a tittle in my heart against it, but I desired the Lord that I might be kept in it." During the next few weeks, Fox came and went, making three important converts, Thomas Lawson of Rampside, James Lancaster of Walney Island, and Leonard Fell of Baycliff. Thomas Lawson was a minister, and a man of learning, who afterwards followed the profession of schoolmaster, and became a noted botanist.[1] James Lancaster became closely associated with Fox in some of his travels, and was evidently a sterling character. Leonard Fell was a man of a loving spirit, the same age as Fox, who visited Scotland three times, and gave faithful service to the Quaker church.[2] Meanwhile, James Nayler and Richard Farnsworth reached Swarthmore, having followed in the track of Fox, enquiring after him from place to place. They were able to help Margaret Fell in her spiritual struggle, and this seems to have reached its crisis about two weeks after she first met Fox, when a strange working of Divine power came upon her, similar, no doubt, to "the power" of which we have already had instances in Yorkshire.[3] "The power of the Lord entered upon me," she says, while Fox tells us[4] "the Lord's power seized upon Margaret Fell and her daughter Sarah and several of them."

A week later the Judge came home across the dangerous sands which gave the only approach from Lancaster. A party of captains and magistrates, all in a great state of anger, met him on the sands, and told him that the Quakers had bewitched his family, and taken them out of their religion, and must be packed off or all the country would be undone. He came to the Hall greatly offended,

[1] See Smith's *Catalogue of Friends' Books*, sub nomine; and note in *Camb. Journ.* i. 408.

[2] For MS. particulars of Leonard Fell see Dev. Ho. Portfolio 2, No. 7.

[3] Margt. Fell's account in *Journ.* ii. 513.

[4] *Journ.* i. 121.

sorely troubled with his wife and the whole household, but Farnsworth and Nayler discoursed with him and persuaded him to be still and weigh things before he took any action, and in this way somewhat pacified him.

"And then," says Margaret Fell, "was he pretty moderate and quiet, and his dinner being ready, he went to it, and I went in and sat me down by him. And whilst I was sitting, the power of the Lord seized upon me: and he was stricken with amazement and knew not what to think, but was quiet and still. And the children were all quiet and still and grown sober, and could not play on their music that they were learning, and all these things made him quiet and still. And then at night George Fox came: and after supper my husband was sitting in the parlour, and I asked him if George Fox might come in, and he said, Yes. So George came in without any compliment, and walked into the room, and began to speak presently, and the family and James Nayler and Richard Farnsworth came all in, and he spoke very excellently as ever I heard him, and opened Christ and the apostles' practices which they were in, in their day. And he opened the night of apostasy since the apostles' days and laid open the priests and their practices in the apostasy, that if all in England had been there I thought they could not have denied the truth of those things. And so my husband came to see clearly the truth of what he spoke, and was very quiet that night, and said no more and went to bed."[1]

In the course of the conversation, the Judge asked Fox if he was the man whom the Yorkshire magnate Luke Robinson had been commending among the Members of Parliament, and Robinson's favourable opinion no doubt weighed with him. The next morning, a Friday in July, the Ulverston minister Lampitt did his best in the Swarthmore garden to influence Fell against the Friends, but with little result. Some of them were in the house, discussing where they could hold a meeting, and of his own accord he offered them the use of the Hall.

"And then," says Margaret Fell, "notice was given that day and the next to Friends, and there was a good large meeting the first-day, which was the first meeting that was at

[1] Margt. Fell's account in *Journ.* ii. 513. Cf. Margt. Fell's *Works*, pp. 2, 3, and *Journ.* i. 122, 123.

Swarthmore, and so continued there a meeting from 1652 till 1690. And my husband went that day to the steeple-house, and none with him but his clerk and his groom that rid with him, and the priest and people were all fearfully troubled."[1]

The visitor to Swarthmore Hall can still see the dining-hall where Friends held their meetings, and the little justice-room adjoining, where the Judge transacted his legal business, and would often sit, it is said, with door ajar, to hear the Quaker-preaching.[2] Overhead is the guest-chamber, and a window, once a door, from which tradition tells us Fox would sometimes preach when the congregation crowded out the dining-hall. The Hall, with its fervent mistress and large-hearted master, became both an "asylum," or place of shelter, and a "focus," or family-hearth, for Quakerism in its early days.

Thomas Fell protected the new movement, but he never identified himself with it.* He showed many kindnesses to Friends, and shielded them from persecution: his wife says that during his last illness he became more than usually loving to them, having been always a merciful man to God's people. But the same breadth of judgment which enabled him to appreciate the deep spirituality of Quakerism would also give him unity with true-hearted men outside the Quaker pale, and he no doubt preserved to the last the catholicity which had thrown Swarthmore open to ministers and religious people of all kinds.

It says much for the spiritual insight and experience of Judge Fell that he was able to recognize the essential sanity of the new truth in spite of the extravagance of statement and the excitement of conduct which accompanied it. Fox, with his intense fervour and prophetic authority, had been received into the Swarthmore family almost as a new Messiah. There is extant a letter[3] to

[1] Margt. Fell's account in *Journ.* ii. 514.

[2] Sewel (edn. 1811), ii. 573.

[3] The letter is in the Spence MSS. vol. iii. fol. 24. A facsimile and somewhat incorrect transcript are given in *Quakerism Examined*, by Jno. Wilkinson, 1836 The letter is signed by Margt. Fell and her two eldest daughters, Margaret and

him from Margaret Fell and other members of the household, which shows the excesses of language into which ardent devotees might be led. It is in substance an earnest plea for the return to Swarthmore of the young prophet, but contains passages of perilous rhapsody:

Our dear father in the Lord . . . we thy babes with one consent being gathered together in the power of the Spirit, thou being present with us, our souls doth thirst and languish after thee, and doth challenge that right that we have in thee, O thou bread of life, without which bread our souls will starve. O for evermore give us this bread, and take pity on us whom thou hast nursed up with the breasts of consolation. . . .

O our dear nursing father, we hope thou wilt not leave us comfortless, but will come again: though that sorrow be for a time, yet joy comes in the morning: O our life, we hope to see thee again that our joy may be full; for in thy presence is fullness of joy, and where thou dwells is pleasures for evermore. O thou fountain of eternal life, our souls thirsts after thee, for in thee alone is our life and peace, and without thee have we no peace: for our souls is much refreshed by seeing thee, and our lifes is preserved by thee, O thou father of eternal felicity.

In several other letters of this kind received by Fox, the offensive phrases have been struck through,[1] but here there is no note of dissent, although the paper bears endorsements in his own handwriting, probably made at some later date when he was arranging his papers.[2]

Bridget, and by Thos. Salthouse, Ann Clayton (Cleaton), Mary Askew, and Wm. Caton. Short messages from the four younger daughters, Isabel, Sarah, Mary, and Susanna, are added, and an urgent postscript from Margt. Fell pressing Fox for a further visit.

[1] I may instance the following: Mary Howgill to Fox, 1656, cited in *F.P.T.* 201 *n.*; Thos. Curtis to Fox, 1659, Swarthm. Colln. iii. 87; Richd. Sale to Fox, 1655, Swarthm. Colln. iv. 211; Thos. Holme to Fox, 1655, Swarthm. Colln. iv. 244. In other cases no erasure occurs, *e.g.* Mary Prince to Fox, 1656, Swarthm. Colln. iv. 58; Ann Burden to Fox, Swarthm. Colln. iii. 102. Other cases are given in the envenomed Anti-Quaker writings of the end of the seventeenth century, *e.g. The Snake in the Grass*, 1698 edn. pp. 114, 115.*

[2] The following very early letter from Fox to Margt. Fell (Swarthm. Colln. iii. 186, with covering letter from Audland) may be the reply to this; in any case it shows the kind of reply he probably made: "Dear and tender and loving sister in the truth of God, my tender love in the truth of God to thee and all the rest of thy family in the truth. Walk in the truth of God, and in that which keeps you pure to God: and the everlasting God of power and truth keep you to Himself in His truth, to whom be praise and honour and glory for ever. The Lord doth show much of His love and power here amongst us, to Him be praise for ever, to the confounding of the deceit for the simple ones' sake and making His power known and thy words are fulfilled. I can say little of coming over."

It is charitable to suppose that the letter was the first he received from Margaret Fell, and was kept as a precious memento rather than for its contents. Perhaps it is not possible for us to put ourselves in the writer's place. The new spiritual experience had exalted her life, and had caused her to rest herself in the young prophet's larger personality, which she felt to be possessed by the living spirit of Christ. In giving expression to this feeling in an intimate letter, she inevitably made use of the Biblical phraseology alone familiar to her, and in her gush of feeling and poverty of vocabulary seems to have lost a due sense of the value of the words used. Such a document reveals the tendencies which in their acute form produced the disaster of James Nayler's fall. If the country-side had seen it, it would have confirmed the belief that Margaret Fell was bewitched and that Fox was a blasphemer. His actions indeed at this time aroused the fiercest likes and dislikes. The iconoclast was sometimes idolized and sometimes stoned. The following, from the so-called *Short Journal*, shows the spirit in which he moved from place to place:

> I went into Kendal market and spoke to the people at the market time. I had silver in my pocket, and I was moved to throw it out amongst the people as I was going up the street before I spoke and my life was offered up amongst them . . . and the power of the Lord was so mighty and so strong that people flew before and run into the shops, for fear and terror took hold upon them. I was moved . . . to tell them the mighty Day of the Lord was coming upon all deceitful merchandize and ways and to call them all to repentance . . . and so passed through the streets, and when I came to the town's end I got upon a stump and spoke to the people, and so the people began to fight, some for me and some against me, and so after awhile I passed away without any harm.[1]

A few weeks later—we are now at the end of September 1652—Fox returns to Swarthmore and finds the Furness people embittered against him.[2] He attempts to speak in Ulverston church and is mobbed; and Justice Sawrey,

[1] *Short Journ.* 21, 22. [2] *Journal*, i. 132.

"the first stirrer up of cruel persecution in the North," hands him over to the constables to be whipped and put out of the town. They take him to the moss-side, give him a blow or two with their willow-rods and leave him to the rude multitude, who beat him with hedge-stakes and holly bushes till he falls senseless on the wet common. He stands up again "in the strengthening power of the Eternal God," and stretching out his arms over them bids them strike again. A mason with a walking rule-staff takes him at his word, and numbs his arm with a cruel blow, but Fox looks at it in the love of God, for he says, "I was in the love of God to them all," and the arm is strong again. With unflinching courage he goes back through the daunted people into Ulverston market. A soldier*takes his part, saying, "Sir, I am ashamed that you should be thus abused, for you are a man."[1] A fortnight later a pistol is snapped at him, but does not go off; and in Walney Island he is knocked down and half-drowned by a rabble of men, who charge him with bewitching his new adherent, James Lancaster. He gets back to the mainland, where he is roughly handled by a crowd who cry out, "Knock him on the head." There is a warrant out against him*for blasphemy, but Judge Fell returns again to Swarthmore, and it is not served. Fox, however, rides over with Fell to the Lancaster sessions on the 18th October[2] to answer it. The main charge was that he affirmed himself to be equal with God,[3] but the evidence when sifted out by Judge Fell's questions proved untrustworthy. Fox[4] himself said:

> . . ., that was not so spoken that I was equal with God, [but] He that sanctifieth and he that is sanctified are all of one, they are one in the Father and the Son, and of His flesh and of His bone, this the scripture doth witness, and ye are the sons of God, and the Father and the Son are one.

---

[1] *Journ.* i. 133, and *Short Journ.* 24, 25.

[2] The date is supplied by James Nayler's letter of the 30th October given in *Journ.* i. 140.

[3] See *The perfect Pharise under Monkish Holines*, 1654 edn., p. 3; cf. the Lancashire Petition, *infra*.

[4] A verbatim report of much of the trial is given in the *Cambridge Journal*, i. 63–68, one of the inserted illustrative documents.

To the charge that he said he was the judge of the world he replied, "The saints shall judge the world, whereof I am one," and, when asked if he believed himself as upright as Christ, he said, "As He is, so are we in this present world: the saints are made the righteousness of God." Full liberty was given him to speak, and he declared his message with great power. At the ensuing assizes the opposing justices informed the judge against him, but Colonel William West, the Clerk of Assize, refused to make out a warrant and offered up body for body and his estate for Fox, so stopping the judge's mouth.[1] A number of Lancashire justices and ministers now petitioned the Council of State against Fox and against Nayler, who also had been busily publishing the Quaker message in North Lancashire. But again their ragings were impotent, for Fox and his friends obtained a copy and sent their answer up to London, while the petitioners, owing to the cost, never sent the petition up at all.[2] The proceedings occasioned "Saul's Errand to Damascus, with His Packet of Letters from the High Priests against the Disciples of the Lord, etc.," London 1653, by Fox and others, which deserves careful notice. The book contains an admirable Preface to the Christian Reader by an expert hand, hoping that "the Lord will never suffer that monster persecution again to enter within the gates of England's Whitehall," and suggesting that the loyalty to the Commonwealth of the contrivers of the petition is by no means above suspicion. The petition is printed, denouncing Fox and Nayler for subverting religion and the ordinary relationships of life, in a fashion which reminds us of the charges against the early Christians. Moreover, they

> . . . have drawn much people after them: many whereof (men, women and little children) at their meetings are strangely wrought upon in their bodies, and brought to fall, foam at the mouth, roar and swell in their bellies. And that some of them affirmed themselves to be equal with God, contrary to the late Act, etc.

Accordingly the Council is desired to take some speedy

[1] *Journ.* i. 143; *Short Journ.* 72.

[2] *Short Journ.* 27.

course for suppressing these evils. There is a schedule which amongst other things charges Fox with professing himself to be equal with God, to be the eternal judge of the world and to be the Christ, the Way, the Truth, and the Life. Neither Fox nor Nayler refutes the charge about the strange workings—foamings and the like—at Quaker meetings, a charge for which in that age of religious excitement there was no doubt a good deal of foundation. Fox replies to the more serious charges, as he had done at the quarter sessions, by denying that he had ever made such statements in the sense that George Fox was equal with God or that George Fox was Christ, but he insists that the new life, the spiritual man, is the Lord from heaven and that Christ is one in all His saints. Fox's words, even in this answer, are open to misconstruction. The following especially was laid hold of:

> Where He [that is, Christ Jesus] is made manifest, the works of the devil are destroyed and there He speaks and is king, and is the way, and is the truth, and is the life . . . and he that hath the same spirit that raised up Jesus Christ is equal with God. And the scripture saith that God will dwell in man and walk in man. As Jesus Christ, which is the mystery, hath passed before, so the same spirit takes upon it the same seed and is the same where it is made manifest. According to the flesh I am the son of Abraham, according to the Spirit the Son of God, saith Christ.

Fox, and others of the early Friends, had a vivid sense of personal union with their living Lord, but they coupled this experience of the indwelling Christ with a doctrine of perfection that betrayed them, during the first exhilaration of the experience, into extremes of identification with the Divine. They believed that inspiration gave infallibility, a belief that men have often held with respect to the writers of scripture, and they had to learn, with the help of some painful lessons, what we are learning to-day about the writers of scripture, that the inspired servant of God remains a man, liable to much of human error and weakness. The subject is dealt with temperately, considering the controversial virulence of the day, in a little book called *The Quakers' Wilde Questions*, London, 1654, written by Richard Sherlock, the chaplain to Sir Robert Bindloss of Borwick, near Carnforth, in order to protect Lady Rebecca Bindloss from being beguiled as Margaret Fell had been. He treats the Holy Spirit as bestowed on man, not in His personal essence but only in His qualifications, and it is significant to note his evident feeling that if the bestowal of a personal Spirit be admitted the position taken by Friends was not an unreasonable one.

> For our new sect of Enthusiasts, had they the Spirit of God as they pretend abiding in them and speaking in them personally and essentially, this blasphemy must necessarily follow, that they are equal with God, in respect of the Spirit in them, as themselves affirm it, though not as George [Fox], Robert [Widders], etc.[1]

He is on stronger ground when he says, too sweepingly no doubt, but still with some measure of truth:

> This [light within us], say they, is the only Judge we must follow, the Pilot we must steer by, the Voice whereunto we must give ear, the only sanctuary to which we must fly for resolution, never remembering how this sanctuary is profaned by continual acts of spiritual fornication or idolatry therein committed; whilst instead and even in opposition to [the] God and Spirit of all truth they enshrine and idolize their own fond, vain and lying imaginations.[2]

It was this inadequate recognition of the earthly character of the vessel that was responsible for most of the excesses of early Quakerism.

[1] P. 66. I have filled out the names.

[2] P. 112.

CHAPTER VI

FURTHER WORK IN THE NORTH

(1653–1654)

The next day we came through the country into Cumberland again, where we had a General Meeting of many thousands of people atop of an hill near Langlands. A glorious and heavenly meeting it was; for the glory of the Lord did shine over all; and there were as many as one could well speak over, the multitude was so great. Their eyes were fixed on Christ, their Teacher, and they came to sit under their own vine, insomuch that Francis Howgill coming afterwards to visit them, found they had no need of words. . . . A great convincement there was in Cumberland, Bishopric, Northumberland, Westmorland, Lancashire, and Yorkshire, and the plants of God grew and flourished so, the heavenly rain descending and God's glory shining upon them, that many mouths were opened by the Lord to His praise, yea to babes and sucklings He ordained strength.—GEORGE FOX, *Journal*, i. 182 (anno 1653).

AFTER the Lancaster assizes Fox spent the midwinter of 1652-53 at Swarthmore, whence he issued several strongly worded letters to those who had persecuted Friends. Meanwhile the Westmorland clergy had roused themselves, and were petitioning the justices against Nayler, Fox, and Howgill. Nayler found the Kendal people hostile, and in November he and Howgill were taken before a justice at Kirkby Stephen and were committed to Appleby gaol.[1] At the January sessions Nayler was charged with blasphemy for saying that Christ was in him, and that there was but one Word of God. The striking account he gave of his spiritual experience convinced, as we have seen, one of the justices, Anthony Pearson, as he sat on the Bench, and another justice, Gervase Benson, was already a Friend. There was clearly

[1] For the trial see Nayler's *Works*, pp. 1-16. See also Besse, *Sufferings*, ii. 3-6. Cf. *F.P.T.* p. 248, and letter, Nayler to Margt. Fell, Swarthm. Colln. i. 85.

no blasphemy within the Act, but a majority of the justices, law or no law, continued Nayler and Howgill in prison to answer the petitions that had been presented, and they were not released till Easter 1653. In beautiful words Nayler writes from his prison:[1]

> Dear hearts, you make your own troubles by being unwilling and disobedient to that which would lead you safe. There is no way but to go hand in hand with Him in all things, running after Him without fear or considering, leaving the whole work only to Him. If He seem to smile, follow Him in fear and love, and, if He seem to frown, follow Him and fall into His will, and you shall see He is yours still,—for He will prove His own.

Anthony Pearson, of Ramshaw Hall, near St. Helen's Auckland, Durham, was a justice in three counties and a notable recruit to the Quaker Movement.[2] He was a young man of twenty-five, a native of Lancashire, who had been secretary to one of the chief Parliamentary leaders, Sir Arthur Hesilrige, and served as Clerk and Registrar to the Committee on Compounding. He took an early opportunity of seeking out Fox at Swarthmore, and was much impressed with him and with the Fell household, "a family walking in the fear of the Lord, conversing daily with Him, crucified to the world and living only to God." The letter containing the above[3] was written in May 1653, and shows him adrift from his old religious moorings but not yet anchored in the new experience. It throws so clear a light on the difference between Quakerism and the "notional" or doctrinal religion of the day that I make no apology for a full quotation.

> I have long professed to serve and worship the true God, and, as I thought, above many sects attained to a high pitch in religion. But now, alas, I find my work will not abide the fire: my notions were swelling vanities without power or life: what it

---

[1] Nayler to Fox, Swarthm. Colln. iii. 66 (February 1653).*

[2] See particulars of his life in Jno. W. Steel's *Early Friends in the North*, 1905, pp. 8–11; life in *Dict. Natl. Biography*; and note in *Camb. Journ.* i. 470.

[3] Swarthm. Colln. i. 87, and iii. 33, printed in *Letters of Early Friends*, p. 10 *n.*, and, less correctly, in *Fells of Swarthmoor Hall*, p. 71.*

was to love enemies, to bless them that curse, to render good for evil, to use the world as using it not, to lay down life for the brethren, I never understood: what purity and perfection meant I never tasted: all my religion was but the hearing of the ear, the believing and talking of a God and Christ in heaven or a place at a distance, I knew not where. Oh, how gracious was the Lord to me in carrying me to Judge Fell's to see the wonders of His power and wisdom. . . . I was so confounded all my knowledge and wisdom became folly: my mouth was stopped, my conscience convinced, and the secrets of my heart made manifest, and that Lord discovered to be near that I ignorantly worshipped. I could have talked of Christ in the saints the hope of glory, but it was a riddle to me: and truly, dear friend, I must tell thee I have now lost all my religion and am in such distress I have no hope nor foundation left. My justification and assurance have forsaken me, and I am even like a poor shattered vessel tossed to and fro without a pilot or rudder, as blind, dead and helpless as thou canst imagine. . . . What it means to wait upon God I cannot apprehend, and the confusions in my own spirit, together with the continual temptations from without are so great, I cannot understand nor perceive the small still voice of the Lord.

In accordance with a desire expressed in this letter, Nayler, his former prisoner and now his spiritual guide, visited him at Ramshaw in July,[1] and had a meeting at which several were convinced. Pearson was with Fox in the course of the summer, and for some years continued a zealous Friend, travelling long distances in the service of truth, taking a leading part, as we shall see, in matters of organization, continually using his best efforts to mitigate the rigour of the authorities, writing the standard Quaker book against tithes, and throwing his house open to ministers. He kept up his active interest in politics, and probably shared the dissatisfaction of his leader, Sir Arthur Hesilrige, with the Protectorate. In the autumn of 1654 he attended some of the meetings of the plotter Wildman, presumably on behalf of Hesilrige, one of the men who was expected to help.[2] In August 1659 Howgill found him immersed in his affairs, and wrote:[3]

[1] *F.P.T.* 88.

[2] Gardiner, *Hist. of Commth. and Prot.* iii. 229 *n.*

[3] Howgill to Burrough, Durham, 8th Augt. 1659, Dev. Ho., A.R.B. Colln. No. 60.

I pity Anthony; there is a good thing in him if he did keep out of the world's spirit, for that betrays him and hurts him, however at present he is low and diligent at meetings.

At the end of the same month Howgill wrote [1] that Pearson was a Commissioner for the militia, and would have raised the country round Kendal against the Royalist insurgents in Lancashire, but was thwarted by others. After the Restoration, he was informed against [2] for this action and for corresponding with disaffected persons, but successfully cleared himself. He says:

I confess amongst others I was drawn into opinions in religion, which in those days transported me into excesses—zeal in young years commonly exceeding knowledge—which made my carriage offensive to many, being forward to assist my own party, which I then took to be the most honest and harmless. And in this I hope I may expect a favourable censure, being ignorant of the doctrine and discipline of the Church of England and of the order and decency of ecclesiastical government and only nursed up with the chimerical notions of those giddy times, wherein I confess I was too apt to soar with the highest.

Having thus temporized, he became under-sheriff at Durham, and died a true son of the Church of England about 1665. Ramshaw Hall is occupied by a farmer, but is still much as it was two hundred and fifty years ago.[3] Anthony Pearson's last years of compromise and compliance should not make us forget that he sacrificed much of his strength and means to the Quaker movement, and placed his capacity for affairs at its service during the first critical period.

We now return to the summer of 1653. Nayler's work in Durham (then usually known as Bishopric) was followed up in October by a visit from Thos. Holme of Kendal.[4] A little later in the year Audland and Burrough came into the county. Audland wrote: [5]

[1] Howgill to Burrough, Kendal, 22nd Augt. [1659], Dev. Ho., A.R.B. Colln. No. 169. I supply the year from internal evidence. See *post*, p. 461.

[2] J. W. Steel, *op. cit.* p. 10, and *Extracts from State Papers*, Second Series, p. 138.

[3] J. W. Steel, *op. cit.* p. 11, with illustration.

[4] *F.P.T.* 89.

[5] *F.P.T.* 89, and *The Memory of the Righteous Revived*, p. 68. As Audland and Burrough are together (see the letter), and it is headed "soon after he was gone forth in the ministry," it may be placed here with confidence.

The harvest here is great, even all the fields are white, and all the dumb dogs, and idle shepherds, drones and loiterers runs, quakes, trembles and flies before us, but the sword of the Lord is in the hands of the saints, and this sword divides, hews and cuts down deceit, and so way is made for the pure seed to arise and reign above all, which conquers all. . . . I really see the Lord will raise up to Himself a pure and a large people to serve and worship Him in spirit and in truth.

Howgill and other Westmorland Friends also assisted. Burrough, "a brisk young man of a ready tongue,"[1] laboured in the county for some months, only returning to Kendal in February 1654. He speaks[2] of "abundance convinced of the Truth, and among the priests is a fire kindled: they are all in an uproar." He urged Fox to come for a few meetings, and suggested a General Meeting for religious fellowship at Shap in Westmorland. Fox's visit to Anthony Pearson's and to Durham and Northumberland probably followed in March.[3] Ann Audland had some trying experiences in Durham about the same time.[4] Altogether we find not less than thirteen "First Publishers of Truth," to use the Quaker phrase, at work in Bishopric during these nine months, clear evidence of a systematic campaign. Ramshaw Hall was the base of operations, and the clergy took alarm at the success of the new movement, as they had done in North Lancashire and in Westmorland. *The perfect Pharisc under Monkish Holines*, published by five Newcastle ministers in 1653, was designed as a preservative against the blasphemies and delusions of the Quakers. The chief of these ministers was Thomas Weld from Massachusetts, who had been foremost in the proceedings in 1637, which drove Mrs. Anne Hutchinson and others to Rhode Island.[5] Nayler replied to this book, and his answer called forth "A Further Discovery of that Generation of men called Quakers," a pamphlet printed at Gateside

[1] Thos. Ellwood's *Life*, 1714 edn. p. 19.
[2] Burrough to Fox, 7th February 1654, Swarthm. Colln. iii. 14.
[3] *Journ.* i. 180.
[4] See her life in *Piety Promoted*, part iii. p. 200, which says "about the beginning of 1654," *i.e.* March or April.
[5] See *The Quakers in the American Colonies*, p. 5.

(Gateshead) in 1654. Pearson's influential position no doubt shielded Friends from persecution, and the new movement spread rapidly. In Northumberland, on the other hand, the doors were closed on Friends. In April 1654 Burrough and Atkinson had found the county most inhospitable: they were put out of Alnwick and Berwick, and at one place were suspected of being horse-thieves; the people, says Burrough, were "the rudest, wild, savage people as ever I saw."[1] This wild nature is illustrated by an incident dated February 1655.[2] Some Friends spoke to the minister at Hasington; the country people fell on them and almost killed one or two, who, going out of the church, fell on their knees and prayed God to pardon the people, for they knew not what they did. Then they spoke with such force to the crowd that they left off beating the Quakers and began fighting among themselves.

In Durham the planting of the new seed was done by the men and women who had now gathered round Fox. He himself took a larger share in the work in Cumberland. Swarthmore had continued his centre till the latter part of July 1653,[3] but he then goes into Cumberland, whither his friend James Lancaster had already preceded him.[4] Fox says in his vivid way,[5] much as he afterwards said when entering Scotland, "I saw the sparks of life rose before I came into it, and a multitude of people the Lord had there." At Bootle[6] he finds an enraged minister and a turbulent people, who attempt his life. At Embleton

[1] Letter to Nayler, 25th April 1654, under cover of letter from George Taylor to Margt. Fell, Swarthm. Colln. iv. 170. About the same time Audland and Halhead underwent imprisonment for a time at Newcastle.

[2] Whitelocke's *Memorials* (1732 edn.), p. 618. Perhaps Easington, County Durham. See *F.P.T.* 90.

[3] The *Journal* is here innocent of all dates. The following are, however, ascertained *aliunde*: (*a*) John ap John's memo. of his visit to Fox shows that Fox was at Swarthmore as late as 21st July 1653 (John ap John Supplmt. to *J.F.H.S.* p. 6). (*b*) Fox is stated to have been at Thos. Bewley's at the beginning of August (see *F.P.T.* p. 47), but this should be the end of July, since his seven weeks' imprisonment at Carlisle began on Monday 1st August (see *A True Discovery of the Ignorance . . . of . . . Magistrates about Carlile*, by J[ohn] C[amm], 1654). He was still in prison on 11th September (see Rawlinson's letter to Margt. Fell in the *Camb. Journ.* i. 120). (*c*) Fox was at Pearson's (*Journ.* i. 181) beginning, say, March of the year 1654 (*Piety Promoted*, pt. iii. p. 200).

[4] *F.P.T.* 33.

[5] *Short Journ.*

[6] *Journ.* i. 159.

he has a great meeting, to which above a thousand persons flocked as to a horse-fair.[1] Fox stood on a seat in the church, largely declared the word of life to them for nearly three hours, and hundreds were convinced.[2] He held a similar meeting on the following Sunday at Brigham, and naïvely tells us that the minister "knew that the people was taken with truth in the country, and they would have comed to have heard me rather than him."[3] Most of this congregation joined Friends, including, after a time, the Baptist minister himself, John Wilkinson, who is to be distinguished from the "First Publisher" of the same name, the future Separatist.[4] Fox now, towards the end of July 1653, comes to Haltcliff Hall, the seat of Thomas Bewley. He was a man of about fifty-eight,[5] already obedient to the Spirit of God in his heart, and with his family at once received and championed the new truth.[6] Soon afterwards Fox reaches Carlisle, where he speaks his message to the Baptists in the Abbey, to the garrison in the castle, to the people in the market, and, finally, to the magistrates and others in the cathedral.[7] There his words cause a great tumult; people quiver and tremble; some say the cathedral itself is shaking, and it requires the help of friendly soldiers to keep Fox from the mob, who throw stones and shout, "Down with these Roundhead rogues." The next day he is had before the bench.

And one sware one thing and another sware another thing against me. And they asked me if I were the son of God. I said, "Yes." They asked me if I had seen God's face. I said "Yes." They asked me whether I had the spirit of discerning. I said, "Yes, I discerned him that spoke to me." They asked me whether the scripture was the word of God. I said, "God was the word, and the scriptures were writings, and the word was before writings were, which word did fulfil them." And so they sent me to prison.

For the third time the charge against Fox is that of blasphemy. The High Sheriff, Wilfrid Lawson, seems to

[1] *F.P.T.* 33; *Short Journ.* 29.
[2] *Journ.* i. 163.
[3] *Short Journ.* 30; *Journ.* i. 164.
[4] *F.P.T.* 34 and *note*; *ibid.* 70.
[5] See Besse, *Sufferings*, i. 132.
[6] *F.P.T.* 47.
[7] *Journ.* i. 166, etc.; *F.P.T.* 31; and for the examination before the magistrates, *Short Journ.* 32, 33.

have been greatly incensed against him. Fox is put in the dungeon among felons and moss-troopers, and bears almost incredible hardships from cruel gaolers and loathsome surroundings.

"The gaoler," he says,[1] "continued exceeding cruel, so that he beat Friends and friendly people exceedingly with great cudgels, as if he had been beating a pack of wool. And I could get up to the grate where sometimes I took my meat, and the gaoler was offended and came in a rage with his great staff, and he fell a-beating of me though I was not at the window at the time and cried, 'Come out of the window,' though I was far enough off it. And as he struck me, I was made to sing in the Lord's power; and that made him rage the more. And then he fetched a fiddler, and brought [him] into the dungeon, and set him to play, and when he played I was moved in the everlasting power of the Lord God to sing; and my voice drowned them, and struck them and confounded them, that [it] made them give over fiddling and go their ways."

Fox, as we shall remember, had already been convicted at Derby under the Blasphemy Act,[2] and on conviction for a second offence would be sent to gaol till the next assizes, and, if there convicted, would have been banished out of the Commonwealth, and for failing to go, and we may be sure that George would never have budged a step, he would have suffered "as in case of felony without benefit of clergy." Translated out of the legal jargon, this meant that he would have been hung, and accordingly at the assizes all the talk was that Fox was going to be hanged. The judges, however, did not put him on his trial, but left the case to the magistrates. Gervase Benson and Anthony Pearson wrote a fiery letter to the Carlisle authorities, and, what was more to the point, the Nominated Parliament in London, which sat from 4th July to 12th December, heard that a young man was to die for religion. This Parliament, according to

[1] *Camb. Journ.* i. 126.

[2] 1650, cap. 22 (Scobell, pt. ii. p. 124). Margt. Fell's letter to Col. William West, printed in her *Works*, pp. 40-45, and also in the *Cambridge Journal*, i. 116-120, says: "They intend banishment to George or else to the taking away of his life, if it be in their power, now at their sessions; for the Judges left him to them to proceed against according to the Act; and Lawson was in hopes to have gotten his life now taken away at the 'sizes."

our great seventeenth-century historian,[1] touched the high-water mark of Puritanism in Church and State, rejecting, on the one hand, all mundane influences and rights over the individual conscience, and upholding a purely voluntary system of religion, and, on the other, in spite of its unrepresentative character, willing to enforce its own policy in defiance of the national will. When Cromwell, at the end of its brief rule, resumed the powers which he had delegated to it, it was preparing to abolish tithes, and there was also alarm lest the universities should be destroyed, in accordance with the doctrine of William Dell, the Master of Caius—which was also that of Fox—that university teaching was useless for producing spiritual ministers of religion.[2] A list of the members has been preserved, divided into those favourable or unfavourable to the "godly learned ministry and universities." It is interesting to find in the more extreme list the names of several, who in the next few years either received or became Friends.[3] Such a Parliament was likely enough to interfere with the Carlisle authorities. Margaret Fell wrote up to Col. West, who had befriended Fox at Lancaster assizes, and was one of the Lancashire Members,[4] and a letter was sent from Westminster to the sheriff and magistrates. They anticipated its arrival, however, by releasing Fox, after he had been in custody seven weeks.[5]

About this time we have an interesting incident which shows the jealousy with which the Quaker apostle guarded his reputation among his own friends. Gervase Bennett, his persecutor at Derby, was a member of the Nominated Parliament, and had reported in London that Fox had been imprisoned in Derby for saying that Christ who died at Jerusalem was a rogue. Fox thereupon sent three Westmorland Seekers—Widders,

[1] Gardiner, *Hist. of the Commth. and Prot.* ii. 340.

[2] *Ibid.* ii. 322 *n.*, and Fox, *Great Mistery*, p. 113.

[3] Gardiner, *Hist. of the Commth. and Prot.* ii. 308 *n.* Robert Duncon and Edward Plumstead (Suffolk), Dennis Hollister (Somerset), John Swinton and Alexander Jeffries [Jaffray] (Scotland) seem to have joined Friends, while John Anlaby (Yorks), John Herring (Herefordshire), and Col. Willm. West (Lancashire) were at one time or another well-wishers.

[4] Letter in Margt. Fell's *Works*, pp. 40-45, and *Camb. Journ.* i. 116-120.

[5] See Besse, *Sufferings*, i. 127.

Halhead, and James Taylor—to Derby to make full inquiry into the facts, and they took a copy of the mittimus and of his examination before the magistrates, and procured a certificate from a minister present at the examination, who said that the alleged words had never been spoken. After thus clearing himself to the Westmorland Seekers, he wrote a letter of severe reproach to his slanderer, "for all the country people and the town and the priests and gaoler cleared George from thy lies and slanders."[1]

Fox spent the rest of 1653 mostly in Westmorland and at Swarthmore, but in the spring of 1654 visited Cumberland on his way to and from Durham. Others actively cultivated the new field; Dewsbury, Widders, and Lancaster were the most prominent and the most maltreated, but we read also of service by Audland, Holme, John Blaykling, Howgill, and Nayler.[2] A meeting was settled in 1653 at Peter Head's of Pardshaw, the first in Cumberland,[3] "and many were convinced of the Truth, [so] that the houses could not contain them, but they met without doors for many years on a place called Pardshaw Crag, and abundance of people crowded to the meetings." The Crag was a broken ridge of mountain limestone with several sides to it, which allowed Friends to find shelter in windy weather. After a time the meeting was divided into four in winter, which were held at different Friends' houses. In the summer Pardshaw Crag continued to be resorted to for nearly twenty years, till the building in 1672 of a meeting-house at the foot of the ridge. John Burnyeat was among those now convinced. Brought up[4] to believe that though he sinned the guilt of it would not be charged on him but imputed to Christ, and Christ's righteousness be imputed to him, the light to which he turned showed him the need of a Saviour to save from the power of sin, as well as the need of the blood of a

[1] *Camb. Journ.* i. 5.

[2] *F.P.T.*, Cumberland account.

[3] *F.P.T.* 37, 41; cf. Whitehead's *Christian Progress*, p. 124, and article in *Friend*, 10th March 1893. The present meeting-house, built in 1727, has over the stable entrance the "door-head" of the 1672 house.

[4] See Burnyeat's *Works*, pp. 1-11.

sacrificed Christ to blot out sin and of faith in His name for the remission of past sins. His invented notional faith was overthrown and found to be an Adam's fig-leaf apron in which he could not abide God's coming. He and others who had been reached now began to mourn after a Saviour and to look for a Deliverer. Often meeting together, they minded the Light of Christ in their hearts with a holy resolution to obey the Lord's will at all costs, and through much spiritual conflict came to know the wonderful power from on high revealed among them. Their meetings became times of great delight in the Lord, even when no word was spoken, and Burnyeat says the power of the Lord "wrought sweetly in our hearts, which still united us more and more unto God, and knit us together in the perfect bond of love, of fellowship and membership, so that we became a body compact, made up of many members, whereof Christ Himself became the Head." This account of the stages by which the Light of Christ in the heart changed high-professing Calvinists into a society of Children of the Light is worth giving in an abridged form, because it is typical of much of the work that Fox and his followers were now doing. But in several places in Cumberland* as in Westmorland the people had already moved far towards the Quaker experience before the new message was published among them.[1] Thus at Wigton in 1653 there was a little community of persons separated from the national worship and often sitting together in silence who joined Friends; at Bolton there was a people that was seeking the Lord and had left the dead way of worship then professed, and at Abbeyholme some zealous Roundheads had kept meetings in their houses before the coming of Friends and readily embraced the new truth. Many of the Cumberland meetings date their commencement from this year 1653, and Friends grew strong in numbers. Fox's experiences at Carlisle throw a clear light on the conditions under which Quakerism was making rapid way in the North of England. An atmosphere of qualified

[1] For the cases given see *F.P.T.* 52, 56, 73.*

religious liberty prevailed during the whole of the Commonwealth period, which favoured the new growth. But especially during the early years of the period, say from 1650 to 1654, the balance of power rested with men of advanced religious views, many of whom were not unfriendly to the Quakers and their opinions. These men were ruling over a distracted England with the help of the army, and were not likely to give support to the godless rabble and the Royalist or Presbyterian authorities who raged against the new sect of enthusiasts. Fox and his followers would indeed be regarded as a wing of the dominant religious party, and until the influence of this party in the State waned, the views of the Quakers and their opposition to a State ministry found in many quarters a ready acceptance.

Meanwhile the work in Yorkshire had gone on. Dewsbury, Farnsworth, and Nayler, when not engaged elsewhere, continued their zealous service. Farnsworth wrote in June 1653:

> The Lord carries on His work mightily in [these] parts and He is fitting labourers to send forth and hath fitted some already. . . . If my brother George was here now he might say, Who hath begotten me all these.[1]

John Whitehead proved a powerful helper, establishing meetings in Whitby and at several places in Cleveland, "for he declared the truth through their markets and many believed."[2] The Westmorland Seekers who had joined the movement were also active in Yorkshire.

In one other district, namely, Cheshire and the borders of Wales, work had also begun. The celebrated mystical preacher, Morgan Lloyd, the Independent minister of Wrexham, had a good deal of sympathy with the views of Fox.[3]

> "One cause," he wrote to Baxter, "of our present woeful Babylonish contention is the want of right apprehensions of the

---

[1] To Margt. Fell, Swarthm. Colln. iii. 47.

[2] *F.P.T.* 298.

[3] For these particulars and others respecting Morgan Lloyd see *A Hist. of the Older Nonconformity of Wrexham*, by A. N. Palmer, 1888, pp. 28, 22.*

Godhead in His Christ and Spirit. Neither shall man agree in God till the fleshly mind, that perks up in man's heart to judge of God's mind, be mortified. And in that the Quakers say well, as I think."

He insisted in his teaching that God and the Spirit were the only substances, the only things that were real.

Substance is every spirit: and the seen world is but a shadow of the unseen which pervades it: and the body also is but a shadow, and like as the clothes-horse of the spirit, or the sheath of the sword which shall endure for ever.

In July 1653 he sent two of his congregation into the north to inquire about Friends. One of them, John ap John, warmly embraced the new teaching.[1] In October, John Lawson of Lancaster and Hubberthorne went to Wrexham and attended a church-meeting there. The Quaker preachers, as was often the case, behaved with more zeal than charity, and were taken to task for speaking against one of the ministers; "the priest was silent, Richard laid more judgment on him: the priest sat sobbing." They reported[2] to Margaret Fell that the great idol, known as the Church at Wrexham, called themselves the people of God and saints, and said that Christ was in them, and had a high form of words, but denied the power of God and lived in pride, envy, and covetousness. Their visit, conducted in this spirit of judging, had little result, and they failed to recognize the open-mindedness, faithfulness to conviction, and freedom from convention which distinguished Morgan Lloyd's own deeply mystical character.

In Cheshire they fared better, and Separatist communities supplied the nucleus of meetings which were settled at Malpas and Morley. At Malpas on the Welsh border Lawson found one or two persons already convinced. His visit exhibits very vividly the clash of crude Quaker experience with established Puritanism. The ardent Quaker went to the church with four newly

[1] See his memo. in John ap John Supplmt. to *J.F.H.S.*, and Nayler to Fox, Swarthm. Colln. iii. 60.

[2] See letters Jno. Lawson to Margt. Fell, Swarthm. Colln. iv. 66, and iv. 69.*

convinced Friends. Soon the ecstatic state known as "the power" came on one of them, stopping the priest and making the people wonder and bless themselves. The man was put out, but came in again, and Lawson, who had left the church, says: "Presently I heard them all of an uproar, beating and haling my friend out of [the] steeple-house, for he had the power very fiercely as ever I saw any." The rest of that Sunday was a time of wild excitement, and the people spent Monday also in baiting the strange Quaker who, they no doubt believed, had bewitched their townsfolk. The Friend who had been seized with the power defended Lawson from the mob, and when they told him that his wife lay in a swoon at her count or nearby and was like to die, he replied, "Her blood be upon your heads, I will not leave my friend to you to murder him." Lawson was at last carried to the stocks and kept there four hours. He had liberty for a meeting with the Separatist community, about thirty in number, but was then thrown into Chester prison for six months with two of the newly convinced Malpas Friends. He writes:

> The people of this city come many to see us, I am made to speak the word of the Lord to them, which causeth often the power of the Lord to raise in my two friends, [and] makes the world to wonder at it.

Hubberthorne visited Malpas and the Separatists there seem to have divided into two parts, one meeting together and speaking their own words as before, the other waiting on the Lord without words. He also reached a separated community at Congleton, of whom he wrote in May 1654, about six months after his first visit: [1]

> About Congleton and Leek there is a people drawing in, where we have had some meetings, and many high separates and strong oaks that ways are convinced by the power of truth. . . . Send some Friends this ways as shortly as may be—but some are not fit for the work of the Lord in these parts, for they are a wise people, and must be comprehended and keeped out, for in their subtlety many would be approved of.

[1] *F.P.T.* 18, and Hubberthorne to Fox, Swarthm. Colln. iv. 1.

This is not a request for a man of great learning, but rather for labourers of deep spiritual experience who could take these high professors into a region where the emptiness of their notions would be made manifest.

In November 1653 Hubberthorne had been committed to Northgate prison at Chester on frivolous grounds, and while there convinced Thomas Yarwood, a great Puritan professor and preacher,[1] who soon carried the new teaching to Seekers at Mobberley, afterwards Morley meeting, "whose custom was, when met together, neither to preach nor pray vocally, but to read the scriptures and discourse of religion, expecting a farther manifestation."

Thomas Holme and some young women, Elizabeth Fletcher, Elizabeth Leavens, and Jane Waugh, came early in 1654 to assist in the work in Cheshire and South Lancashire. The Friends were zealous and often under strange workings of "the power," the people rude and violent, the authorities alarmed at what they could not understand. For example, the people returning from church look in at the Quaker meeting and see persons trembling and crying. The mayor is told, and sends an officer, who is much afraid, and faints when he arrests Holme.[2] Holme lies on the prison floor, having been commanded by the Lord to deny his bed. There at midnight the power of the Lord comes upon him and sweet melody is within him and he is compelled to sing.

> And the power was so great it made all my fellow-prisoners amazed, and some were shaken, for the power was exceeding great, and I scarcely know whether I was in the body, yea or no, and there appeared light in the prison and astonished me, and I was afraid, and trembled at the appearance of the light, my legs shook under me: and my fellow-prisoners beheld the light and wondered, and the light was so glorious it dazzled my eyes.[3]

The same thing was repeated on the following night, and in the morning he was made to sing and was brought to shed many tears to see the unspeakable love of God.

[1] Hubberthorne to Margt. Fell, Swarthm. Colln. i. 339, and *F.P.T.* 18.
[2] Holme to Margt. Fell, at the end of March 1654, Swarthm. Colln. i. 189.
[3] Holme to Margt. Fell, about 5th April 1654, Swarthm. Colln. i. 190.

It was amid fervours of this kind that the gospel of the Inward Light manifested itself in Cheshire, and the Quaker community that came into being suffered from the overwrought spiritual conditions under which it had been fostered. Holme himself was a man of little judgment, and was imprisoned in 1655 for going naked through the city as a sign. He found much discord among Friends in prison, "they being so many together of an equal growth [and] wanting one to stand over all the rest." Two Friends especially, Thomas Yarwood and another, had wounded whole meetings by their spirit. "Many a heavy burden I had of them," he says, "before I got them under foot."[1]

Richard Sale, a constable who had been convinced in 1654, may represent to us the zealous indiscretion of these early days.[2] He writes in 1655[3] a letter full of highly extravagant phrases about Fox, and about this time had gone through Derby streets as a sign, barefoot and barelegged, dressed in sackcloth, with ashes on his head, sweet flowers in his right hand and stinking weeds in his left, the people struck into astonishment, though some set their dogs at him. In 1657, to complete our account of him, he went through Eastgate St., Chester, at midday with a lighted candle in his hand to show the uselessness of candlelight worship.[4] He had the courage of his convictions, and several times suffered terribly in Northgate Prison, where he was put for three, four, five, and eight hours together into a hole in the rock, called Little Ease, which had a breadth of seventeen inches, a depth of about nine, and a height of not more than four feet and a half. Being a corpulent man, he could not be put into the horrible cell without violence, four men having much ado to thrust him in, in doing

[1] To Margt. Fell, 28th August 1655, Swarthm. Colln. i. 197.

[2] John Lawson to Margt. Fell, Chester, 15th February [1654], in Swarthm. Colln. iv. 68; cf. *Letters of Early Friends*, p. 86. Sale came from Hoole, in the county of Cheshire, and freed Hubberthorne from passing home as a vagrant by burning the pass. His occupation was tailoring (Mittimus in Swarthm. Colln. iv. 113).

[3] 28th October, Swarthm. Colln. iv. 211.

[4] To Margt. Fell, 11th March 1657, Swarthm. Colln. iv. 114.

which they crushed him till the blood gushed from mouth and nose. These barbarities caused his body and legs to swell, and so weakened his health that, after his last torture, he languished about two months and then died in August 1658.[1]

The map at the end of the book shows roughly the places where meetings had been settled by the beginning of the year 1654.[2] The chief convincement has taken place in Yorkshire, Westmorland, North Lancashire, Cumberland, and Durham, to take them in the order in which during 1652 and 1653 they were reached by the message of Fox: but there were also Quaker communities of rather older standing in some of the North Midland counties. We know little of the work done here during the two years that saw the wonderful expansion of Quakerism in the North. Fox, as we have seen, had gathered companies of "Children of the Light" in Nottinghamshire, Leicestershire, Derbyshire, Warwickshire, and Lincolnshire, but there were no centres of life to compare with those that sprang up in Yorkshire, Westmorland, and Cumberland.

Farnsworth, a man of great energy, found time for frequent service in the North Midlands during 1653.[3] In one such visit he held meetings in the Isle of Axholme (Lincolnshire), spent half a week among Friends at Sturton and three nights at Mansfield, where, he says, Friends "grow very precious," and then went on to Skegby, the home of Elizabeth Hooton. At another time he is in Derbyshire, disputing with priests at Chesterfield.[4]

Mansfield and Skegby were the chief Quaker centres. At Mansfield in 1653 a Mr. John Firth had been invited into the town as a minister, "a very high deceiver,"

[1] Besse, *Sufferings*, i. 101.*

[2] The map is based on the statements in *F.P.T.* supplemented from other sources. At all the places marked persons who afterwards took a leading part in the work of the Society had been convinced, but in a few cases we cannot be sure that settled meetings were already gathered. At this period the meetings were held at Friends' houses or in the open air.

[3] Farnsworth to Fox, 1653, Swarthm. Colln. iii. 52.

[4] Farnsworth to Fox, November 1653, as internal evidence shows, Swarthm. Colln. iii. 51.

Farnsworth calls him,[1] who was "tabled" or boarded for a quarter at a Friend's house, where Farnsworth disputed with him for three hours till he was "much cut and confounded" and the other Friends present were "made very bold every one to take a bout with him." In July 1654 a number of the inhabitants petitioned the Protector for his regular appointment, not only on account of his gospel principles and good affection to the Commonwealth, but also because they had been destitute of a minister for upwards of five years, "and the common enemy of mankind, taking occasion thereby, hath poisoned the spirits of very many with that erroneous spirit of Quaking, whereby the interest of Satan hath increased more and more in the said town."[2]

The division caused by the Proud Quakers and the strength of the Ranters in the North Midlands prejudiced the growth of Friends, and we find Nayler in November 1654 speaking of "much coldness in those parts,"[3] and Margaret Killam, who travelled through Mansfieldside in 1655, reporting "much deadness thereaways." Later in the same letter, however, she speaks of the Lord 'rising the dead and bringing again that which was driven away in the cloudy and dark day."[4] Fox, in more sanguine mood, a few months previously, had felt that "a great people the Lord had thataways."[5] When he at length went south, in the summer of 1654, leaving "the North fresh and green under Christ their Teacher,"[6] he spent the rest of the year in going through South Yorkshire and these North Midland counties, confirming the churches, before passing on to the fresh work in the South of England that was opening out to Friends.

The strength of the new evangel lay in the six Northern Counties. There the Leicestershire shoemaker

[1] To Fox, 1653, Swarthm. Colln. iii. 52.

[2] *Extracts from State Papers*, First Series, pp. 2, 3.

[3] To Fox, 7th November 1654, Swarthm. Colln. iii. 74.

[4] To Fox, year by internal evidence, Swarthm. Colln. i. 374. The sentence also speaks of a town where Fox had worked with a man of his trade, but is somewhat obscurely worded on this point.

[5] *Camb. Journ.* i. 150.

[6] *Journ.* i. 189.

had found the receptive soil for his message, largely among Separatist and Seeking communities, who counted institutions and organization nothing in comparison with the need of winning Christ for themselves. The turnings and overturnings in Church and State had indeed for the time deprived established institutions of their usual stability and show of authority, and had made a unique opportunity for the emergence of the non-institutional types of religion. Side by side with the doctrinal systems of Presbyterians, Independents and Particular Baptists, and in fierce conflict with them, Quakerism could spring up and flourish, calling men to the eternal inward realities and to lives of unswerving devotion to the light.

CHAPTER VII

QUAKERISM AT THE BEGINNING OF 1654

We met together often and waited upon the Lord in pure silence, from our own words and all men's words, and hearkened to the voice of the Lord, and felt His word in our hearts to burn up and beat down all that was contrary to God; and we obeyed the Light of Christ in us . . . and took up the cross to all earthly glories, crowns and ways, and denied ourselves, our relations and all that stood in the way betwixt us and the Lord. . . . And while waiting upon the Lord in silence, as often we did for many hours together, . . . we received often the pouring down of the Spirit upon us . . . and our hearts were made glad, and our tongues loosed, and our mouths opened, . . . and the glory of the Father was revealed; and then began we to sing praises to the Lord God Almighty and to the Lamb for ever, who had redeemed us to God, and brought us out of the captivity and bondage of the world, and put an end to sin and death,—and all this was by and through and in the Light of Christ within us.—EDWARD BURROUGH, Epistle to the Reader, prefixed to Fox's *Great Mistery*.

AT this point we may turn aside for a time from watching the hurrying drama of a victorious cause in order to consider the life and practice of the newly born Quaker communities. Group-life of the simplest kind began inevitably and naturally from the first; indeed, it was characteristic of Fox that he won men to an acceptance of his message, not merely as individuals but most often in groups. The Mansfield "Children of the Light," the Balby circle, the great Preston Patrick community, the Swarthmore household, the groups scattered up and down Cumberland and Cheshire, are illustrations of this, and it seems probable that Quakerism has always consisted of compact bodies of Friends in a limited number of localities. These groups, as we have seen, consisted most often of pre-existing church-fellowships, spiritually prepared for the message of Fox. They were composed mainly of persons who had already dissociated themselves from established Churches, but had found living union with one another because of common convictions and a common search. The experience of the indwelling light of Christ gave them a new ground of fellowship, sure and abiding, and drew them off still more completely from the world's ways of darkness and from all that was outward in the religion of the Churches. These men and women felt themselves to belong to a new order of life in which all things were seen in changed but far truer values. As sharers together in this great experience, they were closely knit to one another in a unity of spirit of which those around them knew nothing.

Fellowship then, of a most intense kind, naturally resulted both from the origin of Quakerism, as a matter of history, in already existing groups, and from the centripetal force inherent in the doctrine of the Inward Light. But this does not mean that Fox and his fellow-workers deliberately set about founding a new sect. The fresh truth, in those early years, abundantly proved itself suitable to every variety of circumstance and order of mind. It was a message of universal significance, and was proclaimed as a gospel for all men; those who received it were the true flock, those who rejected it followed false shepherds or preferred the husks of the world. Such a word as "sect" is quite inadequate. Fox, in one of the first of his printed papers (1653), addresses himself "to all that would know the way to the kingdom, whether they be in forms, without forms or got above all forms." Farnsworth, in the same year, published *The General-Good to all People, or the Lord's free Love running forth freely to his own People in these latter days.* Quakerism was not founded as a sect: its first followers regarded themselves as the seed of God springing up in the midst of a perverse generation. Others might label them with the nickname "Quaker," by way of derisive distinction, but the very vogue given to this name shows how carefully Friends had avoided describing themselves by terms with a denominational meaning. Their own names, of which the chief were "Children of the Light" and "Friends in the Truth," or "Friends," belonged equally to all disciples with a living experience of Christ, and were not descriptive terms that would be naturally accepted or used by others.[1]

The universal claims made with the utmost sincerity by the first Quakers go far to explain their untiring zeal and wonderful success, and to account for their early extravagances and their unsparing aggressiveness. The inward spiritual life which pulsed through them compelled action, especially in the period of what may be called "nascent" energy which belongs to a new truth in the first years of its discovery. Friends were under a necessity to express themselves. They were continually driven to bear their witness in the markets and the churches: they plunged with zest into the controversial debates which were a chief interest of that Puritan age: they flooded England with the violent religious pamphlets which formed the sensational literature of the Commonwealth period. They put themselves in unflinching and confident opposition to much of the worship and the way of life round them, and had the courage and the consistency to give their Christian experience an all-round application to every department of life. Above all, the inward life laid hold so strongly on many that, leaving their outward callings, they formed themselves into what they regarded as a camp of the Lord, and devoted their lives to the publishing of the truth. Fox in a well-known passage[2] says that by the spring of 1654 "a matter of seventy ministers did the Lord raise up and send abroad out of the North countries." According to Margaret Fell, some twenty-four came from Westmorland, Furness, and North Lancashire before the middle of 1653.[3] A Westmorland account[4] says that by the end of this year about thirty labourers were raised up out of their meetings.

[1] I have already referred to the use of the word "Quaker," *ante*, p. 57, to the word "Friend," *ante*, p. 73, and to the phrase "Children of the Light," the earliest of all, *ante*, p. 44.

[2] *Camb. Journ.* i. 141. *Journ.* i. 190, puts the number at sixty.*

[3] Testimony to Fox, in *Journ.* ii. 515.

[4] *F.P.T.* p. 249.

Quakerism indeed produced a spiritual army, strong for warfare, before it developed a church organization. Fox himself was unwearied in service. His followers felt it their duty to take every opportunity of spreading the light. The churches were then much less restricted in use than is the case now,—at Pickering, for example, the church was used as the sessions-house,[1]—and the "First Publishers" came into frequent collision with the authorities through speaking in them. This practice was widespread, though Friends usually kept within the law as it stood prior to August 1656[2] by waiting to testify until the sermon was over. In Durham in 1653 nine "steeple-houses" were thus visited on one Sunday.[3] They also did much preaching in private houses, at a time when this was a strange thing,[4]—a setting up of "Jeroboam's calves' houses," the Ulverston minister called it,—and they frequently, and in some places habitually, held crowded meetings in the open air—another innovation. Fox and Farnsworth, as early as 1652, gave wise advice as to these:[5]

See that when ye appoint your meetings in any open place, in the fields, on the moors, or on the mountains, that none appoint meetings in your own wills, for that lets in the wills of

---

[1] *Journ.* i. 92.

[2] The Act 1 Mar. st. 2. cap. 3, punished malicious disturbance of a preacher in his sermon or when celebrating Divine service. In *The perfect Pharise under Monkish Holines* (1654 edn.), p. 47, Friends are asked, "How they can now of late forbear till our public worship and exercise be concluded? At their first breaking forth it was otherwise; but since they have found that their speaking in the time of our public work is punishable by law they can now be silent till we have closed up the work." The account of Fox's visit to Bootle, Cumberland, in July 1653, as given in the *Short Journ.* 27, 28, shows the legal position clearly. In the morning he says, "I was moved to speak in his time, he uttered such wicked things, and therefore, for the Truth's sake, I was moved to speak to him, if I had been imprisoned for it." In the afternoon he writes, "I sat me down and heard till he had done, though several Friends spoke to him in his time. So, when he had done, I began to speak to him . . . and he began to oppose me. I told him his glass was gone, his time was out; the place was as free for me as for him; and he accused me that I had broken the law in speaking to him in his time in the morning, and I told him he had broken the law then in speaking in my time." The Lord's Day Act, 1656, cap. 15, strengthened the law against Friends. See *F.P.T.* p. 349, and *post*, p. 450.*

[3] Thos. Rawlinson to Margt. Fell, Swarthm. Colln. iii. 15. I infer the locality.

[4] *Journ.* i. 90, 130.

[5] The extract is from Fox, *Epistles*, No. 14. Farnsworth's similar advice, signed R. F., is in Dev. Ho., Saml. Watson Colln. p. 126.

the world upon the life of Friends, and so ye come to suffer by the world. But at such meetings let the wisdom of God guide you, that some may be there to preserve the Truth from suffering by the world, that all burdens may be kept off and taken away, —so will ye grow pure and strong. And when there are any meetings in unbroken places ye that go to minister to the world take not the whole meeting of Friends with you thither, to suffer with and by the world's spirit, but let Friends keep together and wait in their own meeting-place, so will the life (in the Truth) be preserved and grow. And let three or four or six that are grown up and are strong (in the Truth) go to such unbroken places, and thresh the heathenish nature, and there is true service for the Lord.

These varied forms of aggressive work were done by the individual under a sense of personal guidance, but were often suggested by some Friend of spiritual authority. As Robert Barclay afterwards put it:[1]

Great lowliness and simplicity of heart was upon such that were newly convinced of the truth, and deep humiliation of spirit and subjection to the power both in themselves and in those who were over them in the Lord and had gathered them into the truth.

Fox, Farnsworth, and Dewsbury exercised a real leadership. Numerous instances of this could be adduced. Aldam, for example, in a letter written at the end of 1653,[2] rejoices that Fox is to view all books before they are printed, and urges him to send forth his threshing instruments to thresh upon the mountains as the wisdom of God may guide. Margaret Fell also took almost at once a place of unique service, becoming "a tender nursing mother unto many."[3] Disabled by family duties from going about herself, she kept open house for travelling Friends, so that sometimes there were Friends at Swarthmore from five or six counties at once.[4] She made it her business to create and to maintain close relations of personal friendship between herself and most of the leaders of the new movement. The extent of her correspondence is amazing, and her careful preservation of the letters received enables

[1] *Anarchy of the Ranters*, sect. 2.
[2] Swarthm. Colln. iii. 39.
[3] Thos. Camm's testimony at beginning of Margt. Fell's *Works*.
[4] Wm. Caton, *Life*, 1689 edn. p. 8: quoted *ante*, p. 98.

us to-day to write much of the early history of the Society, as few such books can be written, from the best of all sources, intimate contemporary documents.[1] She took a leading part in the establishment, development, and administration of the fund collected at Kendal "for the service of truth," the accounts of which were regularly rendered to her from 1654 to 1657, and are still preserved.[2] They begin 1st June 1654, at the time when the Mission to the South, of which we shall speak in the next chapter, was undertaken, and for the first few months the only receipts came from the Westmorland Seekers and from Margaret Fell herself. Towards the end of the year, however, she secured a wider support for the Fund by means of the following appeal in a letter which went into North Lancashire and Cumberland:[3]

Our Friends in Westmorland hath borne the heat of the day, and many have been sent forth into the service from hence, and that hath caused the burden to lie heavy upon the rest of the Friends hereabouts and most of all of our Friends at Kendal, our dear brethren Geo. Taylor and Thos. Willan, who have been very serviceable . . . to the whole body,—to those that have been sent forth into the ministry and to them that have suffered imprisonment, and for books and several other things. . . . So I knowing at this time that they are out of purse, I see in the eternal unchangeable light of God that all . . . who are of the body ought to . . . administer freely according to their abilities, as they have received of the Lord freely,—for Jerusalem which is above is free, which is the mother of us all, and who is there, is one;—therefore, that there may be some money in a stock for disbursing . . . either to Friends that go forth into the service

1 See Appendix B on Swarthmore documents.

2 In the letters from Geo. Taylor and Thos. Willan to Margt. Fell in the Swarthm. Colln. The *J.F.H.S.* vi. pp. 49-52, 82-85, 127, 128, has printed a series of disbursements made from this stock. The account at bottom of p. 50 does not belong to this series, and the third in series of the accounts (bottom of p. 51) is repeated in the account on p. 82. See *post*, pp. 317, etc.

3 Thirnbeck Colln. No. 1, per transcript lent by Wilfrid Grace, of Bristol. See the letter in abridged form in *Fells of Swarthmoor Hall*, pp. 84, 85. As printed in Margt. Fell's *Works*, pp. 56-59, the personal details are blurred. In the parchment-bound volume in Dev. Ho., Portfolio 9, there is an Answer by Margt. Fell to "Ambrose Appleby or any others who stumbles at the note." saying that it is contrary to scripture, in which she justifies the course she had taken. Appleby lived at Startforth, near Barnard Castle (*F.P.T.* 88). It is not quite clear to what "note" of Margt. Fell's he takes exception.

or to prisoners' necessity, I . . . am moved of the Lord to acquaint you with it, that in your several meetings in this part of Lancashire and Westmorland, excepting the town of Kendal, and at their several meetings in Cumberland, and so to be gathered and sent to Thos. Willan and Geo. Taylor to be disbursed according as the Lord requires, and that the burden may not lie upon them more than others.

In the following year substantial sums were also received from the Bishopric and from Yorkshire, being, I think, donations to the Westmorland stock from similar stocks established in these two counties.[1] The frugal wants of the Publishers of Truth were thus supplied, and they were provided with the necessary outfit of clothing for their long and arduous service. Money was also spent in the relief of prisoners and the purchase of books. Friends refused to pay tithes, as being forced payments for the maintenance of a professional ministry, but they approved a voluntary provision for the needs of those whose service prevented them from earning a livelihood. Fox, for example, writes in 1653:[2]

If any minister of Jesus Christ . . . who said, freely ye have received, freely give,—comes to our houses and minister unto us spiritual things, we will set before him our carnal things: and he that soweth unto us spiritual things, it is the least that we minister unto him of our carnal things.

Hubberthorne, writing in 1659 on the maintenance of ministers, says:[3]

Let every one that will preach the gospel live of the gospel, and not upon any settled or State maintenance . . for the cry of the honest and godly people of this nation is to have a free ministry and free maintenance, and are willing freely to maintain those that minister unto them the word and doctrine.

In this as in other things a sound spirit of discernment had to be used. We find Farnsworth in an early "Order

[1] Thos. Willan to Margt. Fell, Swarthm. Colln. i. 239, says of the first Yorkshire contribution, "received from John Killam which they had to spare besides what as would serve for their own necessities in that country"; and a letter of Samuel Watson's, 8th June 1657 (Swarthm. Colln. i. 389), speaks of a collection ordered from Balby.

[2] *Epistle*, No. 29. Cf. Thos. Budd's opinion, *post*, p. 387.

[3] *Works*, p. 234.

to the Church given forth by the Holy Ghost"[1] warning against those that go about in idleness. "If they will not work and labour with their hands, but say they are unfree, it is nothing but flesh and deceit that would be at ease, let such be noted and cause that they abide at some place and labour."

From the organization of the new movement for aggressive purposes we pass to its internal development. Here the new truth manifested a wonderful constructive energy, quickly finding expression in a consistent body of principles and building up for itself, no doubt with the help of existing materials, such simple institutions as it required. The Inward Light was itself the artificer of the Society of Friends, but of necessity was coloured by the Puritan medium through which it was transmitted, for its children, like the prophets of other days, remained in many things the children of their age.

In considering this constructive side of early Quakerism, we are surprised to find the wide variety of questions upon which substantial agreement was quickly reached. The distinguishing views of Friends are found to be, as a matter of history as well as of theory, corollaries which flowed naturally from the main proposition. That this should have been the case exhibits the boldness and consistency of the early Friends in the strongest light. Seldom has a great spiritual truth been followed along its untried consequences with surer and more resolute steps. The claims of the Inward Light demanded a separation from all that was outward in religion, and left no place for a man-made ministry or for reliance on the external features of Baptism and the Lord's Supper. But the leaders showed conspicuous courage in so completely laying aside these venerable institutions and relying instead upon the inward spiritual provision of whose substance they were only the shadows. The courage was theirs because it was rooted in experience: they knew the Divine ordination, they were baptized with the washing of regeneration and renewing of the Holy Ghost, they had

[1] Dev. Ho., Saml. Watson Colln. p. 36.

found their spiritual food and communion in Christ Himself. As Fox put it in one of his papers:[1]

> They who are made ministers by the will of God, their word is God, their light is Christ, their Church is in God, their record is the Spirit, their original is the Word which was before all tongues, their gospel is the Lamb of God. . . . The saints' baptism is with one Spirit into one body . . . the bread which the saints break is the body of Christ and the cup they drink is the blood of Christ.

The courage was theirs because it was rooted in experience, but the experience had been a plant of slow growth. The communities of Seekers who accepted the message and the prophetic leadership of Fox were already, as we have seen, separated from the world's worship and dry religious formality, and were maintaining their fellowship and spiritual life by meetings for waiting on the Lord, in silence, or fervent prayer, or religious conference, as they were led. When they came to know the indwelling life of Christ, for which they had been waiting, their meetings continued, but were now radiant with a new joy. Transfigured into newness of life, they became, more vividly than before, seasons of creaturely silence and spiritual spontaneity, times of living fellowship and communion, warm with the central fires of Divine love. We still feel something of their glow as we read the description given by Burrough at the head of this chapter. Young Caton says that those at Swarthmore were so delightful that some of the household waited on the Lord nightly after the rest of the family had gone to bed.[2] George Whitehead, then a lad of fifteen, describes a meeting at Sunnybank, near Grayrigg, in Westmorland, where nothing very impressive was said, but there seemed to him a great working of the power of the Lord. After a time he saw a young girl go out crying, and followed her. She sat down on the ground crying bitterly, "Lord, make me clean, O Lord, make me clean." This touched his heart more than all the speaking had done, and more than all the preaching he had ever heard, and was a certain testimony to him of the Lord's power.[3]

[1] Swarthm. Colln. ii. 5.

[2] *Life* (1689 edn.), p. 7.

[3] *Christian Progress* (1725 edn.), p. 3.

Other points of early Quaker practice seem to have come into general acceptance almost at once, though we might have thought they would only gradually have established themselves. I refer to such matters as the refusal of "hat-honour," and other conventional courtesies, the use of the plain language, the simplification of dress, the changed designation of the months and the days of the week, and the refusal of oaths. The cases of divergence on these points are very few, and, while admitting the congruity of these practices with the fundamental spiritual experience of Friends, other causes must also have been at work to secure the uniformity that prevailed. Four may be suggested as the chief: (1) The advanced preparation of the Seeker communities on many of these questions; (2) the predominant Puritan bias of those who joined the new movement; (3) the commanding influence exerted by the pattern-conduct of the leaders; (4) the earnest zeal with which, like the Galatian Christians, those who were convinced sought to carry out to the full the requirements of their new faith. On some of these questions, however, we find traces of a time when variations of practice existed. Fox himself had used the "heathen" names of the months as late as 1650, writing, "Upon the fourth day [of] March the power of the Lord spread over all the world in praise."[1] Others of the leaders frequently use these names, also Monday, Tuesday, Wednesday, and the like, up to the middle of 1654.[2] As to the days of the week, a sentence in a letter from Fox in 1653[3] had no doubt a great effect: "My dear brethren in the covenant of life, keep to

[1] See the original in Swarthm. Colln. vii. (Jas. Backhouse Colln.), 93. In Fox's printed *Epistles*, p. 7, "March" has been corrected to "the first month," and there is a corresponding correction in the original by a later hand. Baptists sometimes used numbers for the months in the same way. See the ***Broadmead and Fenstanton Records.****

[2] For instances of the ordinary names of the months, see, *e.g.*, Farnsworth to Margt. Fell, 7th Jan. 1653, in Swarthm. Colln. iv. 83; Farnsworth to Margt. Fell, 8th June 1653, in Swarthm. Colln. iii. 47; Howgill and Camm to Margt. Fell, 27th March 1654, in Dev. Ho., A.R.B. Colln. No. 20; and Howgill and Camm to Fox, same date, in A.R.B. Colln. No. 127. For instances of the ordinary names of the days see, *e.g.*, Jno. Lawson to Margt. Fell, autumn of 1653, in Swarthm. Colln. iv. 66; and Burrough to Nayler, 25th April 1654, in Swarthm. Colln. iv. 170.

[3] *Epistles*, No. 48. The reference is, of course, to the days of the Creation.

Yea and Nay, and call the days first-day, second-day, third-day, fourth-day, fifth-day, sixth-day and seventh-day, as they were given forth and called by God in the beginning."

The use of the plain language, "thee" and "thou" instead of "you," was of general usage from the first, although Margaret Fell, in her letter to her husband, February 1653,[1] seems to address him with both "you" and "thou."

The spiritual leadership which impressed upon the new religious fellowship a common body of experience and a common practice on a wide variety of subjects was quite equal to the task of developing an organization, so far as this became necessary. As early as the end of 1652, as we have seen, Dewsbury had settled a General Meeting once in three weeks in the East Riding of Yorkshire, and the Westmorland Seekers, before they received the message of Fox, held a General Meeting at Preston Patrick once a month.[2] An early letter of Farnsworth's[3] gives detailed instructions for General Meetings once a month throughout the West Riding, specifying in a most interesting way the constituent meetings that are to form each General Meeting, and naming responsible Friends who are to see that the General Meeting is duly arranged; and, he adds, "see that you be there and observe the order, and let not the earth hinder or keep back, but keep to the pure that it may guide you and lead you on in the true diligence and obedience." These instructions may probably be connected with the important letter, addressed to Friends by Dewsbury some time in the year March 1653-54, and countersigned by Fox.[4] It is, says the letter, the word of the living God to His Church that in each meeting there should be chosen "one or two who are the most grown in the power and life," who shall take the care and charge over the flock of God in that place. These Friends, to whom no name is given, were to see that a meeting was held, "according to the rule that hath

[1] *Fells of Swarthmoor Hall*, p. 44 (Shackleton Colln. No. 1).

[2] *F.P.T.* p. 244.

[3] Dev. Ho., Boswell Middleton Colln. p. 26.

[4] Printed in Dewsbury's *Works*, pp. 1-4, "writ in the year 1653." Also in the Swarthm. Colln. iii. 19, signed "W. D., G. ff.," and endorsed in George Fox's writing, "from W. D. to Friends about 1653." Cf. Smith's *Life of Dewsbury*, 1836, p. 62 *n*.

been given forth," once a week or oftener, in addition to the first-day meeting, and that a General Meeting was held with other Friends in the district once in two or three weeks. They were also to watch over one another to see that those who came among Friends walked orderly, according to their Christian profession, and if any walked disorderly, they or other discerning Friends were to deal plainly with them, so as "to raise up the witness, to judge and cut down the deceit, that their souls may be saved." If the disorderly life continued, open reproof when the Church met together was to follow,—a questionable piece of advice, afterwards reversed,—and, if this failed, such persons were to be charged to depart from among Friends, and were to be cast out, "until they repent and turn to the Lord to walk in obedience to that which is pure." Further, the Friends chosen to watch over the flock were to see that there were none in outward want in the Church, and that all walked orderly in their places and callings, and when any differences arose they were to judge between Friends and end it in righteousness, with help, if necessary, from other Friends of discernment.

It will be seen that in this incipient stage of Quakerism the stress was laid (1) on securing times of religious fellowship, and (2) on securing efficient spiritual leadership. The General Meetings were evidently meetings for all the Friends of a district, held primarily for religious fellowship, when the scattered groups of Children of the Light could feel their hearts burning within them as they met with one another and with their Lord. The spiritual leadership came in the first place from the men like Fox, Farnsworth, Dewsbury, and Nayler, who were the apostles of the movement. But the men of spiritual power, who became many of them itinerating Publishers of Truth, also exercised leadership, according to their gifts. We find Farnsworth, for example, in the letter of instructions already referred to, saying to Christopher Taylor,[1] brother of Thomas Taylor:

[1] At the end of 1654 he had been savagely treated in Appleby gaol, where he was imprisoned with other Friends. See document in Swarthm. Colln. i. 14,

As thou art in those parts be at the General and Monthly Meetings, and as thou art moved to go abroad be diligent and faithful to the pure of God in thee, and bold, and the Lord God of power be with thee.

In addition to these there were also, it is clear, local leaders to whom a special responsibility for the Church was committed. We need not suppose that they were formally appointed. In many cases they must themselves have stood forward as the persons round whom the groups of Friends gathered; it was enough that they had the confidence of the leaders of the movement and of their own neighbours. In other cases the service may have been laid upon them by their neighbours or by one of the itinerating leaders. The manner of selection was unimportant, the essential point was that the office of "elder," as it came to be called, was recognized.

The special place of influence given to the "elders" and the travelling Publishers of Truth has close analogies with the practice of the General Baptists.[1] We have already seen that the earliest corporate expression of Quakerism occurred in Baptist surroundings, and it is easy to see how naturally the Baptist type of church-government, *mutatis mutandis*, might affect the new movement. The General Baptists held:

. . . that though it is most certain there were several things proper and peculiar to the first and chief Apostles, not to be pretended at all by their successors, the subordinate messengers, yet it is also true that many things pertaining to their office as itinerant ministers are of perpetual duration in the Church with respect to that holy function, and consequently to descend to those who were to succeed them as travelling ministers, to plant Churches and to settle them in order, who are as sheep without a shepherd.[1]

also letter to gaoler in Dev. Ho., Boswell Middleton Colln. p. 10, "let this be read at meetings amongst Friends." Cf. account, wrongly dated, in Besse, *Sufferings*, ii. 6. For Christopher Taylor see Jno. Whiting, *Persecution Exposed* (1715 edn.), p. 166.

[1] Grantham's *Christianismus Primitivus*, Book II. chap. ix. p. 119, London, 1678, cited from Barclay's *Inner Life*, p. 353. Barclay works out the connection carefully. Vavasor Powell, the fervid Welsh preacher, created a band of missionary preachers about 1646, and became known as the "metropolitan of the itinerants."

Accordingly, a travelling ministry came into use, whose work was to plant Churches, ordain officers, set in order things that were wanting in all the Churches, defend the truth, and travel up and down to perform the work.[1] These "messengers of the Churches" had the position of elders, and the other elders of the Church, chosen usually by an association of the Churches in a particular district, were also men with a gift of teaching.

It is in connection with the "elders" that we first hear of Monthly Meetings for business. Fox says:

> In 1653 in Cumberland many of the Elders came to me at Swarthmore in Lancashire, and desired that they might have a Monthly Meeting to look after the poor and to see that all walked according to the Truth, &c., and they had a meeting settled there for the same purpose.[2]

We have evidence that a Monthly Meeting was soon after established for the Durham meetings.[3] A paper has been preserved, signed by sixteen Friends, amongst others Anthony Pearson, John Langstaff, and Andrew Rawe, stating that those who were met together "do think it convenient that some of every meeting do meet together the first seventh-day of every month beginning with the third month," that is, May 1654, "and to declare what necessities or wants are seen in their several meetings, there to be considered on by Friends, and as necessity is seen so to minister." Then follow directions as to a collection for the poor to be taken up on a first-day and paid over to John Langstaff.

In this way two kinds of periodical meetings for spiritual fellowship and church-affairs—namely General Meetings for a district, and select Monthly Meetings—seem to have grown up quite naturally out of the

[1] See Hooke, *Orthodox Creed*, art. 31, cited from Barclay's *Inner Life*, p. 354. Cf. Dr. Rufus M. Jones, *Studies in Mystical Religion*, p. 426.

[2] See *Letters of Early Friends*, p. 312—in the document, "Concerning our Monthly and Quarterly and Yearly Meetings, etc.," written by Fox, August 1689. Cf. *Journ.* ii. 247. The date (1653) is not in *Camb. Journ.* ii. 316.

[3] Swarthm. Colln. ii. 17, printed in Bowden's *Histy. of Friends in America*, i. p. 209. Fox endorses the document, "The setting up the men's meeting in Bishopric, 1653." As it provides for a first meeting in 3rd mo. (May), and work in Durham had not begun in May 1653, the date must be 1654. Fox was in Durham, March 1654.

occasions of the time. The arrangement of both kinds of meetings must have rested upon the Friends charged with special duties, whom we have called Elders. Indeed, when we have said that the first organization of Friends in the North of England depended on spiritual leadership, exercised by the apostles of the movement and the itinerating Publishers of Truth, and locally through Elders and the meetings which they arranged, we have gone as far in the way of definite statement as seems possible. It was sound insight which caused the leaders of Quakerism to create the minimum of organization and to allow the spiritual life of the movement its freest possible development. Instead of relying on organization, they relied on the deep unity of experience and spirit which bound together the Children of the Light.

Where it was necessary to make outward arrangements, the practical genius of Quakerism soon showed itself. At a very early date a system of registration was set on foot by Fox for the due recording of births, marriages, and burials. In the case of Friends, no baptisms took place, and no clergyman officiated at marriages and burials: no record of these great domestic occurrences was made in any parish register, and a new system became a matter of urgency. Some existing register books are stated to date back as early as 1650,[1] but a continuous record would hardly begin so soon as this. It was quite usual for pre-Quaker entries*to be inserted in the books. Thus in the cover of a Westmorland Register, No. 1598, we find an entry of Edward Burrough's birth on 1st March 1632, that is 1633 New Style, baptized in Kendal on the 3rd; and in the Warwickshire Registers, No. 1175, the baptism "so-called" of Ambrose Crowley is given in 1635. One Yorkshire entry of death is said to be as early as 1570. After the Registration Act of 1837, the existing Quaker registers, so far as they were procurable, were deposited in Somerset

[1] See on the whole subject *Some Special Studies in Genealogy*, 1908; article by Josiah Newman on "The Quaker Records." In this article he gives the earliest dates at which births, marriages, and deaths begin for each of the county districts.

House, where they can still be consulted, but before they were placed there a complete alphabetical index was compiled in duplicate, one copy of which is in the Society's Library at Devonshire House.*

"It is," says Josiah Newman, "the most complete and beautifully kept record of its kind belonging to any religious denomination throughout the world. It forms a striking monument to the genius of George Fox, and is, in a way, remarkably typical of the careful, conscientious Quaker of to-day."

In the matter of marriages, however, something beyond a system of registration was necessary under the old English law, now altered by the Marriage Act of 1836 (6 & 7 Will. 4, c. 85). The English law contemplated not only a contract between the parties but a celebration in church, and here the Quaker in obedience to conscience had to run the risk of being a law-breaker. The absolute necessity for a celebration in church was, however, only established by a legal decision given long after the days of Fox—the celebrated decision of the House of Lords in 1844 in the case of *Queen* v. *Millis*.[1] Prior to this decision it had been commonly considered that, while the religious sanction depended upon the celebration in church, the requirements of the law were complied with by a contract between the parties, followed by an actual living together, and the House of Lords itself was equally divided on the point, three law lords taking one view and three the other, so that the case was only decided by the help of a maxim of procedure designed for such a contingency. The validity of Quaker marriages had been generally regarded as established by a *nisi prius* case at Nottingham in 1661,[2] and after the decision in *Queen* v. *Millis* an Act was passed (10 & 11 Vict. c. 58) validating these marriages *ex post facto*. In considering how Fox handled the subject, it has also to be remembered that in 1653

[1] 10 *Clark and Finnelly*, p. 534.

[2] Fox, *Journ.* i. 520. Sir Matthew Hale considered that "all marriages made according to the several persuasions of men ought to have their effects in law," and on one occasion stretched a point so as to avoid pronouncing a Quaker marriage illegal. Gilbert's *Life and Death of Sir Matthew Hale* (1721 edn.), p. 44.

the requirement of celebration in church was for the time being superseded by another. An Act had been passed on 24th August of that year declaring that only marriages solemnized before a Justice of the Peace would be recognized by the State.[1]

Fox gave forth a paper on marriages as early as 1653.[2] According to the abstract in his *Journal*, under date 1667, he advised Friends to lay their intentions

> . . . before the faithful in time, before anything were concluded, and afterward publish it in the end of a meeting, or in a market,[3] as they were moved thereto. And when all things were found clear, they being free from all others and their relations satisfied, then they might appoint a meeting on purpose for the taking of each other in the presence of at least twelve faithful witnesses.

A thoroughly regular system was, however, only gradually established. Full publicity and a solemn act of contract were secured by the procedure adopted by Friends, though it was not, as we have seen, in strict conformity with the law. Thomas Robertson of Grayrigg,[4] one of the First Publishers, would have liked the magistrates to have been informed of the marriage at the time when it took place, so as to take away all offence; but it was not possible to admit marriage *by* the magistrate. In Fox's view[5] the right joining in marriage was the work of the Lord only, and could not be done by priest or magistrate; it was the Lord's work, and those who were present were only there as witnesses. But after the marriage a Friend might carry a copy of the certificate to the magistrate if he desired to do so.

It must not be supposed that even in this first period the new fellowship was free from internal difficulties. The fresh sense of indwelling spiritual life, which betrayed Fox

[1] Scobell, ii. 236; Gardiner, *Hist. of Commth. and Prot.* ii. 292.

[2] *Journ.* ii. 88. The Swarthm. Colln. ii. 34 contains a letter "about 1653" to Kendal Friends against secret proceedings; and a letter of Thos. Willan and Geo. Taylor to Margt. Fell, 26th February 1655 (Swarthm. Colln. i. 214), wishes "less of that were practised amongst Friends."*

[3] Banns were at this period sometimes published in the market-place, *e.g.* at Beverley in 1656.

[4] Swarthm. Colln. iv. 206.

[5] Fox, *Epistles*, p. 281.*

himself into occasional extravagances, sometimes worked havoc in less stable characters.* Much feeling was aroused against Kendal Friends in May 1653 by the disordered conduct of one John Gilpin, who had been strangely wrought upon at one of their meetings.[1] In November 1652 the infant community in Furness was seriously compromised by James Milner, a tailor,[2] who, after a fourteen days' fast, prophesied, amongst other wild fancies, that Wednesday the 1st December would be the Day of Judgment, and Thursday the 2nd December would be the first day of the new creation, when a four-cornered sheet would come down from heaven with a sheep in it. He and another Friend of a like "airy" spirit drew some after them, and we are not surprised to find that Fox was sorely exercised, and in a fast for ten days on Truth's account. He wrote a wise letter to Friends,[3] that their minds should not go out from the Spirit of God into their own notions. In this he recognizes that they might depart from the truth into their earthly wills, and so give room "for the enchanter and sorcerer and the airy spirit." Accepting the current dualistic view of the universe, he says:

> Dwell in the pure and immortal, and wait upon the Living God to have your hope renewed, and to be renewed again into the image of God, and [to have] the image of the devil defaced and the Prince of the air cast out,—for he lodgeth in the mind that doth despair, and in that mind that doth presume.

He found himself able to distinguish this airy spirit from the impulse under which Friends acted when moved to testify in churches.

> To speak of truth when ye are moved, it is a cross to the will; if ye live in the truth which ye speak ye live in the cross to your own wills.

But as soon as Friends left the cross and that which was pure and eternal and let in that which was mortal, to

[1] See *The Quakers Shaken, etc.*, London, 1655.
[2] *Ibid.*; also referred to in the Lancashire Petition and in *Saul's Errand* and Fox's *Journal*, i. 158.
[3] Fox, *Epistles*, No. 32; cf. No. 20.

be servants to it, there the image of God in them would come to be lost.

While the advice given by Fox was excellent for the purpose in hand, and is a striking proof of his sober bent of mind, it did not cover the whole ground. Infirmities of judgment and gusts of emotional impulse and nervous exaltation beset the religious enthusiast in his hours of supremest self-devotion as well as in his moments of self-willed wisdom—the imperfections of his human personality intrude themselves even when he is bearing the cross. The high doctrine of spiritual guidance held by the early Friends did not allow for this. They were disabled by their point of view from perceiving or discountenancing the extravagances connected with the testifying of truth in churches and market-places, and in particular with the testifying by signs after the manner of the old Hebrew prophets. As early as the end of 1652 Fox wrote approvingly to the people of Ulverston of the most extreme form of this testimony:

. . . the Lord made one to go naked among you, a figure of thy nakedness, and of your nakedness, and as a sign amongst you before your destruction cometh, that you might see that you were naked and not covered with the truth.[1]

A hostile pamphlet, printed in 1654, gives particulars of eight cases of this kind at Kendal, Hutton, and Kirkby Stephen in the years 1653 and 1654,[2] and such testimonies were more frequent during the early years of the movement than has been commonly allowed. Some Friends, notably William Simpson of Lancashire and Richard Robinson of Wensleydale, had this service frequently laid upon them. William Simpson, according to a vagrancy pass,[3] came from Sunbree, in the county of Lancaster, probably Sunbreak, near Swarthmore, and was of low personage, brown-haired, and aged in 1657 about thirty years. Fox tells us:[4]

[1] *Journ.* i. 153; cf. letter in Swarthm. Colln. ii. 12, and *The Great Mistery*, pp. 77, 217, 233.

[2] "A Further Discovery, etc.," Gateside, 1654, pp. 83, 84.

[3] Dev. Ho. Portfolio 5, No. 51. Cf. *Camb. Journ.* ii. 67. When a person convicted as a vagrant was sent to his home from constable to constable he was to be provided with a pass for purposes of identification. See *F.P.T.* p. 347.

[4] Quoted from *F.P.T.* 365.

He went three years naked and in sackcloth in the days of Oliver and his Parliament, as a Sign to them and to the priests showing how God would strip them of their power, and that they should be as naked as he was, and should be stripped of their benefices. All which came to pass after King Charles the Second came in. And moreover he was made oftentimes to colour his face black, and so black they should be and appear so to people for all their great profession. And then when it came to pass he was made to put on his clothes again, who was made before many times to go through markets to priests' houses and to great men's houses and magistrates' houses and to Cambridge stark naked. And the Mayor of Cambridge put his gown about him, being sensible there was something in the thing. And he was made to go through London naked, and he was obedient unto the heavenly command, and often ventured his life and it was given up: who many times did receive many stripes upon his naked body with thorn bushes, so that when his service was done, Friends were forced to pluck the thorns out of his flesh: but he was carried over all by the mighty power of God.

At Oxford, and very probably on the other occasions, the act was done with great solemnity, after the approval of local Friends had been obtained, one or two of them accompanying him and carrying his clothes.[1] At Oxford some of the scholars would have taken Simpson before the magistrates, but some soldiers reproved them, saying, If he went naked, let him, what was that to them—a remark which shows that they were not shocked by the incident.[2] The use of this sign appears somewhat less extravagant when we remember that it belonged to an age which was familiar with the brutal practice of punishing vagrants—including travelling Publishers of Truth, both men and women—by stripping them naked from the middle upward and openly whipping them till the body was bloody.

Richard Robinson, of Countersett in Wensleydale,[3] was four years younger than Fox, and the first in the dale to receive the Quaker message in 1652. His house became the meeting-place for Friends, and he developed a con-

[1] Cf. case at Leeds (1655) given in Besse, *Sufferings*, ii. 95.

[2] *F.P.T.* 213.

[3] His house is still standing. See illustration in *Richard Hubberthorne*, p. 12, in Friends Ancient and Modern Series (1911).

cern for proclaiming the truth in churches, markets, and law-courts, doing this systematically in the North Riding and in Durham, and going as far afield as York, Nottingham, and London, where he spoke in Cheapside, Leadenhall Market, St. Paul's Churchyard, and the Courts at Westminster. Sometimes he went almost naked as a sign to the people.

"He travelled much on foot," we are told, "being a lusty, strong man of body, and likewise finding it to be more agreeable to his service in those public places, the roughness of the people in those times considered, for he was forced to lay sometimes out of doors in the fields, and to travel in the night as well as the day, and in winter seasons as well as summer, without shrinking from the violence of weather. And after this manner the Lord led him on his way through many rough and untrodden paths: but the Lord's power was with him and supported him through them all; and notwithstanding the many blows and strokes he got by staves and clubs, several of which were broken upon him with such violence that pieces thereof flew up into the air."[1]

Going naked as a sign was not disowned by the Quaker leaders. Nayler[2] says that the Friends who acted in this way acted contrary to their own wills, and this phrase illuminates the position. The wild prophecies and notions of James Milner had been condemned by Fox, because they were prompted by the earthly nature: here, on the other hand, there was a real crucifixion of the will on the part of the honest-hearted men and women concerned. They only undertook the service under a strong sense of religious duty. One Friend writes: "I have strove much, and besought the Lord that this going naked might be taken from me, before ever I went a Sign at all."[3] They felt themselves to be the prophets of a new religious era. The word of the Lord burned within them and demanded expression in speech and action. Saturated with Bible knowledge, they there found examples for their own conduct. In this matter of testifying truth by signs,

[1] *F.P.T.* 307, 308, 311, and, for passage cited, 313.

[2] Paper in *A Woe against the . . . People of Kendall*, 1654, cited from *F.P.T.* 366.

[3] Solomon Eccles' *Signes are from the Lord*, 1663, cited from *F.P.T.* 366.

Old Testament prophecy and apocalyptic imagery were rich in fitting phrase and authoritative precedent. They read, for instance, that Isaiah (chap. xx.; cf. Micah i. 8) walked naked and barefoot three years for a sign and a wonder upon Egypt and upon Ethiopia. Dr. George Adam Smith translates the word "naked," "unfrocked," that is, without the prophet's robe of sackcloth, and it is interesting to find that this interpretation was already urged against Friends in 1654.[1] They, however, took the passage literally, and, desiring to show that Cromwell, his Parliament and priests would be stripped of their power, acted again, as they supposed, the sign of the prophet, all the more zealously because their natural feelings shrank from obedience to the Divine command. While, then, we may deplore the crude literalism of Quaker practice on this question as on some others, we should recognize the devoted spirit of obedience which lay behind it, and its naturalness under the circumstances and the conditions of thought of the first Friends.

The practice reveals to us more clearly than anything else the prophetic character of early Quakerism. The leaders of the movement, it is evident, did not think of themselves as the founders of a new sect. They were far more concerned, in these early years, with proclaiming what they called the Day of the Lord. They were Publishers of Truth—men and women to whom the word of the Lord had come, and who must declare it at all costs through town and country, university and hamlet, in church and sessions-house, from market-cross and prison-window, to Cromwell and his officers, to the magistrates and ministers, and to all sorts and conditions of men. Their primary business as pioneers was this work of message-bearing, this broadcast sowing of the seed on every soil: the message was regarded by them as one of universal scope, though the spiritual Israel gathered out of the nation might alone respond to it.

The most potent message, however, was given by the

[1] "A Further Discovery, etc.," p. 87.

daily life of these first Friends. George Fox, in a notable passage of his *Journal*, says:[1]

At the first convincement when Friends could not put off their hats to people, nor say you to a particular, but thee and thou; and could not bow, nor use the world's salutations nor fashions nor customs—and many Friends being tradesmen of several sorts—they lost their custom at the first, for the people would not trade with them nor trust them. And for a time people that were tradesmen could hardly get money enough to buy bread, but afterwards, when people came to see Friends' honesty and truthfulness and yea and nay at a word in their dealing, and their lives and conversations did preach and reach to the witness of God in all people, and they knew and saw that they would not cozen and cheat them for conscience' sake towards God:—and that at last they might send any child and be as well used as themselves at any of their shops, so then the things altered so that all the inquiry was where was a draper or shop-keeper or tailor or shoemaker or any other tradesman that was a Quaker: then that was all the cry, insomuch that Friends had double the trade beyond any of their neighbours: and if there was any trading they had it, insomuch that then the cry was of all the professors and others, If we let these people alone they will take the trading of the nation out of our hands. . . . And this was from the years 1652 to 1656 and since.[2]

It was this power of Quakerism to penetrate the whole of life that was the greatest of its credentials. None could dispute the validity of a Christianity which resulted in consistent and Christ-touched lives. In such lives, amid all their imperfections, the Inward Light was justified of its children.

[1] *Camb. Journ.* i. 138; cf. *Journ.* i. 185.

[2] Cf. an important passage in Geo. Fox, *Doctrinals*, p. 74, *post*, p. 523, as to fixed prices;* also the case of Wm. Edmondson, *post*, p. 211.*

CHAPTER VIII

THE MISSION TO THE SOUTH

(1654)

From the dales and fells and from the country-sides of the North went out a band of preachers whose names are hardly known to the historian, but whose lives and teaching had the deepest influence on seventeenth-century England. Simple yeomen most of them, whose message came more strongly through the spoken word than the written page: men whose writings make difficult reading after two centuries and a half of time, but of whose spirit we can in some measure get glimpses in the brief spiritual autobiographies which not a few left behind them, and in the "testimonies" which their friends published after their death to bear witness to the truth for which they had lived.—T. EDMUND HARVEY, *The Rise of the Quakers*, p. 71.

THE new faith that had been cradled in the nooks and corners of the North was now to prove its worth in a wider world, where it would find less generous welcome. The envious priests had said, "The Quakers would not come into any great towns, but lived in the fells like butterflies."[1] There was some truth in this. Just as the secluded highlands of Judaea were the fit home for the earnest hearts waiting for the redemption of Israel, among whom Christ was born,[2] so, in the stirring Commonwealth times, the country districts of the North furnished receptive soil for the Quaker message, which could not appeal to a larger audience until it had rooted itself strongly in these favourable spots. Many of the travelling ministers in later years must have felt like Richard Roper of Cartmel, who wrote to Margaret Fell:[3] "Truly Friends in the North is rare and precious, very

[1] *Journ.* i. 413; cf. *Short Journ.* 34.
[2] Sanday's *Outlines of the Life of Christ*, pp. 22, 23.
[3] 20th October 1656, Swarthm. Colln. iii. 131.

few I find like them: yet this I declare to thee not to them, lest they should be puffed up." But now the time had come when the message must spread to the more thickly peopled districts, if it was to make its mark on the religious life of England. The distribution of population has greatly altered since 1654. It is estimated[1] that, out of a total population of about five millions, less than one-seventh belonged to the counties north of the Humber; now out of a population eight times as great one-fourth comes from these counties. The North was then in its infancy as a manufacturing district, and was regarded as the wildest part of the country,

> . . . where the Peel-towers were still useful refuges, where the judges on circuit needed a strong guard of troops, where the magistrates had to raise armed men to protect property, and the parishes kept bloodhounds to hunt down robbers.[2]

This reputation, however, was beginning to be ill-deserved, and the pacification of the Scottish border, combined with the spread of education and the greater security of tenure, had much improved the position of many of the northern dalesmen. H. S. Cowper tells us, respecting the Furness district,

> . . . about 1650 a fashion for rebuilding set in with such vigour that during the ensuing sixty years nearly every homestead appears to have been rebuilt, or adapted to the new fashion, and furnished throughout.[3]

The same was probably the case in neighbouring districts —for example, the visitor to Camsgill near Preston Patrick can still see the panel carved

C
I M
1647

which shows the date at which John and Mabel Camm built their house. The Publishers of Truth who came from these Northern Counties were often men of prosperous yeoman stock, and in any case had the substantial support of men of this class.

[1] Traill's *Social England*, iv. 648 (illustrated edn.). [2] *Ibid.*

[3] *The Oldest Register Book of the Parish of Hawkshead*, p. xxviii.

Not only was the Commonwealth population divided differently from our own as between North and South, it was also much more largely rural and much less urban. At least two-thirds is now urban, at least two-thirds was then rural. York was the capital of the Northern Counties, Leeds and Kendal had importance for their cloth manufacture, and Newcastle and Sunderland for their coal; but the chief towns and industries were in the South. London had a population of half-a-million; Bristol, the principal seaport, had about 30,000; Norwich, with a similar number of inhabitants, was still the largest manufacturing city. The Publishers of Truth would now make these three places chief fields of their service, showing something of the same concentration of effort at strategic centres which marked the extension of Christianity through the Roman Empire under the leadership of Paul.

Fox says of the early summer of 1654:

> And so when the Churches was settled in the North, and the Lord had raised up many and sent forth many into His vineyard to preach His everlasting gospel, as F[rancis] H[owgill] and E[dward] B[urrough] to London, J[ohn] Camm and J[ohn] Audland to Bristol through the countries, Richard Hubberthorne and G[eorge] Whitehead towards Norwich, and Thomas Holme into Wales, that a matter of seventy ministers did the Lord raise up and sent abroad out of the North Countries.[1]

In the *Ellwood Journal* the number is altered to sixty; the seventy has, I suspect, a connection with our Lord's Mission of the Seventy, but either number should be taken as a round figure; the significant thing in Fox's statement is that it marks a new point of departure in the history of Quakerism. A camp of the Lord had been gathered in the North and would now carry its conquering message to the rest of England.

It would be interesting, if we could do so, to trace the origins of the great enterprise. Gervase Benson had been

[1] *Camb. Journ.* i. 141, and *Journ.* i. 190. Geo. Taylor, writing to Margt. Fell, Kendal, 11th Sept. 1658 (Swarthm. Colln. i. 303), says 'three-score and ten ministers was within the mark, for there were then seventy-three.' I think he means in Westmorland, Cumberland, and N. Lancashire alone. Cf. p. 132.

in London in November 1653, and wrote,[1] "There are many hereaways inquiring after Friends in the North and the truth made manifest in you and much writing for and against the priests." A few months later, in the spring of 1654, Camm and Howgill went up from Westmorland on foot to see Oliver Cromwell and declare to him the message of the Lord.[2] Twelve days after their arrival they procured an interview, but found him "too wise in comprehension and too high in notion to receive Truth in plainness and demonstration of the Spirit." He questioned with his carnal reason whether their message was the word of the Lord, and argued strongly for the priests. "[He] pleads for every man's liberty and none to disturb another, and so he would keep up himself by getting or keeping favour with all." They found him in a grey rough coat "not worth three shillings a yard": he had heard that Camm and Howgill were plain men and "condescended" to them, offering money or anything they needed, and at last desiring them to leave him as he was tired with business. In their report of this interview to Margaret Fell, they say, "He holds that all the worships of this nation is the worship of God, but the blind cannot judge of truth." The two Friends further declared the word of the Lord to Cromwell by letter, and then returned to the North. During their stay in London, they found few with whom they could have fellowship.

> The pure simplicity is lost: all have eaten of the tree of knowledge and so is puffed up in knowledge and stumbles at the cross,—nor they have not so much as heard of a cross, but lust and pride and all manner of filthiness, such as cannot be declared. O the rich and boundless love of God unto us the people of the North, who hath separated us from the world, and from the pollutions of it, and hath gathered us together into the unity of the Spirit.

We may picture these two plain North-countrymen

[1] *Letters of Early Friends*, p. 2 (Swarthm. Colln. iv. 32).

[2] Letter asking for interview, Swarthm. Colln. iv. 115. Letters giving particulars of interview, Dev. Ho., A.R.B. Colln. Nos. 20, 127; letters to Cromwell after interview, Sewel, 1811 edn. i. 139, and Camm and Audland's *The Memory of the Righteous Revived*, pp. 1-10; letter to Fox after return, A.R.B. Colln. No. 39.

viewing the city and its liberal-minded ruler much as Christian and Faithful viewed Vanity Fair. But they go on to say, "There is some that is convinced of the Truth, some few simple hearts, and for their sakes we shall stay some few days." This visit must have laid the foundations of work in London, for we now hear of meetings at Simon Dring's house in Watling Street and at Robert Dring's in Moorfields. Two Quaker women from the North were the heralds of the message.[1] One of them, Isabel Buttery, came, I think,[2] from Wakefield; the name of the other is not given in our sources. They had with them the paper written by Fox, "To all that would know the way to the Kingdom," which when printed they dispersed abroad to all who would receive it. Amor Stoddart and a few more were already convinced, and the circulation of this paper added others to the small company of Friends, amongst whom were two women, Ruth Brown, afterwards the wife of William Crouch, and Ann Downer, daughter of the vicar of Charlbury. At the meetings the two women from the North now and then spoke a few words.

A letter dated 27th June[3] shows that the help of Friends from the North was at this time eagerly expected by the little flock. Though they were regarding the Lord rather than any creature, still they looked daily for some one out of the North to come and stay in London, for where there was but childishness there could be nothing but stammerings. The harvest was great if there were the labourers. Word should go to those who were to come to London that they should make haste.

Before this letter was received the Mission to the South was already on foot. The six first pioneers were Burrough and Howgill, Camm and Audland, Hubberthorne and Thomas Ayrey of Grayrigg meeting. They started out together at the end of June, but divided their forces in

[1] See William Crouch, *Posthuma Christiana*, chap. ii., also *F.P.T.* p. 165.

[2] It is evident from the letter next referred to that Isabel Buttery was well known to Nayler, and she is therefore probably the Isabel living by Nayler to whom Farnsworth sends love in a letter in Swarthm. Colln. i. 372.

[3] Alexander Delamain and John Bridges to Thos. Willan, Swarthm. Colln. iii. 93, printed in *Letters of Early Friends*, pp. 5-10, not completely.

Lancashire. Howgill and Burrough went direct to London, Hubberthorne spent a fortnight in Oxford on his way, while Audland and Ayrey went by Chester and the edge of Wales to Bristol and so to Exeter and Plymouth, reaching London early in August,[1] where plans were laid for more systematic work. Audland's flying visit to the West of England had been encouraging. At Bristol he had spoken at a Baptist and at an Independent meeting,[2] and at Plymouth he was received "of many who were waiting for the Lord's appearance" and stayed four or five days.[3] His companion, Thomas Ayrey, however, like another Mark, began to faint and abandoned the mission, and for the rest of his life was but a weak and faithless man who could not stand to suffer for truth.[4] Hubberthorne's experience at Oxford was less promising. Two Quaker girls from Kendal, Elizabeth Fletcher and Elizabeth Leavens, had preceded him by a few days.[5] Elizabeth Fletcher, then a girl of sixteen, and "a very modest, grave young woman, yet contrary to her own will or inclination, in obedience to the Lord, went naked through the streets of that city, as a sign against that hypocritical profession they then made there, being then Presbyterians and Independents, which profession she told them the Lord would strip them of."[6] Both girls also went into the colleges and churches, preaching repentance and declaring the word of the Lord.[7] Their conduct subjected them to savage treatment from the "black tribe of scholars" and to a whipping from the authorities, the mayor refusing to be a consenting party. Hubberthorne stayed a fortnight, and narrowly escaped similar usage.

[1] Thos. Camm's accounts in his Testimony concerning Camm and Audland in *The Memory of the Righteous Revived* (1689), and *F.P.T.* 266, need some correction. Burrough and Howgill came together to London (*F.P.T.* 165), Hubberthorne and Camm seem to have followed separately (*F.P.T.* 211, 212).

[2] *The Memory of the Righteous Revived*, p. 133; cf. *F.P.T.* 10.

[3] *F.P.T.* 77.

[4] *F.P.T.* 266. Ayrey, however, was in London in August, Farnsworth to Margt. Fell, Swarthm. Colln. iii. 49, and went on to Cambridge, Gervase Benson to Margt. Fell, Swarthm. Colln. iv. 35.

[5] See *F.P.T.* 209, 258; Hubberthorne's *Works*, pp. 41-44; Besse's *Sufferings*, i. 562.

[6] Thos. Camm's account of Elizth. Fletcher in *F.P.T.* 259.

[7] *F.P.T.* 209.

He was able, however, to distribute Quaker pamphlets and to hold one or two meetings, at which a number of persons were convinced.[1] Six months earlier two Friends, Elizabeth Williams and Mary Fisher, had been cruelly flogged at Cambridge, and Elizabeth Williams had been ducked at Oxford.[2] Clearly, in the two universities, the Quaker message, with its scorn of human learning, would only find utterance amid much persecution. Camm, visiting Oxford from London a little later, confined himself to private meetings and escaped ill-treatment. He made a notable convert in Thomas Loe, an Oxford tradesman, who in after years would be the means of William Penn's convincement.[3]

Meanwhile, early in July, Howgill and Burrough had reached London, Howgill a man of thirty-three, Burrough only twenty-one.

> A report spread about the city that there was a sort of people come there that went by the name of plain North-country ploughmen, who did differ in judgment to all other people in that city.[4]

They were lodged by Robert Dring, a linen-draper in Moorfields, and gained a hearing by declaring their message in meetings of Waiters, Independents, and Anabaptists, and then appointing meetings of their own. Howgill[5] gives a graphic account of the early work in a letter dated 1st August. "By the arm of the Lord," he says, "all falls before us, according to the word of the Lord before I came to this city, that all should be as a plain." They had

[1] *F.P.T.* 211.

[2] Besse, *Sufferings*, i. 84; *F.P.T.* 209, and *post*, p. 294. Her companion at Oxford was Thos. Castle. These Friends were afterwards imprisoned at Stafford and proved so unsatisfactory that Burrough requests Fox to "call them in when they come out of prison." (Letter, Dev. Ho., A. R. B. Colln. No. 161; to be dated 8th May 1654). Burrough calls them Thos. Castley and Elizth. Williamson. For Castley see also *Perfect Pharise, etc.*, p. 45, and "Further Discovery, etc.," p. 84.

[3] *F.P.T.* 212. The letter of Howgill's of 1st August cited below shows that Camm went from London, and that Hubberthorne was making a preliminary visit to Cambridge at the same time.

[4] *F.P.T.* 163.

[5] This important letter (no year given, but clearly belonging to 1654) is, I think, only preserved, with a number of other letters from Howgill, in a modern copy in Dev. Ho. (Port. 3, No. 83, p. 58). See also a letter of Hubberthorne's written to Margt. Fell about same time, in Wm. Caton Colln. (Dev. Ho., Jas. Bowden's copy).

been to the greatest Churches and fellowships they could hear of, and had confounded them all, and the Puritan professors were giving it out that the Quakers had agreed to come a thousand strong to break their Churches. During the week they had held a meeting at their lodgings to which some "high spirits" came, whose smooth words they denied, and, says Howgill, "we were made in much power to speak, and our words clave the rocks, that many cried, and some were taken in the power to the great astonishment of the rest." Another day Howgill had been to the Glasshouse, in Broad Street, the mother-congregation of the Particular Baptists, but could not get leave to speak, though he had some little dispute and left queries to be answered by the whole Church. Burrough and Hubberthorne meanwhile went to the Waiters. On the Sunday, Howgill was moved to go to a society of Seekers; he found them one after another "reconciling scriptures," and, after three of them had spoken, rose with the words "I thank thee, O Father of heaven and earth, that thou hast hid these things from the wise," and so spoke above an hour, and many women cried bitterly, and some of the company were much confirmed in their faith. From this meeting he returned to a great meeting which Burrough was holding, where the mighty power of God was seen and hundreds were convinced. Their chief difficulty was to get the convinced persons separated from the crowds that came to hear. They "threshed" among these crowds diligently and with wonderful results.

They found the city full of pious persons, high flown in wisdom and notions, who spent their time in putting questions on religion to one another and in discussing things of which they had no experimental knowledge.[1] Many of these great professors were at an end of all, and had outrun all. Amid the confusion of sects, the Waiters, the Seekers, and some of the Ranters showed most readiness to receive the Quaker message. At first, indeed, it was looked on by most as a bare notion, like the many

[1] The religious condition of London is taken from early letters of Gervase Benson, Pearson, Burrough and Howgill, in *Letters of Early Friends*, pp. 2, 11, and 15; Benson's letter is in Swarthm. Colln. iv. 32.

others that were being promulgated, but soon began to sink into the hearts of many as a thing of living experience. Howgill and Burrough preached after a new fashion, using few words and speaking to the conscience so as to raise up the witness to truth in their hearers' hearts and bring them under judgment. This directness and simplicity were in refreshing contrast with the fashion of the day. "Living words from living men" make their appeal in every age. By the end of July, Pearson, who had been in London to see Cromwell, found that some deep ploughing had been done by the plain North-countrymen. "Great is the harvest like to be: hundreds are convinced and thousands wait to see the issue, who have persuasions that it is the truth."[1] Pearson's account of his interview with the Protector[2] shows how high was the claim of Quakerism at this time. It was the Lord's work, and to oppose it was to resist the Lord.

I showed him what great things the Lord had done in the North, which was going over England, and should pass over the whole earth. And I let him see how the Lord had carried on the work in a figure without, in the time of the late wars, and that all the deliverances [of that time] was for the seed's sake, which then lay in bondage, and not for his nor any person's [sake], or interest of men: and how that the Lord had now revealed the substance, and opened the figure, and raised up the seed, to whom the kingdom belongs for ever. And now was the Lord coming to establish His own law, and to set up righteousness in the earth, and to throw down all oppressors. And I showed him that now the controversy should be no more between man and man in wars and fightings without, for the seed was redeemed out of all earthly things, and that nature whence wars arise (which are from the lust and for the lust), and that now he that withstood should resist the Lord.

From the first Howgill and Burrough threw themselves into the work with unflagging energy. We continue to hear of three or more large meetings every week[3] to which many of all sorts flocked, of strong fightings with

[1] See Pearson's letter to Fox, 30th July, *Letters of Early Friends*, p. 13.

[2] Pearson to Fox, 18th July, Swarthm. Colln. iii. 34.

[3] See Burrough and Howgill to Margt. Fell, 29th Augt., *Letters of Early Friends*, p. 15 (Wm. Caton Colln.); do. to Aldam, 19th Sept., p. 41, wrongly dated 1656; Howgill to Widders, 23rd Sept., p. 18 (Swarthm. Colln. i. 89).

the most eminent religious societies in the city, of visits to churches for declaring Truth, and of incessant labours among the multitudes, so that they were often at a stand where to get bread to satisfy so many. It is evident that the pioneer work was pursued with a refreshing freedom from the trammels of routine, and that the men who came from the North not only spoke like the Apostles with a provincial accent, but had much of the primitive apostolic fervour in their work. They were under a Divine compulsion to speak the things which they had seen and heard, and in their simple earnestness confounded the religious wisdom of London. An early letter from Margaret Fell "to Francis Howgill and the rest in London" shows her deep interest in the Mission: "You are all dear unto me," she writes, "and you are all present with me, and are all met together in my heart."[1]

The little band of First Publishers met in London early in August to compare their impressions and to decide on further action. It was arranged that Howgill and Burrough should stay in the city, "to maintain the war" there, corresponding with the others, consulting with fresh Publishers from the North, and in a general way supervising the whole Mission. Camm and Audland would go to Bristol and the West, while Hubberthorne set out for Cambridge and Norwich where others were soon expected to join him.[2]

The work in the Eastern Counties, the stronghold of the Parliamentary party, may be first considered. A short imprisonment at Cambridge[3] prevented Hubberthorne from going forward towards Norwich till October. At Wymondham he spoke in church after the sermon, and as a result entered Norwich as a prisoner, where he lay for six months, chiefly for contempt of court in not putting off his hat. George Whitehead, who would prove an indefatigable champion of Quakerism through his long life, reached the city a few weeks later and had liberty

[1] Dev. Ho., Wm. Markey Colln. [2] *Letters of Early Friends*, p. 15.

[3] Hubberthorne to Burrough, Swarthm. Colln. iv. 5. For the early work in Norwich see Besse, *Sufferings*, i. 486, 487; Hubberthorne's letters in Swarthm. Colln.; Whitehead's *Christian Progress*.

till December, when he was imprisoned on similar pretexts. He came from Orton in Westmorland, and was at this time a young man of about nineteen, who had been convinced at Grayrigg a year or two previously. He was well educated, and had done some teaching.[1] Two other Friends from the North, Christopher Atkinson and James Lancaster, came about the end of November, and were also imprisoned as disturbers of the peace, on the plea that they could show no lawful cause for their coming but only to declare the Truth. Others followed and shared the same fate. The Norwich authorities, law or no law, evidently intended to stifle the new movement. Hubberthorne had some excuse for writing:[2]

> I am called to [be] amongst a people where the gospel hath not been preached nor no man hath laid a foundation to build upon but are all aliens and strangers to the life of God.

He calls the townsfolk[3]

> . . . the most wrangling, mischievous, envious, malicious people that ever I came amongst, who are wholly bent to devise mischief one against another to destroy all the appearances of righteousness in any where it appears.

A few in the city were, however, convinced by the testimony and suffering of Friends, and a meeting was gathered at the house of Thomas Symonds,* a master-weaver.[4] By May 1655 most of the Friends had been released, and there were meetings at six or seven places in the district besides Norwich.[5] Young Whitehead's work had been the most successful. At Mendlesham in Suffolk, prior to his imprisonment,[6] he had found an honest-minded people, dissenting from the parish priests and their worship, who met together with preachers of their own and would become a congregation of Friends content to wait upon the Lord together in silence to receive life and teaching from Him. Robert Duncon, a

[1] *Christian Progress*, pp. 2, 75.
[2] To Fox, 13th Nov. 1654, Swarthm. Colln. iv. 235.
[3] To Margt. Fell, 15th Mar. 1655, Swarthm. Colln. i. 347.
[4] Geo. Whitehead, *Christian Progress*, 1725 edn. p. 24.
[5] Richard Clayton to Margt. Fell, 23rd May 1655, Swarthm. Colln. i. 29.
[6] *Christian Progress*, p. 31.

tanner, brother-in-law to Thomas Symonds, was the leader of this community of Seekers, and Edward Plumstead, senr., was the most noted of their preachers. These two men were presumably the Robert Duncon and Edward Plumstead, whose names are found among the Suffolk representatives to the Nominated Parliament of 1653, marked as belonging to the more extreme party in that Parliament.[1] Their adhesion to the new movement must have greatly assisted it.

After his release from Norwich, Whitehead held a great meeting out of doors in an orchard near Woodbridge,[2] and preached for nearly five hours from a joint-stool. This was the first and foundation meeting in that part of Suffolk. At several places he proved himself a skilled antagonist in disputes with Antinomians, Ranters, and parish priests.

On the whole, however, the Eastern Counties were proving refractory to the strenuous Quaker attack, probably because of the assured dominance in them of the current types of Puritanism. Norwich for some years had been a stronghold of the Fifth Monarchy men,[3] who held that only the godly were fit to govern, the Church should be the sole depository of civil power. Boatman, the preacher to the large congregation at St. Peter Mancroft, held this view and had such influence that two years later, at the Parliamentary election at the end of 1656, ineffectual attempts were made by the Government to stop his preaching. It was for speaking after one of his sermons that George Whitehead had been mobbed and thrown into prison—a merciful rescue, for, as he afterwards wrote,[4] "in those days prisons and gaols were made sanctuaries and places of refuge and safety to us from the fury of the tumultuous mob." Another circumstance which retarded the work of Friends round Norwich was the lapse into immoral life, in the summer of 1655, of one of the First Publishers, Christopher Atkinson, then in Norwich gaol. In order to

[1] Gardiner, *Hist. of the Commth. and Prot.* ii. 308 *n.*

[2] *Christian Progress*, p. 60.

[3] Gardiner, *Hist. of the Commth. and Prot.* i. 29, iv. 267. *Ante*, p. 18.

[4] *Christian Progress*, p. 57.

clear the Truth, his written confession and condemnation of himself were taken and read in the meeting of Friends, and he was then cast out from among them, or, as we should now say, was disowned.[1]

The West of England gave the Quaker message a readier entrance. Indeed, there is nothing in the history of Friends that has more of the Pentecostal character about it than the story of the early work at Bristol. Camm and Audland left London on the 25th August, and, after visiting Oxford and planting the truth in Puritan Banbury,[2] reached Bristol a fortnight later, intending to go forward after a time to Hereford. At Bristol they were received by an important community of Seekers, of whom we have this description:[3]

> There were many which were seeking after the Lord, and there were a few of us that kept one day of the week in fasting and prayer; so that when this day came we met together early in the morning, not tasting anything; and sat down sometimes in silence, and as any found a concern on their spirits and inclination in their hearts they kneeled down and sought the Lord; so that sometimes, before the day ended, there might be twenty of us might pray, men and women, and sometimes children spake a few words in prayer; and we were sometimes greatly bowed and broken before the Lord in humility and tenderness.

Again we have to note the wonderful preparation for the Quaker experience in these seeking souls who thus spent one day a week in fasting and prayer and in waiting for the day of redemption. Camm and Audland came to such souls as the messengers of the Lord, sent in answer to prayer. We are no longer surprised to hear that their work, during these September days,[4] was of a

[1] Rich. Clayton to Margt. Fell, 12th July 1655, Swarthm. Colln. i. 30.

[2] *F.P.T.* 212, 208. Also Audland to Burrough and Howgill, 9th Sept. [1654], in Dev. Ho., A.R.B. Colln. No. 158.

[3] Chas. Marshall's *Works*, 1704 edn. d3, verso.

[4] For the early work in and around Bristol see the important letters of Camm and Audland to Burrough and Howgill, 9th Sept. [1654] and 13th Sept. (1654, as the day of the week, "4th day," shows), in Dev. Ho., A.R.B. Colln. Nos. 158, 157. Also particulars in *The Memory of the Righteous Revived* (1689), p. 134, and Chas. Marshall's account in his Testimony to Camm and Audland in *The Memory of the Righteous Revived* and elsewhere. Also *F.P.T.* 10, 104, 226; and *The Cry of Blood*, by Geo. Bishop and others (1656).

marvellous character; "every day is but a meeting," wrote Audland, "and as the work is great, the power is greatest in us that ever we knew." They write on 9th September, two days after their arrival:

Here is a pretty many convinced of the Truth . . . they are much come down into themselves since we were here . . . they are the most noble of any that we have met withal. . . . The work of the Lord is great hereaway: the people hungers after life: they groan to be delivered: they meet every day: if we go into the fields they follow us: from us they cannot be separated: if we sit silent a long time, they all wait in silence: the Lord will do a great work amongst them, and raise up a pure people to place His name in.

Camm a few days later says:

"This day the people in the city who are our friends"—*i.e.* the Seekers—"met together to seek the Lord as they call it . . . we bore them long till the power of the Lord took hold upon us both and I was forced to cry out amongst them, My life suffered and if I did not speak I should be an example amongst them. And in much tenderness I spake unto them and silence was amongst them all, and much tenderness and brokenness. . . . They have many of them cast off their beautiful garments which was without"—this reminds us of the burning of ribbons at Malton. . . . "We are with them from six in the morning: they will come to us before we get up: and unto eleven or sometimes one at night they will never be from us. Go into the fields they will follow us, or go into any house, the house will be filled full, so that we cannot tell how we should get from them. The Lord hath subjected them all under us, and they are as fearful to offend us as a child is to offend its loving father."

We have vivid accounts of the first Sunday's work, 10th September 1654. One of the Seekers, Charles Marshall, a lad of seventeen, had been with Camm and Audland in the country in the early morning, about a mile and a half from the city, to a little spring of water, where he had often spent many solitary hours seeking the Lord, and here they sat some time and drank of the spring. After some hours of the morning were spent, a great travail of spirit took hold of the two Friends, and Audland said, trembling, "Let us be going into the city." They found that the house in Broadmead where they were staying was filled with people and also the street, but an old man offered the use of his field, called Earlsmead, and the people trooped into it "like an army." After Camm had spoken, Audland rose, "and all my limbs smote together and I was like a drunken man because of the Lord and because of the word of His holiness, and I was made to cry like a woman in travail." Young Marshall tells us he stood up

"... full of dread and shining brightness on his countenance"—transfigured before the crowd—"lifted up his voice as a trumpet and said, I proclaim spiritual war with the inhabitants of the earth, who are in the Fall and separation from God, and prophesy to the four winds of heaven. And these words dropped amongst the seed: and so went on in the mighty power of God Almighty, opening the way of life. But, ah! the seizings of souls, and prickings at heart which attended that season: some fell on the ground, others crying out under the sense of opening their states, which indeed gave experimental knowledge of what is recorded (Acts ii. 37). Indeed it was a notable day, worthy to be left on record, that our children may read and tell to their children."[1]

The same afternoon Camm and Audland were at the Fort among the soldiers, the Royal Fort on St. Michael's Hill, "the greatest meeting that ever I saw," says Audland. On the Tuesday five hundred people flocked to a "gallant" meeting three miles out of the city: the next day they met at the Red Lodge, a fine old house at the corner of Lodge Street, which is still standing; on the Friday they had a meeting at Filton by invitation of the parish minister. They went among Baptists and Independents, thrusting themselves in, according to the *Broadmead Baptist Records*,[2] and were evidently warmly welcomed by the soldiers, as was often the case. A hostile critic[3] says that "having nothing else to do [they] struck in with them in their quaking."

The news from Bristol stirred Howgill and Burrough, who wrote exultantly from London:

[1] Testimony in *The Memory of the Righteous Revived* (1689).
[2] P. 44 (published by Hanserd Knollys Society, 1847).
[3] Farmer's *The Great Mysteries of Godlinesse and Ungodlinesse*, 1655, Preface.

We have received letters from our dear brethren . . . the mighty power of the Lord is that way: that is a precious city and a gallant people: their net is like to break with fishes, they have caught so much [there] and all the coast thereabout: mighty is His work and power in this His day. Shout for joy, all ye holy ones, for the Lord rides on in power to get Himself a name.[1]

At the end of September Camm and Audland returned to the North for a short visit, travelling via Hereford and Chester.[2] A letter from Hereford to the newly convinced Bristol Friends (to be read "amongst Friends at the Meeting")[3] exhorts them to dwell in the Light and in the pure fear of the Lord, and they will then know "the gentle leadings of the Father, and the green pastures and the still waters, and the dew from above upon the tender plants, and the watering of the plants."

During Camm and Audland's absence, Howgill and Burrough visited Bristol, and the great work went on with crowded meetings every day. On Sunday 29th October, about a week after their arrival, a meeting of some 2000 people was held at the Fort, the people so thronging the Quaker Publishers that they could only get away from them with great difficulty.[4] The ministers and magistrates took alarm, and on the Monday closely questioned them. Their claim to an immediate call from God was challenged, and they were charged with meeting in a tumultuous way, but one of the magistrates bore witness that there had been many godly honest people present without tumult. At last, say Howgill and Burrough,

. . . they commanded us to depart out of the town, but we were bold and said, We were free-born men, and we knew no law we had transgressed, and therefore we should not be at any man's will, but when He moved us that called us, we should, and come in again as He moved. So we passed away, and all the people

[1] 19th Sept. 1654, *Letters of Early Friends*, p. 41, correcting 1656 to 1654. Cf. Burrough and Howgill to Fox, 25th Sept., Dev. Ho., A.R.B. Colln. No. 156.

[2] See *The Memory of the Righteous Revived*, pp. 40–50. Meetings were held at Hereford at Capt. Jno. Herring's house, a Member of the Nominated Parliament. See also Holme to Margt. Fell, Oct. 1654, Swarthm. Colln. i. 195.

[3] *The Memory of the Righteous Revived*, p. 40.

[4] Howgill and Burrough to Margt. Fell, 1st Nov. 1654 (*Letters of Early Friends*, p. 219, from Wm. Caton Colln.), gives full account. Cf. Besse, *Sufferings*, i. 39.

were silent, and the priests and the magistrates were enraged. We stayed till night and then went out of the city; and this day we were moved to come in again and to walk in the streets.

This episode, so apostolic in its spirit, shows the stuff of which the Quaker Publishers were made. They stayed till after Camm and Audland's return about the middle of November,[1] having had several meetings of about 3000 people. The city was now in a highly excited state. Camm writes:[2]

We have here in Bristol most commonly 3000 to 4000 at a meeting. The priests and magistrates of the city begin to rage, but the soldiers keep them down. . . . And many captains and great ones of the city are convinced and do believe in us and that we are of God, and all within ten miles of the city round about the people is very much desirous after truth. . . . Yea, at any point we come, we can have 400 or 500 or even 1000.

In Bristol then, during these stirring autumn months, a great spiritual awakening had roused the city. The opposers of Friends admitted the multitude of their followers and their success in prevailing with people to lay aside rich apparel and worldly contentments.[3] An interesting anonymous letter in the Clarke papers[4] shows that the awakening was something quite out of the ordinary.

In Bristow I have heard was a high spirit of expectation of God's pouring out His Spirit, which now they judge is answered in the generation of the Quakers, and multitudes there are taken herewith, and the eminent in profession of grace too. I write this by way of caution, the Lord help us to be watchful and faithful to the end.

These outside opinions may be supplemented by the vivid picture which Charles Marshall draws of this "glorious morning" of Bristol Quakerism.[5]

[1] Burrough to Margt. Fell, 15th Nov. 1654, Wm. Caton Collection (Jas. Bowden's copy at Dev. Ho.).

[2] Letter in Barclay's *Inner Life*, p. 309. I conjecture that it belongs here: the situation is too developed for the date in September suggested by Barclay.

[3] Farmer's *The Great Mysteries of Godlinesse, etc.*, 1655 edn. p. 88.

[4] 19th December, vol. iii. p. 14.

[5] See Testimony in *The Memory of the Righteous Revived* (1689).

We received the gospel with a ready mind, and with broken hearts and affected spirits, and gave up to follow the Lord fully. . . . Oh! the strippings of all needless apparel, and the forsaking of superfluities in meats [and] drinks: and in the plain self-denying path we walked, having the fear and dread of God on our souls that we were afraid of offending in word or deed. . . . Our meetings were so large that we were forced to meet without doors and that in frost and snow.

The new movement attracted a number of the Baptists. The Broadmead Church, begun in 1640, lost about twenty members, or a fourth of its strength. These twenty followed the lead of Dennis Hollister, a grocer in High Street, who had been one of the extreme Members of the Nominated Parliament, and, according to the *Broadmead Baptist Records*,

" . . . staying at London had sucked in some principles of this upstart locust doctrine," and "came home from London, with his heart full of discontent and his head full of poisonous new notions, as was discerned by some of the members of the Church. And he began to vent himself, and at one meeting of the Church, after he came down, he did blasphemously say, the Bible was the plague of England."

When the Quaker Publishers came to Bristol, Hollister received them into his house, and closed in with their doctrine, "and thought to have drawn away all the congregation after him, as he superbiously did use that word, John xii. 32, 'will draw all men unto Me.'"[1] It was in his orchard that the great meetings at Bristol were held.[2]

Other leading persons joined with Friends. There were the soldiers, Captain Beal, who commanded at the Fort, and three others who became prominent Friends,

[1] For this paragraph see *Broadmead Baptist Records*, pp. 42-57. The writer, Edward Terrill, then a young man of twenty, expounds the situation thus: "But Satan, seeing the abundance of light of reformation in this nation, . . . made use of popish Jesuits to creep abroad, up and down, in England. Under the guise of professors of truth [they] spread about many damnable errors and heresies, beguiling some unstable professors. Thereby Satan deceived many profane people to embrace their upstart notions of Quakerism, under a pretence of a great degree of holiness, by hearkening to the light within, which they called Christ, laying aside the manhood of our blessed Redeemer. . . . Thus smoke out of the bottomless pit arose, and the locust doctrine came forth, as it is written, Rev. ix. 2, 3, 4."

[2] My authority is Wm. Tanner's opinion to this effect in *Three Lectures on Friends in Bristol and Somerset*, p. 75. See *post*, p. 384.

Captains Edward Pyott, George Bishop, and Thomas Curtis, the last a woollen-draper who lived at Reading.[1] Thomas Gouldney, grocer, and Henry Row were well-to-do merchants; Josiah Coale, Barbara Blaugdone, and Charles Marshall became leading ministers.

The growing excitement of feeling in the city led to riots in December.[2] The rage of the unruly Bristol apprentices had been stirred against Friends by Ralph Farmer, the zealous Presbyterian minister of St. Nicholas, and they mobbed Camm and Audland on Bristol Bridge. Next day three of the rioters were arrested, and they rose again to the number of fifteen hundred and forced the magistrates to discharge their companions. The officers of the garrison had intervened, being well affected to Friends, and fearing that the strong Royalist party in Bristol would assert itself—indeed, shouts for King Charles had been raised by some of the rioters. The disturbances were reported to London, and the action of the Protector, after some ambiguity, so far inclined against Friends that Farmer could write[3] with thinly veiled insolence:

> Awhile ago there came to this city of Bristol certain Morice-dancers from the North, by two and two, two and two, with an intent here to exercise some spiritual cheats, or (as may well be suspected) to carry on some levelling design. . . . I was coming to you with a supplicatory epistle. But His Highness, by breath from his mouth, hath driven away these northern locusts from us, and given a command for the remove of their abetters and favourites. . . . And surely, Sir, His Highness hath gained much upon the hearts of our citizens by this act of grace and duty. We were made believe these men had countenance from him, which, upon my knowledge, made our magistrates here so backward to be quick with them and to deal so severely (and justly) with them, as they have been dealt with in other places. And therefore I rejoice that you breathe so good an air at court. . . . 'Tis not for his honour nor safety that every petty captain should dally with his commands and ride away from their obedience to them.

---

[1] Convinced at Bristol, *F.P.T.* p. 8.

[2] See Besse, *Sufferings*, i. 39, and Sewel, i. 143. Both accounts are taken from *The Cry of Blood*, by Bishop, Gouldney, Row, Pyott, and Hollister (1656).

[3] The Epistle dedicatory to John Thurloe, Secretary of State, dated 1st Jany. 1655, prefixed to Farmer's *The Great Mysteries of Godlinesse and Ungodlinesse*, 1655.

It is not quite clear why Farmer thought it no longer necessary to upbraid the Protector for his sympathy with sectaries, but Camm and Audland were away from the city for a time, and some change was perhaps made in the personnel of the garrison.[1] * He hints plainly enough that by favouring the Quakers the soldiers were abusing their power and making the citizens malignant to the Government. The Quakers, he writes, are spiritual jugglers, who speak, indeed, of God and Christ and the scriptures, but mean a light, a God, a Christ, scriptures and ordinances all within you only, and so within you that those without you are not worth looking after. They must have come to Bristol on Antichrist's errand, for Lancashire and those parts are as famous for Papists as they are for witches. He goes on to buttress up this fancy by suggesting, shrewdly enough, that Quakerism is tainted with the popish tenets of universal grace, freewill, satisfaction by our own sufferings, justification by inherent holiness, ability to keep the law, perfection and the real presence. The good man had persuaded himself that the Quakers, though professing themselves to be mechanics, might be Papists in disguise. Was there not a Jesuit who had masqueraded as a converted Jew, and had preached his notions among the Anabaptists and belittled the scriptures? Before the ink of Farmer's pamphlet was dry, his suggestion had taken visible shape. An information was sworn[2] alleging that some of the Quaker preachers in London were Franciscan Friars, and that in the previous autumn they had spoken of coming to Bristol. The Bristol magistrates, believing it "to be very probable and much to be suspected that the persons so lately come hither are some of those that came from Rome as aforesaid," ordered diligent search to be made for any of the Quaker leaders,[3] while the famous William Prynne from his retirement at Swainswick, near Bath, spread the libel broadcast through England in his pamphlet "The Quakers

[1] Grigge's *The Quakers' Jesus* (1658), p. 34, says that the absence of the Governor of the garrison had left Capts. Beal and Watson in chief command.

[2] See *The Memory of the Righteous Revived*, p. 129.

[3] See Besse, *Sufferings*, i. 40.

Unmasked, and clearly detected to be but the Spawn of Romish Frogs, Jesuites and Franciscan Fryers, sent from Rome to seduce the intoxicated Giddy-headed English Nation."

Owing to the temporary absence of Camm and Audland, the matter was dropped, and the Bristol Friends grew into strength, with little interruption from the authorities. The dangerous Royalist elements in the city probably made it inexpedient to repress the Quakers who were strongly Puritan. When in Bristol, Audland and Camm spent themselves without stint. In July 1655 the service was the greatest that Audland had ever seen.[1] In the autumn [2] he reports that Friends are precious and grow in the life and are in sweet order also in the country round about. He spends Sundays for the most part in the city, where meetings are very full and in much peace. During the week he visits country meetings, many of which are well settled. It is of these years of lavish service that Audland used to say:

> Ah! those great meetings in the Orchard at Bristol I may not forget. I would so gladly have spread my net over all, and have gathered all, that I forgot myself, never considering the inability of my body,—but it's well, my reward is with me, and I am content to give up and be with the Lord, for that my soul values above all things.[3]

Camm, who was the older man, poured forth his life in the service with equal devotion, his weak constitution wasted away in consumption, so that for several years before his death (in January 1657) he could not walk half-a-mile at a time, and after a meeting would seem as one ready to be dissolved.[4]

Summing up the work of the Westmorland Publishers in the South, we find that by the end of the year 1654 they had won a wonderful entrance for the Quaker message in and around London and in Bristol and the

[1] Letter to Howgill and Burrough in Dev. Ho., A.R.B. Colln. No. 58.*

[2] Two letters to Margt. Fell in Wm. Caton Colln. dated 20th Oct. 1655, and 17th Nov. (1655), taken from Jas. Bowden's copies at Dev. Ho.

[3] Thos. Camm's Testimony to John Camm and John Audland in *The Memory of the Righteous Revived.*

[4] *Ibid.*

neighbourhood, and had strenuously laboured, though with less success, in the two universities and at Norwich. It remains to consider the similar service undertaken by the Yorkshire leaders. Aldam was not released from prison till the beginning of December, and Nayler seems to have spent the year in the Northern Counties,—there is a graphic journal of six weeks of his travels among the Swarthmore Papers,[1]—but Dewsbury and Farnsworth were earnest in pioneer work. Dewsbury had passed the spring in York Castle on a charge of seducing the people, and on suspicion of blasphemy, though never brought to trial.[2] On his release in July he had arranged his outward affairs,[3] and after some service in Yorkshire started for the South. During the next five months he published his message, though not without interruption from the authorities, through the North Midlands, especially at Derby, Lincoln, Newark, Nottingham, Leicester, and Wellingborough. Everywhere he had large meetings, and found a "tender people coming towards Zion." At Wellingborough Thomas Andrews, the minister of the place, charged him with deceiving the people by telling them there was no original sin. Some weeks after, being again in the town, he challenged the minister in church to make good his accusation, and was taken before a neighbouring justice, who committed him to Northampton gaol. He was not allowed to see a copy of the Mittimus, but the professed charge seems to have been suspicion of blasphemy. The justice had found on him a paper, couched in high language, addressed to Cromwell, upbraiding him for the unrighteous laws by which God's people were being persecuted, and telling him, in the name of the Lord, that if he still hardened his heart, none should deliver him out of God's hand, "which will speedily perfect my pleasure upon thee, for the time is not long ere

[1] Swarthm. Colln. iii. 6.

[2] Besse, *Sufferings*, ii. 91, gives full details, taken from Dewsbury's "The Discovery of the Great Enmity of the Serpent" (*Works*, p. 26, etc.). See also Smith's *Life of Dewsbury*, p. 69, etc.

[3] See letter in Smith's *Life*, p. 76 (Swarthm. Colln. iv. 133); and for his Northampton imprisonment, and the events leading up to it, "The Discovery of the Great Enmity of the Serpent."

I accomplish what I have spoken, except thou repent."[1] This paper and the nervousness of the authorities at this time as to plots[2] were no doubt the real cause of his detention. At the trial, in March 1655, Judge Wyndham rated Dewsbury soundly for not staying at home, "but thou must go abroad in the country and in these parts to delude the people and to make a disturbance. . . . If thou and Fox had it in your power, you would soon have your hands imbrued in blood."[3] It was not until January 1656 that Dewsbury was released, by which time the political situation had changed and the Protector's personal government had greatly developed. Boteler, Cromwell's Major-General for the Northampton district, told him that it had been "the purpose and intent of the Lord Protector to suppress this way, which had taken little effect, and now he would try further in releasing them."[4] Marmaduke and Joseph Storr and other Friends shared his imprisonment for longer or shorter periods, and a great convincement took place in the district. The stiffness of Friends in refusing to procure their liberty by giving bond for good behaviour, and in declining money towards their support in prison, much "confounded their adversaries,"[5] and Dewsbury, as often in his life, found his prison bars served the truth better than any pulpit. Shortly before his imprisonment he had made one notable convert in Justice John Crook*of Beckerings Park, near Ampthill,[6] whose house became a centre for Friends, and already by January 1655 we hear of Friends all along the 35 miles from Market Harborough to Ampthill, and of a mighty thirst raised on every side.[7]

[1] *Works*, pp. 4-8.

[2] See Gardiner, *Hist. of the Commth. and Prot.* iii. 226, etc. Some were Levelling, others Royalist. Pearson and Capt. Bishop seem to have sympathized to some extent in the objects of Wildman's Levelling plot. See Gardiner, iii. 228 *n.*

[3] Besse, *Sufferings*, i. 522, and Smith's *Life*, p. 94.

[4] *F.P.T.* 198.

[5] See especially Dewsbury to Margt. Fell, 3rd Sept. 1655, Swarthm. Colln. iv. 139 (Smith's *Life*, p. 100).

[6] See *F.P.T.* 6. and *J.F.H.S.* i. 41 *n.*

[7] See Dewsbury's letters, Jan. 1655, giving account of his trial at the quarter-sessions in *Works*, p. 386; Dev. Ho., Boswell Middleton Colln. p. 8 (addressed "to all the *elders* of the church of the living God scattered in Yorkshire"); and *J.F.H.S.* i. 40, which are different but parallel accounts; also Jno. Whitehead's letter, *J.F.H.S.* i. 42.*

Farnsworth had received the news of the great work in London with exultation,[1] and with Thomas Goodaire zealously carried on the campaign in the North Midlands during the rest of the year, keeping touch with Dewsbury. He found near a hundred that kept constant at one meeting in Warwickshire—no doubt Baddesley—and vividly describes his work: [2]

> [The Lord] hath raised up a pretty sweet people in these parts: there is near a hundred that keep constant at one meeting in Warwickshire, and there is many at Leicester and thataways, and towards Lichfield and towards Swannington the river begins to divide into three heads: we had three meetings the last first-day and sweetly carried on. We are throng in our harvest. I have had two set meetings with the priests . . . and they are even teared to pieces: the sword is sharp, the horse swift, the rider active, the armour proved. . . . I had three great battles while Thomas was absent, one sore battle with the great Baptists in Staffordshire [27th September at Harlaston near Tamworth], but conquered Goliath, . . . down, down they fall. . . . We shall divide into three or four heads and march about, but I believe I shall stay with the camp, for the arrows and bullets are shot at me on every side, yet I have a good headpiece that a sword cannot enter.

It was in this spirit of fearless confidence that the Puritan sects were everywhere being attacked by the new evangel. We cannot be surprised at the authorities regarding it as a disruptive force.

[1] To Margt. Fell, 13th Augt. 1654, Swarthm. Colln. iii. 49.
[2] To Friends, Dev. Ho., Saml. Watson Colln. p. 44.

CHAPTER IX

FURTHER WORK IN THE SOUTH

(1655)

We endeavour to give people no cause for stumbling in anything, lest the work we are doing should fall into discredit. On the contrary, as God's servants, we seek their full approval—by unwearied endurance, by afflictions, by distress, by helplessness; by floggings, by imprisonments; by facing riots, by toil, by sleepless watching, by hunger and thirst; by purity of life, by knowledge, by patience, by kindness, by the Holy Spirit, by sincere love; by the proclamation of the truth, by the power of God; by the weapons of righteousness, wielded in both hands; through honour and ignominy, through calumny and praise. We are looked upon as imposters, and yet are true men; as obscure persons, and yet are well known; as on the point of death, and yet, strange to tell, we live; as under God's discipline, and yet we are not deprived of life; as sad, but we are always joyful; as poor, but we bestow wealth on many; as having nothing, and yet we securely possess all things (2 Corinthians vi. 3-10).—From Dr. WEYMOUTH'S *The New Testament in Modern Speech.*

FOX had spent the later months of this memorable year, 1654, in Yorkshire and neighbouring counties, confirming the Churches. From Thomas Stacey's at Cinderhill Green, about August,[1] he issued a letter of counsel and cheer to the Quaker Publishers of Truth. Late in December 1654 he arranged a meeting at Swannington in Leicestershire, which was attended, amongst others, by Aldam and Farnsworth, Camm probably and Audland and Capt. Pyott from Bristol, and Burrough and Howgill who were passing north from London.[2] This "concourse of two

[1] Dewsbury, who was not released from York till 24th July, seems to have been with Fox at this time. See letter to Margt. Fell, Swarthm. Colln. iv. 144. The letter of counsel is in *Journ.* i. 190, and the *Camb. Journ.* i. 142 says it was issued from Cinderhill Green. According to Norman Penney, *Camb. Journ.* i. 423, the place is now called Handsworth Grange.

[2] See *Journ.* i. 199. For Camm's name, see Geo. Taylor to Margt. Fell, Swarthm. Colln. i. 210.

hundred Quakers at least"[1] disquieted the authorities, who did not understand the object of the rendezvous and suspected plots. The Ranters, who had great strength in the North Midlands, made some disturbance, and Fox challenged them to come forth and try their God. They "sung and whistled and danced," says Fox,[2] "but the Lord's power so confounded them that many of them came to be convinced." A visit to his relations at Drayton followed, and some busy weeks of controversy with ministers. His travelling companion, Alexander Parker, from the Bowland district, had been convinced in 1653. He was at this time twenty-five years old, well educated, and a man of gentlemanly carriage and deportment, who became one of Fox's closest personal friends.[3] He writes how the people came to the disputes at Drayton,[4] "as if they had come to a bull-baiting or the like, and haled and tewed and hurried George up and down, who, like a king, reigned over them and trod upon their necks, and the power was over them and we had the victory, though the world saw it not."

At the end of one day's dispute Fox writes:[5]

> A great shake it was to the priests and my father in the flesh thwacked his cane on the ground and said, "Well," said he, "I see he that will but stand to the truth it will carry him out," though he was an hearer and follower of the priests.

Meanwhile the Protector had been informed[6] that the Quakers and Cavaliers were joined together in a plot to rise in arms against him, and accordingly at Whetstone, on 11th February,[7] Fox was arrested by Colonel Hacker,[8]

[1] See letters in Thurloe, *State Papers*, iii. 94, 116, under dates 9th Jany. and 21st Jany. 1655.*

[2] *Journ.* i. 199.

[3] *F.P.T.* 306, and John Whiting's *Persecution Exposed* (1715 edn.), pp. 184, 185. Cf. *J.F.H.S.* viii. 30, where Dilworth Abbatt suggests that Chipping in Lancashire was his birthplace. His letters in the Swarthm. Colln. are of great value.

[4] To Margt. Fell, 1st Feby. 1655, Swarthm. Colln. iv. 234. See also *Journ.* i. 200-207, and *Short Journ.* 36-38 for some additional facts.

[5] *Camb. Journ.* i. 158; *Journ.* i. 206.

[6] Aldam's account in Dev. Ho., Boswell Middleton Colln. p. 33.

[7] For date, see Parker to Margt. Fell, 22nd February 1655, in *Letters of Early Friends*, p. 21, from Wm. Caton Colln. As Gardiner, *Hist. of the Commth. and Prot.* iii. 263 *n.*, points out, the date in Dr. Hodgkin's *Geo. Fox*, p. 108, is wrong.

[8] For Colonel Francis Hacker see note in *Camb. Journ.* i. 424. His wife and sister became Friends.

and taken to the Marshalsea at Leicester. We have a curious picture of his stay here.[1] Dippers, Separatists, and Ranters came to visit him, and he spoke to their several conditions of heart, although he had never seen them before. Some said he was a "witch," others demanded by what power he knew these things. Fox replied that God had revealed His Son in him, who knew all things. Then they said, Was he the Son of God. The answer Fox gave follows the lines with which we are already familiar. "I said, I was no more; but the Father and the Son was all in me, and we are one." He went on to appeal to the light in his hearers' hearts, and amongst others Jacob Bauthumley, the notorious Ranter,[2] with whom Farnsworth and Dewsbury had contended,[3] witnessed that what had been spoken was the eternal truth.

Colonel Hacker would have been content with a promise from Fox that he would go home and keep no more meetings, but as he could not thus limit his freedom he was sent up to London.* Here he was lodged at the Mermaid, "over against the Mews at Charing Cross," and on the 5th of March[4] the Protector required from him a written promise that he would not take up arms against the Government. The reply which he was "moved of the Lord" to give is quite explicit on this point, though full of high language, beyond what would be tolerable now. An extract will sufficiently show the nature of its contents:

I, who am of the world called George Fox, do deny the carrying or drawing of any carnal sword against any or against thee Oliver Cromwell or any man; in the presence of the Lord

[1] The account by Fox is in Swarthm. Colln. vii. 171, and is endorsed "Sufferings at Leicester, 1653." It clearly belongs to this date, both from internal evidence, and by comparison with a letter from Richd. Weaver to Margt. Fell, in Swarthm. Colln. i. 91.

[2] For Bauthumley, see *Studies in Mystical Religion*, pp. 472, 473, 474.

[3] See Dev. Ho., Saml. Watson Colln. p. 162 (4th Jan. 1655), and Dewsbury to Fox, Swarthm. Colln. iii. 22 (no date).

[4] See documents in Swarthm. Colln. ii. 2 (Thos. Aldam's handwriting). See also *Camb. Journ.* i. 161 (and note, i. 425), where the letter is given in its original form, not as toned down in *Journ.* i. 209. Also in Dev. Ho., Boswell Middleton Colln. pp. 32, 33, with valuable supplementary particulars by Aldam. A facsimile of the letter from the *Camb. Journ.* is given as a frontispiece to Elisha Bates's adverse *Appeal to the Society of Friends*, 1836.

God I declare it, God is my witness: by whom I am moved to give this forth for the Truth's sake, from him whom the world calls George Fox, who is the son of God, who is sent to stand a witness against all violence and against all the works of darkness. . . . And my kingdom is not of this world, therefore with the carnal weapon I do not fight, but am from those things dead, from him who is not of the world, called of the world by the name George Fox, and this I am ready to seal with my blood . . . from him who to all your souls is a friend, for establishing of righteousness and cleansing the land of evil-doers, and a witness against all wicked inventions of men and murderous plots. . . .

The following day he saw the Protector, who showed himself moderate, saying at the end with tears in his eyes, "Come again to my house, for if thou and I were but an hour in a day together we should be nearer one to the other," and adding that he wished him no more ill than he did his own soul. Cromwell told Fox's gaoler, Capt. Drury, that Fox was not a fool, and that he had never seen such a paper as the one he had written.[1] The interview served to clear Friends from several of the wild rumours current about them, and Fox was able to satisfy Cromwell in the matter of plots. But the uncompromising sincerity of the Quakers and their militant attitude towards the dominant Puritan sects made them a strangely disturbing element in the Commonwealth, and it is not surprising that the authorities looked on them with disfavour. Circumstances were forcing Cromwell to govern England more and more by absolute rule, and disturbances of all kinds must be repressed. He was a sincere upholder of religious liberty, but the unsettlement of the nation compelled him to insist that it should be a liberty within the limits of good order. Three weeks prior to the interview with Fox a proclamation had appeared which Gardiner calls "the charter of religious freedom under the Protectorate."[2] The large and sincere phrasing of the opening sentences justifies this title, but the gist of the document is in the later part, which laments the rude and unchristian disturbance of

[1] *Camb. Journ.* i. 168.

[2] *Hist. of the Commth. and Prot.* iii. 260; cf. *F.P.T.* 350.

ministers, practised, contrary to just liberty, by divers men lately risen up under the names of Quakers, Ranters, and others. The proclamation strictly requires "that they forbear henceforth all such irregular and disorderly practices: and if, in contempt hereof, any person shall presume to offend as aforesaid, we shall exteem them disturbers of the civil peace, and shall expect and do require all officers and ministers of justice to proceed against them accordingly." This proclamation, implemented by the Instrument of Government, was a powerful persuasive to persecution. George Whitehead, with good reason, complained of the way in which Quakers and Ranters were coupled together.[1] Where was any justice or equity or judicial proceeding, he cries, thus to compare an innocent people with the scandalous, and thus to reproach or recriminate them upon informations and evil reports. But it seems probable that at the date of the proclamation the sobriety of the Friends, as compared with the Ranters, was not understood in London, and it was supposed that their high claims to spiritual light meant a claim to live without any law but their own wills. When Fox was set at liberty, the false intelligence current about Friends caused him to be an object of curiosity to the London crowd. His piercing gaze, his silver buttons (in reality alchemy), his leather breeches, his rumoured witchery of people with ribbons, were the talk of the town. Henry Walker, whom Fox calls Oliver's "newsmonger," was especially scurrilous in his newsbook of *Perfect Proceedings*.[2] Fox, on his side, looked out on the gay city with his keen eyes and saw its frivolity.[3]

"What a world is this," he wrote, ". . . women plaiting the hair, men and women powdering it, making their backs look like bags of meal. . . . If he have store of ribbons hanging about his waist, and at his knees, and in his hat of divers colours, red or white or black or yellow, and his hair be powdered, then he is a

[1] *Christian Progress* (1725 edn.), pp. 38-44.

[2] See article in *Friends' Quarterly Examiner*, Oct. 1910, by J. B. Williams.*

[3] *Journ.* i. 219. The *Cambridge Journal*, i. 175-177, is a little rougher in the phrasing, and while attributing the piece to Fox, has at the end the name of Thos. Rawlinson, as though he had assisted in it.

brave man, then he is accepted, then he is no Quaker. . . . Likewise the women, having their gold, their spots on their faces, noses, cheeks, foreheads, having their rings on their fingers wearing gold, . . . having their ribbons tied about their hands and three or four gold laces about their clothes, this is no Quaker, say they. . . . Now are not all these that have got their ribbons hanging about their arms, hands, back, waists, knees, hats, like unto fiddlers' boys? . . . O these are gentlemen indeed, these are bred up gentlemen, these are brave fellows, and they must take their recreation for pleasures are lawful. And these in their sports set up their shouts like unto the wild asses. . . . These are bad Christians and show that they are gluttoned with the creatures and then the flesh rejoiceth."

It was less than twelve months since the message of the plain North-country ploughmen had first reached the capital.[1] Already in October 1654[2] Howgill had written, "Our burden is great, we cannot get any separation for the multitude: and so Friends do not much know one another: and we cannot conveniently get any place to meet in, that Friends may sit down." Early in 1655 part of an ancient great house within Aldersgate was taken for a meeting-place, which was called the Bull and Mouth meeting, from the sign of the inn that occupied the other part of the building. This "new hired great tavern chapel," as opponents called it,[3] held a thousand people, presumably standing. Here Howgill and his younger companion Burrough, that "son of thunder and consolation," diligently laboured, "threshing" among "the world." William Crouch gives a vivid account of Burrough's work at a typical Bull and Mouth meeting:[4]

I have beheld him filled with power by the Spirit of the Lord . . . when the room which was very large hath been filled with people, many of whom have been in uproars, contending one

[1] The early work in London is well told in Wm. Beck and T. F. Ball's *London Friends' Meetings* (1869). Many of the letters in the Swarthmore and Wm. Caton Collections relating to London are printed in A. R. Barclay's *Letters of Early Friends* (1841). The other main sources are *F.P.T.* 163-166; Wm. Crouch's *Posthuma Christiana* (1712); and Richard Hawkins's *Brief Narrative of the Life of Gilbert Latey* (1707).

[2] In *Letters of Early Friends*, p. 27 *n.*

[3] See *The Quacking Mountebanck*, 1655 (title).

[4] *Posthuma Christiana* (1712 edn.), p. 26.

with another, some exclaiming against the Quakers, accusing and charging them with heresy, blasphemy, sedition and what not, . . . others endeavouring to vindicate them and speaking of them more favourably. In the midst of all which noise and contention, this servant of the Lord hath stood upon a bench, with his Bible in his hand, for he generally carried one about him, speaking to the people with great authority from the words of John vii. 12, "And there was much murmuring among the people concerning Him," to wit Jesus: "for some said, He is a good man: others said, Nay; but He deceiveth the people." And so suitable to the present debate amongst them that the whole multitude were overcome thereby, and became exceeding calm and attentive, and departed peaceably and with seeming satisfaction.

Of Burrough's undaunted courage a striking instance is given.[1] In Moorfields he came upon an excited throng of journeymen and apprentices gathered round a wrestling ring, in which a lusty young fellow, the victor in many bouts, was challenging any one to try a fall with him. Burrough stepped into the ring and, looking austerely and gravely about him, faced the expectant crowd and told them that man was made for something higher than the display of brute force; he was meant to fight, in comradeship with other fellow-soldiers, in the service of Christ. We feel that such a man would have felt at home in the rough work of saving men of strong animal passions by fellowship and friendship which has to be done in our own day.

The strenuousness of the Quaker propaganda in London is shown by the taking of the Bull and Mouth premises. A responsibility was felt, "to have some settled meetings for the sake of those who yet sat in darkness, that they might come and hear the truth declared and be turned to the Lord."[2] Burrough and Howgill, in March 1655, give the following account of their usual work on the Sunday:[3]

[1] See Sewel, i. 137 (1811 edn.), and Croese, p. 70 (Latin 1695 edn.), p. 52 (English 1696 edn.).*

[2] *Life of Gilbert Latey*, p. 10.

[3] To Margt. Fell, *Letters of Early Friends*, p. 25 (from Wm. Caton Collection).

We get Friends on the first-days to meet together in several places out of the rude multitude . . . and we two go to the great meeting-place which we have, which will hold a thousand people, which is always nearly filled, to thresh among the world; and we stay till twelve or one o'clock, and then pass away, the one to one place and the other to another place where Friends are met in private; and stay till four or five o'clock.

In the following month,[1] we hear of two great places for a threshing-floor, besides five or six meetings every first-day for Friends, and a meeting set up a little beyond Whitehall, near Westminster. The regular holding of meetings for "threshing" among the world is a distinctive feature of the early London work. The advice of Fox and Farnsworth [2] respecting such meetings seems to have been followed, the main body of London Friends being encouraged to keep to their retired meetings, and a few, fitted for the work and strong in the truth, undertaking this more arduous service.

Friends were also eager protagonists in the public religious disputes which were then in fashion. Howgill, for example, says: [3]

All the priests and all the gathered congregations in the city preach against us and are bent in great rage, and print lies and incense people much. E[dward] B[urrough] and I have ordinarily two public disputes with the heads of them, and they lose their numbers so fast they know not what to do; yet the city is pretty calm and quiet, and wisdom begins to grow among Friends, and divers are moved to go forth in the ministry.

The effect of all this work was considerable. "A great shatter," wrote Parker in May,[4] "is among all the forms and gathered Churches . . . and many are inquiring after the truth." The rapid settlement of a number of meetings, at private houses or on hired premises, shows the success which attended the propaganda.

George Fox had thrown himself with zest into the

[1] Howgill to Margt. Fell, *Letters of Early Friends*, p. 35, from Wm. Caton Colln. To be dated April; cf. Howgill and Burrough to Margt. Fell, dated London, 3rd April 1655, in Wm. Caton Colln. (Dev. Ho., Jas. Bowden's copy), though this date needs correcting, I think, to 30th April.* [2] *Ante*, p. 133.

[3] To Margt. Fell, 21st May 1655, *Letters to Early Friends*, p. 32, from Wm Caton Colln.

[4] To Margt. Fell, *Letters to Early Friends*, p. 30, from Wm. Caton Colln. 267.

London work. It was his first visit to the city since he had become the apostle of England's spiritual awakening. Friends, says Parker, "begin to know George, though at the first he was strange to them; and one thing they all take notice of, that if George be in the company, all the rest are for the most part silent." He took part in the Bull and Mouth meetings, where we hear of him,[1] his voice and outward man almost spent among the crowd. He also had disputes with Ranters, Baptists, Muggletonians, and others. His most important service, however, at this time seems to have been the fortnight at the end of March which was spent at Justice Crook's house at Beckerings Park in Bedfordshire,[2] where he had full opportunity of conference with Audland and Lancaster, Benson, Thomas Stubbs, and others.

During this spring of 1655 London was the headquarters of the rapidly widening work. The extant letters to Margaret Fell[3] show the close touch maintained from the city with the Publishers of Truth throughout the South of England. These were almost always working two and two, after the example of the mission of the first Seventy (Luke x. 1). In some cases the field of work was already marked out, though even here there was nothing that could be called settled residence in one place. Thus Burrough and Howgill were in London, Camm and Audland at Bristol, John Story and John Wilkinson (the two future Separatists) in Wiltshire. In other cases fresh ground was being broken, and fresh workers from the North were coming forward, and accordingly we are told of a direction rather than of a locality.[*] John Stubbs and Caton are moved to go towards Dover, Richard Clayton and Thomas Bond towards Norwich and into Suffolk, Miles Halhead and Thomas Salthouse towards Plymouth, John Slee[4] and Thomas Lawson into Sussex,

[1] Burrough and Howgill to Margt. Fell, *Letters of Early Friends*, p. 27.

[2] See *Journ.* i. 225, and Parker to Margt. Fell, 3rd April 1655, Swarthm. Colln. i. 161 (also in part in *Letters of Early Friends*, p. 28). The *Journal* says at Luton, but this note of place is not in the *Camb. Journ.* i. 180, and Parker had a dispute at Bedford, near Beckerings Park, but twenty miles from Luton.

[3] See *Letters of Early Friends*, which contains a series from London, from which the following particulars are taken.

[4] *Camb. Journ.* i. 420.

Robertson and Ambrose Rigge into Surrey and Kent, Lancaster and Thomas Stubbs into Bedfordshire. As these Friends passed through London, Howgill and Burrough supplied their needs; Howgill writes, for instance, in April:[1]

I shall take care for the supplyment of Friends in these parts, while I am hereaway, and truly I fear lest the burden should be heavy upon the North, for the charge is great, and our camp great.

In reply to this six pounds is sent from the Kendal Fund, draining it dry for the time.[2]

We may now follow in the footsteps of some of the Quaker Publishers. In March the message was carried into Kent[3] by John Stubbs, an old Commonwealth soldier of some learning, who had been convinced while Fox lay in Carlisle gaol,[4] and "all his imaginary light" put out,[5] and William Caton, a lad of eighteen, who had acted as tutor and secretary in the Swarthmore household. At Dover they were protected from the rage of the authorities by a shoemaker Luke Howard, who a few months later was the instrument, with George Harrison of Sedbergh, in the convincement of the great political agitator John Lilburne. Lilburne was then lying in Dover Castle, and wrote to his wife in December, referring to Friends as "those preciousest, though most contemptible, people called Quakers, the truly beloved objects of my soul."[6] In 1657 Hubberthorne found him "zealous and forward for the truth," with "a sight and comprehension which is deep,"[7] and he closed his stormy career in August of that year, "bearing a testimony for Truth, both by writing and speaking, unto his death."[8]

[1] Howgill to Margt. Fell, *Letters of Early Friends*, p. 35, from Wm. Caton Colln.

[2] Willan and Taylor to Margt. Fell, 14th April, Swarthm. Colln. i. 219.

[3] See *F.P.T.* pp. 130-146; Caton's *Life*, cap. 6; letter printed in Barclay's edition of *Life*, at p. 20; and "A True Declaration of the Bloody Proceedings of the Men in Maidstone . . . 1655."*

[4] *Journ.* i. 189.

[5] Stubbs to Margt. Fell, in *Camb. Journ.* i. 121. He was born about 1618, and had been a Baptist and a "preacher up of the water till he came to Christ the Light." See Testimony by Fox in Dev. Ho. Portfolio 16, No. 58.

[6] *F.P.T.* 144, 145.

[7] To Fox, Swarthm. Colln. iv. 14.

[8] *F.P.T.* 145; Gardiner, *Hist. of Commth. and Prot.* iv. 2, 3. For further particulars see Sewel (1811 edn.), pp. 211-215, and *Dict. Natl. Biography.**

At Folkestone a notable convert was made in Samuel Fisher of Lydd, a man of learning and controversial skill who had surrendered his lectureship in order to join the Baptists. When Stubbs and Caton reached Maidstone, the law against vagrants was put in force against them in its most savage form. The authorities[1]

> . . . searched them narrowly, and took away their money, Bibles, gloves, knives, inkhorns and paper and such like things as was in their pockets from them, and then had them into a room where they were stripped naked and their necks and arms put in the stocks; and there cruelly whipped with cords in a bloody manner in the sight of many people, which forced tears from the tender-hearted that were there, to see the execution done. And when they had thus cruelly proceeded, they fastened irons upon them with great clogs of wood, and put them in amongst transgressors.

A few days later they were despatched off home under the Vagrancy Act, from constable to constable, but, as happened in other cases, the constables grew weary of their charge, and left the Friends to themselves. They thereupon returned to Maidstone, testified in the church, and passed away unscathed, for "God chained down the red dragon" of persecution at that time. This first visit to Kent resulted in the settlement of several meetings, "and all was as a green field of corn springing up."

The Eastern Counties still proved stony soil for Quakerism. By May 1655 the Norwich prisoners had been mostly released. Hubberthorne and George Whitehead resumed their active service, while Howgill, Burrough, and Fox paid short visits. At the end of July, Whitehead[2] was passing towards London with Richard Clayton and John Harwood, a Yorkshire Friend, who afterwards became a troubler of the Quaker Israel. Clayton put a paper on the church-doors at Bures, near Sudbury, and the other two took occasion to speak to the people who had gathered round. Clayton was whipped as a vagrant, while Whitehead and Harwood were thrown into Bury

[1] See *F.P.T.* 139; and for the Vagrancy Act, st. 39 Eliz. cap. 4, see *F.P.T.* 346.

[2] George Whitehead, *Christian Progress* (edn. 1725), pp. 67-98.

prison, where they were joined a month later by George Rofe, a glazier of Halstead,[1] who had asked a question of a minister after his sermon, and later in the year by George Fox the younger and a Cambridgeshire Friend, Henry Marshall. Fox had been convinced by Whitehead at Mendlesham, and is distinguished from his great namesake by the epithet "younger"—that is, younger in convincement. Both he and Rofe became gifted ministers during their imprisonment.

Suffolk had replaced Norfolk as a centre of persecution. The prisoners would not submit to the gaoler's extortions, and accordingly lay "in the common ward among felons, in a low dungeon-like place, under a market-house, our poor lodging being upon rye-straw, on a damp earthen floor, though we were therewith content, and the place sanctified to us." Here they were shamefully maltreated and were kept prisoners, on the slenderest grounds, till October 1656, when a special order for their release came from the Protector. A Westmorland Friend, Margaret Sutton, travelled to Bury, and offered the judge to lie in bonds so that Whitehead might go free, or to lay down her life for him[2]—an incident which sets in a strong light the mutual love of Friends.

In the neighbouring county of Essex the sufferings of another young man, James Parnell, had a fatal issue. Parnell[3] was a well-educated lad from Retford, born there in September 1636, small in height and mean in appearance, but of high zeal and courage. When about fifteen, the power of the Lord was made known in his heart; he turned from the professors and the world, and his relations disowned him.[4] He sought for a people with whom he might have union, and found one, "a few miles from the town where I lived, whom the Lord was

[1] For Geo. Rofe see *F.P.T.* 129 *n.*

[2] Besse, *Sufferings*, i. 662.

[3] For Parnell's life see his collected *Works*, edn. 1675; references in *F.P.T.* (Essex); *Life of Jas. Parnell*, by Charlotte Fell Smith, 1906; article on Parnell by Dr. Thos. Hodgkin in *Friends' Quarterly Examiner*, July 1906; and sketch of life in *Palestine Notes and Other Papers*, by Jno. Wilhelm Rowntree, 1906, pp. 126-129. I have added or corrected a few details.

[4] *Works*, p. 233, etc.

a-gathering out of the dark world, to sit down together and wait upon His name." I suggest that this refers to the Tickhill and Balby group of Friends some twelve miles away, the rather as a message of love by Farnsworth to "little James" occurs in a letter to Fox in 1653, and seems almost certainly to relate to Parnell.[1] If this is so, he was no doubt sent by this group of Friends to make acquaintance with Friends in the North. A visit to Fox in Carlisle gaol confirmed his faith.[2] In the summer of 1654 he found himself at Cambridge, stirred to visit the university town by the cruel flogging that had befallen his friends Elizabeth Williams and Mary Fisher. There he was thrown into prison for publishing two papers against the corruption of the magistrates and of the priests; but at the second quarter-sessions, at the end of September, the jury only found against him that the papers were his, and three days later he was sent out of Cambridge as a vagrant.[3] Six months' work in Cambridgeshire and the neighbourhood led up to fierce disputes with the Baptists at Fen Stanton, and afterwards at Cambridge, Littleport, and Ely. In the Isle of Ely, "that island of errors and sectaries,"[4] he had great meetings, marked by his usual impetuous fervour.[5] "In much power was I carried forth to the binding and chaining of the heathen and the reaching of the witness, so that many was convinced." At Soham he spoke in the church after the minister had done; but a Littleport man created a good deal of offence by going naked as a sign, and Parnell again found himself in Cambridge gaol, though freed the next day by a friendly justice. Essex was thenceforward to be his field of work—a county where there was a leaven of waiting people, who were weary with running to and fro. After visiting Halstead,

[1] Swarthm. Colln. iii. 52. The endorsed date, 1653, is confirmed by internal evidence.
[2] *Journal*, i. 172.
[3] See *Works*, p. 237, and Hubberthorne's letter in Swarthm. Colln. iv. 5, and another to Margt. Fell, dated 27th Sept. [1654] in Wm. Caton Colln. (Dev. Ho., Jas. Bowden's copy).
[4] Edward's *Gangraena*, 1646 edn. 2nd div. p. 29.
[5] See Parnell's letter to Burrough and Howgill, 18th May [1655], in Dev. Ho., A. R. Barclay Colln. No. 29.

Coggeshall, and other places, he reached Colchester, which, through the immigration of Protestant Dutch refugees, had become an important manufacturing town, but was much demolished by the siege of 1648. The record of a day's work at Colchester shows the unsparing energy of the "quaking boy," as the people called him. There is a meeting in his lodging, then he speaks at church after the sermon, in the afternoon addresses a thousand people out of a hayloft window in John Furly's yard, and in the evening disputes with the town-lecturer and a Baptist Seventh-day preacher. It was at Colchester, as he came out of St. Nicholas' Church, that the lad was struck with a great staff and told to "take that for Jesus Christ's sake," to which he replied meekly, "Friend, I do receive it for Jesus Christ's sake."[1] Ten days' work in the town resulted in numerous convincements, amongst others that of Steven Crisp, then a young man of twenty-seven, of whom we shall hear again. Parnell now goes to Coggeshall, and on the 12th July 1655 attends with his usual courage a meeting specially convened to fast and pray against the errors of the Quakers. Feeling ran high that day, and the preacher, who was an Independent, did not spare his language. When he had done, Parnell began a reply, and a disturbance followed. He was arrested by the Puritan magistrates for causing a riot, and committed to Colchester Castle. When the assizes at Chelmsford came round, he travelled the twenty-two miles amongst felons and murderers, in a party of six hooked together on a chain day and night. The judge was a partial, overbearing man, but he could not persuade the jury to convict, and therefore took the law into his own hands and fined Parnell £40 for contempt of the magistracy and the ministry, saying, presumably with reference to the Proclamation of the preceding February, that the Protector had charged him to see that he punished such persons as should contemn either. Sent back to Colchester, Parnell wrote a beautiful letter[2] to his Essex Friends:

[1] Cf. the similar incident recorded in the early part of the *Life of John Roberts.*

[2] *Works*, p. 292.

As I had a time to preach the Truth amongst you, to the convincement of many, so also now I have a time to seal the same with patient suffering in the bonds of the gospel, that you may see that it is no other but what we are made able and willing to seal with patient suffering, yea, with our blood, if we be called to it. . . . Be willing that self shall suffer for the Truth, and not the Truth for self.

These last noble words express the spirit not only of Parnell, but of many another Quaker sufferer. At Colchester he was most harshly treated, and put

. . . in the Hole in the Wall, which is very high from the ground, and where the ladder was too short by six foot, and when his friends would have given him a cord and a basket to have taken up his victuals in they would not let them . . . but he must either come up and down by a rope (or else famish in the Hole), which he did a long time. But after a long suffering in this Hole, where there was nought but misery as to the outward man, it being no place either for air or smoke, and James being much benumbed in his naturals, as he was climbing up the ladder, with his victuals in one hand, and coming to the top of the ladder, catching at the rope with his other hand, missed the rope and fell from a very great height down upon stones, by which fall he was exceedingly wounded in the head and arms and his body much bruised and taken up for dead. Then they put him in a little low Hole called the Oven (which place was so little that some bakers' ovens have been seen bigger than it, though not so high) without the least air, hole or window for smoke.[1]

Eight months of such imprisonment wore away the strength but not the spirit of the young man. In December[2] he was able to write to Dewsbury, also in prison, and say, much as Paul said in Philippians i. 12-14, "These bonds have been very serviceable, to the piercing of the hearts of many, and the discovering of the spirits of my persecutors, and the confirming of these in the Truth that were convinced. . . . They have laboured to make my bonds grievous, but my strength the Philistine knows not." At the beginning of April 1656[3] he

[1] *Works*, Ellis Hookes' Testimony.

[2] *Letters of Early Friends*, p. 224. The original is in the York Records, Dewsbury corr. fol. 18.

[3] The date usually given is 4th May, based no doubt on the date 5th May attached to the "true copy of the verdict" at the coroner's inquest. But, in

died, and was buried in the castle-yard. "Here I die innocently," he said at the close to Thomas Shortland, who had offered to lie in prison for him while he restored his strength at a Friend's house; "now I must go: will you hold me?" and so fell into a sweet sleep for about an hour and drew breath no more. His persecutors had called him "the railing fellow in the Castle, a wandering star, to whom is reserved the blackness of darkness for ever," but were now ashamed of their work, and sought to cover it up by the verdict procured at the inquest, which ran as follows:

> We do find that James Parnell through his wilful rejecting of his natural food for ten days together, and his wilful exposing of his limbs to the cold, to be the cause of the hastening of his own end; and by no other means that we can learn or know of.

This tale was circulated in a pamphlet,[1] and turned into a ballad,[2] though promptly answered by Friends.[3]

Parnell was not, strictly speaking, the first Quaker to die in prison,[4] but he was the first of the company of

view of the other evidence, it is clear that this copy was made some weeks after the actual verdict. The true date is 10th April, and is given in *The Diary of the Rev. Ralph Josselin*, 1616-83, edited for the Royal Historical Society by E. Hockliffe, 1908 (see *J.F.H.S.* vi. p. 41): "April 11. Heard this morning that James Parnel the father of the Quakers in these parts, having undertaken to fast forty days and nights, was *die* 10 in the morning found dead; he was by jury found guilty of his own death, and buried in the Castle yard." A letter of Thos. Willan's, dated 26th April 1656 (Swarthm. Colln. i. 272), says, "Jas. Parnell died in Colchester prison about 20 days since." The ballad dates the death in April. See also Whitelocke's *Memorials*, edn. 1732, p. 636. Firth, *The Last Years of the Protectorate*, i. 82, wrongly says "May."

Ralph Josselin refers in his *Diary* to the Coggeshall disturbance, July 1655, and says many feared the Quakers would ruin Cromwell, but in his opinion it took more than words to alter governments.

1 "A True and Lamentable Relation of the most desperate death of Jas. Parnell, Quaker," by Henry Glisson and others, 1656.

2 "The Quaker's Fear, etc." (Broadside with three woodcuts), 1656, by L[awrence] P[rice].

3 "The Lamb's Defence against Lyes, etc.," by Thos. Shortland and others, 1656.

4 The Swarthmore Colln. iii. 91, contains a document concerning one William Peares, which is endorsed by Fox, "died in prison at York, about 1654." This William Peares signs with others a letter from Aldam to Fox from York prison in Swarthm. Colln. iii. 36, and also the printed paper, "False Prophets and false Teachers described"; see Smith's *Catalogue of Friends' Books*, i. 5. The document endorsed by Fox says of Peares: "The cause of his imprisonment was because he was moved to strip himself naked, a figure of all the nakedness of the world. . . . It was the naked that suffered for the naked truth, a figure of your nakedness."

Publishers of Truth to seal his witness with his life, and his name appropriately comes first in the early collection of Quaker "Testimonies" known as *Piety Promoted*.[1] His blood proved a fruitful seed, and Colchester became one of the strongholds of Quakerism.

The year 1655 was a time of much active service and much persecution in the Midland Counties. Dewsbury lay a prisoner at Northampton, but Farnsworth and others were untiring in their work. Worcestershire at this time acknowledged the celebrated Richard Baxter as its religious leader. A great Comprehensionist, he had succeeded in setting on foot a Worcestershire Association which united together Presbyterians, Independents, and many Episcopalians. In the religious confusion of the period such a plan found imitators, and by the beginning of 1657 the system had spread to fourteen counties.[2] But while Baxter was "distinguished for his charity towards those from whom he differed in non-essentials," he was also known "for the controversial vigour with which he assailed extreme opponents."[3] His sword was sharp against Anabaptists and Separatists, who, in his opinion, had withdrawn themselves from the unity of Christ's Church. Still worse in his view were the Quakers.

> The Quakers among us are the ignorant, proud, giddy sort of professors, first made Separatists or Anabaptists, . . . and then drawn further by Popish subtlety, and now headed with some secret dissembling Friars, and by them and by the devil enraged against the ministers of Christ, and set upon the propagating of the substance of Popery.[4]

The poison of Prynne's Bristol pamphlet was working in Baxter's veins. In another pamphlet he says[5] there were

> . . . very few experienced, humble, sober Christians that ever I heard of that turn to them: but it's the young, raw professors

---

[1] *Piety Promoted, etc.*, by John Tomkins, 1st edn. 1701. Camm, who died in Jany. 1657, comes second, followed by the Boston martyrs. The order of the collection is chronological.

[2] Gardiner, *Hist. of the Commth. and Prot.* iii. 26; iv. 24.

[3] *Ibid.* iii. 26.

[4] *The Quakers' Catechism*, 1655, p. C3.

[5] "One Sheet against the Quakers," 1657, p. 11.

and women, and ignorant, ungrounded people that were but novices and learners in the principles, and such as are notorious for self-conceitedness and pride, being wise in their own eyes. And most of all these that ever I heard of were Anabaptists or the members of some such sect, that by their division and error were prepared before.

Baxter, it is evident, had at this time no appreciation of the inward spiritual experience which had come to Friends, and considered them a spawn of presumption and separation. Early in 1655 he had come into sharp conflict with them. On the 21st February,[1] Farnsworth and Goodaire had a "great battle" at Chadwick, near Bromsgrove, with two ministers. The Friends were militant, and followed up the debate by addressing some violently worded queries to Baxter by way of challenge. He offered to reply by word of mouth at their meeting, but they urged a written answer, which he gave at the end of March, beginning his reply with the words "Miserable creatures."[2] A few days earlier, Goodaire had attended the service at Kidderminster, and made a disturbance, Baxter happening to be away ill. As a result, the Quaker was imprisoned for a month at Worcester. Baxter's account of this may be accepted:

. . . whereupon it pleased the magistrate to bind one of you to the good behaviour, for the public disturbance and railing at the magistrate; and upon this you send another paper with an outcry against us as persecutors, when you might know that I was not concerned in the business, and when indeed no man did so much as once ask my advice in it. But as for them that did it, I dare no more accuse them of persecution, than I dare accuse them for persecution who shall burn a thief in the hand. Alas, what impatient souls are you to cry out so much of persecution, when many a poor scold is ducked in the Gumble-stool for words more incomparably sweet and lamb-like than yours?[3]

It is well for us to hear the view of a strong but sincere opposer of Friends, who took no part in the punishment, but did not discountenance it.

In May both Farnsworth and Thomas Goodaire at-

[1] See *F.P.T.* 279 *n.*

[2] *The Quakers' Catechism*, 1655.

[3] *Ibid.* p. 3.

tended a sermon of Baxter's at St. Swithin's, Worcester. Farnsworth says:[1]

> I was moved to speak to them in their time,[2] and great stir there was, and when they had haled me out, the great Rabbi went on, and Thomas stayed till he had done, and then he spoke: but they would not stand, only the city were sore troubled and in so great rage that they intended to have killed Thomas, and yet let me pass up and down the streets. And when the rage was great, the soldiers that had been serviceable in the deliverance of Thomas took us both to their quarters. Then after the priests had done we went and spoke to them in the city, and they would not abide but took horse and rode away. After all that we had a great meeting in the city [in] the afternoon, which did continue till about ten o'clock in the night, and the soldiers were very serviceable to us, and went with us to our lodging.

Baxter on this occasion refused to be drawn into a dispute* with his fierce antagonists and left them in possession of the field. In his printed answers he had required the Quakers to have no more to do with him and had renounced them as heretics.

Goodaire suffered a few days' imprisonment on this occasion, and the two stalwart Quakers left behind them groups of Friends in several of the Worcestershire towns. Their pamphlet, "The Brazen Serpent lifted up on high," is now most deserving of recollection for one phrase, "no crown without the cross,"[3] which may have suggested the title of Penn's celebrated book.

Later in the year Evesham became a centre of persecution. In August the magistrates, at the instigation of the ministers of the town, had imprisoned Humphry Smith and three Evesham men because they would not swear the oath abjuring the papal authority and the doctrine of transubstantiation.[4] Humphry Smith, a man of rare prophetic gift, was the same age as Fox and came from Herefordshire, where, before joining

[1] Letter to Fox, 7th May, Swarthm. Colln. iii. 57; cf. account in *F.P.T.* 275.
[2] See *F.P.T.* 348; to disturb a preacher *in* his sermon was an offence.
[3] Edn. 1658, p. 20. Cf. *post*, p. 431.
[4] This oath was enforced by a proclamation in April 1655. See *Journ.* i. 246, and *F.P.T.* 346.

with Friends, he had been a preacher of such note that a justice had offered him a maintenance. But he replied, "I shall rather go in sheep-skins and goat-skins and eat bread and drink water." Afterwards the judgment of the Lord in his heart withheld him from preaching, and at his last meeting at his birthplace, Stoke Bliss, he told the congregation that his mouth was stopped, but added that if ever the Lord should open it again then he should preach indeed. He passed through deep experiences, but the Light of Christ in his heart made him willing to give up his life to serve the Lord, and, already a Quaker because of his first-hand spiritual experience, he took up his cross of witness to the truth.[1] The Evesham prisoners promptly though injudiciously printed a broadside representing their case to the Protector.[2] At the quarter-sessions in October the Recorder had many of the signatories before him, rated them severely for coming into court with their hats on,[3] and for setting their hands "to a scandalous paper against the magistrates of the town," and fined them heavily. Later in the month the mayor broke up a meeting in the street, and put six Friends in the stocks for attending it. The Friends who had been fined remained in prison for refusal to pay, and were brutally treated by a savage gaoler, who would have liked to hang them all, and thought he could do as he pleased, since no lawyer durst take their part. The place had already earned the name of "the persecuting town of Evesham" when in the middle of November two women Friends from Westmorland, Margaret Newby and Elizabeth Cowart, came to it. After a large meeting at Captain Edward Pittway's, they went to visit the prisoners. The townspeople were excited against the Quakers, and when one of the women began to address them she was arrested and put in the stocks. As

[1] See his pamphlet, "Man Driven Out of the Earth and Darkness," 1658.

[2] Printed with the quarter-sessions' proceedings in Besse, *Sufferings*, ii. 50-55.

[3] Friends justified themselves by the precedent of the children in the fiery furnace, in "their hats" (A.V.), as George Fox did at Launceston in the following year (*post*, p. 232). The word used in Danl. iii. 21 may mean "turban" (so A.V. and R.V. margin), so that the answer was a cogent one.

they were taking her away, the other spoke, under strong feeling. The story can be given in her own words:[1]

A Friend did hold me in her arms, the power of the Lord was so strong in me, and I cleared my conscience, and I was moved to sing, and Friends was much broken and the heathen was much astonished. And one of them said that if we were let alone we would destroy the whole town. And the mayor came . . . and took hold on me, and Friends did hold me and strove with him, and at length he tore me from them, and . . . put both my feet in the same stocks it being the fifth hour at night, and said we should sit there till the morrow, being the market day, and we should be whipped and sent with a pass [*i.e.* as vagrants] to our own country, and charged us we should not sing, and, if we did, he would put both our hands in also. Nevertheless we did not forbear, being both moved eternally by the Lord to sing in the stocks, each of us both legs in, and so remained till the tenth hour the next day. And then the mayor . . . sent his officers to fetch us out, the which officers said that these stocks were prepared for George Fox, against he came to the town, and then . . . we were by the officers conveyed away on the backside of the town.

This barbarous exposure for seventeen hours on a freezing November night occasioned the sickness and death of Margaret Newby two years later. Not being allowed a seat, the two women had been forced to lie on their backs on ground lower than the stocks.[2]

The excessive violence of the Evesham magistrates was a scandal which attracted the attention of the authorities. In March 1656 the nine prisoners were released and their fines remitted by the Protector, and Major-General Berry, a kind-hearted man, wrote to Thurloe that he could not understand either their faults or their fines.[3] There was much mortification in the town over the turn things had taken, and much reluctance to give effect to the order. Berry was obliged to summon the magistrates to Worcester,[4] where

[1] Margt. Newby and Eliz. Cowart to Margt. Fell, 25th Nov. 1655. Swarthm. Colln. i. 359; a remarkable document.*

[2] For foregoing account see above letter, Besse, *Sufferings*, ii. 50-60, *F.P.T.* 268 (where Margt. Newby's companion is called Gilpin by mistake) and 282. See also Alfred W. Brown's *Evesham Friends in the Olden Time*, 1885, pp. 54-102, a carefully written book, and note in *Camb. Journ.* ii. 472.

[3] Thurloe, *State Papers*, iv. 613. Cf. *post*, p. 449.*

[4] *F.P.T.* 283.

he told them that Friends being a peaceable people should and must be protected in their religion, and at the same time admonished Friends not to disturb the national ministers in their worship. Furthermore, instead of printing their sufferings, they should have written to the Protector, who might have stopped the persecution to prevent the cry of it getting about the nation. These moderate views were Cromwell's own, but it was not only at Evesham that their application was interfered with by Quaker zeal and local intolerance. Baxter was present at this interview, saying nothing, but standing by the fireside with his hat over his eyes.

Farnsworth meanwhile had zealously continued his work. He and Nayler held a great controversy at Glentworth near Gainsborough (31st May) with a body of persons called Manifestarians or Mooreans, from their leader Thomas Moore, with whom George Whitehead and other Friends afterwards crossed swords.[1] This obscure sect had been gathered by Moore at King's Lynn and in adjacent parts of the Fen Country, and included some persons of tender spirit whose leanings towards Friends had embittered Moore against the Quaker Publishers of Truth. Farnsworth ineffectually challenged their leaders to go preaching with him for a fortnight, neither party taking any sustenance but a little spring water or looking in a book during that time.[2] This extravagant conception of spiritual guidance is characteristic of the man. In an early letter of his to Fox, he had said:[3]

I am out of all friends and creatures whatsoever and lives only by faith in the sense of the love and power of the Lord and

---

[1] For this controversy see Killam to Margt. Fell, 9th June 1655, Swarthm. Colln. iv. 88. In the Dev. Ho. Saml. Watson Colln. there is a paper on the tenets of the Manifestarians, p. 210, and a vindication by Farnsworth of what he had said, dated 5th June, p. 210, etc. For the pamphlet war which ensued see Smith's *Bibliotheca Anti-Quakeriana*, p. 293. In 1658 George Whitehead, Jno. Whitehead, and Geo. Fox, Jr., renewed the conflict. See *Christian Progress*, edn. 1725, pp. 169, etc., *Bibliotheca Anti-Quakeriana*, p. 295, and *post*, p. 304.*

[2] Dev. Ho., Saml. Watson Colln. p. 208.

[3] Swarthm. Colln. iii. 51, 12th Nov. 1653. Caton had a similar experience; see his *Life* (edn. 1689), p. 37.

readeth in the Revelation much, and often that is the book that I preach out of. I am as a white paper book without any line or sentence: but as it is revealed and written by the Spirit, the Revealer of secrets, so I administer.

In the autumn we find him at Banbury. This Puritan town had been visited by Camm and Audland a year before, and in January 1655 their wives came and carried on the work.[1] Ann Audland had cried out to the Banbury vicar, "Man, here see the fruits of thy ministry," and was asked what he had said which was untrue. She replied that when men were out of the doctrine of Christ all they spoke was untruth, and though they should say "the Lord liveth," they would swear falsely. On this she was bound over on the grave charge of blasphemy, which kept her in the town and neighbourhood for some months, and many were convinced. Jane Waugh, one of John Camm's serving maids, quite illiterate but on fire with the Quaker message, shared her imprisonment and ill-usage. The trial in September of "that prating woman Audler," as the great Lord Saye and Sele called her, disappointed the intolerant authorities. The Deputy-Recorder proved moderate, and when the jury refused to find her guilty of blasphemy she was simply required to give bond for good behaviour. Refusing this, she and Jane Waugh passed the winter in the prison:

. . . a close, nasty place, several steps below ground, on the side whereof was a sort of common shore that received much of the mud in the town, that at times did stink sorely; besides frogs and toads did crawl in their room and no place for fire, yet . . . God's presence and peace being with them, made their nasty, stinking gaol a palace.[2]

Ann Audland wrote to Margaret Fell:[3]

[1] See *F.P.T.* 208 and Dev. Ho., A. R. Barclay Colln. No. 158. Particulars of the Banbury persecution are given in *The Saints' Testimony Finishing through Sufferings*, 1655, the various papers in which are in sad chronological confusion. Ann Audland's Trial is also reported in a letter from Audland to Margt. Fell, 1st Oct. 1655, in Swarthm. Colln. i. 391.

[2] Account in *Piety Promoted*, iii. 205.

[3] Letter dated 1st Jany. 1656, in Wm. Caton Colln. (Dev. Ho., copy by Jas. Bowden). Margt. Fell had written a letter of encouragement to the prisoners dated 24th Dec. 1655, preserved in the parchment-bound volume in Dev. Ho, Portfolio, No. 9.*

This is indeed a place of joy, and my soul doth rejoice in the Lord. I continue a prisoner in Banbury, but I witness freedom in the Lord.

Many leading Friends had attended the trial,[1] and chief of all Richard Farnsworth. On the following Sunday a Banbury woman spoke in the church against what had been done, and was dragged off to gaol with a mob following her. The mayor and a justice were at the head and met Farnsworth in the street, who refused to uncover, and was thereupon clapped in prison. His trial by the Borough Bench is as instructive a piece of its kind as we possess. After long debate on such various topics as immediate revelation, swearing, and women's preaching, the mayor, who wanted to rid the town of a Quaker firebrand like Farnsworth, told him that if he would pay the gaoler's fees and be off that night he might go free. He would not engage to do either of these things, and accordingly suffered an eight months' imprisonment, during which, while preaching to the people through the prison grating, he convinced John Roberts of Siddington, near Cirencester, the hero of one of the raciest of Quaker journals.[2]

Fox meanwhile had been rapidly visiting the newly-opened-up work in the South of England. His energy, undaunted courage, verging at times on recklessness, and above all his commanding personality, everywhere carried his cause to triumph and confounded his adversaries. June was spent in Kent, where he confirmed the work begun in March by Stubbs and Caton. He passed on to Sussex, where Thomas Lawson, John Slee, and a Friend named Thomas Laycock had been in May,[3] and held a great meeting at Ifield, at the house of Richard Bonwick,

[1] *Piety Promoted* says they threatened that she should be burned. *The Saints' Testimony, etc.*, p. 41, says she was in danger of life. This could not be under the Blasphemy Act of 1650, but must have been under the idea that blasphemy was heresy and punishable within the writ *de haeretico comburendo*, an opinion confuted by Whitelocke in Nayler's Case, Cobbett's *State Trials*, v. col. 825.

[2] *Some Memoirs of the Life of John Roberts*, written by his son Daniel Roberts, and dated from Chesham, June 1725. First printed, 1746. Smith's *Catalogue* specifies thirty editions up to 1867.

[3] The *Journal* is supplemented by *F.P.T.* 233-237. For Laycock's sufferings see Besse, *Sufferings*, i. 708.

which became the first settled meeting in the county. In July he was at Reading, the home of Captain Curtis, who had been convinced in the Pentecostal days at Bristol. The place had at this time the name of being a microcosm of all sorts of heretical opinions.[1] Here a great part of the town came to a meeting in George Lamboll's orchard, and Fox also disputed with Baptists and Ranters. After a short stay in London he went on at the end of the month to the difficult Eastern Counties. At Coggeshall the justices, who a fortnight before had imprisoned Parnell, rode up fiercely to Fox as he was walking in the fields after a great meeting.[2] George turned and looked at them, and they slunk away. He had large meetings at Colchester, Mendlesham, Wramplingham, and Lynn. Going on to Cambridge, the students rose against him, incensed as they were with a man who scouted University learning. Fox's personality again defended him.

> "I kept," he says, "on my horseback, and rid through them in the Lord's power. Oh! said they, he shines: he glisters: but they unhorsed Captain Amor Stoddart before he could get to the inn. . . . And the people of the house asked me what I would have for supper, as is the usual way of inns. Supper, said I, were it not that the Lord's power was over these rude scholars, [it] looked as if they would make a supper of us and pluck us to pieces. For they knew I was so against their trade, which they were there as apprentices to learn, the trade of preaching, that they raged as bad as ever Diana's craftsmen did against Paul." [3]

After another visit to London, Fox went into the Midlands as far as Derbyshire, where he conferred with Balby Friends. Thomas Killam accompanied him into Worcestershire,[4] and he had a great meeting at Chadwick on the side of a hill. Hearing of the Evesham persecutions and of stocks a yard and a half high prepared for his coming, he spent a night in the town, visited the

[1] See citation from Simon Ford's Assize Sermon at Reading in 1653, given in note to *Camb. Journ.* i. 430.

[2] *Camb. Journ.* i. 185. The date is given in G. Whitehead's *Christian Progress*, edn. 1725, p. 65.

[3] *Camb. Journ.* i. 190.

[4] *F.P.T.* 276.

prisoners, and rode away just as the magistrates were coming to seize him. At Worcester he had a dispute with Clement Writer, the clothier who became notorious through attacking the infallibility of the Bible.[1] He wished him to confirm his message by miracles. Edward Bourn, the Quaker physician of Worcester, has preserved a vivid reminiscence of Fox as he rode out of the city.[2]

In our discourse together on the road before our parting, he spake of the glory of the first body, and of the Egyptian learning and of the language of the birds, and of what was wonderful to me to hear; so that I believed he was of a deep and wonderful understanding in natural, but especially in spiritual things. . . . [He] said we should reign over the town, and pressed E. B. much to keep up our meetings. And after Edward Bourne and G. F. parted, G. F. reined his horse about to speak to him and put off his hat, saying, "The Lord Jesus Christ go along with thee," by which E. B. was greatly comforted and refreshed and made glad in the Lord, and went away rejoicing.

Passing on to Warwick, Fox again showed his heroism. The party of Quaker horsemen was mobbed in the streets[3]:

"and so," says Fox, "when we were ridden quite through the market, I was moved of the Lord to go back again into the street to offer up my life among them . . . and so I passed up the street, and people fell upon me with their cudgels and abused me, and struck me and threw the horse down, yet by the power of the Lord I passed through them and called upon the town and the shopkeepers and told them of their immodest state, how they were a shame to Christians and the profession of Christianity."

Further work followed in the Midlands, and then a visit to London about the end of 1655. Fox now set out on an important journey into the West of England, with Captain Edward Pyott of Bristol and William Salt of London for travelling companions. Cromwell's Major-Generals were by this time in office and followed the proceedings of the party with keen suspicion. Goffe, who was in charge of the Sussex, Hampshire, and

[1] *F.P.T.* 276.* [2] *F.P.T.* 278, 276.
[3] *Short Journ.* 41; cf. *Journ.* i. 255.

Berkshire district, wrote[1] that they were "doing much work for the devil," and proposed to lay them by the heels, if he saw a good opportunity. They passed on, however, to Dorset, which was outside his jurisdiction. Fox had done little pioneer work during the previous two years, but here he was on untilled ground, convincing some prominent Baptist leaders at Poole, especially a ship-master, William Bayly, and having large service at Dorchester and Weymouth. In Devonshire the soil had been already broken by Miles Halhead of Underbarrow and Thomas Salthouse, one of the Swarthmore household, who, more than any other of the First Publishers, became the Apostle to the West. These two men had left London in March 1655, and on their way held the first Quaker meeting in Reading on the Broad Face Bowling Green, convincing Joseph Coale.[2] Going forward into Devonshire, they were kept a fortnight in Exeter prison as vagrants, and then sent back towards their homes. They renewed their journey westward, however, and reached Plymouth in the middle of May.[3] Here they gathered a meeting, but their plain speech angered the chaplain of a frigate, and they were brought before the magistrates, who sent them to Exeter as disturbers of the peace against the Protector's proclamation of February, the Quakers refusing to give bail. The patent insufficiency of this charge was eked out with an alleged breach of an ordinance against duels, challenges, and provocations.[4] It has to be recognised that at this period of the Protectorate the executive authority, strong in the force of military support, dealt out penalties at its own will and pleasure, without definite rules laid down beforehand, and without adequate security for the release of the innocent.[5] In this case the mayor wrote to the Major-General of the district, Desborough, that the behaviour of Halhead and Salthouse was most unchristian, for, besides their contempt of authority, all the time they were in prison they never

[1] Thurloe, *State Papers*, iv. 408.
[2] *F.P.T.* 8.
[3] *F.P.T.* 77.
[4] See Besse, *Sufferings*, i. 146-148.
[5] I quote from Gardiner, *Hist. of Commth. and Prot.* iii. 339.

sought God by prayer at any time, nor gave thanks for their food. They were men who held many sad opinions, wandering up and down and venting them to the disturbance of good people.[1] In Exeter Bridewell they lay till May 1656, for non-payment of a fine laid upon them, harshly treated, and hardly suffered to see their Friends or provide for their necessities.

They were followed by Margaret Killam of Balby,[2] who also visited Reading on her way and shepherded the young Church at Plymouth with Barbara Pattison, though suffering a two months' imprisonment at the end of the year. She was barbarously carried ten miles towards Exeter, with her arms pinioned behind her and her feet tied under the horse she rode on.[3]

Fox and his party were in an enemy's land in these Western Counties.[4] They passed through Devon without molestation and entered Cornwall, "a dark country"[4] not yet visited by Friends. Their method was to inquire from place to place for the honest and well-inclined, whose desires were to fear God.[5] At Marazion Fox overheard some one say that they should be examined before they went away, and resolved to stay till he had been examined.[6] From this place he wrote one of his fervid religious appeals, to be sent to the seven parishes at the Land's End. It came to the hands of Major Ceely, who took the party into custody at St. Ives on the 18th January 1656. As they left Redruth, Fox was moved to go back to speak to the people, which the guard of soldiers swore he should not do, "but," says Fox,[7] "the truth brought all under, for they rode after me with their pistols, and they rode and I rode, and I discharged myself,

[1] See account in Sewel, i. 193-203, especially p. 200 (edn. 1811). The original authority is *The Wounds of an Enemy in the House of a Friend*, 1656. See also two letters of Salthouse to Margt. Fell, 1st June 1655 and 28th May 1656, in Wm. Caton Colln. (Dev. Ho., Jas. Bowden's copies), and Salthouse to the justices, Swarthm. Colln. iii. 180. Cf. *Extracts from State Papers*, First Series, p. 4.

[2] Jno. Killam to Margt. Fell, 9th June, Swarthm. Colln. iv. 88.

[3] Besse, *Sufferings*, i. 148.

[4] *Short Journ.* 42.

[5] *F.P.T.* 20, giving the names of the principal Friends convinced. Cf. *Journ.* i. 265, and *post*, pp. 375, 396.

[6] *Journ.* i. 266.

[7] *Short Journ.* 43 and *Journ.* i. 268.

and when I had done, I passed with them." They met Desborough on their way to Launceston; the captain of his troop knew Fox and spoke to Desborough on their behalf, but the Major-General was a hard man and slighted them.[1] A word from him would have saved Fox from the horrors of Launceston gaol, where he was now to undergo the worst and most memorable of his imprisonments.

At this point we may pause in our narrative. The evangel of the Light of Christ in the heart had now been preached through the length and breadth of England, from Berwick to Dover and from Norwich to the Land's End. The seed had been sown broadcast over every kind of soil, and in the good ground had brought forth abundantly. Groups of Friends were to be found in almost every county, and in some favourable centres in the South there had been a great convincement. The first planting of Quakerism in England had taken place amid the astonishment and rapidly growing hostility of the authorities, whose attempts at suppressing these men who turned the world upside down were again and again disconcerted by the energy and fearlessness of the Publishers of Truth. But the strenuous service was already a costly one to Friends. The message had made triumphant progress through the land, yet in the hour of its success, in this winter of 1655-56, the three chief apostles of the movement, Fox, Farnsworth, and Dewsbury, were in prison, also Halhead and Salthouse, Whitehead and Parnell, Humphry Smith, Ann Audland and others, while men like Camm and John Audland were burning themselves out in the intensity of their service. We shall expect some slackening in the work, some withdrawal of aggressive energy to the urgent needs of defence against persecution and the no less pressing claims of shepherding the flock and building up the Church.

[1] *Short Journ.* 43.

CHAPTER X

THE WIDER OUTLOOK

Sound, sound abroad, you faithful servants of the Lord, and witnesses in His name, . . . and prophets of the Highest, and angels of the Lord! Sound ye all abroad in the world, to the awakening and raising of the dead, that they may be awakened, and raised up out of the grave, to hear the voice that is living. For the dead have long heard the dead, and the blind have long wandered among the blind, and the deaf amongst the deaf. Therefore sound, sound ye servants and prophets and angels of the Lord, ye trumpets of the Lord, that you may awaken the dead, and awaken them that be asleep in their graves of sin, death and hell, and sepulchres and sea and earth, and who lie in the tombs. Sound, sound abroad, ye trumpets, and raise up the dead, that the dead may hear the voice of the Son of God, the voice of the second Adam that never fell; the voice of the Light, and the voice of the Life; the voice of the Power, and the voice of the Truth; the voice of the Righteous, and the voice of the Just. Sound, sound the pleasant and melodious sound; sound, sound ye the trumpets, the melodious sound abroad, that all the deaf ears may be opened to hear the pleasant sound of the trumpet to judgment and life, to condemnation and light.—GEO. FOX to Friends in the Ministry, 1669 (*Journ.* ii. 111).

WE have described the first preaching of the Quaker message throughout England. Before continuing the main narrative, the beginnings of work in Wales, Ireland, and Scotland must be sketched, so that we may gain a better understanding of the immense initial energy of the new movement, and of its universal mission.

We have already recorded Morgan Lloyd's inquiries after Fox in 1653, and Lawson and Hubberthorne's visit to Wrexham. John ap John, one of Lloyd's messengers, became the centre of the first Quaker group in North Wales, and the first sufferer in the Principality, the offence being that he asked the minister at Swansea if he were a minister of Christ.[1] This was in October 1655,

[1] Besse, *Sufferings*, i. 735. For Jno. ap John see *J.F.H.S. Supplmt.* No. 6.*

and the magistrates were urged to have the devil whipped out of him, but contented themselves with sending him to prison. He had already convinced a number of persons in Monmouthshire and Glamorganshire, including Walter Jenkins of Pontypool, a Justice of the Peace who visited Fox in Leicestershire in the autumn of 1655 with another justice, Peter Price, of Presteign.[1] Three Welsh-speaking Friends out of the North had effected a considerable convincement in Radnorshire, drawn from the Baptists whose congregations were in a shattered state.[2] Thomas Holme, of Kendal, whose service in Cheshire we have noticed, became, however, the chief labourer in Wales. He had married another Publisher of Truth, Elizabeth Leavens, in the autumn of 1654, and in January 1656 went into South Wales, whither his wife and Alice Birkett of Kendal had preceded him. By April there were ten or eleven places where Friends met together in small companies.[3] Cardiff became the centre of his work, but in June Holme went into Pembrokeshire, or Little England beyond Wales, and found much to encourage him at Tenby, Pembroke, and Haverfordwest, then the largest town in the Principality.[4]

Wales was, generally speaking, hostile to Puritanism. In 1650 an Act had been passed for the propagation of the Gospel in the Principality, by depriving malignant and scandalous clergy of their cures and establishing a preaching ministry in their room. Vavasor Powell was the most notable of these Puritan preachers, and with his Welsh eloquence and genuine sincerity made many converts. As early as 1639, when a young man of twenty-two, he had adopted the career of a travelling evangelist in Wales, and though he spent the first years of the Civil War in London, he resumed his work about

[1] *F.P.T.* 322, *Journ.* i. 251; and for Walter Jenkins, Dewsbury to Margt. Fell (1660), Swarthm. Colln. iv. 134, and *J.F.H.S. Supplmt.* No. 6, pp. 33-35.

[2] Holme to Fox, 27th Feby. 1656 (year by internal evidence), Swarthm. Colln. iv. 247.

[3] *Ibid.* and Holme to Margt. Fell, 10th Dec. 1655 (year by internal evidence), Swarthm. Colln. i. 194, and a third letter in April, Swarthm. Colln. i. 203. For Holme's marriage see letter to Margt. Fell, Swarthm. Colln. i. 195.

[4] To Margt. Fell, Swarthm. Colln. i. 204.

1646, gathering round him a band of missionary preachers, and becoming known himself as the "metropolitan of the itinerants." He disliked Cromwell's usurpations, and by 1654 had joined the Baptist section of Independents, holding to some degree Fifth Monarchy views. But in spite of his work there were many districts left in great religious destitution. Major-General Berry in 1656 reported from Brecon: "One great evil I find here, which I know not how to remedy, and that is the want of able preachers. Certainly, if some course be not taken, these people will some of them become heathens."[1] Holding these views he protected Friends,[2] and would see in the travelling Publishers of Truth an application of Powell's itinerating system.

Though Powell had little sympathy with the Quaker position, his congregations seem to have been the chief source out of which sprang the groups of Friends in Mid Wales. On one occasion two women Friends came among them, while they were breaking bread, and spoke with so much fear and humility that the Elders at first allowed them liberty, but, on their speaking a second time, Powell told one of the members, Thomas Ellis, to take them away. He was unwilling to do this, until they had fully cleared themselves, but at last took them into an adjoining room and said to them in the true Seeker spirit, "Friends, you see how we are met together here: we are like the prodigal who was spending his portion, and we have a little yet unspent; and, when we have spent all, we must return to our Heavenly Father and come to you and your way."[3] This Thomas Ellis, some years later, in 1662, became fully convinced and assisted in the spread of Welsh Quakerism. Richard Davies, the Welshpool hatter, author of a racy journal, was another member of Powell's congregation. He openly professed Quakerism in 1657, and separated from Powell, who became angry and preached much against the

[1] Gardiner, *Hist. of Commth. and Prot.* ii. 36, 249, iv. 32, and notice of Powell in *Dict. Natl. Biography*.

[2] Holme to Margt. Fell, 3rd Mar. (I think 1656), Swarthm. Colln. i. 201.

[3] Richard Davies, *Life* (edn. 1771), pp. 81-83.

Quakers. Davies attended one of his meetings at Cloddiecochion, near Welshpool, and was allowed to give his message once, but, when he began again, was led out by a near relative, William Lewis, who owned the house, and sat under an ash tree on the common, mourning the darkness that had come upon a people who had formerly been tender in spirit. The word of the Lord came to him, "that though they put me out of their house, yet in time they would come to own Truth, and that house should be a meeting-place for Friends." [1] William Lewis joined Friends in 1662, and his house was in fact used regularly for meetings for at least forty years.[2] In this year a considerable number of Powell's people in Montgomeryshire and Merionethshire were convinced, as will be recorded in its place. Powell himself was in prison for preaching, where he remained with short intervals until his death in 1670. He held Davies and his wife in high esteem, on one occasion leaning out of his prison window and saying, "Behold Zacharias and Elisabeth, it was said of them, That they walked in all the commandments of God blameless." [3]

In tracing the early Welsh work, we are struck by the number of justices who were convinced, as, for example, at Presteign, Pontypool, Cardiff, and Tenby. In anti-Puritan Wales, justices would no doubt be appointed whose Puritanism could be relied on, and these earnest-minded men would belong, for the most part, to the advanced wing, which was favourable to Quakerism. Fox, who visited Wales in 1657, does not give a good account of the morals of the people. One town was full of Independents, "but a very wicked town and false. We bid the innkeeper give our horses a peck of oats, and no sooner had we turned our backs but the oats were stolen from our horses." At another town he turned his back for a moment on the ostler, and on looking round again found him filling his pockets with the provender. "A wicked, thievish people," he says, "to rob the poor dumb

[1] Richard Davies, *Life* (edn. 1771), p. 39.

[2] *Ibid.* p. 68.

[3] *Ibid.* p. 69.

creature of his food: I had rather they had robbed me."[1]

William Edmondson, a man of singularly sterling character, was the founder of Irish Quakerism.[2] An old Cromwellian soldier from Westmorland, three years the junior of Fox, he had settled in Ireland about the year 1652. He had already been attracted to Quakers in Chesterfield, and in the year 1653, when in the North of England on business, heard James Nayler speak, whose words were not many but powerful, and reached "the witness," so that he returned to Antrim a convinced Friend. Many professors of religion came to jangle and contend with him, and spoke evil of the way of truth, which troubled his spirit, though it worked for good because it raised much talk as to Friends, their ways, manner, and behaviour, and caused sober-minded people to inquire into their principles and faith. Major Bousfield, who came from Garsdale near Sedbergh, where he had entertained Fox, exhorted him to be cheerful and merry and not to be cast down with his soul's troubles; but they soon burst out afresh, and Edmondson felt something in him that withstood the work of God, which had to be slain and crucified by the Lord's judgments, and by the daily cross of Christ Jesus. Then he saw that Bousfield and others of a like spirit rested in a talk and notion of religion, without the true cross of Christ, and were at ease in a form of godliness without the real work of the power. Removing to Lurgan, he and his brother began the first settled meeting of Friends in Ireland in 1654. At the end of 1655 he came to Baddesley in Warwickshire to see George Fox, and carried back with him a beautiful message[3] to the infant Church.

In that which convinced you wait: that you may have that removed you are convinced of. And all my dear Friends dwell in the life and love and power and wisdom of God, in unity one with another and with God: and the peace and wisdom of God

[1] *Journ.* i. 374, 375.

[2] See Rutty's *History of . . . Quakers in Ireland*, 1800 edn. p. 75, etc., and Wm. Edmondson's *Journal*, 1715, and other editions. He was born at Little Musgrave.

[3] Fox, *Journal*, i. 257.

fill all your hearts, that nothing may rule in you but the life, which stands in the Lord God.

When these few lines, presumably in Fox's own laborious script, were read to the little group at Lurgan, the power of the Lord seized on all in the room—they were mightily shaken and broken into tears and weeping. As Edmondson says:

In those days the world and the things of it were not near our hearts, but the love of God, His truth and testimony lived in our hearts: we were glad of one another's company, though sometimes our outward fare was very mean, and our lodging on straw: we did not mind high things, but were glad of one another's welfare in the Lord, and His love dwelt in us.

The progress of the meeting was slow: in 1656 about ten persons met at Lurgan and a dozen at Kilmore, the people of the district being thick, dull, and sottish.[1] The Quaker stiffness in using the plain language and refusing hat-honour was here as elsewhere a great offence and it is interesting to read that

The keeping to one price in selling of goods and to the first asking without abatement was a great stumbling-block to most sorts of people, and made them stand at a distance from buying for some time, until they saw further into the justice of the manner thereof.[2]

The first visit to Ireland by English Friends seems to have been paid by James Lancaster, Miles Halhead, and Miles Bateman in the spring of 1654. They only stayed a short time, preaching their message through the towns as they passed along. A six weeks' visit followed from a Pardshaw Friend, named John Tiffin, the first of nine which he would pay.[3] The Whitehaven seamen refused to take him because he was a Quaker, so he journeyed on foot to Liverpool and then to Bristol, some two hundred and fifty miles from his home, where he got shipping. He stayed at Lurgan, and Edmondson travelled with him to several places. Richard Clayton, one of the Swarth-

[1] Edmondson to Margt. Fell, 27th June 1656, Swarthm. Colln. iv. 77.
[2] Cf. *ante*, p. 152. [3] *F.P.T.* 38.

more household, had similar service in Ulster, and one or two other meetings were begun.

Ireland at this time was under the harrow of Cromwell's resolute government. The system of holding down the island by means of English colonies, begun by the later Tudors, had been continued, especially in Ulster, by the Stuart kings. The Civil War aroused the fears of the Roman Catholics and gave the Celtic population a chance of resuming possession of land taken from it. In the name of King Charles, Ireland rose in insurrection, with its attendant cruelties. Cromwell's iron hand had avenged the excesses of these years in the massacres of Drogheda and Wexford. He honestly regarded the Irish as having been led into wicked rebellion by priests and nobles, and set himself to expatriate the military leaders and to confiscate the lands of malcontent proprietors, whom he drove into the wilds of Connaught. Their place was usurped by the settlement of soldiers and new "planters" from England. Quakerism was seeking entrance into a "distressful" land, under military law, whose native population was bleeding from recent conquest and whose garrison and new settlers were for the most part zealous Baptists and Independents.

Numerous visits were paid in the years 1655 and 1656, in the face of much opposition. Edward Burrough and Francis Howgill led the attack. As we have seen, they had been working mainly in London for nearly a year—with wonderful success and in the closest fellowship. The call to Ireland came to them with as much distinctness as it had come 1250 years earlier to Patrick, when, as his "Confession" tells us, he had the vision of the letter containing "The Voice of the Irish." Burrough says that late in the evening on the 28th June 1655 the moving of the Lord came upon him to go to Dublin city, and on the 30th he gave up and submitted to go. Howgill tells us that the word of the Lord came to him on the 7th July, "about the tenth hour, near Islington, a mile off London, when I was waiting upon the Lord, saying, 'Go to Dublin in Ireland with my servant Edward Burrough.'"

We can picture him walking with serious steps in the fields of merry Islington and receiving the inward message.[1]

It was no light thing to leave the growing work in London, which was full of promise and called for inspired leadership; but Fox himself was at this time in the South of England, and Nayler had come to the city and had thrown himself with great zeal and ability into the service. Nayler had written Howgill and Burrough a letter containing criticism, and though this had been at once cleared out of the way when the three met, there may have been reasons which made it seem to be well that the guidance of the London work should pass into other hands for a time.[2] At the farewell meeting at Robert Dring's house there was great brokenness of heart and "the melting power of God."[3] The two Publishers of Truth visited Swarthmore before setting out,[4] and reached Dublin about the middle of August.[5] While Fleetwood had been in Ireland as Lord Deputy, the Baptists had been in high favour, so that soldiers were re-baptized as the way to preferment, but with his departure from Ireland on 6th September their hour of authority passed.[6] Burrough went three times to Baptist meetings at his house, and found him moderate, much like Cromwell; but we are told "the officers have bowed down to the idol Baptism for promotion, for it grew in great fashion awhile here, but now it withers."[7] They had good service in the city, though they found the people proud, careless, and dissolute.[8] Some three weeks after their arrival the two parted in much grief of heart, Howgill going South with a cornet of horse, who was very loving, and Burrough continuing in Dublin, where there were few that hungered after God,

[1] See Dev. Ho., Boswell Middleton Colln. p. 80, for both these.

[2] Howgill to Margt. Fell, 3rd July 1655, Swarthm. Colln. i. 86; cf. Burrough to Fox, 2nd July, Dev. Ho., A.R.B. Colln. No. 37.

[3] Crouch, *Posthuma Christiana*, chap. ii.

[4] Howgill to Margt. Fell, 30th Augt. 1655 (correcting Sept. to Augt.), *Letters of Early Friends*, p. 260.

[5] Thos. Holme to Margt. Fell, 28th Augt. 1655, Swarthm. Colln. i. 197.

[6] Gardiner, *Hist. of Commth. and Prot.* iv. 115 *n.*

[7] Howgill to Margt. Fell, 30th Augt. 1655, *Letters of Early Friends*, p. 260.

[8] *Ibid.*

blindness and deafness possessing all. He writes to Margaret Fell:

With heaviness of spirit I write unto thee, yea and with my eyes full of tears, for I am separated outwardly from my dear beloved brother, F.H., who was my right-hand man in the war, before whom many Philistines have fallen.[1]

Howgill went with his loving cornet

. . . into the heart of the nation, about fifty miles from Dublin, through deserts, woods and bogs, and the desolatest places that ever any did I think behold, without any inhabitant except a few Irish cabins here and there, who are robbers and murderers that lives in holes and bogs where none can pass.[2]

His Quakerism had evidently not cured him of anti-Irish prejudices. At Kinsale, Bandon and Cork, he found openings among the officers and soldiers—a cornet, Edward Cook of Bandon, who served in the Protector's own troop of horse, became a Friend with his wife, and Colonel Robert Phayre,* the Governor of Cork, attended the meetings and said that more was being done by the Quakers than all the priests in the county had done for a hundred years.[3] Howgill was helped in his work by "little" Elizabeth Fletcher, of Kendal.

Meanwhile Burrough had continued in Dublin for a time, "a bad place, a very refuge for the wicked," and had then passed south to Waterford, "for our service," he says, "lies only in great towns and cities, for generally the country is without inhabitant."[4] Here he had great opposition from the Baptist authorities, and was tried as a vagabond and examined for a Jesuit—proceedings which seem to have led Bristol Friends to send a certificate[5]—the earliest of its kind that I have come across—stating that Burrough and Howgill were not vagabonds

[1] Burrough to Margt. Fell (no date), *Letters of Early Friends*, p. 262 (Swarthm. Colln. iii. 17).

[2] To Kendal Friends, Dev. Ho., Boswell Middleton Colln. p. 92.

[3] To Margt. Fell (no date), Dev. Ho., A.R.B. Colln. No. 65; in *Letters of Early Friends*, p. 267. Phayre afterwards became a Muggletonian: see *The Acts of the Witnesses of the Spirit* (1699 edn.), p. 114.

[4] To Margt. Fell, 5th Jany. 1656, in *Letters of Early Friends*, p. 264 (Swarthm. Colln. iii. 16).

[5] Wm. Tanner's *Three Lectures*, p. 92.

or popishly affected, but were well known to the writers as men of godly conversation, always faithful to and active for the Commonwealth—

. . . sound in the faith, having Jesus Christ the Rock of Ages for their foundation, in obedience to whom they have borne their testimony in this nation . . . travelling up and down and preaching the gospel freely, according to the example of the saints recorded in the scriptures of truth.

At Kilkenny he gave a warning to the inhabitants, and was twice among the Baptists and roughly handled by them, but there were a few who received the message.

"We have not spared to wound on the right hand and on the left," he says, "and victory, victory, hath been our word of watch. And though this nation be as the heath in the desert, yet here is a seed and a remnant, for whose sake we are sent."[1]

The attention of the Government was now drawn to the work in the South of Ireland. The Protector's second son, Henry Cromwell, had succeeded Fleetwood, and was commander of the Irish army, and he wrote in February 1656[2] that the most considerable enemy were the Quakers, who began to grow in some reputation in County Cork, their meetings being attended by some of the principal officers, and some of the soldiers being perverted by them, including the Protector's own cornet.

"I think," he added, "their principles and practices are not very consistent with civil government, much less with the discipline of an army. Some think them to have no design, but I am not of that opinion. Their counterfeited simplicity renders them to me the more dangerous."

The following general account which Howgill gives in a letter from Cork, dated 18th February 1656, shows that Henry Cromwell's information was well grounded.[3]

"The word of the Lord," says Howgill, "we have sown all along about a hundred and twenty miles in the principal towns and cities from Dublin west and in the heart of the nation, and

---

[1] To Margt. Fell, 5th Jany. 1656, in *Letters of Early Friends*, p. 264 (Swarthm. Colln. iii. 16).

[2] Thurloe, *State Papers*, iv. 508.

[3] To Fox and Nayler, Dev. Ho., A.R.B. Colln. No. 61.

much is done in so little a time. . . . There is some in Dublin meets together and grows, and at another city called Kilkenny another meeting, and at another city called Waterford many pretty people; at Youghal a seaport town there is a few that meets; at the city of Cork, where I am at present, there is many will hear. I have had great liberty often in public and great contests with Baptists. . . . The Governor is a moderate man and his family is pretty. Many captains and majors and officers hath heard and doth daily. At Bandon Bridge, another market-town, there is a constant meeting of some precious, at Kinsale the Governor is loving, and divers there is convinced and some soldiers: I have had many meetings in the garrison, and the priests are all on a rage and posts up and down with lies, and informs against the officers who have received us, and all is on fire. And they rode a hundred mile and gat an order from the Council at Dublin the eleventh month [Jany.] to examine me and send me bound up to Dublin, but the justices unto whom it was directed sent for me to Cork in love, and after a week-time I went as I was moved, but nothing they will do in it, and the priests hath sent up again to inform against them; and so it is expected to command us all up to before their judgment-seat. E[dward] B[urrough] is at Waterford: I was moved to write to him to come to me with speed; and so if we have our liberty [propose] to pass to another city called Limerick within the nation."

Henry Cromwell had already imprisoned the English Friends then in Dublin, Richard Hickock and Elizabeth Morgan of Chester, James Lancaster, and Rebecca Ward, daughter of Captain Ward; and the refractory conduct of the authorities in the South led to one of them, Major Richard Hodden, the "loving" Governor of Kinsale, being put out of the commission of the peace.[1] In January, Hodden had written a remarkable letter to Henry Cromwell in favour of encouraging Quakers to settle in Ireland.

My Lord, I entreat leave humbly to offer these few words with the enclosed concerning the persons called Quakers, etc. . . . My Lord, I beseech you consider that Reformation is began not finished, and the foundation and principal part thereof spiritual, without which all outward forms are but deceit . . . and it hath been and is hoped that in this waste land may be comfortable habitations for religious Englishmen, if thereunto encouraged,—

[1] Howgill to Margt. Fell (no date), Dev. Ho., A.R.B. Colln. No. 65.

God hath heretofore remembered His servants in their low estate, and it will be your joy, strength and happiness to own such in the Lord. . . . It's like few will be so free and plain with you, which I the rather am for that I have . . . had full knowledge of divers of the before-mentioned persons in England and here. Dear Sir it will never repent you that you encourage virtue and punish vice.[1]

Towards the end of February the orders from Dublin were at last carried out by the High Sheriff, and the two Friends, who were now both at Cork, were taken into custody and brought to Dublin. Nothing specific could be charged against them, but the Council ordered their return to England, which they reached about the beginning of March. They summed up their work by saying, "In short there is a precious work begun, and a seed sown, which shall never die."[2]

Burrough and Howgill addressed a remonstrance to Henry Cromwell,[3] and a challenge to the Dublin priests "to try their God, and their ministry and their worships."[4] Burrough, amongst other papers, sent one "to all the poor desolate soldiers of the lowest rank, who are scattered up and down in this desolate land of Ireland,"[5] which incidentally shows the Quaker testimony against war in process of development.

This Light reproves you in secret of violence . . . and it will teach you not to strengthen the hands of evil-doers, but to lay your swords in justice upon every one that doth evil. And it will teach you not to make war, but to preserve peace in the earth . . . which Light, if you love, it is your command to march by, and your rule to judge by, and weapon to fight withal, and your chief commission for duty.

On the day that they left Dublin, Barbara Blaugdone, a Friend of good education and standing, from Bristol, arrived. She went at once to Henry Cromwell, and when he came into the withdrawing-room and sat down on a couch, she cautioned him "to beware that he was not

[1] Lansdowne MSS. 822, fol. 93. *J.F.H.S.* vii. p. 101.

[2] To Fox, Lancaster, March 1656, *Letters of Early Friends*, p. 270 (Dev. Ho., A.R.B. Colln. No. 176).

[3] Burrough's *Works*, p. 85.

[4] *Ibid.* p. 90.

[5] *Ibid.* p. 93.

found fighting against God, in opposing the truth and persecuting the innocent, but like wise Gamaliel to let them alone, for, if it was of God, it would stand, but if of man it would fall." She seems to have acquitted him of personal hostility, and attributed his action to the advice of evil magistrates and bad priests, delivering her message with such power that she was afterwards told "the deputy was so much troubled and so melancholy that he could not go to bowls nor to any other pastime." [1]

The necessities of military discipline and exaggerated fears as to the political aims of Anabaptists and Quakers caused Henry to base his religious policy on the support of Presbyterians and Independents. Ireland proved a stony soil for the Quaker ploughmen from the North. Nevertheless a succession of earnest men and women went over, and amid much opposition and petty persecution sought out receptive souls and brought to them the message of the Inward Light. Meetings were slowly gathered, and a strong Quaker community began to be established, the seed bringing forth fruit with patience.

Among the converts was William Ames, a king's soldier, who had turned Baptist and Parliamentarian, and soon after his convincement became a pioneer of the Quaker movement in Holland. Many of the new Friends had been Cromwellian soldiers, amongst others Cornet Cook, who was dismissed the army; Corporal Richard Pike of Cork, who came from Newbury, and had the character of a very sober, conscientious man of great courage; Robert Malins of Bandon; Major William Barcroft and Captain William Morris, of Ulster. Others belonged to the "planters" who followed in the wake of Cromwell's army.[2] In a short relation of sufferings in Cork and Limerick, prepared by Cook in 1656, out of thirteen male sufferers ten were soldiers.[3] Quakerism in the army seemed a dangerous infection to Henry Cromwell,

[1] Besse, *Sufferings*, ii. 458, and Sewel (1811 edn.), pp. 188-193, both taken from *An Account of the Travels, etc., of Barbara Blaugdone* (1691). From this it appears that she had kept a school.

[2] See two valuable papers on Irish Quaker Records, by Thos. Hy. Webb, in *J.F.H.S.* iii. 9, 60.

[3] Besse, *Sufferings*, ii. 460.

and the Dutch ambassador in London, eagerly picking up news adverse to the Commonwealth, thought it worth while to report over to Holland of the Quakers that "by their means some mutiny hath happened in the regiment of Colonel Phayre."[1] This may refer to the action of two Quaker soldiers in Major Hodden's company, who refused to go to the public worship, and put up a placard against drunkenness.[2] But it is obvious that the stiffness of Friends on points of conscience ill accorded with military discipline. The difficulties of Friends in the garrison towns are well shown in Colonel Henry Ingoldsby's report of his action as Governor of Limerick.[3] As regards the Quakers belonging to the town, "vipers bred in our bosoms," they have liberty quietly to meet; but if strangers crowd in with them and get crowds about them, then he turns out the disturbers, as he could not be answerable for the safety of the place unless he is at liberty to secure the garrison from "huddles of discontented spirits." In the case of strange Quakers from unknown parts, as soon as they come in at one gate he sends them out at another, never letting them rest a minute in the garrison after he knows who they are. He has issued a proclamation against harbouring strange Quakers and Irish Papists, without giving him notice, and has fined one Friend twenty shillings for breach of the proclamation. He has cashiered Quaker soldiers, not merely for being Quakers, but for disobedience to their officers, etc., and this action has cured above a hundred others "of that aguish distemper they were inclining to." The chief Quakers in the town are Captain Holmes, Mr. Thomas Phelps, and Mr. Richard Pearce, who are stark mad with him for his restrictions, but "methinks if their devotion were so hot for that which I dare not call a religion, the country at large should serve their turn . . . but no place will please them but this."

In Ireland the progress of Quakerism was slow but

[1] Thurloe, *State Papers*, iv. 757.

[2] Besse, *Sufferings*, ii. 460.

[3] To Henry Cromwell, 31st March 1657, Lansdowne MSS. 822, fol. 117, *J.F.H.S.* vii. p. 56. Cf. Besse, *Sufferings*, ii. 463.

sure. About 1656 William Edmondson and some other Lurgan Friends took farms in Cavan in order that they might testify against tithes. Several of these Friends in 1659 moved on to Mountmellick, in Queen's County, and settled a meeting there. At Belturbet the provost imprisoned a party of Friends and put Edmondson in the stocks, much to the dissatisfaction of the people. The governor, who was a Baptist, took no action at first, but finally decided that the Quakers were under the protection of the law, and said he was sorry that they had been so abused.

> "My spirit," says Edmondson, "was borne up in the power of the Lord, as upon the wings of an eagle that day: Truth's testimony was over all their heads . . . and several of them received the Truth and abode in it."

Among the imprisoned Friends was the wife of a Baptist preacher: he came in the morning to look for her, and finding Edmondson sitting in the stocks in the cold winter in the open market-place, was smitten to the heart. He told one of the Baptists with tears in his eyes that he was ashamed of them for suffering conscience to be trodden in the dirt, after so long professing and fighting for it. A Baptist elder, Captain William Morris, who held important civil and military appointments in the district, heard of the day's proceedings, and was much troubled, saying it was a shame for the Quakers to be so abused. Both these men became Friends.[1]

Barbara Blaugdone, who had dealt with Henry Cromwell for his treatment of Friends, went on to Cork, where she had relations, who were alarmed at her religious enthusiasm, "because she sometimes spake to them in so solemn and awful a manner that her speech caused them to tremble: others said she was a witch, and avoided her till their servants turned her out of doors."[2] After sundry adventures she came a second time to Ireland, and was banished the country.[3]

The meeting in Dublin, held at George Leatham's,

[1] Edmondson's *Journal*, 1715 edn. p. 30.

[2] Besse, *Sufferings*, ii. 459. [3] *Ibid.* ii. 461 (Edward Cook's report).

Polegate, was small and weak. When Richard Waller was there, shortly after Howgill and Burrough's banishment, he found about thirty men and women on the first-day, of whom six or eight were pretty faithful, "the rest are convinced, but doth not take up the cross."[1] Waller paid a second visit in 1657 with Richard Roper, and found Dublin Friends burdened with the ministry of a diffuse man named John Craven, whom they rebuked.[2] They went on to a General Meeting at Kilkenny, to which a number of Baptists had come in order to make a disturbance. At Waterford they attended the Assize Sermon, and on Roper saying a few words after the minister had done, the two Friends were thrown into prison.

"Here," they write,[3] "is much service in this nation. Friends are even but unsettled, little of the power they have tasted, it is almost [an] astonishment to them. Many high spirits and high talkers, but little of the power."

Burrough's estimate of the condition of Friends, on reaching Ireland for a second visit in August 1660, is much more favourable. Writing from Cork, he says:[4]

I perceive in this land Friends are generally well, and Truth grows in victory and dominion . . . and through the rage of men and above it all the little flock is preserved in its beauty.

Thomas Loe, of Oxford, was one of the most devoted labourers in Ireland. His first visit seems to have been paid as early as the autumn of 1655, for Burrough writes from Dublin at this time:

Here is a Friend come from England, since I wrote this, from Oxford, who saith he was moved to come, and I believe it: I am refreshed by him.[5]

In 1657 he came a second time, travelling on foot from Munster to Dublin, where he declared the

[1] To Margt. Fell, 30th March 1656, Swarthm. Colln. iii. 133.
[2] To Margt. Fell, 29th June 1657, Swarthm. Colln. iii. 134.
[3] To Margt. Fell, 24th July 1657, Swarthm. Colln. iv. 23.
[4] *Works*, p. 701.
[5] To Margt. Fell (undated), Swarthm. Colln. iii. 17. *Letters of Early Friends*, p. 264.

Day of the Lord through the streets; "he had blessed service, and many were convinced by him."[1] He also visited Friends in Carlow and Ulster. In 1660 he was again in Ireland. His letter to Fox in August, when amplified out of other sources, gives a vivid picture of Irish Friends, and confirms the opinion formed by Burrough about the same time.[2] For the moment, he says, persecution has slackened and "things are pretty cool." At the time of writing he is in the North, where all is quiet and still and meetings enlarge daily. He came lately from the West, from Cork, Bandon, Limerick, and those parts where persecution had been fierce since the political changes. Whole meetings had been carried to prison in several places, almost in all parts of the nation, yet things were generally well with Friends and meetings fresh and living. A blessed presence was among them, and they were well got over their sufferings, and many were freely given up to bear all things for the Truth's sake. About the middle of the nation, no doubt at Moate or Mountmellick, there was a meeting of forty Friends, most of whom had been lately convinced. The letter closes with a fine passage of personal devotion.

> I am well, and the Lord's blessings and pure presence is with me in my labours, and it is yet on me to stay in this nation, and the thing hath oft run through me, Thou must travel through this storm with Friends here, and I am truly and wholly given up into the will of God.

Loe, however, felt free to return home later in the year, when the tempest of persecution seemed over and the prospect was bright. The Fifth Monarchy rising, as we shall see, blighted these fairer hopes, and a few months after his return he found himself, with many other Friends, thrown into Oxford gaol.

John Burnyeat of Cumberland, another earnest worker in Ireland, spent more than a year there from May 1659 to July 1660, mostly with Robert Lodge of Masham in Yorkshire.

[1] Rutty's *Hist. of Quakers in Ireland* (1800 edn.), p. 105.
[2] Swarthm. Colln. iv. 238, printed in *Letters of Early Friends*, p. 271.

"The Lord," says Burnyeat, "gave us sweet concord and peace in all our travels; for I do not remember that we ever were angry or grieved one at the other in all that time."[1]

They travelled diligently, amid many hardships, for the country was in parts uninhabited, and their testimonies against the "hireling priests" brought them to prison several times. The itinerary includes many of the places where there were settled meetings. In the North, Lisburn, Lurgan, Kilmore, and Grange, near Charlemont, were the chief centres; in Leinster there were meetings in Cavan, Athlone, Mountmellick, Carlow, New Ross, and Wexford, as well as at Dublin; in the South, Limerick, Cork, Bandon, Youghal, and Waterford had meetings. As in England, the new movement gathered groups of adherents in certain places and depended greatly upon the personal influence of men of high Christian character, with the gift of leadership and the capacity for self-sacrifice. The meetings were almost always held in private houses.

Numerous other visits were paid by Friends from England, but the particulars given add little to our knowledge. The Irish authorities were hostile, for Henry Cromwell regarded Quakerism as an anti-social force, and especially subversive of civil government and military discipline.[2] His policy was to counteract the influence of Baptists and Friends by fostering Presbyterianism and Independency. It does not appear, however, that there was any further systematic exclusion of English Friends, although some found a difficulty in persuading the shipmasters to take them. This may, however, have been due to a general objection to take on board such strange persons as the Quakers were generally supposed to be. Richard Clayton, in February 1655, had been turned back through contrary winds on his passage, and the passengers and seamen nearly refused him another passage, for they "said that it was because I was amongst them that they were so much crossed in their journey."[3]

[1] *Works*, p. 28.

[2] See Firth, *The Last Years of the Protectorate*, ii. 155, and *ante*, p. 215.

[3] To Margt. Fell, Swarthm. Colln. i. 27.*

The same superstition may sometimes have impeded the efforts of Friends to spread their message in the Isle of Man. After the Earl of Derby's execution at Bolton in October 1651, for the part he took in the Royalist rising, his Dominion of Man was reduced by the Commonwealth authorities and was governed by William Christian, the "Brown-haired William" of Manx story, and afterwards by James Challoner. In the summer of 1655 we find an entry in the Kendal accounts showing that the sum of £1 : 5s. was given to the brother of Thomas Salthouse, no doubt Robert Salthouse, and another unnamed Friend for the expenses of a visit to the island.[1] James Lancaster and that valiant woman Katharine Evans of English Batch, near Bath, were also in Man, either in this or the following year, and were banished the island, Katharine Evans being taken out of bed by a soldier at ten o'clock at night and carried on shipboard.[2] The authorities, in the spirit which afterwards prevailed in New England, seem to have decided on expelling all Quakers, and in 1656 we hear of Peter Cowsnocke and others being banished and appealing to Sir Thomas Fairfax, who refused his help, although afterwards, on application to Parliament, those who were natives were repatriated.[3] Earlier in the year two Manx Friends, who had been public preachers, went to see Fox in Launceston gaol.[4] I presume one of these was Cowsnocke, who went in June 1658 to Barbados and the American colonies with a party of seven other Friends, and was lost at sea with two Warwickshire Friends in the passage from Barbados to Rhode Island.[5] In 1657 we first hear of William Callow,

[1] *J.F.H.S.* vi. p. 52. Certainly Robert Salthouse; see Annals, 1655, in *Camb. Journ.* ii. 332.

[2] John Whiting's *Persecution Exposed*, 1715 edn. p. 220. For Quakerism in the Isle of Man see a good article by Dr. Thos. Hodgkin, "Ruillick-ny-Quakeryn," in *Friends' Quarterly Examiner*, 1908, pp. 457-495, as supplemented by Wm. Callow's letters in *J.F.H.S.* vi. pp. 6-11. I have added or corrected some details.

[3] Besse, *Sufferings*, i. 269; and Richd. Hickock to Margt. Fell, 12th Nov. 1656, Swarthm. Colln. i. 141.

[4] Richd. Hickock to Fox, 8th May 1656, Swarthm. Colln. iv. 208.

[5] See Cowsnocke's letter, Swarthm. Colln. i. 177; Henry Fell to Fox, Swarthm. Colln. iv. 182; Nicholson to Margt. Fell, 3rd April 1660, Swarthm. Colln. iv. 107, and record cited in Wm. White's *Friends in Warwickshire*, p. 23 (1894 edn.).

of Ballafayle, near St. Maughold, the apostle of Manx Quakerism. He was imprisoned eight weeks for reproving a minister who was abusing the Quakers, and a month for holding a meeting at his house, and with other Friends was distrained on for fines; but the poor of the parish refused to help themselves to the oats which had been taken, though invited to do so by the priest. One man, indeed, took some, and died before he had eaten what he took. This seemed so clear a judgment upon him that the rest of the corn lay till it was spoiled.[1]

Four Lancashire Friends landed safely in Man in 1658,[2] but other Friends failed to reach the island.[3] Meanwhile petty persecution of Callow, Evan Christian, and other Manx Friends continued. Several of them in 1659 were imprisoned for refusing to pay the priest 2d. apiece for the Bread and Wine, a curiously perverted consequence of Eucharistic ritual.[4] Callow and Christian were also imprisoned for refusing tithes.

> "One morning early," says Besse,[5] "as soon as they came on shore, having been all night in the wet and cold at sea, for they were fishermen, they were hurried to prison in their wet clothes, and detained several days in the midst of their herring-fishery, the most advantageous season for their business. This, however designed by their adversary, was not prejudicial to them, for the next night after they were released they caught as many fish as they were able to bring on shore, so that they could do no less than gratefully acknowledge a peculiar Providence attending them."

The treatment of Quakers by the Manx authorities illustrates on a petty scale the persecuting spirit which animated many of the Puritans when they were allowed to act as they pleased, though, in this case, as in England, much fiercer trials came upon the Children of the Light in the Restoration days. It was not, indeed, until 1671 that Callow could write as though the storm were nearly past.

1 Besse, *Sufferings*, i. 269.
2 Waller to Margt. Fell, 20th Feby. 1658, Swarthm. Colln. iii. 132
3 George Taylor to Margt. Fell, Swarthm. Colln. i. 306; and Robert Salthouse to Margt. Fell, 9th Augt. 1658, referring to Anthony Patrickson, Swarthm. Colln. i. 369.
4 Besse, *Sufferings*, i. 270.
5 *Ibid.*

I with my wife and children and all Friends in this island are all well, glory be to God for evermore, and our little meeting quiet and peaceable after our great and long sufferings, everlasting praises be given to our [God] for ever and for evermore. Only some threatenings we do hear of sending us away again, but we are not afraid at their threats: the Lord God of power in the mightiness of His glorious infinite power has delivered us in six, and will be with us in the seven[th], as we abide faithful unto Him, everlasting praises be unto His holy name for evermore.[1]

Scotland was a country even less receptive than Ireland to the new message, although it would one day produce the greatest of Quaker theologians in Robert Barclay and the ablest of Quaker separatists in George Keith. Prior to Cromwell's military occupation of the country, the nobility and the Kirk had been the ruling powers. Presbyterian church-government had won an impregnable position through its success in opposing sovereigns hostile or indifferent to the Reformed religion, and nobles who were eager for personal aggrandisement and brutally callous to the moral advance of the nation. The position was secured by a strong church-organization, which exercised a severe discipline over its members, and discountenanced all tendencies to sectarianism. A dominant type of religion was thus in possession of the country, suited to the dour Scots character, a religion which with all its sternness stood for morality and individual responsibility, and there was none of that confusion of opinions and little of that unsatisfied craving after a more vital experience which prevailed in England. The political situation was an additional reason why the country should be inhospitable to Quakerism or any other southron influence. Cromwell's government appeared to the Scots as a strong military power which menaced their national independence, while the English army, in the opinion of the Kirk, was a hotbed of sectaries and spiritual anarchists. But the Scottish attempt to overthrow Cromwell in the interests of Charles II. had resulted in the defeats of Dunbar and Worcester, and the country lay embittered and humiliated under the heel of the Ironsides.

[1] To Margt. Fell, 23rd Dec. 1671, *J.F.H.S.* vi. p. 11.

As early as 1653 meetings were kept by one Alexander Hamilton at Drumboy and Heads by Clydesdale.[1] Visits from English Friends began soon after,[2] but we are without full particulars. Further meetings were soon settled at Gartshore, in Dumbartonshire, and at Edinburgh. The Kendal accounts contain an Edinburgh entry at the end of 1654, "to James Graime for books, 10s."[3] When Caton and Stubbs visited Scotland at the end of 1655[4] they found things at Edinburgh "somewhat out of order," through the unfaithfulness of some convinced persons who did not live as became the Gospel, but in spite of this they had "gallant" meetings, extraordinarily good service for the Lord, and much convincement. On a second visit with John Grave of Cumberland a few months later (May 1656) Caton found Friends in difficulty as to a meeting-place,[5] and says:[6]

. . . truly the simplicity is much scattered, and the great convincement much lost and many hearts hardened. And exceeding hard it will be to get anything brought forth to perfection amongst them. The gatherings is less than they were when I was here before, and few or scarce any comes into obedience. Here hath been several unwise builders amongst them, which will tend to the ruin and destruction of the whole building, which hath been daubed with untempered mortar.

---

[1] Sewel (1811 edn.), i. pp. 158-159. Drumboy, or Drumbowy, 3 miles S. of East Kilbride, was the home of Hamilton; John Hart lived at Heads in the parish of Glassford. In 1675 a burial-ground was acquired at Shawtonhill half-way between Drumboy and Heads. There were also Friends at Hamilton and at Douglas on the Douglas Water. (See Records of Edinburgh Yearly Meeting, Book U, "A common-place book for Friends of the West, containing their Sufferings, births, deaths, collections, etc.," per transcript kindly lent me by W. F. Miller of Winscombe, Somerset. Cf. *J.F.H.S.* i. 71.) Gartshore is near Kirkintilloch, and Badcow, another centre for meetings, was in the same neighbourhood.

[2] Burrough, in the Epistle to the Reader at the beginning of Fox's *Great Mistery*, mentions "some parts of Scotland" as visited before the Mission to the South in July 1654. When at Berwick with Atkinson in April 1654, Burrough writes, "There hath been something in me as of a cry through some garrisons in Scotland and a warning to the soldiers of the mighty Day of the Lord," and I think it likely that he carried out his intention (Letter to Nayler, Swarthm. Colln. iv. 170). A sentence in a letter of Thos. Willan to Margt. Fell, 26th Nov. 1654 (Spence MSS. vol. iii. fol. 6), confirms this: "Dear sister, Christopher [Atkinson] writes home that they must have the passages of him and Edwd. Burrough of their sufferings in Northumberland and Scotland."*

[3] *J.F.H.S.* vi. p. 50.

[4] See Wm. Caton's *Life* (1689 edn.), p. 27.*

[5] Letter to Lancelot Wardell, Swarthm. Colln. iv. 257.

[6] Letter to Margt. Fell, 27th May 1656, Swarthm. Colln. iii. 187.

During this visit the Scots were afraid of them in the country districts, "looking upon us as if we had been some straggling soldiers," and the service was evidently almost entirely amongst the English garrison: "as for the Scots, they could not endure sound doctrine, but turned away their ears from hearing the truth."[1] In December of this year there were said to be four or five who took part in ministry, especially one William Stockdale who was "finely brought forth."[2] But a few months later John Hall speaks[3] of Stockdale as "highly exalted," and causing trouble in the infant church.

As had been the case in Ireland, Quakerism found most entrance in the army, and again we find that it quickly roused the suspicion and hostility of the military authorities. When Caton[4] was in Scotland at the end of 1655 he had found General Monck seemingly moderate, and had been more than once protected by the English soldiers; but a year later the General had grown suspicious, and wrote to the Protector[5] that the Quakers seemed likely to increase among the forces in Scotland. There were already a few officers and many men who had joined them, and these might prove dangerous and mutiny on slight occasion. A few days later Major Richardson sent Monck word from Aberdeen[6] that John Hall, a young man of nineteen, from Airton in Craven, one of the Quaker Publishers who had been convinced by Gervase Benson,[7] was disturbing the public worship, and was owned and

[1] See Wm. Caton's *Life*, p. 33.

[2] Thos. Willan to Margt. Fell, Swarthm. Colln. i. 293.

[3] To Margt. Fell, 15th Feby. 1657, Swarthm. Colln. iv. 64. Stockdale continued a Friend, removing to Charlemont meeting in the North of Ireland, and afterwards in 1687 to Pennsylvania, where he died in 1693. He travelled much as a minister. (John Whiting's *Persecution Exposed*, edn. 1715, p. 231; note in *Camb. Journ.* ii. 473; *The Quakers in the American Colonies*, p. 449.)

[4] See Wm. Caton's *Life*, p. 28.

[5] Thurloe, *State Papers*, vi. p. 136, dated 21st March 1657.

[6] *Ibid.* vi. pp. 145, 146. This despatch is confirmed by the letter from Hall to Margt. Fell (Swarthm. Colln. iv. 65), endorsed "about 1655," but really to be dated about April 1657. Hall seems to have been the first Quaker to reach Aberdeen, and John Barclay is wrong (*Diary of Alexander Jaffray*, p. 230) in speaking of Burnyeat's visit at the end of 1658 as the earliest. For the earlier part of Hall's Scottish visit see letter to Margt. Fell, Paisley, 15th Feby. 1657, in Swarthm. Colln. iv. 64.

[7] Note in *Camb. Journ.* ii. 476. In after years he kept an inn at Skipton and died in 1719.

lodged by Cornet Ward. The Cornet, it seems, was inclined to Quaker principles, and had said, pointing to the guard of his sword, that, if he became convinced, "he purposed not to make use of any carnal sword, but was resolved for that thing to lay down his tabernacle of clay." No wonder that Monck was told that "these peoples' principles will not allow them to fight, if we stand in need, though it does to receive pay." Hall went on to Inverness, and was put out of the town by the Colonel, after being entertained by his Captain-Lieutenant, a man named Davenport, who was much confirmed in "his principles of quaking, making all the soldiers his equals," so that when the soldiers did their duty to him "by holding off their hats, he bade them put them on, he expected no such thing from them." [1]

After this, Hall was court-martialled at Aberdeen for disturbing the minister and being a vagabond, a Jesuit and a spy, and was turned out of the city. Monck seems to have instructed his officers to discharge from the army any soldiers who were Quakers,[2] and in the autumn, while Fox was in Scotland, there was a drastic purge of two troops in Colonel Robert Lilburne's regiment of horse.[3] One troop was commanded by Captain William Bradford, presumably the Captain Bradford of Yorkshire, who received Fox in the autumn of 1654, and visited Dewsbury in Northampton gaol.[4] The other troop, stationed at Cupar, was under Captain George Watkinson, also a Yorkshireman,[5] who had received Friends in June 1655, and had visited Fox in Launceston gaol. Captain Watkinson and Bradford's Lieutenant, Matthew Foster, were brought to Monck's headquarters at Dalkeith, where they

[1] See Hall's letter, and Thurloe, *State Papers*, vi. p. 167.

[2] Thurloe, *State Papers*, vi. 241.

[3] See the soldiers' statement in Swarthm. Colln. iv. 237. Cf. *Clarke Papers*, iii. 122, and Alexander Parker's Letter, Leith, 13th Jany. 1658, Swarthm. Colln. iii. 140.

[4] See Benson to Margt. Fell (1654), Swarthm. Colln. iv. 35; Fox, *Journal*, i. 195; Dewsbury to Margt. Fell, 15th Oct. 1655, Swarthm. Colln. iv. 141. Norman Penney, note in *Camb. Journ.* i. 423, suggests that he lived near Cinderhill Green, the home of Thos. Stacey.

[5] See John Killam to Margt. Fell, 9th June 1655 (Swarthm. Colln. iv. 88); Parker to Margt. Fell, 19th Augt. 1656 (Swarthm. Colln. i. 166).

remained covered, and were dismissed the army, with seven others, expressing joy at suffering for the truth. Further dismissals also took place about the same time.

These interesting proceedings in the Scottish army of occupation are another illustration of the affinity there was between Quakerism and the religious standpoint of many of the Puritan soldiers, and also show how soon the inevitable conflict came to a head between the spiritual campaign of the Quakers and the carnal warfare by which Cromwell sought to achieve the will of God. They also confirm the conclusion that convincement in Scotland was at first mainly confined to the army. John Hall, at the beginning of 1657, had correctly summed up the position by saying,[1] "There is soldiers straggled up and down which is convinced, and some Scotch people, but little establishment amongst them."

It is always well, if we can, to get an outsider's impression of Quakerism, and we have this, in the case of Scotland, in a lively Leith letter in Thurloe's *State Papers*,[2] dated 28th December 1657. After referring to the activity of the Quaker Publishers, both men and women, the writer, Timothy Langley, says:

> They spare no pains, and voluntarily go into those places where they may meet with most want of outward things, which makes them the more admired, if not adored, at their return by their disciples. They say that they know they shall overspread the face of the earth; and when any oppose their way, they seem to prophesy, and tell them they may oppose the truth for a time, but they know they shall be of the same mind within three years to come. And since the putting of some of them out of the army, they sometimes upbraided the officers and told them that they deny the truth, fearing the loss of their places, otherwise they knew and could defend that many of them are convinced by the light that is within them. Our women Quakers in this town have learned this lesson well of late, and often repeat it to their husbands. They have hired a chamber in this town to meet in, and have another at Edinburgh, so that they meet daily.

[1] Letter to Margt. Fell, 15th Feby. 1657 (Swarthm. Colln. iv. 64).

[2] vi. 708.

They have got a small parcel of Scots into their crew, I think about a dozen, and they have great hopes of gaining a lady in Edinburgh, and boast of many converts in the West.

Howgill and Thomas Robertson spent ten weeks in Scotland in the summer of 1657, when dismissals from the army were already taking place,[1] watering what little there was of the Truth. They give a sinister picture of Scottish affairs.

Oh, this is a dark nation, lost for lack of knowledge . . . one cannot believe a word they speak . . . a stupid, sottish, ignorant people, and yet ripe to do mischief and full of craft to devour . . . and the priests are such cowards, not one will stand nor answer a query . . . and a general hatred there is against the English. And since they have reduced the English soldiers who were convinced, they have let loose the spirits of all the ungodly, both English and Scots, so that it is much—but the eternal power of God that preserves—that any can pass . . . so that the way of truth is much dammed up at present. . . . And them who should have been Friends are altogether strangers, most of them, to silence, and few ever hath known the judgments, neither have tasted of the power, but are careless and out of the fear. . . . Some more comes forth to hear, but the cross they are strangers to as yet: few to receive us in the name of the Lord, although many Friends have passed through the nation in much hardship, I see, and them who would cannot receive us, they are so poor one cannot lean upon them, neither can we stay little in a place.

It was evidently by no means easy for the Quaker Publishers, with their prejudiced English standpoint, to win a hearing from a hostile nation: the army was closed against them, and the small groups of friendly persons were weak in the faith. Howgill sums up the position to Fox by saying,[2] "It is a dark and an untoward nation, and little desire after God, and a false-hearted people and a blood-thirsty."

[1] Howgill to Fox (no date), Dev. Ho., A.R.B. Colln. No. 31, and Howgill and Robertson from Leith, 14th July 1656 (correct to 1657), Dev. Ho. Portfolio 2, No. 77, a letter addressed in an interesting fashion: "Leave this with Thos. Turner, shopkeeper, upon the bridge at Newcastle, to be sent by the first carrier to Geo. Taylor in Kendal, Ironmonger, with care and trust." It is this letter I quote. The year is fixed by the reference to the dismissal of soldiers, as well as by confirmatory entries in May 1657 in the Kendal money accounts.

[2] Dev. Ho., A.R.B. Colln. No. 31, *ubi supra*.

We have, as a matter of convenience, carried the account of the early work in Wales, Ireland, the Isle of Man, and Scotland beyond the year 1656. Still wider fields of service were being occupied by the ardent devotees of Quakerism on the Continent and in the New World. The first important visit to the Continent was paid by Stubbs and Caton in the autumn of 1655, and the attempt to carry the message to America began in 1656, so that work beyond the seas was opening out just at the time when the foremost apostle of Quakerism lay caged in Launceston Castle.[1]

Fox and his two companions, Capt. Edward Pyott and William Salt, began their eight months' imprisonment on 22nd January 1656.[2] The assizes did not take place for nine weeks, and during this interval the prisoners paid for their board and for the keep of their horses, and were fairly treated. Judge Fell, it is interesting to learn,[3] sent a man down to inquire if Salthouse, then in Exeter prison, or Fox had need of anything. Serious-minded people in the district came to see the prisoners, and some were convinced, though others chafed at the plain language and the refusal of hat-honour, and expected to see them hanged at the assizes. The trial drew a great crowd from far and near, and the soldiers and javelin-men had much ado to get the prisoners through the thronged streets into the court. There they stood some time in a hush with their hats on, till Fox said, "Peace be amongst you." Chief-Justice Glyn, the assize judge, insisted on the removal of their hats, and flew into a rage at Fox's arguments on the point, crying out, "Take him away, prevaricator, I'll firk him," that is, "trounce" him. Soon, however, he called them up again, and said to Fox, "Come, where had they hats from Moses to Daniel; come, answer me: I have you fast now." Fox answered as Cartwright had done at Evesham[4] in September, "Thou

[1] See *post*, chap. xvi.

[2] See *Journ.* i. 271, etc., *Camb. Journ.*, and the good account in Dr. Thos. Hodgkin's *George Fox*, pp. 129, etc.*

[3] Salthouse to Margt. Fell, 9th Feby. 1656, Swarthm. Colln. i. 112.

[4] See *ante*, p. 196.

may'st read in the third of Daniel that the three children were cast into the fiery furnace by Nebuchadnezzar's command with their coats, their hose, and their hats on." In the afternoon a paper against swearing, which Fox had circulated, drew down further censures from the judge, and the hat question was again raised. At last the prisoners asked the judge why they had lain in prison for nine weeks, seeing that nothing was objected to them except about their hats. After much difficulty, William Salt was allowed to read the *mittimus*, which alleged a number of vague offences, suited to the arbitrary régime of Major-Generals, such as spreading about papers tending to the disturbance of the public peace, being persons unknown and having no passes for travelling, refusing to give sureties for good behaviour and refusing the oath of abjuration. Major Ceely, who had committed them, said to the judge, "May it please you, my lord, this man," meaning Fox, "went aside with me and told me how serviceable I might be for his design; that he could raise 40,000 men in an hour's warning[1] and involve the nation into blood and so bring in King Charles. And I would have aided him out of the country, but he would not go." Fox pointed out how woefully Ceely's impotent conclusions halted behind his tremendous charge of treason: for he had been willing to help Fox away, and had delayed discovering the pretended plot for nine weeks. If his evidence were true, he also should have been standing in the dock. Instead of ensnaring the Quakers he had ensnared himself. But the Major was not at the end of his inventions. He proceeded to accuse Fox of giving him a blow on the Castle Green, in Captain Braddon's presence, such as he had never had in his life. When the Captain was called in corroboration he bowed his head, but said nothing. He afterwards explained to Fox that Ceely was referring to a passage of words between them. Ceely had said, "How do you do, Mr. Fox? your servant, Sir!" doffing his hat. Fox, in his downright fashion, had replied, "Major Ceely, take

[1] The *Short Journ.* 45 says more credibly, 400 men in a day's warning.

heed of hypocrisy and a rotten heart, for when came I to be thy master and thee my servant? Does servants use to cast their masters into prison?" The judge, who politically was a time-server, but in his judicial character was an able lawyer, and had the reputation of being just and impartial, saw that no reliance could be placed on the evidence adduced, and contented himself with imposing on the prisoners the heavy fine of twenty marks (£13:6:8) apiece[1] for their contempts of court, with imprisonment until the fines were paid. He may have expected payment to be made, but the Quakers, as was their wont, were ready to endure all the horrors of a noisome dungeon rather than compromise their principles. Their stiffness and readiness in argument were the talk of the town, and it was said that the judge and justices were not able to answer back one word in twelve.

As the Friends now felt bound to discontinue their payments to the gaoler, they were thrown into a part of the Castle called Doomsdale, of which Fox gives a horrible description. Few people came out of it alive: it had been used for witches and murderers awaiting execution, and was supposed to be haunted by their spirits: it was ankle-deep in filth, and had not been cleansed, it was said, for a score of years. Overhead was a roomful of thieves, and the prisoners were subjected to unnameable indignities from a savage gaoler, who called them hatchet-faced dogs, and treated them accordingly. Complaint was made to the quarter-sessions at Bodmin, and the justices ordered that Doomsdale door should be opened, and the Friends should have liberty to cleanse it and to buy their meat in the town. After this they were allowed to walk on the adjacent Castle Green, and the rigour of their confinement was relaxed.

Cromwell's chaplain, shrewd Hugh Peters, told the Protector that imprisoning Fox in Cornwall was the surest way to spread his principles, and this seemed likely to be the case. Humphrey Lower, an influential

[1] The *Cambridge Journ.* i. 216 has 40 marks apiece; 20 marks, however, is correct. See Willan to Margt. Fell, 12th April 1656 (Swarthm. Colln. i. 270).

magistrate from near Bodmin; Thomas Lower, Margaret Fell's future son-in-law; his aunt, Loveday Hambly, of Tregangeeves, near St. Austell; and her sister, Grace Billing, were amongst those who came to the prison and were convinced,* and there was a "little remnant" of Friends raised up at Launceston itself.

There was also a continual coming and going of Friends who desired conference with Fox, and these published the Quaker message far and wide. In February, John Killam and Thomas Aldam visited Exeter, where Killam's wife Margaret was in prison, and went on by Launceston to Major-General Desborough on behalf of the prisoners. The Major-General would have set them free on terms.[1] Miles Bateman and Barbara Pattison were also at Launceston about the same time.[2] Later in the spring Audland tells us that many Friends were gone, or going, towards Fox.[3] Amongst others there came a ministering angel, Ann Downer, one of the earliest London converts, who at Fox's request travelled the two hundred miles down into Cornwall on foot, lodged in the town, bought and dressed the prisoners' food, and took things down in shorthand.[4] We may recall the description of Fox's industry given some twenty-five years later by Thomas Ellwood,[5] "that good man, like Julius Cæsar, willing to improve all parts of his time, did usually, even in his travels, dictate to his amanuensis what he would have committed to writing." It was easy to keep such a man in prison, but almost impossible to stop him from uttering his message. The personal devotion he inspired is further shown by the extraordinary action of Humphrey Norton, a Durham man, who for a time seems to have acted in London as correspondent with the Kendal Treasurers of the fund for the service of Truth.[6] In April he wrote to Fox that "the want of thy shewing forth unto Israel lies

[1] Salthouse to Margt. Fell, 9th Feby. 1656 (Swarthm. Colln. i. 112).
[2] *Ibid.*
[3] To Burrough, Bristol, 12th May (Dev. Ho., A.R.B. Colln. No. 110).
[4] Fox's testimony to her in *F.P.T.* 204 *n.*, and *Journ.* i. 283.
[5] *Life*, 1714 edn. p. 321.
[6] See Willan to Margt. Fell, Kendal, 11th Sept. 1655 (Swarthm. Colln. i. 255). For Norton's chequered service see note in *Camb. Journ.* i. 441.

now upon me," and that he was ready to lay down his life for him, and was going to Cromwell to offer himself body for body. The Protector could not, of course, accept this vicarious prisoner, but the offer so struck him that he said to his Council, "Which of you would do so much for me, if I were in the same condition?"[1] Nor was this the only case. Joseph Nicholson of Bootle, in Cumberland, requested an interview with Cromwell[2] "to offer up my body and my life, if it be required, for my brethren which are in prison in several gaols in this nation, at Launceston, Edmundsbury, Bath and Northampton, and if it be required of me to fix of one particular [*i.e.* individual], I know whom the Lord doth set before me."

Fox, indeed, continued the leadership of the Quaker movement from his prison. Thomas Holme, for example, was, as we have seen, gathering a Quaker community at Cardiff in the beginning of 1656. He had married Elizabeth Leavens about fifteen months previously, and, when a child was expected, Margaret Fell had expostulated and objected to the charge of a wife and child being put upon a company of newly convinced Friends. Holme wrote her a letter of excuse, "with tears upon my cheeks and our innocency will be made manifest in time . . . and for the charge . . . thou complains of . . . it is yet to come, and if our going together be the ground of what is against us, the ground shall be removed . . . for we had both of us determined long before thy letter came to keep asunder."[3]

In June, Holme went across the Bristol Channel to Launceston with six Friends from Wales, and spent two days with Fox, who said that his wife should have gone to her friends in the North, but as that was no longer possible, Holme's proposal to place the child in the care

[1] See *Journ.* i. 318, and Norton's letter in the *Cambridge Journ.* i. 245.*

[2] See two letters in Dev. Ho., Boswell Middleton Colln. pp. 153, 154.

[3] Holme to Margt. Fell, 30th April 1656 (Swarthm. Colln. i. 203). This form of asceticism was so far encouraged in New England as to produce a somewhat serious state of things among Friends there in 1659. See *The Quakers in the American Colonies*, p. 69, and letters from Joseph Nicholson to Margt. Fell, Swarthm. Colln. iv. 107 and 108, which show that some of the Publishers of Truth from England had advocated the practice, especially Wm. Brend, Dorothy Waugh and Mary Clark.

of a Cardiff Friend was the best arrangement.[1] Elizabeth Holme herself saw Fox shortly after the child's birth, and seems to have continued her work as an itinerating minister. Holme and his wife were held in high esteem in spite of their impulsive natures and occasional unwisdom. Fox records among the notable events of the year 1655 an unusual service of theirs, which Thomas Willan of Kendal thus describes:[2]

> Thomas Holme and Elizabeth is gone. . . . Truly, we are much refreshed by the voice and sound which the power of God did utter through them, and many can witness the life raised and refreshed, for they were much exercised by the power of the Lord in songs and hymns and prayer, that made melody and rejoiced the heart of some; but being not in wisdom of words altogether made some scruple, especially Friends of Underbarrow, but truly it was that preaching of the cross, which will confound the enticing words of man's wisdom.

The use of song in the meetings of Friends showed a tendency to establish itself in the Kendal district at this time, for in April 1656 Humphrey Norton wrote to Fox[3] that he had been lately at Swarthmore and found many speakers and prayers, and such a singing as the like he had not heard and a lightness among them. The complaint, however, it should be noted, is not against singing under the guidance of the Spirit, but against a flow of utterances of various kinds in a light spirit.

In July, Caton saw Fox and discussed with him a number of important matters. He speaks of him to Margaret Fell[4] as one "who is adorned with glory, power, and wisdom, and keeps his authority and triumphs in his freedom and liberty, which no man can take from him." Fox had in a marked degree that greatness of bearing which belongs to the prophet who inhabits an eternal order of life, and breathes its spirit as his native air. But

[1] Holme to Margt. Fell, 4th June 1656 (Swarthm. Colln. i. 205).

[2] Letter to Margt. Fell (Swarthm. Colln. i. 247); cf. *Camb. Journ.* ii. 326.

[3] *Cambridge Journ.* i. 245. When Margt. Fell heard of this she wrote (Spence MSS. vol. iii. folio 40), "In that thou might have spared thy pains, for they [Fox and Nayler] do know us and see us and feel us in that which thou wanted to judge."

[4] 23rd July (Swarthm. Colln. i. 313).

at the same time he had the qualities of practical statesmanship strongly developed. He was anxious for Caton to go again to Holland and finish his work there, so that he might be free for other service. Caton brought up the work of women Friends, which sometimes caused special difficulties. Fox "said little to it, but that some of them might cease, yet he said they would be glad of women or any in these parts," that is, in Cornwall and Devon.[1] At the end of the letter comes a glowing sentence: "When I am with our beloved, in the enjoyment of him, I enjoy thee and the rest of the family of love of which he is the head, yet hath become servant of all." It is interesting to find the term "family of love" thus used of the spiritual fellowship of Friends, with some consciousness perhaps of the affinities between the Friends and the Familists.

In August, Ames and Stubbs, newly arrived from Holland, reported to Fox,[2] and were sent forward by him to Ireland and Scotland, with a further prospect of work in Flanders, Holland, Germany, and Denmark. Audland also was with Fox for a short time,[3] and Thomas Curtis of Reading visited him and had good service in Cornwall.[4]

There were others who tried to reach Launceston, but were turned back under an order of the Devonshire justices made in July.[5] Henry Fell, who was just starting for Barbados, could not get through, and Thomas Rawlinson, James Nayler, and others were taken up and thrown into Exeter gaol. During these summer months twenty-six Friends became imprisoned at Exeter.

There is a remarkable letter from Fox to Friends in the ministry, belonging to the time of the Launceston imprisonment, which sets in a clear light the unconquerable spirit of the man.[6] I can only quote here a few sentences:

[1] But in Nov. 1656 Arthur Cotten of Plymouth wrote to Fox, "they do not care," in these two counties, "to hear any women Friends" (Swarthm. Colln. iv. 163).

[2] Ames to Margt. Fell, 2nd Sept., Dev. Ho., A.R.B. Colln. No. 3.

[3] *Camb. Journ.* i. 255.

[4] *Journ.* i. 326.

[5] See *The West Answering to the North*, 1657, p. 76.

[6] *Journ.* i. 315.

Let all nations hear the sound by word or writing. Spare no place, spare no tongue nor pen, but be obedient to the Lord God; go through the work and be valiant for the Truth upon earth; tread and trample all that is contrary under. . . . The ministers of the Spirit must minister to the spirit that is in prison, which hath been in captivity in every one, that with the Spirit of Christ people may be led out of captivity up to God, the Father of spirits, and do service to Him, and to have unity with Him, with the scriptures and one with another. . . . Be patterns, be examples in all countries, places, islands, nations, wherever you come, that your carriage and life may preach among all sorts of people, and to them; then you will come to walk cheerfully over the world, answering that of God in every one.

As we read words such as these, we think of the Friends who were setting out for America and Europe, and we realize how the magnetic personality of Fox must have made him the central force of the Quaker community, even when in prison. A spiritual primacy was his by right, and no horizon of service was too wide for his illumined vision. To such a man the prison doors would at last open of their own accord. He would never purge his so-called contempt of court by paying fee or fine: when the time came his gaolers would have to confess themselves beaten, and he would go forth in triumph. This was, in fact, the course of events. Cromwell had throughout been well disposed towards Fox; he had inquired into the barbarous prison treatment meted out to him, and in the summer offered, through Major-General Desborough, to free the prisoners if they would go home and preach no more. Capt. Pyott replied with a vigorous letter[1] containing a noteworthy phrase, asserting "the liberty of Englishmen to travel in any part of the nation of England, it being as the Englishman's house by the law." Desborough visited Launceston and played at bowls on the Castle Green, but left the Friends still in prison. He seems to have handed over the business to Colonel Bennet, who was willing to set the prisoners free if they would pay the gaoler's fees. This again they

[1] *Journ.* i. 318.

refused, and at last, early in September,[1] the prison doors were opened without any fees being paid or conditions imposed. A month later Friends were also freed from Exeter, Dorchester, Colchester, and Bury St. Edmunds.[2]

The eight months during which Fox was a prisoner witnessed important changes in the external and internal condition of the Quaker movement. On the one hand it was now reaching out, amid much persecution, into the New World; on the other it was being seriously compromised in the minds of many sober people by the extravagances of James Nayler and his company. We must now turn to this painful but instructive chapter of Quaker experience.

[1] There is some doubt as to the date. The *Journal* says 13th Sept., in both Ellwood's edition and the Cambridge edition. But a contemporary letter from Alexander Parker to Margt. Fell, dated from St. Austell 13th Sept., clearly specifies 9th Sept. (Tuesday) as the date. See letter, Swarthm. Colln. i. 167.*

[2] See *Extracts from State Papers* (First Series), p. 5.

CHAPTER XI

NAYLER'S FALL*

(1656)

Reader, if you are not acquainted with it, I would recommend to you, above all church-narratives, to read Sewel's *History of the Quakers*. It is in folio, and is the abstract of the journals of Fox, and the primitive Friends. It is far more edifying and affecting than anything you will read of Wesley and his colleagues. Here is nothing to stagger you, nothing to make you mistrust, no suspicion of alloy, no drop or dreg of the worldly or ambitious spirit. You will here read the true story of that much-injured, ridiculed man (who perhaps hath been a by-word in your mouth)—James Nayler: what dreadful sufferings, with what patience, he endured even to the boring through of his tongue with red-hot irons without a murmur; and with what strength of mind, when the delusion he had fallen into, which they stigmatised for blasphemy, had given way to clearer thoughts, he could renounce his error, in a strain of the beautifullest humility, yet keep his first grounds, and be a Quaker still!—so different from the practice of your common converts from enthusiasm, who, when they apostatize, *apostatize all*, and think they can never get far enough from the society of their former errors, even to the renunciation of some saving truths, with which they had been mingled, not implicated.—CHAS. LAMB, *Essays of Elia*, "A Quaker's Meeting."

The difficulties of the doctrine of Inward Guidance are, as James Nayler's experience reminds us, serious and practical. I would suggest that the solution lies in a deeper interpretation of the person and message of Jesus Christ. Apart from the thought of God as we see Him set forth in Jesus, and the common consciousness of truth as revealed in lofty souls who have been touched by His spiritual fire, it is not evident how the faults of individual interpretation are to be corrected. . . . [But] with Jesus as the Gospel, witnessed in the conscience of a civilization infected by His Spirit, I see the balance-wheel to the doctrine of the Inward Light.—J. W. ROWNTREE, *Essays and Addresses*, pp. 244, 245.

IN a previous chapter the account of the work in London was not carried beyond May 1655. Howgill and Burrough had been the chief labourers: they now spent a month in the Eastern Counties, and in July went north towards Ireland, not returning to London until the spring of 1656. Shortly before they left, James Nayler, the most brilliant of the Quaker preachers, had come to the city[1] and threw himself into the work with ardour. He found much clamour against the new movement; at an afternoon meeting which he attended at a Friend's house "hundreds of vain people continued all the while throwing great stones in at the window . . . yet people kept in peace within."[2] Nayler had already shown himself specially skilful in handling the public discussions on religion in which men delighted: at one such dispute in Derbyshire, when the ministers were defeated, the people cried out, "a nailer, a nailer hath confuted them all."[3] He proved well fitted for the great work in London, quickly winning the affection of many. We read, for example, of a zealous Baptist, Rebecca Travers, who went out of curiosity to hear him dispute with the Baptists at the Glasshouse in Broad Street. She

> . . would have been glad to have heard the Baptists get the victory but . . . it proved quite contrary, for the countryman stood up on a form over against the Baptists and . . . she could feel his words smote them, that one or two of them confessed they were sick and could hold it no longer, and the third . . . shamed himself in bringing scriptures that turned against him, and she was confounded and ashamed that a Quaker should exceed the learned Baptists.

This woman accepted the Quaker message, and was especially helped by Nayler's advice to her with respect to the high notions and curious questions of the time: "Feed not on knowledge: . . . it is good to look upon, but not to feed on, for who feeds on knowledge dies to the innocent life."[4] Nayler gained a hearing from the highest circles: at one meeting at Lady Darcy's, many of the court were present, lords, ladies, officers, ministers, though they were hidden away "behind a ceiling."[5]

[1] Sewel (1811 edn.), i. 234, brings him to London at the end of 1654 or beginning of 1655, which is a little too early.

[2] Nayler to Margt. Fell, Swarthmore Colln. iii. 81.

[3] See Fox's *Journal*, i. 252, and letters of Alex. Parker in *Letters of Early Friends*, pp. 37 *n.* and 37.

[4] See Jno. Whiting's *Persecution Exposed*, p. 176, dated wrongly 1654. A letter to Fox from Nayler (Swarthmore Collection, iii. 76), written in the first half of 1656, refers to the Glasshouse debate as a recent thing.

[5] Nayler to Margt. Fell, 3rd Nov. 1655, in *Letters of Early Friends*, p. 38 (Swarthm. Colln. iii. 80).*

Nayler's charm of manner and appearance must have been considerable, though Ellwood, after his terrible punishment, describes him as looking like a plain, simple husbandman or shepherd.[1] He was of ruddy complexion and medium height, with long, low-hanging brown hair, oval face, and nose that rose a little in the middle: he wore a small band close to his collar, but no band-strings, and a hat that hung over his brows.[2] When he was taken into custody at Bristol, there was found on one of his companions a copy of the spurious document known as the Epistle from Lentulus to the Roman Senate,[3] which contains the famous description of our Lord as a man of regular features, grey eyes, and innocent look, with filbert-coloured hair coming down to his shoulders, and a short forked beard of the same colour; and Nayler, it was said, had adapted the fashion of his hair and beard so as to affect a resemblance to this description.

Until Burrough's return in the spring of 1656,[4] he continued the chief Publisher of Truth left in London. The position was one of much spiritual peril. In May 1655, before Nayler came to the city, an old minister named Richard Nelson, with whom he was in controversy, had given him some sharp but prophetic advice.[5]

> Take good heed while thou forbears to have outward reverence of men, as capping and kneeing and the like, that thou steal not men's hearts away from God to thyself, and so lord it on their conscience that they have neither God nor scripture, nor any privilege of their own experience, but take thee as a demigod and to make thee a mental idol, which is a worse kind of idolatry than all that thou reproves,—for this hath more possibility to deceive, if it were possible, the very elect.

Nayler afterwards wrote[6] that he had entered London in

[1] *Life*, 1714 edn. p. 19.

[2] The description in Cobbett's *State Trials*, v. col. 840, from *The Grand Impostor Examined*, agrees with and perhaps suggested the engraving by T. Preston.

[3] For this Epistle of Lentulus see Fabricius, Cod. Apoc. N.T. i. 301. It is translated in Lord Lindsay's *Sketches of History of Christian Art*, 1847 edn. i. 77.*

[4] Burrough was back by 22nd April. See Audland to Burrough, Dev. Ho., A.R.B. Colln. No. 116.

[5] Dev. Ho., Boswell Middleton Colln. p. 2.

[6] Nayler's Works, *To the Life of God in all*, pp. xxxix-xlix.

great fear, foreseeing that something, he knew not what, would befall him there. At first the same presence and power which he had known elsewhere were with him. But following his reason in certain small matters, he allowed his mind to become ensnared by trifles, vanities, and persons, and to lose something of its watchfulness. Thus the light ot Christ in his heart withdrew, and his old life began to revive. In this darkness he sought to be alone that he might cry before the Lord and recover his condition; but in his distraught state he suffered others to lead him and, as he says, "My adversary so prevailed that all things were turned and perverted against my right seeing, hearing, or understanding, only a secret hope and faith I had in my God whom I had served that He would bring me through it." With this brief autobiography of Nayler's spiritual crisis in mind, the attempt must be made to trace the obscure events which led to his fall. In March 1656 he had urged Howgill and Burrough to return to London, where he was pressed with work.[1] In May both he and Burrough were in great service in the city, and in June, at the suggestion of Fox, he paid a brief visit to Yorkshire, and also visited Lincoln to compose a difference there,* still having, it is clear, the full confidence of his friends.[2] The ensnaring of his spirit now took place, "quick and sudden," says Captain George Bishop of Bristol. Martha Simmonds, wife of Thomas Simmonds, and sister of Giles Calvert, the two chief printers of Friends' books, was a woman of much enthusiasm and little judgment, who took an unhelpful part in meetings and engaged in service away from London against the judgment of Friends. She and some other women had been reproved for their conduct by Howgill and Burrough, and went to Nayler demanding justice. When he refused to pass judgment

[1] Willan to Margt. Fell, Swarthmore Colln. i. 268, 274.

[2] Nayler to Margt. Fell, 1st June (1656), Swarthmore Colln. iii. 82; Dewsbury to Margt. Fell, 25th June 1656, Swarthmore Colln. iv. 137, cf. letters in Nayler's *Works*, 703, 705, both of which should, I think, be dated in 1656. Burrough as late as 12th July writes a most loving letter to him from Oxford (Dev. Ho. Portfolio 1, No. 43). Fox dates his "running out" in June; see Annals in *Camb. Journ.* ii. 334.

on his brethren, she fell into passionate mourning and cried out bitterly, "How are the mighty fallen! I came to Jerusalem and behold a cry and behold oppression." Nayler was moved to tears and was struck down for three days into sorrow and sadness, and during all this time the "power" arose in Martha Simmonds. Physically prostrated and overwrought, he became clouded in his understanding, and his regard for the women prevented him from disowning their dividing spirit. After staying three days at Thomas Simmonds' house he was so changed that many Friends, in the crude phraseology of the time, concluded that Martha had bewitched him.[1] At the end of July he went to Bristol for religious service at the time of the St. James' Fair, with a company of two men and two women round him, who began to compromise him and Friends by their extravagant conduct, bowing, kneeling, and singing before him, justifying themselves by the example of the Shunammite woman who fell down at Elisha's feet (2 Kings iv. 27, 37). At the meeting held in the Orchard, Nayler said nothing, but after it was over, Martha began her singing, and the leading Bristol Friends, who perceived his condition, forcibly separated the two. Howgill and Audland were also at Bristol, and tell us how Nayler's party scattered. Friends persuaded him to go towards Launceston to see Fox, and sent with him two sober Friends, John Bolton, a London goldsmith, and Nicholas Gannicliffe of Exeter.* Howgill and Audland went fifteen miles with them, and reported that Nayler said little, "but one while wept exceedingly."[2] Farnsworth about this time wrote from Gloucestershire, "My dear J. N. is as one that is not, but the Lord is faithful who changeth not."[3] Fox had already been informed of the extravagances that had taken place, and was most anxious to see Nayler. By order of the Devonshire justices the roads in that county, as we have

[1] I have drawn my narrative from Geo. Whitehead's account in Nayler's *Works*, viii. etc.; Farmer's *Satan Inthron'd, etc.*, and Bishop's *The Throne of Truth Exalted, etc.*

[2] Dev. Ho., A.R.B. Colln. No. 114.*

[3] To Margt. Fell, Kendalshire, 5th Augt. (Swarthm. Colln. iii. 56).

seen, had been stopped to all Quakers travelling without a pass, and Nayler and Bolton were taken near Okehampton, within fifteen miles of Launceston,[1] and thrown into Exeter gaol, which soon became full of Friends arrested in the same way. Of the critical months spent here we have a good deal of information. At first John Bolton[2] reported Nayler much as he was when they left Bristol, in a fast, very quiet, lying down a great deal, and without the life which he used to breathe forth. This fasting lasted a month, and his fellow-prisoner, Thomas Rawlinson, wrote that he was "standing in the will of God, waiting in his own way. . . . He ate no bread but one little bit for a whole month, and there was about a fortnight . . . he took no manner of food, but some days a pint of white wine and some days a gill mingled with water, but now he eats meat."[3] Rawlinson in this letter asked Margaret Fell not to credit every report which she heard about Nayler, who had foreseen suffering though he knew not how, and was innocent of the things that were spoken and done. A few days later John Stubbs[4] could write:

> James is pretty, and dear to the whole household of God for ever, and the rotten rags and dust which he was covered with is near taken off . . . but some spirits . . . is exalted above him in their own imaginations, and he sees it, but [is] silent under it.

Hubberthorne[5] about this time found him "pretty low and tender" when alone; but when Martha Simmonds who was now at Exeter, came and called him away, he seemed subject to her. This misguided woman had been to Fox at Launceston, singing before him, and nearly causing a scandal. Fox, with his robust common sense had judged her "unclean" spirit, and greatly angered her against him. He wrote[6] to the prisoners at Exeter to

[1] Alex. Parker to Margt. Fell, 19th Aug. 1656, Swarthm. Colln. i. 166.

[2] See letter from Audland to Margt. Fell, 18th Aug. 1656, Swarthm. Colln. i. 12. The names of the Exeter prisoners are given in this letter.

[3] To Margt. Fell, 23rd Aug., Swarthm. Colln. iii. 12.

[4] To Margt. Fell, 2nd Sept., Swarthm. Colln. iv. 27.

[5] To Margt. Fell, 16th Sept., Swarthm. Colln. iii. 153; also Fox to Nayler Swarthm. Colln. iii. 193.

[6] Fox, *Epistles*, No. 110.

mind that which would keep all meek and low, that none of them might be "puddling" in their own carnal wisdom. Under Martha's influence Nayler became alienated from Fox, whom he accused to Margaret Fell[1] of burying Nayler's name that he might raise his own. About this time also one of Nayler's fellow-prisoners, Dorcas Erbury, daughter[2] of the famous Seeker, William Erbury, fell into a swoon and believed herself to have been raised to life by Nayler laying his hand on her head and crying over her, "Dorcas, arise." In December 1654 Francis Howgill[3] had felt himself led to take a lame boy by the hand, and bid him, in the power of God that raised Jesus from the dead, to stand up and walk. He had written to Fox in much perplexity because the attempted miracle had failed. Fox himself, more than once, had been used in this way, and had cured a deformed boy at Hawkshead by laying his hands on him and speaking to him.[4] Nayler was no doubt equally sincere in what he did, and his apparent success must greatly have strengthened the devotion of his followers. Extravagant letters were written to him, especially one by Hannah Stranger, who had been with him at Bristol with her husband John, in which he was styled "the everlasting Son of Righteousness."[5] In the prison some of the women knelt before him, bowing, and singing "Holy, holy, holy."

Fox was released from Launceston early in September, and a week later visited Exeter.* Nayler and some of his companions, according to Fox,[6] did not stay through the meeting held in the prison on the Sunday, and, when Fox prayed, they kept on their hats, being the first, as he notes in his *Journal*, to set that bad example among Friends. On the Monday, Nayler slighted what Fox said,

[1] See letter from Margt. Fell printed below, p. 249.

[2] Farmer, *Satan Inthron'd*, p. 17, says "daughter"; cf. Burton's *Diary*, i. 173. In *State Trials*, col. 837, she is called widow of Wm. Erbury, but as she afterwards refers to her mother, this seems a wrong description.

[3] Dev. Ho., A.R.B. Colln. No. 21 (date by internal evidence).*

[4] See *Camb. Journ.* i. 140, where other strange cures by Fox are also given. Cf. Dewsbury's *Works*, an early unnumbered page.*

[5] Cobbett's *State Trials*, v. cols. 830, 831.

[6] *Camb. Journ.* i. 244, and *Journ.* i. 328.

". . . and was dark and much out; nevertheless he would have come and kissed me,"—as was then the custom between intimate friends,—"but I said, seeing he had turned against the power of God, it was my foot* and so the Lord moved me to slight him and to set the power of God over him. And when he was come to London his resisting the power of God in me . . . became one of his greatest burdens."

Nayler wept, however,[1] and must keenly have felt both Fox's words at the time and the sharp letter which followed and rebuked him for trying to kiss a man against whom he had written false and secret letters. Fox added, "And, James, it will be harder for thee to get down thy rude company than it was for thee to set them up (if ever thou come to know and own Christ), whose impudence doth sport and blaspheme the truth."[2] Fox wrote again from Reading on 12th October,[3] and told Nayler that the responsibility for the scandal and serious division that were being caused lay on him because he would not condemn the proceedings of his company. London Friends, we are told, were for the time like the Church at Corinth, one saying, "I am of James"; another, "I am of Francis and Edward."[4] Howgill and Burrough were in great exercise of spirit, and could scarcely enjoy a quiet meeting. A few days later, on the eve of Nayler's own release, a very different letter, dated 17th October, reached him from Hannah Stranger, styling him "the fairest of ten thousand" and "only begotten Son of God," with a postscript from her husband John, a London comb-maker, which contained the words, "Thy name shall be no more James Nayler, but Jesus."[5] Nayler afterwards wrote[6] that a fear struck him when he received

[1] See letter, Walter Clement to Margt. Fell, 4th Oct. 1656, Swarthm. Colln. i. 181. From *Hidden Things brought to Light*, by Robert Rich, p. 37, it would appear that the phrase used by George Fox, "It was my foot," means "It was my foot he should kiss."

[2] Fox to Nayler, Swarthm. Colln. iii. 195. In the folio vol. at Dev. Ho. of early London documents known as the Wm. Markey Colln., the following occur: p. 120, Burrough to Martha Simmonds; p. 121, Fox to Nayler from Launceston; p. 122, Fox to Nayler after the Exeter visit; p. 123, Dewsbury to Martha Simmonds.

[3] Swarthm. Colln. iii. 193; for its date, see letter, Geo. Bishop to Margt. Fell, 27th Oct., Swarthm. Colln. i. 188.*

[4] Rich. Roper to Margt. Fell, 20th Oct. 1656, Swarthm. Colln. iii. 131. Cf. Audland to Margt. Fell, 18th Augt. 1656, Swarthm. Colln. i. 12.

[5] See Cobbett's *State Trials*, as above.

[6] *Works*, liii.

it, and he put it in his pocket, intending no one to see it, as he could not own its contents. The Order in Council for the release of Quaker prisoners at Exeter, Dorchester, Colchester, Ipswich, and Bury St. Edmunds was made on 2nd October;[1] but in the case of the Colchester, Ipswich, and Bury prisoners we happen to know that the actual release was not dated till the 16th,[2] and they could not have been set at liberty till, say, a couple of days later. On the same allowance of time the Exeter prisoners would not be released till Monday, 20th October. This date makes it unlikely that Nayler could have received either at Exeter or at Bristol, four days later, the strangely worded letter from Swarthmore on the 15th, which Margaret Fell addressed to him at Exeter.[3] Indeed, the preservation of this letter among her papers suggests that it was returned to the sender. Margaret Fell had just received news of the way in which Nayler had slighted Fox three weeks before, and her spirit is greatly grieved.

Since I have heard that thou would not be subject to him to whom all nations shall bow,[4] it hath grieved my spirit. Thou hath confessed him to be thy father, and thy life bound up in him, and when he sent for thee and thou would not come to him, where was thy life then? Was thou not then banished from the father's house, as thou knows thou hath writ to me? And that which showed thee this which was to come I own, but that which banished thee I must deny. And when he bended his knees to the Most High God for the seed's sake, and thou would not bend, nor bow, nor join with him, how will thou

---

[1] *Extracts from State Papers*, First Series, p. 5. Major-General Desborough was to see to the Exeter discharge, to consider how the fines were to be remitted and to take care upon discharging the prisoners that they were sent to their respective homes. It was found to require a special order in Feby. 1657 to take off the fines.

[2] See *ibid.* and Geo. Whitehead's *Christian Progress*, p. 95.

[3] Thos. Salthouse, in 1668, Swarthm. Colln. i. 102, speaks of a letter from Margt. Fell which took nine days from Swarthmore to Bristol. Two letters of Thos. Willan, Swarthmore Colln. i. 270, 280, give seven days as the time taken from Kendal to Bristol, and Swarthmore would be at least a day further. Margaret Fell's letter is in the Spence MSS. vol. iii. fol. 38, and is printed, though not quite correctly, in Wilkinson's *Quakerism Examined*, xii.—a book hostile to Friends.*

[4] This expression also occurs in a letter from Holme to Fox, 6th Augt. 1655 (Swarthm. Colln. iv. 244), but Fox has altered it into "to the power shall all nations bow."

answer this to Him who hath given him a name better than every name, to which every knee must bow? This is contrary to what thou writ to me, where thou saith he is burying thy name that he may raise his own; but it was thy name that stood against him then. And thou writ to me the truth should never suffer by thee; for where the seed suffers, the truth suffers: doth not the seed and all the body suffer by that spirit that holds not the head, but rebels against him? Oh, consider what thou art doing. I am sure the lamb in his suffering is in subjection, not resisting, nor exalting; but in the time of his suffering he is servant to all the seed. And, if thou stood in the suffering for the seed, thou had not resisted him who is the promise of the Father to the seed, who hath said, "Blessed are ye that are not offended in me." Oh, dear heart, mind while it is called to-day what thou art doing, lest thou walk naked and be a stumbling-block to the simple, and be [thou] tender of the truth which thou hath served before and suffered for, which draws thine ear from unclean spirits, which is like frogs which cometh out of the mouth of the Dragon, the Beast, and the False Prophet. These [frogs] was seen when the sixth angel poured out his vial upon the great river Euphrates:[1] read and understand, and return to thy first husband, my dear brother. I can bear all that hath been past, if thou will be subject to the will of the Father; and he who doth the will hath learned obedience and is subject, and I could lie down at thy feet that thou might trample upon me, for thy good; and so I know would he whom thou hath resisted, though to the spirit that rebels it cannot be, for that is not one with the Father. So in dearness and tenderness have I written to thee, my Father shall bear me witness; and I warn thee from the Lord God that thou beware of siding with unclean spirits, lest thou be cut off for ever.[2]

It is necessary to give this letter fully in order to judge it fairly. Its purpose is to win back Nayler by the persuasive power of womanly tenderness to an acceptance of Fox as the prophet of the new movement. It contains indeed high expressions concerning Fox, "him to whom all nations shall bow," "him" to whom has been given "a name better than every name, to which every knee must bow," "him who is the promise of the Father to the seed." But we must remember that in the phraseology of Fox and the early Friends,[3] *all* might

[1] See Revelation xvi. 13.
[2] Compare with letter from Thomas Ayrey, Swarthm. Colln. vii. 98.
[3] I take the phrases from epistles of Fox written in or before 1655. An

know Christ the seed of God in them, which seed was one in them all, and inherited the promise of the Father and had dominion over all that was in the Fall. Accordingly, Margaret Fell's phrases are not intended by her to designate Fox as the Messiah, in the sense of one who possessed uniquely the spiritual life and authority of Christ, but only as conspicuously foremost in the company of men and women who, by virtue of their possession of Christ, the promised seed, were "Children of the Light." Writing in sisterly freedom to a man of the same spiritual experience and vocabulary as herself, she ran no risk of being misunderstood. In a letter to Friends written the next year, when the lessons of Nayler's fall had been learnt, she uses similar phrases this time in a perfectly general sense:[1]

Join with God's pure witness and testimony, and there will be your peace. And here you will know Him who is the Life and the Resurrection; and he that believes on Him, though he were dead, yet should he live; and there is no other name under heaven by which any shall be saved than by that name, which is better than every name, to which every knee shall bow and every tongue confess.

Margaret Fell's letter might well have made a powerful impression on Nayler, had it reached him. As it was, enfeebled by imprisonment and fasting, and smarting under the censures of Fox, he allowed his companions, on his release from Exeter, to behave towards him as their misguided feelings prompted.

"Thus," he wrote at a later date,[2] "was I led out from amongst the Children of Light and into the world, to be a sign, where I was chased as a wandering bird gone from her nest; so was my soul daily and my body from one prison to another."

The company set out towards London, and reached Bristol on Friday, 24th October, having spent the previous

epistle in 1653, Swarthmore Colln. ii. 56, has the following: "The promise is to the seed, which seed is not many but one, which seed is Christ. . . . To the seed all nations shall bow where it is carried up into power."

[1] I have quoted this from the original draft, in the Spence MSS. vol. iii. fol. 10. It is printed in Margt. Fell's *Works*, p. 194.

[2] *Works*, p. xliii.

night at Chew Stoke. According to Capt. George Bishop, they came "with full purpose and resolution to set up their image and to break the Truth in pieces, and to bruise and tread down and beguile and devour the tender plants of the Lord in this His vineyard, as before was given forth."[1] Through Glastonbury and Wells the party passed; a man going bareheaded before Nayler,[2] others at each stirrup and others strewing garments in the way. After these rehearsals the company approached Bristol in similar fashion. A young man bare-headed, a Devonshire youth named Timothy Wedlock, led Nayler's horse through Bedminster along the muddy cart-way; another walked in front; two men followed on horseback, each with a woman behind him, and the eighth of the party, a woman, walked on the raised causeway. As they went along, they sang "Holy, holy, holy, Lord God of Sabaoth." On reaching the Almshouse within the suburbs of the city, one woman alighted and, with the one who had been walking, took the reins of Nayler's horse, Martha on one side, Hannah Stranger on the other, while Nayler himself rode with his hands before him. It was between two and three in the afternoon, raining heavily, and the women were up to their knees in mud; but they trudged along, singing "Holy, holy, holy, Lord God of Israel," with a buzzing melodious noise, not easy to understand, and the women spread garments before Nayler. So the sorry procession passed through Redcliff Gate to the High Cross and on to the White Hart Inn in Broad Street, a house that belonged to two of the Bristol Friends,* Dennis Hollister and Henry Row. A crowd followed, for the whole city was moved. While the women were drying their outer garments at the fire, the magistrates summoned the party before them, still singing "Holy, holy, holy." All were clapped into prison, Nayler, Dorcas Erbury, Martha Simmonds, Hannah Stranger and her husband John,

[1] Capt. Bishop to Margt. Fell, 27th Oct., Swarthm. Colln. i. 188.

[2] The account is taken from the above letter and Cobbett's *State Trials*, v. cols. 802-842. In addition to the report of the proceedings in Parliament, Cobbett reprints *The Grand Impostor Examined* (1656), by John Deacon, and Whitelocke's Opinion as to the death punishment.

Samuel Cater from the Isle of Ely, Robert Crab,[1] and Timothy Wedlock. Friends held a meeting that Friday afternoon, which proved a heart-searching time. Captain Bishop, writing to Margaret Fell, says:

> With us in silence was the presence of the Lord very great, and the Lord went forth with His power to preserve all His lambs and babes in one and to break the powers of darkness and to chain them down, so that Friends are all kept and preserved, none are hurt. . . . And that of God in the whole town witnessed to us and our innocency, even in our enemies, and begat in them a good savour and much moderation and a secret joy . . . that we were clear.

Out of the thousand or more[2] of Quakers then in Bristol not one was concerned in Nayler's proceedings.*

Nayler was examined next day by the magistrates. He said he had not reproved the women, but bade them take heed that they sang nothing but what they were moved to by the Lord. As to the extravagant phrases in the letters found on him, he denied that any such title as "fairest of ten thousand" was due to him, but if it was used of that which the Father had begotten in him, then he owned it. He made similar replies with respect to other titles. Being asked, "Art thou the only Son of God?" he replied, "I am the Son of God, but I have many brethren," and to another question said, "Where God is manifest in the flesh, there is the everlasting Son, and I do witness God in the flesh. I am the Son of God, and the Son of God is but one," that is, but one in all His manifestations. He admitted fasting for fifteen or sixteen days, "without any other food except the word of God," but denied raising up Dorcas Erbury by any power of his own. He added, "The Lord hath made me a sign of His coming, and that honour that belongeth to Christ Jesus in whom I am revealed may be given to Him, as when on earth at Jerusalem, according to the measure.'

[1] I insert this name from Grigge's *The Quakers' Jesus*, 1658, p. 11. Besse includes the name of Robert Crab among the Exeter prisoners, *Sufferings*, i. 149. So also Audland's letter, Swarthm. Colln. i. 12.

[2] "Rabshakeh's Outrage Reproved," cited in Barclay's *Inner Life*, p. 320 *n.*, says, "many more than 700"; Geo. Bishop, *The Throne of Truth Exalted*, p. 4, says "thousands."

When we remember the similar terms in which Fox and the other early Friends expressed their experience of the indwelling Christ, these careful answers do not of themselves suggest that Nayler's mind was unhinged. But an unbalanced mental condition shows itself more often in a weakening of the powers of the will than in a weakening of the powers of perception, and we must regard Nayler's conduct as due in part to a state of mental overstrain and physical prostration.

If madness were the full explanation of the matter, the whole episode might be dismissed in a paragraph, as a thing of little importance. But if, as is the case, we have to deal with the conduct of a man of deep spirituality but clouded judgment,—a leader who mainly differed from the other leaders in allowing himself for a time to be pushed to extremes,—then this passage in Quaker history has great significance. Nayler, as his answers show, even in his hour of darkness, placed a clear difference between himself as a man and the life of Christ manifested in him, and we have to reconcile this point of view with the extraordinary conduct which he countenanced in prison and at his entrance into Bristol. He supplies the key by saying, "The Lord hath made me a sign of His coming." What the women meant in their enthusiasm it is not easy to say, but as far as Nayler is concerned, it is evident that he regarded himself as submitting to be made a sign of Christ's coming, actively engaged in the proceedings to some extent, but mainly taking the passive part of allowing behaviour to be acted towards himself in this character of the Messiah. The entry into Bristol is, in fact, in line with other early extravagances already alluded to, and was intended to bring home with dramatic emphasis the cardinal Quaker doctrine that Christ was come to teach His people Himself and was revealed in His saints. Nayler afterwards, as we shall find, saw that the worship and honour given to his person had been idolatrous in its character, and confessed in the amplest terms the error into which he had been led.[1]

[1] An article by the Rev. Bryan Dale, *Congregational Historical Society*

Thomas Simmonds,* Martha's husband, had not been of the party. He had carried down the release to Exeter, but returned by the direct way to London, and wrote a sensible letter to his wife dated 1st November,[1] pointing out their wrong conduct, especially because when a prompting to speak or act came to any of them singly, often from some earthly dark principle, the whole company would join whether the rest felt the prompting or not. And hence, he said, came all their "cumber and trumpery without," which his soul was grieved to see. He had heard of their proceedings and feared that his wife was chief leader. He adds shrewdly, "If there was such a glory among you, why were *you* not silent, and have let the *people* cry Hosanna, etc. Your work is soon come to an end: part of the army that fell at Burford was your figure." Burford, we note, was where Cromwell suppressed the mutineers in 1649.

The conclusion I have expressed is confirmed by the subsequent proceedings. The Bristol magistrates were at a loss what to do, and wrote to their town-clerk, who was in Parliament and reported the matter to the House.[2] The House appointed a Committee of fifty-five, to consider "the great misdemeanours and blasphemies of James Nayler and others at Bristol and elsewhere, and to examine the truth thereof and to report." The Committee sent for Nayler, who was brought to London with four of his company, Cater, Wedlock, and Crab having been discharged. They sang through most of the towns on the road, to the wonder of those who heard them.[3]

Transactions, March 1903, p. 236, puts nearly the same point in view: "He was the chief actor in a public scene or miracle play which was abhorrent to sober Christians, tended to mislead the people, and to create a disturbance of the peace." "Miracle play" is a term, however, which would be foreign to Nayler's Puritan mind. I am indebted to this suggestive article, though it is incorrect in some details. J. G. Bevan, in his *Life of Nayler*, 1800, p. 74, regards him as receiving the honours done him as not done "to his person, but to that extraordinary manifestation of Christ, which he continued to think he possessed." Masson, *Life of Milton*, v. 68, goes too far in calling Nayler "stark mad."

[1] See Farmer's *Satan Inthron'd*, p. 20, for this letter. Simmonds seems to have wished that Nayler and his company had returned quietly to London, where the Lord, he says, "would have manifested His mighty power amongst us." This indicates that he was himself one of Nayler's followers, and makes his criticism the more significant.

[2] See *The Quakers' Jesus*, by Wm. Grigge, 1658, p. 11.

[3] Taylor to Margt. Fell, Swarthm. Colln. i. 294.

The examination of Nayler elicited answers similar to those which he had given at Bristol. With respect to the raising of Dorcas Erbury, he said that what

> . . . any attribute unto me as to a creature that hath beginning and ending I utterly deny, but that that any see of God in me by the same Spirit that revealed anything to them, that I do not deny. This may serve at one word; for there cannot be a more abominable thing than to take from the Creator and give to the creature. The same power which did raise from the dead, which you read in the scripture, the same Christ, the same anointing according to the measure of Him is manifest in me and no other.

He stated that he looked upon the worship given him as the true honour of Christ, or else he would have utterly denied it, and he had never understood that his companions gave that honour except to God. At the end of the examination he said:

> I do abhor that any of that honour which is due to God should be given to me as I am a creature. But it pleased the Lord to set me up as a sign of the coming of the righteous One; and what hath been done in my passing through the towns, I was commanded by the power of the Lord to suffer such things to be done to the outward [man] as a sign. I abhor any honour as a creature.

We have an interesting sidelight on this examination in a letter of Anthony Pearson's dated Westminster, 18th November 1656.[1] According to Pearson, the whole assembly, except some violent men of the Committee, was strangely astonished and satisfied with the answers. He gives a somewhat fuller version of Nayler's important last answer.

> For any worship or honour he denies that any was due to James Nayler. But if any was moved to give such things to the appearance of God in him, as to a sign of Christ's second coming and being revealed in His saints, the great mystery that hath been hid from ages, he did not judge them for it.

Pearson adds that the testimony given by Nayler was the highest that had been made since the days of Christ.

[1] Swarthm. Colln. iii. 78.

People were in amazement, and wondered what would be the end of it. Friends disapproved of the outward things which had been acted to Nayler, but were tender towards him, and anxious that the matter should make no rent in the Church. Hubberthorne, about the same time, says that Nayler had kept the Committee out of all occasions against him by denying that he was Christ, though Christ was in him. He was, however, still under the power of darkness in the women round him.[1]

The Parliament by which Nayler's case was being dealt with was the second which Cromwell had set up since he became Lord Protector under the Instrument of Government of 15th December 1653. It was a vain attempt to reconcile military power and parliamentary government. When it met in September,[2] he was at pains to defend the arbitrary rule by Major-Generals which he had adopted about November 1655. The institution, he said, had not only preserved the peace of England, but had proved more effectual for discountenancing vice and settling religion than anything done these fifty years. Necessity was its justification. "If nothing should be done but what is according to law, the throat of the nation may be cut while we send for some to make a law." By high-handed measures the Protector and his Council secured the exclusion or abstention of about one-third of the members returned, and thus endeavoured to safeguard the political unity which seemed necessary in the dangers that beset the Commonwealth. One result of the exclusion was to fill the house with Presbyterians and the less tolerant Independents, who were opposed to the Protector's large-minded practice on matters touching religious liberty.[3]

The Parliamentary Committee reported on 5th December, through its chairman, Thomas Bampfield, Recorder of Exeter, who became Speaker of the next Parliament.

[1] London, 25th Nov., *Letters of Early Friends*, p. 45.

[2] Samuel Fisher of Lydd, in Kent, tried to deliver a religious message at the opening ceremony but was hustled out, some crying, "A Quaker, a Quaker, keep him down, he shall not speak." See his *Works*, pp. 1-9.

[3] See Firth, *Last Years of the Protectorate*, vol. i. chap. 1.

Nayler, the report said, had "assumed the gesture, words, honour, worship, and miracles of our blessed Saviour, and His names, incommunicable attributes and titles." The report occasioned lengthy debates, highly significant of the temper and thought of the age.[1] Major-General Skippon, a poor speaker, but a man of stanch courage, who was held in universal esteem, led the attack. The members had sat silent in horror on hearing the report. Then the old man rose to his feet, giving it as his opinion that it was a case of horrid blasphemy, and ought to be punished as such. "It is now come to your doors. . . . I have often been troubled in my thoughts to think of this toleration. . . . Their great growth and increase is too notorious, both in England and Ireland. Their principles strike both at ministry and magistracy. . . . Should not we be as jealous of God's honour as we are of our own? . . . Shall we suffer our Lord Jesus thus to be abused and trampled upon?" The Independent Major-General Boteler, already a persecutor of Friends, followed the Presbyterian Skippon. His ears tingled and his heart trembled to hear such blasphemies, which could not have been intended to be indulged under the notion of a toleration of tender consciences.

Next day Nayler was called to the Bar and questioned by the Speaker. He declared that "there was never anything since I was born so much against my will and mind as this thing, to be set up as a sign in my going into these towns, for I knew that I should lay down my life for it." "I was set up as a sign to summon this nation, and to convince them of Christ's coming. The fulness of Christ's coming is not yet, but He is come now."

After Nayler's withdrawal a vigorous debate began, which lasted on for nine days. Major-General Lambert, who was at this time Cromwell's right-hand man, had urged mild measures: he told the House that he knew

[1] For these debates see Burton's *Diary*, vol. i., and Firth. *Last Years of the Protectorate*, vol. i. chap. iii.

Nayler personally, who had served him as quartermaster, and "was a man of a very unblameable life and conversation, a member of a very sweet society of an Independent Church."[1] Sir Gilbert Pickering, the Lord Chamberlain, pointed out that Nayler did not claim to be Christ, but to be a "prophet, a type, a sign to warn men of the second coming of Christ." The rest of his company were far more guilty of blasphemy than Nayler himself. Lord President Lawrence, who represented Colchester, the scene of Parnell's death, and presided over the Council of State, showed a clear discernment. "I wonder," he said, referring to Nayler's statement that Christ was in him, "why any man should be so amazed at this. Is not God in every horse, in every stone, in every creature? Your Familists affirm that they are christed in Christ, and godded in God. . . . If you hang every man that says Christ is in you the hope of glory, you will hang a good many. . . . I do not believe that James Nayler thinks himself to be the only Christ, but that Christ is in him in the highest measure. This I confess is sad. But if from hence you go about to adjudge it or call it blasphemy, I am not satisfied." Another member of the Council, Walter Strickland, thought Nayler highly deluded, but yet not absolutely a blasphemer. Colonel Sydenham, a fourth councillor, said, "That which sticks most with me is the nearness of this opinion to that which is a glorious truth, that the Spirit is personally in us." "Consider," urged Colonel Holland, member for Lancashire, "the state of this nation, what the price of our blood is. Liberty of conscience, the Instrument gives it us. We remember how many Christians were formerly martyred under this notion of blasphemy, and who can define what it is? I am wholly against the question."

It is clear that some influential voices were raised against the action of Parliament, but the House was in

[1] This, as well as the whole tenor of Nayler's life, rebuts the random charges of immorality made against him in the report. Compare his own explicit denials, *e.g.*, *Works*, p. liv.; Burton's *Diary*, i. p. 46.

no mood to listen. Monck's brother-in-law, Thomas Clarges, cried, "Let us all stop our ears and stone him," and it was at length resolved without a division that Nayler was guilty of horrid blasphemy, and was a grand imposter and seducer of the people.

Debate upon the punishment followed. The Instrument of Government, published at the end of 1653, was invoked, but set aside as having no authority in such a case. It contained the following articles:

> XXXVII. That such as profess faith in God by Jesus Christ (though differing in judgment from the doctrine, worship, or discipline publicly held forth) shall not be restrained from, but shall be protected in, the profession of the faith and exercise of their religion; so as they abuse not this liberty to the civil injury of others and to the actual disturbance of the public peace on their parts: provided this liberty be not extended to Popery or Prelacy, nor to such as, under the profession of Christ, hold forth and practise licentiousness. XXXVIII. That all laws, statutes, and ordinances, and clauses in any law, statute, or ordinance to the contrary of the aforesaid liberty, shall be esteemed as null and void.

Skippon said that Quakers, Ranters, Levellers, Socinians, and all sorts bolstered themselves up under these clauses, but he had heard the Protector say it was never intended to indulge such things, and, if this were liberty, God deliver him from such liberty. George Downing remarked, "As to the Instrument of Government, I hope it shall never be made use of as an argument to let this wretch escape. I am as much for tender consciences as any man, but I deny that this has any share in such liberty." Major-General Goffe, who, we may remember, had proposed to lay Fox by the heels as he passed through Hampshire, declared that he would spend his blood for the Instrument of Government, "yet if it hold out anything to protect such persons, I would have it burnt in the fire."

Though the provisions of the Instrument were thus brushed aside, some difficult questions still remained. How was Nayler's blasphemy to be punished, and had Parliament any jurisdiction to punish? One member urged that by common law, blasphemy and heresy were punishable by death. Others appealed to the statute *de haeretico comburendo*, that is, to the proceedings under the writ of that name against Lollards. Thurloe, on the other hand, knew of no law in force against blasphemy except the Act of 1650. Whitelocke, in a written opinion, took the same view, and if they were correct, six months' imprisonment, or possibly banishment, was the limit of punishment.

The House desired some more rigorous sentence, and decided to take the law into its own hands. We should have expected it to cloak its arbitrary action in the form of law by drawing up a Bill of Attainder against Nayler, or at least by making a general law *ex post facto*, under which he could have been punished retrospectively. But though several of the more experienced members advocated one or other of these courses, neither found favour, because, under Clause XXIV. of the Instrument, all Bills had to be presented to the Lord Protector for his consent. Captain Baynes had already pointed out this difficulty: "We may bring him into a snare unless he heard the matter. His opinion may stick and demur as to the offence; for the Instrument of Government says, All shall be protected that profess faith in Jesus Christ, which I suppose this man does." The House accordingly fell back on a supposed judicial power, about which there was not a word in the Instrument. There was a great deal of bad constitutional law talked on the subject. It was argued that the House of Lords had undoubtedly possessed a judicial power, and as this body was for the time being extinct, its power had devolved on the House of Commons. Goffe went further, and asserted that the ecclesiastical jurisdiction in matters of blasphemy had since the abolition of bishops, also devolved on the Commons.

The punishment had now to be determined. The Old Testament penalty of death was hotly advocated, with much appeal to Leviticus and Deuteronomy, as though these formed part of the Statutes at large. Bampfield proved to his own satisfaction, and that of many of his fellow-members, "that it was the mind of God to punish this offence with death." The "merciful men," however, prevailed, and on 16th December the proposal that a Bill should be brought in to provide a death penalty for Nayler's offence was defeated by 96 votes to 82. Cromwell's second Parliament thus narrowly escaped the disgrace which would have attached to it and to Puritan England if its illegal and arbitrary action had resulted in Nayler's martyrdom.

The punishment actually inflicted was savage enough. When it was proposed to bore his tongue through, President Lawrence objected, but without effect, "You had better take his life: that tongue may afterwards praise the Lord." It was resolved on the 17th that on the following day Nayler should be set on the pillory, in the Palace Yard, Westminster, for two hours, and be whipped by the hangman through the streets to the Old Exchange, London. On Saturday the 20th he was to stand in the pillory at the Old Exchange from eleven to one, where his tongue was to be bored through with a hot iron, and his forehead to be branded with the letter B. Afterwards he was to be sent to Bristol, and carried through the city on horseback, bare-ridged, with his face backwards, and was to be whipped there on the market-day following his arrival. Lastly, he should be imprisoned in Bridewell, London, till released by Parliament, and was there to be kept in solitary confinement, at hard labour, without the use of pen, ink, and paper. When Nayler was brought in to hear his sentence, the Speaker in reading it told him that the House had mingled mercy with justice, as it desired his reformation rather than his destruction. "God," replied Nayler, "has given me a body: God will, I hope, give me a spirit to endure it. The Lord lay not these things to your charge."

The eighteenth was an extraordinarily cold day.[1] Nayler had at least one stanch defender, his fanatical friend, Robert Rich, "the mad merchant," who had

[1] See letter of W[m]. T[omlinson's], Dev. Ho., Box C, for these details.

besieged Parliament with petitions and letters. The House was too wearied with the unprofitable business to listen to his belated applications. On the eighteenth he was at the doors as usual, calling to the members and crying, "The Lord is coming to separate between the sheep and the goats, to gather up the wheat into garners, and to burn the chaff with fire that is not to be quenched." These words, we are told, passed with such a power, mixed some time with singing, that none resisted or gainsaid. He turned into Westminster Hall, singing very loudly, and stood over by the Court of Chancery, where the Commissioners of the Great Seal were sitting, and cried to them "that the land mourned because of oppression." He went on, with a great crowd following, into Palace Yard, and marched still singing round the pillory where Nayler was undergoing his punishment.

After standing in the pillory, Nayler was whipped at the cart-tail along the streets, through the biting air, naked to the waist, with only a white cap on his head. The whip had seven cords, full of knots, and one lash was given (a curious detail) at each of the 310 kennels on the way to the Old Exchange. He spoke no word, only before the whipping began he prayed the Lord to make him go through with it. The bailiffs that rode by the cart behaved brutally, their horses trampling on his feet and crushing him against the cart. His friend Rebecca Travers washed his wounds and reported:

> There was not the space of a man's nail free from stripes and blood from his shoulders near to his waist: his right arm [was] sorely striped, his hands much hurt with cords that they bled and were swelled: the blood and wounds of his back did very little appear at first sight by reason of abundance of dirt that covered them, till it was washed off.[1]

The second part of the punishment was to have taken place two days later. On the morning of the day four persons presented a petition, begging for the respite of a week, which was granted, and five ministers were sent to Newgate to try methods of persuasion. On the 23rd

[1] Sewel (1811 edn.), i. 239.

another petition, signed by eighty-seven persons, Friends and others, in and about London, was presented.[1] Joshua Sprigge,* once chaplain of the New Model, headed the deputation, and the petition, after saying that the respite had refreshed the hearts of thousands and made them see that something besides the terrors of Mount Sinai dwelt on the Parliament, prayed it to remit the remainder of the punishment and to leave Nayler "to the Lord and such gospel remedies as He hath sanctified." The House had only agreed to receive the petition by one vote, and quickly rejected it. "We are God's executioners, and ought to be tender of His honour," said George Downing.

The petitioners turned to the Protector, reciting the facts and requesting

> . . . that you will be pleased according to former declarations and the experience we have had of your Highness' care of this tender interest of liberty of conscience to weigh the consequence of these late proceedings, and according to the 37th Article of the said Instrument and one of the grounds you declare upon in your war with Spain, your Highness will stand up for the poor people of God in this day, in doing whereof your Highness will not do more right to your Petitioners than to yourself and these nations.

Cromwell had been watching the proceedings with growing disapproval, and now intervened by a strongly-worded letter which was read in Parliament on December 26th.

> We, being entrusted with the present government, on behalf of the people of these nations, and not knowing how far such proceeding, entered into wholly without us, may extend in the consequence of it, do desire that the House will let us know the grounds and reasons whereupon they have proceeded.

There is little doubt that the action of Parliament had been grossly irregular. It had no legislative power independently of Cromwell, and its assumed judicial power was usurped for the occasion. Major-General Lambert pointed out that the Protector had good ground for intervening since he was under oath to protect the people both

[1] For this petition and the one to the Protector, see *Extracts from State Papers*, First Series, pp. 21-23.

in freedom of conscience and in their persons and liberties, and was bound to inform himself when these were being encroached upon. Glyn advised a committee to consider precedents.

If we proceed in this manner, judicially, against any man as we please, we . . . take the sole power of judging men without law or against law. It is true such things have been done by Parliaments alone, but never without great regret. . . . It may be of very dangerous consequence to Englishmen to be governed by a court of will.

Colonel Rous, one of the Council, drove the situation home. "If you have done what you cannot justify, you must be whipped for whipping James Nayler." Sir Gilbert Pickering observed, "By this means by a vote of to-day you may pull out a man's eyes, to-morrow slit his nose, or cut off his hands, ears, or tongue."

The majority had certainly good grounds for uneasiness. But they were informed by several members that Cromwell had no wish to have the punishment respited. Whalley, the Protector's kinsman, assured the House that he was not against the sentence. Colonel Markham said that Cromwell abhorred Nayler's crime and did not desire a reprieve, adding, "For my part, if he did not abhor it, I would never serve him." The debate spread into two days, December 26th, 27th, and it was decided to adjourn consideration of the letter and not suspend the remainder of the sentence. The letter was debated again, but no conclusion was reached, and Cromwell, having made his protest, did not further assert his position.

Prof. Firth, in his *History of the Last Years of the Protectorate*,[1] discusses the grave constitutional issues raised by the proceedings of Parliament. The Protector regarded the authority of the House as based on and limited by the Instrument of Government. Parliament, however, seemed disposed to claim the unlimited sovereignty which the Long Parliament had exercised. This claim soon produced an unsettling effect on the army, which saw that the Instrument of Government failed to

[1] Vol. i. pp. 102-104.

limit the authority of Parliament in the interests of individual liberty. Cromwell, in February, recommended his House of Lords' proposal on these grounds. "By the proceedings of this Parliament," he said, "you see they stand in need of a check or balancing power, for the case of James Nayler might happen to be your case."

On Saturday, 27th December,[1] the second part of the punishment took place. Nayler stood in the raised pillory beside the Old Exchange from twelve to two, the three women, Martha Simmonds, Hannah Stranger, and Dorcas Erbury beside him, while his friend Rich was allowed, strangely enough, to step up and place over his head a paper with the inscription, "This is the King of the Jews," thus suggesting the resemblance which he found between Nayler's pitiful punishment and the most solemn tragedy of history.[2]

After standing in the pillory, Nayler's tongue was bored and his forehead branded. "He shrinked a little when the iron came upon his forehead," but behaved throughout with fortitude and patience, and, on being unbound, embraced his executioner. Rich sat bare at his feet, sometimes singing and crying, now kissing his hand, now sucking the fire from his forehead. In after years he said, "I am the dog that licked Lazarus's sores."[3] The people watched bareheaded, struck into silence by the pathos of the scene. Three weeks later, on 17th January 1657, the third act of the drama took place at Bristol.[4] Our authorities help us to follow the course of the procession through the city. Nayler, with his face backward, rode in at Lawford's Gate, and so down to High Street, and over the Bridge to Redcliff Gate. There he was made to alight, and was brought back by St. Thomas Street, being whipped from the middle of this street over the Bridge

[1] The letter of W[m]. T[omlinson] at Dev. Ho., Box C, says expressly, "last seventh-day 3rd 11th mo." (3rd Jany.), but other authorities date the punishment 27th Dec., including Burton, *Diary*, i. 265, who was himself an eye-witness of the proceedings.

[2] See the print attributed to Wenceslaus Hollar, 1607-1677, a prolific and talented engraver.

[3] Geo. Whitehead in Nayler's *Works*, xvii.

[4] Willan to Margt. Fell, Swarthm. Colln. i. 300; also letter in Devonshire House, Box C.

again to the middle of Broad Street, and so into the Taylor's hall. Afterwards he was taken to the city Newgate. The whipping on this occasion was only perfunctory, for a Quaker coppersmith named Jones[1] was allowed to hold back the executioner's hand, so that the strokes fell lightly. One Michael Stamper rode in front, singing most of the way. Several other Friends, men and women, accompanied Nayler, and Rich rode by his side bareheaded and singing, "Holy, holy, holy," as far as Redcliff Gate, where the officers interfered and brought him away. Nayler was now returned to London, and lay in the Old Bridewell awaiting the pleasure of Parliament. At first he was kept close, and was reported to be silent and sullen; but after a few days he asked for food, and was content to work. He was put into "the Hole," a cold, damp, unsavoury place, and was not allowed even a candle. His wife, on 24th February, petitioned[2] that he might have air, fire, and candlelight, and that she might be suffered to attend him and supply him with food suited to his weakened condition. The petition was in part granted and, in March, Hubberthorne could visit Nayler,[3] and found him "loving and much nearer the truth than he was." This was only about nine months from the beginning of his fall, and was quickly followed by a clear perception of the false position into which he had been led.

Before dealing with Nayler's repentance we must revert to the immediate consequences of his conduct on the Quaker movement. There were (1) the discouragement into which his fellow-members were brought; (2) the public scandal and odium caused by the proceedings; (3) the opportunity afforded to wild and turbulent spirits, many of them Ranters, to disturb meetings under cover of Nayler's name; and (4) the division caused among Friends. Contemporary accounts show the discouragement felt by Friends. Edmondson, for example, who

[1] The name is given in *The Quakers' Jesus*, by Wm. Grigge, p. 20.

[2] Barclay's *Inner Life*, p. 426 *n.*, prints the petition, but wrongly refers it to the Exeter imprisonment. It is now printed in *Extracts from State Papers*, First Series, p. 24.

[3] Hubberthorne to Fox, 20th March (1657), Swarthm. Colln. iv. 12.

had been convinced by Nayler, tells us in his journal of his distress—he was then in prison at Cavan—until the thought came to him, "Truth is truth, though all men forsake it."[1] The letters from Fox and others found upon Nayler, and the attitude taken up from the first by Bristol Friends, had cleared them from complicity in the actual offences charged; but the whole affair left on the minds of many men a deep impression of the dangerous tendencies of Quaker principles, which could not be so easily removed. Petitions against the Quakers came from Bristol and the West of England, and from Northumberland, Newcastle, Durham, and Chester, and the Nayler Committee was asked to report upon a Bill to suppress the mischief.[2]

According to the Cumberland member the Quakers met in multitudes and upon moors, to the terror of the people. He referred, no doubt, to the many Cumberland meetings which were kept out of doors, and perhaps specially to some meetings which Audland and Miles Halhead had just been holding on a hill near Ireby and at Pardshaw Crag, both attended by many hundreds of people.[3] A Devonshire member said: "They meet in thousands in our county, and certainly will overrun all, both ministers and magistrates." Other members, Luke Robinson of Thornton Risebrough, for example, objected to a law made specifically against Quakers. The petitions should be considered only in order to see how far the offences alleged involved disturbance of the peace. Parliament proceeded on these lines, and stiffened the law against vagrancy so as to include persons, whether actually begging or not, who were found wandering from their usual place of abode without a good cause that satisfied the magistrate before whom they were brought.[4] Under this law a persecuting justice clearly had the itinerating Quaker ministers at his mercy.

[1] *Journ.* 1715 edn. p. 33.
[2] See Nayler's *Works*, xii.
[3] Audland to Margt. Fell, 1st Nov. 1656, Wm. Caton Colln. (Dev. Ho., Jas. Bowden's copy).
[4] Act 1656, cap. 21, coming into operation 1st July 1657, Scobell's *Collection* pt. ii. p. 477.

The Nayler extravagances were followed by much disturbance of meetings, especially in London. The persons who formed his company, although the chief offenders, had escaped with nothing worse than a short imprisonment, and, excepting Samuel Cater, sank back into the obscurity from which they had emerged a few months earlier. We read in August 1657 that at Salisbury there was "some hurt by some of Martha Simmonds' company which came thereabout to dwell."[1] She died in 1665 on her way to Maryland.[2] Hannah Stranger became Hannah Salter, and in 1669, according to the Bristol records, condemned her conduct, "with all its stratagems, wiles, and practices."[3] In the following year she was in London petitioning the king on Margaret Fell's behalf.[4] Samuel Cater was a young man of Littleport, Cambs., born in 1627, who had been a Baptist Elder, but was convinced by James Parnell, and became one of the leading Friends in the Eastern Counties.[5] He seems to have played a very subordinate part at Bristol. Of Timothy Wedlock and Robert Crab* I know nothing further.

About this time the London meetings were greatly disturbed by those who followed Nayler*—"Ranters and loose persons" Fox calls them[6]—two of whom, known to us as Mildred and Judy, proved especially troublesome. In February 1657 Hubberthorne[7] says that Nayler's women followers sometimes appointed meetings in the most public places of the city, as in the Exchange and at the places where he suffered. He adds: "From the Exchange they [the authorities] sent some of them to prison at Bridewell: they are a great offence to the way of Truth here for the present, but the Truth will work through it

[1] John Braithwaite to Margt. Fell, Swarthm. Colln. iii. 129.

[2] Ellis Hookes to Margt. Fell, London, 7th Apl. 1665 (Swarthm. Colln. i. 45). Smith's *Catalogue of Friends' Books* gives the date 27th 7mo. 1665, which is perhaps an error for 1st mo., *i.e.* March.

[3] Bristol Books, C. 1842, C. 3, per A. Neave Brayshaw.

[4] Hannah Salter to Margt. Fell, 1670, Swarthm. Colln. i. 132. Cf. *Camb. Journ.* ii. 169, and note, ii. 424.

[5] There is a MS. Life of Samuel Cater, by Joseph J. Green, at Devonshire House. See also *Fenstanton Records* (Hanserd Knollys Society), p. 140, etc.

[6] See *Camb. Journ.* ii. 314.

[7] To Margt. Fell, *Letters of Early Friends*, p. 48 (Wm. Caton Colln.).*

all." In February 1658 he speaks of "an impudent lass that said she was above the apostles,"[1] who made it her practice to go to the meetings at the Bull and Mouth and Worcester House. In March,[2] Hubberthorne writes that Mildred tried to keep him from speaking, and at one meeting, which lasted from three to near midnight, she spoke till she was half distracted, her breath spent and her voice gone. The two meetings just named and one in the Strand were especially subject to disturbance by Mildred and Judy.[3] Whitehead says: "Persons of a loose ranting spirit got up, and frequently disturbed our Friends' meetings in London, by their ranting, singing, bawling, and reproaching us, crying out against divers of our faithful ministers and their testimonies in this manner, viz. 'you have lost the power, you have lost the power.'"[4] They cried against Fox and said a higher thing was come out, and in standing against it the Quakers were as bad as the priests[5] In Kent some ran out into "signs and lying wonders" with burning their Bibles and other "actings in the deceit"; but they were brought to own their condemnation.[6] At Cardiff, Fox found a separation among Friends.[7] An attempt had been made to stop the work of Thos. Holme. People came to the meeting and fell down on the floor, and when other ways failed they started singing, and some sat in the meeting in haircloth and ashes.[8] Robert Rich[9] went to Barbados, where he disturbed Friends' meetings with noisy singing. After some years he returned to London, and used to come to a meeting

[1] To Fox, 16th Feby. 1658, Swarthm. Colln. iv. 15.

[2] To Fox, Swarthm. Colln. iv. 12, printed in part in *Camb. Journ.* ii. 460. Fox wrote two characteristic denunciations of Mildred and Judy, which are preserved in the Swarthm. Colln. ii. 42. The one against Mildred concludes: "I say unto thee, pluck in thy horns, James, and [do] not push against the lambs, for the corner-stone is set upon your heads."

[3] Hubberthorne to Fox, 16th Mar. 1658 (year by internal evidence), Swarthm. Colln. iv. 13, printed in part in *Letters of Early Friends*, p. 49, and in part in note in *Camb. Journ.* ii. 460.

[4] Nayler's *Works*, xvi.

[5] See Fox to Nayler, Swarthm. Colln. i. 382.

[6] Hubberthorne to Fox, prior to Augt. 1657, Swarthm. Colln. iv. 14.

[7] *Journal*, i. 360.

[8] Holme to Margt. Fell, 16th Apl. 1657, Swarthm. Colln. i. 196.

[9] Geo. Whitehead in Nayler's *Works*, xvii.

and walk up and down in a stately manner, having a long white beard, and being dressed in a black velvet coat with a loose cloth one over it. When he heard anything that pleased him he would cry, "Amen, amen, amen." He was a man benevolently disposed towards all the sects, and died in 1679.[1] But while Nayler's fall prejudiced the work of Friends in the various ways which I have indicated, its most lasting result was good, for it effectually warned the Quaker leaders of the perils attending the over-emphasis which they had laid on the infallibility of the life possessed by the Spirit of Christ. Henceforth they walked more carefully, heedful of the special temptations which beset the path of spiritual enthusiasm.

William Dewsbury was the chief agent in reconciling Nayler to Friends. Both men had come under the influence of Fox at the same time, and a warm friendship united them. Dewsbury was in London in 1657, and laboured with some of those who had run out.[2] He wrote to Nayler urging him to judge the deceitful spirit that had caused the Truth to suffer,

> . . . then will the Lord give thee dominion over it, to reign in the life. . . . In the suffering with me many wait to hear thee raised up in the light and life, to judge down and reign over this spirit, that hath and doth seek to make disorder and strife amongst brethren. God Almighty in a pure understanding restore all them that have been veiled.

In reply Nayler says that the rents and divisions that have been caused are the great grief of his soul, beyond what can be spoken. Nothing in the world is dear to him but God's truth and His people who live in it, and if he could take up their sufferings he thinks he could submit even to death

But as for that exalted spirit that would break His people

---

[1] See Smith's *Catalogue*, ii. p. 482, where the titles of his various writings are given.

[2] See his letter to Nayler, cited in Smith's *Life of Dewsbury*, p. 146, which seems to fit in here. The full text of the letter and Nayler's reply are to be found in Swarthm. Colln. v. 50, 51. In the early part of his letter Dewsbury attributes Nayler's fall to his coming under the dominion of wilful spirits who abused the grace of God which they had tasted of, and in the deceits of their hearts wrought lying wonders.

and respect persons, I do utterly abhor [it] as the enemy of my Head and Life, whose presence in me hath filled me with love to Him and His people, manifold more than ever I knew before, or can be here expressed.

With this letter Nayler wrote a paper in which he deplored the spirit of disorder which had got head through what the Lord had done with him, and denied that spirit as not of the Lamb.[1] This paper is a strong plea for a peaceable spirit, but does not contain any direct condemnation by Nayler of his own proceedings. He was, however, as the letters printed with it show, in a tender frame of mind. Farnsworth, writing in September,[2] reports him as very loving, humble, tender, and low. A little later, in a paper delivered to the Parliament which had condemned him, and so earlier in date than its dissolution on 4th February 1658, he makes full acknowledgment of his fault, and says[3] that to ascribe the name, power, and virtue of Christ Jesus "to James Nayler (or to that which had a beginning and must return to dust), or for that to be exalted or worshipped, to me is great idolatry, and with the Spirit of Christ Jesus in me it is condemned, which Spirit leads to lowliness, meekness and longsuffering." Cromwell, in the summer of 1658, shortly before his own death, sent his private secretary, William Malyn, to see Nayler.[4] He reported him "under a resolved sullenness, and, I doubt not, in the height of pride," and could not draw him into conversation. Cromwell, it is clear, intended him kindness, and perhaps purposed his release, but Nayler could not disclose his soul to a visitor whose letter shows that he was hostile and unsympathetic to the prisoner.

During this summer Nayler was vainly hoping for a reconciliation with Fox. Parker wrote to Margaret

[1] This paper was issued before the end of July 1657. See Thos. Barcroft's letter to Margt. Fell, Swarthm. Colln. i. 173. A letter from Jno. Stubbs to Margt. Fell, dated 10th Augt., Swarthm. Colln. iii. 152, refers to the letters between Dewsbury and Nayler, and to a general letter to Friends, which is probably this paper. The copy in the Barcroft letter is superior to that printed in Nayler's *Works*, p. xxvii. In Nayler's *Works* the paper is preceded by three short letters, one from Dewsbury, probably written about the same time.

[2] *Letters of Early Friends*, p. 52. For concluding words see *Second Period of Quakerism*, p. 609, note 2.

[3] Nayler's *Works*, xxxv.

[4] Nickolls, *Letters and Papers of State addressed to Oliver Cromwell*, p. 143.

Fell urging her to intercede in the matter.[1] She also received a touching letter from Nayler,[2] in which he said:

Truly for the hardness and unreconcileableness which is in some I am astonished and shaken lest the spirit of Christ Jesus should be grieved and depart. For, if I know anything of it, or ever have done, that is it which naturall[y] inclines to mercy and forgiveness and not to bind one another under a trespass till the uttermost farthing, though this may be just and I do not condemn it. Yet I have felt a spirit which delights more in forgiving debts and seeks all occasion thereto, even where it is not sought to but seeks. And by this spirit I have been able to bear all things while it is with me, else had I not been at this day: so that I complain not as to myself in what I here write, God knows: but my fear is of provoking the justice of God without mercy, through not showing mercy one to another.

The reconciliation had not been effected a year later when Nayler was released by the Rump Parliament on 8th September 1659, after nearly three years' imprisonment.[3] Young Margaret Fell, writing to her mother on the 12th, a Monday,[4] says that Parliament gave his release to Francis Howgill and Edward Byllinge, a leading London Friend; it is pleasant to find Howgill associated in the matter. Nayler attended a meeting of Friends in London, but did not speak in it, and had gone on the Saturday to see Fox. Fox was at Reading, wrestling with his hour of darkness and discouragement, "under great sufferings and exercises, and in great travail of spirit about ten weeks."[5] Nayler wrote to Margaret Fell[6] that he had gone "in tenderness of love, . . . as soon as I was got out of prison,

[1] 15th June 1658, *Letters of Early Friends*, p. 57 (Wm. Caton. Colln.).

[2] Swarthm. Colln. iii. 84, undated.

[3] It is generally assumed that Nayler's imprisonment was continuous, but it is possible that after his paper of confession to Parliament he was allowed to visit his home in the North of England. There is in his *Works*, p. 734, a letter written after his recovery which says, "When I was in the North, it was in my heart to have seen you . . . but on a sudden was I brought back to this city and here I wait the will of our Father, to do or suffer." Geo. Whitehead (Nayler's *Works*, ix.) says that Nayler rehearsed to him his spiritual experiences "as we were walking together in the field at Great Strickland in Westmorland 1657, . . . and this was after he was revived and restored to a measure of good understanding and judgment." Whitehead was at Great Strickland in the winter of 1657-8, but not afterwards during Nayler's life.

[4] See Spence MSS. vol. iii. fol. 56.

[5] *Journ.* i. 444.

[6] *Letters of Early Friends*, p. 58.

hearing he was not well, but I was not permitted to come where he was." He exhibits a delightful spirit in the face of this rebuff. "Which [thing] my adversary rejoiced at, that thereby he might add sorrow to affliction, but my spirit was quieted, in that simplicity in which I went, in that to return; and [the Lord] gave me His peace therein, as though I had had my desire."

It was not till the end of the following January that the long-deferred reconciliation was brought about. Dewsbury had been under a great travail of soul.

> "In fulness of time, I was led of the Lord into London," he says,[1] "according to His will, to behold His appearance amongst His people. . . . Mighty was His majesty amongst His people in the day He healed up the breach which had been so long to the sadness of the hearts of many. The Lord clothed my dear brethren G[eo.] F[ox], E[dward] B[urrough], F[ras.] H[owgill], with a precious wisdom. A healing spirit did abound within them with the rest of the Lord's people there that day . . . and dear J[ames] N[ayler] the Lord was with him."

About this time Nayler went to Bristol,[2] and in a public meeting confessed his offence in a way which tendered and broke the meeting into tears, so that there were few dry eyes, and many were bowed in their minds and reconciled to him. The remaining months of his life were chiefly spent in London. He lived in "great self-denial and was very jealous of himself."[3] We hear of him in great service at William Woodcock's house in the Strand,[4] one of the regular Quaker meeting-places, whither many, "great in the outward," resorted to hear him, so that the place became so full that some who usually attended there had to be asked to meet elsewhere. In October he set out on foot for the North, intending to go home to his wife and children at Wakefield. He was

[1] Dewsbury to Margt. Fell, Swarthm. Colln. iv. 134, cited in Smith's *Life of Dewsbury*, p. 145. The letter has no date, but mentions first-day the 5th, 12mo. (February), and third-day the 7th, which fix it to 1660. The presence in London of Fox, Dewsbury, Howgill, and Burrough is confirmed by a letter in Spence MSS. vol. iii. fol. 51.

[2] Sewel (1811 edn.), i. 244 *n.*, from Jno. Whiting's account.

[3] Sewel, i. 269 *n.*, Jno. Whiting's account.

[4] Hubberthorne to Fox, 24th July 1660, *Letters of Early Friends*, p. 82 (Swarthm. Colln. iv. 19). Nayler sends his love to Fox.

seen by a Friend of Hertford,[1] sitting by the wayside in meditation, and passed on through Huntingdon, where another Friend saw him "in such an awful frame [of mind] as if he had been redeemed from the earth and a stranger on it, seeking a better country and inheritance." Some miles beyond Huntingdon he is said to have been robbed and bound, and was found towards evening in a field and taken to a Friend's house near King's Ripton. Thomas Parnell, a Quaker doctor who lived there, could do nothing for him, and he passed away in the peace of God towards the end of October 1660. He was buried on the 21st in Thomas Parnell's burying-ground at King's Ripton. His last words, spoken about two hours before his death, have been often quoted, and give perhaps the most beautiful expression in the language to the spirit that has passed beyond martyrdom into peace.[2]

> There is a spirit which I feel that delights to do no evil nor to revenge any wrong, but delights to endure all things, in hope to enjoy its own in the end. Its hope is to outlive all wrath and contention, and to weary out all exaltation and cruelty, or whatever is of a nature contrary to itself. It sees to the end of all temptations. As it bears no evil in itself, so it conceives none in thoughts to any other. If it be betrayed, it bears it, for its ground and spring is the mercies and forgiveness of God. Its crown is meekness, its life is everlasting love unfeigned; and takes its kingdom with entreaty and not with contention, and keeps it by lowliness of mind. In God alone it can rejoice, though none else regard it, or can own its life. It's conceived in sorrow, and brought forth without any to pity it, nor doth it murmur at grief and oppression. It never rejoiceth but through sufferings: for with the world's joy it is murdered. I found it alone, being forsaken. I have fellowship therein with them who lived in dens and desolate places in the earth, who through death obtained this resurrection and eternal holy life.

Nayler's time of clouded judgment lasted for less than one year out of the eight of his active work as a Friend. Yet this one year has been often suffered to eclipse the whole of his life. But when we rightly understand the atmosphere of thought in which he moved, we are less

[1] Sewel, 269 *n.*, Jno. Whiting's account.

[2] *Works*, p. 696. *

arrested by the fact that such a fall took place than by the meekness and Christ-like beauty of soul which came to him after this sore discipline. Not in that pitiful procession through the rain at Bristol, but in the spirit of forgiveness and uncomplaining acceptance of suffering which he afterwards showed, was he set before the Puritan England of his day as a sure sign that Christ was indeed come. Nayler's writings deserve more attention than they have received. In style and temper they are greatly superior to most early Quaker literature. One or two pieces, written after his spiritual recovery, are of great force and beauty. I allude in particular to "What the Possession of the Living Truth is,"[1] and "Milk for Babes and Meat for Strong Men,"[2] both of which were written in prison. They have the savour of an experience refined in the crucible of shame and suffering.

> Press into the heavenly spirit with its power to overcome the earthly spirit with its powers. Strive earnestly in the meek spirit to obtain a measure of faith and patience larger than the temptation and that will endure to the end of it, a meekness and love to cover all strife and wrath, a longsuffering to famish all haste and that which seeks its own ease. . . . And so in the cross come to put on Christ Jesus, . . . which is done by sinking down into the heavenly feeling, contrary to the will of the exalted life, whereby you will be overshadowed from above (from whence the Saviour is looked for), to overcome things below.[3]

Before we pass from the fall of James Nayler, it may be well to ask ourselves how far the extravagances of language and conduct which are part of the picture of early Quakerism throw doubt on the validity of the great experience of the Inner Light. We expect a certain exuberance and exaltation to accompany the first manifestations of such an experience, and the intense fervour, which showed itself in "tremblings" of body and in seizings by "the power," will, accordingly, present no serious difficulty to our minds. But we shall not approve some of the other accompaniments of the new experience—the disturbance of ministers, the virulence of controversy, the high

[1] *Works*, p. 425. [2] *Works*, p. 664. [3] *Works*, p. 676.

language in which the new way of life was often described, and some of the conduct connected with the testifying by signs. These things, it is true, were in part the natural outcome of a great sincerity, which could not tolerate shams and empty professions, and of a spiritual experience, fresh, new, and vital, which had become the supreme reality of life to thousands of seeking souls, and in so far we can justify them; but they were also in part a product of the faulty mental environment which belonged to the seventeenth century. We do not now regard the inspiration of prophet or saint as freeing him from the limitations of his own personality and of the age in which he lived: we rather think of the Divine illumination as allying itself with and to some extent coloured by the human personality through which it shines. But, in accordance with the sharp division made by the Puritan age between the undivine natural world, and the Divine world, Friends for the most part thought of the vitalizing experience which came to them as a power which controlled them not in partnership with their own faculties, but independently and infallibly. This explains much of their high language and extreme positiveness of conduct, and also justifies, from their point of view, the literalness with which they followed the prophetic precedents in the matter of Signs.

We may admit that the first Friends held a very imperfect doctrine of human nature. Even here, however, their faith that every man was given a measure of the Divine light of Christ gave them a point of view greatly superior to the current doctrine of man's depravity. But their imperfect conception of human nature is no valid ground for denying the reality of the spiritual experience which possessed them. This great experience is the commanding fact of Quaker history, and we need not be surprised to find that its adjustment to other facts of life was a work of time.

Friends made the true adjustment, from the first, in two most important directions, which at once marked them off from the Ranters and other ill-balanced mystical groups. They refused to admit that unrighteous or immoral conduct could proceed from the light, and, as we have seen, they tested, in doubtful cases, the reality of spiritual guidance by asking whether it pointed to action which crossed the carnal nature. Righteousness and self-sacrifice were their marks of heavenly-mindedness. Further they provided in their "retired" meetings times in which the soul could foster its larger spiritual life in fellowship and in waiting upon the Lord.

With the growth of Quakerism, and under the stress of painful but salutary experience, there was much abatement of the high language, and an increasing use of the corporate sense of the Quaker community as a check upon individual aberrations. This had serious dangers of its own, especially at periods when the corporate enlightenment of the Society of Friends was low, but there is undoubted value in group-guidance when it comes from disciples who are united together in open-hearted intercourse and common study and who are one in a loyal comradeship of worship and service.

We are able, in the present day, to work out a fuller conception of spiritual guidance than our forefathers possessed, especially through recognizing that the intellect is rather a province of man's spiritual nature than something which stands apart from it, and that our own faculties have their important part to play in developing the eye which can make use of the spiritual light. But in their resolute obedience to all the demands which the light made upon them and in their sure insight into truth the early Friends have never been surpassed, and, in spite of all crudities, abundantly justified their name of "Children of the Light."[1]

[1] For a fuller discussion of the whole subject see my *Spiritual Guidance in Quaker Experience* (1909).

CHAPTER XII

CONTROVERSY

The volume [of Fisher's collected works] contains nearly a thousand closely-printed pages, and the contents are clothed in a redundancy of language, lavish even for the long-winded seventeenth century. Laborious and sadly involved sentences, pages bristling with parentheses, and a woeful economy in full stops, make the long paragraphs "heavy travelling" for a twentieth-century reader. So much must be frankly confessed, and it is therefore evident that "wise oblivion" must play its part in any resuscitation of Fisher's writings. But, despite these defects of style, there is much to interest the student of theology in the old pages. Vigorous conviction pulses through the often uncouth phraseology, and little as modern taste may relish the acrimonious controversy of Fisher's time we can at least do justice to the sincerity which prompted its expression.—EMILY J. HART, Paper on Samuel Fisher in the *Young Friends' Review* (May 1906), p. 193.

WHEN Fox was released from Launceston in September 1656 he was moved of the Lord to travel through the country in order to answer the objections of envious Puritans against Friends.[1] Hitherto the ardent First Publishers of Truth had been most often the attacking force, but their success had roused their opponents into fierce hostility, while Nayler's extravagances were causing their central message to be looked upon with suspicion. Fox and his followers were called upon to justify their position, and their answers give us an insight into the religious outlook of Quakerism at a time when its new wine was still bursting the bottles of Calvinism.

Friends had attacked the ministers of the Puritan sects as false prophets and Antichrists. They had published a flood of controversial literature upon the subject. For example, Fox, in 1653, had issued his

[1] *Journ.* i. 335.

"Unmasking and Discovering of Antichrist," and in 1654 "The Vials of The Wrath of God Poured forth Upon the seat of the Man of Sin": Farnsworth in 1653 sent out "A Voice of the first Trumpet sounding an Alarme to call to Judgement," also "A Call out of False Worships," and "A Brief Discovery of the Kingdome of Antichrist, and the downfall of it hasteth greatly," whilst Margaret Fell in 1655 wrote "False Prophets, Antichrists, Deceivers . . . which hath been long hid and covered, but now is Unmasked, in these last dayes, with the Eternal Light which is risen."[1] The enormous title of Dewsbury's contribution in 1655 to this class of pamphlet sufficiently describes its scope. The major part runs as follows:[2]

A true prophecy of the mighty Day of the Lord, which is coming, and is appeared in the North of England, and is arising towards the South, and shall overspread this nation and all nations of the world, wherein the Lord is redeeming Sion forth of her long enthralled captivity in Babylon's kingdom, where she hath been scattered in the cloudy and dark day, into forms and observations, and there kept by the priests and teachers of the world, who ran when God never sent them. Now is the Lord appearing in this day of His mighty power, to gather His elect together, out of all forms and observations, kindreds, tongues, and nations; and is making up His jewels, His mighty host, and exalting Jesus Christ to be King of Kings, to lead His army He hath raised up in the North of England, and is marched towards the South in the mighty power of the living Word of God, which is sharp as a two-edged sword, to cut down high and low, rich and poor, priests and people, and all the powers of darkness in the land, and all the world over, that are fruitless trees that cumbers the ground, defiles the flesh, and walks in disobedience to the righteous law of God, the pure light in the conscience. . . . So shall this nation, and all the nations of the world, be conquered, and the victory witnessed, neither by sword nor spear, but by the Spirit of the Lord.

In the last chapter we saw how Nayler allowed himself to be made a sign of Christ's second coming and being revealed in His saints, and Anthony Pearson's comments on the trial served to show us that Nayler's extravagance

[1] I cite these titles, though with much necessary abridgment, from Joseph Smith's *Catalogue of Friends' Books*, 1867, an invaluable work of reference on all points of Quaker bibliography.

[2] *Works*, pp. 90-114.

came very near to the main stream of Quaker conviction at the time. Friends did regard themselves as the manifestation of Christ to the world after the long reign of apostasy—only that manifestation was made through all in whom the "Seed" reigned, and not through the one man, James Nayler. The Puritan ministers, smarting under the denunciations of the Quakers, had their retort ready. They, too, believed that the Day of the Lord was at hand. It was, indeed, an age of Messianic expectation. The Baptists and the Fifth Monarchy men had prophesied that in 1656 Christ would come and reign upon earth a thousand years.[1] John Reeve and Lodowick Muggleton had, as we have seen, founded a considerable sect by professing themselves the two last witnesses spoken of in Revelation xi., sent to seal the foreheads of the elect and the reprobate before the coming of Jesus. What more natural than to turn upon the Quakers and say that they were the false prophets and Antichrists that should come in the last days. Christopher Feake, the Fifth Monarchy leader, and others published in 1653, "A Faithful Discovery of a treacherous Design of Mystical Antichrist Displaying Christ's Banners"; Joshua Miller, in 1655, "Antichrist in Man, the Quakers' Idol"; James Brown, about 1656, "Antichrist in Spirit unmasked"; and Thomas Moore, Jr., the Manifestarian, in 1655, "An Antidote against the spreading Infections of the spirit of Antichrist." Fox, so far as Nayler's case was concerned, met the outcry by a letter to the Parliament,[2] in which he said in words which leave the main difficulty unresolved, "If the Seed speak, which is Christ, He hath no other name, for the Seed is Christ Jesus, and it is not blasphemy but truth; but, if the seed of the serpent speak and say he is Christ, that is the liar and the blasphemy." In his *Journal* he deals[3] with the general charge that the Quakers were Antichrists at some length by showing that it was

[1] Fox, *Journ.* i. 314. Morgan Lloyd held this view; see *A Hist. of the Older Nonconformity of Wrexham*, by A. N. Palmer, 1888, p. 17 *n.*

[2] Printed in the *Camb. Journ.* i. 266 with date 1st Nov. 1656, also in the Swarthm. Colln. ii. 23. Parts of the letter are similar in phrasing to an epistle to Friends (printed *Epistles* of Fox, No. 130), which may therefore be also dated in November.

[3] *Journ.* i. 336-338.

the men who set up false persecuting worships that compelled obedience and the blind deceivers who perverted the truth that had the marks of Antichrist. For sixteen hundred years, since the apostles' days, an apostasy had gone over all men; but he adds, "In the name and power of the Lord Jesus was I sent to preach the everlasting gospel, which Abraham saw, and was preached in the apostles' days, and was to go over all nations and to be preached to every creature." A great light had sprung up, which carried Friends in the everlasting gospel that was the power of God beyond the apostasy and over the false prophets and Antichrists.

All this, however natural to the religious atmosphere of Puritan England, is remote from the thought of the present day, which is not accustomed to discuss the spiritual outlook in apocalyptic terms. We read to-day, with an uncomprehending wonder, the portentous title of Fox's book, published in 1659, in which he made rejoinder to over a hundred pamphlets directed against Friends. He called it "The Great Mistery of the Great Whore Unfolded, and Antichrist's Kingdom Revealed unto Destruction: In Answer to many False Doctrines and Principles which Babylon's Merchants have traded with, etc." Appended to an admirable Epistle to the Reader, from the pen of Edward Burrough, are some verses, equally barren in metre and in ideas, which show the depths into which artificial modes of thought plunged the plain-spoken Quakers. Burrough says, for example:

The Antichrist, who hath put on, and covered with sheep's clothing,
And long ruled king on nations, inwardly ravening,
Who hath devoured God's heritage and had a kingdom great,
I have seen him made war against, and Truth give him defeat.

. . . .

And the woman that long hath fled into that place of mourning,
And rested in the wilderness, she is again returning,
And her seed is again springing, and shall replenish nations,
And the man-child must come to rule forever through generations,
And when this is all come to pass, oh, then, rejoice and sing,
Ye prophets and apostles all, and heavenly children.

I may be allowed at this point to give a summary account

of the controversial literature which served as ammunition to the opponents of Friends during the heated polemics of the Commonwealth period. Much of it was in the nature of a general attack on the Quaker position; another part consisted of replies to Quaker attacks; other pamphlets reported debates with Quakers; others again attacked particular tenets of Friends; others were full of scurrilous charges, based on the extravagances of a few individuals. A paper war, when once begun, sometimes continued till all the verbal ammunition was exhausted. For instance, Hubberthorne published the report of a public dispute with Thomas Danson, a well-known divine of the day: he replied with "The Quakers' Folly Made manifest to all men." George Whitehead, one of the disputants, retorted with "The Voice of Wisdom uttered forth against Antichrist's Folly and Deceit"; Danson took up the cudgels a second time with "The Quaker's Wisdom descendeth not from Above," and was answered by Luke Howard in "The Devil's Bow Unstringed," as well as by Samuel Fisher, the third of the disputants. One debate thus gave rise to six pamphlets, surely overmuch shedding of printers' ink.[1] Or, again, John Stalham, an Essex minister, begins with "Contradictions of the Quakers"; Farnsworth replies with "The Scriptures' Vindication"; and is answered in "The Reviler Rebuked." Hubberthorne continues with "The Rebukes of a Reviler fallen upon his own head," to which Stalham rejoins in "Marginall Antidotes"; and Fox has the last word in a reply to "Marginall Antidotes," to be found in *The Great Mistery.* He had also commented on Stalham's "Reviler Rebuked," so that we have here one controversial pamphlet growing into seven papers. In this sword-play of thrust and parry the titles chosen were often shrewd hits at the foe. "The Boasting Baptist dismounted and the Beast Disarmed" is answered by "The Quaker quasht and his Quarrel Quelled,"[2] "A Second Beacon Fired" by "The Fiery darts of the Divel quenched,"[3] and "Quaking Principles dashed in pieces" calls forth

[1] For this and other instances see Joseph Smith's *Bibliotheca Anti-Quakeriana*, 1873, an indispensable bibliography of anti-Quaker books.

[2] See under Jonathan Johnson. [3] See under Luke Fawne.

"The Walls of Ierico Razed down to the Ground" and "The Boaster bared and his Armour Put off."[1]

The virulence of these pamphlets, apparent even in their titles, is strange to our less earnest days. We read specimens of them, and find on both sides an intolerance of language that shocks us. Baxter says,[2] with some exaggeration:

> "There is scarce a scold heard among us in seven years' time that useth so many railing words to the basest that they quarrel with as these people," *i.e.* the Quakers, "will use familiarly in their religious exercises against the faithful servants of Christ. Nay, I have had more railing language from one of them in one letter than I ever heard from all the scolds in the country to my remembrance this twenty years. And no servant of Christ who hath learnt of Him to be meek and lowly can believe, if he be well in his wits, that this is the language of the Spirit of Christ."

It is unfortunately the case that the intense conviction and the faithfulness, which gave Friends the courage to publish their message through storms of persecution, were also expressed in unwarrantable interference with the religious practices of others and in harsh and uncharitable condemnation of their lives. The opposers of Friends were often equally unrestrained in their language, and in addition enforced their words with the iron mace of an intolerant law. Some of them poisoned the wells of controversy with the lies of personal slander. The verbal violence of Friends was singularly free both from the spirit of persecution and from the filth of private scandal. Its excesses sprang not from bigotry or malice, but from the honest-hearted conviction of half-educated men who were the champions of a great truth.

We deplore the virulence of these early polemics, yet we should do well to recognize that this insobriety of speech was incidental to an age when religious passion was convulsing Europe. A man's faith mattered to him in those days in a more vital way than seems to be the case now. Puritan earnestness, even with its rough,

[1] See under Enoch Howet.

[2] Baxter's *One Sheet against the Quakers*, 1657, p. 4.

intolerant speech, need not fear comparison with the easy indifference of our Laodicaean age. Dr. Hort[1] says wisely:

Smooth ways of thought are like smooth ways of action: truth is never reached or held fast without friction and grappling.

Moreover, as already pointed out, virulent controversy was the mark of an age which was entering into the enjoyment of religious liberty. It was a great advance for polemic, however violent, to replace persecution.[2]

We have had occasion to refer to several of the chief pieces of controversial literature. On the Puritan side were many redoubtable champions—Baxter and Bunyan, Dr. Owen and Prynne; leading divines such as Samuel Clarke, a member of the Savoy Conference, 1661; Samuel Eaton of Stockport; Samuel Hammond, chaplain to Sir Arthur Hesilrige; Thomas Jacombe, a Trier, or official examiner of ministers; Matthew Poole, the Biblical Commentator, and Richard Sherlock, afterwards Rector of Winwick; also leaders of the Baptists, such as the General Baptists Matthew Caffyn, John Griffith, and Jeremiah Ives, and the chief persons among the Manifestarians, Muggletonians, and Fifth Monarchy men. On the other side we find most of the Quaker leaders engaged, especially Burrough, Farnsworth, Samuel Fisher, Fox, Howgill, Hubberthorne, Nayler, and George Whitehead. Burrough, that "Son of thunder and consolation,"[3] as he is called on the title-page of his collected *Works*, held, I think, the first place in the estimation of his friends. Howgill says of him:[4]

How great an alarum didst thou give in thy day, that made the host of the uncircumcised greatly distressed! What man so valiant, though as Goliah of Gath, would not thy valour have encountered with, while many despised thy youth! And how have I seen thee with thy sling and thy stone—despised weapons as to war with—wound the mighty, and that which seemed

---

[1] *The Way, the Truth, the Life*, p. 171.
[2] *Ante*, p. 17.
[3] In the title of *A Trumpet of the Lord sounded out of Sion*, 1656, he styles himself "A Son of Thunder."
[4] Burrough's *Works* (c2).

contemptible to the Dragon's party, even as the jawbone of an ass, with it thou hast slain the Philistines heaps upon heaps, as Samson.

No one now reads the 900 small folio pages of Burrough's *Works*, and they are no doubt greatly inferior, both in learning and in literary finish, to the writings of Penn and Barclay and Penington, which belong to the next period of Quakerism. Burrough, as his friend Howgill admits,[1] was a young man of no great learning, but he had indomitable courage and a natural eloquence which reached the understandings and consciences of those with whom he conversed. His controversial powers may be illustrated from his discussion in 1656 and 1657 with John Bunyan,* then a man of twenty-eight, who had come under religious conviction a few years previously, and was at the time a deacon and a preacher in the Baptist Society at Bedford. The first book published by the immortal writer of *Pilgrim's Progress* was directed against the Quakers. It was called "Some Gospel Truths opened, according to the Scriptures . . . and also Answers to several Questions, with profitable Directions to stand fast in the Doctrine of Jesus, the Son of Mary, against those blustering Storms of the Devil's Temptations which do at this Day, like so many Scorpions, break loose from the Bottomless Pit, to bite and torment those that have not tasted the Vertue of Jesus by the Revelation of the Spirit of God."[2]

Bunyan laid down that every man as he came into the world received a light from Christ, which made manifest sins against the law, but it did not therefore follow that this conscience or light was the Spirit of Christ or the work of grace wrought in the heart. By turning the mind within to the light which convinces of sin, and closing with something within, the poor soul might be carried headlong to Hell, for the devil might thus be counterfeiting the work of grace. The light convinced of sin, but only of sin against the law: it did not show the soul a Saviour or Deliverer.

[1] Burrough's *Works*, p. before (f). [2] Smith's *Bibliotheca Anti-Quakeriana.*

Burrough makes short work of this attempted distinction:

Thy confusion is seen at large, who wouldst seem to divide between the Light of Christ, which thou confessest is given to every man, and the Spirit of Christ and the grace of God. However thus far I say, the Light of Christ given to every man is not contrary to the Spirit of Christ nor to the grace of God, but one in their nature, and a man cannot possibly love one of them and hate another; neither can any obey one of these and disobey the other, therefore are they one in the union, leading in the same way unto the same end. And where doth the Spirit of Christ give light or the grace of God work or lead, if not in the conscience? And can there be any surer thing for the creature to look to, to walk to life, or to come to God by, than the Light of Christ in the conscience, which thou confessest every man hath that cometh into the world?[1]

Bunyan proceeded to publish "A Vindication" of his book, in which he adopted the common charge against the Quakers that they did not own the historical Christ, and enforced the contention in his first pamphlet that they made no difference between the light with which Christ as God had enlightened all, and the Spirit of Christ which was only given to some. Bunyan asserted that the light from God, which all possessed, was the soul of man, which had a faculty of its own called conscience. After replying at length to these points, Burrough concludes his elaborate answer with a sentence which is a fair specimen of his impassioned, rhetorical style:

Alas, alas for thee, John Bunion, thy several months' travail in grief and pain is a fruitless birth, and perishes as an untimely fig, and its praise is blotted out among men, and it's passed away as smoke: Truth is atop of thee and outreaches thee, and thy formed weapons cannot prosper, and it shall stand forever to confound thee and all its enemies: and though thou wilt not subject thy mind to serve it willingly, yet a slave to it thou must be: and what thou dost in thy wickedness against it, the end thereof brings forth the glory of it, and thy own confounding and shame: and now be wise and learned and put off thy armour, for thou mayst understand the more thou strives the

---

[1] *Works*, p. 144.

more thou art entangled, and the higher thou arises in envy the deeper is thy fall into confusion, and the more thy arguments are the more increased is thy folly;—let experience teach thee, and thy own wickedness correct thee, and thus I leave thee; and if thou wilt not own the Light of Christ in thy own con science, now to reprove thee and convince thee, yet in the Day of Judgment thou shalt own it, and it shall witness the justness of the judgments of the Lord, when for thy iniquities He pleads with thee, and behold, as a thief in the night, when thou art not aware, He will come, and then, woe unto thee that art polluted.[1]

Nayler deserves a place before Burrough if the quality of his work is to be the test. His controversial pieces are not easily accessible, as the Collection of his writings which was at last published by Friends in 1716 omitted most of these, about eighty-six sheets, or I suppose an equivalent of 1000 octavo pages. Those that I have seen are full of good sense, and, for the age, are singularly free from violent language.

Samuel Fisher, with his University education and his varied experience as a Puritan lecturer, and afterwards as a Baptist preacher, was a formidable and learned controversialist. He had heard Caton and Stubbs in Kent in 1655, and his heart responded to their message and to the witness of their innocent lives.[2] His book, "*Rusticus ad Academicos*. . . . The Rustick's Alarm to the Rabbies, Or The Country Correcting the University and Clergy, etc.," was published in 1660, after the Restoration, and is the most important piece of Quaker controversy belonging to the Commonwealth period. It was directed against four eminent Puritan divines: Dr. John Owen, a man of rare force of character, high in Cromwell's confidence; Thomas Danson, minister at Sandwich, Kent; John Tombes, the Baptist divine of Leominster; and the great Richard Baxter. In Fisher's collected *Works*, published in 1679, the treatise occupies 750 pages. William Penn, in a "testimony" to Fisher, thus describes his prowess in this kind of literature:

[1] *Works*, p. 309.

[2] For Saml. Fisher see two carefully written papers by Emily J. Hart, of Scalby, in *The Young Friends' Review*, Feby. and May 1906. I have made use of these and of Fisher's collected *Works*, 1679.

It was so ordered by God's providence that his part fell to be mostly controversial; in which to carry a clear mind and an even hand is very difficult. However, allowing him in some passages the freedom of the prophet Elijah against the prophets of Baal, sometimes exposing absurd things by vulgar terms and proverbs to derision in the view of his ingenuous readers, yet all that kind of rhetoric and learning he had so low an esteem of it, that he often counted it not worthy to be compared to the least degree of Divine wisdom and experience of Christ Jesus. . . In all his controversies he has acquitted himself with that manifest advantage against his adversaries upon the points debated, that, if I were not of the same mind myself, I must offer violence to my understanding if I did not ingenuously resign to the force and evidence of his arguments. . . . In perusing his *Rusticus ad Academicos*, I found the objections of several considerable opposers so closely handled, and so plainly enervated,[1] that my heart was not more affected than my understanding was clearly satisfied of the truth and reasonableness of those principles he defended.

To summarize Fisher's prodigious and diffuse pamphlet is no easy task. Owen had written two English treatises and a Latin tractate on the authority of scripture, Danson "two trifling tractates," Tombes nine sermons "thrust into one treatise," and Baxter had commended this treatise to the public.

The strength of Fisher's argument is directed to showing that the Light of Christ in the conscience and not the external text or letter of scripture is the only firm foundation of the Church's faith, the only true touchstone of all doctrines, the only right rule of all saving belief and holy life, the infallible Spirit's infallible guidance of all that follow Him as their guide. In the Preface to the Reader occurs a passage which, as ruthlessly pruned, gives us a clear view of Fisher's attitude.

And because we do not with the misty ministers of the mere letter own the bare external text of scripture entire in every tittle, but say it hath suffered much loss of more than vowels, single letters, and single lines also, yea, even of whole epistles and prophecies of inspired men, the copies of which are not by the clergy canonized nor by the Bible-sellers bound up, and specially because we own not the said alterable and much altered

[1] Used in the sense, now obsolete, of "destroying the force of arguments."

outward text, but the holy truth and inward light and spirit to be the Word of God, which is living [and] the true touchstone, therefore they cry out against us. Yet the scriptures are owned by us in their due place, and the letter is acknowledged by us full as much as it is by itself, to have been written by men moved of God's Spirit, and to be useful, profitable, serviceable, etc., to be read and heeded.

Owen asserted the sole authority of scripture and its complete integrity, but without defining what he meant by scripture, and Fisher wants to know if he is talking of the original autographs, or of the transcribed copies or of the translations.[1] He puts awkward questions about the canon,—Was it God or was it man that set such distinct bounds to the scripture as to say such a set number of books (excluding the Apocrypha) shall be owned and the rest be rejected?[2]

Who was it that said to the Spirit of God, O Spirit, blow no more, inspire no more men, make no more prophets from Ezra's days and downward till Christ, and from John's days downward forever? But cease, be silent, and subject thyself as well as all evil spirits to be tried by the standard that's made up of some of the writings of some of those men thou hast moved to write already; and let such and such of them as are bound up in the Bibles now used in England be the only means of measuring all truth forever.[3]

He asks whether the Apocryphal books are fit for nothing but to be cashiered; if some of them be but human, yet is there nothing of as self-evidencing efficacy as some of those they own? Who first set the one upon the Bench and the other at the Bar?[4] He commends certain books of the Apocrypha, especially 2 Esdras, dear to the apocalyptic temper of the Commonwealth age, Jeremiah's Epistle, Ecclesiasticus and The Wisdom of Solomon, saying, "Sure I am that book of Wisdom was inspired into the penman that expired it out, from no less than that wisdom which is from above."[5] He inquires after lost books such as the Book of Jasher,[6] and further letters of Paul. He suggests that Clement's

[1] *Works*, p. 194. [2] *Ibid.* p. 269. [3] *Ibid.* p. 270.
[4] *Ibid.* p. 270. [5] *Ibid.* p. 273. [6] *Ibid.* p. 275.

Epistle and that "sweet, short, precious reply" of Jesus to Abgar, king of Edessa, deserve room in the canon as much as Paul's personal letter to Philemon.[1]

Somewhat fuller treatment is given to the Epistle of Paul to Laodicaea, the existence of which Danson, during the public dispute at Sandwich in April 1659, at first denied, until a man stood up and said he had the book.[2] Fisher evidently accepts both it and the letter to Abgar as perfectly genuine.

He next deals with the question of the Hebrew vowel-points, and "traces after John Owen in his treatings and twinings to and fro, in vindication of the integrity of his Greek and Hebrew texts" (p. 395) for more than a hundred pages, making merry over all his far-fetched positions and enjoying himself greatly. He touches at last, according to the uncertain lights of the age, upon problems of higher criticism,[3]

> . . . what thinkest thou of the history of John Mark, which some have in that respect styled *sacrum furtum*, a kind of holy

---

[1] *Works*, p. 277.

[2] Pp. 282-286. Fisher says, The Epistle "speaks out itself and its author whose it is, as well by the style and majesty of it as by the superscription, being both translated and printed in English, as it was found, though not in your Testaments, yet in the oldest Bible that was printed at Worms. And also in a certain ancient MS. of the New Testament text which I have seen and can produce, written in Old English three hundred and forty years since, or above, before the art of printing came up here, by which it's evident that it was owned as canonical in the Church of England in those days, and was, however it came to be since left out, bound up amongst its fellows." The Epistle is now universally recognized to be apocryphal, and is in Lightfoot's words, "a cento of Pauline phrases strung together without any definite connection or clear object." For the Epistle and a full discussion upon it, see Lightfoot's *Colossians and Philemon*, pp. 347-366. The interest of Fisher's reference lies in the fact that the curious tract, "Something concerning Agbarus, etc." (an anonymous and undated tract), also gives the Epistle to the Laodicaeans with the same statement that it was found in the oldest Bible that was published at Worms. Fisher also refers, a few pages later, to the insertion after Luke vi. 4, of the saying of Christ to the man working on the Sabbath (for which the Codex Bezae, D, is the sole authority), again agreeing with the tract, which gives the verse as being, according to "the margent" of a Hollybush Latin-English Testament, 1538, "in one of the Greek copies." Fisher in this dispute repeated it in English "out of the Greek," adding, "in which Greek tongue I have also read it" (p. 286). It seems likely that Fisher himself was the author of this tract. It would be interesting to recover the Hollybush Latin-English Testament, in which he had seen the reading of D. Presumably it was a MS. insertion taken from the Stephen Greek Testament of 1550 or the Beza of 1598. The Hollybush Testament had the name of "John Hollybushe" on the title-page, but was based on the translation of Miles Coverdale.*

[3] *Works*, p. 415, etc.

theft, is it not possible but that it might be some abbreviation of Matthew's story concerning Christ, there being little in it but what is well-nigh word for word in the other?

Modern study of the synoptic problem has exactly reversed this long-prevalent idea, but we could hardly better the further comments of Fisher.

Whether it were Mark writing out of Matthew, or from Peter's mouth, or of himself, as it seemed good to him to set down, it was but a history of such things as he was well acquainted with, either as an eye- or ear-witness thereof, or as one that had it sufficiently attested to for him to undertake to write it out as truth, and so not without an active concurrence of his rational faculties in the reception of what he wrote, as well as not without a moving thereto by the Holy Spirit in which he lived, and in the light of which he saw it might be serviceable.

He enforces this point, as we should do to-day, by reference to Luke's preface, which shows that he wrote,

. . . not upon the account of a mere passive immediate reception thereof from God, . . . but rather at second-hand, as they were heard and believed and understood by him as true matters of fact from such as were eye-witnesses, not without a concurrence of his rational faculties in receiving what he wrote.

Then he asks about duplicate narratives, where one account is transcribed out of the other, but with additions or alterations or ablations.[1] He further tests Owen's theory of supernatural dictation by inquiring how it held with respect to books written by the hand of scribes, as in parts of Jeremiah and in many of Paul's epistles.[2]

A few pages later, Fisher's own enlightened theory of inspiration emerges. Again I must retrench the exuberance of his sentences.

God, who is the Giver of every good gift, using every instrument according to what He hath fitted it for, a beast as a beast, a man as a man, a saint as a saint, a prophet as a prophet, holds the hand of the scribe, so that he would else draw but misshapen characters, and guides, assists and acts in and by him, yet He lets the action bear its denomination from its next and immediate agent, which is not God Himself but men. At the first it was no

[1] *Works*, p. 416. [2] *Ibid.* p. 417.

more immediately from God than the writings of His moved and inspired prophets are at this day, which is as that was but the spiritual man's testimony for God, though specially assisted by Him in it.[1]

Fisher, it will be noticed, shows a much greater sense of the co-operation of the human and the Divine than was felt by his age or by Friends generally. He seems, however, like other Friends of his time, to have undervalued human learning, although himself possessing no small measure of it, and the book contains an extraordinary sentence of 574 words, many of them almost unique, about the verbal quarrels of divines, "twattling away their time to learn in about the gaudy outsides of their horn-books and primers, and brawling about the backside of their Bibles," a sentence which brings in during its spacious course references to various lections, targums, alcorans, Mishnas, Polyglots, and fifty other persons and things.[2]

Fisher followed the bad habit of his contemporaries by closing his book with some doggerel rhymes. It was apparently felt that verse was the final means of discomfiting your literary foes. The forgers of these dangerous weapons little dreamed that their chief use would be to injure and perhaps destroy their own literary fame. Fortunately, in the case of Fisher, in spite of poor verses, rude wit and immense prolixity, his vivacity, learning, shrewdness, and in some points singular breadth of view may well rescue his great work from total oblivion.

Of this book George Whitehead says, "I never heard of any answer or reply made or attempted,"[3] though it should be remembered that after the Restoration the Puritan divines who were attacked had more urgent matters to attend to than polemics with Quakers. The wrong translations pointed out in Fisher's treatise set Anthony Purver (1702-1777), the Quaker Bible-translator, upon his study of Hebrew.[4]

[1] *Works*, p. 424.
[2] *Ibid.* p. 437.
[3] *Christian Progress* (1725 edn.), p. 149.
[4] Smith's *Catalogue of Friends' Books*, i. 615. For Purver, whose translation was published in 1764, see *Dict. Natl. Biography*.

The *Rusticus ad Academicos* shows the prodigious lengths to which the war between the Quakers and University learning was carried. The dogmatism of the theological expert held England in spiritual bondage. "The Rabbi, armed *cap-à-pie* with texts of proof, held the pulpit against all comers."[1] There was no ground for mutual understanding between him and the Quaker. To the Puritan divines the "Children of the Light" seemed "poor, deluded, fanatical, silly souls,"[2] "uncatechized ignorance set off with great confidence," "unlearned and unstable men of low parts and small capacities,"[3] and were looked down upon in the spirit in which the philosophers of Athens looked down upon the babbler Paul, or the Pharisees upon the accursed people who knew not the law. Friends, on the other hand, fell into the opposite error, and laid exclusive stress on the Light within, till they despised human learning, seeing no good in hireling priests who spoke a divination from their own brain, using their knowledge of tongues and stealing the words from their neighbours.[4]

When Cromwell, in 1657, signed a writ for founding a University at Durham—a project afterwards abandoned on account of petitions from Oxford and Cambridge—Fox met the Protector's emissary, and "let him see that was not the way to make them Christ's ministers, by Hebrew, Greek, and Latin and the seven arts, which all was but the teachings of the natural man . . . for Peter and John that could not read letters preached the Word, Christ Jesus, which was in the beginning before Babel was."[5]

The rancorous feeling showed itself in extraordinary fashion both at Oxford and Cambridge. We have already noted the rude treatment meted out in 1654 to the first Quaker Publishers at Oxford, and in 1655 at Cambridge to Fox.[6] We may now complete the story, so far as the Commonwealth period is concerned.

It was as early as December 1653 that Mary Fisher

[1] J. Wilhelm Rowntree, *Essays and Addresses*, p. 5.
[2] John Owen, Fisher's *Works*, p. 205.
[3] Dr. John Gauden, Fisher's *Works*, p. 51, etc., at end of book.
[4] Fox, *Epistles*, No. 42.
[5] *Camb. Journ.* i. 311, 312, and *J.F.H.S.* iv. 128.
[6] *Ante*, pp. 158, 201.

and Elizabeth Williams, after reproving some Cambridge students at Sidney-Sussex college gate, had been stripped naked to the waist and brutally flogged at the Market-Cross, their bodies being slashed and torn exceedingly.[1] In the autumn of 1654, Hubberthorne and Parnell were imprisoned there for a time, and Ann Blaykling, sister to John Blaykling of Draw-well, near Sedbergh, was in prison for several months for disturbing a minister.[2] While there she was visited by Margaret Killam, wife of John Killam of Balby, who in letters to her husband and George Fox gives a vivid account of the behaviour of the students and townspeople.[3]

Upon the seventh-day I was moved to go into the market, and stand upon the cross and speak there, and so passed through the streets, and was moved to go through the colleges, and it were betwixt the eleventh and twelfth hour, and they was at meat at many of the colleges, and the dread and terrible voice of the Lord passed through me, and they rose up and followed us and thrust us out, and so we passed from one to another through the most of them, but they were not suffered to hurt us: but the rude multitude did throw dirt in our faces, and our clothes were almost covered over, but we did receive little harm for the blows and the stones which they flung, the pain was presently taken away.

For several years there were frequent imprisonments of Quakers, and the meetings kept by Friends in their meeting-room in Jesus Lane, over against Sidney-Sussex college, were often turbulent times. In 1658 and 1659 the scholars used to throw stones at the windows and shoot bullets in. William Allen frequently preached, and "they would run through the meeting-house like wild horses, throwing down all before them, halloing, stamping, and making a noise, as if several drums had been beating, to prevent his being heard."[4] In April and May

[1] See Besse, *Sufferings*, i. 84, and the extract from a letter dated 29th Dec. 1653, printed at the end of Nayler's *Churches Gathered against Christ* (1654).

[2] Hubberthorne to Burrough, 27th Sept. 1654, in Swarthm. Colln. iv. 5.

[3] See letter to her husband in Dev. Ho., Saml. Watson Colln. p. 130, and letter to Fox in Swarthm. Colln. i. 2, from which latter the extract is taken.

[4] Besse, *Sufferings*, i. 87. See also Geo. Whitehead's letter to Fox, Chesterton, 11th July 1659, printed in *Letters of Early Friends*, p. 229 (Swarthm. Colln. v. 92).

1660, just at the time of the Restoration, there were riotous scenes, especially on three successive Sundays in May. On the third Sunday they broke the doors and windows and beat Friends with the pieces of board, doing great damage and hurt, and followed Friends to the town's end, beating and stoning them.[1] A letter written on the following day by Alderman James Blackley to London Friends, addressed to Gerrard Roberts, deserves reproduction as an absolutely contemporary piece of graphic history.

CAMBRIDGE, *28th 3mo* 1660.

DEAR FRIEND—My love reacheth unto thee and to all Friends, desiring that prayers be made for us in the Church of Christ, that our faith may be firm and that we may be steadfast and immovable, grounded upon the Rock of Ages, in these shaking times, especially now when the Dragon sends forth his floods of persecution that are ever ready to overwhelm us, if the mighty power of God did not sustain us.

For yesterday, in our meeting-house when we had been together two hours, the soldiers came and set upon us with swords and their staves, and brake in upon us and gat smiths' hammers and brake the windows and doors in pieces, and with shivered boards and window-bars fell upon us and beat and wounded many Friends, that few or none did escape without a wound, and haled every one out, and would not suffer one to stay within the house; only I stayed there to see what they would do. And when the house was emptied of Friends they brake down all the glass windows, the stairs, the forms, benches, chairs, etc., whatever could be broken in the house. The soldiers and scholars began and the rude people in the town made an end. Wm. Allen was much beaten and bruised. This is all for the present from thy friend,

JAS. BLACKLEY.[2]

At a General Meeting on the first Monday in July the abuses reached their height.[3] A mob gathered about the meeting-house, some being the worse for drink, and after hustling Friends as they went into meeting, fell upon them as they were waiting on the Lord,

. . striking at those they could reach, flinging at others, and making an hideous noise, with scoffing, laughing, railing, shouting,

---

[1] *F.P.T.* 13-15.

[2] Dev. Ho Portfolio 1, No. 48.

[3] Besse, *Sufferings*, i. 87.

knocking, drumming upon the boards, and sometimes throwing wildfire and gunpowder into the meeting to drown the sound of that which was spoken to us in the name of the Lord, and continually exercising themselves in one act of mischief or other to make a disturbance and weary us out of the place: and when they saw they could not do it by all those means, they brake and battered down the doors and walls next the street with bolt-hammers and other engines, and . . . called us rebels . . . and used us as if our lives were all at their mercies . . . so that very many of us were sorely hurt and bruised, twenty-two had their blood shed, one so lamed that he was left behind unable to walk abroad, and a woman almost killed by their cruel usage . . . and [they] quite battered down the walls and bays on each side of the meeting-house.

The sister University has an equally shameful record. Anthony Wood says that in the autumn of 1654 Oxford was pestered with the northern Quakers, who were meeting constantly in the lane called the Seven Deadly Sins (now New Inn Hall Street) in an old stone house almost opposite the common gate of New Inn, in which house lived Richard Bettris, surgeon and Quaker. The old stone house is Frewen Hall, where Edward VII. had his residence while at the University.[1] Here the rude Oxford scholars made sport of unresisting Quakers whenever the spirit of persecution was abroad. The following belongs to the year 1658,[2] and is too precise in vile detail to be reproduced in full.

Our usual manner hath been to meet together to wait upon and worship God in spirit and in truth at Richard Bettris' house on first-days of the week about the ninth hour in the mornings and on fifth-days of the week about four in the afternoon, at which times 'twas the constant practice of the scholars there to meet us and act their wickedness and abuses toward us, as pulling of Friends' hair off their heads, and beards by the roots, plaiting their hair into knots, pluck off Friends' hats and throw them at others and then beat them on the heads. They took

---

[1] Chas. E. Gillett brings these facts out in articles in *Oxford Review*, June 11, 12, 1902; copies at Dev. Ho.*

[2] See "The True Relation, etc.," by Lawrence Willyer and others, undated but referred to in 1660 in Fisher's *Works*, p. 261 (extracts in Besse, *Sufferings*, i. 565). Also MS. account of Oxford Sufferings, 1654-1683 (Dev. Ho. Portfolio 5), from which above passage is taken.

one Friend by the neckcloth and held him up from the ground until they had near choked him, and stopped another Friend's mouth ready to strangle him. . . . [They] pull Friends up and down the meeting-room and some out of doors, . . . bring in nettles and thrust them in Friends' faces, throw down forms with Friends on them, bind some with cords and draw them up and down the meeting-room abusing them, tear Friends' clothes, shoot bullets in Friends' faces . . . with a pair of scissors cut one side of a Friend's beard off and left the other remaining, . . . thrust pins in their flesh, ride on Friends' backs. . . . They have brought hogs into our meeting and pulled them about the room to make a noise, and likewise madmen. One Mack of Trinity College brought into our meeting a pistol and cocked it and sware he would shoot Friends . . . they have come into our meetings, whooping and halloing, houghing, scoffing, swearing and cursing and . . . calling for . . . beer and tobacco, calling Friends rogues and whores, dogs, bitches and toads . . . making a noise like cats and dogs, throw squibs into our meeting, squeeze and abuse Friends going in and coming out, break the porch of the door and break the windows of the house.

These barbarities make extraordinary reading, and we can imagine Richard Bettris, in his capacity of surgeon, mending many broken heads when meeting was over. Extravagances of conduct on the part of Friends may have helped to inflame the scholars against them. William Simpson, we shall remember, went naked in ritual fashion through both Universities.[1] But the chief reason for this coarse horse-play was the same as that which caused the craftsmen of Diana at Ephesus to rise against Paul—fear that their craft was in danger. The Quakers were unsparing in their denunciations of University learning, and the hot-headed champions of established religion proceeded, in the spirit of *Hudibras*, to

prove their doctrine orthodox
By apostolic blows and knocks.

A crusade against ceremonial and priestcraft and all paid ministry, conducted by men of earnestness and ignorance, very fallible in their methods and very infallible in their own eyes, might even to-day flutter the dovecotes of Oxford or Cambridge, and lead to rough reprisals. Owen was

[1] *Ante*, p. 149.

Vice-Chancellor of the University during these years of outrage, and comes in for severe handling on the subject from Samuel Fisher,[1] who considers such "arch-abominable and antic actions" fitter for bears and dogs and swine than for the sheep of Christ.

We now return to some of the other early controversialists. It is a considerable descent from the learning of Fisher to the simplicity of Fox. Yet though there is less knowledge, there is more wisdom. The reader who is at first oppressed by the formless immensity of the matter ends by regarding only the massiveness of the thought. Here is a man who believes invincibly in his message, and, while bringing all other men's notions to the test of it, preserves through endless repetitions the freshness and force of his convictions. Proficient in scripture and in mother-wit, and having a great reliance on truth, he proved a formidable antagonist. His chief controversial work, *The Great Mistery of the Great Whore*,[2] with its answers to 100 anti-Quaker publications, has been already referred to. He shows himself ready for every opponent, Baptists, relapsed Quakers, Independents, Brownists, Ranters, Presbyterians, Manifestarians. He seldom deigns to notice the slanders against Friends, using again and again some such phrase as "and as for his lies, they will be heaped upon his own head, and to his own sorrow."[3] Accordingly the book is not rich in personal details. Nor is it a systematic statement of Quaker principles. It is rather a series of rejoinders to unguarded passages in the books adverse to Friends, each passage being printed in italics and followed by its answer. A reprint of one section will show the character of the book better than any description. I will take the section (pp. 262, 263) devoted to John Owen, Fisher's chief antagonist.

[1] *Works*, p. 261. But Owen behaved well to Thos. Taylor. See *post*, p. 395.

[2] Published 1659. The Title follows the mode of thought of the age. So "The Records of the Church of Christ at Warboys" in the *Fenstanton Records, etc.* (Hanserd Knollys Society), p. 267, begin as follows: "Mystery, Babylon, or the Great Whore, spoken of by the blessed apostle John in the Revelation . . . had so deceived the nations of the world . . . that few knew in what manner Churches ought to be gathered and governed."

[3] *E.g.* p. 36.

John Owen, who calls himself *a Minister of the Gospell*, his principles as followeth, in his Catechisme which he gives forth, 1657.

Pr. [Principle]. *All truth concerning God and ourselves is to be learned from the holy Scripture, the Word of God.*

Ans. There was truth learned before the Scriptures were written, and the Scriptures of truth are the words of God, which ends in Christ the Word; and there is no truth learned, but as the spirit doth lead into all truth, which comes from Christ the truth, which was before the Scripture was written: And *the spirit of truth leads into all truth* of the Scripture; And many has the Scriptures, but knows not Christ the Truth, but as the spirit leads them, and reveals them: and so he hath thrown out Christ and the spirit.

Pr. *There is one God in three persons, etc.*

Ans. Where doth the Apostle tell us of three persons, but tells us of Father, Son, and holy Ghost; but thou, out of the Masse-book, and old Common-prayer-book, who are the mutterers about three persons.

Pr. *I am conceived in sin, and born in iniquity.*

Answ. Then thy Parents were not believers, so children unholy; for by nature children of wrath, that is the unconverted state, in the transgression, unbelievers; for they who by nature are children of wrath, are not born of the believers; for the unbelievers are sanctified by the believers, else were their children unholy, but now are they clean.

Pr. *We have not kept the Commandements of God, but are all sinners and transgressors of them.*

Ans. We do believe thee, *John Owen*, and the rest of you, who call your selves Ministers of the Gospell, and yet have not kept the ten Commandements, and would conclude all men in with you to be sinners and transgressors of them. Nay, *John* was separated from you, who said, *He that loves God, keeps his Commandements.* But what, are not you false-witness-bearers that calls your selves Ministers of the Gospel, and covetors after other mens goods, houses, etc.? Are not you committers of Adultery and stealing? Are not you murdering men in holes for goods like a troop of Robbers, as the company of Priests did in the day of the Law and Prophets? Do not you live in dishonouring your parents and God, and taking it to your selves? And do not you all come short of keeping the Sabbath, bearing of burdens, making a fire, gathering your meat when you should be at rest? Are not you all taking God's holy name in vain both in Pulpit, Town-house, Alehouse, Streets, Market-houses, and naming Christs name in your iniquity, so not held guiltlesse?

Are not you all making Images, and graven Images, and hanging them up in your Steeple-houses, and signes, and houses, and gardens, and high wayes, and things above, and things that are beneath? And do you think that people do not believe you, when you tell people in your Catechism, that you have broken all the ten Commandements, when we see your fruits have declared it? And are you not ashamed to set forth such a Catechisme, who say you keep not the Commandements?

Pr. *The Sacraments are the seals of the Covenant of grace.*

Answ. It's God that seals the Son, and sent him into the world, and not outward shadows: And as for thy word *Sacraments*, the Pope was the Author of them in his Common-prayer-book. And as for the rest of thy work in thy book of Catechism, [it] is like unto the old Doctors of the Jewes that broke the commands of God, that loves him not, whom Christ cryed woe against.

This strange book with its mixture of wisdom and incoherence was chiefly prepared about the year 1657. In the annals for that year, bound up in the *Cambridge Journal*,[1] we are told, "also this year G. F. drew up the priests' principles, being collected out of their own mad books." At the end is a remarkable section called "Several Scriptures corrupted by the Translators," which is almost identical with part of the anonymous tract, "Something concerning Agbarus, etc.," which we have seen reason to attribute to Samuel Fisher. The Quaker origin of this part of the tract is shown by the character of the alleged corruptions, of which fifteen out of twenty-three are intended to confirm the doctrine of the Inner Light by giving the Greek preposition ἐν its full meaning of "in," and most of the others support distinctive Quaker tenets. Fox cannot be regarded as the author; but at the end of the list of corruptions, as given in the *Great Mistery*, Isa. ix. 6 is badly printed in Hebrew, without any translation, and Rev. xxi. 7, in Greek, quite accurately according to the *textus receptus*, and this dash of scholarship at the end of his book is quite in Fox's style.

A certain parade of learning was indeed one of his

[1] *Camb. Journ.* ii. 338.

weaknesses.[1] He regarded himself as possessing a spiritual counterpart to human knowledge which qualified him to meet experts on their own ground. He probably picked up a smattering of several languages, including Hebrew, Greek, and Welsh. His curious linguistic tastes are shown with respect to Hebrew by his strange interjection at the Lancaster trial in 1664, when he amazed the court by calling out "Lo-tishshab'un bekŏl-dabar" ("Ye shall not swear by anything"),[2] and by the Hebrew alphabet attached to a page of notes on the Old Testament, part of which is in his handwriting.[3] As to Welsh, when the Scarborough bailiff's son, in 1666, "came to dispute and spoke Hebrew to me, I spoke in Welsh to him and bid him fear God, who after became a pretty Friend";[4] while for evidence of his interest in Greek the insertion of the closing section of *The Great Mistery* may suffice. We shall have occasion later to refer to his connection with that extraordinary book, the *Battle-Door*, for teaching from the example of other tongues the use of the plain language.[5]

Four other principal writers remain for notice—Farnsworth, Howgill, Hubberthorne, and George Whitehead. Farnsworth's works were never collected, although in influence he ranked by the side of Fox. He was a bitter opponent of the clergy, but could on occasion develop a careful and temperately worded argument. Howgill's writings, though often vehement in their style, contain many passages of rare tenderness. He sometimes speaks the language of pure mysticism, as when he says, "I am lost in the incomprehensible being of eternal Love";[6] "I lie down with you in the bosom of eternal love, life, peace, joy and rest forever, where none can make us

[1] For example, his talk with Edwd. Bourn, of Worcester, *ante*, p. 202, *F.P.T.* 278; cf. his challenge to the mountebanks at Lyme Regis (*Camb. Journ.* i. 269). His point of view is shown in the extract from *Journ.* i. 28, printed *ante*, p. 38.

[2] *Camb. Journ.* ii. 78.

[3] See Green's *Short History* (illustrated edn.), iii. 1339. Geo. Whitehead, in *Innocency against Envy, etc.*, p. 16, asserted that Fox "attained both to the reading, writing and understanding of Hebrew." But this is an exaggeration. Cf. Mary G. Swift's article in *J.F.H.S.* vi. 140-145, also 162.*

[4] *Camb. Journ.* ii. 106.

[5] *Post*, p. 496.

[6] *Works*, p. 35.

afraid";[1] but more often he lays stress on the life which comes through the work of Christ in the heart, and on the need for taking up His cross. Hubberthorne and George Whitehead have no distinction either of style or matter, but were reliable and strenuous in controversy. Adam Martindale, who had disputed with Hubberthorne in Cheshire at the end of 1655, calls him "the most rational calm-spirited man of his judgment that I was ever publicly engaged against."[2]

The methods of printing and circulating books pursued by Friends,*and the liberty they enjoyed in these respects, are matters of interest. The Commonwealth secured a large though qualified religious liberty to Englishmen, and liberty of the Press was often allowed, in fact, although severe laws were passed in restraint of printing. The Act of 20th September 1649 forbade the publication of any book or pamphlet without a licence, but in spite of this the unlicensed presses easily kept themselves in existence.[3] In 1652 six of the London booksellers addressed "A Beacon Set on Fire" to the Parliament, directed against Popish and blasphemous books,[4] and in 1654 "A Second Beacon fired" followed from the same hands. In this they spoke of "the dangerousness of great meetings in London of Quakers, whose opinions are blasphemous, paganish, anti-scriptural, and anti-Christian."[5] The Worcestershire Petition of December 1652, which was designed to promote associated work between the Puritan clergy, contained strong denunciations of a London bookseller, Giles Calvert,*whose shop was referred to as an apothecary's shop kept open for the sale of soul-poison.[6] He and his brother-in-law Thomas Simmonds became the chief printers of Friends' books in the early years. Calvert's shop was at the Black Spread Eagle, near the west end of St. Paul's, while Simmonds established himself at the

[1] *Works*, p. 36.

[2] *Life*, in Chetham Society publications, 1845, pp. 115-117. "Of his judgment" is equivalent to "among the Quakers."

[3] Gardiner, *Hist. of Commth. and Prot.* i. 173, 174.

[4] Smith's *Bibliotheca Anti-Quakeriana*, p. 179.

[5] Howgill's *Works*, p. 17.

[6] Fox, *Great Mistery*, p. 235.

Bull and Mouth, Aldersgate. In August 1655[1] commissioners were appointed to put in force the law against unlicensed printing, and in April 1656 some books by Burrough were seized and taken to Whitehall.[2] But we hear little of active interference; and Friends often took the most open methods of putting their books in circulation. Hubberthorne, for example, in July 1660, tells Fox that the answer to a book against Friends has been printed; "and some of them is given abroad in Whitehall, and others of them is sold in divers shops, and some of the women cries them about the streets."[3]

The check, such as it was, upon unwise publications, was not exercised by any public licenser, but by the authority of the leaders. We have already[4] noticed how Aldam, in 1653, approved the proposal that Fox should view all books before they were printed, but other leaders no doubt acted in the same way. Fox, in 1656, simply says, "And all Friends everywhere, take heed of printing anything more than ye are required by the Lord God."[5] One Friend sends her paper to Gerrard Roberts for Francis Howgill or George Fox to see, to be printed after they have read it and given directions.[6] Another Friend, John Whitehead, sends up to Fox and others an answer to the Manifestarians which he wishes printed, and if George Whitehead and George Fox the younger, who were also concerned in the dispute, have anything on their minds, it is to be annexed to the answer he has written. He adds, "If they have already printed an answer, I see not that it can clear me and the Truth unless this come forth also, but I leave it to be ordered in God's will as you may further see meet." He wishes 300 copies to be sent down into Lincolnshire, where there were many Manifestarians, some of whom were shaken with the Truth.[7] In spite of this letter only George Whitehead's replies appear to have been printed.

[1] Gardiner, *Hist. of Commth. and Prot.* iv. 26.

[2] Willan to Margt. Fell, 26th Apl. 1656, Swarthm. Colln. i. 272.

[3] Hubberthorne to Fox, 31st July (1660), Swarthm. Colln. iv. 20; cf. *Journ.* i. 441.

[4] *Ante*, p. 134.

[5] *Epistles*, No. 131.

[6] Dorothy White, Swarthm. Colln. i. 22.

[7] 20th Nov. 1659, Swarthm. Colln. iv. 178.

The cost of printing seems to have been borne at first by Northern Friends. An entry by Fox in his *Journal* in the year 1656 says, "At first the North took 600 of every book and bore all charges."[1] These were no doubt circulated through the different districts. The Swarthmore letters give particulars of several parcels sent to Margaret Fell at Swarthmore. A letter in September 1658[2] speaks of the great charge of books, and proposes ascertaining from Giles Calvert, who has the particulars, exactly how much has been spent. The cost is not entered in the regular accounts rendered from Kendal to Margaret Fell, and in 1659 the Skipton General Meeting directed that each of the county Monthly Meetings should pay for its own books, except books going into other nations.[3]

Although sometimes unequally matched in point of learning, Friends pitted themselves against any antagonist, armed against all comers by their living teaching respecting the Inner Light. Smith, the Quaker bibliographer, in his *Bibliotheca Anti-Quakeriana*, includes about ninety-eight adverse authors during the Commonwealth period, and the names of thirty-seven of these occur in the *Dictionary of National Biography*, clear proof of the importance in their own day of these obscure controversies. The zest with which Friends threw themselves into public disputing and polemics is, in fact, only another evidence of the large claims and wide ambitions of early Quakerism.[4]

[1] *Cambridge Journal*, i. 266.

[2] Taylor to Margt. Fell, Swarthm. Colln. i. 303.

[3] See *post*, p. 328; and for the arrangements in Somersetshire in 1659, *post*, p. 316.

[4] Consult *J.F.H.S.* viii. 148-150, and *Antiquarian Researches among the Early Printers and Publishers of Friends' Books* (1844).*

CHAPTER XIII

CHURCH ORGANIZATION

Being orderly come together, . . . proceed in the wisdom of God . . . not in the way of the world, as a worldly assembly of men, by hot contests, by seeking to outspeak and overreach one another in discourse, as if it were controversy between party and party of men, or two sides violently striving for dominion, . . . not deciding affairs by the greater vote, . . . but in the wisdom, love and fellowship of God, in gravity, patience, meekness, in unity and concord, . . . all things to be carried on; by hearing and determining every matter coming before you, in love, coolness, gentleness, and dear unity; —I say as one only party, all for the Truth of Christ, and for the carrying on of the work of the Lord, and assisting one another in whatsoever ability God hath given; and to determine of things by a general mutual concord, in assenting together as one man in the spirit of truth and equity, and by the authority thereof.—EDWARD BURROUGH, Testimony concerning the setting up of the Men's Meeting in London, *Letters of Early Friends*, p. 305.

IN a former chapter we described Quakerism as it existed in the North at the beginning of 1654, prior to the great extension work which was to carry its message into the farthest corners of England by the close of the following year. We noted the group-life and strong fellowship of the new movement, its nascent energy and universal mission, its guidance by the vital forces of personal conviction and inspired leadership rather than by discipline and organization. We traced the early provision made for the aggressive work of "the camp of the Lord," and the place occupied by the itinerating Publishers of Truth. We brought into prominence the few simple institutions which satisfied the early needs of the Quaker fellowship,—the regular meetings for waiting on the Lord, the local leaders or Elders, the Monthly Meetings of Elders and General Meetings for Friends of a district, and the practical arrangements which were beginning to be made with respect to such necessary matters as the recording of births, and the due solemnization and recording of marriages and burials.

In the period we have now reached, 1656-1660, the central interest of Friends was still in their vision and their mission, but success had brought new responsibilities. "The Lord's truth was finely planted over the nation and many thousands were turned to the Lord,"[1] and the leaders found themselves charged with important duties to the rest of the household of faith.

The methods which had been relied on in the North of England continued to prevail. The life of the community was cherished by the strength of its group-fellowship, centring in meetings for united waiting on the Lord, and its active work still consisted in a militant testimony to the truth for which it stood. The co-ordinating of these groups into one body, inspired with common ideals and going forward unitedly in a common work, continued to depend, so far as outward influences were concerned, chiefly upon the personal influence and incessant work of the itinerating leaders. But group-fellowship and inspired leadership naturally began to clothe themselves with an appropriate organization through which they could readily exert their influence, and as this organization grew into being, the Quaker movement developed not only a propaganda but a religious Society. It would, however, be premature, in 1656, to speak of the Society of Friends. This name is not met with till later:* the earliest reference which I have found is in 1665, and that a doubtful one. In Curwen's "Answer to John Wiggan's Book," published in that year, Wiggan is quoted as having said, in reference to the Light of Christ, "the falling down to this image is that whereby every particular person is matriculated or registered into their Society of Friends."[2] While Friends

[1] Geo. Fox, *Journal*, i. 343 (1656).

[2] P. 67. The quotation from Wiggan by Curwen is in italic type throughout, and capitals are used, though in a day of lavish capitals this counts for little. The quotation is taken from Wiggan's *Antichrist's strongest Hold overturned*, which was printed in two editions in 1665. At p. 49 of presumably the first

were expecting to carry the fire of the Inward Light of Christ over the whole earth, they regarded themselves as the Church of God gathered out of the world, and not as a sect, and we shall find that this conception underlay all their endeavours after church organization.

As an instance of the early Quaker conception, I cannot do better than give the trusts upon which Thomas Hodgson of Danby, in Yorkshire, bachelor, and Elizabeth Hodgson, widow, conveyed the burial-place adjoining the north side of their house in August 1658.[1] It is to be held,

> . . . to and for the only and proper use and behoof of the People of God who are gathered in the light and Spirit of Jesus Christ off from the outward temple made with hands in the time of apostasy (which ignorantly is called a church) and from the will-worship and superstition that attends it, to the Church in God (1. Thess. i. 1), of which Christ Jesus is declared to be the Head (Ephes. i. 22; Ephes. v. 27; Col. i. 18), and to worship God the Father in spirit and in truth according to the scriptures (John iv. 23, 24; Phil. iii. 3), who are the true worshippers of God as aforesaid, though of the world they are reproachfully called Quakers, to and for their only and proper use and service to meet together in and bury their dead at all time and times (as their freedom and occasion shall be) from henceforth and for ever.

The formative influences which gradually change a religious movement into a religious institution are not always easy of analysis. External circumstances and the various forces within the movement itself act and react on one another in a perplexing way. But the problem is one of extraordinary interest. How long will the vital forces of genuine first-hand experience, and of fellowship and personal leadership remain supreme: how soon will

edition, the phrase is printed, "Sotiety of *Friends*," where the italics used for "Friends" show that the word "Sotiety" is still descriptive and not a customary title. The second edition prints, "society of *Friends*." Accordingly in this quotation we seem to have the phrase prior to its crystallization into a title.

[1] See J. Wilhelm Rowntree, *Essays and Addresses*, p. 57. I have consulted a copy of the deed in my possession made by George Dixon of Great Ayton. J. Wilhelm Rowntree says that he has found the same declaration in two other early deeds, so that it was evidently an accepted formula. The parish of Danby was too much out of the way for it to have originated there. Ephes. v. 23 would be a better reference than v. 27.

they become subordinated to tradition and organization and authority? At what point will the preservation of a sect claim more attention than the propagation of a new way of life? How soon will the vision of a new heaven and a new earth fade into the light of common day?

It is one of the objects of the present history to examine the changes of this kind which slowly turned the aggressive Quaker movement of 1654 into the hermit-like Society of Friends of the eighteenth century. Most of them belong to the Restoration period, but a good deal of development in organization and in practice occurred during the five years 1656-1660.

Fox, within a few months of his release from Launceston, held three important General Meetings—one at Thomas Mounce's near Liskeard, a second at Ringwood in Hampshire, and the third at the Seven Stars Inn at Exeter.[1] At one of these he gave forth an important paper[2] of practical counsel. We have seen how the honesty of Friends had increased their trade, often to double what it had been before their convincement, and Fox now warns them of the danger of being clogged with business, "so that ye can hardly do anything to the service of God, but there will be crying, 'my business, my business,' and your minds will go into the things, and not over the things." He warns them against jars and strife, which will "eat out the seed in you," and against preaching in "a brittle, peevish, hasty, fretful mind," and against gossip and "tattling, idle words." The poor and prisoners are to be relieved: meetings are to be held in the life and power and wisdom of the Lord, that all uncleanness may be brought down and rooted out, till all be brought to be a "sweet savour to the Lord God, and in the hearts of one another." Friends are to take heed of printing anything more than they are required of God. They are warned against wandering up and down about needless occasions and of travelling among meetings,

[1] See *Journ.* i. 326, and Thos. Turner's letter to Margt. Fell (Swarthm. Colln. iv. 123) and *Journ.* i. 359.

[2] See Swarthm. Colln. ii. 95, and the paper as printed in Fox's *Epistles*, No. 131.

especially settled meetings, except as they are moved of the Lord. The phrase "silent meetings" is used to distinguish these from meetings with the "world." They are to take heed of slothfulness and sleeping in meetings, and of wronging the world or any one in bargains or overreaching them, and are encouraged to record births and deaths. The paper, it will be seen, is full of that robust judgment and mother-wit which in combination with the deep spiritual experience and enthusiasm of Fox, made him a great religious leader, in spite of all his limitations of education and outlook. In another paper, perhaps written from Launceston gaol,[1] he gives some wise advice as to checking unhelpful ministry in meetings, which has throughout the history of Friends been a matter of delicacy and difficulty. Dewsbury in 1653, in the letter, countersigned by Fox, quoted in an earlier chapter, had approved the public judging in a meeting of persons of disorderly life. This is approved by Fox in the case of openly profane and rebellious persons, where it may be necessary to clear the Truth.

But such as are tender, if they should be moved to bubble forth a few words, and speak in the seed and Lamb's power, suffer and bear that,—that is the tender. And if they should go beyond their measure, bear it in the meeting for peace, and order's sake, and that the spirits of the world be not moved against you. But when the meeting is done, then if any be moved to speak to them, between you and them, one or two of you that feel it in the life do it in the love and wisdom that is pure and gentle from above,—for the love is that which doth edify and bear all things, and suffers long and doth fulfil the law.

Fox, however, desired for Friends, especially in the North of England, where there were fully settled Churches, some action respecting disorderly conduct which should proceed from the united mind of the whole community. We find from a letter of Farnsworth's[2] that a meeting of Elders was arranged at Balby in Yorkshire, in November

[1] *Journ.* i. 344. In the *Cambridge Journ.* i. 223, it is given with some other papers during the Launceston imprisonment.

[2] To Howgill and Burrough from Swarthmore, 4th Oct. 1656 (Dev. Ho., A.R.B. Colln. No. 38).

1656, to give effect to this desire. To this meeting one approved member from each Church in Yorkshire, Lincoln, Derby, and Nottingham was to come to consider of such things as might in the Truth's behalf be propounded. The document issued by this general meeting of elders and approved Friends is still extant.[1] It bears evidence of being modelled on the apostolic letter to the Gentile disciples in Acts xv., and is entitled:

> The elders and brethren sendeth unto the brethren in the North these necessary things following; to which, if in the light you wait, to be kept in obedience, you shall do well. Farewell.

At the end is the subscription:

> Given forth at a General Meeting of Friends in the Truth at Balby in Yorkshire, in the ninth month 1656, from the Spirit of Truth to the Children of Light in the light to walk, that all in order may be kept in obedience, that He may be glorified, who is worthy over all, God blessed for ever. Amen.

The letter is signed by Richard Farnsworth, William Dewsbury, and other Friends. A postscript follows, which is not the least noteworthy part of the document:

> Dearly beloved friends, these things we do not lay upon you as a rule or form to walk by, but that all with the measure of light which is pure and holy may be guided, and so in the light walking and abiding these may be fulfilled in the Spirit,—not from the letter, for the letter killeth, but the Spirit giveth life.

I have elsewhere pointed out[2] that this letter shows that the first Quaker leaders did not invoke their personal authority, but based their claim to give guidance upon their own possession of the Spirit of truth and upon the witness to the Spirit in the hearts of those they addressed. They took the position of inspired leaders, not of spiritual superiors.

The letter itself deals with a number of important practical questions, as may be seen from the following abstract of its contents. Certain peculiarities of style

[1] The full letter is to be found in the records of Marsden Monthly Meeting. I have used a copy made by the late Josiah Forster. An imperfect copy, wrongly attributed, is printed in *Letters of Early Friends*, pp. 277-283.

[2] *Spiritual Guidance in Quaker Experience*, p. 59.

lead me to suspect the pen of Dewsbury, but the substance of the advice was no doubt the joint conclusion of the whole meeting.

Clause 1. The settled meetings to be kept each first-day. General Meetings, as a rule to be on some other day of the week.

" 2. As any are brought in to the Truth new meetings are to be arranged to suit the general convenience, without respect of persons.

" 3. Persons ceasing to attend meetings are to be spoken to. Persons who walk disorderly are to be spoken to in private, then before two or three witnesses; then, if necessary, the matter is to be reported to the Church. The Church is to reprove them for their disorderly walking, and, if they do not reform, the case is to be sent in writing "to some whom the Lord hath raised up in the power of the Spirit of the Lord to be fathers,—His children to gather in the light" so that the thing may be known to the body and be determined in the light.

[Here we have a congregational discipline, in the first instance, with a discipline by the leaders in the last resort.]

Clause 4. Ministers to speak the word of the Lord from the mouth of the Lord, without adding or diminishing. If anything is spoken out of the light so that "the seed of God" comes to be burdened, it is to be dealt with in private and not in the public meetings, "except there be a special moving so to do."

" 5. Collections to be made for the poor, the relief of prisoners, and other necessary uses, the moneys to be carefully accounted for, and applied as made known by the overseers in each meeting.

" 6. Care to be taken "for the families and goods of such as are called forth in the ministry, or are imprisoned for the Truth's sake; that no creature be lost for want of caretakers."

" 7. Intentions of marriage to be made known to the Children of Light, especially those of the meeting where the parties are members. The marriage to be solemnized in the fear of the Lord, and before many witnesses, after the example of scripture, and a record to be made in writing, to which the witnesses may subscribe their names.

Clause 8. Every meeting to keep records of births, and of burials of the dead that die in the Lord. Burials to be conducted according to scripture, and not after customs of "heathen."

„ 9. Advice to husbands and wives, as in 1 Pet. iii. 7. Advice to parents and children, as in Eph. vi. 1, 4.

„ 10. Advice to servants and masters, as in Eph. vi. 5-9.

„ 11. Care to be taken "that none who are servants depart from their masters, but as they do see in the light: nor any master put away his servant but by the like consent of the servant; and if any master or servant do otherwise in their wills, it is to be judged by Friends in the light."

„ 12. Needs of widows and fatherless to be supplied:—such as can work and do not to be admonished, and if they refuse to work, neither let them eat. The children of needy parents to be put to honest employment.

„ 13. Any called before outward powers of the nation are to obey.

„ 14. "That if any be called to serve the Commonwealth in any public service which is for the public wealth and good, that with cheerfulness it be undertaken and in faithfulness discharged unto God, that therein patterns and examples in the thing that is righteous ye may be to those that are without."

„ 15. Friends in callings and trades are to be faithful and upright, and keep to yea and nay. Debts to be punctually paid, that nothing they may owe to any man but love one to another.

„ 16. None to speak evil of another, nor grudge against another, nor put a stumbling-block in his brother's way.

„ 17. None to be busybodies in other's matters.

„ 18. Christian moderation to be used towards all men.

„ 19. The elders made by the Holy Ghost are to feed the flock, taking the oversight willingly, not as lords, but as examples to the flock (see 1 Pet. v. 2, 3).

„ 20. Closing words out of 1 Pet. v. 5.

Such is the oldest church advice on Christian practice

issued by any general body of Friends. The church organization is still of the simplest, consisting of congregational life under the leadership of local elders, and, in the last resort, of the "fathers" of the Church. No Monthly Meetings are referred to. There is as yet no appeal to any authority except that of the light: the central experience of the indwelling life of Christ, which had gathered Friends out of the world into fellowship, was still so generally the living possession of Friends that its vital control held the body together as one organism. But, at the same time, sporadic cases of backsliding and of disorderly life had to be dealt with, and marriages required to be regulated, and the poor to be provided for. To suggest wise lines of action in respect to these matters, and to exhort Friends in their various relations of life to walk worthily of their calling, was all that seemed of urgent necessity to the framers of this document. There is, on the one hand, a tacit acceptance of the main body of Quaker experience and practice, which is assumed to be a ground of union common to all; and, on the other, a refusal to multiply regulations beyond what seemed practically necessary. And, though Friends were at this time incurring the hostility of the State, there is no sign as yet of that indifference to public life which persecution and nonconformity with the practices of the world gradually fostered: on the contrary, the duty of serving the Commonwealth so far as possible is inculcated—a point which must receive careful examination, so far as the materials admit, in a future chapter.

We have another document of a similar kind from a meeting of Friends of four counties, Kent, Sussex, Surrey, and Hampshire, held at The Lodge, Horsham, Bryan Wilkinson's house, two and a half years later, in May 1659.[1] It tenders the following as "counsel and advice."

[1] Printed in *Letters of Early Friends*, p. 283, from a Register Book of a Monthly Meeting in Hampshire. The names of forty-four principal Friends in the four counties are appended, and are given in the MS. copy of the document in the vol. of Yearly Mtg. Epp. 1656-1843, Dev. Ho., Bookcase No. 7. This four-counties General Meeting continued to be held as late as Whitsuntide 1661. See letter from Joseph Fuce to Fox, 25th May, in Swarthm. Colln. iv. 222. It was also held in 1660 at Horsham. See Wm. Caton's *Life*, 1689 edn. p. 59.*

Clause 1. Friends at their several meetings to make collections orderly and timely for the poor or other necessary uses, any surplus to be brought into the general stock for each county.

" 2. Marriages, as in Balby letter, clause 7.

" 3. Births and burials, as in Balby letter, clause 8.

" 4. Burial places to be provided in convenient places distinct from the world, as Friends are moved to it.

" 5. Disorderly walking, etc. As in Balby letter clause 3, but instead of report to Church and reference to leaders, the clause simply provides for report to others that be in the Truth, that it may be known to the body and with the consent of the whole be determined in the light.

" 6. Care to be taken of children, wives, servants, soldiers or others, who are turned out of their places and families for the Truth's sake.

" 7. Friends to keep their General and particular meetings on first-days and at other times, "for they who forsake the assembly of saints lose the unity."

" 8. (*a*) If any be moved to speak in steeple-houses, streets, markets, meetings or beyond the seas, they are not to quench the Spirit.

(*b*) No Friends to judge one another in meetings, but any advice to be given after meeting in private.

(*c*) Friends to take heed of slothfulness and sleeping in meetings.

(*d*) "Live in the power of the Lord that you may be kept in the unity: that all things that are done, may be in the moving power of the Lord God, and nothing out of it."

Two additional clauses are added, after the meeting had been held, but apparently nearly at the same time.

Clause 9. Sufferings of Friends to be gathered up and recorded, the sufferers to report to a recorder in each meeting who is to report to the next General Meeting for the county for record by a county recorder.

" 10. If under clause 1, the county collection prove insufficient to supply the necessity of Friends in the same county, then the other three counties who have any money in their general stock are to contribute.

This document clearly shows the influence of the Balby letter. It is not quite so comprehensive, although it deals with one or two new matters. The advice as to reporting sufferings is no doubt due to the directions given to Friends by Fox in 1657, to keep copies of all their sufferings, whether for tithes, refusing church-repairs, not swearing, not putting off their hats, ill-treatment at meetings, or when moved of the Lord to go to steeple-houses. They were to be laid before the judges on circuit, and also before the Protector, in order that they might be brought home to those who caused the sufferings.[1] Gerrard Roberts, of London, was the person designated by Fox to receive these reports.

Documents similar to the Horsham one were no doubt issued in other parts of the South. There is one, for instance, in a book belonging to Shaftesbury and Sherborne Monthly Meeting, from a General Meeting at Cerne, in Dorset, 18th August 1659, giving advice as to burial-places, registering births, marriages, and deaths, the poor, disorderly walking, books sent down, and collections;[2] and another from a General Meeting for Somersetshire, set up at Glastonbury[3] 27th June 1659, giving similar advice, and adding a direction that if a necessity be laid on any Friend to write or print any book for the service of Truth, the copies are to be first tried and weighed by such persons as are able to judge in the wisdom of God, and the same being approved, the charge of printing, above what is raised by sale of the book, may be borne by the public stock.[4] A month later a full Minute was passed as to marriage procedure, providing for public notice of intention on a market-day in full market, or at a General Meeting, or at the end of the meetings to which the parties belonged. The marriage is to be solemnized at a meeting of not less than ten Friends and registered, and the certificate of marriage is to be shown to some public magistrate

[1] Dev. Ho., Swarthm. Colln. ii. 97, ii. 99; Fox, *Epistles*, Nos. 140, 141.

[2] Per A. Neave Brayshaw.

[3] Wm. Tanner's *Three Lectures*, pp. 61-64, from the Dix MS. Collection.

[4] The date of the Glastonbury meeting is confirmed by a reference in a letter of Thos. Salthouse, dated Somersetshire, 26th June (Wm. Caton Colln., copy by Jas. Bowden at Dev. Ho.).

soon afterwards, thus conforming as nearly as possible to the law then in force.

We have taken these documents in connection with the Balby letter, but they belong to a somewhat more developed organization than prevailed at the end of 1656. The Horsham meeting, for example, is made up of Friends from four counties, each county having its own General Meeting for receiving collections, reports of sufferings, etc., and the surplus collections form a common stock for the four counties. The Balby meeting, on the other hand, was specially summoned for a special purpose.

It is by carefully following out the question of collections that we gain the best insight into the gradual development of organization. At first these were made on personal initiative, afterwards by representatives of districts, finally by a meeting representative of the whole country. Margaret Fell, as we have seen, took a leading part in the establishment of the original fund collected at Kendal "for the service of Truth." This fund dates from 1st June 1654, and we have in the Swarthmore Collection a series of accounts, which, when pieced together, prove to be practically continuous from that date to the end of September 1657.[1] During these three years and four months about £270 was collected and disbursed. The fund was primarily contributed from the particular meetings in Westmorland, Cumberland, North Lancashire, and the Sedbergh district, but £55 in four round sums comes from Yorkshire, and £51 : 13 : 7 in five sums from Durham, or Bishopric. Of the first Yorkshire contribution we are told that it was received from John Killam, of Balby, "which they had to spare besides what as would serve for their own necessities in that country,"[2] a phrase which exactly corresponds with the usage afterwards recommended in the Horsham letter. The money seems to have been collected in response to notes issued

[1] See the series of letters from George Taylor and Thos. Willan to Margt. Fell in Dev. Ho., Swarthm. Colln. Some of the accounts are printed in *J.F.H.S.* vi. pp. 49-52, 82-85, 127-128. Cf. *ante*, pp. 135, 136.

[2] Willan and Taylor to Margt. Fell, 14th July 1655, Swarthm. Colln. i. 239. Yorkshire Friends made their collections from Balby. See Samuel Watson's letter to Margt. Fell, 8th June 1657 (Swarthm. Colln. i. 389).

by the two Kendal treasurers, George Taylor and Thomas Willan, or by Margaret Fell. We have already quoted from the first of these written by Margaret Fell about the end of 1654.[1] A letter from George Taylor[2] sees in it "the eternal love of God to the simple and honest-hearted and that which will leave all the rest inexcusable, glory to the first mover." In March 1655 the need for further funds became urgent, owing to the great work in the South,[3] and Margaret Fell wrote a second letter[4] in which she said:

> Truly dear brethren we would not have troubled you at this time, having troubled you before so lately, but that the necessity is so great, the work so large, and the brethren being gone into so many far and remote places, and now is even the heat of the Lord's harvest, and the burden lies heavy upon Friends here in the north parts at present. . . . So now for the present, dear brethren, offer freely.

In the autumn of this year[5] £5 was received,* which Richard Bowerbank "gave to the Church when he died," one of the earliest charitable legacies left to Friends. The stock was now running dry, and Willan wrote:

> Truly sister this service lies heavy sometimes, and especially how to supply the faithful and truly serviceable, and miss or avoid the maintaining of deceit.

Taylor and Willan seem to have issued the necessary note. It simply said:[6]

> This is to let Friends know that the general stock at Kendal is disbursed and there is great occasion now so many being moved of the Lord to go into other nations and many in prisons.

The result was disappointing, for they wrote to Margaret Fell at the end of December:[7]

[1] *Ante*, p. 135. [2] Swarthm. Colln. i. 211 (25th Dec.).

[3] Willan and Taylor to Margt. Fell, 24th March, Swarthm. Colln. i. 206.

[4] I identify this with the letter to Westmorland, Yorkshire, etc., at the beginning of 1655, in the Dev. Ho., Samuel Watson MS. Colln. p. 202, and in Spence MSS. vol. iii. fol. 7.

[5] Willan to Margt. Fell, 11th Sept. 1655, Swarthm. Colln. i. 255.

[6] Dev. Ho., Swarthm. Colln. i. 304.

[7] To Margt. Fell, Swarthm. Colln. i. 263.

. . . this little note went but as a dead thing amongst earthly and dead spirits. . . . If thou find movings, give them warning of our necessities all, that they that will not hear of one ear may hear of another: for without much beating the hard-hearted will not bow.

In the summer of 1656 there was a difference respecting the Durham contribution between Lancelot Wardell, Anthony Pearson, and the two Kendal treasurers. It is not necessary to give details of what was evidently a mere misunderstanding, but it showed how easily friction might arise with respect to these money matters.[1] One letter[2] incidentally gives the general relation between the Kendal stock and that collected in Durham. Taylor and Willan say that they did not claim any kind of account from Wardell; they were only anxious that any money received should be made serviceable for Truth in the wisest way: but anything received from Durham they would, of course, be accountable for. Wardell did, however, send one paper of accounts to Kendal, showing that out of moneys in his hands he had made payments for travelling Friends, especially in Scotland, precisely similar in character with those made from Kendal.[3]

In September 1656[4] Margaret Fell again wrote to Friends in the North pressing for a liberal collection. In apocalyptic language she spoke of the flying angel (Rev. xiv. 6) who had gone forth to preach the everlasting Gospel, and said:

So, dearly beloved, if there be any bowels of mercy towards the seed which lies yet buried in the graves . . . which no eye pities but the Lord, whose time is a time of love, which [seed] now He is visiting and sending forth His messengers . . . to gather in His elect from the four winds of the heavens, oh, dear hearts, put to your hands to this work . . . and in the fear of the Lord offer freely to His service.

---

[1] The letters are from Wardell and from Willan and Taylor to Margt. Fell, Swarthm. Colln. i. 276-284 inclusive.

[2] Swarthm. Colln. i. 278.

[3] *Ibid.* i. 276.

[4] From a letter endorsed "about 1656," dated 10th Sept. (no date of year), in possession of Wm. F. Miller, of Winscombe, Somerset, who has kindly furnished me with a transcript. The collection is "for providing and maintaining of the brethren with necessaries whom the Lord hath called out of late and is calling out into several nations, as Holland, Barbados, Ireland, Scotland, Flanders, Denmark and Germany, all this within this month and a great part of them North-country Friends." This agrees well with Sept. 1656.

London Friends at an early date set on foot arrangements corresponding with those established in the North. William Crouch[1] tells us that after the taking of the Bull and Mouth premises (1655), the ancient men Friends, to the number of eight or ten, sometimes met together in an upper room, to consider the affairs of Truth, and to make provision to supply all necessary occasions which the service of the Church might require.

Burrough gives a fuller account of the matter.[2] He says that about two years after the beginning of the London work (*i.e.* in the summer of 1656), the Publishers of Truth arranged a meeting of men Friends not in the ministry, to be held once a fortnight, or once a month, at the Bull and Mouth. It dealt with such matters as the provision of meeting-places, the care of the poor, the visiting of the sick and impotent, and the providing of employment for servants turned out of their places owing to their becoming Friends. Such matters, he tells us,

> . . . were not so proper for us of the ministry as for the Friends of the city, neither had we the opportunity of such exercises, being wholly devoted to the work of the ministry, to which we were ordained of God, and were continually exercised in preaching the gospel, in answering books and manuscripts put forth against us, and in disputes and contentions with such as opposed the Truth.

The reasons, it will be noticed, for this men's meeting are practically the same as those which caused the first Apostles to set apart the seven "deacons" for ministering at tables.[3]

We have no account of the collections made under the authority of this meeting, but they were no doubt applied in part for the service of ministering Friends. In 1655, for example, when Howgill and Burrough were in Ireland, London Friends shared the cost.[4] But it is evident that with the greatly widening work, and especially with the growing service undertaken in Scotland and

[1] *Posthuma Christiana*, chap. ii.

[2] *Letters of Early Friends*, pp. 287-310, dated 1662. I cite from p. 299.

[3] Cf. document, dated 1676, in Fox, *Epistles*, pp. 6, 7.

[4] See letter from Burrough in Dev. Ho., Wm. Markey Colln. p. 29.

Ireland and beyond the seas, the resources of the Kendal and London stocks (and any other that may have existed, say at Bristol) would be overtaxed, and steps would sooner or later become necessary for distributing the burden over the whole Quaker community. We may compare the action which Paul took in collecting from the Gentile Churches for the necessities of the poor saints at Jerusalem. And we may note that any such general collection could not fail to have an important influence in drawing Friends together into one body under a growing consciousness of organic unity.

The Annals for 1657, contained in the Cambridge edition of Fox's *Journal*,[1] include the following entry:

> Also this year there was established and ordered for general collections to be for the service of Truth and Friends that travelled beyond seas, through all the nation, which charge had lain mostly upon the Northern Counties before this time,—which was established about the third month [*i.e.* May] 1657.

We are fortunate in possessing letters which confirm this entry, and give a full account of the steps taken.[2] Action was due to Margaret Fell, Howgill, and Burrough, who felt that London Friends were pressed beyond measure, and the needs of the work in other nations were likely to increase. Howgill, with a true perception, saw that a general collection "will make other Friends to know their place in most counties, where in a manner the gospel hath been freely declared to them, so now they may be helpful unto other nations for the Lord's sake, and it will unite Friends' hearts together [to feel] that they can be owned for the service of the Lord." He had propounded the thing to Thomas Aldam, who cordially approved it, had discussed it at Swarthmore with Margaret Fell, Pearson, Gervase Benson, Widders, and some others, and on the 8th May, just before leaving for

[1] ii. 337.

[2] Howgill's letter to Burrough (Dev. Ho., A.R.B. Colln. No. 160) is dated from John Audland's at Crosslands on the evening of the Draw-well meeting; the year is not given, but is certainly 1657. Willan and Taylor's letter to Margt. Fell (Swarthm. Colln. i. 297) is dated from Kendal the following day; the year is given.

Scotland, settled the details at a meeting at Draw-well, near Sedbergh, at which he met with the host, John Blaykling, the two Kendal treasurers, Taylor and Willan, and three Friends out of Durham—Pearson, John Langstaff, and Anthony Hodgson. A letter was prepared to go to every county in the nation, subscribed by Aldam, Widders, Benson, and Pearson,[1] but none in the ministry were to meddle in it. It urged with great force the need of a general collection, "the charge coming on to be great both for furnishing of [Friends], and transporting of them, the passage being hard to get and dear." It asked for a free contribution for the expenses of service beyond the seas into other nations, and to be disbursed for no other end, the amounts to be sent up to London. Howgill helped Pearson to nominate Friends for the several counties of England and Wales, and Pearson undertook to send ten copies of the letter, with an accompanying note of directions, to the ten Friends nominated for the Southern Counties, Margaret Fell sending a similar letter[2] through the Kendal area of Lancashire, Cumberland, and Westmorland. Samuel Watson, of Knight Stainforth, near Settle, writes to her in June, expecting to receive a copy.[3]

I conclude that the action taken later in the year by Fox himself was primarily intended to put this general collection on a regular footing. He says in the *Cambridge Journal*, under date 1656, but the last entry in that year:[4]

And I was moved of the Lord to send for one or two out of a county to Swarthmore and to set up the men's meetings where they was not, and to settle that meeting at Skipton concerning the affairs of the Church which continued till 1660.* . . . And about this time I was moved to set up the men's Quarterly Meetings throughout the nation, though in the North they was settled before.

[1] This letter is, I think, the one preserved in the parchment-covered book in Dev. Ho. Portfolio 9 (p. 68), from which I take the names of the four signatories. It gives Gerrard Roberts as one of the London Friends, though Howgill had suggested that he be excused because of his manifold engagements.

[2] Spence MSS. vol. iii. fol. 9, may be the letter. In this she speaks of the Friends who are going to New England as "willing to offer up their bodies and their lives for the service and will of the Lord."

[3] Swarthm. Colln. i. 389.

[4] *Camb. Journ.* i. 266, 355.

This conference must belong to his visit at Swarthmore in July or August 1657,[1] and the Skipton meeting would be later in the same year. An epistle has been preserved, presumably from this meeting, endorsed in Fox's hand, "from the North to the South at a men's meeting about 1656, from Skipton meeting in Yorkshire." It runs as follows:[2]

From the love of their brethren and seeing that the former paper that went from the North was not owned by all in the South, we were not free to lay anything before them but our own example, but leave it to the movings of the Lord in all: and we were free to acquaint you with what we have done, which keeps us clear, and will provoke others to the same thing: in which we are much refreshed and finds great service in this General Meeting, which we purpose to continue as often as we can: and if all parts and counties in the nation were drawn into the same way of union it would be of great use to the body: and we have also settled a way for collections amongst ourselves, and for ordering other outward things, that all may be preserved in peace and order.

It seems clear, on the face of this letter, that the General Meeting from which it comes is the first of a series, and, if this is conceded, it must be dated in 1656 or 1657, and the reference to the previous letter for a collection shows that it is later in date than May 1657.

In response to the appeal to the counties a general collection was in fact made. We have particulars, the earliest of which belongs to May 1657, of sums paid out by the Kendal treasurers for its purposes, and these moneys are apparently deducted by them from the collection of £40 : 0 : 8, made in the Kendal area of Lancashire, Westmorland, and Cumberland, before it is remitted to London about March 1658,[3] Margaret Fell explaining the course taken in a letter to Pearson,[4] and informing him

[1] The *Journal* itself, as usual, is barren of dates. But the meeting at Wm. Gandy's, referred to in *Journ.* i. 363, was held 28th June (Hubberthorne to Margt. Fell, Swarthm. Colln. i. 353), and Fox went into Scotland on 10th Sept. (Willan and Taylor to Margt. Fell, 12th Sept. 1657, Swarthm. Colln. i. 301, and *Camb. Journ.* ii. 337).

[2] Swarthm. Colln. ii. 18.

[3] Swarthm. Colln. i. 233, and Taylor to Margt. Fell, 3rd March 1658; *ibid.* i. 296.

[4] March [1658], *ibid.* i. 308.

that as the old Kendal stock is now in funds, any debts chargeable to it can be repaid.

Among the Swarthmore papers[1] there is an important statement, without date or name, containing particulars of receipts for "the service of Truth" amounting to £443 : 3 : 5, and disbursements amounting to £490 : 12 : 5. Comparison of this document with the 1657 Annals shows conclusively that the payments made are in respect of service abroad belonging to that year, the same names and places occurring in both lists in practically the same sequence. Money thus spent between March 1657 and March 1658 was almost certainly provided out of this first collection, and we turn with interest to the details. The Kendal area is not represented, their money not having been, I suppose, yet paid over. Yorkshire sends £30, and Durham £21, Cheshire £19 : 5s., and Lincoln £12—a total from the North, including the £40 : 0 : 3 from the Kendal area, of £122 : 5 : 3. The rest of the country contributes £360 : 18 : 5, about three times as much; but neither London nor Bristol appears on the list, for an obviously good reason in the case of London, which had already borne its share of the burden, and probably for a similar reason in the case of Bristol. The Eastern Counties of Norfolk, Suffolk, Essex, Cambridge, and Huntingdon responded generously, contributing £136 : 8 : 1 between them. While it would not be safe to draw wide conclusions from the relative amounts contributed, it may be worth while to place the counties in order of their contributions, as some guide to the districts where Friends were strongest. I omit the six Northern Counties, as these, owing to their former gifts, are not likely to have contributed in proportion to their strength.

The first sixteen are as follows :—Essex, Berkshire, Norfolk, Suffolk, Sussex, Surrey (under the name of Guildford), Cheshire, Cambridgeshire, Somerset, Kent, Cornwall, Oxfordshire (under the names of Oxford and Banbury),

[1] Swarthm. Colln. i. 397. Printed in Bowden's *Hist. of Friends in America*, i. 59, though there attributed to the 1658 Scalehouse meeting.

Lincolnshire, Worcestershire, Buckinghamshire, and Hampshire (under the name of Southampton).

In the following year, 1658, the new system became more clearly defined. An important General Meeting was held at Scalehouse near Skipton on June 24th, attended by forty Friends out of ten counties.[1] There was opposition to the proposal to take a collection for the needs of Friends in the ministry travelling in England, any provision for whom continued to be made out of the local funds. The Friends "wanted information much concerning what was already done, intimating George Taylor's unreadiness or imperfectness in satisfying them in the things propounded to him."[2] The paper or "order" issued by the meeting confines the collection to service beyond the seas. It is a beautifully worded document, which runs as follows:[3]

Having heard of great things done by the mighty power of God in many nations beyond the seas, whither He hath called forth many of our dear brethren and sisters to preach the everlasting gospel,—by whom He hath revealed the mystery of His truth, which hath been hid from ages and generations, who are now in strange lands, in great straits and hardships, and the daily hazard of their lives,—our bowels yearns towards them, and our hearts are filled with tender love to those precious ones of God, who so freely have given up for the seed's sake their friends, their near relations, their country and worldly estates, yea, and their own lives also. And in the feeling we are of their daily wants and sufferings: and do therefore in the unity of the Spirit and bond of truth cheerfully agree, in the Lord's name and power, to move and stir up the hearts of Friends in these counties, whom God hath called and gathered out of the world, with one consent freely and liberally to offer up unto God of their earthly substance, according as God hath blessed every one, to be speedily sent up to London as a freewill offering for the

---

[1] York, Lincoln, Lancaster, Chester, Nottingham, Derby, Westmorland, Cumberland, Durham, and Northumberland. Skipton was a central place for all these counties.

[2] Caton to Margt. Fell, Kendal, 30th June [1658], Swarthm. Colln. i. 317.

[3] I have used a copy taken from an Early Record Book at Kendal, an old thin folio, bound in leather with silk ties, which varies slightly from the copy printed n *Letters of Early Friends*, p. 286 *n.* Cf. the contemporary copy in Dev. Ho. Portfolio 16, No. 1. The Early Record Book is called "Acts and orders of the people of God called Quakers, etc."

seed's sake, that the hands of those that are beyond the seas in the Lord's work may be strengthened and their bowels refreshed, and others that are moved to go may be encouraged and provided for.

And we commit it to the care of our dear brethren of London, Amor Stoddart, Gerrard Roberts, John Bolton, Thomas Hart, and Richard Davis, to order and dispose of what shall be from us sent unto them for the supplies of such as are already gone forth, or such as shall be moved of the Lord to go forth into any other nation, of whose care and faithfulness we are well assured.

And such Friends as are here present are to be diligent in their several counties and places, that the work may be hastened with all convenient speed.

The forty signatories to this "order" do not, no doubt for the reasons already given, include the names of any of the regular itinerating Publishers of Truth, but no weightier list of "solid" Friends from the North could have been compiled. Out of the thirty-eight names which I can identify, fifteen are from Yorkshire, including Thomas Aldam and John and Thomas Killam, five from Durham and Northumberland and from Cumberland, four from Lancashire, three from Westmorland, and two each from Cheshire, Notts, and Derby. One, at least, of the remaining Friends must have been from Lincolnshire, perhaps Peter Crosby.

This collection produced £252 : 11 : 8,* which was sent up to London by George Taylor. It stirred up Friends in the South to like action, for Parker writes from London to Margaret Fell:[1]

Geo. Fox showed me the letter which thou wrote him concerning the meeting at Scalehouse, and he bid me write to thee to certify thee that they are going on with the like work in these parts. To-morrow [14th July 1658] there is to be a meeting at Cambridge for the Eastern Counties: another meeting is to be shortly in or about Bristol for the Western Counties, and another meeting is to be for the Midland Counties as the Lord orders. He is truly sensible of the North, which hath borne the heat of the day, but I perceive [that] he is not altogether against but would have them to be examples to the rest in the freedom of the Lord, and nothing otherwise.

---

[1] 13th July 1658, Caton Colln., copy by Jas. Bowden at Dev. Ho.

In the following year, 1659, also at the end of June (29th), another General Meeting was held at Skipton, attended by thirty-eight Friends out of Yorkshire, Cheshire, Lancashire, Durham and Northumberland, Cumberland and Westmorland.[1] It had been preceded by two meetings, one of ten Friends from Yorkshire, Lancashire, Westmorland, and Cumberland, held at Skipton on 2nd March, and one of twenty-three Friends from Westmorland, Cumberland, Lancashire, and Cheshire, held at Ulverston on 26th May.

At the preliminary Skipton meeting a contribution was offered for the needs of Friends in the ministry who went to Ireland or Scotland, and for Friends in gaol,—the receipts from the several Churches and the disbursements to be reported to the next General Meeting, that any who desired might see the accounts. The Yorkshire contributions were to go to Richard Liddall and Simon Rider at York, and since Durham Friends had disbursed much money for service in Scotland, for which Yorkshire Friends acknowledged their obligation, part of the money was to be sent to the Bishopric, either to George Adamson, of Bishop Auckland, or to Anthony Pearson (we note that Yorkshire and Durham, like the Kendal area, had two treasurers apiece). Any surplus moneys collected from the Northern Counties, after the intended uses were supplied, might be paid to the Kendal treasurers, who were out of purse. The meeting appointed the next General Meeting for 29th June at Skipton.

The Ulverston preliminary meeting arranged in the first place for signatures being collected against the oppression of tithes, and then appointed representatives to the Skipton General Meeting, and directed them to inquire what money had been collected and disbursed since the Scalehouse meeting by the treasurers of the several counties, bearing in mind the shortness of time Friends had at the last Skipton meeting. Should it be found that the Treasury for the North was empty, it was to be replenished at the request of the treasurers by collections

[1] For these three meetings see the Early Record Book at Kendal.

equally in every meeting in each county, the money being sent to Kendal.

The Skipton meeting, thus prepared for, proved an important one. There was no proposal to raise a third national collection, but the suggestion from the March Skipton meeting was proceeded with, and a collection was ordered for all in gaol, whether for tithes or otherwise, and for the needs of ministers in Scotland, Ireland, and other places. The Minute allows us to see that there was now a regular Monthly Meeting system established through the North, not the same indeed as the more localized system afterwards set on foot, but sufficient for the simple needs of the Quaker Churches. It directed that each Monthly Meeting was to care for its own poor, and to pay for the books it required without trenching on the general collection, except for books that were to go into other nations. The Monthly Meetings of Yorkshire, Bishopric, and Cheshire were to keep as much of the general collection as they required at York, Newcastle, and Chester, and were to send the rest to Kendal to George Taylor. Finally, there was a direction for each Monthly Meeting to see that all births, marriages, and burials were recorded. The next General Meeting was directed to be held at Skipton on 5th October 1659.

The Kendal Monthly Meeting, for Lancashire, Westmorland, and Cumberland, met at Kendal on 8th July, and at once put in hand the recording of births, marriages, and burials by agreeing that each particular meeting should keep a register, and a general register should be kept in Cumberland.[1]

The business of the autumn meeting at Skipton was again carefully prepared for, this time by Durham Friends. Twenty Friends, including Anthony Pearson, attended the Bishopric Monthly Meeting held at Durham on 1st October, and addressed to the Skipton meeting a document of great importance, presumably from Pearson's pen.[2]

[1] Early Record Book at Kendal.

[2] Printed in *Letters of Early Friends*, pp. 288-292, from the copy sent to Fox, which is now in Dev. Ho. Portfolio 16, No. 2. The confirmation by the Skipton meeting forms part of this most interesting document, and it no doubt came to

It shows us an organization in the North of England, consisting of particular meetings, County Monthly Meetings, and a General Meeting two or three times in the year, and reveals in an illuminating way the spirit in which any development of organization was approached.

The letter begins with a reference to the truth revealed after the long night of apostasy, and to the "many thousands" already brought into it, and urges Friends to stand fast in their liberty:

> . . . that we be not again led back into the errors of those that went before us, who left the power and got into the form . . . that no footsteps may be left for those that shall come after, or to walk by example, but that all they may be directed and left to the truth, in it to live and walk and by it to be guided, that none may look back at us, nor have an eye behind them, but that all may look forward, waiting in the Spirit for the revelation of those glorious things which are to be made manifest to them.

This fine warning against the invasion of tradition is enforced out of church history, with its many instances of human policy and invention setting up a carnal, worldly religion and worship. The letter accordingly desires

> . . . that none may exercise lordship or dominion over another, nor the person of any be set apart, but as they continue in the power of truth . . . that truth itself in the body may reign, not persons nor forms, and that all such may be honoured as stand in the life of the truth, wherein is the power, not over but in the body,—that our path may be as the way of a ship in the sea, which no deceit can follow or imitate.

After this careful emphasis on the fundamentals of church government, a series of practical proposals is made, obviously designed to put the business arrangements of Friends in the North, and if possible throughout the country, on a more systematic footing. Friends representing neighbouring particular meetings are encouraged to meet together once a month, and Friends from the Monthly Meetings in the North to come together

---

Fox with Aldam's covering letter (Dev. Ho., A.R.B. Colln. No. 73). It is endorsed "To Thomas Doudney, at the Bell Savage in London deliver this, and for him to give or send it to G. F. with speed and care to be delivered to him where he is." A copy is also preserved in Dev. Ho., Samuel Watson Colln. p. 280.

twice or thrice in a year in a General Meeting, "and we wish the like may be settled in all parts, and one General Meeting of England." Each particular meeting should be expected to care for its own poor, to find employment for such as want work, or "cannot follow their former callings by reason of the evil therein"—a significant phrase—and to help parents in the education of their children, "that there may not be a beggar amongst us." If a particular meeting is overburdened, the Monthly Meeting should come to its assistance.

The Monthly Meeting should supply the needs of Friends in the ministry among them, where necessary, and should relieve Friends who are in prison or suffering for the Truth's sake, making collections from time to time for these purposes. If a Monthly Meeting is overburdened, the "General Meeting of Friends in the North" should come to its assistance, "that we may all bear one another's burdens and walk in love as becomes brethren."

Each meeting, whether particular, Monthly or General, should have full disposal of its own collections, "that as Friends according to their freedom do contribute, they may be also satisfied it is laid out by the power and in the wisdom of the body to whom they commit it." In the case of Monthly and General Meeting collections it is important that they should be for the needs of the Churches in general, and not limited for those in the ministry, "who will be as much grieved as others offended to have a maintenance or hire raised on purpose for them." The appointment of two persons at least in all trusts about money had already, as we have seen, been practised in the case of the Monthly Meeting treasurers, and is strongly recommended "for the more clearness of Truth, and satisfaction of Friends . . . that the innocency of the upright may be known and all deceit be prevented." Treasurers should render full accounts under two or more hands to their meetings, "and after every account so made and cleared, all papers to be cancelled,[1] and no further

[1] I correct "concealed" (*Letters of Early Friends*) to "cancelled," following the copy in the Saml. Watson Colln.

remembrance thereof to be had, which may beget many offences in future time, but cannot be of any service to the Truth." This clause explains the non-preservation of these early accounts, though Margaret Fell, happily for the historian, evidently felt at liberty to disregard the recommendation in the case of the accounts which had been rendered to her by the Treasurers for the North during the first period, prior to the establishment of the General Meeting.

The letter concludes by saying that if an agreement can be reached on these matters, which have taken up much time at previous General Meetings, Friends "will see greater things before" them, "which more chiefly concern the state of the Church, and will be of greater service to the Truth, as our Friends who bring this from us may lay before you, as there is freedom and opportunity."

The spiritual perception and practical wisdom of this letter give it a high place among ecclesiastical documents, and at the time it must have powerfully contributed to keeping the Quaker community in the North of England in a healthy condition. When the General Meeting met at Skipton four days later (5th October), the letter "was by all Friends owned and approved, and agreed to be observed, and copies thereof to be sent to all Monthly Meetings."[1] Thomas Killam of Balby, Samuel Watson of Great Stainforth, near Settle, Captain Henry Ward of Sunnybank, near Grayrigg, William Gandy of Frandley in Cheshire, and a fifth Friend, Richard Marge,[2] signed the endorsement of approval, and add:

As to the particular which concerns a meeting of some Friends from all the General Meetings of England, it is desired that Anthony Pearson do forthwith write up to George Fox, Edward Burrough, and other Friends at London, and lay it before them, and if they see it fit, and appoint time and place for it, we do in our names, and as from the body of Friends of

[1] *Letters of Early Friends*, p. 292 *n*. Thos. Aldam was not there himself, but on the 13th forwarded to Fox the "things consented to by many Friends which met at Skipton," and no doubt approved them (Aldam to Fox, Dev. Ho., A.R.B. Colln. No. 73).

[2] Norman Penney thinks that the name in the copy in Portfolio 16, No. 2, had originally been "Large," but had been changed into "Marge."

the Northern parts desire that Gervase Benson, Anthony Pearson, George Watkinson, William Gandy, Samuel Watson, Thomas Aldam, Thomas Stacey, and Richard Johnson attend.[1]

This postscript shows that General Meetings for business purposes were, as we knew from other sources, already becoming a recognized institution in other parts of the country, but, taken with the proposal in the Durham letter, involves the necessary inference that a General business meeting for the whole country was now being proposed for the first time.

This is not the view that has been hitherto taken. The most systematic early account of the institution of Monthly, Quarterly, and Yearly Meetings is that written by George Fox at Kingston-on-Thames in August 1689, "Concerning our Monthly and Quarterly and Yearly Meetings."[2] Not always clearly worded, and written, so far as the present question is concerned, thirty years after the events, when another system of meetings had been established, it must be read with discrimination. After referring to the meeting of Cumberland Elders in 1653, Fox speaks of a meeting of Elders at Swarthmore to settle Monthly Meetings in the Northern Counties, which must, I think, be the meeting at Swarthmore in the summer of 1657, already referred to. He goes on to say—

> And then there was a Yearly Meeting settled at Skipton, in Yorkshire, for all the Northern and Southern Counties, where in the wisdom of God they did see that all walked according to the glorious gospel of God, and that there was nothing wanting among them, and, if there was, one county assisted another, either in relieving the poor, in the Lord's counsel, or in advice in sufferings, or any other matters.

This agrees well enough with the first Skipton meeting in 1657, although there is no reason for supposing that the Southern Counties were directly represented at that meeting. The Skipton epistle, we shall remember, clearly implied that that meeting was the first of a series.

[1] From the MS. copy in Yearly Meeting, epp. 1656-1843, Dev. Ho. Bookcase No. 7. Thos. Stacey was from Cinderhill Green, near Sheffield. Richard Johnson lived at Liverpool (Fox, *Journ.* ii. 114).

[2] *Letters of Early Friends*, p. 310. The missing conclusion is now in the Dev. Ho. Library, and confirms Fox's authorship. See *ante*, p. 42.

The document next speaks of many Elders in the Truth coming from Bristol and London and other places to the series of Skipton Yearly Meetings, and proceeds:

And then the Yearly Meeting was removed to John Crook's and all things there were looked into as before. And many that were there were moved of the Lord to go beyond the seas, and marriages were looked into there and settled, as they had been before at the meeting at Swarthmore,[1] when many Friends met together out of many counties. And after the Yearly Meeting was kept at Balby in Yorkshire, where there were many thousands of people, and likewise at Skipton the same year, by the Elders there ordered from all parts, in the year 1660. And from thence it was removed to London the next year, where it hath been kept ever since, as being looked upon a more convenient place.

This paragraph refers to the Skipton meeting, as Fox knew it, when he attended it in 1660, and he has loosely written, as though there had been a series of meetings at Skipton of the same character, when in fact the 1660 meeting was the first that included representatives from all parts of the country. He also uses the term Yearly Meeting with respect not only to the Skipton meetings, but to the meetings at John Crook's and at Balby, and this has created confusion. But it will be observed that the Skipton meetings are stated to be for Elders, and no such limiting word is used of the other meetings. There were in fact two types of Yearly Meeting, just as there were two types of General Meeting—the meeting attended by ministers and primarily religious in character, and the meeting confined to Elders and chiefly intended for business. This becomes clear if we examine the accounts of the Yearly Meetings at John Crook's and at Balby. The meeting at John Crook's took place at the end of May 1658,[2] and was "a general Yearly Meeting for the whole nation . . . appointed to be held."[3] It lasted

[1] If the Swarthmore meeting was in the summer of 1657, this is likely enough, as John Crook's meeting was in May 1658, and no long space of time would separate action on the subject in the North and South.

[2] *Camb. Journ.* i. 317. This meeting is thought to have been held at his house at Beckerings Park, near Ridgmount, Beds. See *J.F.H.S.* i. 41 *n.*

[3] *Journ.* i. 418.

three days, and was attended by Fox and many Friends from most parts, and a large concourse of others, so that there was "a matter of three or four thousand people."[1] "A glorious meeting it was; and the everlasting gospel was preached, and many received it, . . . which gospel brought life and immortality to light in them and shined over all."[2] But after these large gatherings we have, following the heading in the Cambridge edition of the *Journal*, an address by Fox "spoken to Friends in the ministry particularly," and it was no doubt these Friends who were specially summoned, and not Elders for a business meeting. Another similar General Meeting for ministers was held in London at the Bull and Mouth, and at Horslydown, on Easter Tuesday, 5th April 1659.[3] With respect to the Balby meeting the case is even clearer. We have a letter from Parker to Margaret Fell, written in the preceding autumn,[4] in which he says:

> There is a Gener[al] Meeting spoken of for Friends in the ministry and others t[hat] may be free to come together, if the Lord so order it, [at] Balby in Yorkshire upon that day called Easter Monday. I speak of it to thee, but I leave it to thy wisdom to do as thou art ordered. There be but very few that know of it yet, George [Fox] spoke of it to me on the sixth-day last, and it was concluded upon, so that it cannot well be revoked. So Friends in wisdom may let one another know of it, for there is a service in it and good and true refreshment it is for brethren to behold one another that love may be renewed.

Easter Monday fell on 22nd April 1660, during the tumultuous weeks that preceded the Restoration. But the meeting took place as arranged. "Many thousands of people and Friends was gathered there. And Friends met in a great orchard of John Killam's."[5] "[An officer] came with a troop of horse to our meeting and trumpets sounding, and rode up just to me as I was speaking. . . . So I moderated the man's spirit and told him our meeting was made acquainted a great while before, and persuaded

[1] *Short Journ.* 54 (with some omissions). [2] *Journ.* i. 418.
[3] For this important confirmation of my argument see Wm. Caton's *Life*, 1689 edn., p. 51, and *post*, p. 380.
[4] Chalfont, Isaac Penington's house, 8th Nov. 1659, Swarthm. Colln. i. 168.
[5] *Camb. Journ.* i. 353.

him to be quiet and . . . leave half-a-dozen to see the order of our meeting, and so he did."[1] "And one of the troopers said, Here is more people flock after him than are about my Lord Protector's Court."[2] After describing this great meeting, Fox adds, "the next day we had a heavenly meeting at Warmsworth of Friends in the ministry and several others,"[3] no doubt the meeting of ministers referred to in Parker's letter.

There is nothing, therefore, in the Yearly Meetings at John Crook's and at Balby, or more accurately Warmsworth, to contradict the inference which we drew from the Skipton postscript of October 1659 that the Meeting there proposed of representatives from all the General Meetings of England was the first of its kind. Indeed, as we have seen, General Meetings, other than those in the North, were only being set up in other parts of England, as business meetings, about this year 1659, and therefore no meeting composed of representatives from them could have been previously held.

Fox, Burrough, and Friends of London must have fallen in with the proposal, for the representative meeting was held at Skipton on 25th April 1660, three days after the Warmsworth meeting of ministers. Fox gives an account of the proceedings, less clear than we should like, as he has evidently mixed into it the history of the meeting in previous years.[4] He calls it "a General Meeting of men Friends out of many counties concerning the affairs of the Church." After telling of a Friend who declared truth naked through the town and was beaten, he goes on:

> And at this meeting some Friends did come out of most parts of the nation, for it was about business of the Church both in this nation and beyond the seas. For when I was in the North several years before, I was moved to set up that meeting, for many Friends suffered and their goods were spoiled wrongfully contrary to the law. And so several Friends that had been justices and magistrates and that did understand the law came

1 *Short Journ.* 56.
2 *Camb. Journ.* i. 355.
3 *Ibid.*
4 *Ibid.*

there, and was able to inform Friends and to gather up the sufferings that they might be laid before the justices and judges and O. P. [Oliver, Protector] and his Parliaments before.

And this meeting had stood several years: and at this time Friends was well established upon Christ the Foundation and Rock of Ages, and the truth and life and the power of the Lord was over all, and Friends was informed from this meeting to their Monthly and Quarterly Meetings: so this meeting had done its service, and then all was directed to keep to their Monthly and Quarterly Meetings.

And justices and captains had come to break up this meeting, and then, when they saw Friends' books and accounts of collections concerning the poor, how that we did take care one county to help another, and took care to help Friends beyond the seas, and that the poor need not trouble their parishes, the justices were made to confess that we did their work: and Friends desired them to come and set with them then. And so they passed away lovingly and commended Friends' practice.

And many times there would be two hundred beggars of the world there, for all the country knew we met about the poor, which after the meeting was done Friends would send to the bakers and give them each a penny loaf apiece, be them as many as would. So we was taught to do good unto all, but especially to the household of faith.

And this was the last General Meeting that Friends had there, and then Friends was turned all to the Quarterly and Monthly Meetings as aforesaid, and there to do their business: and many precious papers may be seen that was given forth from this meeting, as in the books of epistles may be seen, and the manner of their collections.

In this account the passage as to breaking up the meeting belongs to the year 1660, but most of the rest seems to refer to the series of Skipton meetings. By Quarterly Meetings we must, I think, understand General business meetings for a district, such as the Skipton meeting itself had been in former years.

From this first business meeting for the whole country there went down to the particular meetings a recommendation for a third collection for the service of Truth, to be sent up to London in the same way as the former two collections. The document[1] shows the wide range of

[1] *Letters of Early Friends*, p. 292 *n.* (Dev. Ho. Portfolio 16, No. 3). Palatine was the German Palatinate; Surinam was then an English possession.

foreign service at this time, and, with a fine confusion of geography, recites

. . . certain information from some Friends of London of the great work and service of the Lord beyond the seas, in several parts and regions, as Germany, America, and many other islands and places, as Florence, Mantua, Palatine, Tuscany, Italy, Rome, Turkey, Jerusalem, France, Geneva, Norway, Barbados, Bermuda, Antigua, Jamaica, Surinam, Newfoundland, through all which Friends have passed in the service of the Lord.

When Fox says that this 1660 meeting was the last General Meeting held at Skipton, he must only be taken to mean that no further General Meetings were held there which exercised a kind of primacy over the rest of the country. There was in fact a General Meeting for the Northern Counties held at Skipton at the same time as the other meeting, and attended by fifteen Friends out of the seven counties, which directed a collection for those not of ability to help themselves, whether from sufferings on account of tithes or other causes. The next General Meeting was to be on 11th October.[1] Of this October meeting we have a record to the following effect in the *State Papers*:

October 11. Agreement made by Friends of Yorkshire, Lancashire, Westmorland, Cumberland, Northumberland, and Durham, at a General Meeting held at Skipton, that a collection be made in Yorkshire, Lancashire, Cheshire, Northumberland, and Durham, to equalize those already made in Cumberland and Westmorland; also that the accounts be brought in to the next General Meeting, March 7.[2]

Fox is no doubt right in saying that after the Skipton meeting the Yearly Meeting was removed to London, as being a more convenient place;[3] and Caton speaks of having been at a General Assembly of the brethren in London held about May 1661.[4] This was probably, like the Yearly Meetings at John Crook's, at the Bull and

[1] Early Record Book at Kendal.

[2] *Extracts from State Papers*, Second Series, p. 118.

[3] Document "Concerning our Monthly and Quarterly and Yearly Meetings" (1689) in *Letters of Early Friends*, p. 313.

[4] To Salthouse, Amsterdam, 21st June 1661, Swarthm. Colln. iv. 275.

Mouth, and at Warmsworth, primarily for Friends in the ministry.

Another General Meeting of the Northern Counties was held at Kendal on the 1st November 1661, when a collection in each county for service abroad was ordered to be made and sent to Gerrard Roberts in London, and Friends hoped there was a like mind in the rest of the nation.[1] We have interesting details of the *modus operandi* of these collections in papers preserved in the Record Office,[2] under date 3rd February 1662. A letter was found on the high-road near Cockermouth, thought to contain suspicious expressions about meetings contrary to the proclamation, and collections which might give opportunity for dangerous designs. The letter was from John Dixon, of Waterend, Loweswater, to Hugh Tickell, a well-known Friend of Portinscale, telling him to send in his month's collection both for London and the country, and informing him that another was ordered for the service of Truth, to be given in at the Monthly Meeting at Thomas Porter's at Quarry Hill, Bolton, near Wigton. On being examined, Dixon explained that they held Monthly Meetings to know what Friends stood in need of relief, in prison or elsewhere. The collection for London was for the service of Truth in Barbados and other places; the other for the service of Truth had a similar object. The meetings consisted of eight or ten Cumberland Friends.

We have now traced the system of business meetings in the North of England almost continuously from their first establishment up to a date well in the Restoration period. The county was in the main the unit of administration; but there was a grouping of counties, at least for some purposes, in what I have called the Kendal area, and for several years the whole North stood grouped together in the General Meetings at Skipton (1657), Scalehouse (1658), Skipton (1659 and 1660), and Kendal (1661), which in some cases were held as General Meetings for

[1] Entry in Y.M. epp., 1656-1843 (Dev. Ho. Bookcase, No. 7). See document in Dev. Ho. Portfolio 16, No. 5.

[2] *Extracts from State Papers*, Second Series, pp. 143-145.*

the North twice in the year. The meetings were not attended by the itinerating Publishers of Truth, but by the Elders sent up from the various districts. While financial provision for the service of Truth occupied a large and, as some thought, an undue part of the time available, the meetings also considered wider questions and developed the Quaker organization so far as necessary. The action of the General Meeting in promoting national collections for the expense of service abroad, in encouraging the setting up of General Meetings in the South, and in initiating the idea of a national business meeting for the whole Quaker community, shows that it was in the hands of men of statesmanlike minds. The organization of Friends in other places was naturally largely guided by the example of the strong Quaker Churches in the North.

The subordinate, and almost accidental place of these meetings in the life of the Quaker community will not have escaped notice. They in no sense superseded the individual or the particular congregation. They did not assume any control over the ministers who exercised spiritual leadership in the Church. They did not attempt to exercise authority. If circumstances had allowed their gradual development the history of the Society might have been materially modified. But they survived with difficulty, if at all, during the stress of persecution in the Restoration period. And it is not surprising to find that, when Fox addressed himself to urgent problems of church government after his release from Scarborough in 1666, he made little use of this earlier system.

In London there were some years of continuous development in the functions of the fortnightly meeting of men Friends not in the ministry which was set on foot about 1656. Burrough, in 1662,[1] describes its constitution very carefully, and it had become an important and well-settled body, with many responsible duties.

It was to consist of men of sound principles and judgment in the Truth of Christ, though with freedom for all Friends in Truth to assist. Its proceedings were to

[1] *Letters of Early Friends*, pp. 287-310.

be conducted in love, coolness,[1] gentleness, and dear unity, as one only party, all for the Truth of Christ. If any matter arose which was beyond the judgment of the Friends assembled, judgment was to be suspended till more Friends, anciently grown in the Truth, should have an understanding of it, and so that Friends in the ministry [2] might be present, assisting in counsel and judgment.

The proper work and service of the Meeting is for the well-ordering of the affairs of Truth in outward things, among the body of Friends, and that a general concord and assent may be among the ancients of them, for the government of the whole, by hearing and considering of things fitting for the advancement of Truth.

If differences arose between any two Friends or between a Friend and a stranger about bargains, debts or the like, the meeting might inquire into it, if the matter were presented to them, and seek to end all such strifes that the body might be preserved in peace and love and not be rent about outward things which were of no moment in comparison with the eternal substance. Records of births, marriages. and burials were to be faithfully kept, but in the case of marriages only when the parties were walking in the Truth of Christ Jesus and of good conversation. Care was to be taken for the poor, and work found for those out of employment, so that while the poor were relieved no idleness or depending on Friends for maintenance might be encouraged. Sufferings were to be preserved and recorded with any remarkable passages in relation to Truth, for the service of that age and for the ages to come.[3]

Side by side with this meeting two women's meetings developed. According to Gilbert Latey, the court-tailor who joined Friends in 1654,[4] the men's meeting, three or

[1] For the full passage, which is a classical description of the spirit in which the business deliberations of a Church should be conducted, see the quotation at the head of the present chapter.

[2] This must be the meaning of the "we" that is used.

[3] Wm. Crouch, *Posthuma Christiana*, chap. ii., confirms Burrough's account.*

[4] *Brief Narrative of the Life of Gilbert Latey*, 1707 edn. pp. 145-149. Crouch, *Posthuma Christiana* (1712 edn. p. 3), says: "Now also some ancient women Friends did meet together . . . to inspect the circumstances and conditions of such who were imprisoned upon Truth's account and . . . the wants and necessities of the poor." This passage is clearly placed in his narrative prior to the Restoration. For the care of prisoners, cf. Thos. Ellwood's *Life*, sub anno 1662.

four years after its establishment, felt the need of this kind of help. Some fifteen of the men were holding their meeting in the upper room at the Bull and Mouth, and they despatched two of their number to Gerrard Roberts' house, where Friends in the ministry were in the habit of meeting. Here they found Fox, Howgill, Burrough, Hubberthorne, and perhaps others, who approved the proposal and convened a meeting of women Friends to take up the matter. Fox writes as though his attention was independently called to the question about the same time.

"I was," he says, "sent for to many sick people. And at one time I was sent for to Whitechapel, about three o'clock in the morning, to a woman that was dying and her child, and the people was weeping about her. And after a while I was moved to speak to the woman, and she and her child was raised up. And she got up, to the astonishment of the people, and her child also was healed. And when I came to Gerrard Roberts' house about eight in the morning, and there came in Sarah Blackbury[1] to complain to me of the poor, and how many poor Friends was in want: and the Lord had showed me what I should do in His eternal power and wisdom. So I spoke to her, to bid about sixty women to meet me about the first hour in the afternoon at the sign of the Helmet at a Friend's house.[2] And they did so accordingly, such as were sensible women of the Lord's truth and fearing God. And what the Lord had opened unto me I declared unto them, concerning their having a meeting once a week, every second-day that they might see and inquire into the necessity of all Friends who was sick and weak and who was in wants, or widows and fatherless, in the city and suburbs. And so they blessed the Lord for the wisdom of God that had settled such a meeting in His power amongst them . . . and great things has been done in their meetings by the Lord's power, and very honourable it has been in the eyes of all the faithful, yea and the world also. . . ."[3]

Both accounts were written long after the events and the critic is naturally disposed to treat them as referring

[1] One of the first women ministers in London. For her association with Nayler and other facts about her, see note in *Camb. Journ.* ii. 484.

[2] Samuel Vosse lived at the Helmet in Basinghall Street.

[3] Document in Fox, *Epistles*, p. 6, dated at the bottom of p. 2, 1676. Also in *Camb. Journ.* ii. 342. I have followed the *Camb. Journ.* text, changing "Blackbourne" to "Blackbury."

to the same meeting; but, curiously enough, two distinct meetings with similar functions, known as the Two Weeks Meeting and the Box Meeting, are found in existence among women Friends in London in the Restoration period.[1]

In the setting up of these meetings we again see the subordination of the business men to the Publishers of Truth, whose full unity was clearly regarded as essential before any step could be taken. The direction continually being given by these leaders was indeed the chief controlling force of the Quaker movement throughout the Commonwealth period. When in London they made Gerrard Roberts' house their headquarters, where they maintained a close fellowship with one another, and could be found by any honest-hearted inquirer who desired access to them.[2]

[1] The question is carefully discussed in Wm. Beck and J. F. Ball's *London Friends' Meetings*, pp. 343-354.*

[2] *F.P.T.* 166.

CHAPTER XIV

ITINERATING WORK OF THE LEADERS IN GREAT BRITAIN, 1656-1660

Dear Friends and Lambs, put on the armour of light and the shield of truth, and the breastplate of righteousness that ye may stand in battle against all the Philistians . . . being led and guided with the Spirit up to God . . . that what ye do beget may be to Him, and into His image, and that which ye do present it may be perfect. . . . Stir abroad whilst the door is open and the light shineth. . . . In the life of God wait . . . that ye may beget to God, that as good plowmen and good thresher-men ye may be, to bring out the wheat.—Fox, *Epistles*, No. 135, to Howgill and Burrough, about 1657.

WE must now glance at the further work of the itinerating leaders during the remaining years of the Commonwealth period. The importance to the Church of their vital and vitalizing influence is everywhere apparent. They brought spiritual freshness and inspiration to the local groups of Friends, and were continually presenting to them the interests and claims of the wider movement. They also out of the maturity of their own experience were able to guide the healthy growth of the new community.

Among Friends of spiritual discernment these services were clearly recognized. Devonshire Friends, for example, depended much on the help of Thomas Salthouse, who devoted himself to work in the West of England. Arthur Cotten, of Plymouth, in March 1659[1] complained to Fox of the destitute condition of Devon and Cornwall, because there were at the time no itinerating ministers in either county, to "pass to and again amongst Friends in dread and wisdom, to stand out of all parties, and that

[1] To Fox, Swarthm. Colln. iv. 169.

to condemn which labour therein," and he wishes that Salthouse could come among them again. When Salthouse paid his next visit in the autumn of 1660, he spent about three months in the two counties, and found Friends "admiring what should be the matter that we had all left them so long." Some envious persons had suggested that the Quaker preachers were all fled for fear.[1] Priscilla Cotten wrote that Salthouse had been very serviceable in riding up and down among Friends at their meetings, and had much refreshed them. She thought there was need of him in the two counties for some time.[2] In all this there is clear perception of the value of inspired leadership. The body tended to become diseased and torpid when there was no active circulation of this life-blood.

Walter Clement, of Olveston in Gloucestershire, writes in the same strain:[3]

> Some disorderly spirits . . . spread themselves hereabouts but prevail little. The country here is pretty open, and if some Friends from the North were here ministering in the life and power of our God, many might be brought in, especially if some little abode and continuance might be here.

On the other hand, we find traces, as early as March 1656, of that jealousy of the itinerating ministers which afterwards appeared at the time of the Wilkinson-Story controversy of 1673. Howgill and Burrough, newly out of Ireland, and Audland, fresh from his service at Bristol, were all in the North, and attended a General Meeting held on Sunday the 16th at the widow Cock's, about a mile out of Kendal at Birkhagg.[4] After they had spoken,

[1] To Fox, Plymouth, 19th Nov. 1660, Swarthm. Colln. iii. 174.

[2] To Margt. Fell, Plymouth, 20th Nov. 1660, Swarthm. Colln. i. 140 She adds, "some Baptise (Baptists) and others have come to meetings." Barclay, *Inner Life*, p. 343 *n.*, cf. p. 373, misreads this as "some baptize."

[3] 20th Oct. 1659, Swarthm. Colln. i. 187.

[4] For this significant episode see a letter from Howgill, Audland, and Burrough to Friends, dated 17th Mar. 1655, *i.e.* 1656 (New Style) in Swarthm. Colln. i. 88. In March 1655 the three Friends were in London, see *Letters of Early Friends*, pp. 25-27, whereas in Mar. 1656 they were all at Kendal, see Geo. Taylor's letter to Margt. Fell in Swarthm. Colln. i. 234, which is dated by comparison with the accts. of the Kendal Fund. For the widow Cock's house see Nayler's *Works*, p. 1, and Besse, *Sufferings*, ii. 13. Hubberthorne had difficulty with Collinson in Sept. 1653, letter to Margt. Fell, Swarthm. Colln. i. 341. For Collinson see also *F.P.T.* 245, and *The Quakers Shaken*, pp. 2, 3.

Robert Collinson, one of the first at Kendal to be convinced, a Friend at whose house meetings were held, denied all that had been said as only a form of words without the life and power, and bade them stay at home and be silent and not go idling up and down, and he further charged them with breaking or putting a stop to the power which had been among Kendal Friends before they came. Some seemed to approve his words, and the three Publishers of Truth, "seeing the simplicity in many betrayed by the deceit," denied what he had said and afterwards issued a testimony against him as a Friend without the wedding garment, in which they exhorted all the Children of Light to deny fellowship with him until he came to repentance. They also urged all to beware of being betrayed by the like transformed appearance which was not the power of God.

Local Friends were sometimes burdened, especially by one or two unsuitable women ministers. Hubberthorne told Fox in 1658 [1] that Mary Howgill, a sister of Francis Howgill,* had been for half-a-year in the Eastern Counties and had done hurt, ministering confusion among Friends, so that some of them would not appoint meetings for her. Burrough, about the same time, found Friends in Bedfordshire and other places burdened by the ministry of a "little short maid" whom he thought more suited for a servant.[2] Ann Blaykling,* sister of John Blaykling, was another who caused trouble.[3] She was imprisoned at Cambridge in 1654, and travelled into several counties in the south. We hear of her in London in April 1655, interviewing the Protector,[4] and she was in prison in Suffolk in 1656 for calling a minister a greedy, dumb dog.[5] Fox includes her in his list of separatists in the following entry:

1657. And Ann Blaykling she run out and gathered a company to work on first-days and not to pay taxes, but they

[1] London, 20th Mar. [1658], Swarthm. Colln. iv. 12. She continued a trouble to Friends as late as June 1660. See letter of Hy. Hall, Jr., to Geo. Fox, Jr., Swarthm. Colln. iv. 177.

[2] To Fox, London, 12th Feby. 1657, Dev. Ho., A.R.B. Colln. No. 36.

[3] *F.P.T.* 252.

[4] Parker to Margt. Fell, 3rd April 1655, Swarthm Colln. i. 161.

[5] Besse, *Sufferings*, i. 662; *Extracts from State Papers*, First Series, p. 20.

must pay the impropriator's tithes: but they came in again, and the rest that did not came to nought.[1]

The Westmorland account of the First Publishers, written about 1708, says,

. . . for want of watchfulness the enemy prevailed to lead her into singularity and whimseys in several things, by which she run out of unity with Friends for several years, yet after came more near to Friends again, and married amongst Friends of the meeting of Sedbergh, and kept to meetings and is yet living.[2]

George Whitehead, writing in 1657 of a visit to the Isle of Ely,[3] throws one last gleam of light on this obscure separation. He reported that Friends there were "pretty well," except for a difficulty among them about tithe, some Friends supporting the payment when the tithe was impropriate, that is, in lay hands. He "was made to judge the thing down, so that several are further brought to deny them."

The later Commonwealth years were times of much spiritual conflict to George Fox. He had not stayed in London throughout Nayler's trial, but made a rapid journey into Lincolnshire and Yorkshire, returning through the Midlands to London by the end of the year. In January 1657[4] he was on the road again, travelling into the South and West as far as Exeter, where he attended an important General Meeting at the beginning of March.[5] From Exeter he returned through Bristol to London, though the fact only emerges after some critical reconstruction of the *Journal*.[6] A visit to Wales followed in June and July, the itinerary of which it is not easy to follow amid the confusion of the authorities; but he visited every county, and the precise order is of little importance.[7] His chief companions were John ap John,

[1] *Camb. Journ.* ii. 314.*

[2] *F.P.T.* 252.

[3] To Fox, 26th Feby. 1657, Swarthm. Colln. iv. 91.

[4] Caton to Margt. Fell, London, 19th Jany. 1657, Swarthm. Colln. i. 314.

[5] Salthouse to Margt. Fell, Plymouth, 3rd Mar. 1657, Swarthm. Colln. iii. 183.

[6] See note, *post*, p. 438.

[7] The known dates are June 1657, Fox was in Wales, A.R.B. Colln. No. 35; 28th June he was at Wm. Gandy's in Cheshire (Hubberthorne to Margt. Fell, Pontymoile, Swarthm. Colln. i. 353). For Wales, the *Journ.* and the *Short Journ.* conflict as to order.

the member of Morgan Lloyd's congregation who had been convinced at Swarthmore in 1653, and Edward Edwards of Denbighshire, who in 1654 was living at Gervase Benson's near Sedbergh.[1] Hubberthorne and Holme were also with him part of the time. The infant church in South Wales had been shaken to its foundations by the controversies occasioned by James Nayler. Holme writes in April 1657:[2]

A witness for the truth of God I stand, out of which some are turned which once was professed witnesses of it, and now doth it oppose . . . and nothing would satisfy them but the stopping of my mouth forever, in which they have not prevailed. . . . I covered their nakedness so long as I could, till they manifested their envy in public meetings. . . . The most of the Welshmen that ministered is gone out of the truth and hath believed a lie. . . . The honest-hearted is preserved in the truth, some is drawn aside which never came to see: they come into our meetings and tumbles upon the floor, and when they can no else stop me from speaking one falls a-singing, and they sit in meetings in haircloth and ashes, and is acted in all manner of deceit and imagination. . . . My endeavour is to keep Friends cool and quiet, and the other will die of itself.

Fox had been told of the trouble when he was in Bristol in March, and his visit to Wales was no doubt undertaken partly with the intention of dealing with the situation at first hand. To use his own phrases,[3] he passed and viewed Wales and there found those who had turned against Truth burst into partics and got up into heaps one against another, till Truth was evil spoken of. At Cardiff he held a great meeting in the Town Hall, to which one justice sent seventeen of his family. Fox sent word to those who had run out after Nayler that the day of their visitation was over, and says grimly, "and they did not prosper noways." Tenby*and Haverfordwest gave the Quaker leader a cordial welcome, though the governor of Tenby threw John ap John into prison for standing with his hat on in the church, while the congregation was singing.

[1] Whitehead's *Christian Progress* (1725 edn.), p. 21.
[2] To Margt. Fell, 16th April 1657, Swarthm. Colln. i. 196.
[3] Fox to Nayler (date uncertain), Swarthm. Colln. i. 382.

Fox asked if the minister himself had not two caps on his head, a black and a white one, and suggested that if his friend turned his hat into a cap by cutting the brim off he would only have one cap on. "Away with these frivolous things," said the Governor. Fox swiftly retorted, "Why then imprison my friend for frivolous things?" On leaving Tenby the mayor, a friendly justice, their wives and a number of others went half-a-mile with the party to the water's side, and there Fox was moved to kneel down with them and pray the Lord to preserve them. Quaker groups already existed at Tenby and Haverfordwest, and the visit must have proved a great cheer.

Pontymoile, near Pontypool in Monmouthshire, was another centre, the leading Friends being Walter Jenkins and Richard Hanbury. Here Fox held a great meeting, and there was a large convincement.[1]

In Radnorshire the largest of his meetings took place.

"There was a meeting," says Fox, "like a leaguer for multitudes, and I walked a little off from the meeting, whilst the people was a-gathering, and there came John ap John to me, a Welshman, and I bid him go up to the people, and if he had anything upon him from the Lord to speak to the people in Welsh he might. And then there came Morgan Watkins to me, who was loving to Friends, and, says he, The people lies like a leaguer, and the gentry of the country is come in, so I bid him go up to the meeting; for I had a great travail upon me for the salvation of the people. And so I passed up to the meeting and stood atop of a chair about three hours, and sometimes leaned my hand off a man's head, and stood a pretty while before I began to speak. And many people sat a-horseback: and at last I felt the power of the Lord went over them all, and the Lord's everlasting life and truth shined over all, and the scriptures was opened to them . . . and all was bowed down under the power of God, and parted peaceably and quietly with great satisfaction, and they said they never heard such a divine in their lives and the scriptures so opened . . . and Christ and the apostles' free teaching set atop of all the hireling teachers: and people turned to Him."[2]

---

[1] *J.F.H.S. Supplmt.* No. 6 (John ap John), pp. 8, 21, 36-38.

[2] I quote from the *Camb. Journ.* i. 273, 274. Ellwood tones down "divine" into "sermon." Fox calls Watkins "Watkison."

The *Short Journal* says that there were many thousands of people at this meeting, and it was reported that if Fox had had another meeting half the country would come in, they were so taken with the Truth.[1]

In the north of Wales the reception was less encouraging. At Wrexham many of Morgan Lloyd's congregation came to them, but "very rude and wild and airy they were, and little sense of Truth they had." One lady in her lightness asked Fox whether she should cut his hair for him, and afterwards boasted "in her frothy mind" that she came behind him and cut off a lock of his hair, "which was a lie."

Fox seems to have divided his Welsh visit by attending a meeting on 28th June of some three thousand persons on the Cheshire side of Warrington, at William Gandy's of Frandley, whose house was the resort of all the travelling Publishers of Truth, and a frequent place for such gatherings. It had been a droughty summer, but after the meeting a great rain fell, whereupon George remarks,

> . . . it was a noted thing generally amongst people that when I came still I brought rain . . . and as far as Truth had spread in the North and South there was rain enough and pleasant showers . . . and the like observation and expectation they have beyond the seas: when there is a drought they generally look for the Quakers' General Meetings, for then they know they shall have rain, and as they receive the Truth and become fruitful unto God, they receive from Him their fruitful seasons also.[2]

His sense of unity with the creation was quite strong enough to make him believe in the meteorological effects of a good Quaker meeting.

When he was clear of Wales he passed north to a few days of sorely needed rest and refreshment at Swarthmore. Since his Launceston imprisonment he had visited most parts of the country, strengthening the groups of Friends amid the fears without and within which assailed them, and he now wrote two important general letters of counsel.[3]

[1] Cf. *Camb. Journ.* i. 274. *Short Journ.* 51.

[2] *Camb. Journ.* i. 273. Dr R. M. Jones tells me that throughout America the tradition still survives that rain will accompany a Quaker Yearly Meeting.

[3] *Journ.* i. 384, 389.

In the first he exhorted Friends to mind the seed of God and to dwell in it: in the second he urged them to be valiant in the day of their trial, and to see that the testimony of the Lord did not fall. When Christ was received into the heart, He destroyed the devil and his works, and cut off the entail of sin.

This angers all the devil's lawyers and counsellors that Satan shall not hold sin by entail in thy garden, in thy field, in thy temple, thy tabernacle. So keep your tabernacles that there ye may see the glory of the Lord appear at the doors thereof.

In another fine passage he says:

We must not have Christ Jesus, the Lord of Life, put any more in a stable, amongst the horses and asses, but He must now have the best chamber, the heart, and the rude debauched spirit must be turned out.

In Westmorland he had large meetings at John Audland's and at Strickland Head. He went to a horse-race, and declared Truth to the gentry there assembled, and a chief constable also admonished them, the sport being at that time illegal.

Fox now paid his first visit to Scotland with Parker, Lancaster, and Widders for companions. Colonel William Osburne, one of the earliest Quaker preachers north of the Tweed, came into Cumberland to guide the party. They set out on 10th September 1657,[1] and Fox says that as soon as his horse set foot across the border the infinite sparks of life sparkled about him, and, as he rode along, he saw that the seed of the Seedsman Christ was sown, but abundance of clods and of foul and filthy earth was above it.[2] The party visited the groups of Friends at Douglas, Heads, Badcow, and Gartshore, where Lady Margaret Hamilton was convinced, who afterwards went to warn Cromwell and Fleetwood of the Day of the Lord that was coming upon them.[3] The Clydesdale Friends had been excommunicated by the Synod at Glasgow, who had

[1] Annals of 1657 in *Camb. Journ.* ii. 337.

[2] *Journ.* i. 412, and similar passage in Fox to Barclay, Swarthmore, 16th Dec. 1675; in *Reliquiae Barclaianae* (1870), p. 3.

[3] There is a letter from her in Swarthm. Colln. iv. 217.

directed that no people in other parishes should bargain with them or entertain them either freely or for money.[1] The Presbyterian ministers followed this up by promulgating the following curses directed against Quaker principles:[2]

(i.) Cursed be all they that say Grace is free, and let all the people say, AMEN.
(ii.) Cursed be all they that say the scriptures is not the word of God, and let all the people say, AMEN.
(iii.) Cursed be all they that say, Faith is without sin, and let all the people say, AMEN.
(iv.) Cursed are all they that say, Every man hath a light sufficient to lead him to Christ, and that within him, and let all the people say, AMEN.
(v.) Cursed be all they that deny the Sabbath Day, and let all the people say, AMEN.

When they heard that Fox was in the country they petitioned the Council in Scotland, and soon after reaching Edinburgh he was ordered to appear before it on Tuesday 13th October. On saying that he was in Scotland "to visit the seed of God, which had long lien in bondage," he was told that he must leave the country by the following Tuesday. Fox took no notice of the order, and, after some further stay in Edinburgh, revisited the Clydesdale Friends, and went forward to other service. He was in the Highlands among the clans—probably only for a few hours—and remarks, "They were devilish and like to have spoiled us and our horses, and run with pitchforks at us, but through the Lord's power we escaped them." At Perth,[3] the Baptists were very bitter, and instigated the Governor to call out the soldiers and banish the party from the town, whereupon, says Fox:

James Lancaster was moved to sound and sing in the power of God, and I was moved to sound the Day of the Lord and the glorious everlasting gospel: and all the streets was up and filled with people: and the soldiers were so ashamed that they cried

---

[1] See The Scotch Priests' Principles in Fox's *Great Mistery* at p. 334, with particulars; cf. *Journ.* i. 404.
[2] The Scotch Priests' Principles in Fox's *Great Mistery*, pp. 335-336.
[3] Fox calls Perth by its alternative name of [St.] Johnstoun.

and said they had rather have gone to Jamaica than to guard us so, and then they set us in a boat, and set us over the water.[1]

Jamaica, with its deadly climate, had lately been taken by England from Spain, and was at this time proving the grave of hundreds of English soldiers. At Perth, Fox was the guest of Captain Davenport, who, as we have seen, entertained Hall at Inverness earlier in the year, and became a Friend.

Fox remained some five months in Scotland, and during December Parker visited Fife, Clydesdale, and the West.[2] The service in Fife lay chiefly among soldiers of the English army of occupation, which was at this time being purged of Quakers. At Badcow there was a growth among Friends and at Heads "a fine sober, growing people," but in face of the hostility of the military authorities and the bitter opposition of the Kirk, it was still a day of small things. The handful of Friends in Edinburgh and Leith consisted chiefly of English and included the wives of some of the officers. Edward Byllinge,* who was then in the army, but was afterwards a brewer at Westminster, was reached by the Quaker message, became reconciled to his wife, and joined Friends. His name appears again in connection with the founding of New Jersey.[3]

Towards the end of February Fox rode South. He knew that warrants were out against him in Leith and Edinburgh,[4] but faced his enemies with characteristic courage. He recounts his passage through Edinburgh as follows:[5]

I bid Robert Widders follow me, and so in the dread and power of the Lord we came to the first two sentries, and the Lord's power came so over them that we passed by them without any examination. So we rid up the streets to the Market Place and by the main guard, and then out at the gate by the

---

[1] *Camb. Journ.* i. 305.

[2] Parker to . . . Leith, 13th Jany. 1658, Swarthm. Colln. iii. 140.*

[3] See *The Quakers in the American Colonies*, pp. 363, 380, and note in *Camb. Journ.* i. 452.

[4] *Journ.* i. 408, confirmed by Thurloe, *State Papers*, vi. 811.

[5] *Camb. Journ.* i. 308.

third sentry, and so clear out at the suburbs, and there we came to an inn, and set up our horses on the seventh-day. So I saw and felt that I rid against the cannon-mouths, pistols, pike-ends [and] sword-points, and so the Lord's power and immediate hand carried us over the heads of them all. And so, on the first-day, we went up to the meeting, Friends having notice that I would be at it in Edinburgh city, and there was a many officers and soldiers, and a glorious meeting it was, and the everlasting power of God was set over the nation, and His Son reigned and shined over it in His glorious power, and all was quiet, and never a one meddled with me.

He returned South through Durham and Yorkshire, visiting Swarthmore and afterwards the North Midlands, where he laboured with some success among the Proud Quakers, who followed Rice Jones. By the end of May he had reached John Crook's house in Bedfordshire, and there attended the Yearly Meeting of Friends in the ministry.[1] The address which he gave shows the spiritual condition of Friends at this date as Fox understood it. Cautions are given against long addresses, against travelling about except as moved of the Lord, and against seeking the praise of men. He says that before all the wicked spirits are got down, which are rambling abroad, Friends must have patience and wait in "the cool life," then all that is contrary will be subjected and the Lamb will have the victory. The importance of the ministry is insisted on, "it is a mighty thing to be in the work of the ministry of the Lord God and to go forth in that; for it is not as a customary preaching but to bring people to the end of all preaching." There are some fine sentences which show the high ideal which Fox cherished for the Quaker fellowship.

Now Truth hath an honour in the hearts of people which are not Friends, so that all Friends being kept in the Truth they are kept in the honour, they are honourable and that will honour them: but if ye lose the power, ye lose the life, they lose their crown, they lose their honour, they lose the cross which should crucify them, and they crucify the just, and, by losing the

[1] *Journ.* i. 418-427, and *Camb. Journ.* i. 317, from which I quote. See *ante*, pp. 333, 334.

power, the Lamb comes to be slain. And so, as it is here, it will have so in other nations, for all Friends here are as one family—the seed, the plants, they are as a family.

The summer of 1658 was spent in London and the neighbourhood, but, after this, it is difficult for a time to follow the course of Fox's life, for the *Journal* becomes strangely confused and fragmentary, and continues so until the months immediately preceding the Restoration. The order of many of the paragraphs differs in the *Cambridge Journal* and the printed *Journal* edited by Ellwood, and in both forms there are insertions which clearly belong to earlier dates.[1] Fox was in London till about 20th August 1658, when he saw the Protector for the last time, and felt a waft of death go forth against him.[2] The news of Cromwell's death on 3rd September reached him in Essex, whereupon he returned to the city and remained in or near it through the winter. In June 1659 we hear of him in Kent with Edward Burrough,[3] and on 17th July[4] he went to Mitcham in Surrey to face a rude throng who were shamefully maltreating Friends. A fortnight earlier they had broken into the meeting, dragged Friends out one by one upon the Common, and punched and driven them along till a neighbour received them into his yard. With splendid pertinacity the Quakers proceeded with their meeting, but, when one of them began to speak, he was drenched with a pailful of muddy water, and when the congregation stood bareheaded at prayer, stones were thrown at them, and after meeting the mob pursued them a great way, stoning them. On the following Sunday they had daubed the Friends with dirt and filth, and then cried out, "How like witches they look." When Fox came he had a table

[1] The paper about the suffering Protestants in Piedmont given in *Journ.* i. 434 belongs to 1655, the day of humiliation was on 14th June, and in the *Camb. Journ.* i. 335 the paper is dated at the end 16th June, but is headed at the beginning 1656, a mistake for 1655. The paragraphs about Thos. Aldam in the *Journ.* i. 446 also belong to 1655; cf. *Letters of Early Friends*, pp. 34, 28.

[2] *Journ.* i. 440.

[3] Parker to Margt. Fell, 22nd June 1659, in *Letters of Early Friends*, p. 69. Burrough had been to Dunkirk with Saml. Fisher in May.

[4] I identify without difficulty the incidents in *Journ.* i. 442, 443, with the sufferings at Mitcham related in Besse, *Sufferings*, i. 689

set in the close where the meeting took place, and stood on this with a Bible in his hand. He spoke home to the consciences of the people and under his potent personality they became ashamed and quiet. He tells us that at this time he was "very weak," and shortly after he went to Reading, where he seems to have lain at the house of Thomas and Ann Curtis for ten weeks in great travail of spirit. It was his hour of darkness and, through his sorrow of mind and exercise of spirit, his face was changed and he looked pale and thin.[1] Envious people said, "the plagues of God were upon him." This year 1659 is often spoken of as "the year of anarchy." Its distractions and confusions, the internecine struggles of Puritan parties "plucking each other to pieces," the hardening of men's spirits in the growing strife, and the ominous outlook, all these oppressed and well-nigh crushed the spirit of Fox. He saw the downfall of Puritanism taking place through the wounds of its own friends, and it seemed to him the Nemesis which so often attends the arrogance of a dominating party in power.

> "I saw," he says, "God would bring that atop of them which they had been atop of, and that all must be brought down to that which did convince them before they could get over that bad spirit within and without."

Yet at last when he had travailed with the witness of God which the Puritan parties had quenched, and had got through with it and over all the hypocrisy, and had seen how it would be turned under and down and how life would rise over it, then he came to have ease and the light shined over all.*

> "So," cries Fox ecstatically, "with heart and voice praise the name of the Lord, to whom it doth belong, and over all hath the supremacy. And the nations will I rock, being on them atop."[2]

---

[1] *Journ.* i. 447: also for the Reading travail of spirit, *Journ.* i. 444, and *Camb. Journ.* i. 341, 347, which places the materials differently. According to Audland's letter to Wilkinson and Story, 1st April 1655, in Dev. Ho., A.R.B. Colln. No. 28, Curtis lived "at the sign of the George."

[2] *Camb. Journ.* i. 343.

He returned to London about the end of October, and during the latter part of the year visited the Eastern Counties, coming back to the city in January 1660, when his long-deferred reconciliation with Nayler took place. It is not, I think, a mere fancy which finds once more in the *Journal* at this point the old note of triumphant power that has been lacking during the preceding months, and the account again broadens out into a full and orderly narrative. The hurt done to the Truth by Nayler's extravagant actions must have wounded Fox deeply, and he found it hard to forgive, till his own spirit, we may conjecture, became hurt and his service was checked. But when he had been reconciled to his repentant brother, he knew again the full tides of spiritual strength.

Fox now goes into the South and West of England, holding blessed meetings. At Dorchester they took off his hat and examined his hair, expecting to find traces of the Jesuit tonsure. He returned through Bristol and the Midlands, paid a visit to his relations at Drayton, and went North to the Yearly Meeting of ministers at Balby in April, which he had arranged for in the previous autumn. From this he proceeded to the Yearly Meeting at Skipton, and so on to Swarthmore.

To Fox himself these three years must have been years of disappointment. There was a hardening in the Puritan character which made it less susceptible to the Quaker message than in the days of eager religious zeal which had preceded. The Kingdom of God which seemed so near at hand in the first freshness of his service had receded, although at the same time he felt that it had been received and realized in thousands of hearts that had opened to the Light of a living Christ.

The service of the other Quaker leaders can be passed over more lightly. The beautiful close of Nayler's life has already been told. While he was suffering his savage punishments, in the opening days of the year 1657, John Camm, one of the apostles of Quakerism in Bristol, had passed away, aged about fifty-two.[1] He had been in a

[1] *F.P.T.* 254.

consumption for some years, and as early as December 1655 wrote from Bristol to his old Westmorland friends, "Now I wait ready to be offered up, being in great weakness of the outward body but in much peace and quiet in the inward."[1] With indomitable courage he continued his itinerating work, though often unable to get on or off his horse without help.[2] His last days were spent at Camsgill, in much spiritual strength. "My outward man," he said, "daily wastes and moulders down, and draws towards his place and centre, but my inward man revives and mounts upward towards its place and habitation in the heavens."

His bosom friend and spiritual yoke-fellow John Audland continued to give the strength of his service to Bristol, though we hear of him also in Cumberland, Westmorland, Durham, and London. Howgill also travelled widely. In the early autumn of 1656 he went through the West Midland Counties, having meetings in the principal towns;[3] in the summer of 1657 he spent ten weeks in Scotland with Thomas Robertson,[4] in the summer of 1659 he was with John Audland in Durham and Cleveland, and afterwards went to Kendal.[5] But his writings and other evidence show that during the years 1658 and 1659 he was also a good deal in London. The year of anarchy moved him profoundly: he saw how the Puritans had lost their fervency and zeal and were become dry and content to make a covenant with death. England seemed to him like a dismasted hull, ready to be blown with every gust of wind upon every rock. Through fair pretences of liberty and freedom, and sanctity and holiness, people had been led up and down like horses and tossed up and down like a tennis ball. The old tenderness to the appearance of God's truth had gone, and in its place there was hypocrisy and deceit. Friends alone had kept their integrity and their first love, and

[1] Dev. Ho., Boswell Middleton Colln. p. 103, and *The Memory of the Righteous Revived*, p. 36.

[2] For the last passages of Camm's life see his son Thos. Camm's Testimony in *The Memory of the Righteous Revived*.

[3] Letter to Fox, Burford, 21st Sept. 1656 (Dev. Ho., A.R.B. Colln. No. 33).

[4] *Ante*, p. 231.

[5] Letters in A.R.B. Colln. Nos. 60 and 169.

had sought the good of the nation.[1] Burrough continued his unwearied service, chiefly in London and the neighbourhood, to which he had returned by May 1656, after his exile from Ireland. In the summer of 1657 he became involved in a dispute with Richard Mayo, the minister at Kingston-on-Thames. He was tendered the oath of allegiance, but was finally committed for misdemeanour in saying that he would prove that Mayo preached damnable doctrine and error. Mayo also sued him for £200 damages. He spent some weeks in prison, but the action, after dragging on for more than a year, was abandoned.[2] Burrough through these years of Puritan decline continued to utter his message with an air of unshaken authority. His writings are diffuse, but full of energy and assurance. He challenged the Pope, for example, in a letter beginning, "Thou Mountain, hear the word of the Lord God, thus saith the Lord God unto thee, I will lay thee low, I will break thee down."[3]

In May 1659 he visited Dunkirk, then in English hands, with Samuel Fisher. Their chief object was to warn the Papists, Jesuits, and Friars, "and that company of idolaters," and to sound the mighty Day of the Lord among them. Their discourses with the Friars and Jesuits in the town produced little effect, and it is of more interest to note that they had good service among the English army, and Burrough says, "I must commend the spirit of our Englishmen for moderation, more than the men of any other nation." He wrote a letter to the army which breathes the atmosphere of Milton's sonnet beginning, "Avenge, O Lord, thy slaughtered saints," rather than the non-military spirit of the Quaker. They were to return to their old righteousness and not to look back for rest and ease till they had visited Rome and avenged the blood of the guiltless through all the dominions of the Pope. Whether the Lord will take

[1] For these sentences see "One warning more unto England," in Howgill's *Works*, pp. 333-343.

[2] Besse, *Sufferings*, i. 688, 689; Burrough's *Works*, pp. 375-385; Burrough to Fox and Howgill, 25th Augt. 1657, Swarthm. Colln. iii. 18; and Edward Cook's *Short Account* of the Trial of the Action on 31st July and *Second Account* of Second Trial on 25th Sept. 1658.

[3] *Works*, p. 472.

vengeance by Himself without an instrument, or through their instrumentality, he does not know, but the time of vengeance is near, and he believes it will be done through the men of the English nation, if they are faithful.

"For what are these few poor islands that you have run through," he says, "and laid many mountains low, they are but little in comparison of the great part of Christendom in which idolatry and grievous oppressions do abound, which the hand of the Lord is against and which He will take vengeance upon. . . . It is the Lord's work, I know, to make men truly religious, but yet the Lord may work by you, to break down the briars and thorns and rocks and hills that have set themselves against the Lord."[1]

In the Restoration year he visited Bristol for about two months in the early summer, where he had "precious service," and then spent some time in Ireland, until February 1661, travelling to and fro some two thousand miles, with free passage in the principal towns and cities.[2]

Hubberthorne was much in London, and bore the brunt of the time of disorder and difficulty which followed Nayler's fall. His letters are one of our chief sources of information, and he showed himself, as Burrough wrote after his death, "a good companion in all conditions, not soon moved into passion of either grief in adversity or of joy in prosperity."[3] He continued a close interest in the Eastern Counties, and also visited the Midlands, Wales, and Cheshire.[4]

George Whitehead, another earnest labourer in the Eastern Counties, had been released from Bury St. Edmunds shortly after Fox came out of Launceston. A brutal flogging which he suffered at Nayland in Suffolk in the following April moved the people to tears and raised in him that elevation of feeling which has so often attended martyrdom.

[1] *Works*, pp. 537-540.* [2] *Works*, pp. 701, 767.

[3] Testimony at beginning of Hubberthorne's *Works*.

[4] He was in the Eastern Counties in the spring of 1657 and again for three weeks in the autumn (Letter to Fox, 7th Apl., Swarthm. Colln. iv. 10, and to Margt. Fell, Swarthm. Colln. i. 353; also to her on 22nd Sept., Dev. Ho., Jas. Bowden's copies of Wm. Caton Colln.). For his other movements see letters, Swarthm. Colln. i. 353, iv. 16, iv. 17; *Journ.* i. 451-453; and Geo. Whitehead's *Christian Progress*, p. 108.*

'It is also very memorable to me," he says, "how wonderfully the Lord, by His Divine power, supported me, even at that very instant while they were inflicting their cruelty . . . that even then my spirit was raised and my mouth opened to sing aloud in praises to the Lord my God, that He counted me worthy to suffer for His name and truth-sake."[1]

During the summer of 1657 he went into the West Midlands with Hubberthorne and afterwards to the North, delayed on the way by a fever, and received by his parents as a returning prodigal. The winter was spent busily among northern Friends, and he then returned to his work in the Eastern Counties, where he proved himself fearless and formidable in many public disputes. The vigour and importance of his work may be traced by the reader of his *Christian Progress*, an interesting journal, though much inferior to that of Fox.

Thomas Taylor, the old leader of the Westmorland Seekers, moved about chiefly in South Lancashire and the North and West Midlands, though with some service in Yorkshire. He underwent imprisonments at Appleby, York, Leicester, and Coventry,[2] and proved both in suffering and in service his sterling character. Says one of his friends:

. . . when he had been going on the road, he commonly had a word of caution to professor and profane, and some of his old hearers who did not receive truth, I have seen him speak to them on the market-day in Kendal-street, and sometime go to their houses to exhort, admonish, and reprove as the Lord directed, or, if he had been travelling on the highway, and seeing boys playing on the first-day in the summer time, and their parents or old people sitting besides them, he would preach to them; so that he was always concerned for God's glory.[3]

The work of Farnsworth, Dewsbury, and the other Yorkshire leaders may now be referred to. Farnsworth was released from Banbury in April 1656,[4] and took a

[1] Geo. Whitehead's *Christian Progress*, p. 106.

[2] See Christopher Taylor's and Fox's Testimonies in Taylor's *Works*; also *Works*, pp. 6, 47-49, and for Appleby imprisonment, Besse, *Sufferings*, ii. 6-8.

[3] Robert Barrow's Testimony in Taylor's *Works*.

[4] Audland to Burrough, 26th April, in Dev. Ho., A.R.B. Colln. No. 116, and Taylor to Nayler, 28th April [1656], in Swarthm. Colln. iii. 32.

principal part in the important meeting at Balby in the following November. He seems to have worked chiefly in Yorkshire, and we hear nothing of the fervent service in which he rejoiced in the first years of "publishing Truth." The scanty materials do not enable us to ascertain the cause of this, but the first planting of Quakerism was done, and the Church at home may have claimed all his strength. He wrote three or four pamphlets during these years.

With Dewsbury the case is different. His long imprisonment at Northampton had held him bound when the rest of the army of the Lord was in full charge upon the enemy. But the years that succeeded his release in January 1656 were for him rare years of freedom, during which he visited Friends throughout Great Britain, his ministry being everywhere in much demonstration of the Spirit and of power. If we had a continuous record of his service, it would reflect a magnetic personality more tender than that of Fox, but almost equally impregnated with high courage and inspiration. To piece together his portrait from our fragmentary materials is one of the most grateful tasks that fall to the lot of the Quaker historian. After a short stay in his home at Wakefield, he went into Essex, probably seeing James Parnell in prison, and returned to Northampton in May.[1] A General Meeting was being held in a field of William Lovell's, a mile out of the town, and had been broken up by the authorities.[2] Dewsbury continued it, six soldiers standing in the field meanwhile with their horses and arms. When Dewsbury knelt in prayer they dragged him away, but he knelt down again on the road, and as he prayed the soldiers' hearts failed them and they allowed him to return to the field and finish the meeting. He seems to have spent the rest of the year in Lancashire and Yorkshire,[3] and, as I infer from the style, was the writer of the

[1] Ann Dewsbury to Margt. Fell, 1st Mar. 1656, Swarthm. Colln. iv. 142; Dewsbury to Margt. Fell, 1st June, Swarthm. Colln. iv. 143. He had written a loving letter to Parnell before his release from Northampton; see Parnell's reply in *Letters of Early Friends*, p. 224.

[2] Dewsbury's letter of 1st June, and Besse, *Sufferings*, i. 529.

[3] Dewsbury to Margt. Fell, Wakefield, 25th June 1656, Swarthm. Colln. iv. 137.

document issued from the meeting of elders at Balby in November. In the spring of 1657 we find him again in the South, writing a wise letter from London,[1] in which he urges Friends not to abuse their liberty and to "keep out the dead airy spirit that utters words out of the life, and brings in a dead formality which burdens the seed of God." After a visit to the Eastern Counties, he reached Kent in May, and on 3rd June was able to go aboard the *Woodhouse*, then lying in the Downs, and bid Godspeed to the devoted band of Friends who were starting on their memorable voyage to the New England colonies.[2] His high spirit, at a time when Nayler's proceedings had clouded the fortunes of the Quaker movement, is shown in a letter written from Kent.[3] "Before one of you that is in the Resurrection and Life in Christ," he says, "shall a thousand flee, and five put ten thousand to flight, for you in the Life are the host of heaven." He now passed into the West of England, reaching the Land's End by the middle of September, and then turning homewards.[4] At Loveday Hambly's house at Tregangeeves Dewsbury held a large meeting, and "had the sight of many Friends from most parts of the county."[5] At Torrington, in Devonshire, he was had before the mayor and justices, and charged as a Jesuit and a vagabond. They asked him how he came to be a minister of Christ, and his answer made one of the justices weep, and when he came before them again the chairman of the bench tore up the *mittimus* which had been made out, and told Dewsbury he was a free man. He held great meetings in Somerset and Wiltshire, also one at the house of Nathaniel Cripps[*] of Tetbury on the Gloucestershire border. Here we get a charming glimpse of his sympathetic nature. The wife of John Roberts of Siddington attended the meeting, in

[1] *Works*, p. 166.

[2] Dewsbury to Margt. Fell, 3rd June 1657, Swarthm. Colln. iii. 24, and account of voyage printed in Bowden's *Hist. of Friends in America*, i. p. 63.

[3] *Works*, pp. 170, 171.

[4] Ambrose Rigge to Margt. Fell, Basingstoke, 22nd Augt. 1657, in Dev. Ho., Crosfield MSS.; *F.P.T.* 83; and letter to wife cited in next note.

[5] See *F.P.T.* 22, 27, and for the Torrington episode, etc., Dewsbury's letter to his wife in *Works*, pp. 172-174; original in Swarthm. Colln. iv. 145, with covering letter to Margt. Fell from wife dated Wakefield, 3rd Nov. 1657.

great trouble because her husband, who had narrowly escaped a long imprisonment, was gone to speak faithfully to the persecuting justice.[1] After the meeting was over Dewsbury walked to and fro in a long passage groaning in spirit, and by and by came up to the distressed wife, and, laying his hand on her head, said, "Woman, thy sorrow is great: I sorrow with thee." Then, walking a little to and fro, as before, he came to her again and said, "Now the time is come that those who marry must be as though they married not, and those who have husbands as though they had none, for the Lord calls for all to be offered up." His words came as a message from God, and she went home comforted, there to learn that her husband had found the justice tender and willing to receive his message. After a short visit to Bristol, Dewsbury went into Wales at the end of October; and at this point we lose sight of his service for nine months, until the important journey which he made to Scotland in the autumn of 1658, from the 13th of August till the end of October.[2] He rode as far as Berwick, and then with his companion, Samuel Thornton, bought shoes for themselves and went forward on foot "with great joy." It was harvest-time, and during the first day's journey they met with hundreds of people, and published Truth to them in the fields and highways. He visited Edinburgh, and after making a circuit among the Clydesdale Friends, and through Glasgow, returned to the capital, again speaking along the roads as he journeyed. "Some hundreds of miles," he says, "in a short time, the Lord led me on foot, with much joy, for the seed's sake." Captain Langley duly informed Secretary Thurloe of the coming of these Yorkshiremen,[3] under whose influence the Quakers, becalmed for a season, were congregating again. He

[1] See *Some Memoirs of the Life of Jno. Roberts*, where, however, no date is given. But the incident must belong here.

[2] For this visit see *Works*, p. 176; Dewsbury to Margt. Fell, Leith, 23rd Sept. 1658, in Swarthm. Colln. iv. 146, printed not quite correctly in Smith's *Life of Dewsbury*, pp. 165, 166; and George Watkinson to Fox, Leith, 23rd Oct. 1658, in Swarthm. Colln. iv. 214.*

[3] Cf. letters of 22nd June, 19th Sept., 23rd Nov. in Thurloe, *State Papers*, vii. 194, 403, 527.*

recounts the latest tale about them, how Sarah Knowles, wife of a captain, had gone on foot, as on a pilgrimage, to "one Margaret Fell, who lives about Lancashire, who they say is Judge Fell's wife, and that she is one that is past the cloud, and hath liberty to wear satins and silver and gold lace, and is a great gallant." Dewsbury disapproved this pilgrimage, and wrote to Margaret Fell to send the woman home with a man and horse as soon as possible—"the Truth is under suffering until she be in her family again."

At Leith, at the end of September, George Watkinson, the Yorkshire captain who had been dismissed the army in the autumn of 1657, joined Dewsbury and travelled North with him as far as Inverness. They met with a good reception in their pioneer work, and Dewsbury's ministry, as always, made a deep impression. At Aberdeen, where a few years later he was to plant the most important Quaker community in Scotland,* a merchant and his wife entertained them going and returning, and were very tender and well satisfied.

During 1659 we may suppose that Dewsbury worked in Yorkshire. At the end of the year he came south to London, bent upon effecting the long-delayed reconciliation between Fox and Nayler.[1] From London he addressed an important letter to Friends, urging them to "watch, watch to the light," to be punctual at meetings, and to be faithful in the use of spiritual gifts, whether praises, prophecy, or exhortation.[2]

After the reconciliation between Fox and Nayler had been happily accomplished, Dewsbury went through Surrey to Bristol, which, with the growing hopes of the Cavalier party, was at this time in a highly excited state. He found the 'prentices and the mob in possession of the streets.[3] Their leaders determined to break up a meeting at Edward Pyott's on Tuesday 7th February 1660. One of them said he would cut the Quakers' God as small as

[1] *Ante*, p. 274. [2] *Works*, pp. 176-180.

[3] Dewsbury to Margt. Fell, dated 1660 by internal evidence (Swarthm. Colln. iv. 134). It is printed, though at the wrong place, in Smith's *Life of Dewsbury*, pp. 145-146, 149-152.

herbs to the pot, but on going to the guard for a halberd they refused him one, and in the quarrel that ensued he was wounded. The meeting was held, and "was precious," says Dewsbury, "in the life of our God, who filled His tabernacle with His glory, in which Friends parted with joy in the Lord." In the evening, however, the enraged mob attacked the house, Dewsbury being within with some New England Friends, who, under the barbarous laws of the Massachusetts colony, had been banished from their families under pain of death. These were presumably Nicholas Phelps, Samuel Shattuck, and Josiah Southwick, banished in May 1659, who had reached Bristol via Barbados.[1] The news of the martyrdom at Boston of William Robinson and Marmaduke Stephenson, at the end of the previous October, had just been received,[2] and we can picture the group of grief-stricken Friends within and the wild mob outside. Dewsbury says:

> We were bowed down before our God, and prayer was made unto Him, when they knocked at the door. It came upon my spirit it were the rude people, and the Life of God did mightily arise, and they had no power to come in till we were clear before our God. Then they came in setting the house about with muskets and lighted matches, so after a season of time they came into the room where I was, and Amor Stoddart with me: I looked upon them when they came into the room [and] they cried as fast as they could well speak, "we will be civil, we will be civil." I spake these words, "see that you be so." They run forth of the room and came no more into it but run up and down in the house with their weapons in their hands, and the Lord God, who is the God of His seed, . . . caused their hearts to fail and they pass[ed] away, and not any harm done to any of us.

The next day Dewsbury and some leading Bristol Friends walked through the mob to George Bishop's house, round which a crowd was gathered.

> The majesty of our God struck their hearts and they all stood gazing upon us: little was spoken but that some said That

[1] See *The Quakers in the American Colonies*, pp. 77, 78.

[2] See Parker to Margt. Fell, Devonshire, 26th Feby. 1660, Swarthm. Colln. i. 169: "Of late we received letters out of New England, etc." The letter is printed in note to *Camb. Journ.* ii. 376.

is one of the Quakers' speakers. So we had a precious time with Friends and I passed away with much clearness and freedom from the city of Bristol, Friends being very precious in the dominion of the Life of God.

Dewsbury went forward to Tewkesbury and Evesham, where his itinerary again fails us. Our glimpses of his work have, however, been enough to reveal the greatness of the man.

The itinerating ministers were the vanguard of Quakerism. They needed an indomitable courage for their work, and bore, even in the Commonwealth days, the brunt of persecution. When they were at liberty, their strength was spent by incessant labours and the heavy care of the Churches. Some, like Farnsworth, failed to sustain the ardour of their first service. Others, like Camm and Audland, wore themselves out to an early death. A few lost their spiritual balance and became disaffected or apostate. The campaign from its commencement was largely fought by officers, and during the fierce persecution of the Restoration period, as we shall see in a future volume, the losses of leaders were terribly severe, and threatened the whole movement with ruin. But even during the Commonwealth some of the brightest and bravest were stricken down. We have already told the martyrdom of James Parnell. This chapter will fittingly close with the story of George Harrison's sufferings and untimely death. He was a young man out of the North, from Killington, near Sedbergh, who went South on his spiritual knight-errantry in the spring of 1656,[1] and did good service in Kent. A man of insight, he met John Lilburne, the seasoned political agitator, with the words, "Friend, thou art too high for Truth," and the message gave Lilburne, in his own phrase, "such a box

[1] The Kendal accounts (Swarthm. Colln. i. 273) contain an entry of 10s. to "Geo. Harrison at his going south," followed by one of 9s. to Stephen Hubbersty, both under date May 1656. For the Kent incident see *F.P.T.* 143-145, also Thos. Robertson to Margt. Fell, 4th Augt. 1656 (Swarthm. Colln. iv. 204). For London, Hubberthorne to Margt. Fell, 2nd Sept. 1656 (Dev. Ho., Jas. Bowden's copy of letter in Wm. Caton Colln.). For the closing passages of his life see Besse, *Sufferings*, i. 661; *Piety Promoted*; *J.F.H.S.* vi. 172, vii. 2 (where I correct the commonly received date of his death).

on the ear" that he could never get from under it. He was already being influenced by Luke Howard, and ended his stormy life as a Friend. In September, Harrison was in London, but shortly after passed on into Essex with Stephen Hubbersty. After a time of service here he declared Truth through the streets of Bury St. Edmunds, was refused entertainment at the inns, and had to ride abroad that night, at the cost of a severe chill. It was the beginning of December, and the two strangers went on to Haverhill, where Anthony Appleby lodged them, though a rabble collected outside his house and threw stones at the door till midnight. Next morning the mob succeeded in breaking in, whereupon they dragged out the two Friends

> . . . and most desperately did beat them to the ground, kicking them in a sad manner, driving them along the town, halloing them and stoning them all along to the end of the town, and this did not the townsmen seek to prevent but set others on.

Harrison was thrown into a fever, and travelling on with difficulty to Coggeshall, died there a few weeks later. Dewsbury's noble service would continue through thirty-six years of imprisonments and labours, Harrison's was consummated in eight months. The Quaker Publisher worked faithfully through the twelve hours of his day, whether long or short, content alike with cloud and with sunshine, if only he might be found walking in the light.

CHAPTER XV

SURVEY OF THE GROWTH OF QUAKERISM

(1656–1660)

Quakerism is nothing unless it be a communion of life, a practical showing that the spiritual and material spheres are not divided but are as the concave and convex sides of one whole, and that the one is found in and through the other. It emphasizes the fact that the church is a body of common men and women, that worship is part of living, and that the whole of life is sacramental and incarnational.—JOAN M. FRY, *The Communion of Life*, p. 11.

WE now pass from the activities of the First Publishers to the domestic history of the movement, and shall find it convenient in our survey to follow the growth of Quakerism in the order of its planting.

The materials for tracing the development in Yorkshire are scanty, but the fact that over five hundred Yorkshire Friends were imprisoned in the general imprisonment shortly after the Restoration shows the strength of the movement.[1] While Richard Cromwell was Protector, a Petition was addressed to him from Leeds, Wakefield, and Bradford, setting out that these populous places had been miserably perplexed and much dissettled by the unruly sect of the Quakers, who made it their common practice to meet by hundreds near the places of worship, and confidently declared that in a short time they would be in a majority.[2]

We gain some idea of Yorkshire Quakerism, especially in its strength of local leadership, if we pass under review the names of the fifteen persons who represented the

[1] Besse, *Sufferings*, ii. 99-103, gives the names.

[2] *Ibid.* ii. p. 98. Cf. document in Thurloe, *State Papers*, vii. 242, dated Leeds, 7th July 1658.

county at the General Meeting at Scalehouse in June 1658, which ordered a collection for service beyond seas. The mother-church of Balby sent Thomas Aldam and John and Thomas Killam, men of stanch service and ripe judgment. A sufferer himself, Aldam was zealous on behalf of suffering Friends, and his death in June 1660 was a heavy loss. John Killam lent his orchard for the great meeting at Balby on Easter Monday 1660, and was first Treasurer of the Yorkshire fund for the service of Truth. His wife Margaret travelled and suffered much. Thomas Killam was another sterling character, who travelled at one time in the Midlands. From Cinderhill Green came Thomas Stacey, an earnest labourer, and from Halifax Captain Thomas Taylor, to be distinguished from his more celebrated namesake.[1] From the Wakefield district came Gamaliel Miller. Miller and Taylor are among the elders named by Farnsworth for the West Riding meetings in the early document referred to in a former chapter.[2] The Settle district sent James Tennant of Scarhouse,[3] who received Fox on his way from Pendle to Sedbergh, and Samuel Watson of Knight Stainforth, to whose industry we owe a valuable MS. volume of early Quaker documents, now at Devonshire House. Watson was several times harshly handled for speaking in churches, and in September 1655 was for ten days silent and fasting, except for water, apples, and nuts. He was a man of note, whose service and writings deserve to be remembered.[4]

Richmond had three representatives, Francis Smithson, Robert Gosling, and Philip Swale of Hartforth, the lawyer whose papers, now in the custody of the Devonshire House Library, throw so clear a light on the early history of the Swaledale and Westmorland Seeker communities. Cleveland, where there was a large body of Friends, only sent one delegate—John Ratcliffe, of Danby. Lastly, there were three men from the East Riding: Marmaduke

[1] Fox, *Journ.* i. 189, 195, 469; ii. 77, 105.

[2] *Ante*, p. 140.

[3] *F.P.T.* 305; cf. Fox, *Journ.* i. 111, and ii. 77, 105.

[4] Besse, *Sufferings*, ii. 97, 99; Smith's *Catalogue*; Dev Ho., Saml. Watson Colln. p. 277. He died in 1708.

Storr, of Owstwick, a man of substance; Gregory Milner, of Cottam-on-the-Wolds; and Thomas Thompson, of Skipsea, a local leader of whom we have already heard.

It would be easy, though perhaps wearisome to the reader, to compile a much longer list of principal Friends in Yorkshire, many of whom were active in their own districts and occasionally engaged in wider service. Roger Hebden, the woollen-draper of Malton, for example, suffered at Newton, near Tadcaster, at Newport Pagnell in Buckinghamshire, and at Northallerton, for speaking to ministers, and in 1660 passed up to London through the Eastern Counties, returning by the Midlands, and then going with Samuel Watson into Scotland and home through Cumberland.[1]

We take next the Westmorland and Furness area, where Friends were in great strength, though many of their ablest members had given themselves to the wider publishing of Truth. The names of the meetings occur over and over again in the Kendal accounts of the "Treasury of the North," between 1654 and 1657.[2] Strickland Head, afterwards divided into Strickland, Penrith, and Shap,[3] was the most northerly meeting, kept for some years on the common both winter and summer, and a convenient centre for General Meetings. Here, at Newby Stones, the learned Thomas Lawson established himself by the year 1659 as the first of the distinguished line of great Quaker schoolmasters.[4] Grayrigg came next, and the small meeting of Ravenstonedale; and we then come, in the edge of Yorkshire, to the important meeting of Sedbergh, held at Richard Robinson's at Brigflatts and at the houses of other Friends and sometimes out of doors. The little meeting of Hutton between Sedbergh and Kendal need not detain us, but Kendal

[1] See *A Plain Account of Roger Hebden*, 1700.

[2] For many of these particulars see Westmorland section of *F.P.T.* by Thos. Camm, pp. 241-273.

[3] Geo. Whitehead, *Christian Progress*, pp. 124, 125; cf. Fox, *Journ.* ii. 15.

[4] Howgill took his son to him in 1659, letter to Burrough, 22nd Augt., in Dev. Ho., A.R.B. Colln. No. 169, year by internal evidence. Lawson was still a schoolmaster thirty years later, letter to Fox, 20th April 1689, in Dev. Ho., A.R.B. Colln. No. 42.

itself was an influential centre of Quakerism.* The meetings were held at various houses, sometimes for five or six hours at a time, and were accompanied, at least in the early years, with some excitement and extravagance.[1] Beyond Kendal on the Windermere side was Underbarrow or Crook, and beyond Windermere, in the Furness Fells, lay Hawkshead, possessing a burial-ground of its own at Colthouse as early as 1659.[2]

South of Kendal came the mother-church of Preston Patrick,* with its burial-ground at Birkrigg Park, acquired by the beginning of 1657.[3] A delightful letter from Camm, dated 6th December 1655, addressed to this and other Westmorland meetings, may be quoted. It warns Friends against "sitting down by the way, and getting into the comprehension before the life."

> "There is your castle," he says, ". . . in the living measure of the living God, where the living is refreshed with the fresh streams which flows out from the eternal fountain of love which refresheth the city of God, which city you are, as you abide in your measures."[4]

South of Preston Patrick, in Lancashire, were Yealand-and-Kellet meeting, and Lancaster, and on the Furness side the three meetings of Swarthmore, Poolbank, and Cartmel, all held in private houses. Swarthmore was the most important of these. Margaret Fell's hospitality and friendship made her house a place fragrant with fellowship and inspiration. Caton again and again uses such expressions as the following about Swarthmore: "Where I found always refreshment in the fulness of the Father's love, which abounded much among us in that blessed family."[5] On one occasion Judge Fell came home with his servants and found the shed so full of the horses of strange

[1] See hostile account in *The Quakers Shaken*, 1655.

[2] For a "miracle" here, see *Camb. Journ.* i. 140; *ante*, p. 247.

[3] *F.P.T.* 254.

[4] *The Memory of the Righteous Revived*, pp. 29-39. The date is corrected and completed from a MS. copy in the Boswell Middleton Colln. at Dev. Ho., p. 103. Preston Patrick is named first, as being Camm's own home. The sentence quoted resembles one of the Sayings of Jesus found in 1903.

[5] Caton's *Life*, 1689 edn. p. 57. Poolbank was in Westmorland just outside the Cartmel district.

guests that he told his wife this was the way to be eaten out of hay.[1] At the end of the year, however, they had a surplus to sell. Humphrey Norton, in 1656, as we have seen,[2] thought the meeting deficient in weight, and I think it quite likely that the fervent temperament of Margaret Fell and the glow of fellowship experienced by Friends gave it sometimes a character all its own. Judge Fell died in 1658 in October,[3] and the Quaker community was no longer protected from persecuting magistrates and priests. During the dark days of 1659, while Fox lay in anguish at Reading, a strange exercise came upon the Swarthmore household, as described in the following letter of Caton's, endorsed by Fox, "how the children fasted":

> Friends here are well, and great and marvellous is the work of the Lord in this family, where several have been exercised and yet are in fasting. Bridget Fell fasted twelve days, Isabel hath fasted about seven and is to fast nine, little Mary hath fasted five, and a little maid that is a servant in the house called Mabby hath fasted twenty. And one Mary Atkinson, of Cartmel, hath fasted above twenty, and two more in this family are exercised in the same thing. And, blessed be the Lord, they are and have been generally wonderfully preserved, and some of them are come very well through it, and others are kept in the faith and patience, and all is pretty well, blessed be the Lord.[4]

Little Mary would be about nine or ten years old.*

Cumberland was another important district where several groups of Seekers had joined the new movement.[5] From Carlisle, however, Friends were for many years excluded by the authorities, except as prisoners. Thomas Bewley of Haltcliff Hall had bought them a house in the Abbey, but in Richard Cromwell's time they were driven out by the soldiers, and soon after were shut out from the city by the magistrates. About the year 1674, John Watson, of Wigton, went naked into Carlisle on a

[1] Sewel, i. 130. [2] *Ante*, p. 237.

[3] Margt. Fell's *Works*, p. 3; Smith's *Catalogue*, i. 602.

[4] Swarthmore, 23rd Oct. 1659, Swarthmore Colln. iv. 267. For Mary Fell's strange warning to the Ulverston minister Lampitt, see *Camb. Journ.* i. 231, and note i. 439.*

[5] For Cumberland, see *F.P.T.* 30-75.

market-day, in sign that though they had thrust Truth out at their gates, it should enter again; and at last, after the Toleration Act, a meeting was begun in 1693 and a meeting-house was built in 1702.[1] A similar policy was pursued at Newcastle-on-Tyne, where, at the end of 1657, a large room was taken by William Coatsworth, of South Shields, and others; but the mayor and his officers broke up the first meeting, and escorted the Quakers to the "blew stone" on Tyne Bridge, which marked the limits of his jurisdiction, and charged them in the name of the Protector to hold no more meetings at their peril. On a first-day soon after, a meeting was attempted out of doors by the river-side, and the Friends were again dragged off to Tyne Bridge. Then the Guildhall was hired, which was outside the liberty of the town; but Samuel Hammond, one of the authors of *The perfect Pharise under Monkish Holines,* induced the hall-keeper to break his bargain, and the meeting had to be held on the hill-side, also outside the liberty.[2] George Whitehead was there, and spoke for two or three hours, in so loud a voice that he could be heard from the Castle Green, where he was standing, over the Tyne into Gateshead. Coatsworth was so chagrined over the business that "he let in too much grief and trouble of mind, insomuch that it did somewhat discompose him, so that in a hurry"—that is, an agitation of mind—"he took horse to ride to London in all haste to speak to Oliver Cromwell." He was taken ill on the road, and died at Durham, but before his end was "made sensible he had not stood in the cross, nor been so watchful as he ought to have been." Fox was in Newcastle a few weeks later, but the ministers and aldermen, who had reproached Friends with living in the fells like butterflies, declined to allow a meeting, and he had to content himself with one at Gateshead.[3]

Cumberland, one of the wettest of counties, was remarkable for the number of meetings regularly held out of doors. George Whitehead says:[4]

[1] *F.P.T.* 30-32, 53, 71, 72.
[2] See Geo. Whitehead's *Christian Progress*, pp. 126-130.
[3] *Journ.* i. 413.
[4] *Christian Progress*, pp. 124, 125 (1657).

> Our Friends in those northern countries were greatly enabled to bear the cold and all sorts of weather, when they had their meetings on the commons and mountainous places for several years at first. I remember when it has rained most of the time, at some meetings where we have been very much wetted, and yet I do not remember that ever I got any hurt thereby, the Lord so preserved and defended us by His power.

The great meeting of Pardshaw was held out of doors on the Crag, as described in a former chapter.[1] In this district, says Fox, "most of the people had so forsaken the priests that the steeple-houses in some places stood empty."

John Wilkinson, of Brigham, had few hearers left in the three churches where he preached, so substituted a meeting in his own house, and afterwards a silent meeting after the manner of Friends; but at last so few were left that he would come to Pardshaw Crag, where Friends had a meeting of several hundred people, and would walk about the meeting like a man that went about the commons to look for sheep.[2] After Fox's visit in September 1657 he himself joined Friends, and after a time of "waiting in deep silence till the Lord opened his mouth," helped greatly in the extension of Quakerism in Cumberland.[3] Another important meeting, known as Isell, had its centre at Settraw Hill, a few miles north-west of Cockermouth; and Broughton, east of the same place, was held for some years at Standing Stone, on Broughton Common. Bolton meeting, which served the district between Wigton and Isell, had been formed out of a congregation of Seekers, and was held "sometimes upon the hills without and sometimes in houses and barns, as it pleased the Lord to make way for His truth in the hearts of His people." Scotby again began by a few Friends from neighbouring parishes meeting on Warwick Moor. One of these had his house burnt, and a subscription was taken up by Friends for his assistance.[4]

In South Lancashire there were several strong groups of Friends.* A letter from Thomas Taylor to Nayler early

[1] *Ante*, p. 120. [2] *Journ.* i. 392. [3] *F.P.T.* 39, etc.
[4] Willan to Margt. Fell, 12th Sept. 1657, in Swarthm. Colln. i. 301.

in 1655 shows in interesting fashion how the intelligence department of Quaker extension work operated. At Manchester, Nayler should consult with Isaac Moss. Henry Woods of Tottington,* near Bury, will welcome a visit. At Blackburn there is one John Culby a Friend, and John Edge a well-wisher. At Haslingden he will find John Robinson, a shopkeeper and a "pretty Friend," — the Friends there and about Rossendale-head meet together though only weak, and a visit from a Friend grown in the Truth would be serviceable.[1] Manchester meeting owed its origin to Thomas Briggs of Bolton-le-Sands, near Carnforth, who had been convinced by the answers Fox gave to the Bolton minister Jaques at the Lancaster sessions in October 1652. Briggs went to Manchester to declare in church against the minister, and was haled out and put in a dungeon on the bridge, where the Lord was so with him that he sang for joy.[2] There was no settled meeting at Liverpool,[3] but Knowsley meeting begun by Holme about the end of 1654 served the district. On one occasion the whole meeting, which met that day at Peter Lawford's house in Huyton, was placed under guard till ten o'clock on Monday morning, when it was taken in a body before Justices of the Peace.[4]

We now pass to the South of England, and follow the growth of Quakerism in London, Norwich, and the Eastern Counties, Bristol and the West, the Midlands and the Southern Counties. London became one of the strongest centres, and apart from the proceedings in Nayler's case, justified in these years Milton's fine panegyric, proving itself "a city of refuge, the mansion-house of liberty."[5] When the storm of persecution at last descended at the beginning of 1661, after the Fifth Monarchy rising, the strength of the Quaker community is shown by the fact

[1] Swarthm. Colln. iii. 31; cf. similar letters of intelligence in *J.F.H.S.* i. 40-43.*

[2] For Thomas Briggs, see *An Account of Some of the Travels and Sufferings of . . . Thomas Briggs* (1685), and Jno. Whiting, *Persecution Exposed*, 1715 edn. pp. 133-137.

[3] Oliver Sansom, under date 1676, says there had been no meeting held in Liverpool for sixteen or seventeen years (*Life*, 1848 edn. p. 178).

[4] *F.P.T.* 147-151, and paper by Richard Cubham in *J.F.H.S.* v. 104; original in Swarthm. Colln. iv. 42.

[5] *Areopagitica.*

that some five hundred Friends were swept into prison, a number only exceeded in this short but fierce persecution by the tale of sufferers from Yorkshire.[1]

Besides the Publishers of Truth from the North, a number of London Friends, men and women, became powerful ministers. There was Ann Downer already referred to;[2] Sarah Blackbury, who began the meeting at Hammersmith, and was the close friend of Nayler and afterwards of Hubberthorne;[3] Ann Gould, who travelled in the North of Ireland and in Essex;[4] and Nayler's convert, Rebecca Travers, whose husband, William Travers, was a tobacconist at the sign of the Three Feathers in Watling Street, and whose sister, Mary Booth, also lived there.[5] Of the men we may mention William Bayly, the Baptist shipmaster of Poole, who had been convinced by Fox,[6] and both travelled and wrote largely; William Brend or Brand, one of the Quaker messengers to New England; and three tailors, Gilbert Latey, of whom we shall speak presently, and Richard Greenaway and John Giles, who travelled together in Oxfordshire and other counties.[7]

The widespread Quakerism of London is best shown by giving some of the curiously minute details which are preserved as to the various places where "retired" meetings or public meetings were regularly held. The earliest of these, as we have seen, were kept at Simon Dring's house in Watling Street, and at Robert Dring's in Moorfields.[8] Several other persons also opened their houses

[1] Besse, *Sufferings*, i. 366, 690.

[2] *Ante*, pp. 157, 235.

[3] *Life of Gilbert Latey*, p. 14; paper *re* Nayler in Swarthm. Colln. i. 41; also account of Hubberthorne's death by her at beginning of his *Works*. For the part she took in setting up the women's meeting for the poor, see *ante*, p. 341.

[4] Edmondson's *Journ.* (1655), and *F.P.T.* 97.*

[5] *Ante*, p. 242; G. Whitehead's *Christian Progress*, p. 292.

[6] *Ante*, p. 203.

[7] Thos. Ellwood's *Life*, anno 1661; *F.P.T.* 102, 161, 206, 207, 220.*

[8] My authorities for these paragraphs are the same as those given, *ante*, p. 182. There is some confusion as to the residences of the two brothers Dring, but it is clear from Alex. Delamain's contemporary letter in *Letters of Early Friends*, p. 9, that Simon then lived in Watling Street, close to St. Paul's, and that Robert lived in Moorfields. A letter of Margt. Killam's (Swarthm. Colln. ii. 28) was written 15th May 1655 "at Robert Dring's house at Moorfields." *Life of Gilbert Latey*, p. 7, confirms this, adding that Simon afterwards removed to Moorfields. Robert's house was the more frequent meeting-place. See *F.P.T.* 163, and *Letters of Early Friends*, p. 8.

for regular meetings, usually on "first-day" afternoons—including Samuel Vosse at the sign of the Helmet, Basinghall Street; Humphrey Bache, goldsmith, at the sign of the Snail, Tower Street; Gerrard Roberts, wine-cooper, at the sign of the Fleur de Luce, St. Thomas Apostles; and John Elson, carpenter, at the sign of the Baker's Peel, Clerkenwell. Gerrard Roberts had been convinced at a public meeting held for a time at Glazier's Hall, in Thames Street, and became the leading London Friend in all matters of business. His house was the residence and head-quarters of the Publishers of Truth who were in the city. Elson's workshop passed into the hands of Friends and developed into Peel Meeting-House, which is still a centre of Quaker activity.* The Baker's Peel was no doubt the Baker's pole or "peel" with a broad flat disk at the end used for thrusting loaves into the oven and withdrawing them from it. There was also a meeting in Whitecross Street, in the garden of a widow named Sarah Matthews, and another at the house of Sarah Sawyer, at the end of a winding blind alley known as Rose and Rainbow Court, off Aldersgate Street. Gilbert Latey speaks of this as the first meeting for the public settled in London, though it was almost immediately overshadowed by the bold venture made early in 1655, when the Bull and Mouth premises were occupied. There was a second great place used as a "threshing floor" at this time, and also one in Westminster.[1] This second place was, I think, Worcester House in the Strand, where Nicholas Bond, a Friend connected with the Court, had lodgings. A retired meeting in this district was held at William Woodcock's house in the precincts of the old Savoy Palace. In 1658 the Bull and Mouth and the Worcester House meetings were the principal public meetings and the ones chiefly disturbed by Nayler's followers. At the beginning of this year these two meetings were, as Hubberthorne expresses it, "left for the world"—that is to say, a few Friends of power in the ministry attended them in order to preach the Quaker

[1] Howgill to Margt. Fell, dated March 1655 (*Letters of Early Friends*, p. 35, from Wm. Caton Colln.).

message, and the main body who had attended at the Bull and Mouth held a meeting instead at the Helmet (Saml. Vosse's) at 9 A.M., while those who attended at Worcester House met instead "in the Strand at the new meeting place [probably the Savoy], which is a large convenient room."[1] The Worcester House meeting must, however, have been closed soon after this—probably on the removal to Greenwich of Nicholas Bond, who provided a place for Friends there in the Palace or King's House, near his new lodgings, until the King resumed possession at the Restoration. During the last years of the Commonwealth, the meeting at the Savoy became overcrowded, and another was begun in July 1660 at Elizabeth Trott's in Pall Mall.[2] Margaret Fell stayed here, as her letters show, during her long visit to London soon after the Restoration. There were at the time very few houses in Pall Mall except on the side next St. James's Park ; on the other side there was a great row of large elm trees, with open fields beyond.[3] This meeting was established with the assiduous help of Gilbert Latey, then a man of thirty-two. He was what we should now call a court-tailor, "being still in great business in the world and concerned by reason thereof with persons of considerable rank and quality, who would have their apparel set off with much cost and superfluities of lace and ribbons."[4] He could not undertake this "superfluous part" of his trade any more, for it ministered to pride. The sacrifice cost him his custom, and he parted with many of his work-people and expected to become a journeyman tailor himself. Cross-bearing, however, strengthened his faith, his mouth was opened in the ministry, he carried his message into some of the London churches, and busied himself earnestly on behalf of suffering Friends. He addressed an outspoken remonstrance to tradesmen, and especially those of his own business,[5] against cheating and

[1] Hubberthorne to Fox, London, 16th Feby. 1658, Swarthm. Colln. iv. 15.

[2] Hubberthorne to Fox, London, 24th July 1660 (*Letters of Early Friends*, p. 83), and *Life of Gilbert Latey*, p. 59. For the beginning of the meeting see letter, Margt. Fell to Fox, 17th July, in *Camb. Journ.* i. 373.

[3] *Life of Gilbert Latey*, p. 65.

[4] *Ibid.* p. 19.

[5] *Ibid.* pp. 36-48.

furnishing themselves with stock dishonestly come by, and keeping it in their shops "in whole bundles of remnants and pieces." He blamed them for inventing vain fashions and failing "to beget people into true moderation and out of pride." "People," he says, "look like apes and fools, that it is even a shame to see them how they are gone out of true moderation into foolish toys and fancies, not like to sober men and women." This straightforward, sympathetic Cornishman had with all his Quaker simplicity a courtly breeding which won him the friendship and help of many of his customers, and enabled him to be of great service to Friends during the terrible times of persecution in the Restoration period.

We return to our review of the early London meetings. A meeting at Westminster, at the house of Stephen Hart, in the New Palace Yard, is frequently mentioned, and was perhaps the "great place, as big as Bull and Mouth, near the Abbey," spoken of in one of Burrough's letters.[1] It was an audacious thing, as Friends found,[2] to set up a meeting at the doors of Parliament. On the Surrey side there were at first a great many meetings in private houses.[3] Towards the end of August 1654, about six weeks after arriving in the city, Howgill and Burrough had held a meeting in Southwark in a large room where the Baptists met on Sunday—several of them were there and many hundreds of people.[4] They had thus come into contact, we may suppose, with the earliest congregation of the Particular Baptists, the Southwark Society, once Congregational under the leadership of Henry Jacob.[5] It is likely enough that some of these Baptists formed the nucleus of the Quaker Church in the Borough. In any case meetings soon sprang up, one in a little parlour in

[1] To Howgill, London, 24th Sept. 1658, *Letters of Early Friends*, p. 59: original in Dev. Ho., A.R.B. Colln. No. 40.

[2] See *post*, p. 471.

[3] For most of the following particulars see *F.P.T.* 166, 167. I correct Robert Benbucke to Robt. Benbricke. The account was prepared by Walter Myers for Southwark Monthly Meeting in 1706.

[4] Burrough and Howgill to Margt. Fell, London, 29th Augt. 1654, *Letters of Early Friends*, p. 17.

[5] *Studies in Mystical Religion*, p. 415. Cf. *ante*, p. 12.

a yard at the sign of the Two Brewers at the upper end of Bermondsey Street, where a young man lived named William Shewen, who became "somewhat concerned in the controversy with the Baptists, and answered that mountebank in religion, Jeremy Ives";[1] others at Bankside, especially "a pretty large and serviceable meeting" at Thomas Hackleton's, near the Falcon, which developed on a neighbouring site into what became known as the Park meeting; another at Robert Benbricke's in the Borough; and, to name only one more out of several, a meeting held in the large garden of a widow named Mary Webb in Jacob Street. This meeting was pretty large, and some time after she built some houses near the Artillery Wall on Horslydown, and with the assistance of Friends put up a meeting-house behind them. In Easter 1659 a General Meeting for ministers from all over the country was arranged in London. The morning meeting was held on the Easter Tuesday (5th April) at the Bull and Mouth; in the afternoon a great concourse of people resorted to the meeting-place at Horslydown, where, within and without doors, it was thought some hundreds heard the word of truth.[2] Horslydown meeting became a centre of fierce persecution in the Restoration period, until demolished in 1670 by order of the King in Council.

In the East of London two meetings only need be mentioned, one at Mile End, at the house of Captain James Brock, the parent of the well-known meeting at Ratcliff, the other at John Oakley's, in Wheeler Street, Spitalfields, near to the spot where, after long intermission of Quaker work, the Bedford Institute now stands. The meeting began in an upper room, then a second room was added, then as it grew it was sometimes held out of doors, afterwards a tent covered with sail-cloth was set up in the garden, and finally a meeting-house was built, which Gilbert Latey preserved from destruction in 1670 by his shrewdness in putting in a tenant as occupier.

[1] John Whiting's *Persecution Exposed* (1715 edn.), p. 239.
[2] Caton's *Life*, 1689 edn. p. 51.

The foregoing particulars show the vigour and spontaneity of the London work, and the missionary spirit in which the Quaker message was being proclaimed to the turbulent and often hostile world. The unsettlement that attended Nayler's extravagances added greatly to the cares of the Quaker Publishers of Truth. But they persevered with faith and courage through every difficulty A letter of advice written by Burrough in 1659[1] is addressed to the special needs of London Friends.

> As for those rebellious and treacherous and deceitful lying spirits amongst you, which may trouble you, as they have formerly done, to the great dishonour of the Lord, I wish they were cut off as for the Truth's sake, yet I exhort you to bear them with patience, and not to heed them, nor be troubled at them, but account of them as disorderly and out of the body: and fret not in yourselves because of the wicked—such things be but for a time, but Truth is forever, and they that walk therein their fruits shall never wither. And let Friends keep their private meetings on the first-days with diligence, and none to run abroad without fear, but as they are moved of the Lord.

The Eastern Counties developed some strong groups of Friends, especially at Colchester. When the great persecution befell there in the year 1663, about sixty Friends were thrown into the town prison[2] without the meeting being effectually broken up. Friends had already been given a burial-ground in Moor Elms Lane,[3] but were then meeting in a hired house. The tenancy expired in the midst of the storm, and with calm assurance they forthwith set about building a very large meeting-house to the amazement of the town in general. During the Commonwealth period there had been little persecution in Colchester, though a good deal in the county. In 1658, however,[4] a wealthy tradesman, Edward Grant, a Friend of sixty-five, was cruelly beaten by troopers, dying a month afterwards. Fox uses a remarkable expression with respect to Colchester Friends, saying, "Many of

[1] *Works*, p. 543.
[2] "Sixty of the richest Friends," *F.P.T.* 100.
[3] C. Fell Smith's *Steven Crisp, etc.*, p. 49.
[4] *F.P.T.* 94.

these people had been of the stock of the martyrs."[1] This must refer to the numerous Marian martyrs or to the Protestant Dutch refugees who came to the town in the reign of Elizabeth, or perhaps to both. Colchester was described by John Evelyn in 1656 as "a ragged factious town, now swarming in sectaries," and it is not surprising that Friends gained a firm footing. Steven Crisp, convinced by Parnell in the summer of 1655, and a man of education, was the leading Friend, by trade a weaver of the "unsophisticated" serges and bays for which the town was famous.

"I was," he says, "hewen down like a tall cedar. . . . The eye that would or at least desired to see everything was now so blind that I could see nothing certainly but my present undone and miserable state."[2]

In 1659 he visited Scotland, the first of many journeys as a travelling minister.

The early meetings at Colchester were persistently disturbed by one or two persons. The account gives so vivid a picture of the times that it may be transcribed nearly in full:[3]

One Worster, a glover, when Truth first brake forth amongst us, . . . frequented the meetings at Colchester above a year, and would commonly be babbling or speaking against Truth, and speak most part of the meeting, whether it was a silent meeting or that a public Friend was declaring, but at last was tired out. . . . After him was another molester . . . one Jacob Cassier, a Dutchman . . . and his way for some months was only to walk to and fro in the meeting, till a Friend speaking to him . . . from that time forward he fell into babbling many words against Friends' doctrines and principles in the meetings, till it was the time to go to his own worship, and then would depart.

Ipswich was, I think, one of the towns shut against Friends. Fox had a little meeting there, "very rude";[4] and when George Whitehead held meetings at Timothy Grimble's in January 1659, the jury of the town promptly made presentment that Grimble had harboured "divers dissolute, idle, loose, lewd and suspected persons, dis-

[1] *Journ.* i. 232.
[2] *Works*, 1694 edn. p. 17.
[3] *F.P.T.* 103, by John Furly the younger.
[4] *Journ.* i. 232.

turbers of the public peace, . . . commonly called Quakers."[1]

Norwich, the largest manufacturing city in England, had shown itself, we shall remember, inhospitable to Friends. A meeting of some strength was maintained though it had its internal difficulties. At the beginning of 1657[2] George Whitehead found Friends "pretty faithful, though them few that formerly have caused division be high, and scarce comes among Friends."

Essex, Norfolk, and Suffolk made generous contributions to the 1657 collection for the service of Truth, taking three out of the four first places in the list of counties. George Whitehead speaks warmly of many of the local leaders: Robert Duncon of Mendlesham, "my dear friend"; Robert Ludgater, senr., a glover of Great Coggeshall, "our dear, ancient and faithful Friend"; John Hubbard, senr., of Stoke Ferry, "our loving, honest Friend"; Henry Kettle, senr., at one time Mayor of Thetford; Captain John Lawrence of Wramplingham, a man of wide influence; Captain William Barber of Gissing, "our ancient and faithful Friend"; William Alexander of Needham, "an honest young man"; and Robert Grassingham of Harwich.[3] We must think of each of these men as the centre of a group of honest-hearted Friends, meeting regularly for their simple worship, witnessing by life to the reality of the Christ of their inward experience, opposing with courage and acerbity the pretensions of priests and the fashions of the world, suffering without flinching imprisonment and the spoiling of their goods, and greatly refreshed from time to time by the ministry and fellowship of the travelling Publishers of Truth. Among the most helpful of these was William Allen,* a barber-surgeon of Cambridge, who was imprisoned for nearly a year in Colchester Castle. His gaoler had treated Parnell cruelly, but now showed himself moderate, and allowed his prisoner to go abroad about the town and country, and even for

[1] *Christian Progress*, 1725 edn. p. 138.

[2] To Fox, Yarmouth, 26th Feby. 1657, Swarthm. Colln. iv. 91.

[3] *Christian Progress*, 1725 edn. pp. 135 and 207, 235, 249, 251, 26, 30, 133, 139

a short time to Cambridge—a liberty which proved much to the advantage of Truth.[1] Seventeenth-century imprisonment, though loathsome beyond description in many ways, was frequently mitigated by the indulgence of a lenient gaoler, and the well-known case of Bunyan can be paralleled again and again out of Quaker annals.

At the end of 1660 Allen travelled with Henry Fell,[2] and they had very many precious meetings. The following, relating to Aldeburgh, carries us back to the first fervour of Quakerism.

> "Here," writes Fell, "is a mighty power stirring. . . . The Friends in the town came where I lay the last night, and I spoke a few words amongst them, where many of them were much shaken with the power and cried out. Though there was some mixture with it, yet there is a true power which I had much unity with."

Turning next to the work in Bristol, we may recall the surprising statement that there were thousands of Quakers here at the time of Nayler's fall.[3] Fox had visited the city for the first time four weeks earlier. He attended the Sunday morning meeting in Broadmead, and in the afternoon went to the "threshing" meeting in Dennis Hollister's Orchard in the Friars, where some thousands assembled. At this time the prospect of a dispute with a "jangling Baptist," Paul Gwin, sometimes drew ten thousand persons.[4] Fox was in Bristol twice in 1657, but did not spend another Sunday there till March 1660. Friends had been turned out of the Orchard, and he asked the mayor and aldermen to let them the Town Hall on Sundays for twenty pounds a year, to be distributed to the poor. Failing to secure this he went to the Orchard, where a rabble of soldiers and tipsy people interrupted the meeting, one man swearing to kill and cut down the preacher. When within two yards of Fox he began jangling with some Friends. "And so," says Fox, "of a sudden I saw his sword was put up and gone, and the Lord's power came over all and chained him and

[1] *F.P.T.* 98 (1658). Cf. *post*, p. 398.
[2] To Margt. Fell, 2nd Dec. 1660, Swarthm. Colln. i. 78.
[3] *Ante*, p. 253.
[4] *Journ.* i. 328-330.

them, and we had a blessed meeting."[1] Before leaving the place he held a General Meeting at Edward Pyott's of many thousands, including Baptist and Independent teachers, and "all was quiet, for most of the sober people came out of Bristol to it, and the people that stayed in the city said the city looked naked."

There had been little persecution in Bristol. When Commissioners for the militia were appointed in August 1659, no less than seven Bristol Friends were named in the Act of Parliament, a circumstance which caused them many heart-searchings, but shows the standing of the leading Friends, and their assured loyalty to the Commonwealth.[2] There were, however, some internal difficulties—friction between some of the Friends,[3] and trials in January 1659 from "Singers," whose envy against Friends was so great that they would have murdered, if it could have been done secretly.[4] Speaking generally, however, the work in Bristol went forward steadily. In 1664 a persecuting mayor hoped to banish four hundred Quakers during his year of office, a figure eloquent as to the strength of the community.[5]

Devon and Cornwall had several groups of Friends* at Cullompton, Plymouth, Exeter, Kingsbridge, and some other places in Devon, and at Falmouth, the Land's End, Truro, Liskeard, and elsewhere in Cornwall; but the magistrates were embittered, Nayler's extravagances "made a great tumult in the minds of many weak Friends,"[6] and the work was carried on with difficulty. Salthouse, Bewley, and Parker did good service up and down the district, and Fox went as far as Land's End in February 1660, and delivered his soul against the wrecking customs of the country, which, he observed, were far below the practice of the heathen of Melita.[7] In Somerset, where

[1] *Camb. Journ.* i. 348; *Journ.* i. 462-464.

[2] Parker to Fox, 7th Augt. 1659, Swarthm. Colln. iii. 143; cf. *post*, p. 388.

[3] Clement to Margt. Fell, 5th June and 20th Oct. 1659, Swarthm. Colln. i. 184, 187.

[4] Benj. Mainard to Margt. Fell, 1st Jany. 1659, Swarthm. Colln. i. 142.

[5] Besse, *Sufferings*, i. 51.

[6] Salthouse to Margt. Fell, 30th Jany. 1657, Swarthm. Colln. iii. 185.

[7] *Journ.* i. 459. He says that they called shipwrecks "God's Grace," and plundered the wreckage, not caring to save life, but he says nothing of the charge sometimes made that the Cornishmen caused wrecks by showing false lights.

Salthouse also laboured the Quaker movement was strong, largely through the convincement of Baptists. At the beginning of 1661 there were no less than two hundred and ten Friends in gaol at Ilchester, only seven of whom were women.[1] We have a list of forty Friends, "at most of whose houses meetings were kept," and several of these were men of much spiritual power.[2] There were John Pitman and Jasper Batt of Street, who had "fed on husks" among the Baptists,[3] while Batt later earned the special aversion of the Bishop of Bath and Wells as the greatest seducer in all the West.[4] There were John Anderdon, the Bridgwater goldsmith, who was turned Quaker in London in 1658 by some words of Howgill;[5] Christopher Bacon, of Venice Sutton in the Poldens, the Royalist soldier who had been convinced at a Quaker meeting in 1656, to which he had gone as a scoffer;[6] and Thomas Budd, of Martock, near Yeovil, formerly a Baptist parish priest.[7] Here, as elsewhere, internal difficulties began to appear, especially a judging spirit, which showed itself about the time of Nayler's fall.[8] There were also cases of Friends who ran well for a time, but then fell away, in particular John Collens of Lydford, near Ilchester;[9] Thomas Morford of English Batch, a man of excitable temperament;[10] and Robert Wastfield of Brislington, near Bristol, a Commonwealth soldier, a travelling minister, and a writer.[11]

The success of the Quakers sometimes greatly enraged their opponents. We read of a large meeting of seven or eight hundred in Thomas Budd's orchard which was broken into by five ministers from neighbouring parishes and a rabble armed with pitchforks and long staves. One man

[1] Besse, *Sufferings*, i. 587, and special index of names.
[2] *F.P.T.* 227; cf. 224.
[3] See title in Smith's *Catalogue*, i. 424, to their "Truth Vindicated, etc." (1658).
[4] Whiting's *Persecution Exposed* (1715), p. 108.
[5] *Ibid.* pp. 130-133.*
[6] *Ibid.* pp. 13-15.
[7] *F.P.T.* 228.
[8] Howgill to Fox, 21st Sept. 1656, A.R.B. Colln., Dev. Ho., No. 33.
[9] *F.P.T.* 228, and Smith's *Catalogue*.
[10] *F.P.T.* 228, and his letters in Swarthm. Colln.
[11] *F.P.T.* 228, and Smith's *Catalogue*.

rode full speed into the meeting "as full of rage and madness as a wild bull in a net." The priests urged on the mob, but refused to dispute; for, quoth one, "we are men and men of order and it is infinitely below us to dispute under a tree." Three weeks later the soldiers were there and dispersed a meeting of two or three hundred persons, taking Salthouse and Budd into custody. Budd, who had been a minister, was asked about tithes, and said, "If any are free to give their tithes, I have nothing against it." He made a stout defence before the authorities,

> . . . we had our clothes torn, some spat upon our heads, others threw cowdung, sticks, and dabs of earth at us, and afterwards our Friends that spake were haled and pulled down from their places. Therefore, as you are set to do justice upon offenders, so I desire that you will make inquiry after such of them as were guilty of that tumult, and let the innocent enjoy their freedom.[1]

Wilts had fewer groups of Friends, but was the main field of John Wilkinson's and John Story's labours, these Friends confining themselves more than other First Publishers to one district. Here, again, a number of Baptists were convinced. "Many falls from them; they have no courage left," says Wilkinson in one letter.[2] There was little persecution from the county magistrates owing, perhaps, to the influence of Justice Edward Stokes of Tytherton Lucas and Justice Nathaniel Cripps of Tetbury.[3] But the town of Marlborough committed several cruelties. One Friend was whipped and imprisoned twenty-one weeks for offering to lie in prison in the place of Barbara Blaugdone; two women were publicly flogged; and an eminent tradesman, Thomas Lawrence, who had employed the poor of the place for some years and spent much money on the public workhouse, was turned out of

[1] For these proceedings (in April 1657) see "A True Testimony, etc." (1657), by Wastfield, Besse, *Sufferings*, i. 578-582, derived from this; and letter from Salthouse to Margt. Fell, Street, 13th April 1657, Swarthm. Colln. iii. 163.

[2] To Burrough and Howgill, Bristol, 6th Feby. [1656], year by internal evidence, Dev. Ho., A.R.B. Colln. No. 162.

[3] Fox had a great meeting at Justice Stokes', see *Journ.* i. 330, 331, and Clement to Margt. Fell, 4th Oct. 1656, Swarthm. Colln. i. 181.

this post on becoming a Quaker, without any allowance for what he had spent on the poor.[1]

Gloucestershire was strong in Quaker groups. The full account extant with respect to Nailsworth illustrates the way in which many of these grew up.[2] A meeting of Seekers had existed there for some years, and when Humphry Smith visited the place in 1655, "most of those meeters came to hear . . . and were mightily affected with him, believing it was the way of truth, and many in and about Nailsworth were convinced." At the Bristol end of the county, meetings had been early settled at Olveston and Winterbourne,[3] and produced several leaders, Walter Clement, who travelled more than once to the North and maintained correspondence with Margaret Fell;[4] Elizabeth Smith the future wife of Miles Hubbersty;[5] Christopher Holder, a well-educated man of good estate who repeatedly visited America;[6] and Josiah Coale, another American labourer, a great preacher and mighty in prayer.[7] Thomas Thurston, who did service in America, but became a Separatist, was also, I think, from these parts.[8] Holder and Thurston were the first to preach the Quaker gospel in Gloucester. The meeting began with three men, Henry Ridall, John Jayes, and John Edmonds, and their wives. Edmonds records its early history in a quaintly worded document, rich in flavour.[9] Elizabeth Morgan, of Chester, who bred dissension in Bristol meeting in 1655 by her unwise conduct and exalted spirit and led George Bishop astray for a time,[10] came

[1] Besse, *Sufferings*, ii. 37-39.

[2] *F.P.T.* 106-107.

[3] *F.P.T.* 104.

[4] Swarthm. Colln. includes eleven of his letters.

[5] *F.P.T.* 264.

[6] *The Quakers in the American Colonies*, p. 46, etc.

[7] Sewel (1811 edn.), ii. 230; *The Quakers in the American Colonies*, p. 74, etc.

[8] *F.P.T.* 109.

[9] *F.P.T.* 109-111.

[10] See letters Willan to Margt. Fell, Kendal, 11th Sept. 1655, Swarthm. Colln. i. 255; Thos. Rawlinson to Margt. Fell, Chadwitch, towards the end of 1655, Swarthm. Colln. iii. 9. Cf. Clement to Margt. Fell, Olveston, 15th July 1656, Swarthm. Colln. i. 179. She went with some Bristol Friends to Fox, who was at Baddesley in Warwickshire, where her conduct was condemned; she was sent back to Bristol to own condemnation of it, and returned home, where in July 1656 she was "pretty low and goes not forth much." At the beginning of 1656 she had been in prison at Dublin (A.R.B. Colln. No. 65). In 1657 she had good service with Elizabeth Fletcher in Ireland (Waller to Margt. Fell, 24th July 1657, Swarthm. Colln. iv. 23).

among Gloucester Friends and in her ecstatic way declared her message to the people very boldly.

And after some time, the powe[r] of God came u[p]on some Friends, which was very strange to the people, and some begin to stand up and to go to see what was happened. . . . Elizabeth Morgan stood before some of them and said, "Ephraim is a heifer unaccustomed to the yoke," and so went on with much boldness in the authority of God's power to the end of the meeting. . . . But after this meeting there was a great noise in the city about the Quaker[s], and [people] said they had bewitched John Edmonds and Henry Ridall and put black strength about their arms, and they said that when it was so done then they had no power to go from that way, and such false scandalous reports they sent abroad. . . . So afterwards we found the people generally incensed against us, and the rude sort would abuse us and throw stones or any other thing they met with, with scoffing and deriding of us, as we went along the streets.*

Leominster was the centre of Herefordshire Friends. A stranger Friend named Thomas Parrish[1] attended the Independent meeting in the year 1655 with the message, "Keep to the Lord's watch." The words were spoken in the power of God, and a silence followed which none of the usual exhorters could break for the awe on their spirits. So after a time he said again, "What I say unto you I say unto all, Watch." Another hush fell on the meeting, though it was a great cross to their wills to sit in silence. At last he spoke, "Where are your minds now, wandering abroad or in the spirit watching with the Lord?" Then he went on and opened out the truth to the hearts of several, especially of one man, probably Morgan Watkins, the narrator of the incident, who had already known the visitations of the Holy Spirit. Of this Parrish I know nothing further: it is just possible, however, that he was the same man as the Thomas Parish, "chaplain to the major," who was among the soldiers discharged by Monck in the autumn of 1657 from Colonel Robert Lilburne's regiment of Horse.[2] In April 1656 Thomas Goodaire held a great meeting in a close

[1] *F.P.T.* 115-117.
[2] Document in Swarthm. Colln. iv. 237; see *ante*, p. 229.

belonging to a free-will or General Baptist, and as the result of further work during the summer settled a considerable meeting, which was held at the house of an attorney, Henry Bedford. John Tombes, the Leominster minister, was a man of note, one of Cromwell's Triers of ministers, with strong views against infant baptism. He entered into violent controversy with many leading Friends, either personally or in print. When Fox and Thomas Taylor were in the town in 1657 they held a great meeting in a field which developed into a dispute with Tombes, who called the Inner Light a natural light and a made light.[1] Fox bid all the people take out their Bibles, for, he writes, "I would make the scriptures bend him though he did not matter of the Spirit."[2] This dispute proved very serviceable to Friends.

Before coming to Leominster, Goodaire had visited Ross,[3] travelling afoot with George Scaife. Here they found a separated people, who often met together, and would sit in silence, without any person being appointed to speak, "but each of them did speak by way of exhortation as [they] had freedom, so that the Lord's power was mightily at work in their hearts, and great openings there was amongst them." A crowded meeting took place in the church, at which Goodaire delivered his message, but the interruptions of a Baptist preacher made a disturbance. The Seekers, including the four town-constables, withdrew with the Quaker Publishers to the church-house adjoining the churchyard, and there listened to the Quaker message, and "embraced the truth in the love of it, especially those as had separated themselves as above, with many more were then convinced, amongst whom were all the four constables. And the generality of the inhabitants in Ross were very kind and loving to them." One of the constables, James Merrick, a tanner, opened his house for meetings, which were held there till the building of a meeting-house in 1676. Again we see the readiness

[1] *Journ.* i. 369-371.

[2] I quote from the so-called *Short Journ.* 55. The *Camb. Journ.* also uses the word "bend," i. 275.

[3] *F.P.T.* 124-127.

with which a Quaker group sprang into being, when it grew out of a community of Seekers. At the beginning of 1661 sixteen men were imprisoned out of Ross meeting, six of them very poor men, having families dependent on their labour.[1] This implies a community of some eighty or a hundred persons at the lowest.

In Worcestershire there were groups of Friends at Bromsgrove, Worcester, Stourbridge, Droitwich, Dudley, Evesham, and Shipston-on-Stour by the end of the year 1655.[2] Evesham continued the chief Quaker centre and the focus of persecution.

One of the Worcester Friends, Susanna Pearson, was betrayed into an extravagance of conduct which gave the enemies of the Quakers their opportunity.[3] In February 1657 a young man, convinced of Truth, became mentally unhinged and drowned himself. After his burial, Susanna Pearson told his mother, who was in great grief, that she would restore her son alive, and went with another woman to the grave and took the corpse out, seeking to raise it to life by imitating the action of Elisha when he raised the son of the Shunammite woman. As this had no effect they went to prayer, but with no better success, and so buried the body again. Baxter made this a charge against the Quakers; it found its way into the newsbooks and was soon published in a black letter tract. Fox endorsed the letter which informed Margaret Fell of the incident with the words "mad whimsey," an illustration of the saving common sense which protected him from complicity with much of the extravagance that from time to time showed itself in others.

Staffordshire developed strong groups of Friends, if we may judge by the fact that there were one hundred and eighty-three imprisonments in 1661 from this county.

[1] Besse, *Sufferings*, i. 255, 256.

[2] *Ibid.* ii. 61, 62.

[3] Willan to Margt. Fell, wrongly dated 1654, Swarthm. Colln. i. 217; "A Sad Caveat to Quakers, etc.," full title in Smith's *Bibliotheca Anti-Quakeriana*, p. 10; Baxter, *Reliquiae Baxterianae* (1696 edn.), pt. i. p. 77. Barclay, *Inner Life*, p. 428 *n.*, wrongly concludes that Susanna Pearson was not a Friend. The name is in Besse, *Sufferings*, ii. 61 (twice), 66.*

The history is obscure, but contains some passages of singular interest. Richard Hickock, the son of old Richard Hickock, the host of the Green Dragon,[1] at Chester, after suffering imprisonment there came into the moorland corner of the county adjoining Derbyshire at the end of 1654. He convinced many persons in Leek and the neighbourhood, and settled several meetings.[2] The Leek magistrates strongly objected to meetings in the town itself; they stationed men with halberds at the door and kept the town's people from coming.[3] A letter from Hickock to Margaret Fell in April 1658 gives a good idea of the work as it had then developed.[4] There is scarcely a first-day meeting in Staffordshire, he says, which has an attendance of less than a hundred, sometimes there will be above two hundred at a meeting. He has had two in Newcastle-under-Lyme and finds it a pretty moderate town. He has also been twice lately among the Ranters at Leek,[5] all their mouths were stopped, only one woman belonging to the Family of Love stood up at the last meeting and opposed. The Baptists are much dashed to hear of the great Quaker meetings in market towns and elsewhere. Hickock wrote a tract to Ranters in 1659, and published another paper in the following year. A few years later,

> . . . giving way to the imaginations of his own heart, [he] was drawn into whimseys, and so lost the knowledge of the eternal power: he degenerated from the Truth and became an absolute apostate, and many that were convinced by him in this county turned back from the Truth also.[6]

From this chequered story we turn to Newcastle-under-Lyme. Here Humphrey Wolrich was the leading

[1] Holme to Margt. Fell (1654), Swarthm. Colln. i. 189.

[2] *F.P.T.* addendum in *J.F.H.S.* v. 165-166.

[3] Hickock to Fox, 8th May 1656, Swarthm. Colln. iv. 208.

[4] Swarthm. Colln. i. 148.

[5] Fox, at the end of 1654, disputed here with Ranters at Thomas Hammersley's of Basford, *Journ.* i. 198.

[6] *F.P.T.* addendum in *J.F.H.S.* v. 165. At the end of 1660, Oliver Atherton, of Ormskirk, went with Jas. Harrison, John Shield, and Richd. Moore through these moorland meetings at the suggestion of Fox. Atherton's account (Swarthm. Colln. i. 134) confirms the above letter and speaks of Hickock as a "dearly beloved friend."

Friend. He had been a Baptist, and in 1659 would be a young man of about twenty-five. An isolated case of baptism, the only one, I believe, in the early history of Friends, occurs in connection with his name. A woman told him that she was moved of the Lord to desire him only to baptize her with water, the spirit by which the Baptists were led not having convinced her. He yielded to her request, and was judged for his action by John Harwood, the future Separatist. Wolrich reported the matter to Fox, and explained his conduct in a pamphlet, whose title sufficiently summarizes the argument:

> The unlimited God, not limited by any of the Children of Light, but by them who are in the darkness and straitness, such would be limiting the unlimited God. Given forth from the Spirit of the Lord in Humphry Wollrich, who was not sent to baptize but to preach the gospel, yet hath baptized one with water for the gospel's sake, and am not without a law to God, yet am made all things to all to gain some to Christ.

Harwood afterwards used the incident as a handle against Fox, who said that he had not utterly denied Wolrich's wrongdoing, for he had simply done such a thing once and no more.[1] This shows that what Wolrich did was against the judgment of Fox, but not a thing which, under its special circumstances, seemed to him deserving of grave censure.

Little need be said respecting other Midland counties. In Nottinghamshire, William Smith, of Besthorpe, near Newark, became a great strength to Friends. He had been a pastor among the Independents, was convinced in 1658, and became an earnest preacher, a frequent sufferer, and a voluminous writer. In Warwickshire, where there were many Friends, the central meeting continued to be that of Baddesley, held at Anthony Bickley's, and frequently visited by Fox and other travelling ministers. This was the district from which Fox came, and it is interesting to find a letter from Thomas

[1] See Wolrich's letter to Fox, Swarthm. Colln. i. 4, and Barclay's *Inner Life, etc.* pp. 372, 373.

Taylor describing the position of Quakerism in the spring of 1656:[1]

> "Friends at Coventry are pretty faithful and increase, and so it is also at Warwick. And Friends at Nuneaton are pretty loving still. There is some going back at Higham"—presumably Higham-on-the-Hill, near Fenny Drayton—"yet the shoemaker, his wife and another continue pretty loving. There is some stirrings of life begun at Hinckley—an apothecary and his wife pretty loving — some others near it inquiring. Baddesley meeting is pretty orderly kept, and Swannington Friends pretty loving and rather an increase than otherwise. . . . The love in those few about Sapcote and Dunchurch-side continues."

Two Friends from Warwickshire, Philip Rose and Edward Teddes, went in 1658 to America, but were lost at sea on the passage from Barbados to Rhode Island.[2] Oxfordshire had some strong centres, especially at Banbury, Warborough, and Henley. At Banbury[3] in the Restoration year there were some forty households regularly subscribing to the current expenses, and as early as 1657 a meeting-house was built at the charge of Friends in the "backside" of James Wagstaff's premises. Among the members was Capt. Henry Phillips, who, as Governor of Holy Island, had been "loving" to Burrough and Christopher Atkinson in the spring of 1654,[4] and to George Whitehead in 1657,[5] and proved a stanch Friend. In 1664 he was praemunired for refusing the oath of allegiance, and spent eight and a half years in prison, being freed by the Pardon of 1672.[6] Shortly after, the Quarterly Meeting paid him £5 "for his pains for recording the sufferings of Friends in the whole county until now."[7] Henley had received the First Publishers in 1658 in the rudest fashion. Guts were thrown at Ambrose Rigge, and when young Joseph Coale, of

[1] To Nayler, 28th April, year by internal evidence (Swarthm. Colln. iii. 32).

[2] Henry Fell to Fox, Swarthm. Colln. iv. 182; Nicholson to Margt. Fell, 3rd Apl. 1660, Swarthm. Colln. iv. 107, and record cited in Wm. White's *Friends in Warwickshire*, p. 23 (1894 edn.).

[3] See accounts at beginning of earliest Banbury Preparative Meeting Minute-Book, and *F.P.T.* 208.*

[4] Burrough and Atkinson to Jas. Nayler, Swarthm. Colln. iv. 170.

[5] *Christian Progress*, p. 125.

[6] Besse, *Sufferings*, i. 569, 573.

[7] 24th Mar. 1674, per C. E. Gillett.

Reading, passed through the streets amid the horse-play of a holiday, a man called out, "Yonder comes a Quaker, throw stones at him," which was accordingly done. "But," says the narrator, who was one of the stone-throwers, "he passed gently on his way, and took no notice of our abusing him."[1] Charlbury had been early visited by Ann Downer, daughter of the vicar, whose pioneer service was followed by a visit from Thomas Taylor. He was also at Oxford, and spoke in St. Mary's after the service was over. For this, he was committed to the Castle, but it is pleasant to learn that Dr. Owen, the Vice-Chancellor, finding that he had been a scholar at the University, released him and paid the gaoler's fees.[2]

Reading, the town of many sects, was the chief Berkshire meeting, the home of Thomas and Ann Curtis, who tended Fox during his illness in 1659. Ann Curtis was a close friend of the Peningtons, and the daughter of a Bristol sheriff, Robert Yeamans, who had been hanged near his door in 1643 for aiding the King.[3]

We close this chapter with a brief review of the Southern Counties. In the case of Kent, the section in the collection known as "The First Publishers of Truth" is almost as detailed and informing as those for Cumberland and Westmorland.[4] The ground, as we have seen, had been broken by "dear William Caton & John Stubbs, of blessed memory." The chief meetings were at Cranbrook, Staplehurst, Dover, and Deal. At Cranbrook and Staplehurst, Caton and Stubbs had found "a very open people,"[5] who wanted to force money on them, but they would not take it. Many of this community of Seekers were convinced and brought to "assemble and sit together to wait upon the Lord in silence, in the measure of that Light of Life in themselves which they turned them unto, to the end that they might come gradually to feel, possess, and enjoy the living substance of what they had long professed." The leader here was

[1] *F.P.T.* 218.
[2] *F.P.T.* 205, 214.
[3] *Journ.* i. 479, and Dr. Hodgkin's *Geo. Fox*, p. 179 *n.*
[4] *F.P.T.* 130-146.
[5] *Account of Ambrose Rigge* (1710), p. 9, shows that he also visited them.

Thomas Howsigoe,[1] who had been an Independent preacher, and proved a "serviceable" man. Caton was with him when he died in November 1660, and wrote that he would be much missed, and there would be more need for Friends to visit the district pretty often than had been the case before.

Luke Howard,* the shoemaker, was the father of Dover meeting. He had championed Caton and Stubbs at the first, and when they left Dover, supplied them with the names of places and persons along the sea-coast likely to receive them.[2] When the newly gathered Dover Friends first began to sit together in silence to wait on the Lord, the Baptist meeting came in a body to the house, and the pastor asked leave to speak.[3] He began with the words, "Beloved, try the spirits, whether they are of God" (1 Jno. iv. 1), and appealed to his audience, including numbers of "the world's people" who had crowded in, to judge the Quakers' spirit and doctrine. Howard met his lengthy invective with the question whether the apostle had addressed his words to the world for them to try the spirits, or only to those called out of the world. The justice of this question reduced the Baptists to silence. "And so the meeting broke up, and the snare broke and Friends escaped."

The Baptists had good reason to be hostile, for the Quaker message attracted many of their best members, amongst others, as we shall remember, the eminent pastor Samuel Fisher. At a meeting at Romney in June 1655, he said to an opposing Baptist, "Dear brother, you are dear and near unto me, but the truth is nearer," and the Baptist replied, "Our brother Fisher is bewitched also."[4] Stubbs, as an old Baptist, found his service "especially amongst the Baptists, so that that former testimony which I had hath been again and again confirmed to me to the great strengthening of my faith."[5]

[1] For Howsigoe see Fox, *Journ.* i. 227; Wm. Caton's *Life*, 1839 edn. p. 91, and letter given in note on same page.

[2] *F.P.T.* 133. Cf. *ante*, pp. 204, 375.

[3] *F.P.T.* 135.

[4] Howard's Testimony to Fisher, Fisher's *Works*; also in *F.P.T.* 142.

[5] To Margt. Fell, London, 10th Augt. 1657, Swarthm. Colln. iii. 152.

Letters of Luke Howard in 1659 give a good picture of the work in Kent,[1] when the vagaries of the shoemaker's spelling are overcome. Further accessions from the Baptists were being made, the word of God grew and prospered, but there were some Friends careless, and some of an unstable character, who had let in Roger Crabb's spirit and were exalted. This Roger Crabb was an interesting character, a vegetarian and water-drinker, the leader of some people called Rationals, and commonly reputed to be a prophet. He lived near Uxbridge, and Thomas Curtis came across some of his company at Kimble.[2]

Sussex, like Kent, contributed Seekers to the ranks of Quakerism. Thomas Robertson in May 1655 brought the message to a community of this kind at Southover, near Lewes, several of whom received it, and their meeting was dissolved.[3] Caton, at the beginning of 1657,[4] had a similar experience, probably among the same community; "A door," he says, "was opened me in a corner of Sussex, where there was several Seekers, so-called: the most part of two meetings were convinced."

Fox, in a vague sentence, speaks of an abundance of Ranters and professors in Sussex and the adjoining counties—men who "had been so loose in their lives that they began to be weary of it, and had thought to have gone into Scotland to have lived privately,"[5] and he says that the Lord's truth caught them all, and they became good Friends. There is some confirmation of this in an undated letter from Thomas Lawson, who speaks of service among Ranters in the south parts beyond London,[6] but it would be unsafe to conclude that there was any general convincement.

In Surrey the chief Quaker centres were Guildford and Godalming and Reigate. There were also meetings near London, especially at Kingston and Mitcham.

[1] To Wm. Caton, Swarthm. Colln. iv. 266, and iv. 256.

[2] See *Dict. Natl. Biography*, and Curtis to Fox, Reading, 8th Jan. 1659, Swarthm. Colln. iii. 87; also Smith's *Catalogue*.

[3] See *F.P.T.* 233-238.

[4] To Margt. Fell, London, 19th Jany. 1657, Swarthm. Colln. i. 314.

[5] *Journ.* i. 230; cf. *Camb. Journ.*

[6] To Margt. Fell, Swarthm. Colln. i. 242, undated.*

Hampshire contained few groups of Friends. Ringwood, Bramshot, Alton, Basingstoke, and Southampton seem to have been the principal centres. The Isle of Wight was difficult ground, but Ambrose Rigge settled a meeting there, though expelled the island.[1] Thomas Morford, who was a Friend of ill-regulated enthusiasm, speaks of the inhabitants as "inveterately malicious against truth," and so fortified with soldiers that as soon as a Friend passed into the island he was forced out. There was however a "dear and precious people of the Lord, though yet kept in fear and bondage of men."[2] As in so many other districts, we now begin to hear of evil influences in the Church itself. One James Attridge, a man from Ireland, "sent a bad smell through the country, which hurt some."[3]

Sussex, Surrey, and Hants persecuted the First Publishers severely. Ambrose Rigge and Thomas Robertson were both from Grayrigg, and young men of about twenty-one in 1655. In July of this year they were at Basingstoke, and were in prison fifteen weeks for refusing the oath of abjuration.[4] When Robertson came again in December, the people were wild and mad against him, and put him into the cage for speaking in the market-place. If he came a third time, a justice vowed to have him flogged, though it cost him as many pounds as Robertson had buttons on his coat.[5] In the following year, he found himself with a number of Sussex Friends in Horsham gaol, in the custody of an indulgent gaoler, who gave him and some others liberty to attend meetings. The gaoler, however, was himself committed to the House of Correction at Lewes, "as a dangerous person for suffering great assemblies of people to have access to and discourse with the said prisoners and to

[1] See *Early Friends in Surrey and Sussex*, by T. W. Marsh, p. 64.

[2] To Margt. Fell, Southampton, 7th Augt. 1657, Swarthm. Colln. iv. 79.

[3] Ambrose Rigge to Margt. Fell, Southampton, 7th Augt. 1660, Swarthm. Colln. iv. 82; Thos. Salthouse to Margt. Fell, Bristol, 3rd Sept. 1660, Swarthm. Colln. iii. 166; cf. Besse, *Sufferings*, i. 692.

[4] Besse, *Sufferings*, i. 228.

[5] Robertson to Margt. Fell, Basingstoke, 30th Dec. 1655, Swarthm. Colln. iv. 205.

disperse among the people dangerous books tending to sedition and disturbance and setting them at liberty without any warrant."[1] Ambrose Rigge was imprisoned in the Isle of Wight, and suffered cruelly at Southampton as a rogue and vagabond, in 1658, the mayor threatening that, if he returned again, he should be burned in the shoulder with the letter R as broad as a shilling.[2] Thomas Laycock, another First Publisher, an old Commonwealth soldier,[3] suffered four imprisonments in Sussex: on one occasion the mayor of Arundel sent him to the Bridewell,

> . . . where they forthwith put on a chain and a lock upon one of his legs, thus lying in a dampy room ten days and ten nights without fire or candle in the coldest of this weather . . . and on the ninth day they violently rent off his clothes and unhumanly did slash him according to the threatenings of the Mayor.[4]

Humphry Smith, from Herefordshire, suffered for twelve months (February 1658–59) in what he calls "this little stinking, lousy, smoky hole at Winchester called the Common Gaol and House of Correction."[5]

Dorset had been visited first by Fox at the end of 1655,[6] when several members of the Baptist community at Poole were convinced. This town and Lyme Regis, Bridport, and Weymouth were the chief Quaker centres, but there were meetings at sixteen places in 1668.[7] There was no part of the country where the vagrancy laws were more frequently put in force against Friends. Humphry Smith spent most of the year 1657 in the county, and with his companion was flogged, on one occasion, just across the Devon border, by order of Thomas Bampfield, member for Exeter, the reporter to the Committee in Nayler's case, and afterwards Speaker of the House of Commons.[8] George Bewley, of Cumberland,

[1] *Extracts from State Papers*, First Series, p. 19.

[2] See *Early Friends in Surrey and Sussex*, p. 65; Besse, *Sufferings*, i. 230.

[3] *Extracts from State Papers*, First Series, p. 17, says, "who hath engaged his life for the just freedom and liberty in the Commonwealth's service."

[4] *Ibid.*

[5] Letter to his son in bound volume of tracts belonging to him, now in possession of Gilbert Gilkes of Kendal.

[6] *F.P.T.* 80; *J.F.H.S.* v. 35.

[7] See particulars in Elizth. B. Rutter's valuable paper, "A Glimpse of Ancient Friends in Dorset," in *J.F.H.S.* v. 39.

[8] *F.P.T.* 86.

was whipped as a vagrant by the bailiffs of Bridport. Going back for his horse and clothes, they had him whipped a second time, and coming again for the same purpose he was given a third flogging, but this time was sent away with his horse and clothes.[1] These are only illustrations which serve to show the temper of the authorities.

[1] *F.P.T.* 84.

CHAPTER XVI

WORK BEYOND SEAS

You people . . . scattered into Barbados, Virginia, New England and other islands thereaways and countries elsewhere . . . to you the mighty Day of the Lord is coming and in His power is appearing amongst you, in raising desires in some of you towards His name, which desires cannot be satisfied with any outward observations and traditions of your fathers . . . let the time past be sufficient: you have followed men who have deceived you . . . no longer look forth, the glad tidings of the gospel of eternal salvation is heard within, in this day of the Lord's mercy, wherein He is teaching His people Himself . . . turn your minds within and examine your hearts, search and try your ways with the Light Christ Jesus hath enlighted you withal, that shows you in your hearts what is sin—that pride and covetousness is sin, lying, swearing is sin, dissimulation, cheating, cosening is sin, vain idle communications, foolish jesting and unbelief is sin."—WM. DEWSBURY, Address issued from Northampton Gaol, 7th Jany. 1656 (*Works*, pp. 156-165).

THE universal mission of the early Friends receives its most emphatic illustration from the outlay in service and money which was devoted to the work of carrying the message beyond seas to the American Colonies, to the Protestants of Holland and Germany, to the Roman Catholics, and even to Jews and Mohammedans. The result, except in the case of the American Colonies and Holland, was altogether disproportionate to the effort involved, although it will be seen that some of these forlorn hopes have added lustrous pages to the annals of Quakerism.

I shall only sketch in barest outline the work in America,* as the rare interest and significance of the story are brought out in detail in the companion volume of the present series, *The Quakers in the American Colonies.* But the work was at first so essentially the natural outgrowth of English Quakerism that some reference is necessary.

The Puritan colonies of Plymouth, Massachusetts, and Rhode Island were in close touch with the Commonwealth authorities. South of these came New Amsterdam, afterwards New York, which was in Dutch hands until 1664. The old colony of Virginia and newly founded Maryland were more royalist in sentiment, as were also the English West Indies, which consisted of the Bermudas, Antigua and adjacent islands, Barbados, Tobago, and in South America, Surinam. Jamaica was added in May 1655, on its capture from the Spaniards by Admiral Penn, the father of William Penn.

The two centres from which Friends worked were Barbados, then in the heyday of its prosperity, and Rhode Island, the isle "of errors" and seat of religious liberty. In Barbados a wealthy sugar-planter, Lieutenant-Colonel Rous, who was a great friend of the Governor, was among the first to join Friends with his son John, and the island soon became, in George Rofe's phrase, "the nursery of the truth."[1]

The pioneer work in America, as had been the case in the South of England, was begun by women—Mary Fisher and Ann Austin reaching Barbados at the end of 1655, and proceeding to Boston in the summer of 1656. The venomous Anti-Quaker pamphlets, written by Calvinist divines who had lived in New England, had already inflamed the Massachusetts authorities against the Quakers, and the two women were summarily expelled, the same drastic treatment being applied to the eight Friends who arrived from London two days later and constituted the main mission. A reinforced party made a second attempt in the summer of 1657, and the narrative of their voyage in the *Woodhouse*, with the Lord leading their vessel, "even as it were a man leading a horse by the head," is assuredly one of the most curious of sea-journals.[2] A sum of £115 : 3s. for freight, pro-

[1] See Letter to Crisp, 16th Nov. 1661, in *Steven Crisp and His Correspondents*, p. 30.

[2] Printed in 1659, reprinted in Bowden's *Hist. of Friends in America*, i. 63-67.

visions, bedding, etc., was paid in connection with this voyage, in the first instance by London Friends, though afterwards, as we have seen,[1] general collections were made for these services beyond sea, and the money was repaid. These collections, from 1657 onwards, show the great interest which was taken by the Quaker groups in England in this wider work. The Friends who formed the mission were themselves in the state of spiritual exaltation which belongs to heroic adventure. One of them writes:

> The Lord God of Hosts is with us, the shout of a King is amongst us. . . . His power has led us all along, and I have seen His glory and am overcome with His love. Take no thought for me, for my trust is in the Lord, only be valiant for the truth upon earth.[2]

The party made land at New Amsterdam, afterwards New York, where some of them went ashore, though most went on to Rhode Island, where they were received with joy. With this hospitable citadel of freedom as the base of operations, they penetrated in ones and twos into the New England Colonies, undaunted by the increasingly severe laws which were enacted against them. Banishments, savage floggings, brandings, and imprisonments failed to abate their zeal, and their ranks were strengthened by Friends from Rhode Island and Barbados. John Rous, of Barbados, in a letter dated from "the Lion's Den called Boston Prison," on 3rd September 1658,[3] reports that Truth is spread through the colonies for two hundred miles, and there are many convinced, some of whom have gone forth as travelling ministers, and "they," he adds, "do more grieve the enemy than we, for they have hope to be rid of us, but they have no hope to be rid of them." Friends at this time were strong at Newport, Rhode Island, and at Sandwich in the Plymouth Colony; and at Salem, in Massachusetts, there were "several pretty Friends in their measures."

[1] *Ante*, pp. 321-325.

[2] Bowden, i. 58 (letter of Jno. Copeland).

[3] To Margt. Fell, Swarthm. Colln. i. 82, printed in Bowden i. 118-121.

A pre-Quaker spiritual movement had existed in all these places, as is shown in detail in *The Quakers in the American Colonies*, where the beginnings of the Quaker groups are also traced. At Sandwich and Salem persecution was fierce, though at first the authorities in the Plymouth Colony, founded by the Pilgrim Fathers, were less intolerant than the stern Calvinists of Boston.

In October 1658 the Massachusetts rulers, at the instigation of John Norton, of Boston, passed by the narrowest of majorities a new act against "the cursed sect" of Quakers, under which they could be banished upon pain of death if they returned. The crisis of persecution followed this enactment. A third party of eight Friends had by this time crossed the Atlantic. Six Salem Friends had been already banished under the new law, and their acceptance of banishment stirred William Robinson, who had come over in the *Woodhouse*, and Marmaduke Stephenson, who came with the third party, to give up their lives in order to test the bloody laws of Boston. Banished in September, they sought sanctuary with the remnant of Friends at Salem, and returned to Boston four weeks later, accompanied by several Salem Friends, one of whom carried linen with her in which to wrap the dead bodies of those who were to suffer. Sentence of death was passed on Robinson and Stephenson, and on Mary Dyer, of Rhode Island, who had also been banished and had returned. On Thursday 27th October 1659 they walked with transfigured faces, hand in hand, to the gallows on Boston Common, a mile from the town, where the two men suffered martyrdom, but Mary Dyer, at the last moment, was reprieved. In May 1660 her dauntless spirit led her again into the "lion's den" of Boston. This time there was no reprieve. After her death a member of the General Court uttered one of those bitter scoffs which prove the truest of all epitaphs, "She did hang as a flag for others to take example by." A fourth martyr, William Leddra, of Barbados, suffered in March 1661.

Popular odium and the fall of Puritanism in England shook the position of the Massachusetts persecutors, and they avoided further hangings of Quakers, by substituting flogging from town to town for the capital punishment. A little later their cruelty recoiled on themselves. English Friends had dragged the works of darkness to light, especially in the book which George Bishop published in the early part of 1661, called *New England Judged.* Burrough saw the King, and told him that there was a vein of innocent blood opened in his dominions, which, unless stopped, would overrun all. Charles issued a mandamus to the New England authorities, and entrusted its delivery to an exiled New England Friend, Samuel Shattuck. The Friends in prison were released, and it was judged prudent to send a deputation to England to moderate the royal displeasure.

The opposition between Quakerism and rigid Calvinism, which was masked in England by the tolerant principles of Cromwell, showed itself without reserve in the theocratic government of Boston. Purity of doctrine, worship, and religion was the thing beyond all else which its rulers desired to safeguard. Only under compulsion would they tolerate heretics in Massachusetts. The battle with Calvinism, owing to the Restoration, was never fought to a finish in England, but here it was waged to the death, and the ultimate victory rested with Friends. Accordingly, the New England chapter of Quaker history is essential to a right understanding of the full consequences of the Quaker movement.

The work in Rhode Island, from an opposite point of view, is also of much significance. For we can here see how Quakerism could develop in an atmosphere of complete religious liberty. Especially do we learn how Friends addressed themselves to the manifold duties of government which came to them. In Virginia and Maryland the early service of Friends met with much success, but presents no features of equally commanding importance.

We pass now to the Continental work,* which lay partly in Protestant, partly in Roman Catholic, and partly in Mohammedan countries.

Holland,* and especially Amsterdam, was the home of religious liberty. The Dutch Republic had been founded in 1579 on a basis of toleration, and became, as we have seen, the natural place of refuge for persecuted Nonconformists and Separatists. The spirit that long prevailed in Holland is well shown in a letter addressed by the Amsterdam Chamber of the West India Company about 1657 to its Director Stuyvesant, at New Amsterdam, who had been persecuting the Quakers:[1]

> "The consciences of men," they say, "ought to be free and unshackled, so long as they continue moderate, peaceable, inoffensive and not hostile to government. Such have been the maxims of prudence and toleration by which the magistrates of this city have been governed; and the consequences have been that the oppressed and persecuted from every country have found among us an asylum from distress. Follow in the same steps and you will be blest."

Through adhesion to these principles the United Provinces became the breeding-ground of new religious ideas, out of which issued the currents of latitudinarian and pietist thought which were at this time modifying the religious atmosphere of Europe. The Quaker movement itself was related to contemporary spiritual movements in Holland, especially that of the Collegianten.

In May 1655 Howgill speaks of some young London Friends with "movings" for Barbados, and of Stubbs and Caton having movings for Holland.[2] In June Caton paid a short visit to Calais, and then planned with Stubbs a brief pioneer journey to Holland. After many delays the two Publishers left the Tyne at the beginning of September.[3] On landing at Flushing they were moved by the power of the Lord "to publish His eternal truth in and through their streets, whether they could understand or no." After some service among the English and Scottish congregations

[1] Fiske, *Dutch and Quaker Colonies in America*, i. 236.

[2] *Letters of Early Friends*, p. 33.*

[3] Annals in *Camb. Journ.* ii. 325. A still earlier Continental visit is glanced at in a letter from Burrough and Howgill to Fox, 25th [Sept. 1654], which says, "Our brother Christopher Atkinson and two women took water towards France six days since" (Dev. Ho., A.R.B. Colln. No. 156). As Atkinson was at Norwich by the end of November (*ante*, p. 163), the visit must have been a short one.*

at Flushing and Middleburg, they came to Rotterdam and met with a company of Dutch and English merchants. "The power spoke," writes Stubbs; "they were terrified and chained and confessed to the truth." "Oh!" says Caton, "alas, how did we suffer for want of a good interpreter, for he that interpreted for us not being true and faithful . . . the hearers or some of them especially came rather to be incensed against us, than to be won or gained to the truth,—howbeit the witness of God answered to the truth of our testimony in some."[1] In the summer of 1656 a fuller publishing of the Quaker message took place, William Ames spending ten weeks in Holland and Stubbs a month.[2] At Rotterdam Ames was threatened as a Jesuit: at Amsterdam the minister of the congregation of English Brownists thrust him out and shut the door upon him. Later in the visit he and Stubbs had a "precious memorable meeting at Amsterdam," and a silent meeting was begun at Rotterdam. A number of persons were convinced at the places visited. From details given by Stubbs to Margaret Fell it appears that their expenses in Holland were about £11, of which only about £2 : 10s. was on meat and drink, and he adds, "Thy care in the Lord is for us all, and if I do not spend my portion and allowance in His dread and pure fear in moderation and much temperance, woe is me." Caton speaks of similar frugality when with Stubbs in 1655.[3] The visit was evidently a time of seed-sowing, and some persons in Amsterdam, then one of the greatest cities in Europe, welcomed the Quaker message. The city had been called in 1608 by Bishop Joseph Hall "a common harbour of all opinions, of all heresies."[4] Ames, who had been a Baptist, found favour with the Dutch Baptists, but Stubbs, another ex-Baptist, was less to their liking.[5] Ames, it seems,[6] had

[1] Wm. Caton's *Life* and Stubbs' account, Dev. Ho., A.R.B. Colln. No. 12.

[2] Stubbs to Margt. Fell, 2nd Sept. 1656 (Swarthm. Colln. iv. 27); Ames to Margt. Fell (Dev. Ho., A.R.B. Colln. No. 3).

[3] *Life*, 1689 edn. p. 21.

[4] Mullinger, *University of Cambridge*, iii. 158.

[5] Sewel (1811 edn.), i. 232. Wm. Sewel was born at Amsterdam, 1654, and may be regarded as an original authority on all Dutch matters.*

[6] Croese (1696 edn.), p. 60.

been a marine under Prince Rupert, in the Admiral's own ship, in which there were many Dutchmen, from whose conversation he had gained some knowledge of the language.

In the autumn of 1656 Caton paid a second visit, and was received with gladness at Amsterdam, where some of the newly convinced persons interpreted to the rest what he said. At Rotterdam, however, he was obliged to give his message in Latin, which was then put into Dutch. Here some people, convinced by Ames, were already under the name of Quakers running into extremes, both in words and writings.[1] Caton, a young man of nineteen, felt overwhelmed, for a number of high conceited professors attended the meetings, and several of them were more disposed to teach others than to be taught themselves. Their leader was one Isaac Furnier, who, Sewel tells us, lived as another Diogenes, using a split stick for a pair of tongs, making it a matter of holiness to employ the most blunt language he could think of, and constantly saying, "My spirit testifieth." He is called by Sewel a passionate and giddy-headed man, whom the true Quakers would not own, though he translated their books, and would also preach among them. At last he left them, and turning Papist fell into a dissolute life. Caton after a time found himself at Middleburg with a young man from England who knew both languages. The young man attended some of the meeting-places in the city, and raised a great rage against the Quakers, so that they were both imprisoned, and after some harsh treatment were shipped off to England, which they reached in November.

In Holland, with its many sects, it would seem that the Quaker Publishers did not at first succeed in attracting persons of serious, well-balanced minds, but rather, as Sewel puts it, whimsical people, more inclined to novelties than to true godliness. The soil here was not stony as it had been in Ireland and Scotland, but shallow, bringing forth rank and short-lived growths.

Nayler's extravagances caused strange reports every-

[1] Sewel, *loc. cit.* and Caton's *Life*.

where about Friends,* and the next visitor to Holland, Christopher Birkhead, a shipwright and mariner of Bristol, came into conflict with the English congregation at Middleburg, and was sent for two years to the house of correction.[1]

Early in the year 1657 Ames paid a second visit with Humble Thatcher, the young man who had helped Caton.[2] The magistrates of Amsterdam were stirred out of their usual tolerance by the rumours abroad, comparing the Quakers, for instance, with the enthusiasts of Münster, and the two men were banished the town for not putting off their hats.[3] The visit, however, was not fruitless, for at this time Ames convinced two Flemish Baptists, Jacob Sewel and his wife Judith Zinspenning, the parents of the Quaker historian.

"They," he says, "with two or three more, were the first orthodox Quakers in Amsterdam, orthodox, I say, because I very well remember what a strange and odd sort of people about that time did flock to the Quakers in this country." [4]

Caton came to Amsterdam in April, and spent some seven weeks in shepherding the infant Church, distracted by the suspicions of the authorities and by the unruliness of some of its members, especially an Englishwoman, Ann Gargill, who, according to the Annals in the *Cambridge Journal*, had already carried the Quaker message to Portugal.[5] He visited other towns, but returned again and again to Amsterdam, where the number of Friends increased and meetings began to be kept in good order, though the rude multitude who crowded in were often troublesome. After a year in Holland he went back for a time to England.

Ames meanwhile continued on the Continent. The Mennonites and the Collegianten supplied most of the recruits to Quakerism. The Mennonites, so named from

[1] Sewel, i. 281; cf. i. 250. Besse, *Sufferings*, ii. 395. For Birkhead, see note in *Camb. Journ.* ii. 481.

[2] Sewel, i. 283; Ames to Margt. Fell, 17th Apl. 1657, Swarthm. Colln. iv. 28. Stubbs gives some account of Thatcher in a letter to Margt. Fell, 10th Augt. 1657, Swarthm. Colln. iii. 152, and says that he had been in service with Caton.

[3] Sewel, i. 283, and letter of Ames cited above.

[4] Sewel, i. 284.

[5] *Camb. Journ.* ii. 326. For Ann Gargill see note in *Camb. Journ.* ii. 468. A letter in the Swarthm. Colln. i. 6, A. G. to Fox is, I suspect, by her. For Caton's visit see his *Life*.*

Menno Simons, the Reformer of the Anabaptist movement,[1] had been the parents of the General Baptist Churches founded in England by Thos. Helwys and John Murton, and offered a promising field for the propaganda of men like Ames and Stubbs, who had been Baptists themselves. The Collegianten had absorbed many Mennonites, but originated among the Arminians or Remonstrants, whose views were condemned in 1619 by the Synod of Dort. At Warmond, near Leyden, the Remonstrant minister had been ejected, and meetings for devotional purposes had been begun there and at Rynsburg and another village by four brothers named Van der Kodde. They were called "free-speech meetings" or "collegianten," owing to the large liberty of prophesying which was allowed in them to all spiritually-minded persons.[2] Sewel, at the end of his *History*, prints a Collegiant tract called "The Light on the Candlestick," which lays the whole stress of religion upon the Inward Light, in terms which might have been penned by a Quaker. The Collegiant practices also show striking points of resemblance with those of Friends, as well as some points of difference. Ames opposed both Mennonites and Collegianten, because in spite of their close approach to Quakerism in many respects, "he still judged their way of worship, especially their disputations and will-worship, to be out of the way of the Lord."[3] He seems to have felt towards them much as Friends in England felt towards Baptists and Seekers.

The relations with Quakerism of the celebrated Dr. Galenus Abrahamsz are probably typical of the sympathetic but non-committal attitude maintained by many persons belonging to the more spiritual of the Dutch sects.[4] Born in 1622, he studied medicine and alchemy,

[1] See *Studies in Mystical Religion*, by Dr. Rufus M. Jones, pp. 393-395.

[2] For the Collegianten, see Barclay's *Inner Life*, pp. 89-92; article by Isaac Sharp (translating Pastor Sippell of Marburg) in *Friends' Quarterly Examiner*, 1910, pp. 299-301; and "De Rÿnsburger Collegianten," by J. C. Van Slee, Haarlem, 1895, as communicated to me by D. Mulder of Herwen.

[3] Sewel, ii. 57.

[4] For these particulars I am indebted to lectures on Quakerism in Holland, prepared by D. Mulder, of Herwen, and delivered at Woodbrooke, Birmingham, in 1906, which are the fruit of much careful research.

and settled in Amsterdam as a doctor in 1646. His father was a Mennonite minister, and his own gift of eloquent speech was exercised among the Flemish Mennonites and the Collegiants. With the help of his friend David Spruyt he published in 1659 a statement of theology of the Seeker type called "The Nineteen Articles," to which, says a hostile writer, all kinds did gather, as Millenarians, Fifth Monarchy men, Socinians, Boehmists, pretended prophets, dreamers and visionaries, mystical philosophers, fanatics, Quakers, etc., in a word all who were out of conceit with their former religion and were allured by the doctrine of free-speech.

Galenus had a good deal of intercourse with the Friends who visited Holland, and in one of his pamphlets claimed that he had always upheld them and had shielded them from trouble. Ames he compared to a musician who played a very melodious tune, Stubbs to a disturber of the harmonious music, though Ames afterwards displeased him by his unsparing zeal.[1] Some years later he disputed through an interpreter with Penn and Fox, and, says Fox, "He was then very high and very shy, so that he . . . bid me Keep my eyes off him, for, he said, they pierced him." In 1684, however, he met Fox again, and "was very loving and tender, and confessed in some measure to Truth: his wife also and daughter were tender and kind, and we parted from them very lovingly."[2]

The Quaker influence in Holland is not to be measured by the number of persons who definitely associated themselves together in Quaker groups. Besides these there were wide circles, especially among the Mennonite sects and the Collegianten, who accepted the Quaker teaching without leaving the religious fellowships to which they belonged. The maintenance in Holland of a Quaker mission was accordingly a matter of much importance.

Ames was a man of great boldness, as is shown in an incident belonging to March 1659.[3] Returning from a meeting near Gouda, he was mobbed by a crowd who

[1] Sewel, i. 232.
[2] Fox, *Journ.* ii. 401; cf. 402.
[3] Sewel, i. 342.

shouted out, "Quake, quake, quake," and pelted him with stones and clods. The minister, hearing the noise, came out, and explained to Ames that the people were not accustomed to behave in this way to honest folk; "but," said he, "I believe you [to] be a deceiving wolf that comes among the sheep to seduce them, and therefore they cry so." Ames, insisting on proof of this charge, was locked up in the Rotterdam Bedlam as a madman, but three weeks later was invited by the deputy-governor of the house to break prison. He was, in fact, let out on the following day, but went to the dike-grave who had committed him, and returned to Bedlam on hearing that he was supposed to have broken out. Sewel adds, "I truly believe he would rather have died than to have spoken a lie."

Caton paid a fourth visit to Holland in the spring of 1659, and had good service, being by this time familiar with the language. He found Friends well settled, and the meetings in good order, with strangers coming to them more frequently than formerly. At Amsterdam, to avoid uproars by the mob, and consequent interference by the authorities, he arranged that the meeting should be kept now at one house and now at another.[1] The chief centre in Holland was in the capital, but there were also a Quaker group at Rotterdam, a "little flock" at Leyden, and meetings at Haarlem and Alkmaar.[2]

Shortly after the Restoration, when the storm of persecution burst over English Friends, through their supposed share in the Fifth Monarchy rising, there was a ground-swell of rage against them in Holland, and Caton reported that a mob was intending to raze to the ground[3] the large garret of a tanner's house which was then used as the Amsterdam meeting-place.[4] The city, however, maintained its enlightened policy, and drew from him a few years later a well-earned eulogium:[5]

Methinks it is very commendable for to see, as I have often seen in this city, how that Calvinists, Lutherans, Papists,

[1] Sewel, i. 339. [2] Caton's *Life* (1689 edn.), pp. 61, 63.
[3] Letter in *Life* (1839 edn.) p. 97. [4] Sewel, i. 340.
[5] To Jas. Moore, Amsterdam, 19th Oct. 1665, in Caton's *Life* (1839 edn.), p. 139.

Baptists of divers sorts, Jews, Friends, Arminians, etc., go in peace, and return in peace, and enjoy their meetings in peace, and all are kept in peace in the city, and that without any trouble to the rulers of the city.

The chief minister from among the Dutch Friends during these early years was Judith Zinspenning the mother of Sewel the historian. She was a Baptist who had been drawn into a deeper religious experience through the preaching of Dr. Galenus Abrahamsz, and became convinced with her husband under the teaching of Ames and Caton. She was so well esteemed that the Collegianten, on one occasion, allowed her to address them, saying, "It is true, friend, we do not allow women to speak in the Church, yet we bear that respect to you, that we give you the liberty of speaking." Even in her girlhood her keen interest in sermons had made her father say that he wished she were a boy, for then she might become an eminent instrument in the Church. She often visited the outlying meetings at Alkmaar, Haarlem, and Rotterdam, and her death in 1664 was a heavy loss to Friends. A sentence from one of her epistles was no doubt very applicable to the weak and struggling condition of these Dutch meetings.

Dear Friends, keep your meetings in the fear of the Lord, and have a care that your minds are not drawn out to hear words outwardly; but stand in the cross to that which desireth refreshment from without: and when at any time ye feel but little refreshment, let it not enter into your hearts that the Lord is not mindful of you, but centre down into yourselves, in the pure light, and stand still therein: then it may be ye will find the cause why the presence of the Lord is departed from you for some time, and ye, putting away the cause, shall enjoy the Lord again to your comfort.[1]

With the establishment of Quakerism in Holland, a base was provided from which Protestant Europe could be reached.* In the summer of 1657[2] Ames and George

[1] Sewel, ii. 161-169.

[2] The date is ascertained by a paper of Rofe's in the Crisp Colln. No. 49 (July 1657) and a letter of Willan's to Margt. Fell (Swarthm. Colln. i. 301) dated 12th Sept. 1657.

Rofe, the Halstead glazier, visited Griesheim in the Palatinate, near Worms, a village which was a Mennonite centre. Here some persons were convinced and the rabble became excited against Friends, so that the authorities directed that no one should entertain them, and they lodged in barns and stables, until Ames procured an interview with the Prince Elector at Heidelberg, who heard him favourably and gave leave to Friends to travel in his country and reside there.[1] On a second visit paid a year later by Ames and a London Friend named John Higgins, the Prince Elector again showed himself cordial,[2] and Caton in 1661 gives the same report of him. Charles Louis, at the Peace of Westphalia, had been restored to the Lower Palatinate, desolated and depopulated by the Thirty Years' War. His toleration was a part of the easy-going philosophy which caused him to invite Spinoza to a chair at Heidelberg University. The Princess Elizabeth, disciple and friend of Descartes and the future friend of Penn and Barclay, was at this time living at Heidelberg, and her singular breadth of intellect must have exerted powerful influence in the Court. She now came into touch with Friends for the first time and received Ames favourably.[3]

The Quaker group at Griesheim had an interesting history. Sufferings for refusing to bear arms or to contribute towards the charge of the militia, for reproving the priests, for working on a holy day, and for tithes, came on the members of the group much after the fashion of the petty persecution rife in England.[4] They were mostly vine-growers, and when Caton and Ames visited them in 1661, "we continued some time," says Caton,[5] "helping them to gather their grapes, it being the time of their vintage." The meeting was kept up until 1686, when all the members removed to Pennsylvania,[6] to the Germantown Settlement, where to their undying

[1] Sewel, i. 340, and Besse, *Sufferings*, ii. 450.
[2] Sewel, i. 341.
[3] Sewel, i. 341 says the "Prince's sister" received him kindly.
[4] Besse, *Sufferings*, ii. 450-455.
[5] *Life*, 1689 edn. p. 65.
[6] Crisp Colln. No. 131.*

honour they joined in the first great protest by a religious body against slavery.

Ames also travelled widely in other parts of Germany. We hear of him at the end of 1658, in Friesland and going on to Hamburg.[1] In 1661 he spent some time in the Palatinate and visited Bohemia, where there was no liberty of conscience, travelling on by Brandenburg to Danzig and Poland. He found the Poles much like the Irish: they would kill a man for ten shillings. At Danzig some were convinced, and he got entrance among the Baptists. This pioneer work did not at first result in the formation of Quaker groups, though a few years later, in 1662, a meeting was begun at Embden in East Friesland, and we hear of persons convinced in Hamburg in 1660.[2] As early as the summer of 1657 two Westmorland Friends, William Wilson and Reginald Holme, had visited this important free city,[3] and in 1658 John Hall may have passed through on his journey to Copenhagen, where he was imprisoned. He succeeded, however, in speaking with the King, Frederic III., to whom he gave some books, and, says Caton, "I suppose a good sound is sounded forth by him in that place.[4]

Fox would have sent Caton and Ames on still wider errands. At the end of 1660, when he was issuing epistles to Turk and Pope and even to the Emperor of China, he wrote of a seed of God to be gathered in Russia, Muscovy, Poland, Hungary, and Sweden, but Caton freely told him that he felt no call to go, still having much on him for Holland and the neighbouring lands.[5] A remarkable visit was indeed paid to Hungary and Austria by John Philley and William Moore in 1662, which will be noticed in a future volume.[*]

We take next the attempts which were made to carry the Quaker message to Roman Catholic countries

[1] To Fox, 14th Oct. 1658, A.R.B. Colln. No. 6.

[2] Besse, *Sufferings*, ii. 443, 448; cf. paper in Swarthm. Colln. iv. 39.

[3] See accounts of Kendal Fund, Swarthm. Colln. i. 233, and i. 397 (Bowden, i. 59 *n*).

[4] To Margt. Fell, 15th Mar. 1658, Dev. Ho., Caton Colln., Jas. Bowden's copy.

[5] To Fox, 25th Jan. 1661, Swarthm. Colln. iv. 273.

and the East, a service abundant in persecution but barren in fruit. When Burrough was in Dunkirk in 1659,[1] he showed himself conscious that a preparatory work had been done in Protestant countries in freeing men from the spiritual tyranny of Rome, and recognized that until this liberation was effected the message of Quakerism could have little entrance. Caton, visiting Calais in 1655,[2] was burdened with the idolatry, as he considered it, of the Roman Catholic worship, though through ignorance of the language he could not bear his testimony against it. Friends had shared the intense feeling which swept over England in this year when the news of the Vaudois massacre reached the country. Cromwell appointed 14th June as a day of humiliation, and a house-to-house collection was taken up by the minister and churchwardens in most parishes. Fox protested against setting apart a day, but promised the contributions of Friends, which were taken up by Friends themselves over a great part of the North, but in some places were given through the national collection.[3] In Jany. 1657 we hear of two Friends, names unrecorded, who were in Paris half-starved with cold and hunger, and said that "they were ambassadors from the Lord to the Duke of Savoy . . . they despaired not of the gift of tongues, and the Lord had told them they should have success."[4]

Quaker Publishers of Truth, furnished with books and an intense faith in their mission, began to find their way into Roman Catholic lands.* In April 1657 two Friends, John Harwood and George Bayly, tried to reach France, but on the passage the Captain found that they regarded themselves as led over by the Spirit for the conversion of souls and were willing to lose their lives for their religion, and on consideration thought it best to bring back such religious firebrands to England.[5] Harwood was a York-

[1] See *Works*, p. 537, etc. [2] *Life* (1689 edn.), p. 20.

[3] See his letters in *Camb. Journ.* i. 335 (wrongly dated), and Swarthm. Colln. ii. 93, and the references to the collection in letters of Thos. Willan to Margt. Fell in the Swarthm. Colln., also Annals, 1655, in *Camb. Journ.* ii. 326.

[4] *Extracts from State Papers*, First Series, p. 24.

[5] *Ibid.* p. 28. The extract calls them "John" and "George."

shireman, who had suffered imprisonment at York in 1652, and afterwards at Bury St. Edmunds with Rofe and George Whitehead; Bayly, a young London shopkeeper, had also suffered for speaking in church.[1] Later in the spring they reached France, and soon found themselves in difficulties. Harwood got entrance into several religious houses, and found them under a great veil of ceremony and superstition, pleading for the antiquity of their Church, but ready enough to confess the light of Christ within them. He was, however, thrown into the Bastille, where he was kept without books or ink, though he had a French Bible from a fellow-prisoner and began to learn French.[2] Bayly also was cast into prison in Paris and died there in the autumn,[3] after pitiful sufferings. Harwood was released about the same time, and returned to England, where we find him in controversy with the Muggletonian Lawrence Claxton, and after the Restoration in prison at Southwark.[4] Earlier than this, however, he seems to have lost the confidence of his brethren through some irregular proceedings with a widow towards marriage, and nursed a grievance against Fox and others for their censure of his conduct. Fox goes so far as to say that Harwood "sought to take away G.ff's life, but the Lord confounded him."[5] He was probably a man of ill-balanced judgment, for in 1660 he is spoken of as "high in his comprehensions," and one who should keep silence in the Church.[6]

In the early part of 1658 William Salt, of London, Fox's fellow-prisoner in Cornwall, reached France, and was imprisoned at Morlaix for sending papers to the magistrates. He showed the exalted spirit which we find again and again in the Quaker missionaries beyond sea, and wrote home:

1 Besse, *Sufferings*, i. 361 ; *F.P.T.* 157 ; Dev. Ho., A.R.B. Colln. No. 155.

2 Letter to Luke Howard of Dover, 28th June (Swarthm. Colln. iii. 96).

3 Annals in *Camb. Journ.* ii. 337 Sewel, i. 283 ; and for date Hubberthorne to Fox, 19th Nov. (no year), Swarthm. Colln. iv. 9, and Willan to Margt. Fell, 12th Sept. 1657 (Swarthm. Colln. i. 301).*

4 See Smith's *Catalogue*.

5 See Geo. Whitehead, *Christian Progress*, p. 98, Smith's *Catal. Supplmt.* and *Camb. Journ.* ii. 314, and note at ii. 462.

6 Grace Barwick to Fox, Swarthm. Colln. iv. 174.*

. . . the sound is gone forth of a seed brought forth which shall spread over the nations . . . Herod and all Jerusalem . . . are troubled and in confusion, some saying, he speaks well, it is not to be denied, others saying he is an innovator of new religions, and of a new law, a perturbator of the public peace, etc.

The Greffier of the town is said to have designed his death, but through the intervention of the English ambassador, he was released, though so emaciated by confinement and want that he was become like the skeleton of a man.[1] He does not seem to have returned to England until the autumn of 1659, and in 1661 we hear of him in Holland trying vainly to get passage to the East Indies.[2] Later he became involved in the Perrot separation and lost touch with the main body of Friends.

We must now go wider afield. The year 1657 saw several attempts to carry the Quaker message to the shores of the Mediterranean, among people strange in customs, in language, and in religion, with whom the Northern enthusiasts had few points of sympathy. One of the most heroic of these adventures was that undertaken by George Robinson, a young man of London, in the autumn of the year 1657.[3] Going by sea to Leghorn, then the port for English trade with the Levant, he went forward in a French vessel to St. Jean d'Acre, and on to Joppa. Except as a pilgrim he could not have easy access to Jerusalem, and on refusing to go in this way was turned back at Ramleh, and sent again to Acre, where a French merchant lodged him for three weeks. Robinson, however, procured passage to Joppa a second time, and started out for Jerusalem on foot. At Ramleh two Friars of the convent laid hold of him and hurried him

[1] See letters from Salt in Dev. Ho. Portfolio 17, and Besse, *Sufferings*, ii. 395. A reference to Salt occurs in a letter from Hubberthorne to Fox, London, 20th March (Swarthm. Colln. iv. 12). He had then been a prisoner two months. This letter must, I think, be dated 1658 on a balance of internal evidence.

[2] For his return, see Luke Howard to Caton, 9th Oct. 1659, in Swarthm. Colln. iv. 266; for the East Indies see letters of Caton, 21st June and 7th July 1661, in Swarthm. Colln. iv. 275 and i. 326.

[3] See accounts in Besse, *Sufferings*, ii. pp. 392-394; and more fully in Sewel, i. 292-297. The accounts say Ramoth except in one place in Sewel where the place is called Ramla. They are taken from the printed account at end of "A True Account of the . . . Sufferings of K. Evans and Sarah Chevers," 1663. Was he related to the Wm. Robinson martyred at Boston?

away, but with their connivance he was taken by two Turks, who led him off into a mosque. This profanation of a mosque by a Christian put him in peril of his life unless he became a renegade. A crowd collected, and the priests asked him if he would turn Mohammedan, and hold up one of his fingers in token. One of them urged him to say "Christ is bad," but he answered that he knew Him to be good, and was His servant. So they grew angry and threatened to take his life, dragging him away to be burnt to death with camel's dung. While awaiting his end with a retired mind, the Turks continued to debate the matter, and at last a grave ancient Turk came up to him and said that he should not be burnt. They then recorded in a book that he was no Roman Catholic, but of another religion, and the old Turk took him home. A few days later the envious Friars sent a party of horse to carry him to Gaza, where they had prejudiced the Pasha against him. But the Pasha, learning of their malice, obliged them to convey Robinson safely to Jerusalem, where he was lodged, we gather, in a convent of Irish Friars. The next morning a Friar came to him, and asked if he would become an obedient child, and go to visit the Holy Places according to their custom: he answered "No." No persuasions moved him, he said that for the present he had no business calling him to visit them, and under no circumstances would he visit them as a matter of worship. At last they told him that whether he went or not he must pay the customary fee of twenty-five dollars to the Turk, but this he refused to submit to. So he was taken before the Turkish authority, and asked the cause of his coming to Jerusalem. He answered that he came by command of the God of heaven and earth, whose great and tender love was manifest in visiting them, and whose compassionate mercy was such that He would gather them in this the day of His gathering. Having thus cleared his conscience he was willing to leave the city: the Friars were ordered to carry him back to Ramleh, whence he made his way to England.

Other Friends set out with the idea of reaching Jerusalem, but it is doubtful if any of them were successful.[1] The Levant afforded no facilities for itinerating Publishers of Truth. The English consuls and merchants regarded them as fatuous and futile visionaries to be headed back at every opportunity, while at Roman Catholic ports they landed at the risk of falling into the merciless clutches of the Inquisition. The money cost of the journeys was considerable, the danger to life and the spiritual wear and tear were very great, and there were no direct results in convincements. The significance of these visits lies in the evidence they give of the high claims made by the Quaker message and the reckless devotion of the messengers. There was never a more complete scorn of consequence and circumstance.

The chief mission of the year 1657 started somewhat earlier than the date assigned to George Robinson's departure. I hope to tell its story with more completeness than was possible to earlier writers, though there is still some obscurity. The accounts of the first general Quaker Fund for the service of Truth abroad[2] contain items under the head of Turkey amounting to £177 : 5 : 7, which belong to this mission. The party, when we hear of it at Smyrna, consisted of six persons, three men and three women. The three men were all, I think, from Ireland—John Perrot from Waterford,[3] John Luffe from Limerick,[4] and John Buckley, whom it seems most natural to connect with Samuel Buckley, of Kilkenny. When Luffe writes to Gerrard Roberts from Smyrna in December 1657[5] he asks for a further supply of money,

[1] See Barbara Blaugdone to Fox, Swarthm. Colln. iii. 194, and Thos. Hayman to Fox and Burrough (1657), Swarthm. Colln. iii. 124. He speaks of "a Friend come to Plymouth to go with me to Jerusalem," perhaps Robinson.

[2] Bowden, *Hist. of Friends in America*, i. 59.

[3] A letter of Thos. Morford's, dated 6th May 1659 (Swarthm. Colln. i. 26), speaks of a visit to Perrot's wife and children two miles from Waterford.

[4] Rutty's *History of Friends in Ireland* (1800 edn.), p. 85. He is also called Jno. Love.

[5] The authorities for the mission are as follows: (*a*) Perrot's published papers (see Smith's *Catalogue*); (*b*) his MS. letters and papers in Swarthm. Colln. vol. v., especially three letters—To Friends in Ireland, Zante, 7th Sept., To Friends, Venice Lazaretto, 16th Mar. 1658, and To Burrough, Venice Lazaretto, 26th Mar.; (*c*) an important set of abstracts of papers relating to foreign service

and says, "Ireland should be accountable for what thou sendest, as J[ohn] P[errot] did motion in a letter to them to be at all our future charge." The women were Mary Fisher, Mary Prince, and Beatrice Beckly.

Perrot had been a Baptist, and was convinced by Burrough when in Ireland.[1] He became the leader, at a later date, of the first serious Quaker separation, and on that account the following estimate of his character by Ellwood[2] must be read with reservation. "This man came pretty early amongst Friends, and too early took upon him the ministerial office, and being though little in person yet great in opinion of himself, nothing less would serve him than to go and convert the Pope." Luffe, if we may credit the curious account preserved of his martyrdom, had visited and been expelled from New England, and had also spent some time in Seville; Mary Prince, who was from Bristol, and Mary Fisher had both attempted to carry the message to Boston and had been banished the colony. Beatrice Beckly is not otherwise known to me. The party reached Leghorn on the 29th July, and had free service for about a fortnight among English, Jews, and Roman Catholics. They met with much hostility from most, but the English Agent was loving, and one of the oldest French merchants in the town offered help in translating their books and as interpreter. The Jewish Synagogue was visited, and a number of Jews came to Perrot and Luffe for conference and seemed convinced. On the 18th August Perrot was called before the Inquisition and closely questioned, but was not detained. The party set sail again on the 20th, intend-

---

which has recently come to light at Dev. Ho., Portfolio 17, containing Letter from Luffe to Gerrard Roberts, Smyrna, 10th Dec. 1657, followed by the copy of a printed account of his martyrdom, three letters from Perrot to Burrough, dated Leghorn, 17th Aug., Zante, 7th Sept., and Venice, 16th Mar. 1658, and three letters from Stubbs and Fisher to London, dated 2nd May, 18th June, and 7th Augt. 1658; (*d*) documents in Thurloe's *State Papers*, vii. 32, 287; (*e*) account of Mary Fisher in Sewel, i. 433-435; (*f*) Croese, 1696 English edn., pp. 270-276. The commonly received date of 1660 for Mary Fisher's visit to the Sultan must be corrected, and it is clear that she was not alone on the greater part of her service, as has been generally assumed.

[1] Burrough to Dring and Roberts, Waterford, 21st Jany. 1656, Dev. Ho., Wm. Markey Colln.

[2] *Life*, 1714 edn., p. 241.

ing to make their way to Jerusalem. At Zante they divided, Perrot and Buckley going forward across the Morea, the others continuing their voyage by way of Candia to Smyrna, which they reached on 18th November. Perrot and Buckley visited Corinth and Athens, but were delayed in Negropont by the exactions of a Pasha, and did not join the main party at Smyrna till the end of the year. The English consul discouraged their idea of going "to convert the Grand Signior," that is, the Sultan. He treated the party kindly, but was very urgent that they should return, and succeeded in starting them home towards Venice. Mary Prince seems to have stayed behind for a few weeks and then sailed via Venice to England. At Smyrna they had been able to do little; Luffe can only say, "The sound [of our] coming is gone through this town among Turks and Jews and all: I am their [wo]nder and gazing-stock, but the Lord is a strong tower."

The party started for Venice, baffled but still intent on their mission. Bad weather compelled the ship to put into Zante, and Buckley, Mary Fisher, and Beatrice Beckly at once landed, so as "to pass into the Morea again into Turkey . . . to go toward Adrianople, where we hear the Turk's Emperor lies with his army, being, as is supposed, six days' journey from the place where they may land." Perrot adds that he left the two women Friends "in a meet estate to proceed," and that Buckley would make his way to Constantinople.

The five or six hundred miles of the land journey to Adrianople, along the Northern shore of the Morea and through Macedonia and Rumelia, would be an enterprise of great difficulty, and it seems more probable that the Friends went across the Ægean from some Greek port. The six days talked of by Perrot no doubt, in any case, stretched into as many weeks. Our next piece of positive information comes from Sir Thomas Bendish, the English ambassador at Constantinople, under date 24th July 1658. He writes:

Nor are all our troubles from without us: some are, as I may say, from amongst us and from within us, occasioned by a generation of people crept in unawares called Quakers, three whereof not long since arrived here from Zante by way of the Morea, whom I suffered with tenderness so long as their comportment was offenceless, but when, at length, becoming scandalous to our nation and religion (which upon this occasion was censured and scoffed at by Papist, Jew, and others of a strange faith) and insufferable also by reason of their disturbances of our Divine exercises and several notorious contempts of me and my authority, I friendly warned them to return, which the two women did quietly, but John Buckley refusing, I was constrained to ship him hence upon the *Lewis*.[1]

I infer that the two women went home quietly because they had discharged their concern, while Buckley resisted because his mission was still unaccomplished. If so, Mary Fisher's famous visit to the Sultan had already taken place, say in May or June 1658.* Sultan Mohammed IV. was a young man of seventeen, whose Viziers revived the military prowess of the Turks, and made them again a menace to Europe. When the Vizier was told that an Englishwoman had come to the camp near Adrianople with a message from the great God to the Sultan, he caused her to be received with state ceremony. She was then a woman of about thirty-five, and was brought before the Sultan, who had his great men about him, as was the custom when an ambassador was admitted to his presence. Bidden to speak her message, she stayed awhile before she began, weightily pondering what to say. The Sultan told her not to fear, but to speak the word of the Lord to them, neither more nor less, for they had good hearts and could hear it. Then she spoke through an interpreter what was on her mind, the Turks listening with much gravity and attention. When she had ended, the Sultan said that he had understood every word, and it was the truth. He invited her to stay in the country, saying that they felt respect for one who had come so far with a message to them from God. He also offered her an escort to Constantinople, which she declined.

[1] Thurloe, *State Papers*, vii. 287

She, having no more to say, the Turks asked her what she thought of their prophet Mohammed. She answered warily that she knew him not, but Christ, the true prophet, the Son of God, who was the Light of the world, and enlightened every man coming into the world, Him she knew. And concerning Mohammed she said that they might judge of him to be true or false according to the words and prophecies he spoke, saying farther, "If the word that a prophet speaketh come to pass, then shall ye know that the Lord hath sent that prophet; but if it come not to pass, then shall ye know that the Lord never sent him." The Turks confessed this to be true, and Mary, having performed her message, departed from the camp to Constantinople, without a guard, whither she came without the least hurt or scoff. And so she returned safe to England.[1]

Far less Christian was the reception given to Perrot and Luffe by the Roman Catholic authorities. They had reached Venice in March 1658, after some trying experiences, and here Perrot had succeeded in speaking to the Doge. Though they still had Jerusalem in mind, they went forward to Rome about the end of April. Within two or three days of their coming they had spoken with some of the English college of Jesuits, who deemed them mad and betrayed them to the Inquisition for bearing testimony against the Pope and his cardinals, Jesuits, priests, and friars. Luffe was reported about the end of the year to have died in prison, but from a copy of an account of his trial, stated to have been published in 1661, it would appear that he was examined before Pope Alexander VII. and afterwards hanged. "Thou pretendest to sit in Peter's chair," said Luffe, according to this account. "Now know that Peter had no chair, but a boat: Peter was a fisher, thou art a Prince: Peter fasted and prayed, thou farest deliciously and sleepest softly: he was mean in attire, thou art beset with ornaments and gay attire: he fished for men to convert them, thou hookest souls to confound them: he was a friend and disciple to Christ, thou art indeed Antichrist." At a later part of the discussion Luffe said, "Every day is a sabbath wherein we can serve God." "Very well," said the Pope,

[1] Sewel, i. 433-435.

"and is there nothing to be done for the remembrance' sake of our Saviour's blessed ascension?" "No, no," replied Luffe, "I have Christ about me and in me, and therefore cannot choose but remember Him continually." When he was led out to execution he spoke many words against Popery, Presbytery, and Anabaptism, as the three paths that led men astray, then he stood pausing awhile in silent prayer, and bid the executioner do his office. His death by hanging is confirmed by a curious sentence in William Penn's *Judas and the Jews*,[1] which speaks of "John Perrot, who, if he had been as faithful as his companion, might with him have been hanged at Rome, . . . to his own comfort, the Truth's honour, and the Churches' peace."

Perrot* languished in prison and was put into the mad-house, from which place he was able from time to time to write letters to Friends. He was a man of imaginative temperament, and as early as his voyage to Smyrna we find a letter from him beginning, "I, John, a servant and disciple of Immanuel, God with us, etc.," in imitation apparently of the apostle John. This became the usual mode of his epistles from Rome, and his great sufferings in that "fountain of blood and seat of cruelty" must have stirred Friends at home deeply. Here, for example, is the title of one paper: "A Wren in the Burning Bush, Waving the Wings of Contraction, To the Congregated clean Fowls of the Heavens, in the Ark of God, holy Host of the Eternal Power, Salutation . . . [from] John, the Prisoner of Christ." During his captivity his mind carried the Quaker revolt against all the customary, traditional ways of worship to an extreme, and "express commandment from the Lord God of heaven" came to him to bear a sure testimony against the custom and tradition of taking off the hat by men in prayer.[2] This did not find favour with the Quaker leaders in England, who placed a clear distinction between "hat-honour" to men and the reverence due to God, and Perrot became the head of a

[1] 1673 edn. p. 17. Cf. *Camb. Journ.* i. 183.
[2] See paper undated in Swarthm. Colln. v. 17.

serious schism, of which we shall speak in a future volume.

His release did not come until the end of May 1661.[1] It was brought about through the help of Charles Bayly and Jane Stokes.* Charles Bayly was a young man of whom we hear in Maryland in 1658,[2] and became a follower of Perrot in his extreme opinions. He accompanied him home by way of Lyon, but was imprisoned in the North of France for speaking to two priests that bowed to an image in the streets. They seem to have travelled part of the way on foot, for when Perrot reached Kent in July his feet were sore with his journey.[3]* Jane Stokes also became a cause of much trouble to Friends.[4]

The mission to Turkey, of which I have now given the strange story, was the chief but not the only one to the South of Europe or the East. Elizabeth Harris, the pioneer of Quakerism in Maryland,[5] and Elizabeth Cowart, who had suffered so cruelly at Evesham, went to Venice in the winter of 1657-8, and seem to have started on their return journey to England while Perrot and Luffe were lying in quarantine in the lazaretto.[6] A few days after these two brethren had gone forward for Rome, Stubbs and Fisher reached Venice on the same perilous errand. Stubbs had left London for Holland in October 1657, and had been followed a few months later by Fisher.[7] They went on towards Rome about the beginning of March 1658, and William Caton writes in his tender way:

[1] Sewel, i. 490.

[2] Robt. Clarkson's letter in Bowden, *Hist. of Friends in America*, i. 340 (Swarthm. Colln. iii. 7).

[3] Joseph Fuce to Fox, London, 3rd Augt. 1661, in Swarthm. Colln. iv. 224.*

[4] Joseph Nicholson, writing to Fox from Barbados, 10th Feby. 1664 (Swarthm. Colln. iv. 155), speaks of her as "lately come after us: she is a very bad spirit indeed." Norman Penney has supplied other references from Robert Rich, *Hidden things brought to Light* (1678), pp. 10, 26; and Hinchman, *Early Settlers of Nantucket* (1901), pp. 130, 317, who says that she was the first Friend to visit Nantucket from England. A MS. list of Friends who visited New England, in my possession, records a visit of Jane Stokes in 1664.

[5] See *The Quakers in the American Colonies*, 266, etc.

[6] Thos. Hart to Willan, London, 28th April 1658, in Swarthm. Colln. iii. 7.

[7] Stubbs to Margt. Fell, Gravesend, 19th Oct. 1657, in Swarthm. Colln. i. 92. Caton to Margt. Fell, Leyden, 15th Mar. 1658, in Wm. Caton Colln., Dev. Ho., Jas. Bowden's copy. For the rest of the journey, see three letters in Dev. Ho. Portfolio 17, No. 74, dated 1st May, 18th June, and 7th Augt.

I with another Friend brought them on their journey about fifty miles and then parted with them, the consideration of which parting caused tears several months before the time came, but how much more abundantly were our hearts broken with the parting itself, which was indeed as if we should see the faces of one another no more in the outward.

After visiting Friends in the Palatinate, they continued travelling without intermission twenty-six days to Venice, which they reached on the 15th April, with about eightpence in their pockets, as soldiers who examined them at a city in the Alps between Germany and Italy had relieved them of their stock of money. London Friends, however, had arranged with a correspondent in Venice to supply the needs of travelling Friends, and they were soon put in funds. They spent some time in spreading the Quaker message by writing and word of mouth among persons of all nations—Turks, Jews, Indians, Papists, and Protestants—and had some entrance, especially among the Jews. They found that the Jews did not deny that the light in the conscience was the chief teacher, and were willing, both in the synagogues, on the Change, and elsewhere to enter into conversation, delighting "to hear of any hopes of an admission for them to live in England, which might tend much to the conversion of some among them, if such a thing might come to pass."[1] After two months' stay in Venice they heard that steps were being taken by the Inquisition to apprehend them. They had already decided to leave the city, and proceeded down the Adriatic towards Rome, which they reached in the middle of July, after eighteen days of perils by sea and land. Here again they found most openness for their message among the five thousand Jews of the Ghetto. Their situation was one of extreme danger; indeed, all the way from England they looked on themselves as going into a place from which none but the Lord could deliver them. It seemed probable to them that, if once their presence in the city were known to the Papists, they would suffer the same

[1] By the beginning of 1656 the Jews were allowed to resettle in England with the approval of the authorities, though their legal status was still equivocal. See Gardiner, *Hist. of Commth. and Prot.* iv. pp. 10-18.

fate as Perrot and Luffe. They remained a month, and are said to have dispersed books among the friars, and to have spoken with some of the cardinals and testified against the Popish superstition.[1] But they did not feel the necessity of bearing testimony at Rome so strongly on them as before, now that Perrot and Luffe were bearing the Quaker witness. They accordingly seem to have refrained from attracting much notice, and returned unmolested to England.

In the following year 1659 two West-countrywomen, Katharine Evans, wife of John Evans, of English Batch, near Bath, and Sarah Chevers, wife of Henry Chevers, of Slaughterford, in Wiltshire, fell into the hands of the Inquisition. Katharine Evans was a woman of indomitable courage, who had already penetrated into places closed against Quakers, such as the Isle of Wight and the Isle of Man, "and," says Whiting, "the Lord promised her to carry her before the mighty men of the earth, to bear His name before them, and she should have the victory wheresoever she went."[2]

They set out for Alexandria and Jerusalem, and at Leghorn got passage in a Dutch ship going to Cyprus, which touched at Malta, then in the hands of the Knights of St. John. They landed and declared their message, though the English consul told them of the Inquisition. Going ashore on the second day they were examined by the Inquisitor and prevented from leaving the island. After spending some time in confinement in the consul's house they were put into an inner room in the Inquisition, "which," they say, "had but two little holes in it for light or air, but the glory of the Lord did shine round about us."

It would be tedious to recount the many examinations to which these devoted women were subjected or the terrible privations which they endured.[3] After nine months they were parted from each other, but managed to keep in communication. They rejected all induce-

[1] Sewel, 1811 edn. i. 433.

[2] John Whiting's *Persecution Exposed*, p. 220.

[3] Besse, *Sufferings*, ii. pp. 399-420, taken from *A Short Relation*, etc., 1662.

ments to make them turn Catholics, and continued to declare their message to all who came within sound of their voices, especially to the persons who resorted to the Inquisition Courts, and to the workmen who were engaged on a new building.

"In our deepest afflictions," writes Katharine Evans, "when I looked for every breath to be my last, I could not wish I had not come over the seas. . . . O the ravishment, the raptures, the glorious bright-shining countenance of the Lord our God, which is our fulness in emptiness, our strength in weakness, our health in sickness, our life in death, our joy in sorrow, our peace in disquietness, our praise in heaviness, our power in all needs and necessities."

In the spring of the year 1661, while the two women still lay at Malta, a second mission to the East was despatched by English Friends, consisting of John Stubbs, Henry Fell, Richard Scosthrop from the Craven district of Yorkshire,[1] and Daniel Baker of London who had been a captain in a man-of-war.[2] Fox tells us that the first three Friends were moved to go towards China and Prester John's country, and no masters of ships would carry them, so at last a warrant was got from the King, but the East India Company refused to obey it. Accordingly they crossed over to Holland, but found the same difficulty there, and had to content themselves with embarking for Alexandria, intending to complete the journey by caravan.[3] They carried with them epistles from Fox, mostly in Latin and English, to the King of Spain, the Pope, the King of France, the magistrates of Malta, the Turk, the Emperor of China, Prester John, and, as a last epistle, one addressed "To all the nations under the whole heavens."[4] There was also a letter from Stubbs and Fell in Latin and English to Prester John,[5]* who, it

[1] See *F.P.T.* 304. Scosthrop is a village half-way between Skipton and Settle.
[2] *Extracts from State Papers*, First Series, p. 46.
[3] *Camb. Journ.* ii. 8, and Fox's Testimony to Stubbs in Dev. Ho. Portfolio 16, No. 58; cf. Wm. Salt's difficulty, *ante*, p. 418.
[4] See Fell to Gerrard Roberts and Fox, 18th June 1661, in Swarthm. Colln. i. 184; and Fox, *Doctrinals*, pp. 171-213. There is also a letter to the Emperor and the House of Austria, which was to go as well to Holland, the Palatinate, Hungary, and Poland.
[5] See Smith's *Catalogue of Friends' Books*. Cf. note in *Camb. Journ.* ii. 380.

should be explained, was at this time identified with the Christian king of Ethiopia. They write as two apostles sent to all nations to visit God's vineyard, and they are satisfied that the Kingdom of Heaven must be known in all nations, though it be only as a grain of mustard seed. The party sailed through the Straits of Gibraltar to Leghorn, and off Alicante in Spain spoke with a captain who had sought the release of the two women at Malta, and without their knowledge had offered to be bound in the sum of £500 that they should not revisit the island.[1] At Leghorn Stubbs and Fell passed on to Alexandria, which proved the limit of their journey. According to the report of the English consul at Cairo, they "did throw pamphlets about the streets in Hebrew, Arabic, and Latin, and, if they had stayed a little longer, it might have set them a-burning." They seem to have been shipped back to Leghorn, with directions to the English there not to allow other Quakers to embark for Egypt.[2] From Leghorn the two Friends travelled, probably on foot, thirty-two days into Germany, and on reaching Heidelberg in the friendly Palatinate were greatly cheered to find Caton there.[3] They were back in England by February 1662. Baker and Scosthrop went eastward for Smyrna and Constantinople, but the Smyrna merchants communicated with the Earl of Winchilsea, who was English ambassador at Constantinople, and he issued a warrant from his court at Pera[4] directing the consul at Smyrna to send the Quakers home, "because we sufficiently have had experience that the carriage of that sort of people is ridiculous, and is capable to bring dishonour to our nation, besides other inconveniences that may redound to them in particular and to the English in general." After a three weeks' stay, therefore, they were shipped back by the same ship in which they had come. At Zante, then an outpost of Venice, Scosthrop fell ill, and

[1] See Fell's letter as above.

[2] Besse, *Sufferings*, ii. 420, 19th July 1661.

[3] Fell to Thos. Salthouse, London, 3rd Feby. 1662, in Swarthm. Colln. iv. 171, and Caton's *Life* (1689 edn.), p. 70.

[4] Besse, *Sufferings*, ii. 418.

died. Fox says, "he went with Daniel contrary to his own freedom, and so that hard-hearted man left him in his sickness, but he lost his condition."[1] I do not think this harsh judgment is justified. There is a letter extant which, after speaking of Scosthrop's illness, adds, "but through the mercy of God he was raised up again,"[2] and it is probable that Baker then went on to Italy, his friend wishing to make another attempt to reach the East, but falling ill again and dying before he could leave Zante. In any case Baker's subsequent conduct disproves the charge of hard-heartedness. For he went from Venice to Leghorn, and there sailed for Malta, determined to secure the release of the two women. He got audience with the Lord Inquisitor, and, addressing him in Italian, said, "I am come to demand the just liberty of my innocent friends, the two Englishwomen in prison in the Inquisition." The Inquisitor replied that they would lie in prison until they died unless a bond for three or four thousand dollars were given that they should never return to Malta. Katharine Evans gives a lively account of this visit in a letter to her husband dated January 1662:

> The Lord God . . . did send His faithful messenger, whose feet are beautiful and face is comely, . . . [who] went to the Lord Inquisitor to demand our lawful liberty, which would not be granted except we could get some English merchants of Leghorn or Messina to engage 4000 dollars that we should never come into those parts again. The Lord, who alone is our Life and Redeemer, moved our dear brother to offer his own body to redeem ours, but it would not be received; then he offered to lay down his own dear precious life for our liberty. Greater love can no man have than to lay down his life for his friend. The Lord will restore into his bosom double: his service can never be blotted out: his name is called Daniel Baker: his outward being is near London—a right dear and precious heart he is.

The letter ends with a memorable phrase which sums up the inward experience of the sufferers at Malta: "the deeper the sorrow, the greater the joy; the heavier the cross, the weightier the crown."

[1] *Camb. Journ.* ii. 8.

[2] Baker and Scosthrop to Fox, Howgill, and Burrough, Dev. Ho. Portfolio 17, No. 74.

Though Baker's visit proved fruitless, other influences were now at work for their release. After the Restoration the Queen-Mother, Henrietta Maria, who was a Roman Catholic, lived for some years in London, and had as Lord Almoner Lord d'Aubigny, a priest in orders, who had much influence in Malta. Gilbert Latey and Fox saw him, and at his instance the two Friends were at length liberated, and after a wait of eleven weeks in the English consul's house were carried home in an English frigate by way of Leghorn and Tangier, reaching England about the end of 1662, after three and a half years' confinement.[1] On their release they knelt down and prayed God not to lay to the charge of the officers of the Inquisition the evil they had done to them, and on arriving in London they went with Latey to thank Lord d'Aubigny for his intercession. He replied with the courtesy of a high-bred and spiritually-minded Catholic: "Good women, for what service or kindness I have done you, all that I shall desire of you is that when you pray to God you will remember me in your prayers."

Meanwhile Daniel Baker continued his voyage home, and found himself wind-bound for a month in the Straits of Gibraltar. A service pressed on him, which, like Jonah, he tried to escape, namely, to go ashore and be made a sign, at peril of his life, against the "idolatry" of the Church of Rome. On Maundy Thursday (6th April 1662, New Style) he came into the church at Gibraltar, then a Spanish town, and found the priest at the high altar, on his knees, adoring the Host. The indignation of God kindled in him against this "idolatry," and

. . . turning his back upon the priest and his dead God, he set his face towards the people, and saw the multitude upon their knees also, worshipping they knew not what. In this posture, spreading forth his arms, he slipped off his upper garment, and rent it from top to bottom in divers pieces, which he cast from him with indignation. Then he took his hat from off his head, as being the uppermost covering of man, and casting it down, stamped upon it with his feet, and appearing in

[1] See Fox, *Journ.* i. 524, and *Life of Gilbert Latey*, pp. 49-56.

sackcloth covering, he with a loud voice thrice sounded repentance, and said that the life of Christ and His saints was arisen from the dead. And so he passed away unmolested, sounding the same message with repentance through the streets till he came to the seaside, where he kneeled down to pray, and gave thanks to the Lord for his wonderful preservation and that He had suffered no man to touch or do him any harm."[1]

This incident may fittingly close our narrative of these Continental efforts. Quakerism reached the Mediterranean shores not in a form which could bring its truths home to the comprehension of the Latin races and the Mohammedans, for this would have needed a sympathy and a knowledge far beyond the powers of the Publishers of Truth, but rather as a sign of some great but mysterious Divine working, which evidenced itself in the courage and pertinacity of those who pressed through every danger even to Jerusalem or into the presence of the Sultan, and in the endurance which overcame even the rigours of the pitiless Inquisition.

[1] Sewel, i. p. 542, taken from a narrative of his travels written in prison.

CHAPTER XVII

RELATIONS WITH THE STATE*

The military rule which Cromwell was never able to shake off endangered the permanence of his system, and must have endangered it even if, as his unreasoning worshippers fondly urge, his span of life had been prolonged for twenty years. It is the condition on which all strong intellectual and spiritual movements rest that they shall be spontaneous. They win their way by force of inward conviction, not by the authority of the State. How earnestly Cromwell desired to set conviction before force is known to all. He had broken the Presbyterian and Calvinistic chains, and had declared his readiness to see Mohammedanism professed in England rather than that the least of the saints of God should suffer wrong. Yet he dared not give equal liberty to all. To the Royalists his person was hateful, alike as the murderer of the King, as the General whose army had despoiled them of their property, and as the violator of "the known laws" of the land. How, then, could he tolerate the religion of the Book of Common Prayer, which had become the badge of Royalism? It is true that the tide of persecution rose and fell, and that it was never very violent even at its worst; but it is also true that it could never be disowned. There was to be complete freedom for those who were Puritans, little or none for those who were not. Liberty of religion was to be coextensive with the safety of the State. It was a useful formula, but hardly more, when the safety of the State meant the predominance of an army, and the head of the State dared not throw himself on a free Parliament to give him a new basis of authority.—S. R. GARDINER, *Cromwell's Place in History*, p. 111.

THE relations of the Commonwealth to the Quaker movement have been already frequently referred to. Fox at the beginning of his mission addressed himself specially to county magistrates and others in authority, in full confidence that his message was what was needed for the government of the State. He was against the hireling ministers, but had no quarrel with the constituted authorities. It was the disturbance of ministers by earnest Friends which first moved Cromwell to active interference. In the spring of 1654 he had explained to Camm and Howgill that religious liberty, as he understood it, meant that none was to disturb another, and the proclamation of February 1655 directed itself against Quakers and Ranters on the ground of this disturbance. This remained the chief grievance in Cromwell's mind against Friends: though their non-compliance with the customary marks of respect to authority alienated his sympathy, and he no doubt approved the policy of cashiering Quakers out of the armies in Scotland and Ireland. So far as his personal conduct went, he allowed Fox to remain covered in his presence,[1] but, when the preacher in Whitehall Chapel was disturbed in his sermon by a Quaker, Cromwell ordered him to be removed and proceeded against before a justice according to law.[2]

Cromwell had several interviews with Friends who reached his presence and often severely taxed his patience. Considering his press of anxieties, we feel that he treated these self-invited guests with a consideration which showed that he recognized their sincerity and the value of the truth for which they stood, even when he did not find himself willing to obey their exhortations. In 1654 Camm and Howgill visited him in his chamber "for the most part of an hour": he spoke most kindly of Margaret Fell, and offered her friends money or anything they needed.[3] When Pearson saw him in July he was walking on the leads on the house-top, and went into a gallery, and when he came to Pearson put off his hat, and in a kind manner asked him how he did. Cromwell listened patiently to his harangue on the great mission of Friends, but was stirred into speech when Pearson began to expose the injustice of the Act of Mary against the malicious disturbance of ministers.

"There," says Pearson, "he stopped me, and began a long discourse to justify that law, and in the meantime came in his wife and about twenty proud women more, and after them at least thirty young fellows, his sons and attendants: and so when I could get to speak I answered not his questions directly, but

---

[1] *Journ.* i. 234.

[2] Whitelocke's *Memorials*, p. 636 (April 1656).

[3] Howgill and Camm to Margt. Fell, Dev. Ho., A.R.B. Colln. No. 20; *ante*, p. 156. The date is 27th March 1654.

spoke to all, and in discourse answered what was material . . . but still he called 'answer me directly,' and so in his will laboured to persuade them against what I said, and told them the Light of Christ was natural, and that the Light within had led the Ranters and all that followed it into all manner of wildnesses."

After further discourse Cromwell grew weary, and Pearson was dismissed, feeling that "there was not the least sign of any honesty left in him, nor any tenderness, though I spoke enough to have broken his heart, but in his pride and loftiness and will [he] cast it off and justified the priests."[1] This was surely a harsh judgment formed under the mortification of a barren interview, and Pearson speaks very differently in November, when he had returned rejoicing from a second interview with a discharge in his pocket for Thomas Aldam, then prisoner in York Castle. He writes:

There was no way for his liberty but to have a discharge under the broad seal. I had an order under the Protector's own hand, and it was not sufficient: he signed three orders with his own hand, and seemed very ready to do it: he stood all the while I was with him with his hat off, and it was much noised abroad, many being present, which made every one [concerned in the business] desirous to have me come before them, all the great men and judges, and I had such ready dispatch by them all as was wonderful. The fees would have come near to £20, but I could not [*i.e.* in conscience] pay any fees, which made it the more strange how ever it was done, only I gave something to the clerks for parchment and wax and some of their pains.[2]

Aldam had been a prisoner two years and seven months,[3] and wrote in 1654 that he was often waiting in spirit at the doors of Cromwell's house as if clothed with sackcloth, standing in sackcloth and weeping over a seed of God which lay in bonds.[4] When he came up to London with Fox in the spring of 1655 he succeeded in seeing the Protector, "cleared his conscience to him, and was made

[1] Pearson to Fox, 18th July 1654, Dev. Ho., Swarthm. Colln. iii. 34; *ante*, p. 161.

[2] Pearson to Margt. Fell, 28th Nov. 1654, Dev. Ho., Swarthm. Colln. i. 216.

[3] *Ante*, p. 68.

[4] To Fox, Dev. Ho., A.R.B. Colln. No. 122.

as a sign to him in rending a linen cap, with which he went to him on his head, and told him all his covering and counsels should be rent in pieces, but his heart is hardened and he cannot believe."[1] Later in the same spring Benson, Pearson, and Aldam saw Cromwell on behalf of imprisoned Friends, and spoke to him on many things: they found him very moderate, and he promised to read the papers which they had prepared.[2]

Cromwell saw Fox several times. At the interview in March 1655, described in a former chapter,[3] he was evidently impressed with the personality of the Quaker leader, and satisfied that he cherished no sinister designs against the Government. They next met in October 1656 as Fox rode into London from Reading after his Launceston imprisonment.

> "When we came near Hyde Park," says Fox,[4] "we saw a great clutter of people, and we espied O. P. coming in his coach, and I rid up to his coach-side, but some of his life-guard would have put me away, but he forbade them, and so I rid down by his coach-side with him, declaring what the Lord gave me to say unto him of his condition and of the sufferings of Friends in the nation, and how contrary to Christ this persecution was, and to the apostles and Christianity, and so I rid by his coach till we came to James' Park gate, and he desired me to come to his house."

Fox soon availed himself of this invitation and went with his companion, Edward Pyott, of Bristol, to Whitehall, where they found the Protector with Dr. Owen, of Oxford, Samuel Fisher's antagonist. After talk about the sufferings of Friends, Fox sought to bring the experience of the Inward Light of Christ home to Cromwell's heart, but he answered him, as he had answered Pearson, that the light within was only a natural light. The fervency

[1] *Letters of Early Friends*, p. 28, Burrough and Howgill to Margt. Fell, London, 27th March 1655, from Wm. Caton Colln. Fox refers to this (*Journ.* i. 446) as though it belonged to the year 1658. But the incident, and also, I think, the laying of Friends' sufferings before Cromwell, belong to the two interviews which Aldam had with Cromwell in 1655.

[2] *Letters of Early Friends*, p. 34, Parker to Margt. Fell, London, 29th May 1655.

[3] *Ante*, p. 180.

[4] *Camb. Journ.* i. 259.

of the Quaker prophet dominated the occasion, for, says Fox:[1]

> . . . the power of the Lord God ris in me, and I was moved to bid him lay down his crown at the feet of Jesus, several times I spoke to him to the same effect. And I was standing by the table, and he came and sat upon the table's side by me and said he would be as high as I was, for the Lord's power came over him. And so he continued speaking against the light of Christ Jesus, and went his ways in a light manner, and then said to his wife and companions, "I never parted so from them before," being judged in himself.

At the end of the following March Fox was in London—though the fact is not apparent on the face of his *Journal*,[2]—and on 25th March saw Cromwell again.* It

[1] *Camb. Journ.* i. 260.

[2] Some reconstruction of the *Journal* is necessary at this point. The *Cambridge Journal* rightly gives the incident, as I quote it, as the first entry of the year 1657 (*i.e.* not earlier than March 1657), but follows it with a journey into Kent, Surrey, etc., which we know took Fox to Kent in Jany. 1657 (Caton to Margt. Fell, London, 19th Jany. Swarthm. Colln. i. 314) to Sussex in Feby. (Caton to Margt. Fell, Steyning, 13th Feby. Swarthm. Colln. i. 315), and to Exeter on 8th March (Salthouse to Margt. Fell, Plymouth, 3rd March, Swarthm. Colln. iii. 183). The *Journals* (*Ellwood*, i. 360; *Camb.* i. 270) bring him from Exeter to Bristol, and then at once into Wales, leaving no room for any further London visit. But a letter of Thos. Rawlinson, Fox's companion throughout this Southern journey, written to Margt. Fell on 26th March (Swarthm. Colln. iii. 11) clearly refers to the Exeter meeting, says that the party was at Bristol four nights, two at Dennis Hollister's and two at Edward Pyott's, had come from Reading on the 24th, and been one day in London. "George has been with Oliver Cromwell since we came." "George Fox has been with Cromwell this day again: and he was very loving." This is first-hand evidence for Fox being in London and having two interviews with Cromwell just at the time that his acceptance of the proffered kingship hung in the balance. It is significant that in the *Cambridge Journal*, i. 327, among material belonging to the summer of 1658, there is an apparent doublet to this incident. This read, according to the first text, afterwards altered, "And so I visited the meetings up and down in London: and some of them was troubled with rude people and apostates that had run out with J[ames] N[ayler] and he was had before the Parliament and I was moved to write to them and to Oliver Cromwell, and much about this time there was a great noise, and laid before him the sufferings of Friends in the nation and in Ireland, and was moved to go again to Oliver Cromwell and told him that they which would put him on an earthly crown would take away his life, and he asked me, 'What say you?' and I repeated the same words over to him again, and he thanked me after I had warned him of many dangers, and how he would bring a shame and a ruin upon himself and posterity [*i.e.* if he accepted the crown]." The reference in this passage to Nayler carries the whole paragraph back to the early part of 1657. It is obviously a general summary of Fox's work in London at this time. The *Ellwood Journal* (i. 431) only gives the incident once, in an abridged form, at this wrong second place. In the early summer of 1658 the question of the kingship was again in debate, but the two accounts are too nearly identical to belong naturally to two interviews separated by more than a year. Having to choose between the two years, we must certainly prefer March

was the day on which Parliament resolved to ask the Protector to assume the office and title of king, a request which, as we may remember, he refused on 3rd April and finally on 8th May.[1] Fox shared the widespread feeling that was hostile to this proposal, and writes:[2]

I met him in the Park, and told him that they that would put him on a crown would take away his life, and he asked me, What did I say? and I said again, They that sought to put him on a crown would take away his life, and bid him mind the crown that was immortal, and he thanked me and bid me go to his house. And then I was moved to write to him and told him how he would ruin his family and posterity and bring darkness upon the nation if he did so, and several papers I was moved to write to him.

He saw Cromwell again the next day, and probably repeated the warning. Fox was enforcing the appeal which Capt. William Bradford, of Yorkshire, addressed to Cromwell on 4th March.[3] Bradford, as we have seen, was in close sympathy with Friends. In the course of his powerful letter he said:

I beg and beseech your Highness, nay again and again, with tears and prayers I beseech you, to consider what you are doing. . . . Consider, my Lord, I beseech you, and weigh between those two parties voting and dissatisfied. Those that are for a crown, I fear you have little experience of them: the other, most of them, have attended your greatest hazards. . . . I am of that number, my Lord, that still loves you, and greatly desires to do so, I having gone along with you from Edgehill to Dunbar. The experiences that you have had of the power of God at these two places, and betwixt them, methinks, should often make you shrink, and be at a stand in this thwarting, threatened change. Good my Lord, remember you are but a man, and must die, and come to judgment; men of high degree are vanity, men of low degree are a lie. My Lord, those in power having parts and near unto you, I fear have much injured you, in not dealing freely with your Lordship, but rather feeding that in you, grasping after

1657, when the question was being hotly debated, and we know from Rawlinson's letter that Fox saw Cromwell twice. Accordingly Ellwood's conflation of the two paragraphs as relating to the summer of 1658 is to be rejected, and room must be made for a visit to London in March 1657.

[1] Firth's *Last Years of the Protectorate*, i. 148-200. [2] *Camb. Journ.* i. 267.*

[3] Nickolls, *Original Letters*, p. 141, quoted in Firth's *Last Years of the Protectorate*, i. 163.

greatness, and aiming at their own self-interest; and so those now free with your Lordship in never so much love may run the greater hazard. My Lord, neither my life, estate, nor relations were ever anything to me in comparison of the public, nor yet is; yet I would not be prodigal of them or your Highness's favour. My freedom proceeds from a large proportion of love and no bye-ends.

Bradford, Burrough, and Fox seem all to have regarded Cromwell as a man eminently raised up by God, whose service, however, would have been much greater if he had been completely faithful. On one occasion Fox wrote in militant language:

O Oliver, hadst thou been faithful and thundered down the deceit, the Hollander had been thy subject and tributary, Germany had given up to have done thy will, and the Spaniard had quivered like a dry leaf wanting the virtue of God, the King of France should have bowed his neck under thee, the Pope should have withered as in winter, the Turk in all his fatness should have smoked, thou shouldst not have stood trifling about small things, but minded the work of the Lord as He began with thee at first.[1]

Fox had one last sight of the Protector, the date about the middle of August 1658.

I met him riding into Hampton Court Park, and before I came at him, he was riding in the head of his lifeguard, and I saw and felt a waft of death go forth against him, that he looked like a dead man, and when I had spoken to him of the sufferings of Friends and warned him as I was moved to speak to him he bid me come to his house, and so I went to Kingston, and the next day went up to Hampton Court, and then he was very sick, and Harvey told me, which was one of his men that waited upon him, that the doctors was not willing I should come in to speak with him, and so I passed away and never saw him no more.[2]

There can be little doubt that Cromwell's moderate carriage towards Friends endeared him to them, and that he and they felt mutual esteem for one another. When his effigy was carried to Westminster Abbey on 23rd November, eleven weeks after his death, Burrough laments the

[1] Dev. Ho., Parchment-bound book in Portfolio 9, p. 79.*

[2] *Camb. Journ.* i. 327.

idolatry, but breaks out into eulogy of the man.[1] He is struck with pity for "once noble Oliver," that he should be thus misunderstood, who had been a great instrument in the hand of the Lord to break down images; and he recalls his former acquaintance with him,

". . . and what a gallant instrument for the Lord he once was, and how many glorious and noble victories God once gave him, and what good parts, and what a gallant spirit there was in him, and," says Burrough, "how once he showed me and declared what the former dealing of the Lord had been upon his soul, and how he was troubled in conscience formerly, and my spirit run through many such things, with a great deal of seriousness and pity."

When Cromwell had seen Fox in Hyde Park after his release from Launceston, he had told one of his wife's maids, a Friend named Mary Saunders, that he had good news for her, for George Fox was come to town.[2] This Friend was a gentlewoman-in-waiting who had interested herself with Cromwell on behalf of suffering Friends, and afterwards married Henry Stout of Hertford.[3] Other members of the Protector's household associated with Friends. A meeting was begun at John Fielder's house at Kingston-on-Thames, near Hampton Court, and "several that then belonged to Oliver were convinced at this meeting, and continued faithful."[4] When Cromwell's favourite daughter Lady Claypole lay on her deathbed, Fox wrote her a tenderly worded letter,[5] which gave her comfort in her state of mental trouble, urging her to "be still and cool in thy own mind and spirit from thy own thoughts, and then thou wilt feel the principle of God to turn thy mind to the Lord, from whom life comes; whereby thou mayest receive His strength and power to allay all blusterings, storms and tempests."

Cromwell's views largely determined the policy adopted by the central authorities, especially during the periods when the personal government of himself and his officers superseded on occasion the law of the land. The Quaker

[1] *Works*, pp. 457-461. [2] *Journ.* i. 332.
[3] George Whitehead, *Christian Progress*, edn. 1725, p. 93. *Camb. Journ.* i. 444.
[4] *Life of Gilbert Latey*, p. 13. [5] *Journ.* i. 432.

movement had hardly attracted notice in London until the year 1653, when the Nominated Parliament heard that a young man, George Fox, was likely to die for religion at Carlisle. This Parliament, as we have seen,[1] contained a strong body of men of advanced religious views, who were not unfriendly to Quakerism. When, under pressure from the officers of the army, it resigned its powers into the hands of Cromwell in December, a military government ensued which proceeded to set limits to itself by the Instrument of Government adopted on 15th December. The Instrument clothed Cromwell with the title of Lord Protector, proposed a single-chamber Parliament constituted on a broadly representative basis,* and able, after a twenty days' delay, to pass bills into law against his will, and constituted a Council of fifteen named persons for executive purposes, irremovable except by a special procedure. Parliament was to meet in September 1654 and sit for five months. Important articles respecting religion (Arts. xxxv.-xxxviii.) were included in the Instrument. Tithes were continued as a temporary provision pending a more satisfactory arrangement. All who professed faith in God by Jesus Christ were to be protected "so as they abuse not this liberty to the civil injury of others and to the actual disturbance of the public peace on their parts," but this liberty did not extend to Popery or Prelacy, nor to licentiousness under the pretence of Christianity.

"Assistance" of Cromwell by his Council was by no means merely nominal. His temperament made him yield to their demands as long as his own mind was not positively made up, although, as the Council debated with closed doors, it spoke to the world with a single voice, and that voice Cromwell's.[2] Moreover, he remained the Lord General, and could appeal from the entanglements of legal forms to the arbitrament of the sword.

Gardiner points out that the seven officers and eight civilians who formed the new Council were of the type

[1] *Ante*, p. 118.
[2] I follow Gardiner, *Hist. of Commth. and Prot.* ii. 337.

which commonly rises to ascendancy after a revolution has run its course—men of practical efficiency opposed to further changes and above all to anything savouring of fanaticism.[1] They would be slow to respond to Puritan ministers who urged systematic persecution of Quakers, but on the other hand would have no sympathy with men who were turning the world upside down, and would seldom interfere when the law of the land was wrested in the hands of persecuting justices to the destruction of persons whom they regarded as followers of an impracticable visionary.

The Council of State seems to have had its attention first called to Friends in the middle of June 1654, when it received information of tumultuous and numerous meetings in Derbyshire by Quakers, which, it was supposed, might give opportunity to disaffected persons to prosecute their designs. Accordingly a letter was sent down to Colonel Saunders to scatter the meetings and prevent them in future, and to apprehend any notoriously disaffected persons who might be present.[2] The interference authorized is, it will be noticed, solely on the ground of possible plotting against the Government, and it was the same reason which caused the meeting at Swannington in January 1655 to be looked upon with suspicion, and to be followed by the arrest of Fox.[3]

When Parliament met in September 1654, the Quaker preachers had begun their strenuous campaign in the South. The members were very different in character from those that formed so strong an element in the Nominated Parliament, being, in the main, "opposite both to the new anabaptistical and levelling judgment."[4] Grave differences quickly rose between them and the army respecting the Instrument of Government, and the situation became so strained that at the first legal moment, namely at the end of five lunar months, on 22nd January 1655, Cromwell dissolved them. On the question

[1] Gardiner, *Hist. of Commth. and Prot.* iii. 3.
[2] *Extracts from State Papers*, First Series, p. 1.
[3] See *ante*, p. 177.
[4] Gardiner, *Hist. of Commth. and Prot.* iii. 177 *n*.

of religious toleration this Parliament had shown strongly reactionary tendencies. It was ready to subvert one of the main objects of Cromwell's policy, the policy of protecting religious minorities willing to submit to the existing authority in the State. At one point the intolerance of some members wrung from the Protector the celebrated saying, afterwards used by William Penn, "When shall we have men of a universal spirit? Every one desires to have liberty, but none will give it."[1]

Freed from the embarrassment of a Parliament, the Protector and his Council attempted to win popular support by the moderation of their policy. Oliver had protested to the House that he had no wish to protect "profane persons, blasphemers, such as preach sedition, the contentious railers, evil speakers, or persons of loose conversation,"[2] and the reports of the proceedings of Quaker enthusiasts which were now reaching London, as well as their conduct in the city itself, envenomed opinion against them, and brought them colourably under the Protector's censure. Accordingly the Proclamation of 15th February 1655, already referred to, was issued,[3] which, after reiterating Cromwell's views on religious liberty, required "Quakers, Ranters, and others" to avoid disturbing ministers, and, if they offended against the Proclamation, directed all officers and ministers of justice to proceed against them accordingly.

It is at this point that anything in the nature of a policy of persecution first shows itself. There had been, indeed, as previous chapters have recorded, a number of imprisonments by local justices, acting on their own initiative or at the instance of aggrieved ministers. The disturbance of ministers in their sermons and alleged blasphemies were the most usual grounds of complaint—the Quaker was frequently guilty of the first, and his innocence of the second, though clear to himself, was not easy of proof to a prejudiced and unsympathetic judge, who put the worst construction possible on unguarded

[1] Gardiner, *Hist. of Commth. and Protect.* iii. 220. Cf. Wm. Penn, *Works*, 1726 edn. i. 230. [2] *Ibid.* iii. 251. [3] *Ante*, p. 180.

statements about the indwelling life of Christ. When the Publishers of Truth began their vigorous itinerating work, they exposed themselves to a fresh form of oppression, the savage application of the Act of Elizabeth (St. 39 Eliz. cap. 4) "for punishment of rogues, vagabonds, and sturdy beggars."[1] The brutal flogging of Mary Fisher and Elizabeth Williams at Cambridge in December 1653 was probably the earliest case of Friends suffering under the Act, but in 1654 and 1655 it became one of the readiest means of acting against the Quakers. This sporadic persecution, however, was essentially local in character, and in many cases, as we have noticed, the soldiers, representing the central government, interfered on behalf of Friends.

The 1655 Proclamation, though so carefully guarded in its language, had the inevitable effect of stimulating the forces of intolerance. In April 1655 Howgill wrote:[2]

> Cromwell . . . is full of subtlety and deceit: will speak fair, but he hardens his heart, and acts secretly underneath. Our army is most scattered and broken and cast into prison: I know none almost at liberty but George and Alexander, Edward and I and Gervase,[3] and except John Stubbs and William Caton, John Wilkinson and John Story, and it is like they cannot be long out: yet truly the power of the Lord is over all.

Such a letter shows the impression felt at the time, and is more trustworthy than any attempt to gauge by statistics the growth of persecution. We begin to find phrases like the following in our *Acta Martyrum*: "apprehended here as disturbers of the public peace and for divers other high misdemeanours, against a late proclamation," etc.;[4] or this, spoken by the Judge to James Parnell, "that the Lord Protector had charged him to punish such persons as should contemn either magistrates or ministers";[5] or this from a Daventry Justice, John Farmer, who said

[1] *F.P.T.* 346.
[2] To Margt. Fell from London, undated, *Letters of Early Friends*, p. 35 (Wm. Caton Colln.). Internal evidence fixes the date.*
[3] George Fox, Alexander Parker, Edward Burrough, Gervase Benson.
[4] Mittimus of Salthouse and Halhead, 28th May 1655, Besse, *Sufferings*, i. 146.
[5] Autumn of 1655, Besse, *Sufferings*, i. 191.

he acted "by that law that says, all Quakers must go to prison," a good specimen of magisterial sapience.[1]

In April 1655, after the Royalist rising, a proclamation was issued announcing that the law would be enforced which required persons suspected of Roman Catholicism to take an oath abjuring the Papal authority and the doctrine of transubstantiation.[2] Although the oath was directed against Roman Catholics, the widespread idea that Quakers were Jesuits in disguise frequently caused it to be put to them, and in other cases, as Fox says,[3] "envious magistrates made use of that oath as a snare to catch Friends in, who they knew could not swear at all." At the end of May it was tendered to Salthouse and Halhead at Plymouth, but as the proclamation gave no authority to imprison those who refused it no committal was made on that charge.[4] At Basingstoke in July, however, Thomas Robertson and Ambrose Rigge spent fifteen weeks in prison for refusing it,[5] and the tendering of the oath became thenceforth part of the recognized ritual of persecution. It was also found to be easy for that most elastic of offences, contempt of court, to be proved against the Quakers, since they refused the tokens of respect required in courts of justice. The following colloquy between Dewsbury, one of the noblest of the early Friends, and Sir Matthew Hale, the greatest ornament of the English Bench in the Commonwealth and Restoration periods, shows the inevitable conflict of view on this point:

Judge. Now I see what thou art, and thy vizard and form of fair words is seen, that thou art not the man thou pretendest to be.

Dewsbury. Vizards and formality I deny, but the power of God I own and witness, in which I stand, and am subject to it, and to the ordinance of man for conscience' sake.

---

[1] This is placed in the year 1655 in Besse, *Sufferings*, i. 529. The name of the justice, which merits preservation, is given in *Extracts from State Papers*, First Series, p. 9. On another occasion he offered his voice to take away a Friend's life, when the offence was only punishable, if proven, with six months' imprisonment.

[2] Gardiner, *Hist. of Commth. and Prot.* iv. p. 18, and the Ordinance of 1643, cap. 15.

[3] *Journ.* i. 246.

[4] Besse, *Sufferings*, i. 146.

[5] *Ibid.* i. 228.

Judge. Now thou art commanded, Take off thy hat.

Dewsbury. Honour is not in pulling off the hat, but in obeying the just commands of God, which is according to the will of God, and my hat offends not any: but who are offended at it may take it off, I shall not resist them. But there is not any scripture that expresses any honour to be in putting off the hat.

Judge. What? Must we do nothing but what is expressed in scripture for our apparel what we shall put on?

Dewsbury. Yea, the scripture saith, Let your adorning be with modest apparel.

Judge. Art thou judge, that thou standest covered, and wilt not uncover, as other prisoners do?

Dewsbury. What I do, God is my witness I do it not in contempt to any, but in obedience to the power of God for conscience' sake.[1]

Hale, as always, behaved moderately on this occasion, but more self-important judges, jealous of their authority and insensible to the conscientious scruple of their prisoners, visited the refusal of hat-honour with severe penalties.

The insurrectionary movements in the first half of 1655 urged the Government to strong measures. As Gardiner observes, "In later times Parliament would have suspended the action of the Habeas Corpus Act, and have thereby empowered the Executive to take exceptional measures for the safety of the State."[2] The course taken was to place the country under the military regime of the Major-Generals, who held office from about Nov. 1655. During the period of arbitrary government which followed, the personality of the Major-Generals and their instructions from Whitehall counted for much more than the law of the land. Boteler, in charge of Northampton, Huntingdon, Bedford, and Rutland, was the most violent persecutor among the eleven, and was sharply reproved by Fox as the Quaker leader came out from one of his interviews with the Protector.[3]

Goffe in Berkshire, Sussex, and Hampshire was, as we

[1] Besse, *Sufferings*, i. 520, 521 (Northampton, March 1655).

[2] *Hist. of Commth. and Prot.* iii. 315.

[3] *Journ.* i. 333. For Boteler's proceedings see *Extracts from State Papers*, First Series, p. 8. Cf. *F.P.T.* 198, and Besse, *Sufferings*, i. 529, 530.

have seen, hostile, though his descendants would be found amongst the leading families of Irish and American Friends.[1] Haynes in the Eastern Counties held the Quakers in opprobrium and contempt: "concerning which party of men," he wrote, "these parts are greatly molested and [they] have considerable meetings, yet not so feared by myself as by some ministers, who stick not to say they will be soon ripe to cut throats. Truly I think their principles would permit them, if they durst."[2] Worsley, who held rule in Lancashire, Cheshire, and Stafford, found himself much troubled with Quakers.[3] His attitude towards them was, however, greatly changed by attendance at a dispute with ministers held in a great chamber at the Bull in Preston, on 4th March 1656.[4] The Major-General seems to have presided, supported by the Commissioners for securing the peace of the Commonwealth. His opening speech showed a strong bias against Friends, due to the information given him by envious ministers. Audland, Pearson, Parker, Gervase Benson, Thomas Lawson, and William Adamson (of Liverpool) were among the Friends present, and they answered all the charges made against them by the priests. Then they claimed the right of putting questions to the ministers. Samuel Eaton of Stockport, a leading divine in the North, who, like so many other opponents of the Quakers, had been in New England, would not stay to have the tables turned on him, but the others remained.

"Where," says Parker, "we had a gallant charge upon them and got the victory through the love of our God. And the Major-General was very loving: and when he passed forth did take Gervase Benson by the hand, and afterwards all the rest vanished and fled away: and we got their places, and sat us down, some of us in the place where the Major-General sat, and others in the priests' places: and all went away, and we were left alone and had

---

1 "Irish Quaker Records," by Thos. H. Webb, in *J.F.H.S.* iii. p. 65.

2 For Goffe, see *ante*, p. 202; for Haynes, Thurloe, *State Papers*, v. 187 (Bury, 5th July 1656).

3 Thurloe, *State Papers*, iv. 333 (31st Dec. 1655).

4 For this incident see Parker and Audland to Fox, Lancaster, 7th March 1656 (Dev. Ho., Swarthm. Colln. i. 1). The letter is actually written by Parker.

the day,—all were dashed and silent. The next morning Anthony Pearson writ a note to the Major-General and went to his chamber, and he was very loving to them, and confessed he never saw the like meeting so Christianly carried on : and said he had received full satisfaction in all things, and further said of his own accord if anything came against us he would act nothing before he had acquainted us with it. And he further said he expected all those things would have been proved against us, which now he sees the contrary, and that many things are cast upon us which is not true, and said he would take equal care to protect us as upon any other."

Berry, in Wales and the West Midlands, was another fair-minded man: we have already noted his conduct at Evesham,[1] and Holme wrote that he had spoken much on behalf of Friends and had imprisoned two beadles for putting two Friends out of the town of Monmouth and had reproved the mayor sharply.[2] Desborough, in the West of England, showed himself at first hard and unsympathetic towards Fox,[3] but afterwards softened. In February 1656, while the Quaker leader was awaiting trial at Launceston, Aldam and John Killam interviewed the Major-General, and he offered liberty to the prisoners at Launceston and Exeter if they would promise good behaviour. The answer of the Exeter prisoners told him that they stood in the will of God, and chose rather to suffer than to purchase outward freedom by making a covenant with death, and bringing themselves into inward bondage.[4] Again in August, at Cromwell's instance, he offered to set Fox and his companions free if they would promise to go home and preach no more, and as they refused this urged them at least to promise to go home "if the Lord will." Fox, in a characteristic letter, replied that he knew it to be the will of God for him to go and speak at some other place, and so could not give even this conditional promise truly, but if Desborough opened the prison doors without

[1] *Ante*, p. 197.

[2] To Margt. Fell, probably 1656, 3rd March (Swarthm. Colln. i. 201).

[3] *Ante*, p. 205.

[4] Salthouse and Halhead to Margt. Fell, Exeter, 9th Feby. 1656 (Swarthm. Colln. i. 112).

condition (as was afterwards done), then they could go.[1] Later in the year he set free Walter Clement of Olveston, after having tried, without success, to get from him a similar undertaking. For this liberation there was a special reason. At the Parliamentary election in the summer of 1656, certain Gloucester citizens were Desborough's stanch supporters, and afterwards used their influence on Clement's behalf.[2] The incident shows the respect in which many an honest Quaker was held by his neighbours.

The attitude of some of the other Major-Generals can be gathered from their speeches during the Nayler debates. Skippon, who had charge of London, was violently hostile, and vied with Boteler and Goffe in urging extreme measures; Lambert, on the other hand, was moderate, and through his deputies, Howard and Lilburne, administered the North of England in the same spirit.

The Parliament which Cromwell found it necessary to summon in the summer of 1656 was, like the Puritan party in general, less tolerant than the Protector himself. In Nayler's case, which we have examined in a previous chapter, it acted in the most high-handed manner and narrowly escaped the odium of ordering a martyrdom. It passed several Acts which increased the stringency of the law, although not directed expressly against the Quakers. The oath abjuring Papal authority was made more searching.[3] The offence of travelling on the Lord's Day was extended to all persons vainly and profanely walking on that day.[4] Of more consequence to Friends was the extension of the Act of Mary (1 Mar. st. 2, cap. 3), which already punished the malicious disturbance of a preacher in his sermon, or while celebrating divine service. Regular attendance at worship was now required under a fine of 2s. 6d., and the offence of disturbance was extended to include disturbing a minister in the "duty"

[1] *Journ.* i. 318, etc., and Parker to Margt. Fell, 19th Augt. 1656 (Swarthm. Colln. i. 166).

[2] Clement to Margt. Fell, 4th Oct. 1656 (Swarthm. Colln. i. 181).

[3] Act of 1656, cap. 16 (Scobell's Colln. pt. ii. p. 443).

[4] The Lord's Day Act, Act of 1656, cap. 15 (*ibid.* p. 448).

of his place, or in going or returning, or causing any public disturbance on the Lord's Day in any such place.[1] Finally, the Vagrancy Act was extended to all persons wandering without sufficient cause, although not taken begging.[2]

Fox, who should have been in a position to know, estimates that in 1656 "there were seldom fewer than one thousand in prison in this nation for Truth's testimony,—some for tithes, some for going to the steeple-houses, some for contempts, as they called them, some for not swearing, and others for not putting off their hats, etc."[3] The figure is, however, almost certainly an over-estimate, for the Declaration delivered by Friends to Parliament on 6th April 1659[4] only gave a total of about two thousand persons who had suffered imprisonment during the preceding six years, and many of these imprisonments were for short periods only.

Cromwell's Second Parliament, we shall remember, after it had disposed of Nayler, reassembled towards the end of January 1657, and was occupied during the spring with constitutional proposals, especially the abortive one asking the Protector to take the title of King. Its work issued in the document known as The Petition and Advice,[5] which was to be a Parliamentary substitute for the Instrument of Government, whose military origin could not be forgotten. The Protector was asked to nominate his successor, and to call Parliaments consisting of two Houses. The clauses affecting religious liberty were narrower than those of the Instrument, and could be readily used against Friends. One clause desired him to punish according to law persons who openly reviled the godly ministers or their assemblies or disturbed their services, and requested his consent to such further laws as should be made in that behalf (clause 10). Another asked that a confession of faith should be settled,

1 The Lord's Day Act, Act of 1656, cap. 15.
2 Act of 1656, cap. 21 (Scobell's Colln. pt. ii. p. 477).
3 *Journ.* i. 343.
4 Besse, *Sufferings*, i. p. iv.
5 For this and the Additional Petition and Advice, see Gardiner's *Constitutional Documents of the Puritan Revolution*, p. 447, etc.

and that there should be religious liberty for persons professing faith in God the Father, Son, and Holy Spirit, and acknowledging scripture to be the revealed Will and Word of God, but so that the liberty should not extend to Popery or Prelacy, or horrible blasphemies, or licentiousness, or profaneness under the profession of Christ (clause 11).

Parliament adjourned on 26th June 1657, and re-assembled seven months later. The interval was occupied with the complicated work of re-modelling the Council, as requested in the Petition, and creating the Second Chamber proposed by it. Major-General Lambert, who had been Cromwell's right-hand man, but disliked the new constitution, disappeared for the time from public life. When Parliament met in January 1658 the tenour of their debates and the rapid growth of disaffection at home and peril abroad led to their sudden dissolution on 4th February, and for the last seven months of the Protector's life he continued to govern, with the help of his Council. The new constitutional régime was in fact never operative except to a limited extent.

So far as the repression of Quakerism went, the rude persecution of the local justices continued to be more or less mitigated from Whitehall. We have in the *State Papers* an interesting illustration of the way in which the Council acted in one such case at the end of 1656.[1] The petitions were referred to a Commission, which went down to the locality and held a three-days' inquiry, reporting that the imprisonments in question were illegal. The report was read in the Council, and referred to a sub-committee to consider, and upon their report being received two of the sub-committee were ordered to speak to the Major-General of the district about the business. This led to the discharge of the prisoners.

With Cromwell's death on 3rd Sept. 1658 the con-

[1] See *Extracts from State Papers*, First Series, pp. 14-20. Thos. Moore, a Surrey gentleman, was one of the referees, and may be the Friend, Thos. Moore, of Heartswood, near Reigate, the Justice of the Peace who had been convinced by Fox in 1655, and settled a meeting at his house. See also Besse, *Sufferings*, i. 708, 709, and Robertson to Fox, Horsham gaol, 9th May 1656 (Swarthm. Colln. iv. 200); Robertson to Margt. Fell, 4th Augt. (Swarthm. Colln. iv. 204).

ditions for a strong Government ceased to exist. Oliver had been Lord General as well as Lord Protector. But Richard Cromwell had no standing with the army, and, when he and his Parliament insisted on Fleetwood commanding under him as his Lieutenant-General, the army forced him on 22nd April 1659 to dissolve Parliament, and a month later he abdicated, and the Protectorate came to an end.

A few weeks after Oliver's decease, Friends in London and the Home Counties sent to the Council a list of 115 Friends then in prison, and of nine who had died in gaol, and a circular letter was sent down to each of the thirty-four prisons where Friends lay requiring particulars of the offences for which they had been committed. At the end of November, when most of these returns had been made, a Committee of the Council reported in favour of releasing more than forty persons and of sending down a draft letter to justices which would effect the discharge of some of the rest. This letter was no doubt sent, and is a judicious persuasive to mildness, though bigoted and intolerant justices would probably disregard it. It shows a real desire not to strain the law against Friends by taking advantage of their conscientious scruples, and a consciousness on the part of the central authorities that Quakers were not persons disaffected towards the Government.[1]

After referring to the several addresses received, the letter continues:

His Highness and the Council, though they are far from giving any countenance to the mistaken principles or practices of such men, especially in their disturbance of godly ministers or in any affronts put upon magistrates, whose dignity ought to be maintained, yet, finding that the same doth for the most part proceed rather from a spirit of error which hath seduced them than from a malicious opposition to authority, in which

---

[1] See *Extracts from State Papers*, First Series, pp. 37-93. It is evident that the draft presented with the Committee's Report for sending to justices (see pp. 90, 91) is the draft letter to justices printed in an inadequate and wrong context, pp. 33, 34. The date I gave to this draft in *F.P.T.* 351, following the *Calendar of State Papers*, should be corrected to 27th Nov. 1658.

case they—especially such among them as are otherwise of sober conversation—are to be pitied and dealt with as persons under a strong delusion, who choose rather to suffer and perish than to do anything contrary to their, though ungrounded and corrupt, principles: therefore His Highness and the Council have thought fit to recommend their condition unto your prudence to take such course for the discharge of such of them as are in prisons within your county as, having put a discountenance on their miscarriages, their lives may be preserved, divers of them having died in their imprisonments. And that out of a tenderness towards such poor deluded persons you would as much as in you lies endeavour to prevent their running into such contempts for not giving that civil respect, which they owe to you as magistrates when they are brought before you, by causing their hats to be pulled off beforehand, or that for such contempts such punishment may be inflicted as may rather discountenance their folly than endanger their lives, His Highness and the Council judging it safer, in dealing with persons whose miscarriages arise rather from defects in their understanding than from malice in their wills, to exercise too much lenity than too much severity.

During the last weeks of Richard's short-lived Parliament, namely, on 6th April 1659, a remarkable Declaration was presented by Friends to its Speaker—Thomas Bampfield, a man violently hostile to Friends. It gave particulars of the cases of 144 Friends then in prison, and of 21 who had died, and a summary narrative of the sufferings of 1960 within the previous six years. A few days later, on 15th and 16th April, 164 Friends from London and other parts assembled themselves in Westminster Hall, and sent in to the House a paper offering their bodies, person for person, to lie in gaol in the place of their imprisoned friends.[1] When considerable persecution began in 1655, Fox had urged Friends to take this course:[2] "As Christ hath laid down His life for you, so lay down your lives one for another. Here you may go over the heads of the persecutors, and reach the witness of God in all." We

[1] See the documents in Besse, *Sufferings*, i. iv-vi, and *Letters of Early Friends*, pp. 62-69. The editor, A. R. Barclay, treats the Committee appointed in May as a direct consequence of the Appeal. By May, however, the Parliament to which the appeal was addressed had been dissolved, and the "Rump" of the Long Parliament had taken its place.*

[2] *Journ.* i. 248.

have already noted action of this kind on behalf of Parnell and George Whitehead, and of Fox himself. It was now done on a large scale, in a spirit of devotion which entitles the action to rank among the golden deeds of history—those deeds which glow with the flame of a pure and unselfish love. The paper said:

> We, in love to our brethren that lie in prisons and houses of correction and dungeons, and many in fetters and irons, and have been cruelly beat by the cruel gaolers, and many have been persecuted to death, and have died in prison, and many lie sick and weak in prison and on straw, so we, in love to our brethren, do offer up our bodies and selves to you, for to put us as lambs into the same dungeons and houses of correction, and their straw, and nasty holes and prisons; and do stand ready a sacrifice for to go into their places in love to our brethren, that they may go forth, and that they may not die in prison as many of the brethren are dead already. For we are willing to lay down our lives for our brethren, and to take their sufferings upon us that you would inflict upon them And if our brethren suffer we cannot but feel it, and Christ saith it is He that suffereth and was not visited. . . . We, whose names are hereunto subscribed, being a sufficient number to answer for the present sufferers, are waiting in Westminster Hall for an answer from you to us, to answer our tenders [of our bodies], and to manifest our love to our friends, and to stop the wrath and judgment from coming upon our enemies.

The Paper and Declaration were both read in the House, and after debate the House declared its dislike of the scandal cast on magistrates and ministers, and ordered the Friends who had assembled to go home and apply themselves to their callings, and submit to the laws and the magistrates. Three of the Friends—Thomas Moore, John Crook, and Edward Byllinge—were brought in to the bar, and after the sergeant had taken off their hats, the Speaker dismissed them with this unsympathetic answer.

The list of those who thus offered is on many accounts most interesting. More than two-thirds of the names appear again in the pages of Besse's *Collection of the Sufferings of the People called Quakers*, especially during the early years of fierce persecution in the Restoration period. Those who offered themselves on behalf of their brethren were not of the stuff to shrink when their own hour of trial came.

The list includes the men of substance and position in the Quaker community—London goldsmiths like Humphrey Bache and John Bolton; Richard Crane, a distiller in Aldersgate Street; Edward Byllinge, a Westminster brewer: Quaker leaders like Amor Stoddart, Steven Crisp of Colchester, George Bewley, Alexander Parker, and Thomas Rawlinson were among the number: there were probably at least two dozen others who were the principal Friends in their own localities, and in several cases their houses were the places where the meetings were held. Thomas Moore and John Crook had been in the commission of the peace; Stoddart, Byllinge, and Thomas Curtis of Reading had served in the army. In addition to London and the neighbouring meetings, Surrey, Sussex, Berkshire, Bedfordshire, and Essex contributed their quota, and there are a few names from further afield, perhaps those of Friends who happened to be in London at the time. Although the offer failed of acceptance, there is no reason to doubt its seriousness or the willingness of the Friends who offered to suffer the vicarious punishment proposed. The list contains the names of some who afterwards withdrew from the main body—notably John Pennyman and, for a time, Benjamin Furly. It deserves a more minute analysis and examination than can be given here.

Prior to the formal abdication of Richard Cromwell in May 1659, forty-two members of the Rump had on the 7th May constituted themselves a Parliament at the invitation of the soldiers. The Rump was, we shall remember, the name given to the part of the Long Parliament left after Pride's Purge in 1648, which had been itself forcibly dissolved by Cromwell in April 1653. It now took up the phantom of power for a few months, and had the temerity to declare all Oliver's acts illegal, and to resolve that all who had collected taxes for him must repay the money. The officers, many of whom had been Major-Generals, with arbitrary powers delegated to them by the authority of Cromwell, soon found that they had no use for such a body, forcibly brought its sittings to an end on 13th October, and resumed their military rule.*

This Rump Parliament seemed likely to do something for liberty of conscience. On 10th May it appointed a Committee to consider the cases of persons imprisoned for conscience' sake, and how they might be discharged; and on the following day Friends delivered in their paper of sufferings, and it was referred to the Committee.[1] It is quite likely that on this occasion also an offer of substituted imprisonment was made.[2] In Fox's *Journal* we have a reference to this Committee, of which the great Sir Henry Vane was chairman.[3] This remarkable man had been one of the chief Commonwealth leaders until the dissolution of the Long Parliament in 1653—a step which he had strongly disapproved. He had a principal hand in the abdication of Richard Cromwell, and was now striving to keep Parliament and the army in touch with each other. He was a religious enthusiast, with whom Fox had held long discourse at his house at Raby Castle early in 1658, till Sir Henry "fell into a great fret and a passion that there was no room for truth in his heart," and, but for the presence of Anthony Pearson, he would have put Fox out of his house as a madman.[4] George had a provoking way with him at times. Many Friends who were prisoners were brought up to London before this Committee, and although Vane scrupled about letting them come before him with their hats on they seem to have been given a fair hearing. Parker, writing on the 22nd June, says:[5]

The Committee of Parliament are most of them very moderate, and examine things very fully; and whether they do anything or nothing as to the enlargement of Friends, it is

---

[1] *Letters of Early Friends*, pp. 67-69.

[2] Fox in the *Cambridge Journal* says (i. 334): "Many being in prisons at this time, several was moved to go to the several Parliaments, sometimes about two and three hundred at a time, and to offer up themselves," etc.

[3] *Journ.* i. 443.

[4] See full account in *Camb. Journ.* i. 312-314.

[5] To Margt. Fell, *Letters of Early Friends*, p. 69.

serviceable that the wickedness of greedy and covetous men are brought to light. Much cannot be expected of men in that nature, for though there be a change of name, yet the old nature is still standing,—earth enough there is to make another mountain,—but whatever the consequence be, this I know and feel, that Truth hath great advantage, and an open door is further made for spreading the Truth abroad.

Some of the prisoners were freed,[1] and the Rump also showed an inclination to take away tithes, in furtherance of which Friends had collected an important petition, "from many thousands of the free-born people of this commonwealth." We hear of it at the meeting of Friends from Westmorland, Cumberland, Lancashire, and Cheshire, held at Ulverston on the 26th May,[2] when names were appointed in each meeting to "take the subscriptions of all those persons that will give in their testimony against the oppression of tithes, that the same may be returned to London with all possible speed." It is clear that others besides Friends were applied to; for instance, two were appointed for Kendal "to go through the town." A memorandum says that by 25th June 3773 persons had given in their names from this district. The same work was done in Durham and Yorkshire, and probably elsewhere, and at the end of June Gervase Benson, Anthony Pearson, Thomas Aldam, and a number of other Friends came up to London[3] and presented the petition to Parliament, where it was read on 27th June. It had more than 15,000 signatures, and a supplemental paper presented from women on the 20th July bore 7000 additional names.* There was a strong body of opinion in Parliament favourable to the suppression of tithes,*and this was no doubt one reason why the Royalist rising of Sir George Booth in Cheshire was openly or covertly supported by the Presbyterian priests.[4] After this had

[1] Fox, *Journ.* i. 444, confirmed by Hubberthorne, *Works*, p. 280.

[2] Early Record Book at Kendal. See the papers to the Parliament, 27th June and 20th July, catalogued in Smith's *Catalogue of Friends' Books*, ii. 260, under heading "Parliament".

[3] Parker to Margt. Fell, 22nd June, *Letters of Early Friends*, p. 71.

[4] See an interesting letter from Howgill to Burrough, Kendal, 22nd Augt. (Dev. Ho., A.R.B. Colln. No. 169), and Hubberthorne, *Works*, p. 280. Howgill calls them "the black band, the priests' party." Anthony Pearson's

been put down by Lambert, the Rump was itself excluded by the officers, and in October a military government, with a so-called Committee of Safety, attempted to control the increasing confusion of affairs. Burrough, writing in November, addresses himself "to the present rulers of England, whether Committee of Safety, so-called, Council of Officers, or others whatsoever."[1] The attempt proved a complete failure; as the soldiers quarrelled, and the taxes were paid less readily than when a civilian government had existed. Accordingly the Rump was recalled on December 26th.

Friends were zealous with the Committee of Safety as they had been with the various Parliaments. A somewhat confused passage in the *Life of Gilbert Latey*[2] shows that he and a number of Friends made another offer of substituted imprisonment to this Committee. Hubberthorne[3] tells us the situation as it was in November of this year 1659. The officers talk and debate of things, but that, he says, is the most they do. They talk of dealing with tithes, and a suggestion has been in debate to reduce the 9000 parishes in England to 3000, and to provide these with a state-maintenance. Among the chief officers are certain ambitious, self-seeking

account in his own defence may also be consulted (*Extracts from State Papers*, Second Series, pp. 135-141). Booth's muster at Warrington at the beginning of August was made upon the pretext of suppressing a rising of the Quakers. This was a plausible pretext, as fear of a rising of Quakers and Anabaptists was in the air (Thurloe, *State Papers*, vii. p. 704, cited *infra*, p. 480). Henry Newcome tells us how the lying rumour was circulated. See *Life of Adam Martindale* (Chetham Society), p. 132 *n.*, and cf. p. 137. Martindale "feared God would not prosper a business the foundation whereof, as to the practic part, was so much laid in lying and deceit." Newcome knew that the Quakers "were very insolent and troublesome, yet was unsatisfied that the thing was true that they were up in arms." Howgill gives the number who mustered as a thousand at the most, with a hundred priests, but this was an under-estimate. Robt. Widders rode among them with a twig in his hand and told them, a few days before their defeat, that the Lord with His rod of iron would break them to pieces, see *Life* (1688), p. 27, but even a sympathizer like Martindale expected their rout, for "it must be little less than a miracle if raw undisciplined men, as the greater part were, . . . should be able to stand before Lambert's men, who were veteran soldiers."

[1] Burrough, *Works*, p. 588.

[2] The Rump had set up this Committee of Safety. *Life of Gilbert Latey*, p. 29, says that the offer "could not be accepted, and being towards the latter part of Cromwell's time, persecution still raged, etc."

[3] To Margt. Fell, London, 21st Nov., *Letters of Early Friends*, p. 71, from Wm. Caton Colln. ; cf. Hubberthorne's *Works*, p. 280

men, though some of the inferiors have honest intents if they could bring them to pass. Colonel Rich, Colonel Ashfield, and Sir Henry Vane would do something, but their views are rejected, while at the same time the chief officers dare not bring their own views to a vote because they know that the general part of the inferior officers wish for liberty and honest things.

In this year of continually changing authorities the political prospects of Quakerism varied from month to month.* If Sir Henry Vane had succeeded in establishing a stable equilibrium between the Rump and the army an era of religious liberty might have been inaugurated. The hopes of Friends ran high during the last weeks of May. On the 17th, at the request of Parliament,[1] Gerrard Roberts and Thomas Moore wrote down to the counties for three lists—the first of persecuting justices, the second of moderate men, and the third of Friends fit to serve the Commonwealth as justices, and lists were sent up within a few days from many districts. These are preserved in the *State Papers* and are of much interest.[2] The Northamptonshire document, for instance, is signed by nineteen Friends and specifies three Friends of competent estate who might be made justices, seven other men of substance, not Friends, who were against persecution, and eleven persecutors. The names are not only classified but characterized,—William Lovell, one of the Friends, is "a man of a noble, bold spirit"; of the persons favourable to Friends one has publicly declared himself to own them; another would never have any hand against them; a third is really convinced and his hand is against tithes. The opposers are described in bitter terms. Of Boteler

[1] See *A Loving and Friendly Invitation to all Sinners to Repentance* (1683), per Norman Penney.

[2] See *Extracts from State Papers*, First Series, pp. 6-13; Second Series, pp. 105-115. The Northamptonshire and Dorset papers are clearly placed in wrong order and belong with the others. Cf. my note in *J.F.H.S.* vii. 150. The other districts making the return are Berkshire, Essex, Somerset, Worcestershire, the Kendal area, Nottinghamshire, Derbyshire, Cheshire, Isle of Ely, Lancashire, Hampshire, and Radnorshire. Hampshire has no fit Friends, but all the other lists suggest one or more names; in the case of Somerset as many as thirteen names are sent up. Thos. Curtis sends two names from Berkshire (George Lamboll and Andrew Wright), but adds "not an oath on any account will be taken by them."

of Oundle, the former Major-General, we read, "There might be a great volume writ of the wicked tyrannical actions of this man in the last four years. A shame to the nation." Of another, he "said he hoped to have a place at God's right hand in heaven for his punishing the Quakers, and wished he had more power in his hand. A proud man and a bloody persecutor. A shame to true magistracy." Of a third the writer says, "Let us be delivered from bloodthirsty men." Another "hath cast the law of God behind his back." Another is "a bitter man, and hath said that none were fit to live in the Commonwealth that dissented from the priests of England."

The Dorsetshire paper specifies twelve persons who are persecutors and great enemies to Truth, and six other justices who are thought to be of the same spirit, but have not had such occasion to manifest themselves. A list is given of fifteen moderate men who are against persecution, and of four Friends capable of the place of justices. But there is also a singular paragraph containing advice as to the militia troop, as follows: "John Strood, High Sheriff of the county, a cavalier; James Dewey, Commander of the Militia Troop, a very bad man and a persecutor; John Lea, Cornet of the same troop, a priest-ridden man, neither of them fit for that command. We judge Richard Channing, of Cattistock, to be fit to command that troop, and John Pitman, of Sherborne, a fit man for the Cornet's place; they are men well affected to the Commonwealth. Richard Channing hath been an approved Captain, as is well known, and John Pitman hath been a stout and faithful Lieutenant in the State's service already."

The suggested names in the Dorset paper are evidently those of non-Friends, but when Commissioners for the militia were appointed in August, seven Friends were chosen in Bristol,[1] and in the North of England Anthony Pearson was a Commissioner, and at the time of the Cheshire Royalist rising "would have raised the country

[1] Parker to Fox, Wiltshire, 7th Augt., Swarthm. Colln. iii. 143.*

but all the justices and Commissioners were so backward they would not meddle."[1] A Royalist source speaks of him as having been "Adjutant-General to Lambert in the business of Sir George Booth," but this he denied.[2] At Bristol Parker says that Friends were in some little strait about acting; for himself he was under a great weight about it, not knowing what to advise, and desiring to have a word on the subject from Fox. One of Fox's epistles written during this year of anarchy sufficiently shows his attitude on this difficult question.[3] Friends, he says, are dead to all carnal weapons, and stand in a power which takes away the occasion of wars. They should pay taxes to the rulers, who are to keep peace, for the sake of peace and the advantage of Truth. But they cannot bear and carry carnal weapons under the several forms of government, "but have paid their tribute, which they may do still for peace' sake, and not hold back the earth, but go over it; and in so doing, Friends may better claim their liberty." In January 1660 Fox definitely advised Francis Gawler of Cardiff to this effect.[4] Francis Gawler had written that Fleetwood had made his brother John Gawler, who was a justice, Lieutenant-Colonel in a regiment of militia-foot that was being raised. John Gawler, as a Friend, did not want to meddle in it if there were any objection. His colonel was loving to Friends and very desirous to have them in his regiment, but Friends did not feel free, except one who had joined as a private soldier, and another, Matthew Gibbon, who had partly engaged to be a captain, with whom Friends were tender, knowing he had no bad end in it, but thought he might be serviceable for Truth. An endorsed note on this letter says, "Which G. F. forbad, and said it was contrary to our principles, for our weapons are spiritual and not carnal."*

In Anthony Pearson's case no advice seems to have

[1] Howgill to Burrough, Kendal, 22nd Augt., Dev. Ho., A.R.B. Colln. No. 169. George Fell was asked in August by the Council "to raise a troop of horse . . . for the service of the Parliament and the safety of Lancashire and parts adjacent" (*Extracts from State Papers*, Second Series, p. 116).

[2] *Extracts from State Papers*, Second Series, p. 136.

[3] *Epistles*, No. 177.

[4] To Fox, Cardiff, 26th Jany. 1660, Swarthm. Colln. iv. 219.

been sought, but Howgill evidently felt some difficulty, for he wrote from Kendal: [1]

I was not with A. P. in these parts, lest it should be said in something I sought myself to be advanced in some public affairs, which hath been said by divers of me, although without ground or cause at all, and so I forbore, being altogether dead to those things. . . . Friends here are quiet, and meddles in none of these things.

A fortnight earlier [2] Howgill had written that Pearson was hurt by getting into the world's spirit which betrayed him. But though this may well have been the case, it is clear that Pearson was in full unity with Friends in October, when he signed and probably prepared the important letter from the Bishopric addressed to the General Meeting at Skipton, and he was chosen at Skipton on 5th October to consult Fox and other Friends as to a General Meeting for the whole country.

After this last fine piece of service to the Quaker community Anthony Pearson disappears from our story. There is a letter from Margaret Fell, apparently late in 1659, which warns him to beware of the betrayer which lies near him,[3] and shows her consciousness that he was slipping back into the world. Pearson, during his years of Quakerism, had retained his keen political interests, and his activity in 1659 against the Royalists had compromised him. In an hour of weakness and fear he made terms with the Royalist power [4] that sent his political leader, Sir Arthur Hesilrige, to the Tower, and his friend, the great Sir Henry Vane, to the block. There is, however, no record, so far as I am aware, which suggests bitter personal feelings towards him on the part of Friends, or towards Friends on his part. His name dies away in silence.

At this point we may pass in review the general relations of Friends with the Commonwealth authorities, leaving the story of the opening months of 1660, prior

[1] Howgill to Burrough, Kendal, 22nd Augt., Dev. Ho., A.R.B. Colln. No. 169.

[2] To Burrough, Durham, 8th Augt., A.R.B. Colln. No. 60.

[3] Spence MSS., vol. iii. fol. 52, 53.

[4] See *ante*, p. 114.

to the Restoration, to be told in the next chapter. It is clear that to a large extent the Quakers belonged to the Puritan party that was in the seat of power. On the one hand they were anti-Prelatical, and the Papist tendencies sometimes imputed to them dissolved before the most cursory examination. On the other hand they carried the Puritan devotion to a religious life to a point which often seemed an extreme of insensibility to the world. Their religious views brought them into violent collision with the state-ministers and afterwards with the magistracy, and these two parts of the Commonwealth Government strove to keep them down as self-willed and dangerous enthusiasts. But the soldiers, who were religious enthusiasts themselves, usually supported them, and the central Government, which relied largely on military information, and contained men, notably Cromwell himself, who could appreciate the greatness of the Quaker conception, dealt with the cases that came up to them in an opportunist but on the whole a tolerant spirit. The neighbours of Friends, meanwhile, learnt to value them as sterling members of the community, in spite of their strange scruples of conscience, and it is evident to any one who turns over the pages of Besse's *Sufferings* that the actual persecution which occurred was local and capricious. Allowing for all possible imperfections in the record,[1] it is not without significance that Durham, the district protected by Anthony Pearson's influence, has only one paragraph of earlier date than 1660. London, apart from Nayler's case, only names five sufferers prior to 1658, while the persecution in Bristol and Cumberland was very small considering the number of Friends in these parts. According to an old Quaker tract, "there hath suffered imprisonments, putting in the stocks, whippings, loss of goods, and other abuses for keeping a good conscience towards God and man, before the King came into England, 3170 persons."[2] The number seems appallingly large,

[1] The Commonwealth sufferings given in Besse could, in some districts, be largely extended and supplemented from other sources.

[2] Lord Somers' Colln. vii. 246 (1660).

and testifies to the intolerance of many Puritan magistrates, but much of the persecution was petty, and those who died under their sufferings up to April 1659 numbered only twenty-one, compared with at least 300 during the Restoration period.[1]

A community that is in active dissent from the world round it tends to become a state within the State, and the pressure of persecution strengthens the tendency. The Quaker Publisher had a world-wide message, but the Children of the Light who accepted it formed a gathered Church that was very clearly separated from the rest of the population, notably by their separate meetings and by the outward marks of simple dress, plain language, and the refusal of customary ceremonies and marks of social respect. Like the early Christians described in the Epistle to Diognetus (sect. 5), it might be said of them that "they find themselves in the flesh, and yet they live not after the flesh. Their existence is on earth, but their citizenship is in heaven. They obey the established laws, and they surpass the laws in their own lives." Accordingly the business of working side by side with persons of another way of life was at no time an easy one: sons who became Friends left their homes, and servants their masters; soldiers were dismissed from their regiments; justices were removed from the Bench; the world went one way and the Quaker community another. It was only to a limited extent that the Friend found himself free to accept service for the Commonwealth, as the Balby letter of November 1656 had advised him to do. His general attitude was that of a prophet who saw the evil and rebuked it, and he was more concerned with the principles than with the forms of government. The methods of his warfare were not carnal, and the authorities learnt at last that the Quaker was no plotter, though they had constantly to endure from him the high language in which

[1] The Declaration delivered to the Speaker on 6th April 1659 specifies 21 persons who were imprisoned and persecuted to death. The Index in Besse's *Sufferings* of those who died under their sufferings contains 366 names. Of these only nine, I think, died out of England, leaving an ample margin above 300 to cover the cases of death during the year from April 1659 to the Restoration.*

he sought to make them rule for God. Burrough, for example, a young man of twenty-six, addresses the Committee of Safety in November 1659[1] as Christ's ambassador, by special authority and commission from Him. My Master, he says, is a mighty prince, and subjection belongs to Him alone from them and from all men. He has shown great favour to the little island of England, and has a purpose of love towards it, and doth purpose in His season to take it into His own hand, and to sway the Government thereof with His own sceptre, and to set up righteousness alone, and to overthrow all oppressions and oppressors. True it is He hath been long banished as it were by the force of Satan and Antichrist, and all the nation hath been out of right order, and laid waste and barren of good fruit. In another paper in December[2] he apostrophizes "the present distracted and broken nation of England," and well describes the attitude of Friends amid the confusion of the times (I abridge the too luxuriant verbiage).

We are not thy enemies, but we desire thy repentance that thou mayest be healed: we have not the spirit of mischief and rebellion in our hearts towards thee, neither are we for one party or another, nor do we war against any by carnal weapons: neither shall we ever provoke the nation against us, otherwise than by our righteous and holy walking. And we do declare that we are not for men nor names, nor shall we join with this or that sort of men, but as they act righteously alone: nor anything that yet appears can we fully embrace, for they are all corrupted in their ways, and that cursed spirit of self-seeking seems to be the rule of their principal actions, and we rather yet choose to suffer by all than to lose our integrity and innocency by joining to any in their unjust ways: for we reject all places of corrupted honour and we are yet kept free. Alas, what is there effected to this day? What true liberty to subjects more than was many years ago? What oppressions taken off from the people, what establishment in Government? The most of the men that have yet appeared on the throne, they have rejected the word of the Lord, and what wisdom is there in them,—only the policy and subtlety and wisdom of this world. We are utterly out of hopes of this party or the other party, for we know

[1] *Works*, pp. 588-597. [2] *Ibid*, pp. 598-606.

whatsoever men profess they cannot rule for God in our nation till that themselves be reformed and ruled by Him, and have the Spirit of God poured upon them for such a work. For what is a King, and what is a Parliament, what is a Protector, and what is a Council, while the presence of the Lord is not with them? And we are not for names, nor men, nor titles of Government, but we are for justice and mercy and truth and peace, and true freedom, that these may be exalted in our nation, and that goodness, righteousness, meekness, temperance, peace, and unity with God and one with another, that these things may abound. And we are not for such and such names and titles of government that promise fair things and perform nothing; but if a Council, if a Parliament, if any one man or a number of men whatsoever, shall have the Spirit of the Lord poured on him or them to govern this nation, under such only shall the nation be happy and enjoy rest, and the righteous rejoice, when tyranny and oppression shall be clean removed, strife and contention and self-seeking utterly abandoned, and when peace and truth flows forth as a stream, and the Lord alone rules in thy rulers, and under such a government only shalt thou, O Nation, be happy, and thy people a free people.

This fine passage admirably expresses the political standpoint of the early Friends alike in their intense interest in righteous government, their peaceable submission to the existing authorities, their want of sympathy with any of the influential parties, and their somewhat exaggerated claim to know the Divine mind.

CHAPTER XVIII

THE RESTORATION YEAR

(1660)

As concerning those late overturnings . . . be not ye troubled nor shaken in mind because of these things. There is a secret hand working in and through all these overturnings; and they come not to pass without the knowledge of the Lord, for making way for greater things, which the Lord hath to bring to pass in this nation: for much is yet to be thrown down, before truth and righteousness be set up. My advice and counsel is that every one of you, who love and believe in the light, be still and quiet, and side not with any parties, but own and cherish the good wherever it appears, and testify against the evil in all wherever it appears, not like the children of this world, warring with carnal weapons against flesh and blood to destroy men's lives, but like Christians with spiritual weapons warring against spiritual wickedness . . . not striking at creatures, but at the power that captivates the creatures, that so the creatures may be redeemed from the bondage of corruption into the glorious liberty of the sons of God.—ALEXANDER PARKER, Letter of 14th January 1660, in *Letters of Early Friends*, p. 368.

THE swift overthrow of Puritanism is at first sight one of the strangest passages in English history. When Oliver died, his Government stood at its greatest height of power. "Abroad his arms had been successful and his influence decisive; at home all opposition and intrigue, Royalist and Republican alike, had been beaten down, and his hold over the army remained unshaken."[1] But in reality Cromwell, who had struck down King and Parliament when they stood in the way of what he believed to be the interests of the nation, had failed to rear any stable government in their stead. His rule at the last was an unsanctioned military absolutism; the Commonwealth of England rested on force and not on consent. As soon as his supreme personality was withdrawn, it was inevitable

[1] *Cambridge Modern History*, iv. 448.

that the nation should seek to supersede the military rule of the army, but unlikely that it could do so effectually. Richard Cromwell and his Parliament were only supported by the officers until they attempted to control the army by the civil power, and the Rump of the Long Parliament, which the soldiers set up in May, was also expelled when it refused their demands. Then the army leaders, at the end of 1659, tried to rule directly, without any civilian authority, but in turn found themselves helpless, unable to agree or to collect the taxes. The situation naturally and rapidly drifted into anarchy.*

Monck, who was the General in Scotland, dissociated himself from the arbitrary proceedings of the English army. He had been bred, as he said, in Holland, "a Commonwealth where soldiers received and obeyed commands, but gave none," and threw himself on the side of the civil authority. The central consideration in his mind was not the form of government, but whether the law or the sword should be supreme. "I am engaged," he wrote, "in conscience and honour to see my country freed from that intolerable slavery of a sword government, and I know England cannot, nay will not, endure it." Accordingly he husbanded his resources, conciliated the Scots so that he might reduce the garrison to the lowest point, and made ready to come South and intervene.

In December 1659 Lambert and Monck were watching each other on the Scottish border, while the general council of officers was debating the form of a new constitution. The movement for a free Parliament was continually gaining in strength. The fleet declared against the army leaders, and many of the troops showed themselves disaffected. Monck crossed the border, and Lambert's army melted away before him. Fleetwood sent the keys of the House to Speaker Lenthall, and the Rump resumed its sittings. The residue of the Long Parliament which had acquired this nickname of the Rump had long ceased to possess any authority, and petitions came in from the counties demanding the restoration of the other members who had been purged out, as the first step to the assembling of a full and free Parliament. Meanwhile Monck steadily moved South, keeping his own counsel. Thomas Salthouse writes from York in January:[1]

> These strong overturnings and sudden shakings that have happened of late in the nation doth not as yet move nor shake the mountain of the Lord's house, nor much hinder Friends from meeting together. . . . George Monck was received as a prince the last week in this city, and is marched southward with his army. . . . This city is kept by men that adheres unto him, and what they stand for and prosecute time will make manifest: we only mind our work, which the Lord calls us to, and wait to be guided by His counsel.

At the end of the month he drew near London, and was warmly received by the Republican Leaders.* He soon saw the impracticable character of the Rump and the dislike in which it was held by the nation, and joined in the demand for a representative Parliament. As a first step he secured the re-admission of the secluded Long Parliament members, but the House thus enlarged was dissolved on 16th March, forty days prior to the assembling of the free Parliament now to be elected.

The whole country was by this time in a ferment, and the long-repressed Royalist elements asserted themselves with more and more confidence every day. The Quaker letters of the period are full of allusions to the growing excitement of feeling. At Bristol in February "the 'prentices with the rude people were up, running with naked swords . . . up and down the streets, so throng that it were hard to pass thorough them . . . some beating their masters and not suffering the shops to be opened, threatening Friends who opened theirs, not regarding the mayor or any of his officers, but did what was permitted as they see good in their own eyes." At Worcester "the rude people were up in much madness and making fires in the streets."[2] At Gloucester the town was very rude and divided, one part of the soldiers for the King and the other for the

[1] To Margt. Fell, York, 18th Jany. 1660, in Dev. Ho., Jas. Bowden's copy from Wm. Caton Colln.

[2] For these cases see Dewsbury to Margt. Fell, dated by internal evidence, in Swarthm. Colln. iv. 134.

Parliament. At Tewkesbury, Evesham, and Worcester Fox never saw the like drunkenness as there was during the election.[1] Many asked him what he thought of times and things. He replied that "the Lord's light shined over all, and His power was set over all." In London,[2] at the beginning of February, Monck's soldiers, who we shall remember had been purged of Quakers, abused Friends badly, especially at their meeting in the Palace Yard, Westminster, so that Pepys writes, "Indeed the soldiers did use them very roughly, and were to blame." Edward Byllinge gives a graphic account:

. . . we were pulled out by the hair of the head, kicked and knocked down, both men and women, in such a manner not here to be expressed. Many were the knocks and blows and kicks myself and wife received, and this was done by General M[onck]'s foot, who came into the meeting with sword and pistol, being, as they said, bound by an oath to leave never a sectarian in England.

Byllinge was kicked into the kennel in front of the house, and was knocked and kicked across the Palace Yard to the door of Westminster Hall. The House was sitting and he sent in a complaint, and afterwards saw General Monck. He denied giving any order to the soldiers, and Byllinge told him that since he and his army had come to town, Friends could not pass through the streets without being abused; indeed they had not been so abused in London for many years, and never by the soldiers. The soldiers, as we have seen again and again, were favourable to Friends, but the Scottish army was evidently of a different temper.* Hubberthorne also complained, and on the 9th March Monck made an order requiring the soldiers to "forbear to disturb the peaceable meetings of the Quakers, they doing nothing prejudicial to the Parliament or Commonwealth of England." In the North the state of things is well shown by the military

[1] For these cases see Fox, *Camb. Journ.* i. 352.

[2] See *Letters of Early Friends*, pp. 73-82, namely, Henry Fell to Margt. Fell, 7th Feby.; Byllinge to W. M., Feby. (Swarthm. Colln. v.); Hubberthorne to Margt. Fell, 20th March; Hubberthorne to Fox, 29th May (Swarthm. Colln. iv. 18).*

régime which prevailed at the time of the Balby meeting towards the end of April, when a troop was sent from York to disperse the meeting, and Caton, returning South with Thomas Salthouse, was taken by the soldiers to Nottingham, where the two Friends were examined, before being allowed to continue their journey.[1] Caton says that travelling became somewhat difficult, for watches were set with a strict order, as he was informed, to take up all suspicious Quakers, Baptists, and Papists.[2] At Warrington soldiers had broken up a meeting at which he was present, and forced Friends out of the town, but they gathered again on the roadside and had a sweet and precious meeting there, till the soldiers came again with muskets and spears and gave Caton a beating with them; after which, in the indomitable Quaker way, he returned into the meeting again, "which afterwards," he says, "we kept a certain time to our great refreshment in the Lord, whose power and presence did exceedingly appear amongst us, for as our suffering at that time was greater than ordinary, even so was our refreshment in the Lord."[3]

During the forty days' interval between the two Parliaments the government of the country was in the hands of Monck and the Council of State, then composed almost entirely of Presbyterians. They were ready to bring in the King on Presbyterian terms, but Monck refused to promote their proposals, saying that he had promised the nation to leave all to the decision of a free Parliament. At the same time, however, behind the backs of the Council he made preliminary overtures to Charles on his own account, and advised him to make the necessary concessions as acts of his own free grace rather than by any formal treaty with the nation. The King's advisers readily accepted the suggestion, but decided, while granting in general terms the concessions which Monck proposed, to refer to the wisdom of Parliament their precise limits and the responsibility of carrying them into effect.

The result of these deliberations took shape on the

[1] *Life*, 1689 edn. p. 58. Cf. Thos. Salthouse to Margt. Fell, 3rd. Sept. 1660, in Swarthm. Colln. iii. 166.

[2] *Ibid.*, p. 59.

[3] *Ibid.*, p. 57.

4th April in the Declaration of Breda.[1] The important paragraph in this Declaration on the subject of liberty of conscience ran as follows:

And because the passion and uncharitableness of the times have produced several opinions in religion, by which men are engaged in parties and animosities against each other (which, when they shall hereafter unite in a freedom of conversation, will be composed or better understood), we do declare a liberty to tender consciences, and that no man shall be disquieted or called in question for differences of opinion in matter of religion, which do not disturb the peace of the kingdom, and that we shall be ready to consent to such an Act of Parliament as, upon mature deliberation, shall be offered to us, for the full granting that indulgence.

In this as in all other parts of the Declaration there is a full and constitutional recognition of the dominance of Parliament, and, in spite of the word of a King, the actual securing or denying liberty of conscience would depend, as events showed, upon the composition and temper of the Restoration Parliaments.

While the Declaration was preparing the elections were taking place amid scenes of great excitement. A few of the small boroughs returned Republicans, but the King's friends swept the counties. The majority, however, were dissenters from the Anglican Church. A week after the Convention Parliament met the Declaration was presented to them, and was received with enthusiasm. A week later, on 8th May, King Charles was proclaimed, and by the end of the month (29th May) he entered the capital. We have lively accounts in the Quaker letters of the feeling in London. On the day when the King was proclaimed Caton writes:[2]

. . . the concourse of people that have been in the streets this day have been innumerable; the shouting for joy hath been so exceeding great among the people at times that the sound of many trumpets could scarce be heard, nay the bells themselves could not sometimes be heard, but the noise hath been exceedingly confused, like unto the noise of many waters.

---

[1] Gardiner's *Constitutional Documents of the Puritan Revolution*, pp. 465-467.

[2] To Thos. Willan, Swarthm. Colln. iv. 261, printed in *Life*, 1839 edn. p. 87.

Hubberthorne says:[1]

> This day did King Charles and his two brethren James and Henry come into this city. Charles is of a pretty sober countenance, but the great pride and vanity of those that brought him in is unexpressable, and he is in danger to be tempted to those things which he, in himself, is not inclined unto: the great excess and abomination that hath been used this day in this city is unexpressable.

Already the spirit of persecution was abroad among the Cavaliers, who were disposed to break up Friends' meetings on the ground that they were tumultuous assemblies. At Harwich the mob came in on Friends, shouting out, "The King is now coming, who will hang or banish you all." The magistrates imprisoned two of the Friends for speaking words "much reflecting on the government and ministry, to the near causing of a mutiny," and, on informing Parliament of their action, were directed to send them up to London, and were thanked for their care in the matter.

In the Vale of White Horse the county militia broke up a meeting and threw some of the Friends into a pond, acting solely by warrant of the sword; in Dorset, Gloucestershire, Merioneth, and Wiltshire meetings were dispersed, and Friends abused by soldiers of the militia; at Cambridge and Norwich the mob got out of hand, and made havoc of the Quakers.[2] Mention has already been made of the proceedings at Cambridge;[3] at Norwich the apprentices behaved in similar fashion, disturbing meetings

> . . . with throwing of stones, breaking the windows, which is to the value of forty foot of glass, thumping us on the back and breast without mercy, dragging some most inhumanly by the hair of the head, and spitting in our faces, abusing both men and women, with other violent and unseemly actions unfit to be mentioned, also with throwing of fire and drawing blood several times, and several of them getting upon the table, have violently thrown themselves down upon the heads of men and women, and have taken the mire out of the streets and have thrown it at the Friends.[4]

---

[1] *Letters of Early Friends*, p. 82, from Swarthm. Colln. iv. 18.

[2] For there instances see Besse, *Sufferings*, under the several counties.

[3] *Ante*, p. 295.

[4] Letter of 2nd June in Besse, *Sufferings*, i. 488.

George Fox, as we have seen in a former chapter,[1] had attended the important meetings at Balby, Warmsworth, and Skipton, which were held towards the end of April 1660. He went on to a General Meeting at Arnside, and so to Swarthmore.[2] A few weeks later he was arrested and taken to Ulverston, where he was closely watched all night by an alarmed and superstitious guard for fear he should have gone up the chimney, and next day was led on horseback sixteen miles across the sands to Lancaster by a troop of horse.

"The spirits of people being mightily up when I came in the town," says Fox, "I stood and looked upon them, and they cried, 'Look at his eyes,' and, after a while, I spake to them, and they were pretty sober." He was committed to prison as a person "generally suspected to be a common disturber of the peace of this nation, an enemy to . . . the King, and a chief upholder of the Quakers' sect, and that he, together with others of his fanatic opinion, have of late endeavoured to make insurrections in these parts of the country and to embroil the whole kingdom in blood," and the gaoler was directed to keep him prisoner till released by order from the King or Parliament. Margaret Fell went up to London to see what could be done, and towards the end of June succeeded in seeing the King and handing him a paper describing the sufferings and principles of Friends.[3] In July she saw him again[4] with Ann Curtis, of Reading, whose father, when Sheriff of Bristol, had been hung for siding with the Royalists. The King "showed much love to her [Ann Curtis], and she said she had now a request to him, he axed her what it was: she said she had a dear friend in Lancaster Castle whom she had been to see, and she desired her person might be accepted for his, or else that he might be brought

[1] *Ante*, p. 356.

[2] *Journ.* i. 471-488, and *Camb. Journ.* i. 358, etc., give full particulars of the arrest and imprisonment. See also account in Swarthm. Colln. iv. 39. May Day is the date in *Short Journ.* at Dev. Ho. The *mittimus* was dated 5th June.

[3] See her *Works*, pp. 202-210.

[4] For this interview see Margt. Fell's letter in *Camb. Journ.* i. 372. The letter refers to the *habeas corpus* by the terrifying appellation of "horposs scorpions."

up with his accusers to before him, and he might be judge in the cause, and he gave command to his secretary to issue forth an order to that purpose." The King gave proof of his own goodwill in the matter on this and on other occasions, but the royal prerogative did not, of course, extend to interference with the course of justice, and the most that could be done was to issue a writ of *habeas corpus*, which directed the sending of Fox to London for trial. The hollowness of the serious charge that had been made against him was shown by the sheriff allowing him to go up to London with one or two Friends, on his bare promise to appear before the judges on a certain day. He left Lancaster towards the end of September, and during his three weeks' progress to town held meetings and visited Friends after his usual fashion. He reached the city in October, during the execution of the regicides, and when the charge was read against him in the King's Bench, the four judges, says Fox,

> . . . lift up their hands, and I stretched out my arms and said, I was the man that that charge was against, but I was innocent as a child concerning the charge, and had never learnt any war postures, and did they think that if I and my faculty[1] had been such men as the charge declares that I would have brought it up with one or two of my faculty against myself, for . . . I had need of being guarded with a troop or two of horse.

With Fox's consent the judges sent the case on to the King and his Council, who set him at liberty within the next day or two.

The efforts of Margaret Fell and others during the summer of 1660 had gone far towards satisfying the authorities of the loyalty of the Quakers. Hubberthorne, for example, had a long talk with the King on such topics as oaths, the Inner Light, the sacraments, personal inspiration, obedience to magistrates, and the manner of worship. In the course of this conversation the King said, "Well, of this you may be assured, that you shall none of you suffer for your opinions or religion, so long

[1] It deserves note that "society" would have been the natural word if it had then been in use.

as you live peaceably, and you have the word of a king for it, and I have also given forth a declaration to the same purpose, that none shall wrong you nor abuse you."[1] Meanwhile, the meetings of Friends were held for the most part without interference; "glorious, great meetings we had," says Fox, "and the everlasting Truth shined, and many flocked in unto Truth."[2]

The latter half of this year, 1660, was indeed full of promise.[3] The King favoured toleration, and was sincerely anxious to give effect to the promise in the Declaration of Breda, as well as pledged to the Pope and the Catholic Princes to repeal the penal laws against Roman Catholics. It seemed, indeed, probable that a religious settlement would be arranged upon the basis of a union between the two wings of the Royalist party, the Presbyterians and the Episcopalians. On 25th October the King's Declaration was published, proposing a kind of limited episcopacy, in which the bishops would have been assisted and advised by elected presbyters. It was proposed to include in the Act a proviso authorizing Independents, Anabaptists, and others to meet together for public worship so long as they did not disturb the public peace, a clause which would have given Quakers as great a degree of liberty as they had enjoyed during the Commonwealth period. In consequence of Presbyterian opposition, led by Baxter, the Bill dropped.* As to Papists, the opposition said that all that was wanted was the enforcement of the penal laws against them. With respect to sectaries, Baxter distinguished the tolerable parties from the intolerable.

Fox tells us how these halcyon days affected Friends.

"About this time," he says, "the King was willing that one sort of the dissenting people should have their liberty, and that we might have it as soon as any, because they were sensible of our sufferings in the former Powers' days. And some Friends had their liberty to go into the House of Lords before them and the Bishops: so Friends had their liberty to declare their reasons why they could not pay tithes, nor swear, nor join with the other

[1] Hubberthorne's *Works*, pp. 268-272; also in Sewel, i. 428-432.
[2] *Camb. Journ.* i. 384.
[3] See *Cambridge Modern History*, vol. v. chap. v., by C. H. Firth.

worships, nor go to the steeplehouses, and they heard them very moderately, . . . and there was about seven hundred Friends in prison upon contempts to Oliver Cromwell and Richard and their government, when the King came in, and he set them all at liberty."[1]

At the end of November a Committee of the Council was appointed to examine into the sufferings of Quakers and to prepare a proclamation about them; and on the 14th December Thomas Moore, of Surrey, a former justice, was admitted to the King and Council on behalf of Friends.[2] Before he was called in, it was debated whether he should have his hat "taken off gently by the door-keeper or the clerk," but the King was against this, and Moore was told: "You may go up, it is the King's pleasure that you may come to him with your hat on." The King repeated his intention that Friends should enjoy their meetings peaceably and be protected, as long as they lived peaceably and quietly in the kingdom; and on Moore pointing out that the magistrates would not take notice of the King's intention unless it was published by proclamation, he replied, "Leave it to me," bidding them stay awhile and they would see. It is evident that at this time full toleration for Friends was intended, although no statute conferring it could be passed in the Convention Parliament, which was then at the point of dissolution. But there were difficulties to overcome, especially the one of assuring the loyalty of Friends without forcing on them an oath of allegiance. We have two letters from Bristol at the end of November which show the feeling of the authorities against any tampering with the oath.[3] In that city there were many who refused it.

"No Quaker, or hardly any Anabaptist, will take those oaths, so that the said oaths are refused by many hundreds of those judgments, being persons of very dangerous principles.... Sir," the writer continues, "these I had almost said monsters of men with us are very, yea, more numerous than in all the

[1] *Camb. Journ.* i. 384, 385.

[2] Swarthm. Colln. iv. 196, printed in *Letters of Early Friends*, pp. 92-95.

[3] Richard Ellsworth to Secretary Nicholas, 21st Nov. and 24th Nov., in *Extracts from State Papers*, Second Series, pp. 120-122.

West of England, I dare say, on this side London. And here they all centre and have their meetings, at all seasons till nine of the clock at night, and later,—sometimes above a thousand or twelve hundred at a time,—to the great affrighting of this city, as to what will be the consequent thereof, if not restrained, or should a suspension of the said oaths be to them given."

Just as Farmer, a few years before, had expressed his disgust at the tolerant policy of Whitehall, so in these letters the Government is told that if certain persons are excused the oaths there will be much discontent and repining. The Baptist congregations submitted an engagement which they judged as full as the oath;[1] and Friends made an offer, declaring that they could not swear, but testifying that they owned the King to be the supreme magistrate and chief ruler, to whose just commands they would at all times yield due obedience in the Lord. Nor would they plot against his person or the peace of the kingdom, but would be ready by all lawful means to preserve his just authority. They add: "If he shall require aught of us, which for conscience' sake we cannot do, we shall rather choose patiently to suffer than sin against the God of our life; nor can we, or shall we, rise up with carnal weapons to work our own deliverance, but in patience and well-doing commit ourselves unto the Lord."[2] The proposal apparently was that this engagement should be given by six principal Friends in each county, on behalf of themselves and other Friends.

Everything seemed in a fair way to settlement; indeed, Fox, with perhaps some exaggeration, says that an instrument confirming the liberty of Friends was drawn up and only awaited signature,[3] when, in the opening days of the year 1661, the Fifth Monarchy rising in London re-awakened in the authorities their nervous dread of the extreme Puritan sects, and led to the most wholesale of all the imprisonments of unoffending Quakers. An era of persecution began, which would test the faith and fibre of Puritan England to the utmost, and the easy-

[1] *Broadmead Baptist Records*, p. 70.
[2] *Extracts from State Papers*, Second Series, p. 122.
[3] *Journ.* i. 490.

going tolerance of Charles would give way more and more completely to the narrow bigotry of a Cavalier Parliament. The history of Friends during this time of suffering will be told in a future volume.

During the succession of changes which attended the downfall of the Puritan régime, Friends, with one or two exceptions, took no active part in the shaping of affairs, though they exerted themselves with each form of government in turn to secure conditions which would allow them freedom for the practice and propagation of their faith. Anthony Pearson was, as we have seen, an exception, and Alexander Parker, in one of his letters, speaks of two Friends who were charged with having helped Lambert's soldiers to capture some of Sir George Booth's men after the failure of the Royalist rising in Cheshire in the summer of 1659. He says:

> I do perceive that they were at the place, and whether the soldiers did force or command them to go, I know not, but better had it been if all had been kept still and quiet in those times, for because of the forwardness and want of wisdom in some is one great cause of our present sufferings.[1]

There were, however, wild ideas abroad as to the designs of Friends in their great meetings. One Puritan bookworm, name unknown, whose only wish was a tranquil life, speaks in July 1659 of Quakers and Anabaptists arming everywhere, and adds:

> My interests [are] so balanced that, unless a conquest be made by Quakers, which can never last a month in settlement, or by Charles Stuart, which is improbable, I shall have the same quiet abode among my books, and frank entertainment by some of the foremost men in power that I now enjoy.[2]

At York a dangerous rendezvous was feared;[3] meetings were dispersed, the meeting-house door was nailed up; and in the spring of 1660 the Mayor gave orders to the watch not to let any Friends come into the city, and any who came on their ordinary business were brought before

[1] To Fox, Nantwich, 7th Augt. 1660, Swarthm. Colln. iii. 145.
[2] Thurloe, *State Papers*, vii. p. 704.
[3] Bp. Kennet's *Register*, edn. 1728, p. 7.

him, and sent out by another gate.[1] The steady persistence with which Friends carried through their arrangements for meetings, even during times of public commotion, disquieted the authorities, who suspected sinister designs. We have already seen how, at this critical time, George Fox was arrested on suspicion; and it may have been thought prudent to keep him in confinement for a while as a hostage for the good conduct of others. Until the new Government had been fully accepted by the country, it was naturally nervous as to possible plots.

The care of Friends to avoid political entanglements did not imply any want of courage. Wherever the Government oppressed their consciences—as in requiring an oath of allegiance, or in preventing them from meeting for worship—they opposed themselves to the unrighteous law in scorn of consequence. But they were at this period indifferent to the form of government. Their point of view was theocratic rather than democratic on the one hand, or royalist on the other. Nayler, writing during the beautiful close of his chequered life,[2] tells us that all kingdoms and peoples ought to belong to the Lord and His Christ, and to be guided and governed by the law of the Spirit in their consciences. In every form of authority that appeared Friends had waited for the face of Jesus their righteous King and Saviour; and with great sufferings their souls had travailed to see if there were any who would receive His anointing and govern by His power, and would order and be ordered in His counsel; and they had been evil entreated by many contrary spirits for seeking to set up His kingdom in rulers, teachers, and people. They had been unable to join with any of the powers that had risen up, because they heard not the voice of the Holy One in the midst of these Parliaments, Protectors, Priests, and Rulers; nor was His Spirit the strength of their counsels, but they sought the arm of flesh, and to make themselves strong by flattery and deceit and not by truth, and they ruled with violence and

[1] *F.P.T.* p. 320.

[2] *Works*, pp. 602-642, "An account from the Children of Light, etc.," signed by Nayler and Hubberthorne.

cruelty and not with the sword of God, which is judgment and justice.

"And sometimes," he goes on to say, "we have felt some tenderness in some of them, when they have been low, little and in fear, in which we had some hope and gladness to hear the voice of simplicity and truth, though but brokenly, so that we could then have said, They were not far from the Kingdom of God, but, turning away the ear from the Spirit of truth in them, and consulting with fleshly wisdom, and carnal reason likely to make wise and to accomplish their self-ends, how soon hath Truth fallen in them, and blindness and hardness of heart come over them again worse than before, which, being showed us of God, we could not but deny them also to be of God."

The noblest Puritans had also in many cases believed in a theocratic rather than a democratic ideal of government. Cromwell himself, at the suggestion of Harrison, had replaced the Long Parliament in 1653 with the Nominated Parliament, constituted not of elected representatives of the nation, but by selection of those judged most fit to rule for God. He had harangued them in fervent words, telling them that after a time the people would be fit to exercise the liberty of election, and meanwhile "convince them," he said, "that as men fearing God have fought them out of their bondage under the regal power so men fearing God do now rule them in the fear of God, and take care to administer good unto them."[1] The Parliament thus constituted proved an impracticable body, and its failure involved the defeat of the theocratic principle as opposed to the representative. It is true that at the time the immediate effect was to throw all the powers of the State, for practical purposes, into the hands of Cromwell, who became Protector; but the Protectorate, though derived from the army, was always intended to rest on a Parliamentary basis. No adjustment between the Puritanism of the army and the Parliamentary system necessary for giving utterance to the national mind was, indeed, effected during the Protectorate, and it was this unsettled problem and the consequent demand from the

[1] Cited from Gardiner, *Hist. of Commth. and Prot.* ii. p. 287.

country for a full and free Parliament which, as we have seen, led to the Restoration. In Cromwell himself the Puritan theocratic principle had found meanwhile its greatest expression. Milton stated his position in glowing words which must have corresponded closely with the Protector's own aspirations.

> To rule by your own counsel three powerful nations, to try to lead their peoples from bad habits to a better economy and discipline of life than any they have known hitherto, to send your anxious thoughts all over the country to its most distant parts, to watch, to foresee, to refuse no labour, to spurn all blandishments of pleasure, to avoid the ostentation of wealth and power—these are difficulties in comparison with which war is but sport; these will shake and winnow you; these demand a man upheld by Divine aid, warned and instructed almost by direct intercourse with Heaven.[1]

The Puritanism of Cromwell was continually tempered by his own moderate and tolerant character, and by the practical sagacity of himself and his officers. If we would see the full effect of the doctrine that the good and wise were alone to be entrusted with power we must turn to the New England Colonies or to the extreme claims of the Fifth Monarchy men.

The New England Colonies of Plymouth and Massachusetts were theocracies fashioned after the Jewish model, in which there was a complete identification of Church and State. Only those were received who accepted the rigid Calvinism which prevailed; other persons were regarded as mutinous and factious, and told that New England was no place for them. The wise tolerance of such a leader of men as Cromwell was replaced by the bigotry of the Puritan minister and the over-zealous heat of the godly magistrate.

The Fifth Monarchy preachers, who reached a position of great influence at the time of the Nominated Parliament, went still further, and claimed to restore the Law of Moses as the law of the land, in preparation for the coming of the Fifth Monarchy of Christ. When this

[1] Cited from Gardiner, *Hist. of Commth. and Prot.* iii. p. 168.

came, office and authority would be given to the saints alone, and all institutions which were derived from William the Conqueror, who was identified with the Little Horn of Daniel's prophecy, would be abolished.

Between all these theocratic systems and the theocracy of Quakerism there was a great gulf fixed. Cromwell and his Parliaments imposed their Puritanism, their rule of the godly, on England by force, never securing a real national sanction for their rule. An army in being was continually enforcing the Commonwealth. The New England authorities made the power of the State the instrument through which to carry out the intolerant rule of the Church. Their theocratic system had no doubt the general consent of the colonists, but there was no room in it for minorities. The Fifth Monarchists, again, were eager to grasp the sword and force their countrymen to accept the salutary government of the saints. It was this, indeed, that made them both during the Protectorate and in 1661 a dangerous element in the body politic. But the Quakers resolutely excluded compulsion from their scheme of the Kingdom of God.

"Force and compulsion," said John Audland,[1] "may make some men conform to that outwardly, which otherwise they would not do, but that is nothing of weight, their hearts are never the better, but are rather worse, and more hypocrites than before . . . for it is God alone by His powerful word of life operating in the hearts of people that changeth them . . . and it's out of man's power, and that which God doth not require of men at this day, to force by penalties and carnal weapons to this or that worship. . . . How then? How must we do . . . that people might be brought to one way to serve God? . . . Come forth then with spiritual weapons, mighty ones, in the power of the gospel of Jesus Christ . . . let us see . . . your love to enemies, your self-denial, your subjection to the cross of our Lord Jesus . . . this is the way to bring people to be of one mind in the Truth, this is God's way, this is the way the saints walked in, this is the way we love and desire."

[1] *The Memory of the Righteous Revived*, pp. 204-209.

CHAPTER XIX

FRIENDS IN PRIVATE LIFE

I continued . . . four years, mostly following my outward calling and attending and waiting upon the Lord in the workings of His holy power in my heart, both in meetings and at other times, wherever I was, or whatever I had to do, for I found that, as my heart was kept near the power, it kept me tender, soft and living : and besides I found, as I was diligent in eyeing of it, there was a constant sweet stream that run softly in my soul of divine peace, pleasure and joy, which far exceeded all other delights and satisfactions. —JOHN BURNYEAT, *Works*, p. 20.

The bearing of the cross is a true part of the Christian's life. . . . When we walk in the love and will of our Father, sacrifice may indeed be turned as by a heavenly alchemy into a glad expression of our sonship. Yet the highest service is often bound up with sacrifice that must be made with effort and with pain. In the days of the early Friends their ministry rested on such an experience, and it was this that gave them power with their hearers. Let us not hesitate to face sacrifice to-day in whatever form it comes to us, whether it affects our course of life, or our social or business aims, if by so doing we may enter more deeply into the place of power.—*Epistle* (1911), from LONDON YEARLY MEETING OF FRIENDS.

WE have now carried the story of the Quaker movement from its beginnings in the apostolic mission of Fox to the North of England down to the new opportunities and perils which confronted it upon the Restoration of monarchy, parliamentary government, and episcopacy. Before attempting a general review of the position, we shall enrich our knowledge of the inner significance of the movement if we turn aside from the missionary work and the external history of Friends to the private life of the individuals who made up the Quaker groups scattered over the land. We shall gain thereby some fresh sense of the extraordinary place played in the life of the first Friends by the enduring of hardship for the sake of inward peace and the service of Truth. Their eyes were filled with light and their hearts with joy, but their feet trod daily the way of the cross with their Lord.

Already the Quaker was becoming widely known not only for his peculiarities of dress and address, but for that collectedness and integrity of character which distinguished him as one who kept close to his unseen inward Guide. Lord Langdale, for example, after the Restoration, writes from Yorkshire to Secretary Nicholas, "they are persons of most exemplar regular course of life, free from all debauchery or almost other offence to their neighbours, yet extreme strict to the rules of their profession, accounting any persecution an honour to their calling."[1]

There is a very suggestive letter written from London at the end of June 1654, when the coming of the Quaker "Publishers" was daily expected, which shows how the practice of Quakerism did violence to the ordinary course of life. I do not know that the writer, Alexander Delamain,[2] continued a Friend, but this does not affect the picture he draws. He was an apprentice, and his master inquired the reason why he absented himself from family prayers and other "duties." The answer was ill-calculated to mend matters, for it charged the master with being a hypocrite, and thereupon the man burst into a passion, and flew at him with his fists, striking him and crying, "Thou wretch, thou makes me tremble—thou wicked wretch, thou rogue." A minister was called in to give the 'prentice good advice, but Delamain called him a hireling, and the angry master threatened to tear up his indentures and forfeit his right to become a freeman of the city.

There were many similar cases up and down England. When Richard Davies, of Welshpool, then an apprentice at Llanfair, first began to use the plain language, his master was not offended at it, because he saw the truth of it, and that it ought to be spoken to every one, but his

[1] 3rd Jany. 1661, *Extracts from State Papers*, Second Series, p. 124.

[2] *Letters of Early Friends*, pp. 5-10, from Dev. Ho., Swarthm. Colln. iii. 93. There was a Muggletonian named Alexander Delamain, who may have been the same man.

mistress, standing more on her dignity, took a stick, and gave him such a blow on his bare head that it was sore for a long time; indeed she so far forgot herself as to swear that she would kill him, if she should be hanged for it, though before this she seldom, if ever, had given him an angry word.[1] His parents were told that he was gone distracted, and that they ought to send for some learned men to come and restore him to his senses. So Davies went to see them, and they were much disturbed at him for not going down on his knees to ask their blessing, or bowing to them and taking off his hat. His father had already threatened to leave him nothing, and soon turned his back on him. The mother, however, came tenderly towards him, and looked well on his face, and saw that he was her child, and had not been bewitched into some other likeness, as had been reported, and, after some talk, went to her husband and told him to be of good cheer, for their son would yet be a comfort to them. One of Davies's companions met with harsher treatment from his parents, and, because he would not conform himself to "that dry, dead and formal praying that his father used, his father rose from off his knees when he was at prayer, and took a staff, and did violently beat his son, and, against natural affection, he took a lock and chain, and chained him out of doors in a cold frosty night."[2] Davies, and three other young men of like opinions, agreed that they should meet together for waiting on the Lord, but none of them had a house of his own to meet in. So they met on a hill in a common, which was central for them all, they living some miles from one another.

"There," he says, "we met in silence, to the wonder of the country. When the rain and weather beat upon us on one side of the hill, we went to the other side. We were not free to go into any neighbours' enclosures, for they were so blind, dark and ignorant that they looked upon us as witches, and would go away from us, some crossing themselves with their hands about their foreheads and faces."[3]

---

[1] *Life*, 1771 edn. p. 23. [2] *Ibid.* p. 33. [3] *Ibid.* p. 41.

It was quite usual for young men who joined the Quaker movement to be disowned by their relations. We may instance the cases of Burrough, Rawlinson, Rigge, and Parnell. It became a recognized part of church-work [1] to take care of persons turned out of their places and families "for the Truth's sake." Young Thomas Olliffe, of Brampton, in Northamptonshire, for example, afterwards Governor of New Jersey, wrote to Fox in 1658 that his parents wished him to provide for himself, because he was a trouble to them, "being," he says, "out of their life and cannot join with them in their customs, but rather deny them in obedience to the Lord, but I have not freed[om] to go from them according to their wills." [2]

The case of Ellis Hookes, who seems to have come from Odiham, in Hampshire, and became the official clerk to Friends,[3] illustrates vividly the domestic persecution which befell them. In 1657 he went with a letter to his mother, who was at Sir William Waller's house at Stanton Harcourt, in Oxfordshire. Lady Waller, a high religious professor, thought to convert him from his Quaker notions, and had him into her chamber. She took his hat off his head, locked the door, and rated him soundly. He remained silent until she cried out that now his hat was gone his religion was gone, and he could not speak, but only hum. Then he angered her still more by saying unceremoniously, "Woman, shew thyself a sober woman." She fell to beating him about the head and pulling his hair, saying that she was never called Woman before. When she had wearied herself, the young man spoke a second time, "Woman, I deny thy religion that cannot bridle thy tongue nor thy hands," a speech that only added fuel to her passion. She commanded her man and her son to stand before Hookes and keep him up in a corner of the room, where she continued to beat him, and called for a stick, as her fists

[1] See *ante*, pp. 315, 320, 330.

[2] See letter in Swarthm. Colln. iv. 166. For Olliffe, see *The Quakers in the American Colonies*, p. 385.

[3] See Norman Penney's careful account in *J.F.H.S.* i. pp. 12-22. He left a gift to the poor of Odiham, and had an uncle living there.

were sore. After a time he said, "Instead of showing thyself a sober woman, thou hast showed thyself more like a beast." At this insult to his wife, Sir William Waller, who had hitherto taken no part, struck the Quaker down with a blow on his head, and they all cried, "Out of the doors with him." He was thrust out and sent off, bareheaded, and deaf for a week with the blows which he had received. Moreover, his father was written to the next day to have nothing to do with his son, but to turn him out of doors, which he did, though he must afterwards have relented, for on his death in 1672 he left him a considerable fortune.

A case which we can follow in even more detail is that of young Thomas Ellwood,[1] who lived at Crowell, in Oxfordshire, under the Chilterns. Bred as a country gentleman, he was thrown into friendship with the Penningtons, whom his father knew. They lived at the Grange in Chalfont St. Peter, Buckinghamshire, about fifteen miles from Crowell. Near here, at a farm called the Grove, which had formerly been a gentleman's seat, and had a large hall, Ellwood attended his first Friends' meeting in December 1659. Burrough and Nayler were present, and Ellwood, then a young man of twenty, sat on a stool by the side of the long table on which Burrough and, presumably, the other ministering Friends were seated. Ellwood says, "I drank in his words with desire, for they not only answered my understanding but warmed my heart with a certain heat, which I had not till then felt from the ministry of any man." In the evening, after supper at the Grange, the servants were called in, and all sat down in silence. After a short time, Burrough began speaking about the universal free grace of God to all mankind, and Ellwood's father was drawn into a defence of the current Calvinism. Nayler also joined in the conversation, handling the question with great clearness and force. The Crowell party returned home on the following morning—father, son, and younger

[1] See *The History of the Life of Thos. Ellwood*, by himself, first printed in 1714, with a supplement by Joseph Wyeth, and frequently reprinted.

sister—and when they were gone, Burrough said to the Peningtons, with shrewd insight, "As for the old man, he is settled on his lees, and the young woman is light and airy, but the young man is reached and may do well if he don't lose it." Ellwood soon heard of another Quaker meeting, this time at High Wycombe, seven miles away. He determined to attend it, but let his greyhound run by his horse, so that it might be thought he had gone coursing. With his sword at his side, and his fine black clothes on, the young squire sat on the first empty seat, just inside the door, and, when the meeting was over, stepped out quickly to his inn, and rode home, without his absence being noticed by his father. This second meeting was like the clinching of a nail, confirming and fastening what he had previously heard. Light began to break forth in him, discovering the evil growths of his heart, and judging the evil by the law of the spirit of life in Christ Jesus, so that he could no longer go on in his former ways and course of life. The vanity of superfluity in apparel was shown him, and he took off his lace, ribbons, and useless buttons, and ceased to wear rings. He saw the evil of giving flattering titles to men—a custom in which he had been a ready master—and he also felt himself required to put away the practice of baring the head and bowing the knee in salutations, and of saying "you" to a single person, "contrary to the pure, plain, and single language of truth." In fact, the new light in his conscience obliged him to those changes in his mode of life which involved the most complete crucifixion of himself and the most unsparing devotion to the truth. At first, however, he made a difference in his own mind between his behaviour towards his father and towards other people, fearing lest he should do amiss in withdrawing the filial honour due to parents.

During this time of gradual spiritual illumination, his father, who was a county magistrate, sent him to the quarter sessions at Oxford to deliver in the recognizances for keeping the peace, etc., which he had taken, and to bring him an account of the proceedings. On the way he met Burrough, but as both rode in montero-caps, with the ear-flaps down to shelter them from the cold, they passed without recognizing one another. When they met a few days later, they recollected each other's dress, and Ellwood thought how gladly he would have had Burrough's encouragement to faithfulness during that difficult day's exercise at Oxford.

At the sessions a knot of acquaintances had come round him, two of them old Thame school-fellows of his, one a scholar in his gown, the other a surgeon, and the third of the party a country gentleman whom he had long known. They saluted Ellwood in the usual way, putting off their hats and bowing and saying, "Your humble servant, sir." He stood without moving his cap or bending his knee, much to their amazement, until at length the brisk young surgeon clapped him on the shoulder, saying with a laugh, "What, Tom, a Quaker?" "To which," says Ellwood, "I readily and cheerfully answered, 'Yes, a Quaker.' And, as the words passed out of my mouth, I felt joy spring in my heart, for I rejoiced that I had not been drawn out by them into a compliance with them, and that I had strength and boldness given me to confess myself to be one of that despised people." That evening he went to his father, bareheaded as usual, and gave him an account of what had passed at the sessions, and on the following day, desiring to visit the Peningtons again, he acquainted his father with his intention, who tried in vain to dissuade him. He attended a monthly General Meeting at Wycombe, where Burrough spoke with much power, and now the light in his heart convinced him that the honour due to parents did not consist in ceremony but in a ready obedience to their lawful commands. When he reached home, his father was out; but on his return, Ellwood stepped towards him with head covered, and said, "Isaac Penington and his wife remember their loves to thee." The father in an angry tone said, "I shall talk with you, sir, another time," and so left him for that night; but next morning, seeing his son come before him with his hat on, he fell on him with both his fists in a transport of passion, plucked off his hat and threw it away. All his hats—and even his montero-cap—were lost in the same fashion, and young Ellwood took such a cold in his head that he was laid up as a kind of prisoner for the rest of the winter. Whenever he had to speak to his father, though he had no longer an offending hat, his use of the plain language proved an equally powerful irritant, and the father would be sure to fall on his son with his fists. Once he said, "Sirrah, if ever I hear you say 'thou' or 'thee' to me again, I'll strike your teeth down your throat." As Ellwood would not join in the occasional family prayers, he was on one occasion thrashed in the presence of the servants.

The Peningtons at length visited Crowell and persuaded the father to let Ellwood return with them. After a six weeks' stay at Chalfont he came home, and found his father somewhat more moderate. Ellwood says:

> . . . that day that I came home I did not see my father, nor until noon the next day, when I went into the parlour where he was to take my usual place at dinner. [Then he said] but in a milder tone than he had formerly used to speak to me, "If you cannot content yourself to come to dinner without your hive on your head (so he called my hat) pray rise and go take your dinner somewhere else." Upon those words I arose from the table, and, leaving the room, went into the kitchen, where I stayed till the servants went to dinner, and then sat down very contentedly with them. Yet I suppose my father might intend that I should have gone into some other room and there have eaten by myself. But I chose rather to eat with the servants, and did so from thenceforward, so long as he and I lived together. And from this time he rather chose, as I thought, to avoid seeing me, than to renew the quarrel about my hat.

His father, however, still sought to keep him from meetings, especially after the beginnings of persecution in the Restoration year. Ellwood stole from the house one morning and his father came after him, and, says Ellwood, when he "gained ground upon me, I somewhat mended my pace. This he observing, mended his pace also, and at length ran. Whereupon I ran also and a fair course we had, through a large meadow of his, which lay behind his house and out of sight of the town. He was not, I suppose, then above fifty years of age, and, being light of body and nimble of foot, he held me to it for a while. But afterwards, slacking his pace to take breath, and observing that I had gotten ground of him, he turned back and went home, and, as I afterwards understood, telling my sisters how I had served him, he said, 'Nay, if he will take so much pains to go, let him go, if he will.'" Shortly after, the Crowell household was broken up, and Ellwood went to London as reader to the great John Milton in his blindness.

It will be evident that taking up the cross of Quakerism with regard to such matters as the plain language and hat-honour involved a very real separation from the world. The gospel words were found true, "I came not to send peace, but a sword. For I came to set a man at variance against his father . . . and a man's foes shall be they of his own household" (Matt. x. 34-36). In that ceremonious age Quaker plainness seemed not only ill-bred but deliberately offensive. The hat was at this time commonly worn in the house and in church, but not during prayer nor in the presence of superiors. Lord Clarendon says that in his younger days he never kept on his hat before those older than himself (except at dinner), nor when grace was said at meals.[1] To be uncovered before any one was, accordingly, a distinctive mark of deference. It was the same with the plain language. When Lord Coke desired to anger Raleigh at his trial, he had addressed him with the insulting words, "All that Lord Cobham did was at thy instigation, thou viper: for I thou thee, thou traitor." But "thou" was the regular form of speech to inferiors, long after "you" had become customary between persons of equal rank. Fuller lays down the usage thus—"We maintain that 'thou' from superiors to inferiors is proper, as a sign of command; from equals to equals is passable as a note of familiarity; but from inferiors to superiors, if proceeding from ignorance, hath a smack of clownishness;

[1] See note in *Camb. Journ.* ii. 482; also *F.P.T.* 285 (cited *ante*, p. 198). Friends were careful to take off their hats in prayer. See *ante*, pp. 202, 247, 354.

if from affectation, a tone of contempt." For a servant to address his master with "thou," or a son his father, was therefore a gross affront and an act of insubordination, and we need not be surprised at the angry scenes which followed. It should be remembered, however, that in the North of England "thou" was, and still is, the regular form of familiar speech, and cases of offence would in this part of the country seldom occur.

With Fox and his followers "the determination to 'thou' all men was not a piece of capricious trifling. It flowed from the principle which pervaded his whole conduct, the desire of piercing through the husk and coating of forms in which men's hearts and souls were wrapped up, and of dragging them out from their lurking-places into the open light of day."[1] By refusing the homage of the hat, and the customary titles of honour, by using the plain language and declining to pledge healths, Fox was witnessing for reality in life and was applying a test to the Puritan professors by which their patience and kindliness and moderation were tried. He was at the same time putting the followers of Quakerism to a test, which inured them to reproach, taught them to despise the false standards of the world, and led them into the way of the cross. But though these stringent testings resulted, the plain behaviour practised by Friends was above all due to their single-hearted dedication to what they understood was required of them by God, and to the sense that with Him there was no respect of persons. Howgill and Penn and Barclay[2] all make use of a passage in the letter to the Roman matron Celantia, attributed to Jerome (*Epistles*, No. 148, edn. Vallarsi):

Heed not thy nobility, nor let that be a reason for thee to take place of any; repute not those of meaner extraction to be thy inferiors, our religion admits no respect of persons, nor doth it lead us to value the outward condition of men, but their inward frame and spirit: it is hereby that we pronounce men noble or base. With God, not to serve sin is the only freedom, and

[1] *Guesses at Truth*, 1878 edn. p. 127.

[2] Howgill's *Works*, p. 489; Penn's *No Cross, No Crown*, cap. ix.; Barclay's *Apology*, Proposition xv. Cf. Penn's Pref. to Fox's *Journ.* xxxi.

to excel in virtue is to be noble. . . . Besides it is a folly for any to boast his gentility, since all are equally esteemed by God. The ransom of the poor and rich cost Christ an equal expense of blood. Nor is it material in what estate a man is born, since all are equally new creatures in Christ.

The witness of Friends was accordingly a standing rebuke to the world and to Christians for their emphasis on those differences in rank and position which amount to nothing in the sight of God. In the early ages of Christianity, the sense of brotherhood among the disciples of Christ had been so strong as to dissolve all social distinctions, and there was something of the same experience among the early Friends. Servants in the households of Friends became in many cases Publishers of Truth; women were given their sphere of work as well as men; men of standing, like Gervase Benson, were content to call themselves "husbandmen";[1] citizens of position offered themselves as prisoners in the place of their friends; the Quaker groups took the burden of relieving their own poor; the Quaker slave-holder in Barbados, at a time when the oppression involved in slavery was still unperceived, was at least made alive to his responsibilities. The moral alertness of Fox's mind is well illustrated by his letter in 1657 "to Friends beyond sea that have Blacks and Indian Slaves." God, he says, is no respecter of persons, He has made all nations of one blood, and enlightened every man that came into the world. The gospel is glad tidings to every captivated creature under the whole heavens. And so, recognizing these things, Friends are to have the mind of Christ, and to be merciful as their heavenly Father is merciful.[2]

The witness of Friends on points of speech and dress thus touched some of the greatest issues of life, and is not to be treated as an excrescence on their main message. We ought rather to feel that the main message, under the conditions of that age, could not have been uttered in its purity and force if Friends had shrunk from giving it fearless application to these parts of life.

[1] *F.P.T.* 251. [2] *Epistles*, No. 153.

Scoffers naturally found it easy to ridicule this side of Quakerism. Baxter calls these things "silly cavils."

> They go about the world to preach down hour-glasses, and pulpits and tithes, and the title of Master; do you think that the salvation of the world doth lie upon this doctrine? They come to preach down ribbons and lace and points and cuffs; O glorious and excellent doctrine for children to make sport with."[1]

Mary Penington, in her years of spiritual darkness, heard of Friends having risen up in the North, but learnt nothing about them, except that they used *thee* and *thou*, and, she adds, "I saw a book of plain language, wrote by George Fox, as I remember, which I accounted very ridiculous, and so minded them not, but scoffed at them in my mind."[2] Her recollection seems at fault, and the piece she saw was, perhaps, Farnsworth's *The Pure Language of the Spirit of Truth . . . or Thee and Thou . . .* published in 1655. Fox, however, is associated with the most remarkable of all vindications of the plain language, the small folio published in 1660 under the title "A Battle-Door for Teachers and Professors to learn Singular and Plural, etc." The Horn-book of our ancestors, often called a "battledoor" from its shape, consisted of a square piece of wood with a handle, the square of wood having on its face a sheet of paper, often protected by a horn plate, on which were printed the rudiments of learning, namely, the alphabet, small and large, a simple syllabary, the numerals and the Lord's Prayer. The first line began with a Cross and was styled the Christ-cross row,[3] and with the Lord's Prayer gave a religious character to this primer of dame-school education. The Quaker "Battle-Door" was in the same way intended as a primer for the scholars and divines of England, to prove to them by a wealth of instances that the plain language had always been the true way of speech.[4] The main part of the

[1] "One Sheet against the Quakers" (1657), p. 6.

[2] See Mary Penington's *Experiences*.

[3] So in *Don Quixote* Sancho Panza says, "To be a good governor, it is sufficient to know the Christus." In Italian the Horn-book was called "La Santa Croce," and is so termed on the Italian page of the "Battle-Door."

[4] Cf. Fox, *Epistles*, No. 191 (1660).

book consisted of detailed proof of this from about thirty-five languages, many of which were set out in "battledoor" shaped frames, containing a brief statement on the point in the foreign language with an English translation, and, in the handle of the "Battle-Door," this sentence in the foreign language, "The Light which Christ hath enlightened you withal, believe in, that the anointing within you you may know to teach you. George Fox." In the case of some of the more abstruse languages, as Coptic and Armenian, the authors had a sentence or two in English, followed by the foreign alphabet, in type cut, no doubt, expressly for the book. On the Coptic page, for example, we read:

The Ægyptian Language, which is called the Coptick Language, they have also a distinction betwixt Singular and plural, which may condemn the spiritual Ægyptians who have lost distinction through pride and Ambition, who will neither practice plain and simple Language themselves, nor will suffer others, but will persecute them: Therefore let the spiritual Egyptians, who will persecute people for using *thou* to one and *you* to more than one read a few Examples in the Egyptian Tongue, but first see the Letters, as followeth.[1]

The learning in the book was due to John Stubbs and to Benjamin Furly,* of Colchester, whose names appeared after that of Fox on the title-page; but Fox was regarded by many as laying claim to it because his name was put to the sentence in the handle of the "Battle-Door" in various languages, and because he had said in the Preface, with his curious sense of possessing a spiritual super-knowledge,[2]

All languages are to me no more than dust, who was before languages were, and am comed before languages were and am redeemed out of languages into the power where men shall agree: but this is a whip and a rod to all such who have degenerated through the pride and ambition from their natural

[1] For the list of languages see the full title in Smith's *Catalogue*. The "Battle-Door" contained at the end a section on the bad words taught in certain current school-books, intended as a rod and whip to the schoolmasters who used such books. Consult *J.F.H.S.* xv. 31-32.

[2] *Ante*, p. 302. Fox's name was not put to the Preface, but it is evidently by him.

tongue and languages; and all languages upon earth is but natural [*i.e.* undivine] and makes none Divine, but that which makes Divine is the Word which was before languages and tongues were.

The book itself, according to Fox, made a great stir, and was certainly among the strangest products of the press.

"Some of them," he says,[1] "was given to the King and his Council, and to the Bishop of Canterbury and of London, one apiece, and to the universities, and many bought them up, and the King said it was the proper language of all nations. And they asked the Bishop of Canterbury what he thought of it, and he was so astonished at it as he could not tell what to say to it, for it so confounded people that few after was so rugged against us, for saying *thee* and *thou* to a single person, which before they was exceeding bad against us for, and in danger many times of our lives, and often beat for using those words to some proud men, who would say, 'Thou'st thou me, thou ill-bred clown?' as though their breeding lay in saying *you* to a singular, which was contrary to all their accidence and grammar, and all their teaching-books that they had taught and bred up youth by. But this *thou* and *thee* was a fearful cut to proud flesh and self-honour, though they would say and give that to God and Christ which they would not receive to themselves."

There is an interesting undated letter from Stubbs to Fox, which shows that Stubbs was chief author, and saw the book through the press. It breathes an unrestrained devotion to the Quaker apostle, then in prison, that sufficiently accounts for the over-emphasis laid on Fox's share in the work.[2]

[1] *Camb. Journ.* ii. 7, which simply says, "About this time the Book called the Battle-Door was given forth." In the *Ellwood Journ.* i. 513, the sentence is added, "John Stubbs and Benjamin Furly took great pains in the compiling of it, which I put them upon; and some things I added to it," and there is a parenthetical addition that the book was published "while I was prisoner in Lancaster Castle." It looks as though these changes were made to dissociate Fox from the primary responsibility for the form of the book. He had been severely criticized for having his name to it. See *J.F.H.S.* vi. 140-145, article by Mary G. Swift on "Geo. Fox's Knowledge of Hebrew."

[2] Devonshire House, Crosfield MSS. The words as far as "full of glory" are cut off the letter, but are restored from a copy inside the cover of the "Battle-Door" belonging to the Thompson Colln. at Dev. Ho. The letter contains interesting particulars as to the circulating of the book, and speaks of London Friends who had borne the cost of printing and were to be reimbursed out of the sales.

My dear everlasting אָב ['ab, *i.e.* Father] which my life exceedingly reverences, and when I enjoy thee it's unspeakable and full of glory, I have finished the book: these few words[1] which thou wrote with thy own hand to me, which was to put to the Battle-Door, Richard [Hubberthorne] neglected to give me them till the book was printed, yet I fear thy words as a natural child. I thought once to have writ them in, but I see it would be too tedious, and so I got them printed alone and pasted that bit to the latter end of the book, and set thy name to them. I have much labour about correcting the errors in the book: I have made an errata for some and the rest corrects with the pen, thou wilt see the book is well I hope. . . . I endeavour now to get them away to several parts in the nation, they have been much inquired after.

The Quaker manner of life, as remarked in a previous chapter, tended from the first to isolate the Quaker groups from the world round them, and to give to the members of these groups a special kind of corporate life. When Ellwood first went to a meeting in London, in the Restoration year, the mob were very abusive and mishandled Friends as they came out of meeting. But they left Ellwood alone, as being no Quaker, because he wore a large montero-cap of black velvet, the skirt of which was turned up in folds, beyond Quaker simplicity, "and this," says he, "put me out of conceit with my cap."[2] Even at a time when the message of Quakerism was being addressed to all men, and it had neither the aims nor the name of a sectarian Society, the community became a world apart, governed by its own laws of the kingdom of God, and unflinchingly nonconformist not only in doctrine but in life. A type of character was developed so strong, or rather so God-centred, that the men and women who possessed it could, in Fox's phrase, "shake all the country in their profession for ten miles round." They spoke and lived "with authority and not as the scribes." Dewsbury, as we have seen, awed the mob and the soldiers by his prayers; Fox again and

[1] In the Dev. Ho. and the Scalby Library copies which I have inspected the "bit" is pasted in at the end. It charges the Pope with first setting up in his pride the usage of saying *you* to one person.

[2] *Life* (1714 edn.), p. 79.

again showed himself one of those "men whose very look and voice carry the sentence of honour and shame"; Farnsworth, Howgill and Burrough, Audland and Camm went on confidently from victory to victory. Nor is this note of authority found only among the Publishers of Truth; it gave a singular influence to the personality of many less-gifted local leaders, up and down the land. When Walter Clement, of Olveston, was imprisoned at Gloucester in 1656, many in the city interested themselves in his behalf, being much troubled and offended at the persecution to which he was subjected: when Richard Davies, the Welshpool hatter, came before the High Sheriff, his behaviour was such that the High Sheriff continued loving to Friends all his life, and the townspeople accompanied Davies home, after he had been released, with great rejoicing. William Edmondson, the apostle of Quakerism in Ireland, had experiences such as the following. He is in an inn among some troopers, and says:[1]

> When I thee'd and thou'd them in our discourse they were very angry, and one of them swore, If I thou'd him again, he would cleave my head, but, in our discourse, when it came in its place, I thou'd him again, and he, starting up in anger, drew his sword, but one of his corporals sitting by him stopped him, and commanded him to put up his sword, for there should be no cleaving of heads there; [and] so caused the troopers to go to their quarters, but he stayed with me discoursing late in the night, and was convinced, being tender, received the truth and came to meetings.

John Roberts, of Siddington, incurred the anger of a justice, who called him "Sirrah" and feared to sleep in his bed lest Quaker fanatics should come and cut his throat; but when John was released from gaol he made it his first business to beard the justice at his house, found him tender, warned him of his wickedness, and so wrought on him that he said, "I am sorry I have done you wrong: I will never wrong you more," and so in much love they parted.

Such instances as the above could be easily multiplied.

[1] *Journal* (1715 edn.), p. 27.

A titled lady, whom Roberts insisted on bringing to a meeting at his house, at last, because of his importunity, ordered her coach and six to be got ready, saying, "John's like death, he'll not be denied." The Quaker would not be denied, his principles were held with an extraordinary tenacity, he stood not on a sandy foundation of notions but on a rock of experience, and, thus founded, the man was sure and steadfast. His fellowship with the truth outweighed all friendship with the world. As John Gratton wrote, when he came into contact with Friends a few years later,

> . . . these people were despised, persecuted and suffered deeply beyond others, for others could flee from sufferings and conform a little sometimes, but these abode and stood, though the winds blew and the rains fell and the floods beat upon them, for the Lord enabled them to stand and outstand it.[1]

Of this type of character, able to do all things through Christ strengthening him, we may take Isaac Penington as an example, especially as we know something of him and his wife in the intimacy of their private life. Born in 1616, he was the eldest son of Sir Isaac Penington, Lord Mayor in 1642 and 1643, representative of the city in the Long Parliament, one of Charles's judges, though declining to sign the death-warrant, and a member of the Council of State. The son might have said, like Paul, that after the straitest sect of his religion he had been brought up a Pharisee. He calls himself a man of sorrow and affliction from his childhood, and had been sedulous in the faithful practice of a sombre Puritanism. He became conscious, however, that the current religion, for the most part, was only talk compared with what the first disciples had felt, enjoyed, possessed, and lived in. This led him into a separation from the world's worship, and he associated with a gathered society—a group of Independents—from whom he received spiritual help, though they leant too much to the letter and form. Darkness, confusion, and scattering came upon them, and Penington himself was sorely broken and darkened.

[1] *Journal* (1779 edn.), p. 53.

"At that time," he says, "when I was broken and dashed to pieces in my religion, I was in a Congregational way, but soon after parted with them, yet in great love, relating to them how the hand of the Lord was upon me, and how I was smitten in the inward part of my religion, and could not now hold up an outward form of that which I inwardly wanted, having lost my God, my Christ, my faith, my knowledge, my life, my all."

He was now a Seeker, hearkening for any truth which might appear or break forth in others, but seldom meeting with anything which aroused the least answer in his heart. At last he met with some Quaker writings, which he cast a slight eye upon and disdained, as being too weak and poor; and when, some time after, he was thrown into the company of Friends, though their words reached to the life in his soul, and caused a great love to spring to them, yet his reason trampled them down as a silly, contemptible generation. Penington himself was an expert writer; in 1649 he gave a "Glimps of the Heart of Man . . . Drawn with a dark pencill by a dark hand in the midst of Darkness"; in 1650 he committed to the press "Severall Fresh Inward Openings"; in 1651 he treated of the "Life of a Christian," as a lamp kindled and lighted from the love of Christ, and discovering its source by the purity, integrity, and fervency of its love to others who were partakers in the same life; while in 1654, to name only one other of his pre-Quaker pamphlets, he published "Divine Essays," with a lamenting and pleading postscript. His pride of intellect and his culture would prejudice him against the formless Quaker writings and the plain Quaker Publishers of Truth; and it speaks strongly for the sincerity of character which belonged to Penington and his wife that they opened their hearts to truth in such uncouth guise.

One day, whilst walking in a park, husband and wife were stopped by a newly convinced Friend, who cried out against their gay clothes, and, in spite of their scoffing reply, drew them into discourse about the light and grace which had appeared to all men. The Friend was no match in argument with Isaac Penington, and sent two others better qualified, Thomas Curtis of Reading and William Simpson of Lancashire, who talked with the Peningtons on the following day, and, says Mary Penington, "their solid and weighty carriage struck a dread over me." Thomas Curtis had a message which went beyond all inquiry or objections, "He that will know my doctrine must do my commands." She saw that it was by removing what was contrary to God's will in her and by obeying His requirings that she could alone learn the way of truth, and during the next few months she addressed herself to this strait path of inward experience. In her high social position she was in great exercise, as she says,

. . . against the taking up the cross to the language and fashions, and customs, titles, honour and esteem in the world; and the place I stood outwardly in and my relations made it very hard: but, as I gave up out of reasoning or consulting how to provide for the flesh, I received strength, and so went to the meetings of those people I intended never to meddle with, and found them truly of the Lord. . . . I had heard the objection against them that they wrought not miracles, but I said they did great miracles in that they which were of the world and in fellowship with it came to turn from it. . . . Oh, the joy that filled my soul at the first meeting in our then habitation at Chalfont I have a fresh remembrance of, in the sense the Lord had given me to live to worship Him in that which was undoubtedly His own, and that I need put no stop to my spirit in it, but swim in the life and give up my whole strength to that which melted and overcame me that day.[1]

Meanwhile a similar work was going forward in Isaac

[1] I have already described Mary Penington's early experiences. See *ante*, p. 13, etc. The preceding paragraphs are taken from her *Experiences*, the first part of which was written by herself before 1668. They are of great religious value, and were first published in a summary form at Philadelphia, 1797, and in London, 1799. They were printed in full in London (1821) under the title, *Some Account of Circumstances in the Life of Mary Penington, from her Manuscript, left for her Family.* There is a useful reprint of this edition, 1911, Philadelphia, The Biddle Press; London, Headley Bros., under the title, *Experiences in the Life of Mary Penington.* It contains an introduction and notes by Norman Penney, including a bibliography. From this it appears that the extant MS. copies differ somewhat from the printed text, and we are told of an original MS., now lost sight of, "which lay concealed near forty years behind the wainscoting of a room at Wm. Penn's house at Worminghurst in Sussex." I have used a MS. copy in a book of letters, etc., 1662-1794 (Lloyd Colln.), belonging to me, as the text of this copy (made after 1778) is certainly rougher and more primitive than the printed text of 1821. A fresh collation of the extant MS. copies should be made the basis of any further edition.

Penington's case. At the end of January 1658 Hubberthorne had a General Meeting among Friends in Buckinghamshire, and says, "Isaac Penington and his wife grow in the knowledge of the truth: they were there and others of his family."[1] It is perhaps this meeting to which Penington refers when he tells us that words of truth from the Spirit of truth reached his heart and conscience, opening his state as in the presence of the Lord. He said in his heart, "This is He, this is He, there is no other: this is He whom I have waited for and sought after from my childhood, who was always near me, and had often begotten life in my heart, but I knew Him not distinctly, nor how to receive Him or dwell with Him."

Parker says that he first saw Penington at a meeting at Reading in 1656;* and William Penn places his attraction to Friends in 1657, when "it pleased the Lord to send him a Peter . . . and many Aquilas and Priscillas came after, who instructed him in the way of God more perfectly."[2] It was not, however, till the great General Meeting at John Crook's, in May 1658, that Penington became fully satisfied and publicly joined Friends,[3] and it was no doubt the powerful ministry of Fox himself which completed his convincement.

He had at once to face the bitter hostility of his father and friends. The question of hat-honour bred hard feelings, and his father wrote that he no longer had any comfort in him, to which he replied by urging him to pierce into the nature of things and not to set up shadows instead of the truth.[4] The whole course of Isaac Penington's spiritual quest illustrated this advice—with him there had been a noble spirit of inquiry which through mourning and darkness desired truth and never swerved from the search. It was fitting that so great a seeking should have been crowned with a great finding, not indeed

[1] To Margt. Fell, London, 2nd Feby. 1658, Jas. Bowden's copy at Dev. Ho., from Wm. Caton Colln.

[2] Testimonies of Parker and Penn prefixed to Penington's *Works*.

[3] Testimony of Parker.

[4] *Memoirs of the Life of Isaac Penington*, by J. Gurney Bevan, 1830, pp. 49-53, a book which may still be consulted with profit.

of outward ease or success, but of inward blessing. We may describe it in Penington's own glowing words, in a passage which gives classic expression to the central Quaker experience. To understand it we must remember that by "seed" he meant a part of God's nature,* capable of growth, which was brought into the heart of man.

Some may desire to know what I have at last met with. I answer, "I have met with the seed." Understand that word, and thou wilt be satisfied, and inquire no further. I have met with my God, I have met with my Saviour, and He hath not been present with me, without His salvation, but I have felt the healings drop upon my soul from under His wings. I have met with the true knowledge, the knowledge of life, the living knowledge, the knowledge which is life; and this hath had the true virtue in it, which my soul hath rejoiced in, in the presence of the Lord. I have met with the seed's Father, and in the seed I have felt Him my Father, there I have read His nature, His love, His compassions, His tenderness, which have melted, overcome and changed my heart before Him. I have met with the seed's faith, which hath done and doth that which the faith of man can never do. I have met with the true birth, with the birth which is heir of the kingdom and inherits the kingdom. I have met with the true spirit of prayer and supplication, wherein the Lord is prevailed with, and which draws from Him whatever the condition needs, the soul always looking up to Him in the will and in the time and way which is acceptable with Him. What shall I say? I have met with the true peace, the true righteousness, the true holiness, the true rest of the soul, the everlasting habitation which the redeemed dwell in. And I know all these to be true in Him that is true, and am capable of no doubt, dispute or reasoning in my mind about them, it abiding there where it hath received the full assurance and satisfaction And also I know very well and distinctly in spirit where the doubts and disputes are, and where the certainty and full assurance is, and, in the tender mercy of the Lord, am preserved out of the one, and in the other.[1]

In these deeps of spiritual experience Penington found sure anchorage for his storm-tossed soul.

[1] This passage, with much else of the preceding account, is from a paper dated Aylesbury, 15th May 1667, given in Ellwood's testimony prefixed to Penington's *Works*. For other autobiographical data, see Bevan's *Memoirs*, pp. 21-32. Maria Webb's *Penns and Peningtons* tells the story of the two connected families in an attractive way.*

He soon made use of his ready pen on behalf of the truth he had espoused, and commended the Quaker message to the world in a style more polished than had yet been used. He was himself both skilful and curious in pronunciation,[1] being evidently a man of taste, and with him may be said to begin the more adequate literary presentation of Quakerism which a few years later was to enlist the vigorous mind of Penn and the learning of Barclay. In 1658 he published "The Way of Life and Death Made manifest"; and in 1659 four considerable papers appeared, "The Scattered Sheep sought after," "Babylon the Great Described," "The Jew Outward, being a Glasse for the Professors of this Age," and "The Axe laid to the Root of the old corrupt-Tree." Ellwood also commenced author in 1660 with "An Alarm to the Priests," the only piece written by him for some years. Its origin, as stated in his *Life*, throws light on the genesis of much of the sharp polemical writing of the time. He says that he saw the horrible guilt of those deceitful priests who made a trade of preaching, and deliberately kept their hearers in darkness so that their own deeds might not be discovered.

> Against this practice of these false teachers, the zeal of the Lord had flamed in my breast for some time, and now the burden of the word of the Lord against them fell heavy upon me, with command to proclaim His controversy against them.[2]

He judged the service too heavy for his age and experience, but the burden continuing with still greater weight, he rose from his bed and, in the dread of the Lord, committed to writing that which was dictated to him to write. This done, though the sharpness of the message was distasteful to him, the peace of God filled his heart, and he felt it right to print. George Fox the younger saw the paper, and told Ellwood that it was the priests' portion and they must bear it.

Ellwood gives us glimpses into the Peningtons' home life:

[1] Ellwood's *Life*, 1714 edn. p. 201.
[2] *Ibid.* p. 77.

"We stayed dinner," he says, recounting his first visit to them before he had become a Quaker, "which was very handsome and lacked nothing to recommend it to me, but the want of mirth and pleasant discourse, which we could neither have with them, nor by reason of them with one another amongst ourselves,—the weightiness that was upon their spirits and countenances keeping down the lightness that would have been up in us. We stayed notwithstanding till the rest of the company took leave of them and then we also doing the same returned not greatly satisfied with our journey nor knowing what in particular to find fault with."

Of another visit, however, after his convincement, he says:

We spent much of the evening in retiredness of mind, our spirits being weightily gathered inward, so that not much discourse passed among us, neither they to me, nor I to them offered any occasion. Yet I had good satisfaction in that stillness, feeling my spirit drawn near to the Lord and to them therein.[1]

It would be a matter of great interest if we possessed for this first period of Quakerism still further detailed accounts of the lives of typical groups of Friends scattered over the country. But we know enough to see that the sense of fellowship was very close, making the times of meeting together occasions of deep spiritual refreshment and joy; we recognize the great importance to the community of the travelling "Publishers" who were continually moving about from place to place; we are aware of a spiritual dignity which enabled the Quaker to be himself, without pretence, in any company; we find warm domestic affection, but little softness and no frivolity; we may regret the neglect of art and of learning, but we feel stronger in our own manhood for the lives of these spiritual pioneers,—lives occupied with the faithful discharge of responsibilities, crowned with the happiness of work worthily done, fierce in their witness for truth, but tender in love to man, tested and purified in the fires of suffering and self-sacrifice, yet not without the abundant consolations of inward spiritual joy.

[1] *Life*, pp. 15, 43.

CHAPTER XX

QUAKERISM AT THE END OF 1660

Our work in the world is to hold forth the virtues of Him that hath called us; . . . to forget our country, our kindred, our father's house, and to live like persons of another country, of another kindred, of another family: not to do anything of ourselves and which is pleasing to the old nature: but all our words, all our conversation, yea, every thought in us is to become new. Whatever comes from us is to come from the new principle of life in us and to answer that in others; but we must not please the old nature at all in ourselves nor in any one else. . . . We are also to be witnesses for God and to propagate His life in the world, to be instruments in His hand to bring others out of death and captivity into true life and liberty. We are to fight against the powers of darkness everywhere, as the Lord calleth us forth. And this we are to do in His wisdom, according to His will, in His power and in His love, sweetness and meekness.—ISAAC PENINGTON, *Works*, 1784 edn. i. 91.

MANY of the developments in Quakerism which are of most significance to the student of Church history had not taken place by the year 1660.* The Quaker groups were already vividly conscious of their special fellowship with one another, but they still regarded themselves as a spiritual Israel within the nation rather than as a separated sect. Organization and Church discipline were as yet only in an incipient stage, and, as we have seen, the personal leadership of strong local Friends and of the itinerating Publishers of Truth was the main dominating and regulating influence. The pattern conduct of these leaders was still a thing of living example and inspiration and had not become a matter of orthodox tradition, as would be the case when the first generation of Friends began to pass away. A unique instrument for spiritual education was afforded by the meeting for worship. It was in these early years the most potent agent for what we should now call the "intensive" work of the Church, though not altogether free from the beginnings of formalism. Its effect in helping seeking hearts to conscious communion with God and in training the spiritual faculty and consolidating character may be judged from the beautiful letter of advice written by Alexander Parker in 1660:[1]

> The first that enters into the place of your meeting, be not careless, nor wander up and down either in body or mind, but innocently sit down in some place and turn in thy mind to the light, and wait upon God singly, as if none were present but the Lord, and here thou art strong. Then the next that comes in, let them in simplicity of heart sit down and turn in to the same light, and wait in the Spirit, and so all the rest coming in in the fear of the Lord sit down in pure stillness and silence of all flesh, and wait in the light. A few that are thus gathered by the arm of the Lord into the unity of the Spirit this is a sweet and precious meeting, where all meet with the Lord. . . . Those who are brought to a pure, still waiting upon God in the Spirit are come nearer to the Lord than words are . . . though not a word be spoken to the hearing of the outward ear. . . . In such a meeting, where the presence and power of God is felt, there will be an unwillingness to part asunder, being ready to say in yourselves, It is good to be here, and this is the end of all words and writings, to bring people to the eternal, living word.

Richard Davies, the Welshpool hatter, had his introduction to a Friends' meeting at Shrewsbury in 1657.[2] He went first to the house of John Millington, outside the town, where there was much brokenness of heart, though but few words. When Sunday came, there was a meeting at a place called the Wild Cop, which, though silent from words, was a time when the word of the Lord, says Davies, "was as a hammer and a fire, it was sharper than any two-edged sword, it pierced through our inward parts, it melted and brought us into tears, that there was scarcely a dry eye among us, the Lord's blessed power over-shadowed our meeting and I could have said, that God alone was Master of that assembly." William Britten, a Bristol Friend, formerly a national minister and then a Baptist preacher, published in 1660 a pamphlet

[1] *Letters of Early Friends*, p. 365.
[2] *Life*, edn. 1771, p. 34.

called "Silent Meeting, A Wonder to the World," in which he analyses with acuteness the value of silence as an aid to self-criticism and sound spiritual judgment.

> He is no true minister of Jesus Christ, but [he] who is led forth by His Spirit; and such we rejoice to hear declaring the things of God. Otherwise, upon meeting, we sit silent in the tongue, yet having a heart full of praises, where we worship God in Spirit and truth, who makes our bodies temples for the same Spirit, not speaking by hearsay and human arts, but lay all that down, when earthy thoughts, earthy words and earthy works are all laid aside and the temple within us is ready, the light of Christ shining in it, and the Lord with a further manifestation of His love enters it by His eternal power, whereupon we can truly say that the Lord's presence is amongst us, feeding His flock and making us feel the power of an endless life.

He then speaks of keeping spiritual watch, "If thou seekest to reap the pure benefit of silent meetings . . . silence all in thee that is evil, by that eternal power of God," and goes on to say, "When the work, word, or thought is thus stayed by the watch, then bring it to the spiritual touchstone, for trial whether it be good or no, for oftentimes Satan and flesh covers vices under the names of virtues. . . . Thirdly, use the spiritual scales to weigh, ponder or consider all things to be spoken or done, before they pass from thee." The illuminating and educational value of silent meetings lay in the high spiritual results that attended such processes of reflection and meditation, when the issues of right and wrong were weighed in the balance of the sanctuary. Where there was warm fellowship and an earnest seeking after truth, the meetings, alike in their silence and utterance, were times of refreshment and vision, in which Friends had rich communion with one another and with God. But the vacant and the indolent mind needed more of teaching ministry than was commonly found in them. The lack was not felt in the first days of power; indeed, the pioneer Publishers of Truth were men of such deep experience and full Bible knowledge that their addresses could not fail to contain much opening up of truth, even though they laid the stress of their message upon obedience to the Inward Light. But many of the utterances were deficient in positive teaching, and in this direction, as in some others, the Quaker meetings, with all their vitality, were already showing signs of the weaknesses which developed later.

Fox, as we have seen, as early as 1656,[1] warned Friends to "take heed of slothfulness and sleeping in your meetings, for in so doing ye will be bad examples to others and hurt yourselves and them."

Similar advice was given in another epistle of the year 1658,[2] which Fox directed to be read in all the meetings of Friends, and it was repeated in the Horsham document of May 1659. Dewsbury, early in 1660,[3] urges Friends to punctual attendance, not straggling in so that some come when others have been "pretty clear before the Lord to depart"; and Howgill, in 1659,[4] speaks of some who are careless and full and loathe the manna, the least part of which in times past would have been accepted by them. The right holding of meetings was an object of unceasing concern on the part of the leaders. We find much advice as to a worldly spirit and as to the dangers that arise from jangling and judging, and there is a good deal of caution against speaking out of the life. Dewsbury advises, with ripe spiritual wisdom,[5]

. . . when you meet, let your hearts in the light be single unto God, wait to receive His gift in the inspiring of His Spirit, that there be no eye one towards another . . . but all single to God . . . and when the Lord ministers in you any gift, watch that the true birth possess it . . . wait to make thy peace with thy brother, in feeling the word of reconciliation with God in Christ guiding thee to sacrifice upon the altar, and what gift soever thou receivest . . . whether praises, prophecy or exhortation, I am commanded of the God of heaven to lay it upon you that thou quench not His Spirit, but bring thy gift unto God's altar and, in the strength of His life in the light, sacrifice unto Him. So shall thy talent be increased and the babes shall be refreshed. And, dear people of God, be tender over the least breathings of God's Spirit in one another, and all wait to be clothed with a healing spirit.

---

[1] *Epistles*, No. 131.
[2] *Ibid.* No. 169.
[3] *Works*, p. 178.
[4] *Works* p. 172.
[5] *Works* p. 179.

The meetings of Friends were the best index of their vital strength, but it is a matter of some interest to inquire as to the number of adherents who had attached themselves to the new movement by the Restoration year. No accurate statistics are available, but the general imprisonment which followed the Fifth Monarchy rising in January 1661 affords some data for an estimate. About 4200 Friends appear to have been imprisoned in England and Wales, and, while in some cases all the adult men were taken, in several places where Friends were strong this was far from being the case. In Westmorland we hear of 132 imprisonments, but in Cumberland, where Friends were certainly as numerous, there were hardly any. Remembering that very few women were taken, and allowing for the considerable number of men Friends who escaped imprisonment, we may put the number of adult males at 6000 to 8000, and the total number of men, women, and children at from 30,000 to 40,000, out of a population of about five millions. This is confessedly only a rough estimate, and it must be remembered that there was not till much later any formal membership.[1]

Friends were drawn principally from the trading and yeoman classes, though there were also some artisans and labourers, a fair number of merchants, and a few gentry. When Margaret Fell wrote to the King about the Fifth Monarchy imprisonments, she pointed out the loss to the nation, "If you continue and go on to take so many thousands of poor husbands and tradesmen from their husbandry and callings, now in this season of the year when they should plough and sow their ground to maintain their families."[2] These classes supplied the main strength of Quakerism, and the movement, with its plainness of speech and dress, seemed a low and mean thing to persons of education or position. It won its way

[1] The imprisonments in most of the counties are given in Besse. *The Travels of Cosmo through England in 1669*, London, 1821, p. 449, estimates the number of Friends at the Restoration "at upwards of 60,000." I take the reference from Buckle's *Miscellaneous Works*, ii. 377.

[2] *Works*, p. 29.

because it brought to the simple-hearted a spiritual life, filled with sacrifice but filled also with the joy of the Lord, rich in fellowship with Him and with one another, a life whose passion was obedience to the light, whose secret strength overcame all oppression, while its integrity of conduct shamed prejudice and scorn, and whose reward was continually being found in the greatest of all prizes—fuller and more abundant life.

Eight crowded years separated the Restoration from the day when Fox saw from Pendle Hill the vision of a great people to be gathered, and in that time the young enthusiast had become the most powerful religious leader in England, and his spiritual discovery the glad experience of thousands. Truth, when first liberated, possesses a "nascent" energy, and finds elements waiting to combine with it. Accordingly the Apostolic Age of a religious movement is a period of unique interest, a year's swift current carries us as far as a decade of ordinary story. The atmosphere is fresh and life-giving; the persons who have drunk of the new truth have force to mould the world to their purpose; the soul of man, becoming responsive to the inspiring Spirit, springs into heroic being and masters every opposing circumstance. We look back on the first half-century of Christianity with the closest interest, as a time filled with the formative energy of the Holy Spirit, during which the Church gained its universal outlook and swiftly established itself in the great centres of the empire, while at the same time it was learning in the school of the soul's experience the full meaning of the Master's life. We centre study, in the same way, on other periods of spiritual illumination—the missionary era of Irish Christianity, the beginnings of the Franciscans, above all the Reformation—and find them aglow with a wonderful vitality, which marks them off from the days of tradition and institutional rigidity which quickly followed. The nine years of Quaker expansion included in the present volume are a corresponding epoch, which challenges and repays the minutest inquiry.

Let us endeavour to note some of the signs of this apostolic vitality. We mark first a curious counterpart to that spirit of Messianic expectation which prepared the way for Christianity. The swift response to the message of Fox was not only due to the young prophet's fervour and sincerity; it came because the message answered the expectations of the earnest spiritually-minded groups of Seekers, scattered over England, who, like Zacharias, were waiting for the Dayspring from on high to visit them. It was in this spirit that Burrough apostrophized the Northern Counties:

> O thou North of England, who art counted as desolate and barren, and reckoned the least of the nations, yet out of thee did the branch spring and the star arise which gives light unto all the regions round about: in thee the Son [sic] of Righteousness appeared with wounding and with healing . . . out of thee kings, princes, and prophets did come forth in the name and power of the most High, which uttered their voices as thunders and laid their swords on the necks of their enemies and never returned empty from the slaughter.[1]

We note in the second place the strange spiritual exaltation which accompanied the first preaching of Quakerism and reproduced some of the phenomena of the day of Pentecost. The Quakers, like the first Apostles, seemed to their contemporaries to be filled with new wine, men who turned the world upside down, and it must be admitted that the exuberance of their experience again and again betrayed them into excesses of conduct and errors of judgment. The Inward Light which possessed them shone through the medium of minds fallible and often ignorant, and was necessarily coloured with many of the fixed ideas which belonged to the Puritanism of the day. Howgill and Burrough, for example, show no more sympathetic understanding of the Irish and Scots and the Roman Catholics of the Continent than Cromwell himself. Their ideal England would have been as devoid of amusements and art as even the Barebone's Parliament could have wished. But the extravagances and prepos-

[1] *Works*, p. 66, from a paper written in 1655.

sessions of the early Friends should not blind us to the greatness of the new way of life which marked them off from the men round them. To the earnest-hearted Puritan a life of strict religion had meant exact obedience to a Divine law; to the Quaker it became the communion with a living Presence within his heart, so that the earthly life was felt to be a part of the larger eternal life. The dying utterances of many of the early Friends give expression to this intimacy with the Divine in the hour when the veil of flesh is wearing thin. We have already recorded the great words of John Camm:[1] we may refer here to the last sentences of two of the Boston martyrs. Leddra, in his parting letter to Friends, wrote in words of rhapsody, "The sweet influences of the morning-star, like a flood, distilling into my innocent habitation, hath so filled me with the joy of the Lord in the beauty of holiness that my spirit is as if it did not inhabit a tabernacle of clay, but is wholly swallowed up in the bosom of eternity from whence it had its being";[2] and Mary Dyer, as she was led to the gallows, in reply to a taunting question, said, "Yes, I have been in paradise several days."

Friends, in this dominating sense of the spiritual life within them, were able to hold lightly to earthly things, and to see them often in a true perspective. They were continually surprising those round them with the wisdom of heavenly-mindedness, that wisdom which the Lazarus of Browning's great poem possessed:

> He holds on firmly to some thread of life—
> (It is the life to lead perforcedly)
> Which runs across some vast distracting orb
> Of glory on either side that meagre thread,
> Which, conscious of, he must not enter yet—
> The spiritual life around the earthly life:
> The law of that is known to him as this,
> His heart and brain move there, his feet stay here.

Fox, in the spirit of the Hebrew prophets, made this wisdom his one test of right conduct, and applied it with

[1] *Ante*, p. 357.

[2] Besse, *Sufferings*, ii. 217.

courageous faith to mundane affairs. Take in illustration a paper of the year 1661, printed among his epistles to Friends,[1] called "The Line of Righteousness and Justice stretched forth over all Merchants, etc.," which begins:

All Friends everywhere, live in the seed of God, which is the righteousness itself and inherits the wisdom, and is the wisdom itself, with which wisdom ye may order, rule and govern all things which are under your hands . . . and all exchangings, merchandizings, husbandry.

Do what you do, he says, in the wisdom of God, and you will then hurt no one, nor yourselves, for it is pure and preserves pure. Do rightly, justly, truly, holily, equally to all people in all things, that is the word of the Lord to tradesmen, merchants, husbandmen, seamen alike, then the life itself will preach.

"And all," he goes on with sure practical insight, "keep out of debts, owe to no man anything but love. Go not beyond your estates, lest ye bring yourselves to trouble and cumber and a snare: keep low and down in all things ye act. For a man that would be great and goes beyond his estate, lifts himself up, runs into debt and lives highly of other men's means: he is a waster of other men's, and a destroyer: he is not serviceable to the creation, but a destroyer of the creation and creatures, and cumbereth himself and troubleth others and is lifted up—who would appear to be somebody, but being from the honest, the just and good, falls into the shame. Therefore dwell every one of you under your own vine (that know redemption from the earth) and seek not to be great but in that, and dwell in the truth, justice, righteousness and holiness, and there is the blessing enlarged."

He urges Friends not to trade beyond their capacity nor to reach after more than they can perform, for they will then cease to be masters of what they take in hand, and will be at the mercy of chance. They are to keep to their word and day, and to the just measure and weight which avoids all oppression, striving to be rich in the life and kingdom of the world that has no end, rather than coveting this world's riches. "Therefore," he says, "let him that buys or sells or possesses or uses this world be

[1] *Epistles*, No. 200.

as if he did not." The paper closes with two texts out of Proverbs, "He that walketh in his integrity is just, and blessed shall be his children after him"; "Unjust weights and unjust measures, both these are an abomination to the Lord."

The annals of Friends are full of cases which show how vitally conduct such as Fox enjoined was related to the central Quaker experience. Not only in matters of speech and dress but in business life the way of truth was often the way of the cross. Gilbert Latey, the London court-tailor, lost the greater part of his trade because he could no longer trick out his work with the trimmings that the vain world demanded; William Edmondson, the apostle of Quakerism in Ireland, found himself prevented "by a secret hand" from accepting a tempting business opening in Dublin, and from an easy evasion of customs duties, and a little later left shop-keeping and took a farm in order to bear his testimony against tithes; Robert Fowler, the Bridlington shipmaster, ventured his new ship and his own life for the perilous mission to New England.

This integrity of life is well illustrated in the case of Humphrey Bache, the London goldsmith at the Sign of the Snail in Tower Street. In May 1659, three years before his death,* he addressed a pamphlet of rare worth to the Rump Parliament, or, as he styled them, "the old long sitting Parliament who are yet left alive."[1] In this he urged on members the duty of making restitution for moneys corruptly obtained at the expense of the nation, and, as a persuasive to honesty, gave the story of his own spiritual conflict. At the beginning of the Civil War his trade had fallen off, and he had obtained employment under the Commonwealth, being at first engaged at three shillings a day as one of the overseers of the work on the city fortifications. Here he found that petty embezzlement, concealed in the wages sheets, was the practice, and, falling in with it, took about six pounds beyond his

[1] "A Few Words in True Love, etc.," recently reprinted by Jno. Bellows, Gloucester.

salary. After the work was finished, he obtained a place in the Excise at the Custom House, and, he says, "then as I stood in the counsel and dread of God, I stood firm as an iron pillar in the power of God . . . that I could slight the bottles of wine [that] was brought, and what was otherwise offered to ensnare, my heart being single." By degrees, however, he became corrupt like others, on the plea that as members of the Commonwealth he and his fellows had as much right to money as the Commissioners, who had many hundreds a year apiece for sitting some of them a few hours a day. His conscience, however, smote him for what he did; at one time he thought of confessing his unfaithfulness to the Commissioners, at another "to get the pillory set before the Exchange and there stand voluntarily with the money . . . taken unjustly," at another to declare the thing publicly at the Custom House, at noon, when many people would be there. He did in fact cease taking bribes, but his conscience still troubled him.

About this time the Quaker "young men out of the North" came to London, and he heard them several times. On one of these occasions Fox, Howgill, and Burrough were at the Bull and Mouth, and one of them spoke on taking up the cross. The carnal mind, he said, was enmity against God, and was to be crossed by the Light, the Power of God, which would break down the partition-wall of enmity, and bring an experience of reconciliation. This message came home to Bache, and the Light within showed him his unfaithfulness to his trust and made plain to him that though he had ceased to take bribes there was restitution still to be made, 'which truly then," he says, "was near if not full half I had in the outward, having a wife and five children to provide for and not freedom to keep my employment any longer, being convinced it was oppression—the excise then—an[d] no necessity of it, and that I ought not [to] be a servant to any in oppression." Fox came to his house and he opened his mind to him. The young Quaker leader told his host, "he that confesseth and forsaketh his sin shall find mercy." Bache saw that his heart was lifted up in prayer for him, and in this fellowship of spiritual exercise, to quote the words of the pamphlet,

. . . the Lord reached down His right arm of power and touched my heart with His grace and longsuffering and made me willing to submit to His will, deny myself and give up to the Commissioners for Excise the sum of money I received unjustly, which was made plain to me, waiting in the light, to be near one hundred and fifty pound, but it lay on my heart to restore more rather than less, and so I was made free by the power of the Lord and did give back at the Excise Office, London, one hundred and sixty pound.

He goes on to tell how he was brought by the same light to the use of the plain language and to cease to respect persons by putting off the hat, as well as to leave off selling rings and toys to proud and vain people. So, he concludes, "stand in the daily cross to your carnal minds, that iniquity may be rooted out of you by it, and you, through it, [may] be guided into equity."

The holy living required by the Light within involved in many cases either the abandonment or the transfiguration of the employments in which "Children of the Light" were engaged.[1] This comes out very clearly in the case of the army and navy. The army contained many men whose religious earnestness drew them to the Quakers, and the list of ex-soldiers who became Friends includes such names as those of Nayler, Dewsbury, Hubberthorne, Stubbs, John Whitehead, George Fox the younger, Ames, and Edmondson.[2] Many a time, as we have seen, the soldiers protected the Publishers of Truth of the new movement from the mob. But it did not prove possible for a Quaker to remain a soldier.* We have already told how the army in Ireland and Scotland was purged of Quakers, the authorities taking the initiative in the matter, though it is difficult to see how the Friends themselves

[1] Cp. the Durham letter, *ante*, p. 330.

[2] A complete list would be too long for insertion here. There were also a few who had been King's soldiers; Ames, for example, had served both the King and the Parliament.*

could have remained long in their regiments. At this time, however, the question whether a Friend could be a soldier was still in the experimental stage and the dismissals were regarded by the sufferers as pieces of persecution. Here again the stiffness of the Quaker on points of hat-honour and language was often the overt cause of offence, as the following respecting Captain Davenport shows:[1]

> My captain-lieutenant is much confirmed in his principles of quaking, making all the soldiers his equals, according to the Levellers' strain, that I dare say in [a] short time his principles in the army shall be the root of disobedience. My Lord, the whole world is governed by superiority and distance in relations and, when that's taken away, unavoidably anarchy is ushered in. The man is grown so besotted with his notions that one may as well speak to the walls as to him. . . . He hath been under my command almost fourteen years, and hitherto demeaned himself in good order, and many of these whimseys I have kept him from, but now there's no speaking to him, and I do profess I am afraid lest by the spreading of these humours the public suffer, for they [*i.e.* the Quakers] are a very uncertain generation to execute commands, and liberty with equality is so pleasing to ignorance that proselytes will be daily brought in . . . and when I think of the Levelling design that had like to have torn the army to pieces, it makes me more bold to give my opinion that these things be curbed in time.

In the navy the situation proved equally impossible. We hear of a master-gunner on the *Mermaid*, in 1656, who said that no power should command him to fire a gun whereby blood might be spilt, and was discharged as a Quaker or near thereto;[2] and of another gunner in 1657, on the *Assistance* frigate, who was surely a Quaker, for he excused himself for not using flattering titles and then asked for some other employment, so that, to quote his words,

> . . . I may be free to act against all deceit in whosoever it reigns, for I see most men, and especially those in the navy of most ranks and qualities, how they are corrupted and still they will

---

[1] Thurloe, *State Papers*, vi. 167 (Col. Daniel to Monck, 3rd April 1657).
[2] *Extracts from State Papers*, First Series, p. 14, no name given.

remain so till there be a seed of God springing up in them:—till that appeareth they cannot deal justly with God or man.[1]

But the most striking case is that of Thomas Lurting, of Stepney, "the fighting sailor turned peaceable Christian."[2] He served gallantly under Blake in 1657 at Santa Cruz, in the Canaries, when the treasure-galleons of Spain were burnt, and his narrative supplies some vivid details of the great fight. In the ship where he was boatswain there were a few who met together in silence as Quakers, whom he first beat and abused and then grew to love. An epidemic broke out on board, and over forty of the men died, but the Quakers took such care of one another when sick that they all recovered, which gave the captain a favourable opinion of them. When there was any fighting on hand he would say, "Thomas, take thy friends and do such or such a thing." They proved indeed the hardiest men in his ship, but refused to take any plunder. Being come to Leghorn, they were ordered to Barcelona to take a Spanish man-of-war. Lurting's ship opened fire on a castle, and Lurting occupied himself with one corner of the place, the guns of which had found the range of the vessel. He was on the forecastle watching the effect of his shot when it suddenly flashed through him, "What, if now thou killest a man?" Putting on his clothes, for he had been half-stripped, he walked on the deck as if he had not seen a gun fired, and when asked if he was wounded, said, "No, but under some scruple of conscience on the account of fighting," though at that time he did not know that Quakers refused to fight. That night he opened out his new convictions to his friends, who said little, except that, if the Lord sent them well home, they would never go to it again. Soon after, however, one of them went to the captain and asked to be discharged as he could fight no longer. The captain, a Baptist preacher, said he should put his sword through any man who

[1] *Extracts from State Papers*, First Series, p. 27. The writer, Richard Knowlman, was, I suppose, the Ratcliff Friend who, with others, was tried in 1670, immediately after the famous Penn and Meade trial. See Besse, *Sufferings*, i. 426-429.

[2] Tract under this title, published 1710, and frequently reprinted.

declined fighting in an engagement, and, after further words, beat the man sorely with his fist and cane. The time of trial came a little later when the ship was cruising off Leghorn and had cleared for action with a vessel bearing down on them, supposed to be a Spanish man-of-war. Lurting and his friends drew together on deck and refused to go to their quarters. The lieutenant, naturally enough, went to the captain and reported, "Yonder the Quakers are all together, and I do not know but they will mutiny, and one says he cannot fight." The captain, in a fury, dragged Lurting down to his quarters and drew his sword on him. Then the word of the Lord ran through Lurting, "The sword of the Lord is over him, and if he will have a sacrifice proffer it him." Thereupon he stepped towards the captain, fixing his eye with great seriousness on him, at which the captain changed countenance, turned himself about, called to his man to take away his sword, and went off. The ship they expected to fight proved to be a friendly Genoese, and before night the captain sent a message excusing his anger. On returning to England, Lurting took service in a merchantman, but on several occasions he was pressed into the navy, and his conscientious convictions were put to severe proof.*

The continued following of the Inward Light gave Friends a singularly clear judgment on great moral issues. Fox again and again showed a penetrative prophetic insight. At the beginning of his mission he had given a message—after the manner of John the Baptist—to many kinds of persons placed in positions of responsibility, exhorting each to do justly and to forsake oppression. A hundred and seventy years before the reforms of Romilly he had realized the savagery of the English criminal code: he saw the abuses that resulted from the power which the justices then possessed of fixing agricultural wages; he showed himself alive to the duties of slaveholders to their slaves; he denounced unsparingly the luxury of Londoners who were "gluttoned with the creatures."[1] In 1658 Fox wrote a "Warning to all the

[1] See *ante*, pp. 48-50, 495, 181.

Merchants in London and such as Buy and Sell, with an advisement to them to lay aside their superfluity and with it to nourish the Poor."[1] In this he proposed to the merchants that "out of their abundance they would lay a little aside, and have a place provided that all the poor, blind, lame cripples should be put into, and nurses set over them, and looked to, cherished, and seen unto that they do not want: and thus they that could work to work: and this would be a good savour of the city . . . that there should not be seen a beggar walk up and down the streets," but that they might be maintained with a little of the merchants' superfluous wealth. In the same piece he repeated advice as to fixed prices given in 1656,[2] "set no more upon the thing you sell or exchange than what you will have: is it not better and more ease to have done at a word than to ask double or more?" This advice was generally followed by Friends, and entitles them to a high place as pioneers in England of better methods of trading.

In another paper written in 1659[3] he discusses what we should now call the economics of luxury in answer to the question, "How must the poor live if we must not wear their lace, and gold and silver, and ribbons on our backs?" He answers, "Give them all that money which you bestow upon all that gorgeous attire and needless things to nourish them that they may live without making vanities . . . and through that you will live and they will live both." The votaries of luxury, he says, are madmen who destroy on their lusts "the Father's works and the prime of the creatures, which were given forth to be used . . . to the glory of the Creator." The same principle is applied to immoderate eating and drinking; the Quakers can only eat and drink to the glory of God, and "cannot have fellowship with the destroyers and marrers of the workmanship of God and the creation."

In thus identifying religion on the one hand with

[1] *Doctrinals*, pp. 127-130. [2] *Doctrinals*, p. 74. Cf. *ante*, pp. 152, 211.
[3] *Doctrinals*, pp. 157-163 (the first pages so numbered).

personal communion with God and on the other with a life of practical righteousness, Friends were closely associating themselves with the spirit of primitive Christianity and with the type of religion that we call prophetic and "charismatic," by contrast with the priestly and institutional type. The essence of prophecy lay in moral converse with Jehovah.[1] In this converse the prophet learnt the Divine will, and by declaring it to Israel kept alive spiritual intercourse between Jehovah and His people. It brought with it a wonderful illumination on moral issues:

> Ah! but the Word of the Lord is the birth of the soul,
> And it opens its eyes to the morning.[2]

The prophet lived in the strength of this word, and gained from it as his characteristic quality a keenness of vision which penetrated through the show of life to its inner significance, so that he became a SEER, who saw things with a sure knowledge of their true values. If the "word of Jehovah" were withdrawn he felt that the nation would be hopelessly undone. His ideal, as we see beyond question from several Old Testament passages, was a time when all would be prophets,—when "your sons and your daughters shall prophesy, your old men shall dream dreams, your young men shall see visions." It was this ideal which became the inheritance, not even yet fully entered into, of the Christian Church, and Peter regarded it as already in process of realization at Pentecost. "Such prophecy colours all the Apostolic Age and its notions of Divine grace, especially in relation to Christian ministry. To grasp this is to possess the true key to much in primitive Christianity which distinguishes it from later phases."[3]

Quakerism has always been distinctively "prophetic" in character. "The conception of the inwardness of the Kingdom faithfully interpreted, cut at the root of all the shams, all mere conventionalities, all religion by proxy, all unbrotherliness, all injustice, all artificial limitations. Inter-

[1] See W. Robertson Smith, *The Old Testament in the Jewish Church*, pp 283-308 (second edn.).

[2] R. H. Thomas, "The Prophet."

[3] J. Vernon Bartlet's "The Acts" in *Century Bible*, at Acts ii. 18.

preted with sincerity, it worked itself out into a practical gospel, a spiritual and social order transcending all contemporary ideals in its realization of lofty purity, and loving fellowship."[1] The first years of energy were accompanied by a series of acts inspired by the spirit and moulded upon the example of the Hebrew prophets. Messages couched in the phraseology of "Thus saith the Lord," dramatic signs, always earnest and often extravagant, vehement denunciations of false prophets and "hireling ministers"—all alike testified to the Word of the Lord burning within the lives of Friends. But when the sense of infallible Divine guidance somewhat abated, especially after the Nayler episode, and when the day of signs began to give place to less impulsive ways of preaching the kingdom, the essential prophetic elements of Quakerism still continued. The later years of the Commonwealth show only a partial disuse of the first fervent methods, for the pioneer work was still afoot and the universal mission of Friends was not yet greatly contracted. The leaders continued to thunder against the hireling ministers; indeed out of a hundred and thirty-five Friends who were prisoners in the autumn of 1658, thirty-five were sufferers for disturbing ministers. But we begin to hear less of the preaching of repentance through the streets and markets, though this was still done on occasion. With the development of a corporate consciousness on the part of the whole Quaker community there was inevitably a shifting in some degree of the responsibility for witness-bearing in these pronounced ways from the individual to the group, and this no doubt tended to control and to limit these manifestations of an eager spiritual activity. There was also a recognition that the universal message was only likely to take root in receptive soil, and that its wider promulgation was in the nature of a testimony to the world which should not be continually reiterated until it became a witness without power. But service of this kind could still be done under fresh spiritual guidance.

[1] J. Wilhelm Rowntree, *Essays and Addresses*, p. 101.

"If any," wrote Fox in 1658, "be moved to go to the steeple-houses or markets, or to reprove sin in the gate, or to exhort high or low or to reprove them, reason not with flesh and blood, nor quench the Spirit: and, when ye have done, in the same Spirit live, and then ye will have peace and rest and fellowship with God and one with another."[1]

The prophetic character of Quakerism is equally reflected in its early Church arrangements. Organization, at first, was entirely subordinate to the direct spiritual guidance which came to Friends as an inward experience, and was continuously influencing the whole body as it flowed along channels of personal friendship and inspiration from the local leaders and itinerating Publishers of Truth to the less spiritually sensitive. The new movement flourished by virtue of an inner seed of Divine life which brought forth blessed fruits of fellowship and righteousness.

"It was the special privilege of the prophets," says Prof. Sanday,[2] "that they were admitted to the inner counsels of God. And the way in which they were admitted to them was not that they beheld any visible writing upon the wall, but that 'impulses of deeper birth' came to them—impulses deeper and more searching than fall to the lot of common men. . . . The Spirit spoke to them by acting upon and through the inner faculties and processes of their being. And it is in the same manner and through the same channels that He speaks to us."

We find ourselves not in a region of dogma or tradition or external authority, but of the vital and vitalizing relations with God and with one another which filled the Quaker groups with radiant strength.

"Dear brethren and suffering members," wrote Dewsbury,[3] "glad your hearts in the unlimited power of God, that in His strength you reign over all the powers of darkness."

"Always feel a growing in the power of the Lord God that is universal and everlasting," urged Fox,[4] "that every one's lot may fall in the land of the living. . . . Oh the glory of the Lord spreads itself over all. And here as ye abide ye have the savour

[1] *Epistles*, No. 169.
[2] *Personality in Christ and in Ourselves* (1911), p. 46.
[3] *Works*, p. 188. [4] *Epistles*, No. 184, dated 1659.

and can taste your meat in the power of the Lord God, feeding upon every word . . . having your ear open and attentive to His voice: in this ye grow up in the life that is eternal."

"Dear hearts," said Nayler,[1] "it's by the arising of the Almighty we have unity and strength . . . how often doth He revive us with new life . . . and is more in our hearts many times than tongue can utter. And then He brings to a sight one of another, and then in what glory stands His beloved lambs in the eye one of another. . . . Thus doth the Lord often for us and lays us in His bosom together, and removes all evil far from us, and then shews us the spiritual relation that we are in in Him."

"Eye hath not seen, nor ear heard, neither hath entered into the heart of man," wrote Penington,[2] "how and what things God reveals to His children by His Spirit, when they wait upon Him in His pure fear, and worship and converse with Him in spirit; for then the fountain of the great deep is unsealed, and the everlasting springs surely give up the pure and living water."

A reliance on springs of life of this kind rather than on the authority of tradition or system is everywhere the commanding note of the prophetic as distinguished from the far commoner institutional type of religion. Thus in the Apostolic Age[3] the only authority in the Church was the will of Christ, its one Head, and that will, uttered through apostle or prophet, was absolute. The authority of the apostles was dependent entirely on the reality of their intercourse with Christ. But as men especially inspired by the spirit of their Master, they became naturally and necessarily the leaders of the Church, with a controlling influence that was felt in every part of its life.

"Unity and uniformity," says M'Giffert,[4] "were promoted by the itinerant apostles and prophets who were very numerous in the early church . . . [and] travelled from place to place imparting divine revelations and preaching the word of God. . . . Their utterances were listened to commonly as messages from God, and their influence in moulding the conceptions and the customs of the church at large was tremendous. It was very largely through them that unity was preserved between different

---

[1] *Works*, p. 733.
[2] *Works*, 1784 edn. iv. 60.
[3] See M'Giffert's *History of Christianity in the Apostolic Age*, pp. 636-672.
[4] *Ibid.* p. 640.

parts of Christendom, and that it was made possible for communities, even of the most widely sundered provinces, to develop with so striking uniformity. It would be impossible to exaggerate the significance of these travelling apostles, prophets and teachers. . . . It was recognized that they had the right to expect entertainment and support from those to whom they ministered. It was widely regarded indeed as their duty to depend wholly upon the hospitality of others, and to take nothing with them upon their journeys except the bare means of subsistence while going from place to place."

Such a passage might have been written, *mutatis mutandis*, of the early Friends. And when the historian goes on to enumerate other characteristics of the primitive prophetic age of the Church—the intercourse by means of epistles from leaders or from groups of disciples, the spiritual freedom which belonged to the religious meetings, the sedulous charity which cared for the brethren who were in need, the exercise by the whole community of the duty of judging spiritual gifts—we feel again the close parallelism between the spiritual experience of the first century and of the seventeenth. It is as though the early Friends were retraversing the life of the Apostolic Age, and working out under somewhat different conditions the same problems. Quaker history, with its wealth of trustworthy data, becomes, accordingly, a thing of singular interest, if only for the light it throws upon some of the obscure but profoundly important changes that turned prophetic into Catholic Christianity. For amid manifold flux and reflux Friends have maintained prophetic religion as the controlling force in their part of the Church, and have again and again resisted the encroachment of priestly elements. They have, indeed, passed through long periods of traditionalism and institutional rigidity and intellectual poverty, but the living voice of the Spirit has never been wholly silent among them. Their experiences afford much help, both in guidance and in warning, for the task which awaits the Christianity of the twentieth century—the task of transforming institutional religion into a Church of prophetic and apostolic type, whose privilege of intercourse with the living Spirit of

Christ shall be shared by the whole body of Christian men and women, and whose corporate life shall be a true fellowship of discipleship and service. We have too readily assumed that the first vitality attending a new spiritual movement is essentially fugitive and transitory. The wonder and glow of the fresh revelation cannot, indeed, be repeated, but the light itself may come with perennial power to successive generations of disciples, if only their hearts are open to receive it. To bring this about we need to maintain as the controlling forces of the Church the vital relations by which men live—worship, discipleship, fellowship ; we have to lay emphasis not on organization but on brotherly love, not on dogma but on illumination and education, not on official clergy but on the manifold social service for the kingdom of God which should exercise and develop the faculties of countless groups of disciples. In this great revitalizing of Christianity, which is already beginning, the Quaker faith may play a worthy part.

APPENDIX A

THE JOURNALS OF GEORGE FOX

THE *Journal* of George Fox was first printed, some three years after his death, in 1694, in a folio volume, and has been frequently reprinted. The eighth (bi-centenary) edition, published in two octavo volumes in 1891, is convenient for general use, but varies in many small respects from the text as first printed in 1694. My references, unless otherwise stated, are to this edition, but I have restored the 1694 text. In the *Journal* the account of Fox's death is prefaced by the following sentence:

> Thus, reader, hast thou had some account of the life and travels, labours, sufferings and manifold trials and exercises of this holy man of God, from his youth to almost the time of his death, of which himself kept a Journal, out of which the foregoing sheets were transcribed.

This statement, of course, is consistent with a good deal of editorial selection and revision having taken place; nor must it be supposed that the Journal kept by Fox was the only document made use of. It is the object of the present note to show the relation of the *Journal* printed in 1694 to these earlier sources, especially for the period covered by the present volume.

Fox, in a Testamentary paper dated 27th June 1685,[1] named a number of Friends to act as his literary executors, but we know that the principal work on the *Journal* was done on behalf of the "Morning Meeting" by Thos. Ellwood.

In April 1692 we have a minute of the Morning Meeting, which says:

> Two letters from Thomas Ellwood to Steven Crisp relating to dear George Fox's Journal giving an account: he hath transcribed about 200 sheets and hath spent more time in perusal and comparing than writing, by reason whereof he hath got no further than 1666, and desires to know whether he shall bring up what is done

[1] *Camb. Journ.* ii. 347.

now or at the Yearly Meeting [held in May]. The latter is agreed to because he cannot go forward, if he send them up. Steven Crisp is desired to answer him and request him to be here some days before the Yearly Meeting, and bring up with him by coach or otherwise the writings.

A year later Friends were growing impatient at the delay, and Ellwood writes as follows to John Field on 16th April 1693:[1]

I desire thee to acquaint the Friends that dear G. F.'s Journal is, I hope, well near transcribed; for though some years remain still to be digested, yet, being the latter part of his time, they will yield less matter than the former years have done. I am now in the year 1684, and am just bringing him over out of Holland, from his second and last voyage thither. I wish I could have despatched it with more expedition, but can assure Friends and thee I have not neglected it, nor been lazy at it. I have much other public business lying upon me and some private, which may not be wholly neglected, but the main of my time has been spent on this service. As to hastening it to the press, Friends may do as they please, but if I may take leave to offer my advice, I think it were well that the whole were deliberately and carefully read over again, before it be committed to the press; that nothing may be omitted fit to be inserted, nor anything inserted fit to be left out. I left above 200 sheets with W. Meade last summer, which I hope he has looked over since at more leisure than we did then. So that, if Friends be urgent to set the press to work, I dare engage, if God be pleased to give me life and health, it shall not want copy, when they shall be wrought off: yet in a work of this kind I would choose rather to answer expectation in exactness than speed.

In June 1693 the copy was in the hands of the Morning Meeting, who subjected it to careful revision, and its perusal by their committee was not completed till January 1694.

Up to 1676 the materials were ready to Ellwood's hands in the book which Fox calls in his Testamentary papers, "the Great Journal of my life, sufferings, travels and imprisonments." This Great Journal has happily been preserved, and is now the property of Robert Spence, of North Shields, who has generously loaned the MS. to the Reference Library at Devonshire House, where it has been transcribed for publication by the Syndics of the Cambridge University Press.* Their edition preserves all the orthographical and grammatical crudities of the original, and incorporates a number of illustrative documents. It is further enriched with a mass of notes drawn from the treasury of materials at Devonshire House by the Librarian,

[1] *Letters of Early Friends*, p. 213.

Norman Penney. It will be known, I hope, as the *Cambridge Journal*, in honour of the University which has thus made handsome amends for its rough treatment of Fox and other First Publishers of Truth.

The Great Journal, as originally paged, contained 411 pages, of which the first sixteen are missing, and except for a few pages at the beginning is in the writing of Thomas Lower, who was Fox's stepson-in-law, and his fellow-prisoner at Worcester in 1674. Soon after his release, Fox went to Swarthmore, staying there from June 1675 to the end of March 1677. The narrative portion ends with his arrival at Swarthmore, and this, together with other indications, makes it probable that we owe the Great Journal to the Worcester imprisonment, and to these two years of well-earned and sorely-needed rest. On revision by Fox, again with Lower's help, a number of additional pages of narrative were added, and many illustrative documents were inserted, swelling the book to some 940 pages. As thus completed, it seems to have been bound in a rough cover of millboard, and this, with some dilapidation through wear and tear, was its condition when it was rebound with loving care in 1881 by Robert Spence, grandfather of the present owner.

The loss of the first sixteen pages is greatly to be regretted, as we are left with the *Ellwood Journal* of 1694 as our sole authority for Fox's early life and experiences, and for most of his early work up to the beginning of the Derby imprisonment at the end of October 1650. It is clear that the *Cambridge Journal* contained some of this earlier narrative, as it refers to incidents there recorded,[1] and it would have been a great gain to our understanding of the man if this profoundly vital part of his autobiography had been preserved in an untouched form. The numbered pages which are lost from the beginning of the *Cambridge Journal* could not have contained much more than half of the contents of the *Ellwood Journal* for the same period, but, presumably, additional pages of narrative matter were added on revision, as is the case in other parts of the *Journal*.

It is difficult to say how far the *Journal* was first reduced to writing in 1674-1677, and how far it may be regarded as a compilation by Fox from earlier written sources. The opening sentence reads as follows:

That all may know the dealings of the Lord with me, and the various exercises, trials and troubles through which He led me, in order to prepare and fit me for the work unto which He had appointed

[1] *E.g.* the reference in 1655 to the saying of Stephens in *Journ.* i. 51; the reference in 1666 to Reckless, the Nottingham sheriff, of *Journ.* i. 44; the reference in 1662 to the Twycross incident of *Journ.* i. 49.

me, and may thereby be drawn to admire and glorify His infinite wisdom and goodness, I think fit, before I proceed to set forth my public travels in the service of Truth, briefly to mention how it was with me in my youth, and how the work of the Lord was begun and gradually carried on in me, even from my childhood.

This reads as though the early narrative was being written down from recollection mainly, and was on a somewhat different footing from the later narrative of public travels in the service of Truth, and we find a number of indications which support this view.[1] But a different impression is produced in much of the later narrative. Though the *Journal* is barren of precise dates, the sequence of events is often carefully and minutely stated, and where it can be checked *aliunde* is seldom inaccurate, and I have accordingly found it perfectly practicable to synchronize the narrative with the other available authorities, and to provide the *Journal* with an apparatus of dates for most of the period comprised in the present volume.[2] Moreover, the inserted documents which are found throughout the *Cambridge Journal* show a careful preservation of papers by Fox from the first, and we think of him, without difficulty, as a person who would keep by him memoranda respecting the passages of his life. There are periods, however, when the sequence of events becomes confused, especially during the autumn of 1658 and the year 1659.[3] His exercises of spirit were great at this date, and he may for the time have discontinued his memoranda.

Of these earlier materials a few traces remain in the *Cambridge Journal*. For example, in connection with the trial of Fox at the Lancaster quarter-sessions in October 1652, the *Cambridge Journal* has original notes of the trial (i. 63, 67), and a sheet of charges against Fox, and his answers (i. 68).[4] Fox's Testamentary papers speak of "little journals," some of which are extant for the American journey in 1671, 1672, but there is nothing of this kind for the Commonwealth period. We possess,

[1] The notes of time which connect one incident with another are generally vague; reflections and exhortations belonging to a later point of view are plentifully interspersed—*e.g. Ellwood Journ.* i. 10, 11, 13, 17, 18—and there are frequent retrospective phrases. I may instance the following: (i. 4) "one Pickering, a Baptist, and they were tender then"; (i. 18; cf. similar phrase, i. 19) "as the Lord opened them unto me in that day"; (i. 45) "many great and wonderful things were wrought by the heavenly power in those days"; and the reference (i. 49) to the great man at Twycross, "who afterwards was very loving to Friends and when I came to that town again both he and his wife came to see me"; a reference forward to the year 1662, see i. 536.

[2] See pp. 65, 116, 177-179, 200-202, 232-240, 323, 346-356, 438, 475, 476.

[3] See pp. 354-356. Cf. p. 438.

[4] Cf. account of Lancaster imprisonment in 1660 in *Camb. Journ.* i. 367, and Swarthm. Colln. iv. 39, which ends as a contemporary document might, "so this may go among Friends which is some part of the passages."

however, in the Library at Devonshire House, a remarkable document, commonly, though incorrectly, known as the "Short Journal," and so endorsed by Fox himself, which might more properly be called a book of his early sufferings. It begins with the following descriptive sentence:

George Fox, so called of the world, but the world knows neither him nor his name: here are some of his sufferings, that he hath suffered by the world and their professors, priests and teachers, for preaching the truth—Christ that never fell, nor will fall nor change, but ends all the changing figures and types and shadows in Adam in the fall, Christ that never fell, nor never will fall.

The main portion of the document ends with an account of his commitment to Lancaster in 1664, and adds, "and so I was sent to prison, where now I am with eight more." The narrative in this document is therefore some ten years earlier in date than the Great Journal, but on studying it we find that the sections common to the two documents are closely synoptic, though by no means identical. In illustration, take the parallel accounts of part of the Yorkshire journey in 1652:

"SHORT JOURNAL"	GREAT JOURNAL (*Camb. Journ.* i. 30)
And then I was moved towards the land's end in Holderness, and, as I went, I spake thorough	I passed alone, sometimes
the towns and by the seaside, and to people in the fields of the Day of the Lord that was coming upon all ungodliness and unrighteousness, and how that Christ was come to teach His people Himself, and as I was	by the seaside amongst people, and sometimes in the towns, declaring the Day of the Lord unto them and warning of them to repent.
preaching and speaking through a town called Patrington, and as I passed down the town I was moved to bid people to repent and fear the Lord and come off all their false teachers, for the Day of the Lord was coming upon all sin and wickedness, and the priest being in the town street and hearing me, and as I went down the street I spake to the people and some heard and others said that I was mad, and	And so I turned into a town towards night called Patrington, and as I was going along the town I warned the priest that was in the street and people to repent and turn to the Lord
it began to be dark, and I being thirsty I desired drink or milk	and it grew dark before I came to the end of the town, and a

and meat, and saying that I would pay them for it, and they would not, and then I passed out of the town, and some followed me, and asked me some questions about outward things, and I bade them fear the Lord, and prize their time, for I saw their question was tempting, and they left me, and so I passed on, and lay out all the night, and when the day brake I walked when I could see my way and passed towards a town, and in the way there came a man after me to the town, and raised the town and the constable upon me.

great deal of people gathered about me, and I declared the truth and the word of life to them, and after I went to an inn, and desired them to let me have a lodging and they would not, and desired them to let me have a little meat and milk and I would pay them for it but they would not. So I walked out of the town and a company of fellows followed me and asked me what news, and I bid them repent and fear the Lord. And after I was passed a pretty way out of town I came to another house and desired them to let me have a little meat and drink and lodging for my money, but they would not neither, but denied me. And I came to another house and desired the same, but they refused me also, and then it grew so dark that I could not see the highway, and I discovered a ditch and got a little water and refreshed myself, and got over the ditch and sat amongst the furze bushes, being weary with travelling, till it was day. And at break of day I got up and passed on in the fields, and there came a man with a great pike and went along with me to a town, and he raised the town, the constable and chief constable, before the sun was up.

It is evident from such a case as the above that Fox had a clear narrative of travel in his mind many years before the preparation of the Great Journal, and it seems most natural to regard this narrative as already resting on a written basis before 1664. The "Short Journal"* is defective in chronological sequence in some details, though the general arrangement of the sections follows the order of Fox's travels. It has the appearance of being an abridgment made for the purpose of bringing all his sufferings together.

The *Ellwood Journal* is, in the main, a very efficient piece of work. Fox himself had directed his literary executors to revise his writings—"There are many errors and mistakes in the printing and writing of some, which may be mended in the reading of them, and so I desire that all [my writings] may be looked up and carefully printed" (*Camb. Journ.* ii. 348).

We rejoice to-day in having an exact transcript of the Great Journal published in all its irregularity of grammar and spelling, but it was quite necessary that it should be originally printed in more presentable English. It was also natural that Ellwood or "the Morning Meeting"[1] should excise crudities and extravagances of expression, although these are now of singular help to us in giving a true picture of the Quaker community in its early days. The native greatness of Fox asserts itself convincingly through all the ruggedness of the Great Journal, and if there are touches of self-importance and some extravagant mystical language, we feel that they too, under the conditions of the age, were a natural part, such as we should expect to find, of his commanding personality.

[1] See article by Norman Penney on "Geo. Fox's Writings and the Morning Meeting," in *Friends' Quarterly Examiner*, 1902, p. 63.

APPENDIX B

SWARTHMORE DOCUMENTS

THE chief documentary source for early Quaker history consists of the collections of letters and other papers, at Devonshire House, known as the Swarthmore Papers. The main collection (vols. i.-vii.) contains about 1400 original documents, which seem to have been preserved with other similar papers at Swarthmore Hall till the sale of the estate in 1759. A very large number of them are endorsed in George Fox's handwriting, and have evidently been carefully looked through by him, and the Annals of travels and sufferings for the years 1655, 1656, and 1657, which are contained in the *Cambridge Journal*, ii. pp. 325-338, are almost entirely based on these letters. There can be little doubt that they are the historical material referred to by Fox in the Testamentary extract printed as a motto to the present history, and also described in the following further passages from his Testamentary directions:

All the passages of Friends and their travels from the beginning of the spreading of Truth, both in England, Scotland and Ireland and other places beyond the seas, I have them in manuscript among my papers, here at London and at Swarthmore and some of them it's like may be found in Robt. Widders' books of epistles and letters, and some of them may be found in a book that Elizabeth Bland hath of her mother's, and R[ichard] Richardson hath abundance of copies of my papers and letters of passages at the Chamber to beyond the seas, and in England and to the kings—some of them Mark took from me, and besides others that lie in the little drawer under the table: and all them that are mine must be joined to my epistles and papers, and the others which are history and passages [are] to be joined to them, which are to make a history of passages of the spreading of Truth, which will be a brave thing, and Thomas Lower hath many brave epistles and papers of mine, which may come in with the rest, and besides [there are] many epistles and papers which I writ in the counties and never kept copies of, which it's like they may easily be had out of their books from every Quarterly Meeting both in

England and Wales. All the passages of Friends and their travels which they have stitched up at Swarthmore may be gathered up to make a history of. G. ff.

I do order William and Sarah Meade and Thomas Lower to take care of all my books and epistles and papers that be at Benjamin Antrobus's and at R. R.'s Chamber, and those that come from Swarthmore, and my Journal of my life, and the passages and travels of Friends, and to take them all into their hands and all the overplus of them they may have and keep together as a library, when they have gathered them together which are to be printed. . . . G. ff.[1]

The papers which have thus been preserved by the historical instinct of Margaret Fell and George Fox fall into the following classification:

(1) Certain papers of special importance in connection with Fox himself were placed by him with the Great Journal, and are printed with it in the Cambridge edition (1911).
(2) About 200 other papers were handed down with the Great Journal, though never incorporated with it. They were bound up in a separate volume (Spence MSS. vol. iii.) by the late Robert Spence, and are principally letters and epistles by Margaret Fell, many of which are printed either fully or in summary in her *Works*. The volume is on loan at Devonshire House.
(3) Swarthmore Collection, vols. i., ii., iii., iv., containing letters from various Friends, chiefly to Margaret Fell or George Fox. These are at Devonshire House, and were transcribed for convenience of reference by Emily Jermyn, 1866-1869.
(4) Swarthmore Collection, vols. v., vi., formerly belonging to Robert Barclay, author of *The Inner Life of the Religious Societies of the Commonwealth*, and purchased for the Devonshire House Library in 1895. They consist largely of religious epistles, but include some documents of historical importance.
(5) Swarthmore Collection, vol. vii. (James Backhouse vol.), made up almost entirely of documents emanating from George Fox, many of them in his own handwriting, and purchased for the Devonshire House Library in 1907.
(6) A. R. B[arclay] Collection,* consisting of about 250 original letters of early Friends, so named because worked over

[1] Printed in *Camb. Journ.* ii. 349, 350. The directions were given in Oct. 1688. Richard Richardson was Recording Clerk to Friends in succession to Ellis Hookes, and Mark Swanner was a clerk in his office. Wm. Meade married Sarah Fell, and Thos. Lower married another of Margt. Fell's daughters, Mary.

by Abram Rawlinson Barclay for *Letters of Early Friends*. These letters are at Devonshire House, and are mostly addressed to Fox.

(7) Some outlying portions of the Swarthmore Papers are in private hands—belonging to Miss Emma C. Abraham, of Liverpool, a lineal descendant of Margaret Fell (Abraham MSS.); *Abraham Shackleton, of Dublin, another descendant of Margaret Fell (Shackleton MSS.); Wilfrid Grace, of Bristol, another descendant (Thirnbeck MSS.); and William F. Miller, of Winscombe, Somerset (Miller MSS.). The Crosfield MSS., presented to Devonshire House, per John Dymond Crosfield, of Liverpool, also include a number of documents which belong to the Swarthmore Papers.

Remembering the existence of this mass of contemporary correspondence, we are not surprised to find that the accounts of the Kendal Fund from June 1654 to Sept. 1657 include considerable sums for postages, and that there are frequent references to postages in the letters of the Kendal treasurers to Margaret Fell. I cite one dated 26th November 1654:[1]

DEAR SISTER—I read thy letter to be sent to our brother Christopher Atkinson and I am enclosing it to send away by the post, it being but newly comed in, long of the snow. And I have received two parcels of letters from our Friends, but truly the postmaster of London doth use much oppression upon us, for I have paid this evening about 4s. for as much as I have had [at other times] under 3s.: and truly the postman here doth but play upon us here: therefore I was moved to write to our Friends [in London] that they may send all by the carrier, unless it be something of concernment, for the carrier comes every week, and I shall have as much brought me for 2d. as I pay to post 2s. or 3s. for.

It would be a work worthy of the Friends' Historical Society to prepare a Calendar of the Swarthmore Collection,* and, for the purpose of the present history, I have had to do this in a rough way, and to revise the endorsed dates of many of the letters by internal evidence. I have been greatly helped in my work by a transcript of all the historical and biographical portions of vols. i.-iv. of the main Collection which has been made for me from Emily Jermyn's copy by Charles E. Gillett, of Whittington, near Worcester.

The best printed collection of Swarthmore documents is *Letters, etc., of Early Friends*, edited by Abram Rawlinson Barclay, 1841, which is especially rich in letters relating to

[1] Spence MSS. vol. iii. fol. 6.

London. It contains about 150 letters and other documents, largely from the Swarthmore Collection.

A. R. Barclay, in this book, and James Bowden, in his *History of Friends in America* (1850), make use of a Collection of letters (William Caton Colln.), now unfortunately lost,* which A. R. Barclay (p. 18 *n.*) thus describes:

This valuable Collection of early letters, written nearly throughout by William Caton himself, appears to have been intended by him for publication: it has a title-page, dated Swarthmore, 23rd of Sixth month [August] 1659, and a preface signed by himself, dated 7th of Second month [April] 1660; a facsimile of his signature to it is here subjoined.

Barclay prints, in whole or part, twenty-one letters from this Collection, and I have found among James Bowden's papers at Devonshire House copies by him of twenty-three others. A letter from James Backhouse, of York, to Thomas Thompson, of Liverpool, York, 24th 1st mo. 1831 (Dev. Ho., Gibson Bequest MSS. vol. iv.), shows that it then belonged to Thomas Thompson.

The value of this Collection appears from the draft preface, still preserved in the Swarthmore Collection, i. 84, written on the inner pages of a letter to Margaret Fell, London, 22nd June 1659, from A. P., presumably Alexander Parker. This draft preface shows that the book was prepared as a personal gift from Caton to Margaret Fell or some other close friend of the compiler. Caton had come from Holland to England at the end of July, and spent some weeks at Swarthmore, no doubt using A. P.'s letter as a piece of available paper on which to make his draft. The preface runs as follows:

AN EPISTLE TO THE READER

My Friend—The gross darkness which for a long season hath been as a covering for the nations is now expelling and expelled. . . . And therefore was I the more stirred up in my spirit to go about recording of those excellent writings and epistles which are included in the volume, which for the most part are furnished with very remarkable things which are indeed worthy of all acceptation. For, first, the spirit of the Father in all the authors of these epistles gives a very large testimony of the beloved M. F. of her wisdom and care, of her love and faithfulness, of her endowments and virtues etc., secondly, they give a true relation of the acceptation that they have found of the Truth and the opposition which they have met withal against the Truth, thirdly, they show how the Truth got entrance in many places at its first breakings forth, and how all sects combined against it, fourthly, they show how the brethren were moved to go into other nations and what entertainment they found in them, fifthly, they show how that one that was once eminent in the Truth [Jas. Nayler] was overtaken through the strong temptation of the wicked one : and he was through subtlety beguiled in others who declined from the Truth and became great opposers of the Truth, but, by the power of the Lord, in process of time, they were brought down and many of them regained to the Truth ; sixthly, they show and demonstrate many things which fell out and happened in the Church which may be of use even to succeeding generations.

I have laboured and endeavoured, so much as in me [lies] to set them in order ; I mean to record them as they were writ, but, through neglect of citing in what year it was dated, though the day of the month was there, yet in that particular I could not do them so exactly as I desired. Another thing which obstructed me from effecting my desires in the particular before mentioned was they came not all to my hand at once, so that when I had recorded some that had been writ in the year '57 or '58, peradventure there might some come to my hand that had been writ in the year '55 or '56. But however the time when they were writ and the occasion upon which they were writ is to be considered. And withal I thought good to abstract, as it were, the heads of the chief particulars in every epistle and to cite it in the margent, so that without reading the whole epistle over you may partly perceive the scope of it by the contents that I have abstracted out of it. And likewise I have judged it necessary and expedient to make a table for thy readier and better finding out of any of the men's epistles by showing thee at what page they begin ; so, by going to the same page in the book which is in the table, that may conduce thee to his epistles which thou desires to see. The perfecting of these things hath required some diligence, and without some industry they hath not been effected, but indeed it hath been so little tedious to me that I do wish thou could read and peruse them thorough with as little weariness as I have writ them over. Thou may think the volume is large and the epistles many for to be sent to one particular [individual] but, alas, there are many more that this volume could not contain, which peradventure in the Lord's time may in another volume be recorded. Farewell. By a servant of the Truth,

W. C.

ADDITIONAL NOTES

The following abbreviations, beside those mentioned on pp. xi and xii are used in the additional notes:

Ann. Cat. *The Annual Catalogue of George Fox's Papers*, ed. by H. J. Cadbury, 1939.
B.F.H.S(A). *Bulletin of Friends Historical Society (Association)*, begun 1906.
D.N.B. *Dictionary of National Biography.*
E.Q.L. *Early Quaker Letters from the Swarthmore MSS. to 1660*, ed. by Geoffrey F. Nuttall, 1952.
F.Q. *Friends' Quarterly*, begun 1947.
F.Q.E. *Friends' Quarterly Examiner*, 1867–1946.
Second Period. *The Second Period of Quakerism*, by W. C. Braithwaite, 1919 and later editions.

Further examples of local reports on the First Publishers of Truth have come to light and been published in volumes of *J.F.H.S.* as follows: Devonshire (xxvi), Lancashire (xxv, xxxi), London (xxxvi), Middlesex (xiii), Norwich (xviii), Staffordshire (v), Warwickshire (xxxi).

The original manuscript of A. R. Barclay's *Letters, etc. of Early Friends* (1841) is in Friends' Library, London. The work was reprinted in a much larger edition in *Friends Library* (Philadelphia, 1847), xi. 322–449.

PAGE 1

The Puritan Revolution. Since Braithwaite wrote this summary chapter on the religious situation in England from 1628 to 1660 the subject has received extensive study from many angles which bear upon the background of Quakerism. This study has been carried on not only in England but also in Germany and America, notably by Theodor Sippell of Marburg and by two Americans, Professors Roland H. Bainton and Winthrop S. Hudson, and their students.

These studies would provide elaboration and sometimes correction of this chapter, which, however, cannot be attempted here. The following comments can only call attention to some of the trends of recent research, and particularly to the noteworthy general books. Other bibliographical suggestions will be made in the sequel at appropriate places.

Beside other political features of the period the development of ideas of religious toleration is important. W. K. Jordan's *The Development of Religious Toleration in England* (4 vols., 1932–40) ends with the year 1660. It is historical rather than philosophical or theological. Not so Michael Freund's *Die Idee der Toleranz im England der grossen Revolution* (1927) or Johannes Kühn's *Toleranz und Offenbarung* (1923) with a section (pp. 238–270) on George Fox as well as Penn and Barclay.

The relation of economic and social ideas to the religious and political development has aroused much interest, as is shown by the intensive study of Gerrard Winstanley (*Works*, edited by G. H. Sabine, 1941) and the Diggers, and of John Lilburne and the Levellers. More general are W. Schenk's *The Concern for Social Justice in the Puritan Revolution* (1948) and R. B. Perry's *Puritanism and Democracy* (1944). It is hardly necessary to mention the classic general works of Max Weber, Ernst Troeltsch and R. H. Tawney.

To select the religious forebears of Quakerism is a more delicate problem. William Penn once selected as the books forerunning Friends' appearance that a young Quaker should read [J.] Saltmarsh, W. Dell, W. Erberry, [C.] Goad, [R.] Coppin and J. Webster (to Sir John Rodes, October 1693, *B.F.H.S.* iv. 35), while in his preface to Fox's *Journal* he refers especially to the Familists and Seekers as the forerunners of the Quakers. The first list corresponds very closely to the spiritual Puritans studied by J. C. Brauer (see the summary of his thesis in *Church History*, xix. 151–170). Both Sippell (*Zur Vorgeschichte des Quäkertums*, 1920, and *Werdendes Quäkertum*, 1937) and Rufus M. Jones recognize such English predecessors of Quakerism but link them closely with the continental mystics, and Braithwaite followed Rufus Jones. This position is in effect challenged by G. F. Nuttall in his important work on *The Holy Spirit in Puritan Faith and Experience* (1946). He shows how Quakerism is a natural extreme to the whole spectrum of English Puritan thought. The indigenous character of most Quaker phenomena is shown by the heresiographical literature just at mid-century, as in T. Edwards, *Gangraena* (1646–7; cf. A. N. Brayshaw in *J.F.H.S.* viii. 104–106).

Indeed even the British Baptists owe less to the Continental Anabaptists than has commonly been assumed. Their position is largely independent and even antithetical. They grew out of the English separatists. They also, like Friends, belong therefore in a Puritan context.

PAGE 5

Bocking in Essex. The Bocking congregation was not Anabaptist.

PAGE 12

John Smyth. Baptist historians today would dispute the association of English Baptists with Smyth, whom they repudiated. They also reject the view that traces the movement in England to the Anabaptists of the Continent. See for example W. S. Hudson, "Baptists Were Not Anabaptists," *The Chronicle*, xvi. 171–179.

full liberty of conscience. For the General Baptist plea for full liberty of conscience see D. Masson, *Life of John Milton*, iii. 102. But it is not quite true as stated in the text that they "rejected the Calvinist dogmas of original sin and predestination." They did reject the harsher features of hyper-Calvinism associated with the Synod of Dort.

PAGE 18

the less stable products of Puritanism. All the groups here mentioned and some others are described in a hundred pages by C. E. Whiting, *Studies in English Puritanism* (1931), chap. vi, "The Minor Sects." Valuable older works are those of C. Burrage, *The Early English Dissenters in the Light of Recent Research* (1912), and H. Weingarten, *Die Revolutionskirchen Englands* (1868). The same groups, along with Baptists and Quakers, are vividly but differently presented in W. Y. Tindall, *John Bunyan, Mechanick Preacher* (1934).

the Fifth Monarchy men. There is no more recent or fuller account than L. F. Brown, *The Political Activities of the Baptists and Fifth Monarchy Men in England During the Interregnum* (1912).

PAGE 20

Footnote 1. For other literature on the Muggletonians see *Second Period*, p. 244 *n*. 4.

PAGE 22

The Ranters. On the Ranters see Arnold Lloyd, *Notes and Queries*, cxc. 139–141; R. G. Schofield, *B.F.H.A.* xxxix. 63–73; and G. F. Nuttall, *Studies in Christian Enthusiasm*, ch. vi.

PAGE 23

the Family of Love. The term "family of love" is used in an untechnical sense in such passages as when Farnsworth writes to Nayler, addressing Friends generally, "to grow up in righteousness, and act in purity, and walk in humbleness before the Lord, and to be of the household of God, even of the family of love." (Balby, 6th July 1652. Swarthm. Colln. i. 372.)

PAGE 24

The channels through which they influenced George Fox. Most of the writings of Nicholas were early translated into English. In the list of Fox's books that were at his son-in-law's house a few years after Fox died is the folio edition of Henry Nicholas, *Glass of Righteousness* in Dutch or German (*J.F.H.S.* xxviii. 4). The fullest account of this group and of its relation to Friends is still A. C. Thomas, "The Family of Love, or the Familists, a Study in Church History," *Haverford College Studies*, No. 12, 1893, pp. 1–46.

Roger Brereley. Further discussion of the relation of Brereley and the Grindletonians to the Quakers will be found in R. M. Jones, *Mysticism and Democracy in the English Commonwealth*, pp. 79–84 and G. F. Nuttall, *The Holy Spirit in Puritan Faith and Experience*, Appendix I.

PAGE 25

Footnote 3. For a later chapter on the Seeker movement by the same author see his *Mysticism and Democracy in the English Commonwealth* (1932), pp. 58–104.

PAGE 28

The Founder of Quakerism. The right of Fox to this title of Founder has been challenged, and the parallelism of experience of his associates before they joined him, and of others who never became Friends, as outlined in the preceding chapter, indicates that the claims of originality, no matter how sincere, are due to Fox's feeling or that of his admirers. He was spokesman for a spontaneous movement which unconsciously rested on many precedents and predecessors.

It has even been claimed that his supremacy was deliberately promoted, first in the time of James Nayler who for his part seems to have had strong partisan admirers (see ch. xi), and then after Fox's death by his editors and the censorship of the Morning Meeting. As evidence for this view is cited the alleged suppression of some documents no longer extant. See W. S. Hudson, "A Suppressed Chapter in Quaker History," in *Journal of Religion*, xxiv. 108–118, with the reply of H. J. Cadbury (*ibid.* 201–213) and Hudson's rejoinder (*ibid.* 279–281).

George Fox. Among the more recent publications dealing centrally with Fox should be mentioned: Rachel Knight, *The Psychology of George Fox* (1923); R. H. King, *George Fox and the Light Within* (1940); and especially A. N. Brayshaw, *The Personality of George Fox* (ed. of 1933). H. J. Cadbury has edited the *Annual Catalogue of George Fox's Papers* (1939), and *George Fox's Book of Miracles* (1948).

Fenny Drayton. On Fenny Drayton see Jenkyn Edwards, *Fenny Drayton, its History and Legends* (1923). The monument there in commemoration of the birth of George Fox was erected in 1872.

PAGE 30

a just figure of his after ministry and service. For possible echoes of this experience in his writings see Brayshaw, *Personality of George Fox*, pp. 8–13.

Footnote 1. Brayshaw, *Personality of George Fox*, p. 29 *n.* 2, prefers Manchester. The name Gee is found to be not infrequent in the Mancetter (Warwickshire) parish registers of the period. See *J.F.H.S.* xxxi. 41.

PAGE 31

a voice spoke in his heart. In a lost writing Fox is quoted as dating and placing an experience, perhaps this one, on "the 8th of September, 1644 at a place called Atherstone Fair" (*Ann. Cat.* 1, 6, 2A). On Atherstone, cf. *post*, p. 53.

some income of his own. See Brayshaw, *Personality of George Fox*, pp. 29–31, on Fox's financial situation. It has been said that of sixteen references to money noted in Fox's

Journal "only one suggests that he was at all hard up; nearly all the others suggest exactly the reverse" (F. Aydelotte, *B.F.H.A.* xiii. 72).

PAGE 32

Footnote 1. T. E. Harvey on the "Young George Fox and Nathaniel Stephens," *F.Q.E.* 1946, pp. 69–78, gives a friendly picture of this priest. He also summarizes what is known of Fox's "relations." Cf. Matthews, *Calamy Revised,* p. 462.

Footnote 2. See *Second Period,* p. 427 *n.* 3, and Cadbury, *George Fox's Book of Miracles,* pp. 106–108.

PAGE 37

these times of conflict. With what follows compare Brayshaw, *The Personality of George Fox,* pp. 76–77, on "psychic experiences."

PAGE 40

Footnote 3. The reference for Henry More's comment has apparently some error. For Boehme's influence in England and on Quakerism see R. M. Jones, *Spiritual Reformers in the 16th and 17th Centuries,* pp. 208–234. See also W. Struck, *Der Einfluss Jakob Boehmes auf die englische Literatur des siebzehnten Jahrhunderts* (1936), and N. B. Thune, *The Behmenists and the Philadelphians: a Contribution to the Study of English Mysticism in the 17th and 18th Centuries* (Uppsala, 1948).

PAGE 41

Footnote 1. These identities of language between Fox and Boehme are treated as a mark of influence by R. M. Jones, *Spiritual Reformers,* pp. 221–227, but the phrase "the flaming sword" is used by several other Friends, and, after all, it is derived from Genesis iii. 24. Cf. Nuttall, *The Holy Spirit in Puritan Faith and Experience,* p. 16 *n.* 13.

PAGE 43

Footnote 8. The extract, partly quoted, *post,* p. 44 is printed in full in Emily Manners, *Elizabeth Hooton* (1914), p. 4.

PAGE 44

Footnote 2. Possibly George Fox himself is also mentioned by Thomas Edwards without name. Under date of 10th June

1646 he writes: "There is a shoemaker in Coventry or thereabouts, a famous preacher, who goes from Coventry and those parts up and down Gloucestershire, Warwickshire, Worcestershire, preaching and venting erroneous points of Antinomianism, Anabaptism, preaching against tithes, baptism of children. A minister of the City of London being in Gloucestershire heard him preach and heard of his large diocese and perambulations from place to place." (*F.Q.* i. 248.)

PAGE 46

Footnote 1. In this tract several of the company are mentioned by name.

Footnote 2. George Fox addressed a letter of warning and reproof to Rice Jones and his company from Lancaster Castle in 1660 (Swarthm. Colln. vii. 164). But *Journ.* i. 416 shows that they did not long survive the Restoration.

PAGE 52

Footnote 3. Cf. *J.F.H.S.* xix. 24.

PAGE 53

Gervase Bennett and Colonel Nathanael Barton. For Gervase Bennett of Snelston see note in *Camb. Journ.* i. 394; for Nathanael Barton, *ibid.* i. 397.

PAGE 55

Footnote 3. Fretwell died in 1685 (note in *Camb. Journ.* i. 394).

PAGE 56

they struck at his life. For the phrase "struck at my life" see Brayshaw, *Personality of George Fox*, p. 23 *n.* 2. At the time of the episode one of the three spires had been at least partly destroyed (*ibid.* p. 25 *n.* 1).

in his stockings. Fox makes no mention of stockings here. He does mention them later.

a thousand Christians had been martyred there. Fox is quite correct in saying that "the ancient records will testify how many of the Christian Britons suffered there," for many books beside Speed's *Chronicle* tell of the thousand martyrs at Lichfield under Diocletian who "lay cold in their streets." What really kept the tradition alive, if it did not create it, is the name itself which would be understood popularly to mean "field of corpses." For another suggestion, the fabulous Garendon Pool in Leicestershire, whose waters turned blood red, see *J.F.H.S.* xli. 86, 87.

PAGE 58

Footnote 1. There are two editions, but with the same title-page already containing the name Quaker. Braithwaite's interpretation of 1st January 1651 as 1652 New Style may be questioned, for the pamphlet (which is by Thomas Hall; see *D.N.B.*) was occasioned by a debate on 20th August 1650, and was answered 14th July 1651 by Wm. Hartley. It was given an imprimatur as of February 1651. If the date was 1st January 1651, New Style, it puts its printed reference to Quakers even earlier than Braithwaite supposed. Still earlier uses of the word in print or even in manuscript are not known to me. Examples of them when tested have proved erroneous. For this reason the one from the Clarendon MSS cited on p. 57 needs confirmation.

PAGE 60

Thomas Goodaire. For Thomas Goodaire see *Camb. Journ.* i. 399 *n.* He died in 1693.

PAGE 63

Footnote 1. That Nayler joined in London a Baptist conventicle which in turn also expelled him is stated by W. C. Abbott, *Writings and Speeches of Oliver Cromwell*, iv. 319.

PAGE 66

Footnote 3. On Fox's clothing see Brayshaw, *Personality of George Fox*, pp. 26–28, where there are references also to his long hair. To these may be added the remarks of Sewel's *History*, under 1656 and of C. Leslie, *Defence of...the Snake*, ii. 356: "George Fox had a mind to be a Nazirite like Samson and wore long straight hair like rat's tails, just as Muggleton did."

PAGE 67

bewitched people into following him. For charges of witchcraft against Fox and Friends see Index, *s.v.* "Witchcraft"; cf. Brayshaw, *Personality of George Fox*, pp. 68–70. Even John Bunyan took seriously such charges against Friends. See W. Y. Tindall, *John Bunyan, Mechanick Preacher*, pp. 221, 222.

PAGE 69

Justice Hotham. Probably Durand Hotham (1619–91). See *Short Journ.* p. 277. His religious readiness for the Quaker message is shown by his Life of Jacob Behmen (1654) and his preface to *Introduction to the Teutonic Philosophie,* this being his translation of his brother's *Ad Philosophiam Manuductio.* See R. M. Jones, *Spiritual Reformers in the 16th and 17th Centuries,* 1914, pp. 208–213.

PAGE 72

Footnote 1. The Quaker pamphlet to which *The Querers and Quakers Cause* was an answer is *Certain Quaeries and Anti-quaeries Concerning the Quakers (So Called) In and About Yorkshire* (London, 1653). This shows that it was in turn preceded by an Anti-Quaker tract printed at York, containing thirty queries of which No. 25 was: "Whether the men of Malton that burnt their goods because they might be abused by pride, had not better counsel even from Judas, to sell them and give their price to the poor, whereas the fire devoured their goods and charity?" I know no copy of the earliest pamphlet, but one copy each of two different editions of the next earliest. All three tracts were anonymous.

Footnote 4. In view of the July date of the letters in two preceding notes it is clear that this notable episode of burning ribbons at Malton belongs earlier than Thompson writing half a century afterwards recalls it. See E. E. Taylor, "The Great Revival in Malton, 1652" in *J.F.H.S.* xxxiii. 29–31. An attractive account of the earliest period of Quakerism in this section of the East Riding of Yorkshire is included in the paper by Arthur Rowntree on "Quakerism on Moor and Wold" in *J.F.H.S.* xxix. 1–28.

PAGE 77

Footnote 1. Nuttall, *E.Q.L.* No. 129, gives reasons to date this report in 1655.

PAGE 78

The People in White Raiment. The importance of this fortnight, emphasized on p. 86, has been widely accepted, though it might well be extended to a month and so include the visit to Swarthmore mentioned in the next chapter (cf. F. B. Tolles, *The Atlantic Community* (1952), p. 13). It led to naming the year 1952 a tercentenary of Quakerism, and to the pilgrimage held in the north that August, as well as the Friends' World Conference at Oxford and other celebrations elsewhere during the year. A geographical guide published at that time, *The Birthplace of Quakerism, A Handbook for the 1652 Country*, by E. V. Foulds, supplies attractive pictures and identifications of many Quaker homes and sites.

The selection of any date for the birth of Quakerism is arbitrary since the pre-existence of prepared groups, some of them just about Pendle Hill, was a factor in what happened in 1652 (R. M. Jones, "The Date to Commemorate," in *F.Q.* ii. 118–122). Moreover, the early Friends themselves used different dates. William Penn explicitly denied that their "visible beginning (or rather restoration)" was in Lancashire or in 1652 (*Works* (1726), ii. 89). George Fox assigns different dates to different areas. He wrote:

> The Truth sprang up first in Leicestershire in 1644, and in Warwickshire in 1645, and in Nottinghamshire in 1646, and in Derbyshire in 1647, and in the adjacent countries in 1648, '49 and '50, and in Yorkshire in 1651, and in Lancashire and Westmorland in 1652, and in Cumberland and Bishoprick and Northumberland in 1653, and in London and most parts of the nation and Scotland and Ireland in 1654. And in 1655 many went beyond seas where truth also sprang up, and in 1656 Truth broke forth in America and in many other places. (*Camb. Journ.* ii. 338. See H. J. Cadbury, "The Antiquity of the Quakers," *F.Q.* vii. 112–117.)

PAGE 79

Fox sounded forth the Day of the Lord. This phrase "sounded forth the Day of the Lord" occurs here in *Camb. Journ.* i. 40, but not in the Ellwood version. William Penn uses it in his reference to this occasion in his Preface to Ellwood's edition showing that he knew the Journal in unedited form. He wrongly places Pendle Hill in "the hither parts of Yorkshire"; it is in Lancashire.

PAGE 80

Footnote 1. For information on the preparation of Sedbergh separatists see *D.N.B. s.v.* "Giles Wigginton". For the later local situation see the manuscript at Friends House Library, London, "Then and Now. Early Friends' Homes round Sedbergh" by Geoffrey F. and Mary Nuttall.

PAGE 83

Footnote 2. According to Nuttall, *E.Q.L.* p. 52, Gervase Benson had two houses (still standing), Borrat, Sedbergh, and Haygarth near Cautley Crag. They have been confused in this note.

PAGE 84

Fox's Pulpit. A tablet commemorating this gathering on Firbank Fell has been erected near the spot, bearing the following inscription:

LET YOUR LIVES SPEAK

Here or near this rock George Fox preached to about one thousand seekers for three hours on Sunday June 13, 1652. Great power inspired his message and the meeting proved of first importance in gathering the Society of Friends known as Quakers. Many men and women convinced of the truth on this fell and in other parts of the northern counties went forth through the land and over the seas with the living word of the Lord enduring great hardships and winning multitudes to Christ.

PAGE 85

tobacco I did not take. On Fox and tobacco see *ante*, p. 31; *post*, p. 86; *Second Period*, p. 429.

unity with the creation. The phrase "unity with the creation" in Fox reflects his feeling, shared by Thomas Vaughan and by philosophical and theological thought of his time, that except for man, creation was still unfallen, and what God had made was still good. The phrase occurs elsewhere in his writings (Brayshaw, *The Personality of George Fox*, pp. 77–81), but is probably to be connected with his interest in herbs and in medicine, and his references to the first body, and to be interpreted in this broader contemporary context. See G. F. Nuttall, "'Unity with the Creation,' George Fox and the Hermetic Philosophy," *F.Q.* i. 134–143.

PAGE 92

Robert Widders. The correct spelling of the name is doubtless Widder, though throughout this volume the form Widders is employed.

PAGE 93

Footnote 1. A fuller account is given by Elisabeth Brockbank in *Richard Hubberthorne of Yealand: Yeoman—Soldier—Quaker, 1628–1662* (1929).

PAGE 95

the Westmorland Seekers. While the Westmorland Seekers are here emphasized as important for Quaker beginnings one does not know that they were more important than the Seekers elsewhere of whom we know less, for example, in Cumberland (as suggested frequently in *F.P.T.* for that county), and in north-west Lancashire.

PAGE 96

Footnote 2. Cf. a passage in Howgill's "Some Openings of the Womb of the Morning," *Works*, p. 396, which is used by Zentgraff in *Colluvies Quackerorum* (1684), p. 10, in proof that the Quakers proceeded from the Seekers: "We are a great number who have travelled through many dry places and barren wildernesses," etc.

PAGE 97

the groat is there. For Howgill's use of "groat" in this reference to Luke xv. 8 as in sixteenth-century Bibles see *Second Period*, p. 559 *n.*

PAGE 98

Swarthmore. With this chapter may be compared now Isabel Ross, *Margaret Fell, Mother of Quakerism* (1949). "The First Publishers of Truth for Swarthmore," belatedly published in *J.F.H.S.* xxxi. 6–11, gives a full and independent account of the narrative of this chapter. Braithwaite explained in a manuscript note that he preferred the spelling Swarthmore to Swarthmoor (used by Webb, Penney and others) "as being truer to the pronunciation, which lays the stress of the voice on the first syllable and clips the second."

To the quotations may be added the following descriptive account:

> In the same year 1652 in the Government of Oliver Cromwell, the word of the Lord came unto me, saying, Go thy ways to Swarthmore, where my lambs and babes and children of light will be gathered together to wait upon my name: I will feed them with the finest of the wheat, and with honey out of the rock; and with the dew of heaven I will refresh them, that they may grow as plants of my right hand planting, that above all the families of the earth I may rejoice to do them good.
>
> So I...went to Swarthmore, where I found the Lord's people gathered together, to wait upon his name, and the Lord was very good unto that family in feeding them with the dew of heaven, and with the sweet incomes of His love, according to His promise. Glory and honour and living eternal praises be given to the Lord God for evermore. Miles Halhead, *Sufferings and Passages* (1690), pp. 4, 5.

PAGE 99

where there was a great profession of religion. Ross, *Margaret Fell*, pp. 390, 391, refers to five accounts of these days at Swarthmore, three by Margaret Fell herself. From the *F.P.T.* account she concludes that the lecture day at Ulverston steeplehouse was on Thursday, 1st July 1652 and

Fox's first arrival at the Hall on the preceding Monday, 28th June.

another daughter. Margaret Fell's sister apparently married Matthew Richardson, J.P., of Dalton. He died in August 1677, and she outlived him. For many years she had not been in a capacity to deal with business but was the object of a commission of lunacy. See extended note by Norman Penney, the editor, in *The Household Account Book of Sarah Fell* (1920), pp. 543, 544.

Footnote 3. Ross, *op. cit.* pp. 387–389, discusses the tradition of descent from Anne Askew and leaves it as "unproven by any written records though traceable in oral family tradition."

PAGE 100

William Lampitt. For Wm. Lampitt see Nightingale, *The Ejected of 1662 in Cumberland and Westmorland*, especially i. 635, 636; Matthews, *Calamy Revised*, pp. 312, 313.

PAGE 102

George Fell. George Fell (1638–70) was at the time about thirteen. The only son of the family, he did not follow his mother and sisters into active Quaker membership, though he is mentioned with affection by them and their correspondents. His life away from home, his resentment at not possessing the Hall at Swarthmore at his father's death (1658), his marriage to a non-Friend (1660, Hannah Potter, widowed daughter of Edward Cook of London) were among the separative factors. See Norman Penney, "George Fell and the Story of Swarthmoor Hall," *J.F.H.S.* xxix. 51–61; xxx. 28–39; xxxi. 27–35. Cf. *ibid.* viii. 2 (his will); *post*, p. 462 *n.*

PAGE 104

he never identified himself with it. Braithwaite adds a manuscript note: "There is one important letter and two others from George Fox to Thomas Fell in Swarthm. Colln. vii. 73, 67, 74, from which it appears that they were not entirely in agreement at first; as was natural, T.F. had told Fox that he had come to Swarthmore contrary to T.F.'s mind."

PAGE 105

Footnote 1. On adulatory expressions written to or about Fox see Brayshaw, *Personality of George Fox*, p. 154 *n.* 1.

PAGE 107

A soldier. The name of the soldier is given as Leonard Pearson in *J.F.H.S.* xxxi. 8, where this and the following episode are rehearsed in very full detail.

a warrant against him. The warrant was based on signed allegations dated Lancaster, 5th October 1652. The copy of these in the Lancashire County Record Office was published with notes in *J.F.H.S.* xxxix. 15–17. Cf. *Ann. Cat.* 6, 167 A. For the rough draft—"this to be mended"—of Fox's answers to the priests' queries in *Saul's Errand* see Swarthm. Colln. vii. 55.

PAGE 112

Footnote 1. In the same letter Nayler refers to the visit from his wife which "was very serviceable and hath stopped many mouths, and hath convinced them of many lies they had raised....And I myself had great refreshment of her coming, for she came and returned with much freedom and great joy beyond what I in reason could expect, but I see she was sent of my Father and fitted by him not to be in the least a hinderer but a furtherer of his works" (quoted by Fogelklou, *James Nayler*, p. 91). He writes further:

"I see an hair cannot fall from our heads without his will, and he is tender over his, and he calls his to nothing but what is joy to them to suffer. Dear brother, I am here in peace and joy within, and at rest, though in the midst of the fire....I was made after their sessions to refuse their diet, and since to live upon bread and water. ...not that it is any bondage to me, within or without, for it is my liberty whereby the Lord hath set me above all other created things. Oh dear Friends, rejoice with me, for I see that to be taken out of all created things is perfect freedom." (Nuttall, *E.Q.L.* No. 21.)

Fox himself visited the Bishoprick later. See, with special reference to 1657, G. F. Nuttall, "George Fox and the rise of Quakerism in the Bishoprick," *The Durham University Journal*, xxxvi (1944), pp. 94–97.

Footnote 3. Cf. Nuttall, *E.Q.L.* No. 23. The letter is dated 9th May. On 18th May Thomas Taylor wrote to Fox, "Pearson, the justice of the peace, who was on the bench at the first trial of James Nayler and opposed, is much convinced of the Truth since" (*Ibid.* No. 24). See *ante*, p. 62.

PAGE 119

Footnote 3. To the list of M.P.'s favourable to Friends may be added Thomas French (Cambridge). See *Camb. Journ.* ii. 373.

PAGE 121

several places in Cumberland. Wigton and Abbeyholme were among the few Puritan centres. See *Second Period*, p. 353 *n.* 4.

PAGE 122

Footnote 3. There is now a fuller account in E. L. Evans, *Morgan Llwyd* (Liverpool, 1931), in Welsh, and E. L. Evans, art. [in English] "Morgan Llwyd and the Early Friends,' *F.Q.* viii. 48–57. There is also a paper respecting him, which is not quite accurate, in *F.Q.E.* 1919, pp. 23–25, by John E. Southall.

PAGE 123

Footnote 2. For notes on these letters see Nuttall, *E.Q.L.* Nos. 38, 39. On John Lawson see *Camb. Journ.* i. 409. According to "F.P.T. in Lancaster" (*J.F.H.S.* xxxi. 4) he was the first that received Fox there.

PAGE 127

Footnote 1. In accordance with Nuttall, *E.Q.L.* p. 72, the year of his death has been changed from 1657 (Besse) to 1658 (according to the burial registers of Cheshire and Staffordshire, Q.M.).

PAGE 132

Footnote 2. *Post*, p. 155. When enumerated they come to about 66, though Braithwaite admitted there must be a "doubtful margin." See E. E. Taylor, *The Valiant Sixty* (1947). The list is given there in ch. iii, which is based upon the same writer's Presidential Address, *J.F.H.S.* xix. 66–81.

PAGE 133

Footnote 2. See also Index, *s.v.* "Churches, speaking in." Cf. Brayshaw, *Personality of George Fox*, pp. 23, 24 *n.* 3; *Short Journ.* p. 284.

PAGE 139

Footnote 1. Many predecessors and contemporaries of Friends also coincided with their scruple against the non-numerical names, as is abundantly witnessed by their practice, as well as by occasional precept. Continental critics of Quakers noted their practice. See for example, article by H. J. Cadbury on "Heathen Names for Days of the Week and Month," *B.F.H.A.* xvii. 54–58.

PAGE 144

pre-Quaker entries. "1578. 31 Augt. Richard Lindley was baptized this day at Langton, son of Christopher" (*J.F.H.S.* iii. 89).

PAGE 145

the Society's Library at Devonshire House. This Library is now at Friends House, Euston Road. For its history see Anna Littleboy, *History of the Friends' Reference Library* (1920); also in *J.F.H.S.* xviii. 1–16, 66–80. The other copy of the indexes to the Quaker registers was deposited with the Quarterly Meeting involved.

PAGE 146

Footnote 2. This early paper on marriages is referred to in 1675 by Fox, *Epistles*, p. 359.

Footnote 5. Cf. Fox's *Concerning Marriage*, dated September 1659. Quaker marriages in secret were criticized (Swarthm. Colln. i. 214, George Taylor to Margaret Fell, 26th February 1655; cf. *J.F.H.S.* x. 18, 19). The refusal by Quakers to be married by a magistrate led to other difficulties (Swarthm. Colln. i. 357 and 358, Richard Hunter to Margaret Fell, Autumn 1656; cf. *J.F.H.S.* xliv. 80, 81).

PAGE 147

sometimes worked havoc in less stable characters. For an understanding account of the "occasional extravagances" of the early Friends see G. F. Nuttall, *Studies in Christian Enthusiasm: Illustrated from Early Quakerism* (1948). Cf. G. Huehns, *Antinomianism in English History* (1951), ch. ix.

PAGE 152

Footnote 2. On the practice of fixed prices see also *Second Period*, p. 560 *n.* 3; Brayshaw, *Personality of George Fox*, pp. 121–123, and *The Quakers* (1938), pp. 137–139. Fox's recurrent phrase for the practice is to be "at a word." Its technical character probably often escapes the modern reader.

PAGE 163

Thomas Symonds. According to the *F.P.T.* account for Norwich (*J.F.H.S.* xviii. 22–25) Symonds first came under the influence of Friends at Cambridge. With this record may be compared the account of his convincement in his *The Voyce of the Just Uttered* (1656). He is of course to be distinguished from Thomas Simmonds, the London printer, husband of Martha Simmonds.

PAGE 171

they mobbed Camm and Audland. In Bristol MSS, v. 80, is a letter from Audland and Camm to the Bristol magistrates claiming their right and freedom as freeborn Englishmen to be protected by the law.

PAGE 172

some change was perhaps made in the personnel of the garrison. Farmer, like other Bristol citizens, was anxious to get the garrison removed from the city, for other reasons as well as because of its sympathy with Friends. The city council wrote to London laying the blame for the increase of Quakers and for the riots on the continued presence of the military. The immediate result of the appeal was a mandate from Cromwell, 27th December 1654, to Governor Scrope to remove the garrison outside the city and to demolish the castle (Latimer, *Annals of Bristol in the Seventeenth Century*, p. 257). This removal and the resulting cessation of military support for the Quakers reduced the Bristol complaints. (Information from R. S. Mortimer.)

PAGE 173

Footnote 1. Audland writes with equal enthusiasm in September (letters to Howgill and Burrough in A.R.B. Colln. Nos. 157, 158).

PAGE 175

John Crook. On John Crook see H. G. Tibbutt, "John Crook, 1617–1699: a Bedfordshire Quaker" in *Publications of Bedfordshire Historical Record Society*, xxv. 110–128. Cf. *J.F.H.S.* xxiii. 57.

Footnote 7. At this point may be mentioned a collection of letters to William Dewsbury, many of them belonging to the period of 1655, and long preserved at York. They were published as *Letters to William Dewsbury and others*, edited by H. J. Cadbury, *J.F.H.S.* Suppl. No. 22, 1948.

PAGE 178

Footnote 1. These letters were reprinted in *J.F.H.S.* viii. 148–150.

PAGE 179

he was sent up to London. The *Weekly Intelligencer* of Tuesday and Wednesday, 27th and 28th February 1655 gives at this time another of the few early references to Quakerism in the newsbooks:

"This afternoon Fox, the great Quaker, who is said to be one of chief old ringleaders of them was at White-hall, he came out of Leicestershire. Some say he was sent up from thence and divers Quakers were at White-hall following him. They seem for the most part to be the perfect objects of humility and repentance, their aspect as demure as their Habit, so that if they be Lights they are like Lights in a dark Lantern, melancholy without but burning and shining within. The doctrine they profess do seem to answer the character." (British Museum Pamphlets, No. 636, cited by Brailsford, *A Quaker from Cromwell's Army*, p. 82.)

PAGE 181

Footnote 2. Thomas Aldam and others went to Henry Walker's house, but failed to get satisfaction, as reported in Aldam's *The Searching Out of the Deceit*, 1655.

PAGE 183

Footnote 1. For wrestling in Moorfields cf. Pepys's *Diary* (1661, etc.) in *J.F.H.S.* vii. 25, 26.

PAGE 184

Footnote 1. The recovery of the Wm. Caton Colln. shows that the date of the second letter was 30th April as Braithwaite supposed, but of the first letter March, not April as he had thought.

PAGE 185

we are told of a direction rather than of a locality. See also useful particulars by J. Hay Colligan in *J.F.H.S.* vi. 149.

PAGE 186

Footnote 3. Luke Howard, *Love and Truth* (1704), pp. 15 etc. gives some particulars, e.g. p. 16, "I found them eating a little bread and beer without anything to sweeten or relish it." Cf. *post*, p. 407.

Footnote 8. For John Lilburne's final Quaker period see L. V. Hodgkin, *The Shoemaker of Dover* (1943), pp. 44–52. There is a life of *John Lilburne, the Leveller; a Christian Democrat* (1947), by M. A. Gibb. A letter from him to Margaret Fell 27th May 1657 was in the Thirnbeck MSS (printed in *J.F.H.S.* ix. 53–59).

PAGE 195

Baxter on this occasion refused to be drawn into a dispute. For other written controversy between Farnsworth, Goodaire and Baxter see Nuttall, *E.Q.L.* No. 149.

PAGE 197

Footnote 1. Attention may be called to Nuttall's commentary on this letter in *E.Q.L.* No. 200.

Footnote 3. Berry's letter is reprinted in *J.F.H.S.* viii. 156. Cf. *post*, p. 449 and the biography by Sir James Berry and Stephen G. Lee, *A Cromwellian Major General. The Career of Colonel James Berry* (Oxford, 1938).

PAGE 198

Footnote 1. The paper on their tenets mentioned in this note is also in the Swarthm. Colln. vii. 66. See now also Nuttall, *E.Q.L.* Appendix: "The Manifestarian Controversy," pp. 293–297.

PAGE 199

Footnote 3. The untrustworthiness of these copies may be indicated by transcribing from the Wm. Caton Colln. p. 439 the actual wording of the passage quoted: "...this is a place of joy indeed and eternally doth my soul rejoice in the Lord: the rage of the enemies is great, but over their heads in peace and joy can I rejoice. My dear love is to thy family in the Truth. So I continue a prisoner in Banbury but eternal freedom I witness in the Lord."

PAGE 202

Footnote 1. There is a letter from Fox to Writer in Swarthm. Colln. vii. 16.

PAGE 204

in an enemy's land in these Western Counties. Besides the accounts in Besse and *F.P.T.* 20, there is a full narrative of the experiences of Fox and his companions in Cornwall at this time in the book *The West Answering to the North* (1657), which Fox in an unpublished history of Friends assigns to the authorship of George Bishop; see note in *Ann. Cat.* pp. 10, 11. The original manuscript of local sufferings, written by Thomas Lower, was published in 1928 under the title *Record of the Sufferings of the Quakers in Cornwall, 1655–1686.*

PAGE 206

Footnote 1. For this section and later references to Wales see T. Mardy Rees, *A History of the Quakers in Wales and their Migration to North America* (Carmarthen, 1925). See [Edward Bagshaw], *The Life and Death of Mr. Vavasor Powell*, 1671. No modern life of him has been published. See also R. T. Jones, "The Life, Work and Thought of Vavasor Powell", D. Phil. thesis, an unpublished MS deposited in the Bodleian Library, Oxford.

PAGE 214

Colonel Robert Phayre. On Robert Phayre see Firth and Davies, *The Regimental History of Cromwell's Army* (1940), pp. 654–657; Wm. Penn, *My Irish Journal 1669–1670* (ed. by I. Grubb, 1952), pp. 74, 75; *Journal of Cork Historical and Archaeological Society*, 1914.

PAGE 223

Footnote 3. This letter is noted by Nuttall, *E.Q.L.* No. 125 as "of interest as first letter extant from a Quaker in Ireland or anywhere overseas."

PAGE 227

Footnote 2. Elisabeth Brockbank, *Edward Burrough* (1949), makes no allusion to a visit by him to Scotland. In her *Richard Hubberthorne* (1929), p. 153, she gives two references to a visit to Scotland by Hubberthorne, probably later, but otherwise unconfirmed. G. B. Burnet, *The Story of Quakerism in Scotland 1650–1850* (1952), may be consulted (with caution) on pp. 226–231 of this volume. He includes Burrough with visitors to Scotland in 1654 (p. 66), some of whom were certainly later, and he arrives at the date 1650 in his title by including James Nayler's preaching there in the army before he was a Friend. See *ante*, p. 61. Of the "seventy" First Publishers of Truth he says "at least fifty invaded Scotland, the large majority before George Fox himself came north" (p. 15). Certainly Fox himself in his Annals (*Camb. Journ.* ii. 325–338) attributes a great many visits to Scotland to the years 1655–57.

Footnote 4. A full account of Caton's service in Scotland was in the Wm. Caton Colln. (*post*, p. 541), pp. 57–70, but of that collection pp. 51–66 are missing.

PAGE 232

Footnote 2. See also for the following *The West Answering to the North* (1657), and *Short Journ.* pp. 42–47 with notes. On William Salt see *Camb. Journ.* i. 436–437. His name was omitted in *Short Journ.* and in Ellwood, presumably because he joined later with John Perrot and other Separatists. George Bishop of Bristol, the author of *The West Answering to the North*, had written an account to Margaret Fell, 27th August 1656 (*Swarthm. Documents in America*, No. 7, edited by H. J. Cadbury, *J.F.H.S.* Suppl. No. 20, 1940).

PAGE 235

those who came to the prison and were convinced. For a delightful and informative account of this Cornwall group of Friends see L. V. Hodgkin, *A Quaker Saint of Cornwall, Loveday Hambly and Her Guests* (1927).

PAGE 236

Footnote 1. Braithwaite speaks of Norton's offer to become a prisoner in Fox's place as extraordinary, but elsewhere parallels are given, both individual and wholesale. See *post*, pp. 454–456.

Footnote 3. For Fox's own ascetic views of marriage see *Camb. Journ.* ii. 154. Other restrictions on Quakers marrying are mentioned *ante*, p. 146. Cf. M. R. Brailsford, *Quaker Women*, ch. vii, "Husband and Wife."

PAGE 240

Footnote 1. The date of Fox's release as 9th September seems to be fixed by an elaborate discussion by G. F. Nuttall in *F.Q.E.* 1946, pp. 117–121, in which he deals with "The Dating of George Fox's Journey from Launceston to London in the Autumn of 1656" (Besse, *Abstract*, i. 41, 42).

PAGE 241

Nayler's Fall. Two biographies of Nayler have appeared—written appropriately by women, since women had so much to do with his notoriety. They are Mabel R. Brailsford, *A Quaker from Cromwell's Army: James Nayler* (1927), and Emilia Fogelklou, *James Nayler, the Rebel Saint* (1931), translated from the Swedish *Kväkaren James Nayler* (1929). Both writers added new details and drew upon further sources. They have focused attention on the relation between Fox and Nayler. But the last word on the subject has not been said. Among the letters that have come to light dealing with the situation may be mentioned: Fox to Nayler, September 1656 (*J.F.H.S.* xxvii. 34, 35); Hubberthorne to Margaret Fell, Bristol, 4th October 1656 (*J.F.H.S.* xxvi. 13–15); M. T. and Roger Hebden to Dewsbury, 13th June 1657 (*J.F.H.S.* Suppl. No. 22, 1948, pp. 23–25). Cf. list in Fogelklou, pp. 313, 314. For the intervention of other Friends see Ross, *Margaret Fell* (1949), ch. viii, and Brockbank, *Richard Hubberthorne* (1929), ch. xi. G. F. Nuttall has contributed to an understanding of Nayler in the light of his times in his *Studies in Christian Enthusiasm* (1948), ch. v, and in his Presidential Address before the Friends' Historical Society in 1953, entitled *James Nayler: A Fresh Approach, J.F.H.S.* Suppl. No. 26.

The episode's wider implications that deserve further attention include the relation of spiritual guidance and authority (cf. Braithwaite, *Spiritual Guidance in the Experience of the Society of Friends* (1909)); the constitutional problem of the authority of Parliament and of Protector, and the episode's place in the history of religious freedom marking the refusal to use capital punishment in a case of acknowledged blasphemy. The interests and criteria of Friends at that time are not exactly those of our time. Beside the four matters listed on p. 267 there was the danger that the episode would precipitate legislation on blasphemy that would implicate all Quaker acceptance of the Inner Light.

PAGE 242

Footnote 5. "Ceiling" means wainscot or panel.

PAGE 243

Footnote 3. The presence of this letter of Lentulus among Nayler's followers was, he said, unknown to him. Although his critics made the most of it, it was the kind of apocryphon in which Friends were interested. See *post*, pp. 290–291 and 291 *n.* 2; cf. the article mentioned *post*, p. 568 bottom especially pp. 189–191. It was listed in the *Ann. Cat.* (67 H) along with other apocryphal writings found among Fox's papers (61 H to 73 H). This tract was evidently carried by Friends in their Bibles, as by Elizabeth Hooton at Cambridge, Massachusetts, in 1663 (Emily Manners, *Elizabeth* Hooton (1914), p. 43).

PAGE 244

visited Lincoln to compose a difference there. In November Farnsworth was in Lincolnshire composing further differences among Friends (Aldam MSS, quoted in *J.F.H.S.* xxv. p. 52).

PAGE 245

Nicholas Gannicliffe of Exeter. Nicholas Gannicliffe belonged, not to Exeter, but to Lawford's Gate near Bristol, according to note in Nuttall, *E.Q.L.* No. 300.

Footnote 2. The manuscript letter indicates that it was "to her," i.e. to Martha, that Nayler said little.

PAGE 247

a week later visited Exeter. It is now possible to date Fox's movements more exactly. He was released from Launceston on the 9th and arrived at Exeter only on the 20th and saw Nayler in prison. This was Saturday, the day before the Sunday mentioned in the text. The other interview with Nayler occurred on Tuesday, not Monday. See the article by Nuttall cited in additional note to p. 240 *n.* 1.

Footnote 3. The relevant passage is printed in *J.F.H.S.* xxxi. 49 and *George Fox's Book of Miracles*, p. 12. In the original this part of the letter has been heavily crossed out. Overleaf is a long passage in cipher, not yet decoded.

Footnote 4. Cf. Index, *s.v.* "Healing by Friends," and for Fox, Brayshaw, *Personality of George Fox* (1933), p. 90, and Appendix B, and H. J. Cadbury, *George Fox's Book of Miracles* (1947).

PAGE 248

it was my foot. That Fox in saying to Nayler "it was my foot" meant that Nayler should kiss his foot and not his hand is made plain by Robert Rich, *Hidden Things brought to Light*, p. 37, reporting to Fox what he had heard from Nayler "when I went with him from London to Bristol to receive his crucifixion there." Rich says "G.F....held forth thy

[G.F.'s] hand for him [J.N.] to kiss as a testimony of thy favour and of his obedience to thee, which he refusing to do, didst thou not immediately offer thy foot to him, saying, thou wert mistaken, it should have been thy foot and not thy hand?" (Information from manuscript note of Braithwaite.) Cf. *J.F.H.S.* xvii. 44.

Footnote 3. A copy of this letter in the handwriting of George Bishop is extant from the Swarthmore Collection (*J.F.H.S.* Suppl. No. 20; *Swarthm. Documents in America*, No. 8).

PAGE 249

Footnote 3. With Margaret Fell's letter to Nayler may be compared a letter that she wrote to Thos. Ayrey (Swarthm. Colln. vii. 98) who had evidently charged her with making a god of Fox. In general see "Messianic Language in Early Quakerism," an appendix in G. F. Nuttall, *The Holy Spirit in Puritan Faith and Experience*, pp. 181–184.

PAGE 252

a house that belonged to two of the Bristol Friends. The landlord of the White Hart was Nicholas Fox. There is no evidence that he was a Friend. It is perhaps significant that the party went to an inn rather than to a Friend's house.

PAGE 253

not one was concerned in Nayler's proceedings. Bishop, *op. cit.* p. 5, says that Bristol Friends "stood clear of either owning or visiting" Nayler and his associates. Farmer, however, says that "Wathin, a Quaking apothecary, and his wife brought supplies and comforts to them" (cf. Brailsford, *op. cit.* p. 122). John Wathen, apothecary shewed sympathy with imprisoned Friends later (Morford, *Cry of Oppression*, p. 11). There is no evidence that he was a Friend but his widow was. (Information from R. S. Mortimer.)

PAGE 255

Thomas Simmonds. That Thomas Simmonds was also imprisoned is stated by George Bishop in Swarthm. Colln. i. 188, as reported in Nuttall, *E.Q.L.* No. 326.

PAGE 264

Joshua Sprigge. Joshua Sprigge (1618–1684). For biographical details see Beesley's *History of Banbury* (1841), pp. 466–469, also *D.N.B.* For his similarity to Friends and the congeniality of his writings to them see *J.F.H.S.* xxxviii. 24–28, and xlv. 60–63.

PAGE 267

Rich rode by his side. Robert Rich had accompanied Nayler from London. It was during this journey that Nayler reported to Rich the rebuff Fox gave him in refusing to give him his hand to kiss but offering his foot to kiss instead. *Hidden Things Brought to Light*, p. 37 as *ante*, additional note pp. 565, 566.

and lay in the Old Bridewell. The records of Bridewell Hospital refer frequently to James Nayler's physical condition for the first year of his imprisonment, and to the restrictions put upon him. They are printed at length in *J.F.H.S.* xxiii. 25–31, 72–75.

Footnote 1. Richard Jones had been in jail in the previous year for saying that the mayor was a cavalier "more like a horse or an ass than a mayor"—words spoken before he became a Friend but remembered against him afterwards in spite of an apology in court (*Cry of Blood*, pp. 135–137). (Information from R. S. Mortimer.)

Footnote 3. The date of this letter should be given not as 1657 but as March 1658, as is done by Braithwaite himself, *post* pp. 270, 345 *n.* 1, 418 *n.* 1 and by Nuttall, *E.Q.L.* No. 435.

PAGE 269

Robert Crab. Robert Crab was, like Samuel Cater, from Littleport and died in 1656, presumably from the effects of an imprisonment (Besse, *Sufferings*, i. 86). (Information from J. J. Green per *Second Period*, p. 250.)

the London meetings were greatly disturbed by those who followed Nayler. The following note was added by Braithwaite himself to the first edition of the *Second Period*, p. 250: "Robert Rich, *Hidden Things brought to Light*, p. 13, gives the names of the women who disturbed London meetings as Mildred and Judah Crouch and Mary Powel." He added in manuscript that while a Mary Powell is mentioned in the *Middlesex County Records*, iv. 155; 33 Charles II, the more likely identification is "Mary Powell a spinster, domestic servant to Michael Stancliffe who was sentenced to transportation in 1665 (No. 93 in the list mentioned in *Second Period*, pp. 41, 42 *n.*) and died in prison." For a later reference to

Hannah Salter in Delaware, 1679–80, see R. M. Jones, *Quakers in the American Colonies*, p. 419 *n*. There is other reference to her as a resident or property owner in New Jersey. Regarding the name Judah, E. G. Withycombe, *Oxford Dictionary of English Christian Names, s.v.* "Jude", says Judah was used as a woman's name.

Footnote 7. Preceding the words of Hubberthorne summarized or quoted in the text he had written: "And as for J. N. he is in Bridewell and they will suffer few to see him, and then the women when they will not let them in to him, then they fall down and kneel before the wall" (Wm. Caton Colln. p. 375).

PAGE 275

Footnote 2. These famous words of Nayler may be completed by the addition cited from Robert Rich, *Hidden Things Brought to Light*, pp. 21, 22, as is done in *Second Period*, p. 609. Some minor variations occur in earlier printings of the words in pamphlets of Nayler's of 1664 and 1660. See *J.F.H.S.* xli. 3 and xlv. 46.

PAGE 286

his discussion in 1656 and 1657 with John Bunyan. On the Bunyan-Burrough controversy see also E. Brockbank, *Edward Burrough* (1949), pp. 104–111, and W. Y. Tindall, *John Bunyan, Mechanick Preacher* (1934), pp. 45–47. To Tindall we are indebted for recovering a forgotten episode belonging to Cambridge and 1659 in which John Bunyan became involved in an unsavoury charge against two Quakers of bewitching a woman and turning her into a mare (*op. cit.* Appendix). How the Quakers later returned good for evil in securing Bunyan's release in 1672 is not usually mentioned by his biographers. See *Second Period*, p. 85.

PAGE 291

Footnote 2. What the tract "Something concerning Agbarus" does not have in common with Samuel Fisher's work it shares with two pieces at the end of Fox and Burrough's *Great Mistery of the Great Whore* (1659), viz. "Several Scriptures Corrupted by the Translators" and "The Difference between the Old Translation and the New." See the article "Early Quakerism and Uncanonical Lore" by H. J. Cadbury in the *Harvard Theological Review*, xl. 177–204, especially pp. 183–188.

PAGE 297

Footnote 1. Cf. S. Allot, *Friends in Oxford, the History of a Quaker Meeting* (1952); A. M. Gummere, "Oxford and the Quakers", *Penna. Magazine*, xxiii, pp. 273–279.

PAGE 302

Footnote 3. Cf. Brayshaw, *The Personality of George Fox*, pp. 38, 39. For extant or lost holograph writings in Hebrew see *Annual Catalogue*, Nos. 79H to 80, 6H; cf. 12, 68F. A printed sheet of Fox's authorship is extant; see *B.F.H.A.* xxix. 104 (and illustration). Cf. H. J. Cadbury, "Hebraica and the Jews in Early Quaker Interest," an essay in *Children of Light* (ed. by H. H. Brinton, 1938), pp. 135–163; cf. *J.F.H.S.* xv. 31–32.

PAGE 303

The methods of printing and circulating books pursued by Friends. The printing of Friends' books began quite early. Richard Farnsworth wrote to Margaret Fell and others (Swarthm. Colln. iii. 43; cf. *E.Q.L.* p. 13) from Balby, on 2nd December 1652: "There was three hundred of them [books to be distributed] put in print, and Friends is made so bold that they go and reads them in the steeplehouse garths, after they [i.e. the priests] have done, and in the markets, on the cross, on the market-days, and some soldiers is made to go along with them, and stand by them whilst they are reading, and the priests is all on fire, their kingdom must down."

According to Joseph Smith's *Descriptive Catalogue of Friends' Books*, dated pieces occur as early as 1651, separate signed and dated tracts by George Fox in 1652, several each by Farnsworth and Nayler in 1653, and by Burrough, Dewsbury, Howgill and Hubberthorne in 1654.

In undated but early letters Farnsworth writes to Thomas Aldam: "The Truth doth spread much abroad by the books that is in print, and now there is as many written as is sufficient for the downfall of Antichrist's kingdom" (*J.F.H.S.* xix. 109); and Aldam in turn writes to Fox: "Dear brother, I have sent up other four books which my dear brother Richard Farnsworth did send to me. I have sent to London [to be printed]....They are books which will be very serviceable for weak Friends and convincing the world." (A.R.B. MSS, No. 71.) The statement in *D.N.B.* under Nayler that his tract *Spiritual Wickednesse*, and others which Margaret Fell dispatched on 18th February 1653 to her husband in London to be printed formed the first batch of Quaker tracts to be sent to press, is erroneous.

Giles Calvert. On Giles Calvert see *J.F.H.S.* viii. 148–150; xxxv. 45–49, the latter summarizing an unpublished M.A. Thesis at Columbia University (1937) by Altha E. Terry with a full check-list of Calvert imprints.

PAGE 305

Footnote 4. This pamphlet of 1844 was written by Nathan Kite for *The Friend* (Philadelphia (1843)), vol. xvi, from which it was reprinted. Later accounts of Quaker printers and booksellers include A. Littleboy, *History of the Friends Reference Library, with Notes on Early Printing and Printers* (1921); Charles M. Andrews, "The Quakers and their Printers in London" in his edition of *Jonathan Dickinson's Journal* (1945), pp. 209–229; R. S. Mortimer, *J.F.H.S.* xl. 37–49 and in the *Journal of Documentation*, iii. 107–125. Cf. *Second Period*, pp. 418, 419 *n.*

PAGE 307

This name is not met with till later. Not only was the term "Society of Friends" not used in the period covered by this and the following volume, the first occurrences of it have been traced back no farther than the year 1793. See T. E. Harvey, *Quaker Language*, p. 29; *J.F.H.S.* xxxii. 83; and *The Friend* (London), 1900, pp. 525–526. How appropriate it would have been is shown by the actual if accidental use of the term in 1652 by the Quaker forerunner, William Erbury: "Admission [in the formal churches] intimates the Church of Christ to be a corporation, as if there were a common council among them, whereas the Church is a free company or society of friends, who come together, not as called by an outward but freely chosing by the inward spirit" (*The Welsh Curate*, p. 8).

PAGE 314

Footnote 1. There is reference to the General Meeting in June 1660 at Horsham in *Ann. Cat.* 120D. See also under 1658 "a meeting appointed in Gloucestershire, Somersetshire, etc." (3, 71D) and "a General Meeting of Friends out of the several counties of Norfolk, Suffolk and Essex" (3, 72D).

PAGE 318

£5 was received. This £5 was repaid in 1659 to Strickland Head Friends on proof that it had been intended for their poor only (Kendal old Monthly Meeting book of accounts, No. 10).

PAGE 322

which continued till 1660. See also *Ann. Cat.* 5, 20F: "And so the National Meeting at Scalehouse about the Church's affairs did continue from 1657 to 1660."

PAGE 326

This collection produced £252 : 11 : 8. The Kendal Account Book, fols. 2–6, contains particulars of this collection as regards the counties, and also the items from each meeting in the case of Cumberland, Lancashire, Westmorland, Yorkshire (East and North Ridings) and Cheshire. The details given have considerable value.

PAGE 337

Footnote 2. Names of sixteen Friends are given.

PAGE 338

Footnote 2. Cf. *Second Period*, p. 217 *n.* 3.

PAGE 340

Footnote 3. For later developments of London meetings including this Two Weeks' Meeting see *Second Period*, p. 253 *n.*

PAGE 342

Footnote 1. On these women's meetings see *Second Period*, p. 272 and *n.*; A. Lloyd, *Quaker Social History*, p. 109; Cadbury, *George Fox's Book of Miracles*, pp. 46–47; Irene Edwards, "Women Friends of London", *J.F.H.S.* xlvii.

PAGE 345

Mary Howgill, a sister of Francis Howgill. That Mary Howgill was the sister of Francis engaged in publishing the truth is not certain. There was another Mary Howgill from Over Kellet, Lancs., not from Grayrigg. See Nuttall, *E.Q.L.* p. 64.

Ann Blaykling. There is a reference to Ann Blaykling in Bunyan, *A Vindication of Gospel Truths*: "And lest you should think that the Quakers are not such as condemned me and others for preaching according to the Scriptures...

your sister Ann Blackley...did bid me in the audience of many, 'To throw away the Scriptures,' to which I answered, 'No, for then the devil would be too hard for me'" (*J.F.H.S.* xvi. 112).

PAGE 346

Footnote 1. Richard Hubberthorne gives a still later reference to Ann Blaykling "who doth daily harden her heart" (letter to Fox, 7th April 1658, Swarthm. Colln. iv. 10).

PAGE 347

Tenby. For Tenby see Rev. James Phillips in *J.F.H.S.* vi. 185.

PAGE 352

Edward Byllinge. On Edward Byllinge see the essays by L. V. Holdsworth and John L. Nickalls in *Children of Light* (ed. by H. H. Brinton, 1938), pp. 85–132.

Footnote 2. The date should be corrected to 13 January 1658 New Style, as it is given *ante*, p. 229 *n.* 3. If (see Nuttall, *E.Q.L.* No. 425) Fox had already gone for England the sentence below, "Towards the end of February Fox rode South" needs correcting.

PAGE 355

he came to have ease and the light shined over all. His recovery is implied in the cheerful tone of a letter written at Reading 15th October 1659 (*Epistles*, 1698, p. 147).

PAGE 359

Footnote 1. The martial tone of this epistle of Burrough will surprise modern readers, as it disturbed Willem Sewel the Quaker historian. It is dealt with as one of two somewhat contradictory viewpoints in Burrough's thinking in M. E. Hirst, *The Quakers in Peace and War* (1923), pp. 118–120. Cf. Brockbank, *Edward Burrough* (1949), pp. 89–95.

Footnote 4. In 1658 Hubberthorne travelled to the west and twice to Kent, where he saw John Lilburne, who died soon after. Brockbank, *Richard Hubberthorne*, pp. 99–100.

PAGE 362

Nathaniel Cripps. Justice Nathaniel Cripps was having meetings in his house as early as August 1654; J. Audland to Fox 8th August (*J.F.H.S.* xvi. 135) and August 1655, Thomas Holme to George Fox (Swarthm. Colln. i. 197).

PAGE 363

Footnote 2. Dewsbury was moved to return from Scotland 9th October and was at Wakefield by 28th October 1659. See *Piety Promoted*, Part iv (Philadelphia, 1854 ed.), i. 340. If the year 1659 is correct this constitutes a second visit to Scotland. He reached Wakefield shortly before his wife's death. (MS note by W. C. Braithwaite.)

Footnote 3. These are printed in whole or in part in *J.F.H.S.* viii. 165–167.

PAGE 364

he was to plant the most important Quaker community in Scotland. See *Second Period*, p. 331 *n.* 1, where the statement that Dewsbury later planted the community of Aberdeen is corrected in detail.

PAGES 370–1

Kendal itself was an influential centre of Quakerism. Thirty-eight Friends, men and women, contributed to the purchase and walling of the Fellside burial ground at Kendal, acquired as early as 1656. See Kendal Book of Accounts, fol. 7.

Preston Patrick. On Quakerism in the district see Dilworth Abbatt, *Quaker Annals of Preston and the Fylde, 1653–1900* (1931); Elisabeth Brockbank, "The Story of Quakerism in the Lancaster District," *J.F.H.S.* xxxvi. 3–20.

PAGE 372

nine or ten years old. "Nine or ten years old" (Braithwaite) seems too young. The extant evidence as to her birth-date suggests either *c.* 1644 or *c.* 1647. See Friends' London Burial Registers 1719, and Ross, *Margaret Fell*, p. 408.

Footnote 4. The seven young women in the Swarthmore household must have presented a striking phenomenon. Alexander Parker, naming them all in a letter he wrote after the death of their father in 1658, added "seven sisters perfect." Wm. Caton Colln. p. 311.

PAGE 374

In South Lancashire there were several strong groups of Friends. On the origins and growth of Quakerism in Lancashire see B. Nightingale, *Early Stages of the Quaker Movement in Lancashire* (1921).

PAGE 375

Henry Woods of Tottington. Henry Woods of Tottington is said to have migrated to Pennsylvania with many other families (*J.F.H.S.* viii. 100).

Footnote 1. The address of Thomas Taylor's letter is torn but what writing remains suggests that it was to Richard Farnsworth rather than to Nayler. See Nuttall, *E.Q.L.* No. 127.

PAGE 376

Footnote 4. See *J.F.H.S.* ix. 62 *n.*

Footnote 7. John Giles died in prison 29th August 1662 (Besse, *Sufferings*, i. 389).

PAGE 377

Peel Meeting-House, which is still a centre of Quaker activity. Peel Meeting-House was destroyed by enemy action in 1940 and not replaced. For some years before that it was not "a centre of Quaker activity."

PAGE 383

William Allen. For William Allen see *J.F.H.S.* vi. 42.

PAGE 385

Devon and Cornwall had several groups of Friends. See R. Dymond, *Early Records of the Society of Friends in Devonshire* (1873). Beside the account of the Quaker mission in Cornwall (*F.P.T.* pp. 20–28), a very full itinerary is given by James Myers (April 1656, Swarthm. Colln. i. 360, with a precis in *E.Q.L.* No. 258).

PAGE 386

Footnote 5. For further particulars of John Anderdon (1624–1685) see *J.F.H.S.* viii. 17 *n.* Formerly secretary to Maj.-Gen. Hugh Desborough in the West of England, he died a prisoner at Ilchester on 20th March 1685, under sentence of praemunire, and was buried at Bridgwater.

PAGE 389

as we went along the streets. The quotation is from *F.P.T.* pp. 110, 111, written by John Edmonds, as the first person pronoun shows, and in the spelling of West Country pronunciation, here corrected. But "strengh" should be corrected to "string" rather than "strength." For the common charge that Quakers bewitched people by putting string or ribbons on their arms see Brayshaw, *Personality of George Fox*, p. 70 *n.*

PAGE 391

Footnote 3. For bibliography and press report see *Short Journ.* pp. 375–376; *George Fox's Book of Miracles*, pp. 13–15; Thos. Underhill, *Hell Broke Loose or a History of the Quakers* (1660), p. 34.

PAGE 394

Footnote 3. Cf. W. C. Braithwaite, *The First Planting of Quakerism in Oxfordshire* (1908).

PAGE 396

Luke Howard. See now L. V. Hodgkin, *The Shoemaker of Dover, Luke Howard, 1621–1699* (1943).

PAGE 397

Footnote 6. This letter is to be dated on internal evidence about July–August 1655. See Nuttall, *E.Q.L.* No. 168. For Ranters in Sussex see *Camb. Journ.* i. 184.

PAGE 401

the work in America. Singularly little has been published about the mission of Friends to America for the period covered by the present volume, to supplement or correct *The Quakers in the American Colonies*, in the forty years since that volume and this were first published.

Somewhat comparable to the sixty or seventy First Publishers in Great Britain is the list of sixty who went to America, 1656–63, two-thirds of them before 1661 (F. B. Tolles, *J.F.H.S.* Suppl. No. 24, *The Atlantic Community of Early Friends*, 1952, and "The Transatlantic Quaker Community in the Seventeenth Century," *Huntington Library Quarterly*, xiv. 239–258).

The American mission extended from Newfoundland (Hester Biddle) to Surinam (John Bowron) and was limited to British possessions, just as in Europe the Quaker success was limited to the Protestant-Puritan areas.

PAGE 405

the Continental work. For a summary of journeys to the Continent see *Quaker Missions to Europe and the Near East, 1655–1665*, by Bettina Laycock (1950), of which a typescript copy is in Friends' House Library.

PAGE 406

Holland. The early history of Quakerism in Holland has been given in great detail by William I. Hull in his series of volumes in Swarthmore College Monographs on Quaker History, especially the last two published, *The Rise of Quakerism in Amsterdam, 1655–1665* (1938), and *Benjamin Furly and Quakerism in Rotterdam* (1941). In the former are given biographies of Ames and Caton, and the letters referred to in the present volume from them and other early missionaries are quoted quite fully. Quaker theology is presented in its wider context in the Netherlands by C. B. Hylkema, *Reformateurs* (2 vols., 1900 and 1902).

Footnote 2. Fox, recording in 1676 one of his characteristic premonitions (cf. *ante*, pp. 78, 79), says of Holland "the Lord hath a great people to come out in those parts, which I saw in 1651" (*Epistles*, No. 337). Cf. *B.F.H.A.* xlvii, 30–34.

Footnote 3. In fact Atkinson was back from France in London before 14th October, according to a letter of that date from George Taylor and Thomas Willan to Margaret Fell (Swarthm. Colln. i. 209). Cf. Nuttall (*E.Q.L.* No. 88; cf. No. 81) who speaks of this "journey to France, the first taken abroad by Friends."

What may have been the earliest visit to Holland of a Friend is that by Jane Wilkinson. Little is known about it. Fox, who calls her Jane Willinson, dates it in 1654 (*Camb. Journ.* ii. 331) but the Kendal accounts have an entry under 1655: "Jane Wilkinson when she went for Holland—£2. 4. 0." See W. I. Hull, *The Rise of Quakerism in Amsterdam*, pp. 200, 201.

PAGE 407

Footnote 5. For his life see W. I. Hull, *Willem Sewel of Amsterdam, 1653–1720: the First Quaker Historian of Quakerism* (1933). Even some of Sewel's material on English Quakerism is first-hand, since he went in 1668 for a ten months' visit to Great Britain.

PAGES 408–9

Nayler's extravagances caused strange reports everywhere about Friends. On the lasting effects of the Nayler episode in Holland see the extended account of the anti-Quaker Dutch literature based upon it in Hull, *The Rise of Quakerism in*

Amsterdam, pp. 237–254. For similar effects in France, see E. Philips, *The Good Quaker in French Legend* (1932), Index, *s.v.* "Nayler"; in Germany, *Pantheon Anabaptisticum.*

PAGE 409

Footnote 5. The identification of the initials is accepted by Hull, *The Rise of Quakerism in Amsterdam,* p. 276, and Nuttall, *E.Q.L.* p. 309. In spite of the statement in *Camb. Journ.* ii. 468, that "no further account has been found of the visit of Anne Gargill to Portugal" a full summary of it was published in George Bishop's *New England Judged,* Part i, 1661 (ed. 1703, pp. 26–28). For her unruliness in Amsterdam in 1657 see Sewel, who says "how haughty she was, and continued I well remember still" (ed. 1722, p. 162). See also Hull, *op. cit.* pp. 272–278.

PAGE 413

a base was provided from which Protestant Europe could be reached. The general history of Quakerism in Germany is W. Hubben, *Die Quäker in der deutschen Vergangenheit* (1929).

PAGE 414

Footnote 6. For the history of the Griesheim Quakers from 1657 to their settlement in Pennsylvania in 1685–6, see W. I. Hull, *William Penn and the Dutch Quaker Migration to Pennsylvania* (1935), pp. 260–300. Cf. Hubben, *op. cit.* pp. 61–73.

PAGE 415

which will be noticed in a future volume. This mission of John Philley and William Moore to the East is summarized in *Second Period,* p. 216 *n.*

PAGE 416

began to find their way into Roman Catholic lands. Some earlier visits to the Continent than these mentioned by Braithwaite include one to France by George Bayly (1655, *Camb. Journ.* ii. 332; 1656, *ibid.* ii. 334; 1657, *ibid.* ii. 336) and one to France by Christopher Birkhead (1656, *Swarth. Doc. in America,* p. 22; Besse, *Sufferings,* ii. 395; 1657, *Camb. Journ.* ii. 336). But George Bayly's visits may be all one, owing to confusion of dates.

PAGE 417

Footnote 3. Referring to George Bayly's death in Rome, George Fox in an unpublished piece (*Ann. Cat.* "h") says "it was thought they poisoned him."

Footnote 6. Although endorsed by Fox as 1655, this letter should be dated (with Nuttall, *E.Q.L.* No. 563) as 1660, the year in which Harwood "run out." Cf. 54D in *Ann. Cat.* and *Camb. Journ.* ii. 336, where Harwood and Salt are said to have turned apostates from the Truth.

PAGE 423

in May or June 1658. M. R. Brailsford, *Quaker Women*, p. 125, notes that the visit of Mary Fisher to the Sultan must have taken place before 14th June, when the Vizier left Adrianople for Transylvania.

PAGE 425

Perrot. For a Jesuit account of John Perrot in Rome see *J.F.H.S.* xxxi. 37–38.

PAGE 426

Charles Bayly and Jane Stokes. Both Charles Bayly and Jane Stokes seem to have been imprisoned at Rome. See Perrot's letter in Sewel, i. 490, and the postscript to Fox's letter to Friends, London, 22nd August 1661 (Swarthm. Colln. vii. 111): "John Perrot and the young woman that was prisoner with him at Rome are here at this city."

Footnote 3. For fuller details of Perrot's return to England and of the schism associated with his name see *Second Period*, pp. 228–241.

PAGE 429

Prester John. The context in which Fox and others mention Prester John suggests that they shared the tradition of his residence in Asia which "still held sway among the more educated circles of the west." See I. Ross, *Margaret Fell*, pp. 86, 87.

PAGE 434

Relations with the State. The subject of this chapter is continued in *Second Period*, ch. xxi.

PAGE 438

saw Cromwell again. Anne Blaykling and Thomas Morford were other Friends who visited Cromwell this spring. See Swarthm. Colln. i. 161 and iv. 176 respectively.

PAGE 439

Footnote 2. One of Fox's papers of warning to Cromwell is in Swarthm. Colln. vii. 38. Cf. *Ann. Cat.* index *s.v.* Cromwell.

PAGE 440

Footnote 1. This address to Cromwell, signed "George Fox" and with the statement that it was delivered to him in 11th mo. 1657 (presumably January 1658) was printed in E. Burrough's *Good Counsel and Advice Rejected* (1659), pp. 26, 27. With this militant language may be compared that of the 1659 pamphlet *To the Councill of Officers of the Armie and the Heads of the Nation.* It is signed "F. G." and its authorship by Fox has been disputed. But the "F. G." is a not infrequent reversal of initials and the language of the tract resembles Fox's style. It was accepted as Fox's by John Pennyman, Francis Bugg and George Whitehead. Cf. M. R. Brailsford, *Contemporary Review*, Nov. 1915, republished in her *A Quaker from Cromwell's Army* (1927), pp. 23–25; M. E. Hirst, *J.F.H.S.* xv. 146–148, reprinted in her *Quakers in Peace and War* (1923), pp. 120–122; H. J. Cadbury, *B.F.H.A.* xiii. 75–82; xiv. 67, 68; R. M. Jones, *The Friend* (Philadelphia), cxvi. 346; G. F. Nuttall, *The Holy Spirit in Puritan Faith and Experience* (1946), p. 131 *n.* 8. It was included among Fox's writings in the manuscript *Annual Catalogue* (5, 95 E and 6, 130 A *pace* Hirst, p. 122).

PAGE 442

on a broadly representative basis. The novelties of the 1654 Parliament were that seats were redistributed so as to give most members to counties, elected *en bloc*, rather than to boroughs, and the franchise for counties was possession of an estate of the value of £200. In some respects this was a more restricted franchise than the old one. Also all were to be excluded who had acted against Parliament since 1st January, 1654.

PAGE 445

Footnote 2. The actual text of the Wm. Caton Colln. p. 177, now available, gives March as the date of this letter, reads in the third line quoted "almost scattered and broken and cast into prison by the Devil," and adds "many goes to G. F. Kings shall lay down their crowns before him and present their gifts to him."

PAGE 454

Footnote 1. The offer "to lie body for body" was noticed in the newsbook *Mercurius Politicus*, for 14th to 21st April 1659. See *B.F.H.S.* v. 32 for text.

PAGE 457

resumed their military rule. The situation leading to the breach between the Rump and the army may be described more correctly by stating that the Rump on 11th October passed an act declaring it high treason to levy any tax that had not received the approval of Parliament and voiding all acts and ordinances passed since 19th April 1653 which had not received the approval of the present Parliament. Parliament further revoked the commissions of nine leading officers. (Information from Godfrey Davies.)

PAGE 458

7000 additional names. The names of the women were printed with their petition.

favourable to the suppression of tithes. The maintenance of tithes continued only as a result of a tie vote of the House on 14th June and a later vote to continue them unless Parliament found a better way to maintain ministers.

PAGE 460

from month to month. The dilemma of Friends in this period was great; sometimes they were tempted to participate politically, at other times they withdrew into non-partisanship. It has been carefully studied by J. F. Maclear. See his "Quakerism and the End of the Interregnum: A Chapter in the Domestication of Radical Puritanism," *Church History*, xix. 240–271.

PAGE 461

Footnote 1. According to Robert Rich, *Hidden Things Brought to Light* (1678), pp. 28, 29, in an Act of Parliament for the settling of the militia of Westminster only, dated 28th June 1659, no less than five of G. F.'s Friends (all noted Quakers) viz. Nich. Bond, Wm. Woodcock, Amor Stoddart, Richard Davis and Stephen Hart appeared (*Second Period*, p. 18 *n*.).

On Fox's general attitude light is thrown by two papers in Swarth. Colln. vii., Nos. 157 (to Friends at Bristol on Friends as commissioners) and 165 (concerning the Poll Acts). The latter is printed in *The Household Account Book of Sarah Fell*, p. 580.

PAGE 462

our weapons are spiritual and not carnal. From the same later perspective as this endorsement Fox reports his strong opposition to the offers by the Committee of Safety to Friends of great places and commands, and his forbidding the plans of rash spirits among Friends to take up arms or to buy as a place for Friends' meetings the government-owned Somerset House (*Camb. Journ.* i. 334).

PAGE 465

Footnote 1. Braithwaite's text and note here can be misunderstood. He returns to this subject in *Second Period*, p. 115. He quotes 320 as the deaths during the Restoration, but thinks the number should be raised to 450. From sources cited in *B.F.H.A.* xl. 99, we learn that the 21 deaths up to April 1659 become 32 up to the coming of the king, the deaths after that are listed as 14 in 1661, as 57 a year or two later.

PAGE 469

The situation naturally and rapidly drifted into anarchy. The precise sequence appears to have been: On 22nd April Richard was forced by the army leaders to dissolve the Parliament. On 7th May the army leaders were obliged by the under officers and civilian Republicans to recall the Rump. Richard's letter of 25th May is usually taken as his formal resignation from the Protectorate. On 13th October Lambert closed the doors of Parliament. The army leaders with a few civilians like Vane tried to rule until 24th December. On 26th December the Rump sat again. (Information from Godfrey Davies.)

PAGE 470

he drew near London, and was warmly received by the Republican Leaders. The situation in London is not to be so simply described. Monck was not warmly welcomed by the adherents of Lambert, and even the Rump suspected his motives, and their relations were not friendly in the parliamentary changes that followed. (Information from Godfrey Davies.)

PAGE 471

the Scottish army was evidently of a different temper. The hostility of Monck's army to the Quakers is not hard to explain. The Quakers and Baptists were associated in the public mind as "sectarians" and were believed to be supporters of that section of the army that adhered to Lambert. The Quakers and Baptists had in common their opposition to a state church and to tithes to support it.

Footnote 2. The two letters cited to Margt. Fell are from the Wm. Caton Colln.

PAGE 477

In consequence of Presbyterian opposition, led by Baxter, the Bill dropped. The failure to incorporate in law the toleration pledged in Charles's Declaration had political as well as religions reasons. Cavaliers and the officers voted against it and did so apparently in accordance with the King's wishes. (Information from Godfrey Davies.)

PAGE 497

Benjamin Furly. Bibliotheca Furliana, the catalogue of Furly's library published in 1714 after his death and before the auction sale of his books, contains a whole section, pp. 270–284, of grammars and dictionaries of many languages. This library may well have been the source from which the information in the *Battle-Door* was obtained. Cf. W. I. Hull, *Benjamin Furly and Quakerism in Rotterdam* (1941), pp. 137–155.

PAGE 504

at Reading in 1656. Parker's date is more explicitly February 1656/7. A letter from Hubberthorne to Margaret Fell, 5th October 1655, Swarthm. Colln. i. 106, speaks of a meeting at Gaddesden, 12 miles from Isaac Penington's and 12 miles from John Crook's, as though Penington's home was already thought of as a Quaker centre.

PAGE 505

by "seed" he meant a part of God's nature. The use of "seed" is shared by Fox, but it may be doubted if Friends who used it thought of it as something that grows; in the passage immediately following "seed" appears to mean Christ, as it so often does in Quaker writings. See T. J. Pickvance in *J.F.H.S.* xli. 25–28, also G. F. Nuttall, *The Holy Spirit in Puritan Faith and Experience* (1946), p. 158.

Footnote 1. L. V. Hodgkin tells the story in *Gulielma, Wife of William Penn* (1947).

PAGE 508

had not taken place by the year 1660. The developments in Quakerism after 1660 are most fully traced in Braithwaite's companion volume, *The Second Period of Quakerism* (1919). Parallel to that volume and this, and in part dependent on it but on a smaller scale are E. B. Emmott, *A Short History of Quakerism* (1923); Elbert Russell, *The History of Quakerism* (1942); A. Neave Brayshaw, *The Quakers: Their Story and Message* (1927), fifth impression (with a new chapter, 1953); E. Vipont, *The Story of Quakerism* (1954).

PAGE 517

three years before his death. For the death of Humphrey Bache see Besse, *Sufferings*, i. 392. His will, dated 17th August 1662, is given in *J.F.H.S.* viii. 50, 51. He died the next day.

PAGE 519

But it did not prove possible for a Quaker to remain a soldier. It is worth while to emphasize that the authorities in expelling Friends from the army did so not because they were Quakers nor for political reasons but because of their noncompliance with military discipline, and that Friends themselves found other features of army life too distasteful as well as the profession of killing.

Footnote 2. Such a list is now available in M. E. Hirst, *The Quakers in Peace and War* (1923), Appendix A, "List of Soldiers and Sailors who became Friends before the year 1660 (including ex-Soldiers and Sailors)," pp. 527–529. For individuals who had held office in the parliamentary army Firth and Davies, *Regimental History of Cromwell's Army* may be consulted.

PAGE 522

his conscientious convictions were put to severe proof. On Friends' non-participation in war see further *Second Period*, pp. 608–629 and Hirst, *The Quakers in Peace and War.*

PAGE 532

it has been transcribed for publication by the Syndics of the Cambridge University Press. Mention should be made of the revised *Journal of George Fox*, edited by J. L. Nickalls and published in 1952 by the Cambridge University Press; for fuller reference to MS. sources for Fox's *Journal* see vii–ix. In this edition the language of the original Spence manuscripts (miscalled by Braithwaite "The Great Journal"; see *Ann. Cat.* p. 2) is printed in modern spelling and punctuation, supplemented here and there by extracts from the *Short Journal* and from Ellwood, but with the omission of many of the inserted documents and the addition for the final fifteen years of a modern summary chapter by H. J. Cadbury.

PAGE 536

"*Short Journal.*" This manuscript *Short Journal*, collated with another seventeenth-century writing covering the same ground, was edited by Norman Penney with introduction, pp. xxi–xxiii, and notes, pp. 275–293, in *The Short Journal and Itinerary Journals of George Fox* (1925), pp. 1–72. In this edition of the present work page references to this printed *Short Journal* have been added.

The rest of this volume presents for the first time the text of some of the "little journals" but these belong after the period with which we are here concerned. Cf. *Second Period*, p. 433 *n.* 3, and additional note there.

PAGE 539

A. R. B[arclay] Collection. A précis with extracts of the A. R. Barclay Manuscripts is being published in instalments in *J.F.H.S.* beginning with vol. xxvii, 1930.

PAGE 540

Abraham MSS. For the Abraham MSS with which the Shackleton MSS have been merged see a catalogue in *J.F.H.S.* xi. 145–190.

PAGE 540

Calendar of the Swarthmore Collection. This wish has been fulfilled in a very satisfactory way, so far as concerns letters prior to 1661 in vols. i. iii. and iv. of the main collection, by G. F. Nuttall's *Early Quaker Letters* (1952).

PAGE 541

a Collection of letters (*William Caton Colln.*) *now unfortunately lost.* This original William Caton Collection came to light and was purchased by Friends' House Library, London, 1935. It contains 170 letters and papers of which 150 were written in the Commonwealth period. (*J.F.H.S.* xxxii. 67, 68.) The text and the references of the present work derived from the copies of letters by A. R. Barclay and James Bowden can now be corrected from the original.

54°

53°

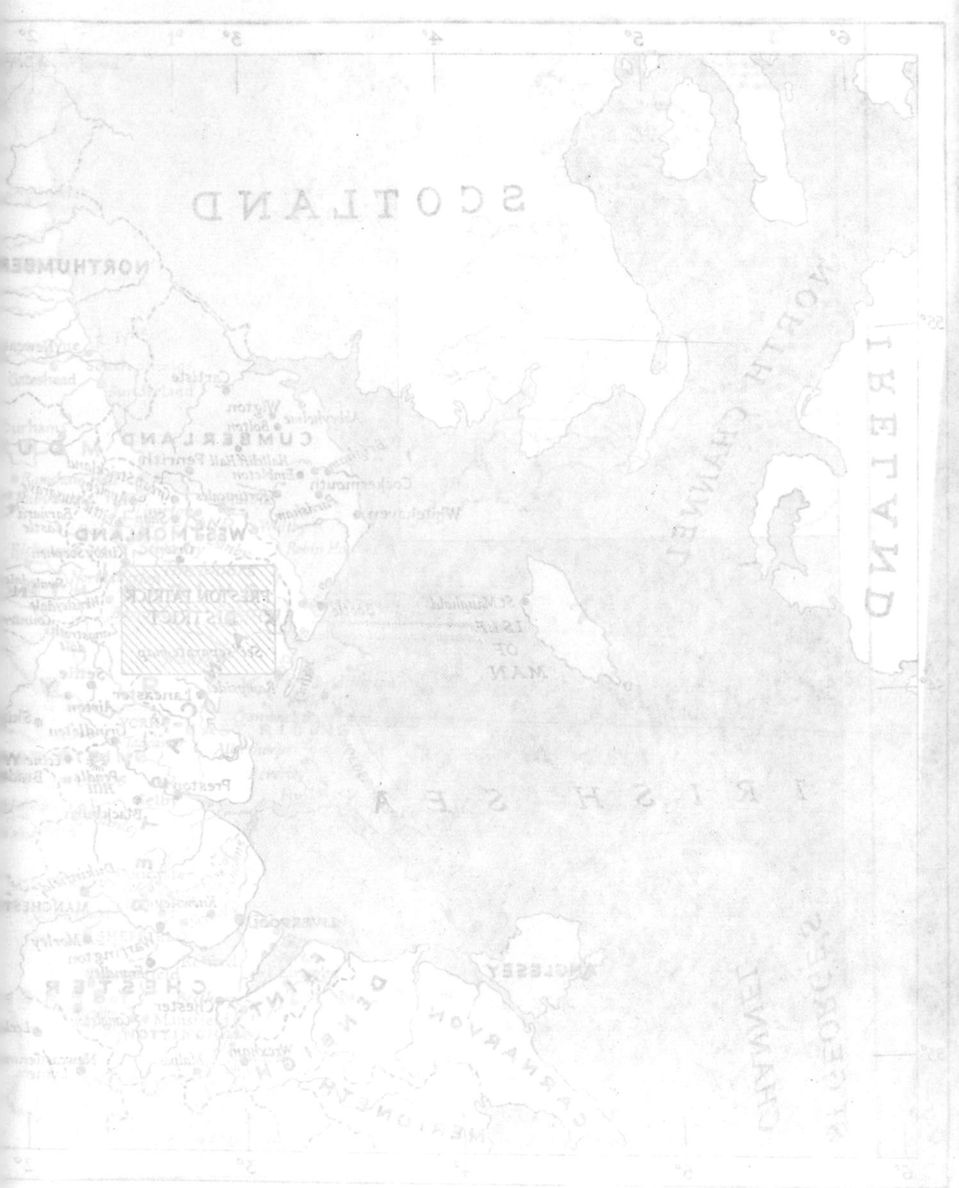